ELITE STUDENT EDITION

5 STEPS TO A 5

AP U.S. History

2018

Daniel P. Murphy
Stephen Armstrong

Mc
Graw
Hill
Education

New York Chicago San Francisco Athens London Madrid
Mexico City Milan New Delhi Singapore Sydney Toronto

1 2 3 4 5 6 7 8 9   LHS   22 21 20 19 18 17 (Cross-Platform Prep Course only)
1 2 3 4 5 6 7 8 9   LHS   22 21 20 19 18 17 (Elite Student Edition)

ISBN   978-1-259-86277-9 (Cross-Platform Prep Course only)
MHID   1-259-86277-1

e-ISBN   978-1-259-86278-6 (Cross-Platform Prep Course only)
e-MHID   1-259-86278-X

ISBN   978-1-259-86279-3 (Elite Student Edition)
MHID   1-259-86279-8

e-ISBN   978-1-259-86280-9 (Elite Student Edition)
e-MHID   1-259-86280-1

The series editor was Grace Freedson, and the project editor was Del Franz.
Series design by Jane Tenenbaum.

McGraw-Hill Education products are available at special quantity discounts to use as premiums and sales or for use in corporate training programs. To contact a representative, please visit the Contact Us pages at www.mhprofessional.com.

CONTENTS

So, you have decided to take AP U.S. History. Prepare to be continually challenged in this course: this is the only way you will attain the grade that you want on the AP exam in May. Prepare to read, to read a lot, and to read critically; almost all students successful in AP U.S. History say this is a necessity. Prepare to analyze countless primary source documents; being able to do this is critical for success in the exam as well. Most important, prepare to immerse yourself in the great story that is U.S. history. As your teacher will undoubtedly point out, it would be impossible to make up some of the people and events you will study in this class. What really happened is much more interesting!

This study guide will assist you along the journey of AP U.S. History. The chapter review guides give you succinct overviews of the major events of U.S. history. At the end of each chapter is a list of the major concepts, a time line, and multiple-choice and short-answer review questions for that chapter. In addition, a very extensive glossary is included at the back of this manual. All of the **boldface** words throughout the book can be found in the glossary (it would also be a good study technique to review the entire glossary before taking the actual AP exam).

The first five chapters of the manual describe the AP test itself and suggest some test-taking strategies. There are also two entire sample tests, with answers. These allow you to become totally familiar with the format and nature of the questions that will appear on the exam. On the actual testing day you want absolutely no surprises!

In the second chapter, you will also find time lines for three approaches to preparing for the exam. It is obviously suggested that your preparation for the examination be a year-long process; for those students unable to do that, two alternative calendars also appear. Many students also find that study groups are very beneficial in studying for the AP test. Students who have been successful on the AP test oftentimes form these groups very early in the school year.

It should also be noted that the AP U.S. History exam that you will be taking may be different than the one that your older brother or sister took in the past. The format of the exam changed in 2015. Further revisions have been made to the 2018 exam. We will outline the test in detail in the first several chapters. Please do not use old study guides or review sheets that were used to prepare for prior tests; these do not work anymore!

We hope this manual helps you in achieving the "perfect 5." That score is sitting out there, waiting for you to reach for it.

INTRODUCTION: 5-STEP PROGRAM

The Basics

This guide provides you with the specific format of the AP U.S. History exam, three sample AP U.S. History tests, and a comprehensive review of major events and themes in U.S. history. After each review chapter, you will find a list of the major concepts, a time line, and several review multiple-choice and short-answer questions.

Reading this guide is a great start to getting the grade you want on the AP U.S. History test, but it is important to read on your own as well. Several groups of students who have all gotten a 5 on the test maintain that the key to success is to *read* as much as you possibly can on U.S. history.

Reading this guide will not guarantee you a 5 when you take the U.S. History exam in May. However, by carefully reviewing the format of the exam and the test-taking strategies provided for each section, you will definitely be on your way! The review section that outlines the major developments of U.S. history should augment what you have learned from your regular U.S. history textbook. This book won't "give" you a 5, but it can certainly point you firmly in that direction.

Organization of the Book

This guide conducts you through the five steps necessary to prepare yourself for success on the exam. These steps will provide you with many skills and strategies vital to the exam and the practice that will lead you toward the perfect 5.

In this introductory chapter we will explain the basic five-step plan, which is the focus of this entire book. The material in Chapter 1 will give you information you need to know about the AP U.S. History exam. In Chapter 2 three different approaches will be presented to prepare for the actual exam; study them all and then pick the one that works best for you. Chapter 3 contains a practice AP U.S. History exam; this is an opportunity to experience what the test is like and to have a better idea of your strengths and weaknesses as you prepare for the actual exam. Chapter 4 describes historical skills and themes emphasized in the exam. Chapter 5 contains a number of tips and suggestions about the different types of questions that appear on the actual exam. We will discuss ways to approach the multiple-choice questions, the short-answer questions, the document-based question (DBQ), and the long essay question. Almost all students note that knowing how to approach each type of question is crucial.

For some of you, the most important part of this manual will be found in Chapters 6 through 31, which contain a review of U.S. history from the European exploration of the Americas to the election of Donald Trump in 2016. Undoubtedly, you have studied much of the material included in these chapters. However, these review chapters can help highlight certain important material that you may have missed or forgotten from your AP History class. At the end of each chapter, you will also find a list of the major concepts, time line of important events discussed in the chapter, and multiple-choice and short-answer review questions.

After these review chapters you will find two complete practice exams, including multiple-choice questions, short-answer questions, and essays. Correct answers and explanations for these answers are also included. Take one of the exams and evaluate your success; review any material that you had trouble with. Then take the second exam and use the results to guide your additional study. At the back of the manual is a glossary that defines all of the **boldface** words found in the review chapters. Use this to find the meaning of a specific term you might be unfamiliar with; some students find reviewing the entire glossary a useful method of reviewing for the actual exam.

Five-Step Program

Step 1: Set Up Your Study Program

In Step 1, you will read a brief overview of the AP U.S. History exam, including an outline of the topics that might be covered on the test itself. You will also follow a process to help determine which of the following preparation programs is right for you:

- Full school year: September through May
- One semester: January through May
- Six weeks: Basic Training for the Exam

Step 2: Determine Your Test Readiness

Step 2 provides you with a diagnostic exam to assess your current level of understanding. This exam will let you know about your current level of preparedness and on which areas and periods you should focus your study.

- Take the diagnostic exam slowly and analyze each question. Do not worry about how many questions you get right. Hopefully the exam will boost your confidence.
- Review the answers and explanations following the exam, so that you see what you do and do not yet fully know and understand.

Step 3: Develop Strategies for Success

Step 3 provides strategies and techniques that will help you do your best on the exam. These strategies cover the multiple-choice, short-answer, and the two different essay parts of the test. These tips come from discussions with both AP U.S. History students and teachers. In this section you will:

- Learn the skills and themes emphasized in the exam.
- Learn how to read and analyze multiple-choice questions.
- Learn how to answer multiple-choice questions, including whether or not to guess.
- Learn how to respond to short-answer questions.
- Learn how to plan and write both types of essay questions.

Step 4: Review the Knowledge You Need to Score High

Step 4 makes up the majority of this book. In this step you will review the important names, dates, and themes of American history. Obviously, not all of the material included in this book will be on the AP exam. However, this book is a good overview of the content studied in a "typical" AP U.S. History course. Some of you are presently taking AP courses that cover more material than is included in this book; some of you are in courses that cover less. Nevertheless, thoroughly reviewing the material in the content section of this book will significantly increase your chance of scoring well.

Step 5: Build Your Test-Taking Confidence

In Step 5, you will complete your preparation by taking two complete practice exams and examining your results on them. It should be noted that the practice exams included in this book do not include questions taken from actual exams; however, these practice exams do include questions that are very similar to the "real thing."

Graphics Used in This Book

To emphasize particular skills and strategies, we use several icons throughout this book. An icon in the margin will alert you that you should pay particular attention to the accompanying text. We use three icons:

The first icon points out a very important concept or fact that you should not pass over.

The second icon calls your attention to a problem-solving strategy that you may want to try.

The third icon indicates a tip that you might find useful.

Boldface words indicate terms that are included in the glossary at the end of the book. Boldface is also used to indicate the answer to a sample problem discussed in the test. Throughout the book, you will find marginal notes, boxes, and starred areas. Pay close attention to these areas because they can provide tips, hints, strategies, and further explanations to help you reach your full potential.

STEP 1

Set Up Your Study Program

CHAPTER 1

What You Need to Know About the AP U.S. History Exam

IN THIS CHAPTER

Summary: Learn about the test, what's on it, how it's scored, and what benefits you can get from taking it.

Key Ideas

✪ Most colleges will award credit for a score of 4 or 5. Even if you don't do well enough on the exam to receive college credit, college admissions officials like to see students who have challenged themselves and experienced the college-level coursework of AP courses.

✪ Since 2015, the exam has had a new format. The new exam de-emphasizes the simple memorization of historical facts. Instead, you have to demonstrate an ability to use historical analytical skills and think thematically across time periods in American history.

✪ In addition to multiple-choice and short-answer questions, the test contains a DBQ (document-based question) and one long essay question.

Advanced Placement Program

The Advanced Placement (AP) program was begun by the College Board in 1955 to administer standard achievement exams that would allow highly motivated high school students the opportunity to earn college credit for AP courses taken in high school. Today there are 34 different AP courses and exams, with well over 4.5 million exams administered each May.

There are numerous AP courses in the social studies besides U.S. History, including European History, World History, U.S. Government and Politics, Comparative Government, Psychology, and Micro and Macro Economics. The majority of students who take AP courses and exams are juniors and seniors; however, some schools offer AP courses to freshmen and sophomores (AP U.S. History is usually not one of those courses). It is not absolutely necessary to be enrolled in an AP class to take the exam in a specific subject; there are rare cases of students who study on their own for a particular AP examination and do well.

Who Writes the AP Exams? Who Scores Them?

AP exams, including the U.S. History exam, are written by experienced college and secondary school teachers. All questions on the AP exams are field tested before they actually appear on an AP exam. The group that writes the history exam is called the AP U.S. History Development Committee. This group constantly reevaluates the test, analyzing the exam as a whole and on an item-by-item basis.

As noted in the preface, the AP U.S. History exam has undergone a substantial transformation that took effect beginning with the 2015 test. New revisions were made to the 2018 exam. The College Board has conducted a number of institutes and workshops to ensure that teachers across the United States are well qualified to assist students in preparing for this new exam.

The multiple-choice section of each AP exam is graded by computer, but the free-response questions are scored by humans. A number of college and secondary school teachers of U.S. History get together at a central location in early June to score the free-response questions of the AP U.S. History exam administered the previous month. The scoring of each reader during this procedure is carefully analyzed to ensure that exams are being evaluated in a fair and consistent manner.

AP Scores

Once you have taken the exam and it has been scored, your raw scores will be transformed into an AP grade on a 1-to-5 scale. A grade report will be send to you by the College Board in July. When you take the test, you should indicate the college or colleges that you want your AP scores sent to. The report that the colleges receive contains the score for every AP exam you took this year and the grades that you received on AP exams in prior years. In addition, your scores will be sent to your high school. (Note that it is possible, for a fee, to withhold the scores of any AP exam you have taken from going out to colleges. See the College Board website for more information.)

As noted above, you will be scored on a 1-to-5 scale:

- 5 indicates that you are extremely well qualified. This is the highest possible grade.
- 4 indicates that you are well qualified.
- 3 indicates that you are qualified.
- 2 indicates that you are possibly qualified.
- 1 indicates that you are not qualified to receive college credit.

Benefits of the AP Exam

If you receive a score of a 4 or a 5, you can most likely get actual college credit for the subject that you took the course in; a few colleges will do the same for students receiving a 3. Colleges and universities have different rules on AP scores and credit, so check with the college or colleges that you are considering to determine what credit they will give you for a good score on the AP History exam. Some colleges might exempt you from a freshman-level course based on your score even if they don't grant credit for the score you received.

The benefits of being awarded college credits before you start college are significant: You can save time in college (by skipping courses) and money (by avoiding paying college tuition for courses you skip). Almost every college encourages students to challenge themselves; if it is possible for you to take an AP course, do it! Even if you do not do well on the actual test—or you decide not to take the AP test—the experience of being in an AP class all year can impress college admissions committees and help you prepare for the more academically challenging work of college.

AP U.S. History Exam

Achieving a good score on the AP U.S. History exam will require you do more than just memorize important dates, people, and events from America's history. To get a 4 or a 5 you have to demonstrate an ability to master primary and secondary sources, construct an argument, and utilize specific historical analytical skills when studying history. In addition, you will be asked to demonstrate your ability to think thematically and evaluate specific historical themes across time periods in American history. Every question on the AP U.S. History exam is rooted in these analytical skills and historical themes. You'll find more information about these analytical skills and historical themes in Chapter 4.

As far as specific content, there is material that you need to know from nine predetermined historical time periods of U.S. history. For each of these time periods, key concepts have been identified. You will be introduced to a concept outline for each of the historical periods in your AP course. You can also find this outline at the College Board's AP U.S. History website. These concepts are connected to the historical themes and analyzed using historical analytical skills.

To do well on this exam you have to exhibit the ability to do much of the work that "real" historians do. You must know major concepts from every historical time period. You must demonstrate an ability to think thematically when analyzing history, and you must utilize historical thinking skills when doing all of this. The simple memorization of historical facts is given less emphasis in the new exam. This does not mean that you can ignore historical detail. Knowledge of historical information will be crucial in explaining themes in American history. Essentially this exam is changing the focus of what is expected of AP U.S. History students. It is asking you to take a smaller number of historical concepts and to analyze these concepts very carefully. The ability to do this does not necessarily come easily; one of the major functions of this book is to help you "think like a historian."

Periods of U.S. History

As noted earlier, U.S. history has been divided into specific time periods for the purposes of the AP course. The creators of the AP U.S. History exam have established the following nine historical periods and have also determined approximately how much of the year should be spent on each historical era:

- **Period 1: 1491 to 1607.** Approximately 5 percent of instructional time should be spent on this period.
- **Period 2: 1607 to 1754.** Approximately 10 percent of instructional time should be spent on this period.
- **Period 3: 1754 to 1800.** Approximately 12 percent of instructional time should be spent on this period.
- **Period 4: 1800 to 1848.** Approximately 10 percent of instructional time should be spent on this period.
- **Period 5: 1844 to 1877.** Approximately 13 percent of instructional time should be spent on this period.

- **Period 6: 1865 to 1898.** Approximately 13 percent of instructional time should be spent on this period.
- **Period 7: 1890 to 1945.** Approximately 17 percent of instructional time should be spent on this period.
- **Period 8: 1945 to 1980.** Approximately 15 percent of instructional time should be spent on this period.
- **Period 9: 1980 to present.** Approximately 5 percent of instructional time should be spent on this period.

On the actual AP test that you will take:

- 5 percent of the exam will relate to issues concerning Period 1.
- 45 percent of the exam will relate to issues concerning Periods 2, 3, 4, and 5.
- 45 percent of the exam will relate to issues concerning Periods 6, 7, and 8.
- 5 percent of the exam will relate to issues concerning Period 9.

Many students are worried when their AP class doesn't get to the present day. As you can see, only 5 percent of the test is on material after 1980; therefore, making it all the way to Donald Trump will not have a major impact on your score.

Structure of the AP U.S. History Exam

The AP U.S. History exam consists of two sections, each of which contains two parts. You'll be given 95 minutes to complete Section I, which includes multiple-choice questions (Part A) and short-answer questions (Part B). You'll have 100 minutes to complete Section II, which includes the document-based question (Part A) and the long essay question (Part B). Here is the breakdown:

Section I
- Part A: 55 multiple-choice questions—55 minutes recommended—40% of the exam score.
- Part B: Three short-answer questions—40 minutes recommended—20% of the exam score. Questions 1 and 2 are required; you can choose between 3 and 4. These questions will address one or more of the themes that have been developed throughout the course and will ask you to use historical thinking when you write about these themes.

Section II
- Part A: One document-based question (DBQ)—60 minutes (including a 15 minute reading period) recommended—25% of the exam score. In this section, you will be asked to analyze and use a number of primary-source documents as you construct a historical argument.
- Part B: One long essay question—40 minutes recommended—15% of the exam score. You will be given a choice between three options, addressing periods 1–3, 4–6, or 7–9. It will be critical to use historical analytical skills when writing your response.

This presents an overview. There will be more information about the different components of the exam later in this book.

Taking the AP U.S. History Exam

Registration and Fees

If you are enrolled in AP U.S. History, your teacher or guidance counselor is going to provide all of these details. However, you do not have to enroll in the AP course to take the

AP exam. When in doubt, the best source of information is the College Board's website: www.collegeboard.com.

There are also several other fees required if you want your scores rushed to you or if you wish to receive multiple score reports. Students who demonstrate financial need may receive a refund to help offset the cost of testing.

Night Before the Exam

Last minute cramming of massive amounts of material will not help you. It takes time for your brain to organize material. There is some value to a last-minute review of material. This may involve looking at the fast-review portions of the chapters or looking through the glossary. The night before the test should include a light review and various relaxing activities. *A full night's sleep is one of the best preparations for the test.*

What to Bring to the Exam

Here are some suggestions:

- Several pencils and an eraser that does not leave smudges.
- Several black pens (for the essays).
- A watch so that you can monitor your time. The exam room may or may not have a clock on the wall. Make sure you turn off the beep that goes off on the hour.
- Your school code.
- Your driver's license, Social Security number, or some other ID, in case there is a problem with your registration.
- Tissues.
- Something to drink—water is best.
- A quiet snack.
- Your quiet confidence that you are prepared.

What *Not* to Bring to the Exam

It's a good idea to leave the following items at home or in the car:

- Your cell phone and/or other electronic devices.
- Books, a dictionary, study notes, flash cards, highlighting pens, correction fluid, a ruler, or any other office supplies.
- Portable music of any kind (although you will probably want to listen as soon as you leave the testing site!).
- Panic or fear. It's natural to be nervous, but you can comfort yourself that you have used this book and that there is no need for fear on your exam.

Day of the Test

Once the test day has arrived, there is nothing further you can do. Do not worry about what you could have done differently. It is out of your hands, and your only job is to answer as many questions correctly as you possibly can. The calmer you are, the better your chances are of doing well.

Follow these simple commonsense tips:

- Allow plenty of time to get to the test site.
- Wear comfortable clothing.
- Eat a light breakfast and/or lunch.
- Think positive. Remind yourself that you are well prepared and that the test is an enjoyable challenge and a chance to share your knowledge.
- Be proud of yourself!

CHAPTER 2

Preparing for the AP U.S. History Exam

IN THIS CHAPTER

Summary: The right preparation plan for you depends on your study habits and the amount of time you have before the test. This chapter provides some examples of plans you can use or adapt to your needs.

Key Ideas

✪ Choose the study plan that is right for you.
✪ Begin to prepare for the AP exam at the beginning of the school year. Developing historical analytical skills, evaluating themes in U.S. history, and studying important concepts take far more time and effort than by simply memorizing facts. The sooner you begin preparing for the test, the better.

Getting Started

You have made the decision to take AP U.S. History. Enjoy! You will be exposed to all of the fascinating stories that make up U.S. history. To be successful in this course, you will have to work much harder than you would in a "regular" high school U.S. history course. You will be required to read more, including reading and analyzing a wide variety of primary source documents throughout the year. In addition, you will be required to utilize historical thinking, to analyze history in a thematic way, and to be knowledgeable of specific concepts that help guide the study of American history. It cannot be stressed enough that the examination for this course that you will take in May is not a test that will simply measure what you "know" about U.S. history; instead, it is an examination that tests your ability to analyze major events, concepts, and themes in American history utilizing specific historical analytical skills.

Being able to utilize historical analytical skills, study history thematically, and develop conceptual thinking are not skills that develop overnight. In fact, it is difficult to develop these skills in the context of one specific course. If you are reading this before you are actually enrolled in an AP U.S. History course, you may want to take the most challenging history courses you can *before* you take AP U.S. History. Try to think conceptually in any history course that you take; it involves integrating historical facts into larger interpretive themes.

Creating a Study Plan

As has already been noted several times, preparing for this exam involves much more than just memorizing important dates, names, and events that are important in U.S. history. Developing historical analytical skills, evaluating themes in U.S. history, and studying important concepts take far more time and effort than by simply memorizing facts. Therefore, it is strongly suggested that you take a year-long approach to studying and preparing for the test.

However, for some students this is not possible. Therefore, some suggestions for students who have only one semester to prepare for the exam and students who have only six weeks to prepare for the exam are included. In the end, it is better to do *some* systematic preparation for the exam than to do none at all.

Study Groups

Many students who have gotten a 5 on the U.S. History exam reported that working in a study group was an important part of the successful preparation that they did for the test. In an ideal setting, three to five students get together, probably once a week, to review material that was covered in class the preceding week and to practice historical, thematic, and conceptual thinking. If at all possible, do this! A good suggestion is to have study groups set a specific time to meet every week and stick to that time. Without a regular meeting time, study groups usually meet fewer times during the year, often cancel meetings, and so on.

THREE PLANS FOR TEST PREPARATION

Plan A:
Yearlong Preparation for the AP U.S. History Exam

This is the plan we highly recommend. Besides doing all of the readings and assignments assigned by your teacher, also do the following activities. (Check off the activities as you complete them.)

IN THE FALL

_____ Create a study group and determine a regular meeting time for that group.

_____ Coordinate the materials in this manual with the curriculum of your AP U.S. History class.

_____ Study the review chapters in Step 4 of this book that coincide with the material you are studying in class.

_____ Begin to do outside reading on U.S. history topics (either topics of interest to you or topics that you know you need more background in).

_____ In your study group, emphasize historical analysis and thematic and conceptual thinking.

FROM DECEMBER TO MARCH

_____ Continue to meet with your study group and emphasize historical analysis and thematic and conceptual thinking.

_____ Continue to study the review chapters in Step 4 of this book that coincide with the material you are studying in class.

_____ Take the diagnostic test in Step 2 of this book to see what the test will be like and assess your strengths and weaknesses.

_____ Learn the strategies discussed in Step 3 of this book. Practice applying them as you study and review for the AP U.S. History exam.

_____ Carefully study the format and approach to document-based questions (DBQs). You will probably have one on your midterm exam in class.

_____ Using the eras of U.S. history you have studied in class, create your own DBQ for two of the units and try to answer it.

_____ Intensify your outside reading of U.S. history topics.

_____ Take two U.S. history textbooks and compare and contrast their handling of three events of U.S. history. What do these results tell you?

DURING APRIL AND MAY

———— Continue to meet with your study group and emphasize historical analysis and thematic and conceptual thinking. Many study groups meet at additional times in the weeks leading up to the test.

———— Continue to study the review chapters in Step 4 of this book that coincide with the material you are studying in class.

———— Practice creating and answering multiple-choice and short-answer questions in your study group.

———— Develop and review worksheets of essential historical content with your study group.

———— Highlight material in your textbook (and in this manual) that you may not understand, and ask your teacher about it.

———— Write two or three essays as they would appear on the exam under timed questions and have a member of your study group (or a classmate) evaluate them.

———— Take the practice tests provided in Step 5 of this book. Set a timer and practice pacing yourself.

You are well prepared for the test. Go get it!

Plan B:
One-Semester Preparation for the AP U.S. History Exam

Besides doing all of the readings and assignments assigned by your teacher, you should do the following activities. (Check off the activities as you complete them.)

FROM JANUARY TO MARCH

_____ Establish a study group of other students preparing in the same way that you are. In your study group you should review essential factual knowledge, but also analyze the essential themes and concepts in the course.

_____ Study the review chapters in Step 4 of this book that coincide with the material you have studied or are studying in class.

_____ Take the diagnostic test in Step 2 of this book to familiarize yourself with the test and assess your strengths and weaknesses.

_____ Learn the strategies discussed in Step 3 of this book. Practice applying them as you study and review for the AP U.S. History exam.

_____ Write two or three document-based and sample multiple-choice questions.

_____ Read at least one outside source (historical essay or book) on a topic that you are studying in class.

_____ In your study group, practice creating and answering short-answer and multiple-choice questions.

DURING APRIL AND MAY

_____ Continue to meet with your study group, and review essential factual knowledge and essential themes and concepts of the course you have taken or are currently taking. Some study groups increase the amount of time that they meet together in the weeks right before the test.

_____ Study the review chapters in Step 4 of this book that coincide with the material you have studied or are presently studying in class. Focus on weak areas you identified in the diagnostic test of Step 2 of this book.

_____ Practice creating and answering sample essays with your study group.

_____ Develop and review worksheets of essential historical content with your study group.

_____ Ask your teacher to clarify things in your textbook or in this manual that you do not completely understand. If you have nagging questions about some specific historical details, get the answers to them!

_____ Take the practice tests provided in Step 5 of this book. Set a timer and practice pacing yourself.

Plan C:
Four- to Six-Week Preparation for the AP U.S. History Exam

 Besides doing all of the reading and assignments assigned by your teacher, do the following activities. (Check off the activities as you complete them.)

IN APRIL

_____ Take the diagnostic test in Step 2 of this book to familiarize yourself with the test and assess your strengths and weaknesses.

_____ Study the review chapters in Step 4 of this book that coincide with any weak areas you identified from the diagnostic exam.

_____ Learn the strategies discussed in Step 3 of this book. Practice applying them as you study and review for the AP U.S. History exam.

_____ Write one sample document-based question (DBQ) as modeled by samples in this manual.

_____ Carefully review the sections of this manual that outline the essential content of each historical period.

_____ If possible, create or join a study group with other students to help prepare for the exam.

IN MAY

_____ Many teachers organize study sessions right before the actual exam. Go to them!

_____ With your study group or individually, review essential content from the course and major concepts of each unit.

_____ Complete another sample DBQ essay and analyze your results.

_____ Review the glossary of this manual another time to help review essential content.

_____ Be certain of the format of the test and the types of questions that will be asked.

_____ Take the practice tests provided in Step 5 of this book. Set a timer and practice pacing yourself.

STEP **2**

Determine Your Test Readiness

CHAPTER 3

Take a Diagnostic Exam

IN THIS CHAPTER

Summary: In the following pages, you will find a diagnostic exam whose content and structure closely matches the "real" AP U.S. History exam. Use this test to familiarize yourself with the actual test and to assess your strengths and weaknesses.

How to Use the Diagnostic Exam

Section I of the AP U.S. History exam contains a multiple-choice section and a short-answer section.

Section II contains the document-based question (DBQ) and an essay question—you will need to pick one question to answer out of the three questions you are given.

55 minutes for 55 multiple-choice questions
40 minutes for three short-answer questions
60 minutes for one document-based question
40 minutes for one long essay question

The purpose of this chapter is to allow you to familiarize yourself with the test and to assess your test readiness in terms of both the skills and the content understanding needed. Try to take this test under testlike conditions; in other words, time yourself and do the test—or at least each section of the test—uninterrupted. Note that in Chapter 5 you will find strategies for each type of question that will allow you to more effectively and efficiently tackle the questions.

When to Use the Diagnostic Exam

This diagnostic test can be helpful to you regardless of whether you are following Plan A, B, or C. Those who chose Plan A should study this exam early in the year so that you will thoroughly understand the format of the test. Look for the types of multiple-choice and short-answer questions early and carefully study the format of the essay questions. Go back and look at this exam throughout the year: Many successful test-takers maintain that knowing how to tackle the questions that will be asked on any exam is just as important as knowledge of the subject matter.

Plan B students (who are using one semester to prepare) should also analyze the format of the exam. Plan B folks: as you begin using this book you might also want to actually answer the multiple-choice and short-answer questions dealing with content you have already studied in class and answer the document-based question and the free-response question and evaluate your results. This will help you analyze the success of your previous preparation for the test.

Plan C students should take this diagnostic exam as soon as they begin working with this manual to analyze the success of their previous preparation for the actual exam.

Conclusion (After the Exam)

After you have studied or taken the diagnostic exam, you will continue to Step 3 of your 5 Steps to a 5. Chapter 5 will provide you with tips and strategies for answering all of the types of questions that you found on the diagnostic exam.

Don't be discouraged and if you answered a lot of questions on the diagnostic exam incorrectly. At this point, the main thing is that you get a feel for the types of questions that you will encounter on the real AP U.S. History exam.

AP U.S. HISTORY DIAGNOSTIC EXAM

Answer Sheet for Multiple-Choice Questions

1 Ⓐ Ⓑ Ⓒ Ⓓ	16 Ⓐ Ⓑ Ⓒ Ⓓ	31 Ⓐ Ⓑ Ⓒ Ⓓ	46 Ⓐ Ⓑ Ⓒ Ⓓ
2 Ⓐ Ⓑ Ⓒ Ⓓ	17 Ⓐ Ⓑ Ⓒ Ⓓ	32 Ⓐ Ⓑ Ⓒ Ⓓ	47 Ⓐ Ⓑ Ⓒ Ⓓ
3 Ⓐ Ⓑ Ⓒ Ⓓ	18 Ⓐ Ⓑ Ⓒ Ⓓ	33 Ⓐ Ⓑ Ⓒ Ⓓ	48 Ⓐ Ⓑ Ⓒ Ⓓ
4 Ⓐ Ⓑ Ⓒ Ⓓ	19 Ⓐ Ⓑ Ⓒ Ⓓ	34 Ⓐ Ⓑ Ⓒ Ⓓ	49 Ⓐ Ⓑ Ⓒ Ⓓ
5 Ⓐ Ⓑ Ⓒ Ⓓ	20 Ⓐ Ⓑ Ⓒ Ⓓ	35 Ⓐ Ⓑ Ⓒ Ⓓ	50 Ⓐ Ⓑ Ⓒ Ⓓ
6 Ⓐ Ⓑ Ⓒ Ⓓ	21 Ⓐ Ⓑ Ⓒ Ⓓ	36 Ⓐ Ⓑ Ⓒ Ⓓ	51 Ⓐ Ⓑ Ⓒ Ⓓ
7 Ⓐ Ⓑ Ⓒ Ⓓ	22 Ⓐ Ⓑ Ⓒ Ⓓ	37 Ⓐ Ⓑ Ⓒ Ⓓ	52 Ⓐ Ⓑ Ⓒ Ⓓ
8 Ⓐ Ⓑ Ⓒ Ⓓ	23 Ⓐ Ⓑ Ⓒ Ⓓ	38 Ⓐ Ⓑ Ⓒ Ⓓ	53 Ⓐ Ⓑ Ⓒ Ⓓ
9 Ⓐ Ⓑ Ⓒ Ⓓ	24 Ⓐ Ⓑ Ⓒ Ⓓ	39 Ⓐ Ⓑ Ⓒ Ⓓ	54 Ⓐ Ⓑ Ⓒ Ⓓ
10 Ⓐ Ⓑ Ⓒ Ⓓ	25 Ⓐ Ⓑ Ⓒ Ⓓ	40 Ⓐ Ⓑ Ⓒ Ⓓ	55 Ⓐ Ⓑ Ⓒ Ⓓ
11 Ⓐ Ⓑ Ⓒ Ⓓ	26 Ⓐ Ⓑ Ⓒ Ⓓ	41 Ⓐ Ⓑ Ⓒ Ⓓ	
12 Ⓐ Ⓑ Ⓒ Ⓓ	27 Ⓐ Ⓑ Ⓒ Ⓓ	42 Ⓐ Ⓑ Ⓒ Ⓓ	
13 Ⓐ Ⓑ Ⓒ Ⓓ	28 Ⓐ Ⓑ Ⓒ Ⓓ	43 Ⓐ Ⓑ Ⓒ Ⓓ	
14 Ⓐ Ⓑ Ⓒ Ⓓ	29 Ⓐ Ⓑ Ⓒ Ⓓ	44 Ⓐ Ⓑ Ⓒ Ⓓ	
15 Ⓐ Ⓑ Ⓒ Ⓓ	30 Ⓐ Ⓑ Ⓒ Ⓓ	45 Ⓐ Ⓑ Ⓒ Ⓓ	

AP U.S. HISTORY DIAGNOSTIC EXAM

Section I

Time: 95 minutes

Part A (Multiple Choice)

Part A recommended time: 55 minutes

Directions: Each of the following questions refers to a historical source. These questions will test your knowledge about the historical source and require you to make use of your historical analytical skills and your familiarity with historical themes. For each question select the *best* response and fill in the corresponding oval on your answer sheet.

Questions 1–4 refer to the following cartoon.

Political cartoon from 1807

1. This cartoon criticizes which policy of President Thomas Jefferson?
   A. The Louisiana purchase
   B. The Embargo Act
   C. The War with Tripoli
   D. Reductions in government spending

2. Jefferson was responding to what situation?
   A. British interference with American shipping and trade
   B. British support for Indians in the West
   C. Aggressive actions by the French Emperor Napoleon
   D. Electoral losses to domestic opponents

3. Which of the following reflects how many Americans responded to Jefferson's policy?

   A. Emigrating to other countries

   B. Advocating military involvement in the Napoleonic Wars

   C. Engaging in illicit trade with foreign countries

   D. Moving to the Western frontier

4. Which of the following most closely resembles Jefferson's policy?

   A. The Open Door in China

   B. The Good Neighbor Policy with South America

   C. Manifest Destiny of the 1840s

   D. Neutrality Laws of the 1930s

Questions 5–8 refer to the following quotation.

Yes, let us pray for the salvation of all those who live in that totalitarian darkness—pray that they will discover the joy of knowing God. But until they do, let us be aware that while they preach the supremacy of the State, declare its omnipotence over individual man, and predict its eventual domination of all peoples on the earth, they are the focus of evil in the modern world. … But if history teaches anything, it teaches that simpleminded appeasement or wishful thinking about our adversaries is folly. It means the betrayal of our past, the squandering of our freedom. So, I urge you to speak out against those who would place the United States in a position of military and moral inferiority. … So, in your discussions of the nuclear freeze proposals, I urge you to beware the temptation of pride—the temptation of blithely … declaring yourselves above it all and label both sides equally at fault, to ignore the facts of history and the aggressive impulses of an evil empire, to simply call the arms race a giant misunderstanding and thereby remove yourself from the struggle between right and wrong and good and evil.

—Ronald Reagan, Address to the National Association of Evangelicals, March 8, 1983

5. The sentiments in the passage above most directly reflect which of the following?

   A. A religious revival in the 1980s

   B. An intensification of the cold war in the early 1980s

   C. A desire to limit the size of government

   D. A distrust of the American military

6. Which of the following would have been most likely to approve the sentiments expressed in the passage?

   A. An antinuclear activist

   B. An atheist

   C. A Democrat

   D. A Republican

7. The sentiments expressed in the passage are most closely linked to which of the following policies?

   A. Strategic Defense Initiative (SDI)

   B. Business deregulation

   C. Encouraging prayer in the public schools

   D. Military cutbacks

8. The sentiments in the passage best reflect which long-standing concern of American presidents?

   A. Support for civil rights

   B. Promoting the separation of church and state

   C. Containment of communism

   D. Expanding the welfare state

Questions 9–12 refer to the following quotation.

They were smart and sophisticated, with an air of independence about them, and so casual about their looks and manners as to be almost slapdash. I don't know if I realized as soon as I began seeing them that they represented the wave of the future, but I do know I was drawn to them. I shared their restlessness, understood their determination to free themselves of the Victorian shackles of the pre-World War I era and find out for themselves what life was all about.

—Colleen Moore, movie star, writing about the 1920s

9. In this passage, Moore is writing about which of the following?
   A. The Ku Klux Klan
   B. Prohibitionists
   C. Flappers
   D. The Model T

10. Many young women of the 1920s expressed their freedom through which of the following?
   A. Political activism
   B. "Mannish" haircuts, new clothing styles, and cosmetics
   C. Living amongst the poor in settlement houses
   D. Rejection of marriage and child-rearing

11. The new freedoms for women in the 1920s were supported by which of the following?
   A. Widespread economic prosperity
   B. Growth in fundamentalist Christianity
   C. A massive movement of women into political offices
   D. Moral reforms like the temperance movement

12. The passage by Moore most directly reflects which of the following continuities in United States history?
   A. Concerns about economic inequality
   B. Efforts to expand civil rights
   C. Worries about political radicalism
   D. Concerns for individual liberty and self-expression

Questions 13–16 refer to the following quotation.

I am for doing good to the poor, but … I think the best way of doing good to the poor, is not making them easy in poverty, but leading or driving them out of it. I observed … that the more public provisions were made for the poor, the less they provided for themselves, and of course became poorer. And, on the contrary, the less was done for them, the more they did for themselves, and became richer.

—Benjamin Franklin, *Autobiography*

13. In this passage, Franklin takes a position similar to which of the following?
   A. Advocates of a market-driven economy like Adam Smith
   B. Supporters of the First Great Awakening
   C. Opponents of British rule in America
   D. Believers in an extensive social welfare system

14. The idea that Franklin expresses in this passage most directly reflects which of the following continuities in U.S. history?
   A. Concern about a religious foundation for society
   B. Belief in individual self-reliance
   C. A distrust of politicians
   D. A desire to expand Social Security

15. Which of the following helped Franklin justify his position?
A. Strong class distinctions in colonial America
B. British efforts to tax Americans
C. A decline in religious beliefs
D. Social mobility in colonial America

16. Which of the following presidents would be most likely to share Franklin's position?
A. Barack Obama
B. Lyndon Baines Johnson
C. Calvin Coolidge
D. Franklin D. Roosevelt

Questions 17–20 refer to the following cartoon.

UNDER THE THUMB.
The Boss. "Well, what are you going to do about it?"

Thomas Nast, *Harper's Weekly*, June 10, 1871

17. Which of the following *best* expresses Nast's perspective in this cartoon?
A. New York City is benefiting from the leadership of Tammany Hall boss William M. Tweed
B. New Jersey is unfairly exploiting New York City
C. The federal government is oppressing New York City
D. Tammany Hall boss William M. Tweed wields too much power in New York City

18. Urban political machines like Tammany Hall derived most of their support from which of the following?
A. Immigrants and lower-class voters
B. The wealthier classes of society
C. Patronage from the federal government
D. Rural voters from outside the city

19. Urban political machines endured for many years because they provided which of the following?
A. Honest and efficient government
B. Help and services for the poor
C. Rights and privileges unavailable outside the city
D. Opposition to the encroachments of the federal government

20. Nast's journalistic perspective can *best* be compared to which of the following?
A. Progressive muckrakers exposing the business practices of the Standard Oil Company
B. Yellow journalists during the period of the Spanish-American War
C. Reporters investigating President Richard M. Nixon during the Watergate scandal
D. Newspaper coverage of World War II

Questions 21–24 refer to the following quotation.

At last they brought him [John Smith] to Werowocomoco, where was Powhatan, their emperor. Here more than two hundred of those grim courtiers stood wondering at him, as he had been a monster; till Powhatan and his train had put themselves in their greatest braveries. Before a fire upon a seat like a bedstead, he sat covered with a great robe, made of raccoon skins, and all the tails hanging by. On the other hand did sit a young wench of sixteen or eighteen years, and along on each side of the house, two rows of men, and behind them as many women, with all their heads and shoulders painted red, many of their heads bedecked with the white down of birds, but every one with something, and a great chain of white beads about their necks. At his entrance before the king, all the people gave a great shout. … Having feasted him after their best barbarous manner they could, a long consultation was held, but the conclusion was, two great stones were brought before Powhatan; then as many as could laid hands on him, dragged him to them, and thereon laid his head, and being ready with their clubs to beat out his brains, Pocahontas, the king's dearest daughter, when no entreaty could prevail, got his head in her arms, and laid her own upon his to save his from death; whereat the emperor was contented he should live to make him hatchets, and her bells, beads, and copper; for they thought him as well of all occupations as themselves. For the king himself will make his own robes, shoes, bows, arrows, pots; plant, hunt, or do anything so well as the rest.

—John Smith, *The General Historie of Virginia*, 1624

21. Which of the following *best* describes the perspective of Captain John Smith?
A. Powhatan and his followers were a backward people.
B. Europeans unfairly looked down on Indians.
C. Indians lacked the vices of the more technologically advanced Europeans.
D. Indian women were the dominant force in their society.

22. Smith's account makes clear which of the following?
A. The people of Powhatan's Confederacy were divided by strong class distinctions.
B. Powhatan's people made important decisions by consensus.
C. Powhatan enjoyed the same sorts of power as a European king.
D. Powhatan's people lived in poverty.

23. Smith's story *best* illustrates which of the following?
A. Indians were unusually cruel.
B. Europeans were usually deceitful in dealing with Indians.
C. The English were foolish to venture into the American wilderness.
D. Indian-European relations often suffered from misunderstanding and suspicion.

24. In the context of this story, Pocahontas can *best* be compared to which of the following women?
A. Susan B. Anthony
B. Sally Ride
C. Jane Addams
D. Amelia Earhart

Questions 25–28 refer to the following quotation.

Let us not wallow in the valley of despair, I say to you today, my friends.

And so even though we face the difficulties of today and tomorrow, I still have a dream. It is a dream deeply rooted in the American dream.

I have a dream that one day this nation will rise up and live out the true meaning of its creed: "We hold these truths to be self-evident, that all men are created equal."

I have a dream that one day on the red hills of Georgia, the sons of former slaves and the sons of former slave owners will be able to sit down together at the table of brotherhood.

I have a dream that one day even the state of Mississippi, a state sweltering with the heat of injustice, sweltering with the heat of oppression, will be transformed into an oasis of freedom and justice.

I have a dream that my four little children will one day live in a nation where they will not be judged by the color of their skin but by the content of their character.

I have a *dream* today!

> —Martin Luther King, Jr., "I Have a Dream" speech, Lincoln Memorial, August 28, 1963

25. Martin Luther King, Jr., in this passage is calling for which of the following?
A. Economic justice for the poor
B. Renewed commitment to the cold war struggle against communism
C. Equal rights for African Americans
D. Special privileges for African Americans

26. In this passage, King points out which of the following?
A. A contradiction between American ideals and American practice
B. A need to create new American ideals
C. The superiority of African American values
D. The futility of hoping for change

27. At the time of King's speech, which of the following would be likely to oppose King's message?
A. A Midwestern Republican Senator
B. A Southern Democratic Senator
C. A Northern liberal
D. A member of the Southern Christian Leadership Conference (SCLC)

28. In this passage, King is addressing which continuity in U.S. history?
A. The struggle for greater economic opportunity
B. A fear of sectionalism in the United States
C. Concerns about moral decline
D. The struggle for individual liberty

Questions 29–32 refer to the following cartoon.

War Department cartoon, 1943
Credit: U.S. Army

29. The message of the cartoon can be *best* described by which of the following?
  A. The invasion of Europe is endangered by inferior weapons.
  B. The war is being lost.
  C. Too many American supplies have been given to allied nations.
  D. Civilians play a vital role in the war effort.

30. Viewing this cartoon would encourage Americans to do which of the following?
  A. Avoid the wasteful use of metal products
  B. Plant a victory garden
  C. Volunteer for military service
  D. Build fewer ships and construct more tanks

31. This cartoon most directly refers to which aspect of the American war effort during World War II?
  A. American efforts to launch a second front in Europe as early as possible
  B. Military operations in the Mediterranean in 1942 and 1943
  C. American industrial production
  D. Efforts to create new and improved weapons systems

32. The message of the cartoon for Americans can *best* be compared to which of the following?
  A. The environmental movement of the 1970s
  B. The boycotts of British goods in the 1760s and 1770s
  C. Abolitionism in the nineteenth century
  D. Consumerism in the 1950s

Questions 33–36 refer to the following quotation.

That whereas your poor and humble Petition(er) being condemned to die, do humbly beg of you to take it into your Judicious and pious considerations that your poor and humble petitioner knowing my own innocence Blessed be the Lord for it and seeing plainly the wiles and subtlety of my accusers by my self can not but Judge charitably of Others that are going the same way of my self if the Lord steps not mightily in I was confined a whole month upon the same account that I am condemned now for and then cleared by the afflicted persons as some of your honors know and in two days time I was cried out upon by them and have been confined and now am condemned to die the Lord above knows my innocence then and likewise does now at the great day will be known to men and Angels I petition your honors not for my own life for I know I must die and my appointed time is set but the Lord he knows it is that if be possible no more Innocent blood may be shed which undoubtedly cannot be avoided In the way and course you go in I Question not but your honors does to the utmost of your Powers in the discovery and detecting of witchcraft and witches and would not be guilty of Innocent blood but for the world but by my own innocence I know you are in the wrong way the Lord in his infinite mercy direct you in this great work if it be his blessed will that no more innocent blood be shed.

—Mary Easty, petition to her judges, Salem, Massachusetts, 1692

33. Mary Easty in this passage is asking her judges to do which of the following?
   A. Stop condemning innocent persons to death for witchcraft
   B. Redouble their efforts to find the real witches in Salem
   C. Separate church from state in their deliberations
   D. Stop their oppression of women

34. Most historians believe that the Salem Witch Trials were the result of which of the following?
   A. The activities of a coven of witches in Salem
   B. Social tensions in Salem
   C. English efforts to enforce religious conformity in Massachusetts
   D. The ideas of the English political philosopher John Locke

35. The religious convictions of Mary Easty and the rest of Salem were shaped by which of the following?
   A. Roman Catholicism
   B. Anglicanism
   C. Quakerism
   D. Puritanism

36. Writers and intellectuals have often compared the Salem Witch Trials to which of the following?
   A. The mistreatment of slaves in the South
   B. Anti-immigrant rioting in the nineteenth century
   C. Government actions in the Red Scares of the twentieth century
   D. The suppression of strikers in the late nineteenth century

Questions 37–40 refer to the following quotation.

Companions in Arms!! These remains which we have the honor of carrying on our shoulders are those of the valiant heroes who died in the Alamo. Yes, my friends, they preferred to die a thousand times rather than submit themselves to the tyrant's yoke. What a brilliant example! Deserving of being noted in the pages of history. The spirit of liberty appears to be looking out from its elevated throne with its pleasing mien and pointing to us saying: "These are your brothers, Travis, Bowie, Crockett, and others whose valor places them in the rank of my heroes." Yes soldiers and fellow citizens, these are the worthy beings who, by the twists of fate, during the present campaign delivered their bodies to the ferocity of their enemies; who barbarously treated as beasts, were bound by their feet and dragged to this spot, where they were reduced to ashes. The venerable remains of our worthy companions as witnesses, I invite you to declare to the entire world, "Texas shall be free and independent or we shall perish in glorious combat."

—Colonel Juan N. Seguin, Alamo Defenders' Burial Oration,
Columbia Telegraph and Texas Register, April 4, 1837

37. Colonel Juan N. Seguin honored the memory of the defenders of the Alamo because
  A. they fought to the death for their cause.
  B. they defeated an invading Mexican army.
  C. they saved New Orleans from the British.
  D. they saved San Antonio from a large war band of Comanche.

38. Colonel Seguin's oration makes it clear that
  A. he thought the defense of the Alamo was a strategic mistake.
  B. many Tejanos (Texans of Mexican descent) favored Texan independence.
  C. he thought the United States was imposing a tyranny on Texas.
  D. he opposed the movement of American settlers into Texas.

39. The defenders of the Alamo gave their lives for what continuity in American history?
  A. The quest for racial justice
  B. The desire for political liberty
  C. The search for social security
  D. Opposition to gun control

40. A dispute over the boundary of Texas led to which of the following conflicts?
  A. The War of Jenkins' Ear
  B. The Quasi-War with France
  C. The Spanish-American War
  D. The Mexican War

Questions 41–44 refer to the following quotation.

When we stormed the Pentagon, my wife and I we leaped over this fence, see. We were really stoned, I mean I was on acid flying away, which of course is an antirevolutionary drug you know, you can't do a thing on it. I've been on acid ever since I came to Chicago. It's in the form of honey. We got a lab guy doin' his thing. I think he might have got assassinated, I ain't seen him today. Well, so we jumped this here fence, see, we were sneaking through the woods and people were out to get the Pentagon. We had this flag, it said NOW with a big wing on it, I don't know. The right-wingers said there was definitely evidence of Communist conspiracy 'cause of that flag. . . . So we had Uncle Sam hats on, you know, and we jumped over the fence and we're surrounded by marshals, you know, just closin' us in, about 30 marshals around us. And I plant the . . . flag and I said, "I claim this land in the name of free America. We are Mr. and Mrs. America. Mrs. America's pregnant." And we sit down and they're goin' . . . crazy. I mean we got arrested and unarrested like six or seven times.

—Abbie Hoffman, Yippie Workshop Speech, 1968

41. Abbie Hoffman and the Yippies were protesting which of the following?
A. McCarthyism
B. The Great Society
C. Legal acid
D. The Vietnam War

42. Which of the following most directly influenced the ideas of Hoffman and the Yippies?
A. Muckrakers
B. The New Deal
C. The New Left
D. The New Conservatism

43. Which of the following most directly influenced the tactics of Hoffman and the Yippies?
A. The Civil Rights Movement
B. The House Un-American Activities Committee
C. The Tea Party Movement
D. The Social Gospel

44. The counterculture of the 1960s sought which of the following?
A. Economic security for the Baby Boom generation
B. Political and military security against the threat of Communism
C. Greater freedom for personal self-expression
D. A return to traditional religious and family values

Questions 45–48 refer to the following image.

Amos Doolittle, "The Battle of Lexington," 1775

45. The British decision to fire on American militiamen at Lexington, Massachusetts, on April 19, 1775, led to which of the following?
A. A controversial court case
B. A series of uprisings against the British government across the colonies
C. A collapse in the support for the Sons of Liberty
D. An invasion by the French in Canada

46. British military commanders always assumed that they would benefit from which of the following?
A. Command of the sea
B. The support of the other European powers
C. Superior air power
D. The support of a majority of Americans for Parliament's legislation

47. When the Americans rebelled against Great Britain, they benefitted from which of the following?
A. The enormous industrial productivity of the United States
B. Weapons that were technologically superior to those of the British
C. The support of most Native American peoples
D. The great geographical extent of the country

48. Militiamen played a key role during the American Revolutionary War by
A. repeatedly routing British Regulars in battle.
B. waging a spectacular campaign of sabotage and commando raids.
C. controlling populations not under the direct supervision of the British Army.
D. buying out the contracts of Britain's Hessian mercenaries.

Questions 49–52 refer to the following quotation.

I arrived at Wichita the 28th, the raid was postponed until the 29th. I took hatchets with me and we also supplied ourselves with rocks, meeting at the M. E. church, where the W. C. T. U. Convention was being held. I announced to them what we intended doing and asked them to join us. Sister Lucy Wilhoite, Myra McHenry, Miss Lydia Muntz, and Miss Blanch Boies, started for Mahan's wholesale liquor store. Three men were on the watch for us, we asked to go in to hold gospel services as was our intention before destroying this den of vice, for we wanted God to save their souls, and to give us ability and opportunity to destroy this soul damning business. They refused to let us come near the door. I said, "Women, we will have to use our hatchets," with this I threw a rock through the front, then we were all seized, and a call for the police was made. There was of course, a big crowd. Mrs. Myra McHenry was in the hands of a ruffian who shook her almost to pieces. One raised a piece of a gas pipe to strike her, but was prevented from doing so. We were hustled into the hoodlum wagon, and driven through the streets amid the yell, execrations and grimaces of the liquor element.

—Carry A. Nation, *The Use and Need of the Life of Carry A. Nation, Written by Herself*, 1905

49. For which of the following causes was Carry A. Nation famous as an activist?
A. Temperance
B. Women's suffrage
C. Trust busting
D. Muckraking

50. Nation can be compared most directly to which of the following?
A. Tecumseh
B. Abraham Lincoln
C. Rosa Parks
D. Hillary Clinton

51. Nation's cause would attain a great victory with the enactment of
A. the Nineteenth Amendment, giving women the vote.
B. the Sherman Antitrust Act.
C. the Social Security Act.
D. Prohibition.

52. The major event that helped pave the way for the triumph of Nation's cause was
A. the assassination of William McKinley.
B. World War I.
C. The Great Depression.
D. World War II.

Questions 53–55 refer to the following quotation.

Be it enacted by the Senate and House of Representatives of the United States of America in Congress assembled, That there be granted to the several States, for the purposes hereinafter mentioned, an amount of public land, to be apportioned to each State a quantity equal to thirty thousand acres for each senator and representative in Congress to which the States are respectively entitled under the census of eighteen hundred and sixty. . . . *And be it further enacted,* That all moneys derived from the sale of the lands aforesaid . . . and the interest of which shall be inviolably appropriated by each State which may take and claim the benefit of this act, to the endowment, support, and maintenance of at least one college where the leading object shall be, without excluding other scientific and classical studies, and including military tactics, to teach such branches of learning as are related to agriculture and the mechanic arts, in such manner as the legislatures of the States may respectively prescribe, in order to promote the liberal and practical education of the industrial classes in the several pursuits and professions of life.

—Morrill Land-Grant Act, July 2, 1862

53. Which of the following was a major purpose of the Morrill Land-Grant Act?
A. To stimulate the excellence of American literature
B. To provide higher education to women
C. To provide support to farmers and working men
D. To address worries about the low educational level of soldiers in the Union Army

54. The Morrill Land-Grant Act reflected the governing philosophy of which political party?
A. The Federalist Party
B. The Republican Party
C. The Democratic Party
D. The Populist Party

55. The Morrill Land-Grant Act can be compared most directly to which of the following?
A. The Homestead Act
B. The Kansas-Nebraska Act
C. The Pure Food and Drug Act
D. The Agricultural Adjustment Act

Go on to Part B ➜

Part B (Short Answer)

Part B recommended time: 40 minutes

Directions: Answer three questions. You must answer questions 1 and 2, and you can choose to answer either 3 or 4. Carefully read and follow the directions for each question. Some will refer to historical sources. These questions will require you to make use of your historical analytical skills and your familiarity with historical themes. These questions do *not* require you to develop a thesis in your responses.

Question 1 is based on the following passage:

The sixteen years of Jefferson and Madison's rule furnished international tests of popular intelligence upon which Americans could depend. The ocean was the only open field for competition among nations. Americans enjoyed there no natural or artificial advantages over Englishmen, Frenchmen, or Spaniards; indeed, all these countries possessed navies, resources, and experience greater than were to be found in the United States. Yet the Americans developed, in the course of twenty years, a surprising degree of skill in naval affairs. ... Not only were American vessels better in model, faster in sailing, easier and quicker in handling, and more economical in working than the European, but they were also better equipped. The English complained as a grievance that the Americans adopted new and unwarranted devices in naval warfare; that their vessels were heavier and better constructed, and their missiles of unusual shape and improper use. The Americans resorted to expedients that had not been tried before, and excited a mixture of irritation and respect in the English service, until "Yankee smartness" became a national misdemeanor.

—Henry Adams, *History of the United States During the Administrations of Thomas Jefferson and James Madison*, 1889-1891

1. Using the excerpt, answer A, B, and C.
   A. Briefly describe Adams' perspective on the American navy during the War of 1812.
   B. Briefly explain ONE historical event or development that supports Adams' perspective.
   C. Briefly explain ONE historical event or development that would challenge Adams' perspective.

Question 2 is based on the following cartoon:

Clifford Berryman, 1936

2. Using the 1936 image, answer A, B, and C.
   A. Briefly explain the subject matter of the image.
   B. Briefly explain the political point of view of the image.
   C. Briefly explain ONE example of a political perspective opposed to the political point of view of the image.

3. Answer A, B, and C.
   A. Briefly explain ONE example illustrating the transportation situation in the United States before the advent of the railroads.
   B. Briefly explain ONE example of a transportation advantage provided by railroads.
   C. Briefly explain ONE example of how railroads influenced American economic, political, or military history.

4. Answer A, B, and C.
   A. Briefly explain how ONE of the following was important for African Americans.
   Dred Scott v. Sanborn
   Plessy v. Ferguson
   Brown v. Board of Education of Topeka, Kansas
   B. Briefly explain how a SECOND of these options was important for African Americans.
   C. Briefly explain ONE example of how the Supreme Court's attitude to African American civil rights changed over time.

STOP. End of Section I.

Section II

Time: 100 minutes

Part A (Document-Based Question)

Part A recommended time: 60 minutes

Directions: Use the documents to answer the question. You may want to spend up to 15 minutes outlining your response and 40 minutes writing the essay that answers the question.

Be sure to provide a thesis that addresses all elements of the question.

Be sure to support your argument with evidence from at least six of the seven documents.

Be sure to support your argument by recognizing and explaining historical complexity, connecting different kinds of historical evidence in a coherent way.

Be sure to base your analysis of no less than four documents on at least one of the following: the point of view of the author, the purpose of the author, the intended audience of the document, the historical context of the document.

Be sure to support your argument by analyzing historical evidence that comes from outside the documents.

Be sure to connect historical evidence supporting your argument to broader historical events or processes.

Be sure to synthesize all the tasks above into a persuasive history essay.

1. To what extent did the Federalist administrations of George Washington and John Adams promote national unity and advance the authority of the federal government?

Document A

Source: George Washington's First Inaugural Address, April 30, 1789

> *I behold the surest pledges that as on one side no local prejudices or attachments, no separate views or party animosities, will misdirect the comprehensive and equal eye which ought to watch over [Congress] so . . . that the foundation of our national policy will be laid in the pure and immutable principles of private morality, and the preeminence of free government be exemplified by all the attributes which can win the affections of its citizens and command the respect of the world.*

Document B

Source: Virginia Resolutions on the Assumption of State Debts, December 16, 1790

> *The General Assembly of the Commonwealth of Virginia . . . represent [that] . . . in an agricultural country like this . . . to perpetuate a large monied interest, is a measure which . . . must in the course of human events produce . . . the prostration of agriculture at the feet of commerce, or a change in the present form of federal government, fatal to the existence of American liberty.*

Document C

Source: Thomas Jefferson's Opinion on the Constitutionality of the Bank, February 15, 1791

> *I consider the foundation of the Constitution as laid on this ground—that all powers not delegated to the United States, by the Constitution, nor prohibited by it to the states, are reserved to the states, or to the people. To take a single step beyond the boundaries thus specially drawn around the powers of Congress, is to take possession of a boundless field of power.*

Document D

Source: Alexander Hamilton's Opinion on the Constitutionality of the Bank, February 23, 1791

This restrictive interpretation of the word necessary is also contrary to this sound maxim of construction; namely, that the powers contained in a constitution of government, especially those which concern the general administration of the affairs of a country, its finances, trade, defense, etc., ought to be construed liberally in advancement of the public good.

Document E

Source: George Washington's Proclamation on the Whiskey Rebellion, August 7, 1794

Whereas combinations to defeat the execution of the laws laying duties upon spirits distilled within the United States . . . have . . . existed in some of the western parts of Pennsylvania; and whereas the said combinations, proceeding in a manner subversive equally of the just authority of government and the rights of individuals; . . . it is in my judgement necessary under the circumstances to take measures for calling forth the militia in order to suppress the combinations aforesaid, and to cause the laws to be duly executed.

Document F

Source: The Sedition Act, July 14, 1798

That if any person shall write, print, utter, or publish, any false, scandalous, and malicious writing or writings against the government of the United States . . . with the intent to defame the said government, . . . then such person, being convicted before any court of the United States having jurisdiction thereof, shall be punished by a fine not exceeding two thousand dollars, and by imprisonment not exceeding two years.

Document G

Source: Kentucky Resolutions, November 16, 1798

Resolved, that the several States composing the United States of America, are not united on the principle of unlimited submission to their general government; . . . that [the States] retain to themselves the right of judging how far the licentiousness of speech and press may be abridged without lessening their useful freedom . . . therefore [the Sedition Act], which does abridge the freedom of the press, is not law but is altogether void.

Go on to Part B ➜

Part B (Long Essay)

Part B recommended time: 40 minutes

Directions: Answer *one* of the following questions. State a thesis that addresses all aspects of the question. This thesis of one or more sentences must be in the introduction or conclusion.

Make use of your historical analytical skills and familiarity with historical themes as you develop your answer.

Support your thesis and substantiate your essay by citing examples of historical evidence.

Relate the topic of the question to broader historical trends or events.

2. Evaluate the extent to which British imperial policy stimulated a desire for independence in America during the eighteenth century.

3. Evaluate the extent to which Manifest Destiny and the Mexican War affected sectional differences in the United States.

4. Evaluate the extent to which the role of the United States as a world power changed between the Spanish-American War and the Cold War.

STOP. End of Section II.

ANSWERS TO THE DIAGNOSTIC EXAM

Multiple Choice

1. B	15. D	29. D	43. A
2. A	16. C	30. A	44. C
3. C	17. D	31. C	45. B
4. D	18. A	32. B	46. A
5. B	19. B	33. A	47. D
6. D	20. C	34. B	48. C
7. A	21. A	35. D	49. A
8. C	22. B	36. C	50. C
9. C	23. D	37. A	51. D
10. B	24. C	38. B	52. B
11. A	25. C	39. B	53. C
12. D	26. A	40. D	54. B
13. A	27. B	41. D	55. A
14. B	28. D	42. C	

Explanations for the Multiple-Choice Questions

1. B. The cartoon criticizes President Thomas Jefferson's 1807 Embargo Act. Following a British naval attack on the American frigate U.S.S. *Chesapeake* that forced the ship to surrender and resulted in removal of four alleged British deserters, many Americans called for war. President Jefferson wanted to avoid war with Great Britain and believed that economic pressure could force the British to change their policy of interfering with American trade and ships. Jefferson persuaded Congress to pass the Embargo Act, which cut off the export of American goods to Europe. The embargo devastated American trade and was very unpopular with many Americans.

2. A. President Jefferson was responding to British interference with American shipping and trade. The British were at war with Napoleonic France and were trying to cut off trade with French-controlled parts of Europe. The British seized American ships that they thought were trading with their enemy, and also impressed American sailors to serve in their navy. Americans deeply resented these policies, which showed no respect for American rights or the flag of the United States.

3. C. Many Americans responded to Jefferson's Embargo Act by ignoring it and engaging in illicit trade, especially with Canada. Jefferson convinced Congress to pass legislation rigorously enforcing the embargo. This made it even more unpopular.

4. D. The Neutrality Laws of the 1930s most closely resemble Jefferson's policy. These laws also regulated American trade to achieve foreign policy objectives. The authors of the Neutrality Laws hoped to keep the United States out of another war by avoiding the conditions that led to American involvement in World War I. The Neutrality Laws stated that once the president recognized the existence of a foreign war, Americans could not make loans to or sell munitions to warring powers, or take passage on belligerent ships.

5. B. President Ronald Reagan's "Evil Empire" speech reflected an intensification of the cold war in the early 1980s. Concerned about Soviet actions in the 1970s, such as the 1979 invasion of Afghanistan, Reagan intensified an arms buildup begun by President Jimmy Carter. Convinced of the essential criminality of the Soviet Union's totalitarian system, Reagan believed that the United States needed to wage the cold war from a position of strength.

6. D. A Republican would have been most likely to support President Reagan's position. Ronald Reagan was a champion of conservative Republican ideas in both domestic and foreign policy.

7. A. The sentiments of the passage are most closely linked to the passage of the Strategic Defense Initiative (SDI), popularly known as the "Star Wars" program. The SDI was a missile defense program proposed by President Reagan and intended to defend the United States by shooting down incoming nuclear missiles. Many critics thought the plan impractical, expensive, and too provocative to the Soviets. President Reagan believed that it offered a way out of the menace of nuclear annihilation. The SDI program, along with Reagan's military buildup, put more pressure on the Soviet Union.

8. C. The sentiments in the passage best reflect the long-standing concern of American presidents to contain communism. The containment of communism had been a cornerstone of American foreign policy since the late 1940s. President Reagan was determined to halt and reverse what he believed was an expansion of Communist influence in the 1970s.

9. C. In this passage Colleen Moore is writing about flappers. Flappers were young women in the 1920s who cut their hair short in a bobbed style, wore shorter dresses, and often experimented with makeup and cigarettes. The flappers represented the growing freedom of women in the United States in the years after World War I and the passage of the Nineteenth Amendment giving women the vote.

10. B. Many young women of the 1920s expressed their freedom through "mannish" haircuts, new clothing styles, and cosmetics. Rather than focusing on politics and social reform, many young women of this period explored their growing independence through an emphasis on social freedoms and self-expression.

11. A. The new freedoms for women in the 1920s were supported by widespread economic prosperity.

Growing economic security gave many people more leisure time and the opportunity to explore greater personal freedoms. The general prosperity stimulated a vibrant cultural life that opened up new ways for women to express themselves.

12. **D.** The passage by Moore most directly reflects concerns for individual liberty and self-expression. Women in the 1920s took advantage of new opportunities to expand their personal freedoms and express themselves more openly.

13. **A.** In this passage, Benjamin Franklin takes a position similar to advocates of a market-driven economy like Adam Smith. The author of *The Wealth of Nations*, Adam Smith defended the principles of modern capitalism. Like Smith, Franklin believed that individuals operating freely in the market can accomplish more than paternalistic government policies can. Franklin believed that the best way to help the poor is to encourage them to help themselves.

14. **B.** The idea that Franklin expresses in this passage most directly reflects a belief in individual self-reliance. Franklin was himself a self-made man. He articulated the self-reliant ethos that became a long-standing American value.

15. **D.** A high degree of social mobility in colonial America helped Franklin justify his position. Most Americans were farmers, or in the few cities businesspeople or artisans. The ready availability of land and a prospering economy opened up many avenues for social advancement. The absence of a privileged aristocracy, along with plentiful avenues to accumulate wealth, made America a land of opportunity.

16. **C.** The president most likely to share Franklin's position was Calvin Coolidge. A man who rose from modest circumstances to the presidency, Coolidge was a believer in hard work and thrift. He insisted on reducing government expenses and resisted interfering with business and the markets.

17. **D.** In this cartoon, Thomas Nast expresses his conviction that Tammany Hall boss William M. Tweed wields too much power in New York City. As the leader of the Tammany Hall political machine that dominated politics in New York City, Boss Tweed used his power to enrich himself and his cronies. Nast was a longtime opponent of Tweed and helped publicize the political boss's misdeeds through his cartoons. Tweed eventually was sentenced to prison because of his crimes.

18. **A.** Urban political machines like Tammany Hall derived most of their support from immigrants and lower-class voters. When they controlled the political structure of a city, machines prospered through the control of city contracts for improvements like sewers and streets. Machine politicians would pocket kickbacks from contractors eager for the work. This money, in turn, funded a hierarchical machine structure that reached into every neighborhood. Local precinct captains would help turn out the vote on election day, keeping the machine in power.

19. **B.** Urban political machines endured for many years because they provided help and services for the poor. In an era before extensive social services and welfare, urban political machines assisted the poor with gifts of food and shelter, and sometimes jobs. In return, the machines expected these people to vote in their favor.

20. **C.** Nast's journalistic perspective can best be compared to reporters investigating President Richard M. Nixon during the Watergate scandal. Nixon, like Tweed, was accused of misusing his office. As with Nast, reporters like Bob Woodward and Carl Bernstein of the *Washington Post* played a key role in exposing a political leader's wrongdoing.

21. **A.** From the perspective of Captain John Smith, Powhatan and his followers were a backward people. Smith sees the Indians as "barbarous." They wear animal skins and paint, and are cruelly ready to execute Smith. The fact that Powhatan makes his own clothes and tools would also lead Smith to see this as a primitive society.

22. **B.** Smith's account makes clear that Powhatan's people made decisions by consensus. After a feast, Powhatan consults with his people and there is a long discussion about what to do with Smith. When the decision is made to kill Smith, only the determined intervention of Pocahontas saves him.

23. **D.** Smith's story illustrates that Indian-European relations often suffered from misunderstanding and suspicion. Smith did not appreciate the concerns of Powhatan's people, and the Indians clearly were hostile to the newly arrived English. Only Pocahontas in this story attempts to bridge the divide between the Indians and English.

24. **C.** In the context of this story, the peace-making Pocahontas can best be compared to Jane Addams. In addition to being a founder of Hull

House in Chicago and a pioneering social worker, Addams was also a vocal peace activist. Addams was awarded the Nobel Peace Prize in 1931.

25. **C.** Martin Luther King, Jr., in this passage is calling for equal rights for African Americans. King gave his "I Have a Dream" speech during the August 28, 1963, march on Washington, when 250,000 people congregated in the nation's capital to express their support for proposed civil rights legislation.

26. **A.** In this passage, King points out a contradiction between American ideals and American practice caused by racial discrimination. Invoking the Declaration of Independence and Constitution of the United States, King in this speech called for all Americans, regardless of their color, to enjoy the inalienable rights of life, liberty, and the pursuit of happiness.

27. **B.** A Southern Democratic Senator would be likely to oppose the message of King's speech. The Democratic party in the South had dominated the region for over a century, and for the most part strongly supported the Jim Crow laws upholding racial segregation. The civil rights laws of the 1950s and 1960s were passed with the overwhelming support of Northern Democrats and Republicans.

28. **D.** In this passage, King is addressing the struggle for greater individual liberty in American history. As King pointed out in his "I Have a Dream" speech, Americans since the founding of the United States have been striving to achieve greater individual liberty for themselves and their families. King saw the civil rights movement as a continuation of that struggle.

29. **D.** The message of the cartoon can be best described as civilians playing a vital role in the war effort. Americans on the home front during World War II were encouraged to see themselves as active participants in the conflict. Food products like meat and sugar and consumer goods like gasoline were rationed. People raised victory gardens and bought war bonds. Many women and African Americans took jobs in war industries. What people did at home was seen as crucial to supporting the fighting men overseas.

30. **A.** Viewing this cartoon would encourage Americans to avoid the wasteful use of metal products. Metals were vital for the manufacture of weapons and ammunition. Civilians collected scrap metal that could be melted down

and used for the war effort. Many consumer goods made of metal, most notably new automobiles, were not available during the war as industries focused on war production.

31. **C.** The cartoon most directly refers to American industrial production during World War II. The United States became what President Franklin D. Roosevelt called the "Arsenal of Democracy" during the war, producing enough weapons and military supplies to equip Americans fighting a global war, while also providing great quantities of Lend-Lease aid to American allies. American industrial output was a major factor in winning World War II.

32. **B.** The message of the cartoon can be best compared to the boycotts of British goods in the 1760s and 1770s. In both cases, Americans were asked to give up goods and make sacrifices to help further a larger cause. In the 1760s and 1770s Americans gave up British goods to exert pressure on British policymakers. In World War II, Americans made sure most metals went to war production to ensure the defeat of Nazi Germany and Imperial Japan.

33. **A.** Mary Easty in this passage is asking her judges to stop condemning innocent people to death for witchcraft. In 1692, a group of girls in Salem, Massachusetts, began acting as if they were possessed. They claimed that they were bewitched. This led to a witch-hunting hysteria that resulted in 20 executions, including the death of Mary Easty. Eventually, the governor of Massachusetts put an end to the witchcraft prosecutions. Years later, the convictions of the people executed and imprisoned during this hysteria were officially overturned.

34. **B.** Most historians believe that the Salem Witch Trials were the result of social tensions in Salem. Massachusetts was undergoing rapid political and social change in the early 1690s. Most of those accused of being witches came from more prosperous families associated with business and trade, while the accusers came from less well-off farming families. Fears about witchcraft probably also reflected anxieties about the shifting social and economic status of people in Salem.

35. **D.** The religious convictions of Mary Easty and the rest of Salem were shaped by Puritanism. Massachusetts was settled in the 1630s by Calvinist Puritans escaping the religious domination of the Anglican Church in England. They

saw their new colony as an opportunity to create a truly godly community. Initially only members of Puritan congregations could vote. Concern that people were falling away from strict Puritan belief probably played a part in the Salem witch hysteria.

36. C. Writers and intellectuals have often compared the Salem Witch Trials to government actions in the Red Scares of the twentieth century. The investigations of Senator Joseph McCarthy in the early 1950s were often compared to witch hunts. Arthur Miller's play about the events in Salem, *The Crucible* (1953), was a critique of McCarthyism.

37. A. Colonel Juan N. Seguin honored the memory of the defenders of the Alamo because they had died for their cause. Seguin had served with Lieutenant Colonel William B. Travis at the Alamo. Seguin was sent with a message asking for help and so was not present when the Alamo garrison was overwhelmed on March 6, 1836.

38. B. Colonel Seguin's oration makes it clear that many Tejanos favored Texan independence. Seguin was a native of San Antonio and had been active in politics. He favored a federal structure for Mexico and opposed the centralizing policies of Mexican President Antonio Lopez de Santa Anna. Federalist Tejanos joined with American settlers to resist the Mexican government. After the Battle of the Alamo, Seguin organized a company of Tejano cavalry that helped protect the Texan army of Sam Houston and fought at the Battle of San Jacinto on April 21, 1836, which secured Texan independence.

39. B. The defenders of the Alamo gave their lives for the desire for political liberty. They were opposed to the efforts of Mexican President Antonio Lopez de Santa Anna to impose a stronger central government on the country. They wanted a return to the Mexican Constitution of 1824, which granted more powers to the Mexican states.

40. D. A dispute over the boundary of Texas led to the Mexican War. The Mexican government refused to recognize Texan independence and was deeply angered when the United States annexed Texas as a state in 1845. The Texans claimed that their southern boundary was the Rio Grande river; Mexico vehemently disputed this. In early 1846, President James K. Polk ordered an American army, under General Zachary Taylor, to the Rio Grande. Mexican troops attacked a detachment of American dragoons on April 25, 1846. The United States responded with a declaration of war.

41. D. Abbie Hoffman and the Yippies were protesting the Vietnam War. Hoffman helped lead the October 21, 1967, March on the Pentagon that drew some 50,000 protesters. Hoffman's actions there were described in Norman Mailer's book *The Armies of the Night* (1968). In August 1968, Hoffman and his Youth International Party (the Yippies) played a prominent role in protests at the Democratic National Convention. When police attacked protesters, riots broke out. Hoffman was one of seven protest leaders, known collectively as the Chicago Seven, who were subsequently indicted for conspiracy and incitement to riot. Hoffman's conviction for incitement to riot was later overturned.

42. C. The New Left most directly influenced the ideas of Hoffman and the Yippies. Central to the formation of the New Left in the United States was the Students for a Democratic Society (SDS) movement organized in 1962. The SDS rejected the old-style authoritarian leftism of the Communist Party. In the 1962 Port Huron Statement, the SDS called for "participatory democracy" that would build a broad social movement for change. Over time, the New Left in the United States would grow increasingly receptive to the countercultural ideals of personal self-expression.

43. A. The Civil Rights Movement most directly influenced the tactics of Hoffman and the Yippies. Civil rights protesters directly challenged racial discrimination by taking nonviolent actions, such as staging sit-ins at segregated drugstore lunch counters. Hoffman and the Yippies engaged in protest theater, such as tossing fake money from a balcony onto the floor of the New York Stock Exchange. What distinguished the Yippies from other protesters was their offbeat sense of humor, which involved such actions as nominating a pig for president in 1968.

44. C. The counterculture of the 1960s sought greater freedom for personal self-expression. Fueled by the great number of young people resulting from the Baby Boom and the disillusionment with authority born of the Civil Rights Movement and the Vietnam War, the counterculture of the 1960s emphasized antiestablishment attitudes. People influenced by the counterculture looked for new ways to live a fulfilling life. Famously, the "hippies" rejected conventional middle class mores, growing their hair long, dressing differently, and experimenting with drugs to expand their consciousness. Books that influenced the counterculture were Jack Kerouac's *On the Road* (1957) and Ken Kesey's *One Flew Over the Cuckoo's Nest* (1962).

45. B. The British decision to fire on American militiamen on April 19, 1775, led to a series of uprisings against the British government across the colonies. As word of the fighting at Lexington and Concord spread across the colonies, British authority collapsed, and American rebels took control of governments, forcing out royal officials. The Second Continental Congress convened in Philadelphia in May and in June appointed George Washington commander of the newly created Continental Army.

46. A. British commanders always assumed that they would benefit from command of the sea. The British Navy was the most powerful in the world. Command of the sea gave the British the strategic flexibility to range up and down the Atlantic coast of the colonies. Until near the end of the war, this was a great advantage. The successful intervention of a French fleet at the Battle of the Chesapeake on September 5, 1781, made possible the isolation and defeat of Lord Charles Cornwallis's British Army at the Battle of Yorktown. Cornwallis's surrender on October 19, 1781, was decisive in convincing the British government to end the war.

47. D. When the Americans rebelled against Great Britain, they benefitted from the great geographical extent of the country. By European standards, the American colonies covered an enormous territory. Much of it was underdeveloped or wilderness. The British did not have the troops to cover all this ground. The British could control some major cities, but they often were isolated and defeated when they ventured into the countryside. A good example of this is the isolation and defeat of General John Burgoyne's army at Saratoga on October 17, 1777.

48. C. Militiamen played a key role during the American Revolutionary War by controlling populations not under the direct supervision of the British Army. While the battlefield performance of militias could be spotty, the militias were very important in maintaining the authority of the American government wherever the British were not present, which meant most of the country. The militias intimidated Loyalists and ensured support for American policies.

49. A. Carry A. Nation was famous as an activist for temperance. After her first husband died of alcoholism, she became a supporter of temperance. Eventually, her methods became more direct and violent as she attacked saloons and their stocks of liquor with rocks and her trademark hatchet.

50. C. Nation can be compared most directly to Rosa Parks. They both took direct action to further their beliefs. While Parks did not act violently, as Nation did, she did sit in the whites-only section of a bus in Montgomery, Alabama, sparking a famous civil rights struggle.

51. D. Nation's cause would attain a great victory with the enactment of Prohibition. A resolution calling for a constitutional amendment prohibiting intoxicating liquor in the United States passed Congress in December 1917 and was ratified by the states in January 1919. Congress passed the Volstead Act in October 1919, which provided an enforcement mechanism for the new amendment. The Eighteenth Amendment went into effect in January 1920.

52. B. The major event that helped pave the way for the triumph of Nation's cause was World War I. The use of grain for alcoholic beverages was restricted by Congress as a war measure because the grain was needed for food. Thus, the consumption of intoxicating liquors was reduced through government action during the war. The spirit of wartime idealism and self-sacrifice also helped spur support for the passage of the Eighteenth Amendment.

53. C. A desire to provide support to farmers and working men was a major purpose of the Morrill Land-Grant Act. The act was the culmination of an effort to give practical assistance to farmers and various types of workers by giving them the most advanced technical education. Most land-grant universities sponsored programs in agriculture and engineering. Examples include Cornell University, Iowa State University, and the Massachusetts Institute of Technology.

54. B. The Morrill Land-Grant Act reflected the governing philosophy of the Republican Party. The Republican Party, with its slogan of "free labor, free land, and free men," not only opposed the extension of slavery but also inherited the Whig Party's willingness to use the government to stimulate economic opportunities. An earlier version of the Morrill Act was vetoed by Democratic President James Buchanan. In the absence of many Southern Democrats during the Civil War, the Republican-dominated Congress passed the Morrill Act. President Abraham Lincoln willingly signed the measure into law.

55. **A.** The Morrill Land-Grant Act can be compared most directly to the Homestead Act.

Republicans supported the Homestead Act, which gave 160 acres of land in the west to Americans willing to settle on it and work it for five years as a way of offering opportunity to "free men." Southern Democrats opposed the Homestead Act because they feared it would block the expansion of slavery. Like the Morrill Act, an early version of the Homestead Act was vetoed by Democratic President James Buchanan. Also like the Morrill Act, the Homestead Act was passed in 1862 and signed into law by President Abraham Lincoln.

Explanations for the Short-Answer Questions

1. **A.** Adams is arguing that during the early nineteenth century and during the War of 1812 the United States Navy distinguished itself. Despite a relative lack of resources and experience, the American navy compared very favorably to its larger competitors. American frigates were more heavily constructed and better armed than comparable ships in European navies. Americans were willing to innovate in naval and military technology. This earned them the grudging respect of their English opponents in the War of 1812. Adams sees this as a sign of "popular intelligence" in the American people.
B. During the War of 1812, American warships like the USS *Constitution*, "Old Ironsides," won a number of famous ship-to-ship battles with British warships. Daring American naval captains like Stephen Decatur became national heroes. American naval forces on the Great Lakes won decisive victories over their British competitors. A fleet commanded by Oliver Hazard Perry won the Battle of Lake Erie on September 10, 1813. Perry reported his victory with the memorable words, "We have met the enemy and they are ours." A fleet commanded by Thomas Macdonough won the Battle of Lake Champlain on September 11, 1814, helping turn back a British invasion of the United States from Canada.
C. Though American naval vessels performed well in individual encounters, the small American navy could not prevail against the numerical superiority of the British navy. By the end of the War of 1812, most of the surviving American warships were blockaded in ports. The

British navy was able to land armies that attacked and burned Washington in 1814, and that threatened New Orleans in late 1814 and early 1815.

2. **A.** This cartoon concerns the "Alphabet Soup" of agencies that emerged during President Franklin Roosevelt's New Deal. Early in the New Deal, Roosevelt and Congress launched a number of new programs and agencies to promote economic recovery from the Great Depression and provide relief to jobless Americans. Pictured in the cartoon are the AAA, the Agricultural Adjustment Administration, which attempted to raise farm prices by paying farmers to take land out of production, the PWA, the Public Works Administration, which launched a series of public works to provide jobs, and the WPA, the Works Progress Administration, which directly hired unemployed workers and set them to work on projects ranging from construction to the creation of murals and plays.
B. The cartoon is sympathetic to Roosevelt and the New Deal, showing the various "Alphabet Soup" agencies as happy children dancing around a smiling father-figure president. The early New Deal was popular, leading to Roosevelt's Democratic Party winning a victory in the 1934 Congressional elections. Despite this, there were challenges to the New Deal coming from both the right and left in American politics. In 1935, the Supreme Court struck down as unconstitutional the National Recovery Administration (NRA) which had attempted to get industries to cooperate in setting standards on such things as prices and

wages. Roosevelt responded with the Second New Deal, and the passage of such laws as the Social Security Act (1935) which set up a system to provide pensions to the elderly, and the National Labor Relations Act (1935) which made it easier for workers to organize unions.

C. There were a number of critics of the New Deal. The Supreme Court invalidated some of the legislation of the First New Deal. Only after a bruising political battle in Roosevelt's second term, during which he lost a lot of political support attempting to pass legislation that would have "packed" the Court with his supporters, did the Supreme Court begin upholding New Deal legislation. Many conservatives opposed the New Deal. Former Democratic New York governor Al Smith was a member of the Liberty League, which believed that the New Deal undermined property rights. From the left, Louisiana Senator Huey Long did not believe that the New Deal was going far enough. He promoted a "Share the Wealth" plan that would give every American a home and a $2500 income. The money for this would come from confiscating wealth from millionaires.

3. A. Before railroads, transportation in the United States was often very difficult. Roads were poor and often badly maintained. Some roads, like the Lancaster Turnpike, completed in Pennsylvania in the 1790s, were exceptions to this rule and economically important. Opposition to federal road construction on state's rights constitutional grounds limited road-building. The best way to travel and transport goods was by water, by sea along the coast and by river in the interior. The Ohio and Mississippi Rivers were major transportation routes, especially after the invention of the steamboat, which allowed movement both up and down stream. By 1860, over a thousand steamboats were operating in the Mississippi River Valley. Canals offered a way to bring waterways to areas not blessed with a convenient river. New York Governor DeWitt Clinton's Erie Canal, completed in 1825, connected the Hudson River and New York City to the Great Lakes. This inaugurated a canal-building craze. By 1840, over 3,300 miles of canals had been constructed.

B. The advantage of railroads was that they were cheaper to build than canals, and tracks could be laid in almost any type of terrain.

The first railroad was constructed in 1828, and by the 1830s railroads were spreading rapidly. In the next two decades the gauges for tracks were standardized, making possible a national railway network. Safety devices improved. In 1859, the Pullman sleeper car appeared, providing a new level of comfort for travelers. Increasingly speedy, safe, and economical, by the 1850s, railroads were becoming the dominant transportation mode in the United States.

C. Before 1840, most Midwestern grain was shipped south down the Mississippi River to the port of New Orleans. With the rise of a thriving railroad network in the Northeast and Northwest, Midwestern grain was increasingly shipped to the big cities of the east. The west and east became increasingly economically interdependent. The growing economic ties between west and east would prove decisive in the Civil War. American expansionists dreamed of a railroad connection between the settled areas of the United States and the Pacific coast. Senator Stephen Douglas of Illinois wanted a transcontinental railroad to start west from Chicago. This northern transcontinental route would have to run through the Kansas and Nebraska Territories. Kansas and Nebraska would have to be organized politically to facilitate railroad construction. The only way that Douglas could win Southern votes for this in the Senate was to overturn the Missouri Compromise, which banned slavery in these territories. Douglas's 1854 Kansas-Nebraska Act provided for the settlers in Kansas and Nebraska to decide the issue of slavery in their territories through popular sovereignty. The Kansas-Nebraska Act outraged many people in the North, who saw it as potentially allowing slavery into what should have been free territory. Popular sovereignty in Kansas devolved into violence, as proslavery and antislavery settlers fought each other. Douglas's scheme to promote a railroad helped bring on the Civil War. During the Civil War, railroads were often vital lines of communication and supply. Occasionally, troops were shipped from one front to another by railroad. As the war went on, the Northern advantage in miles of railroad became increasingly important as the growing industrial might of the North was mobilized for the Union war effort. Railroads became strategic targets during the war. Atlanta, Georgia, was vital to the South as an industrial center and railroad hub. This made it a key target for Union General William Tecumseh Sherman in 1864. When Sherman left Atlanta for his famous march to the sea, his troops made sure to destroy railroad tracks along the way. The Confederacy lacked the industrial capacity to replace these tracks.

4. **A, B.** Dred Scott was a slave in Missouri whose masters had taken him to live in the free state of Illinois and the Wisconsin Territory for several years. Scott went to court to ask for his freedom, arguing that residence in free territory had made him free. In 1857, the Supreme Court in *Dred Scott v. Sanborn* ruled that, as a black slave, Scott could not be a citizen and therefore could not sue in the courts. The Court also ruled that, since Scott was the property of his masters, residence in a free state did not make him free; private property could not be taken from citizens without due process. This reasoning led the Court to rule the Missouri Compromise unconstitutional, opening up the possibility of slaveholders freely taking their slaves anywhere in the country. The Dred Scott decision outraged many Northerners and intensified sectional differences in the 1850s. Following the end of Reconstruction in 1877, Southern states began to institutionalize discrimination against African Americans. Measures such as poll taxes and literacy laws were enacted to keep African Americans from voting. Jim Crow laws segregated whites and blacks in public and private facilities. The 1896 Supreme Court decision in *Plessy v. Ferguson* responded to a challenge against segregation in railroad accommodations in Louisiana. The Court held that segregation was lawful as long as the segregated accommodations were "separate but equal." This decision helped institutionalize segregation in the South; the stipulation that segregated facilities should be equal was ignored. Overturning *Plessy v. Ferguson* became a longstanding goal of the National Association for the Advancement of Colored People (NAACP). The NAACP and its lead lawyer, Thurgood Marshall, took the case of Oliver Brown to the Supreme Court. Brown was unhappy that his daughter could not attend a local school in Topeka, Kansas,

but was instead bussed to an all-black school. In 1954, the Supreme Court in *Brown v. Board of Education of Topeka, Kansas* unanimously ruled that segregated schools were "inherently unequal" and thus unconstitutional. This effectively overruled *Plessy v. Ferguson* and overturned the legal foundations of racial segregation in the United States.

C. Over time the attitude of the Supreme Court moved from hostility to African American rights to support for the African American civil rights movement. In *Dred Scott v. Sanborn*, Chief Justice Roger Taney and the majority of the Court were Southerners. Instead of making a narrow, technical ruling in the case, they intentionally attempted to mount a constitutional defense of slavery. Though Taney had freed his own slaves, he argued that blacks were so inferior to whites they had no claim to the rights of citizens. The Supreme Court, in the aftermath of Reconstruction, helped Southerners establish the Jim Crow regime in the South. In the 1883 *Civil Rights Cases*, the Court struck down the 1875 Civil Rights Act that had given African Americans equal access to accommodations like hotels and restaurants. The Court argued that African Americans were only accorded Fourteenth Amendment protections against discrimination in public facilities; privately owned businesses could constitutionally discriminate in choosing their customers. *Plessy v. Ferguson* continued the process of narrowing the social gains made by African Americans during Reconstruction by offering a constitutional defense of segregation. For years the NAACP chipped away at *Plessy v. Ferguson* in the courts. A victory came in 1944, when in *Smith v. Allwright* the Supreme Court declared all-white political primaries unconstitutional. This was an opening in the effort to end segregation. Earl Warren, who became Chief Justice in 1953, after being nominated by President Dwight Eisenhower, was determined to take a stand against legalized discrimination. He played a leading role in organizing a unanimous decision in *Brown v. Board of Education*. From this point on, the Supreme Court was a supporter of African American civil rights. Fittingly, Thurgood Marshall, who argued the *Brown* case, joined the Supreme Court in 1967, becoming the first African American Supreme Court Justice.

Explanation for the Document-Based Question

The thesis should focus on a historical analytical skill, in this case **Identifying cause and effect**. Support your thesis with evidence drawn from at least six of the seven documents. Analyze more fully at least four of the documents, discussing one or more of the following: the point of view of the author, the purpose of the author, the intended audience of the document, the historical context of the document. As you construct your argument, make connections between the documents. Note differences and agreements between them that help you strengthen your analysis. Be sure to bring in outside knowledge that you can relate to your analysis of the documents and that contributes to your argument. Simply dropping names is not enough. Demonstrate an understanding of the wider context of the subject of the question. With this question such context could include constitutional debates over the limits of federal power, the rise of American nationalism, and the development of the American two-party political system.

Although the Federalists intended to unify the nation and strengthen the federal government, their political and economic policies split the nation into rival partisan factions. Students might note that debates over ratification of the Constitution set the stage for the emergence of political parties by the end of the 1790s. They could briefly discuss the supporters and opponents of ratification, the anti-Federalists, and *The Federalist Papers,* particularly *The Federalist,* no. 10. Students should examine the ideological conflict between loose and strict interpretations of the Constitution, as well as federal versus state authority. They should identify the leading Federalists (Washington, Adams, Hamilton) and Republicans (Jefferson, Madison, Randolph). Document A indicates Washington's desire that Congress may set policy without party division. Students may note, however, that friction stemmed from Hamilton's financial program. They should examine his intention to establish a sound financial foundation for the new nation by creating a national bank, addressing the public debt (Assumption Act, Funding Bill), and raising revenue (excise taxes, tariffs). While Hamilton's program strengthened the federal government, it fostered dissent among the Republicans. Document B reflects Virginia's opposition to the assumption of state debts. Students will note that the conflict over the Bank of the United States in Documents C and D reflects Jefferson and Hamilton's interpretations of the "necessary and proper clause" of the Constitution. Students may also contrast the Republican view of an agricultural economy in Document B, with Federalist support for the Tariff of 1789 and Hamilton's Report on Manufactures. They may note that opposition to the excise tax led to the Whiskey Rebellion. In Document E, Washington states his intention to enforce federal law and implement powers granted under the Constitution. Washington demonstrated federal authority by calling forth the militias from three states to suppress the rebellion. Some students may refer to Shays' Rebellion. Students may begin a discussion of diplomatic policy with Washington's Neutrality Proclamation (1793) and Neutrality Act (1794). They may explain how the neutrality policy survived the challenge of "Citizen Genet." However, Great Britain challenged the policy by seizing American ships. Students should discuss partisan perceptions of Jay's Treaty. They may note that it achieved some of its nationalistic goals regarding the Northwest Territory and promoting commerce with Great Britain. However, they should also address Republican views of its shortcomings. Some students may address Pinckney's Treaty. Students should discuss Washington's views on parties in his Farewell Address. They will note how the election of 1796 yielded a Federalist president (Adams) and a Republican vice president (Jefferson). Students will note how the strife in the executive office reflected party differences in the United States. A discussion of the undeclared naval war with France will reveal the pro-British views of Federalists and pro-French sympathies of the Republicans. Students will discuss how opposing perceptions of the war and the XYZ Affair led to the Alien and Sedition Acts of 1798 (Document F). Students will observe how Madison and Jefferson penned the Virginia and Kentucky Resolutions (Document G), which asserted the theory of nullification. They might conclude how the problems of the Adams's administration led to the election of Jefferson in 1800.

Explanations for the Long Essay Questions

2. The student can begin this essay with a discussion of the French and Indian War, which drove the French off the North American continent, and gave Great Britain control of the eastern seaboard, from Canada to Florida. The defeat of the French vastly improved the security of the American colonists. Neither the western Native Americans nor the Spanish in Louisiana posed much of a threat to them. They no longer needed significant British military protection. Ironically, this was just what the British wanted to give them. The French and Indian War had been the American phase of the Seven Years War, a genuine world war that saw fighting from America to Europe to India. The war had been enormously expensive, and Britain had accumulated an enormous debt that had to be paid down. At the same time, members of the British government wanted to reorganize and rationalize their expanded empire. It seemed reasonable to these men that the Americans help pay for a war that had given them such benefits. The first move in this new policy on the part of the British government came with the 1765 Quartering and Stamp Acts. The Quartering Act required the Americans to provide quarters and support for garrisons the Americans did not feel they needed. The Stamp Act imposed a tax on various transactions and paper products. The Stamp Act outraged Americans because it imposed a tax on them without representation. During the long period of "salutary neglect" which had run from the seventeenth century to the 1760s, the British government had allowed the colonists to largely govern themselves. All colonies had elected legislatures that voted in any needed taxes. Americans conceded the right of the British government to regulate trade, but drew the line at "internal" taxes. In response to the Stamp Act, groups such as the Sons of Liberty appeared to oppose the law. A meeting of representatives from nine colonies at the Stamp Act Congress demonstrated growing colonial unity. In the face of American resistance, Parliament repealed the Stamp Act, but passed the Declaratory Act which asserted Parliament's power to legislate for the colonies. In 1767, Parliament passed the Townshend Acts. These all represented "external" taxes, putting duties on such American imports as glass, paper, and tea. Violators of the acts could be tried in British admiralty courts. Americans were not favorably impressed by these "external" taxes. They were not for regulating commerce, but were clearly intended to raise revenue without American consent. In addition, trying Americans in naval courts and not before juries of their peers was seen as an act of tyranny. Americans resisted the taxes with nonimportation drives. This decreased the amount of American imports from Britain, hurting British merchants. In 1770, all the taxes were dropped but that on tea. That same year a scuffle between a mob of Americans and some British soldiers led to the Boston Massacre. Though the soldiers were acquitted of murder charges, this further poisoned American attitudes toward the British military. In 1773, in an ill-advised attempt to assist the ailing East India Company, the British government gave the East India Company a monopoly on tea sales in America. The sweetener for Americans was that the East India Company tea would be cheaper. This did not assuage the Americans, who saw this as a plot to reconcile them to the tea tax. They resented the imposition of a monopoly on them. Committees of Correspondence organized resistance. In Boston, a group of Americans dressed as Native Americans dumped East India Company tea into the harbor. The outraged British government imposed the "Intolerable Acts," closing the port of Boston until the tea was paid for, giving more power to the royal governor, and limiting the freedom of town meetings. The unrelated Quebec Act angered Americans by giving privileges to the French Catholics in Canada, and seemingly cutting off American expansion to the west. The First Continental Congress denounced the "Intolerable Acts." Much of Massachusetts was defying the authority of the royal governor in Boston. Both sides made preparations for war. On April 19, 1775, British troops attempting to capture an American arsenal exchanged shots with militia, beginning the American Revolutionary War. War came because the British authorities insisted on changing the way that they governed the colonies, and because the Americans insisted on defending what they believed were their traditional rights.

3. The student could begin by briefly looking at the way sectional differences and concerns over slavery had shaped American politics since the Missouri Compromise of 1820. The annexation of Texas was held up for years because many Northern politicians did not want to add to the power of the slave states. President John Tyler finally had to resort to the expedient of joint resolutions in Congress to bring Texas into the Union in 1845. A discussion of Manifest Destiny could reference the Louisiana Purchase of 1803, which gave the United States a claim to territories touching on the Pacific Ocean. The journalist John O'Sullivan coined the term "Manifest Destiny" in an 1845 editorial promoting the annexation of more territory. O'Sullivan's call for the United States to overspread the North American continent captured a popular mood supporting American expansionism. James K. Polk campaigned for the presidency in 1844 as an expansionist, calling for the annexation of Texas as well as for all of Oregon in a territorial dispute with the British. His campaign caught the spirit of Manifest Destiny, and his victory was a mandate for American expansion. Polk compromised with the British over Oregon, but a boundary dispute with Mexico led to war. Militarily the conflict was a triumph for the United States, and in the peace the United States gained California and much of the southwest, increasing the size of the United States by one third. Yet Polk's great achievement also sowed the seeds of disaster. The question of whether slavery would be allowed in the new territories soon arose and helped polarize American politics in the crucial decade of the 1850s. Victory in the Mexican war helped set the stage for the Civil War. Even as the war was in its early stages, in August 1846, a Democratic representative from Pennsylvania named David Wilmot submitted an amendment to an appropriations bill barring slavery from any territory taken from Mexico. The Wilmot Resolution passed the House of Representative twice, and was killed in the Senate. It infuriated Southerners and set the stage for debate in the election of 1848. With Polk declining to run for a second term, the Democrats nominated Lewis Cass of Michigan. Cass first popularized the theory of "popular sovereignty" in the territories. This took the slavery issue

out of the halls of Congress, and left the question to be decided by the people of the territories. For many, this seemed a reasonable compromise, and popular sovereignty would later be taken up by Stephen Douglas in the 1850s. The Whigs fell back on an old formula in 1848, and nominated Zachary Taylor, a popular commander in the Mexican War, who had no overt political philosophy. They kept their platform as vague as possible. A third force in the election was the Free Soil Party, composed of Northern antislavery men. Some were abolitionists who opposed slavery as a moral issue. Others believed that slavery hurt the prospects of free labor. The Free-Soilers nominated Martin Van Buren for president. Their slogan of "Free soil, free speech, free labor, and free men" would reverberate over the next decade. Taylor's heroic appeal won him the election. The Free-Soilers won almost 300,000 votes and may have cost Cass the electoral votes in New York and the election. By the time Taylor took office, the discovery of gold had transformed California. Tens of thousands of people poured into the territory. In 1849, the Californians asked for admission to the Union as a free state. This set off a political crisis. Southerners opposed this rapid move to statehood, and the prospect of another free state crystallized their fears over abolitionist agitation and the Underground Railroad. President Taylor supported the admission of California and asked that discussions of slavery be avoided. This did not have any effect other than angering Southerners. Some Southern "fire-eaters" even talked of secession. Stepping in to avert this danger to the Union was the "Great Pacificator" Henry Clay. Seventy-three years of age and a veteran engineer of compromises since that of 1820, Clay proposed a series of measures designed to offer something to everyone. California would be admitted as a free state. The New Mexico Territory would be organized without reference to slavery. The boundary between Texas and New Mexico would be adjusted. The United States would assume the debt of the Republic of Texas. Slavery would be left alone in the District of Columbia. The slave trade would be banned in the District of Columbia. A fugitive slave law would be enacted. Congress would disavow any authority to interfere with the interstate slave trade. Clay made an impassioned speech on behalf of his compromise. Two other legislative giants also weighed in. The dying John C. Calhoun argued that the compromise did not go far enough in protecting the South. Daniel Webster made one of his most eloquent speeches supporting the compromise. Younger men spoke up. William Seward opposed the compromise because of its provisions protecting slavery. Stephen Douglas played a crucial role lining up votes behind the compromise. The prospects for the compromise improved when President Taylor died suddenly on July 9, 1850. His successor, Millard Fillmore, was a strong supporter of Clay's program. In September the compromise was passed in a series of five bills, with Clay and Douglas putting together different combinations of votes to pass each. In the short run, the Compromise of 1850 saved the Union and seemed to settle sectional differences. But tensions remained strong under surface comity. The Fugitive Slave Law, which opened the North to slave-hunters and which fined and jailed Northerners who helped fugitive slaves, was very unpopular in the North, and fueled antislavery sentiment. The political landscape would shift in the 1850s as the Whig Party disappeared, eventually to be replaced by the antislavery Republican Party. When Stephen Douglas passed his Kansas-Nebraska Act in 1854, the passions raised by the Mexican war would reemerge, and the United States would be set on a course to Civil War.

4. Before the Spanish American War, the United States did not play a prominent role as a great power, despite its burgeoning economic strength. Beginning in the 1880s, the United States did begin building up a modern navy, leading to an interest in

coaling stations in places like Pearl Harbor in Hawaii and Pago Pago in Samoa. Despite this, as late as 1893, President Grover Cleveland would refuse an opportunity to annex the Hawaiian Islands. The Spanish American War of 1898 ushered the United States onto the world stage. After rapidly defeating the obsolescent naval forces of Spain, the United States became an imperial power. Though Cuba, the occasion of the war with Spain, would be given a measure of independence, the United States retained control of Puerto Rico, Guam, and the Philippines. The Philippines, with the magnificent harbor at Manila Bay, were seen as a way station to China, which many Americans hoped would become a major market for American goods. This interest in China led the United States in 1900 to join in the suppression of the antiforeigner Boxer Rebellion. The United States, through its "Open Door" notes, attempted to keep the Chinese market from being closed by colonial powers. This would be the keystone of American foreign policy in China through World War II. In the early twentieth century the United States exerted its power in the western hemisphere, building the Panama Canal and, through President Theodore Roosevelt's corollary to the Monroe Doctrine asserting a right to police the small republics of the Caribbean and Central America. American troops would be repeatedly sent to restore order in countries like Haiti and Nicaragua through the early 1930s. Under Theodore Roosevelt, the United States was accepted into the club of great powers. Roosevelt won a Nobel Peace Prize for helping negotiate an end to the Russo-Japanese War of 1904-1906, and American delegates took part in the 1906 Algeciras Conference. The United States attempted to remain neutral during World War I, while maintaining a profitable trading relationship with Britain and France. Germany's unrestricted submarine campaign brought the United States into the war in 1917. American troops helped turn the tide against Germany on the Western Front. President Woodrow Wilson's Fourteen Points became, for many people around the world, a blueprint for a better postwar world. For a time, as the Treaty of Versailles was being negotiated at Paris in 1919, Woodrow Wilson seemed to be the most influential figure in the world. This power evaporated quickly. Wilson did not prevent the imposition of harsh peace terms on the Germans. His League of Nations failed to win ratification in the United States Senate. The United States did not become isolationist in the 1920s. President Warren Harding hosted the 1921–1922 Washington Disarmament Conference. The 1924 Dawes Plan helped stabilize German and European finances. The Great Depression turned the United States inward. President Hoover did little to oppose Japanese aggression in Manchuria in 1931. President Franklin Roosevelt "torpedoed" the London Economic Conference, attempting to stabilize the international economy so he could focus on fighting the Depression in the United States. Both Hoover and Roosevelt improved relations with Latin America through the "Good Neighbor" policy, which rejected the role of the United States as "policeman" of the Western Hemisphere. The mid-1930s saw the height of American isolationism with the passage of the 1935, 1936, and 1937 Neutrality Laws, essentially designed to prevent another World War I by forbidding Americans to trade with warring countries or travel on belligerent ships. During the late 1930s, President Roosevelt became increasingly alarmed at the aggressions of Japan, Italy, and Germany. Following the outbreak of World War II in 1939, he took steps to allow trade with Britain and France, and began a major rearming program. This military buildup intensified after the defeat of France in 1940. Roosevelt assisted Britain with the Destroyers for Bases Deal, giving Britain old American destroyers in exchange for leases on British bases in the Western Hemisphere. In 1941, Roosevelt persuaded Congress to pass the Lend-Lease Act, allowing him to give military supplies to Britain and other countries fighting Germany. The United States was waging an undeclared naval war on the Atlantic Ocean by late 1941, as the United States Navy helped protect British convoys from German submarines. In the Pacific, Japan launched an all-out war on China in 1937. Following the defeat of France in 1940, the Japanese moved into French Indochina. In 1941, the Japanese established more definite control over Indochina. The United States finally halted its trade in metals and oil with Japan, and demanded that the Japanese end the war in China. The Japanese preferred to fight, hoping to conquer the resources they needed in the British and Dutch colonies of Malaysia and Indonesia. To do this safely, they had to neutralize the American fleet at Pearl Harbor. The December 7, 1941 Japanese attack on Pearl Harbor brought the United States into the Second World War. American military and industrial power proved crucial in defeating Japan and Germany. American policymakers, remembering the failure of Woodrow Wilson at the end of World War I, were determined that the United States would play a constructive role in the postwar world. The United States hosted the new United Nations. The United States played a key role in the 1944 Bretton Woods Conference that laid the foundations of the World Bank, the International Monetary Fund (IMF), and the postwar international economic order. Complicating a postwar settlement was a growing conflict with the Soviet Union, an ally during World War II, but a Communist totalitarian state run by the dictator Josef Stalin. At the end of World War II, the Soviets brutally established their control in Eastern Europe. There was fear that they might try and subvert the pro-American governments of Western Europe. The American policy of containment began to take shape. In 1947, President Harry Truman used a bill to provide support to Greece and Turkey to announce what became known as the Truman Doctrine: the United States would assist any nation threatened by Communism, either by external attack or internal subversion. In 1949, after an abortive Soviet attempt to blockade West Berlin, the United States and 11 other countries formed the North Atlantic Treaty Organization (NATO). NATO gave the signatories collective security against a Soviet attack. The United States, for the first time since the end of the French alliance in 1800, had entered into an alliance with other countries. The United States was now committed to the defense of Western Europe. This would be a cornerstone of American policy for decades to come.

STEP **3**

Develop Strategies for Success

CHAPTER 4

Mastering Skills and Understanding Themes for the Exam

IN THIS CHAPTER

Summary: The exam emphasizes historical analytical skills and a thematic approach to U.S. history. You will need to familiarize yourself with the specific skills and themes listed in this chapter and then be able to apply these skills and interpret these themes using your knowledge of U.S. history.

Key Ideas
- ✪ Just memorizing facts will not be enough to do well on the new exam.
- ✪ You should become familiar with the two historical practices and four historical analytical skills.
- ✪ You should also become familiar with seven historical themes.
- ✪ All the questions on the new exam will be based on one or more of these skills and themes.

The AP U.S. History Exam

If you have taken the diagnostic exam, it should be clear that the questions on the exam—multiple choice, short answer, document-based question (DBQ), and long essay—require you to think in terms of specific historical practices, historical analytical skills, and historical themes. To do well, it is essential that you have a thorough understanding of the two historical practices, four historical analytical skills, and seven historical themes. You should try to regularly utilize them throughout your study of U.S. history. Your teacher will provide you with many activities that will allow you to work with these skills and themes. Whether you are part of a study group or studying alone, you should find additional opportunities to use them while reviewing major events in U.S. history. These skills and themes are the tools you should use to analyze—not just memorize—the information that you are introduced to in your classwork and reading.

Historical Practices, Historical Analytical Skills, Historical Themes, and Exam Questions

Historical Practices

Doing well with questions on the AP U.S. History exam will involve mastering two historical practices.

1. **Evaluation and interpreting historical data.** This involves assessing the significance of different forms of historical evidence and determining its appropriate value for a historical argument, including understanding the distinction between primary and secondary sources. It involves understanding the ways that the perspective of historians is shaped by their particular circumstances and recognizing that there can be many models of historical interpretation.
2. **Creating and assessing historical arguments.** This involves understanding the components of an effective historical argument, recognizing these in the arguments of others, and utilizing them to craft persuasive arguments of your own.

Historical Analytical Skills

Questions on the AP U.S. History exam will all involve one or more of the historical analytical skills in the following list. Be sure you practice these skills as you review for the exam.

1. **Identifying cause and effect.** This involves establishing the relationships between events, determining the ways historical actions and forces influence each other.
2. **Differentiating between change and continuity.** This involves identifying patterns over periods of time and demonstrating how changes and continuities are related to broad historical forces.
3. **Comparing historical events.** This involves relating and contrasting events across time and space, creating contexts by which to evaluate them.
4. **Connecting events to broader historical trends.** This involves linking specific events to wider historical processes taking place around them, showing how they are related to similar occurrences taking place elsewhere.

Historical Themes

All questions on the AP U.S. History exam will relate in some way to the following overarching themes of U.S. History. You'll need to use your historical analytical skills to explain, interpret, and apply these themes of U.S. history.

1. **American identities.** This addresses the development of American nationalism, and within this larger national identity, the emergence of various group identities during the course of U.S. history.
2. **American economies and technology.** This addresses the ways that Americans have structured their economic systems over time, and how technological change has affected economic development in the United States.

3. **American populations.** This addresses the movements to and within the United States by various groups of people.

4. **Political power in the United States.** This addresses the role of government in American history, the understandings Americans have had about the nature of government, and the ways people in the United States have organized themselves to shape the political process.

5. **The United States in world affairs.** This addresses the ways in which the American colonies and the United States interacted with other peoples and governments, in North America and around the world.

6. **The influence of American geography and environment.** This addresses the ways the physical environment and geography of America, including such factors as climate, plants, animals, and natural resources, helped shape the history of the United States.

7. **American culture and conviction.** This addresses the significance of ideas, religious beliefs, and cultural values as formative influences in American history.

To illustrate the ways in which the questions on the new exam expect you to make use of these historical analytical skills and historical themes, let's look at a few examples.

Sample Multiple-Choice Questions

Multiple-choice questions on the exam will often begin with a look at some historical document that you will be asked to read, analyze, and interpret. Following the document below, we'll try some sample multiple-choice questions like those you'll find on the actual test.

> Everybody is talkin' these days about Tammany men growin' rich on graft, but nobody thinks of drawin' the distinction between honest graft and dishonest graft. There's all the difference in the world between the two. Yes, many of our men have grown rich in politics. I have myself. I've made a big fortune out of the game, and I'm gettin' richer every day, but I've not gone in for dishonest graft—blackmailin' gamblers, saloonkeepers, disorderly people, etc.—and neither has any of the men who have made big fortunes in politics.
>
> There's an honest graft, and I'm an example of how it works. I might sum up the whole thing by sayin': "I seen my opportunities and I took 'em."
>
> Just let me explain by example. My party's in power in the city, and it's goin' to undertake a lot of public improvements. Well, I'm tipped off, say, that they're goin' to lay out a new park in a certain place.
>
> I see my opportunity and I take it. I go to that place and I buy up all the land I can in the neighborhood. Then the board of this or that makes its plan public, and there is a rush to get my land, which nobody cared for particular before.
>
> Ain't it perfectly honest to charge a good price and make a profit on my investment and foresight? Of course, it is. Well, that's honest graft.
>
> —William Riordan, *Plunkitt of Tammany Hall*, 1905

Let's look at a sample multiple-choice question based on this passage:

1. The perspective of George Washington Plunkitt expressed in the passage above most directly reflected the attitudes of which of the following?
   A. Progressive political reformers
   B. The owners of big businesses and trusts
   C. Supporters of the Social Gospel
   D. Urban machine politicians

The correct answer is D. George Washington Plunkitt was a leader in New York City's Tammany Hall political machine, and his questionable distinction between "dishonest" and "honest" graft is a justification of the fact that, like many machine politicians, he used his position and insider knowledge to make money at the taxpayers' expense. Note that you have to use historical practices and historical analytical skills to answer the question, including evaluating and interpreting historical data as you interpret the meaning of the passage, and comparing historical events as you weigh the correct answer against responses reflecting contemporary events, such as the rise of progressivism, the growth of big business, and the efforts of social workers and reformers to ameliorate conditions in the cities, including the Protestant leaders preaching the Social Gospel. The question also asks you to reflect on historical themes, such as political power in the United States, because of its obvious political content, and American populations, because the movement of masses of people into rapidly growing American cities in the late nineteenth century was the essential backdrop to the rise of the great urban political machines.

Let's try another multiple-choice question:

2. Given the perspective expressed by George Washington Plunkitt in the preceding passage, which of the following reforms would he be most likely to oppose?
   A. Civil service reform
   B. Abolitionism
   C. Dechartering the Bank of the United States
   D. Creating Social Security

The correct answer is A. As a machine politician who used his position in the city to feather his nest, George Washington Plunkitt vehemently opposed civil service reform, which would replace machine workers on the city payroll with civil servants who would not owe their livelihood and loyalty to political bosses. A historical analytical skill useful in answering the question is connecting events to broader historical trends, necessary in relating Plunkitt's concerns to the movement for civil service reform in the late nineteenth and early twentieth centuries. Grouping events into periods is essential because the other responses to the question date from other times in American history. Correctly answering the question requires you to connect Plunkitt to what was for him a contemporary reform movement. Historical themes that are important for this question are political power in the United States, because once again we are dealing with politics, and American culture and conviction, because this question asks you to reflect on important social ideas in U.S. history.

Sample Short-Answer Question

Now let's try a short-answer question.

1. Answer A, B, and C.
   A. Briefly explain ONE example of a group that contributed to the rapid settlement of the Trans-Mississippi West in the period 1865-1890.
   B. Briefly explain a SECOND example of a group that contributed to the rapid settlement of the Trans-Mississippi West in the period 1865-1890.
   C. Briefly explain ONE example of a way one of these groups influenced the activity of another of these groups during the rapid settlement of the Trans-Mississippi West.

This question asks you to discuss factors in the rapid opening of the West in the period following the Civil War. You can treat the impact of railroads, the emergence of the great open-range cattle empire, and the rise of a new farming frontier. To answer it, you need to use such historical analytical skills as differentiating between change and continuity when you relate one of the options to a broader historical pattern, and identifying cause and effect, as you explore how one of the options affected another. Relevant historical themes are American economies and technology and the influence of American geography and environment as you analyze economic development in the very distinctive climactic environment of the West in the late nineteenth century. The historical theme of American identities would come into play as you discussed the emergence of distinctive cultures among cattlemen and western farmers.

Sample Essay Question

Long essay questions, including DBQs, can draw on all the historical analytical skills, but they often especially test your skill in the historical practices of evaluating and interpreting historical data and creating and assessing historical arguments. Consider a DBQ that begins with the following statement:

Are historians Stephen Armstrong and Daniel P. Murphy correct in arguing that American involvement in World War I was a mistake that could have been avoided if the U.S. government had not insisted on an unrealistic understanding of the freedom of the seas?

In an essay dealing with this position, the historical practices identified above would need to be heavily utilized. Creating and assessing historical arguments and interpreting the past would be important as you weigh the argument of Armstrong and Murphy, putting it into context and evaluating its strengths and weaknesses. As you do this, you will also rely on the historical theme concerning the United States in world affairs.

In Conclusion

What should be clear by now is that the historical practices, historical analytical skills, and historical themes discussed in this chapter are the intellectual framework of the AP U.S. History exam. You ought to be as familiar with these practices, skills, and themes as you are with the facts of U.S. history. Mastery of them will enable you to respond effectively to the questions that you will encounter on the test next spring.

CHAPTER 5

Strategies for Approaching Each Question Type

IN THIS CHAPTER

Summary: Knowing how to most efficiently and effectively attack each type of question on the test will help you score higher on the exam. Learn the question-answering strategies in this chapter and practice applying them to the test questions.

Key Ideas

Multiple-Choice Questions

✪ Multiple-choice questions relate to prompts such as historical texts and images.

✪ The questions test analytical and interpretive skills as well as factual knowledge.

✪ Intelligent guessing will improve your score on the test; there is no penalty for guessing.

✪ There may be more than one possible "right" answer.

✪ Memorizing the facts is *not* enough.

Short-Answer Questions

✪ Short-answer questions ask you to make use of your historical analytical skills and thematic knowledge.

✪ For short-answer questions, it is *not* necessary to develop a thesis statement.

Document-Based Essay Question

✪ Use an appropriate organizational approach: create a thesis and support it.

✪ It is not necessary to spend the entire time writing your answer.

✪ There must be logic to your answer.

✪ Make your essay as readable as possible.

✪ Make sure to comment on all the quotes you include in your essay.

✪ It is not necessary to use every single document, but you must use at least six of the seven documents to construct your argument in order to get the maximum number of points possible.

✪ For at least four documents, address one of the following: the point of view of the author, the purpose of the author, the intended audience of the document, the historical context of the document.

✪ The document-based question will ask you to use your historical analytical skills and thematic knowledge while explaining and interpreting events over longer periods of time.

✪ No document-based question will concentrate on material from before 1607 or after 1980.

Long Essay Question

✪ Use an appropriate organizational approach: create a thesis and support it.

✪ Make an outline before you begin to write.

✪ Pick the question you know the most about.

✪ Watch your time!

✪ The long essay question will ask you to use your historical analytical skills and thematic knowledge while explaining and interpreting events over longer periods of time.

✪ No long essay question will concentrate on material from before 1607 or after 1980.

Reading and Interpreting Primary Source Documents

✪ Be prepared to analyze a variety of primary source documents.

Taking the Exam

✪ Come to the exam prepared but relaxed.

Multiple-Choice Questions

All multiple-choice questions will be tied to a prompt. These prompts may be primary source texts, secondary source texts, or images. For each prompt there will be two to six questions. These questions will require you to interpret source material and analyze it in conjunction with your broader historical knowledge. Remember, you will have 55 minutes to answer 55 questions. This does not give you a lot of time to ponder each question.

All questions on the test will have four possible answers. The following question is an example of the format of questions you may encounter on the exam:

The peace, the freedom and the security of ninety percent of the population of the world is being jeopardized by the remaining ten percent who are threatening a breakdown of all international order and law. ... When an epidemic of physical disease starts to spread, the community approves and joins in a quarantine of the patients in order to protect the health of the community against the spread of the disease. ... War is a contagion, whether it is declared or undeclared. It can engulf states and peoples remote from the original scene of hostilities. We are determined to keep out of war, yet we cannot insure ourselves against the disastrous effects of war and the dangers of involvement. We are adopting such measures as will minimize our risk of involvement, but we cannot have complete protection in a world of disorder in which confidence and security have broken down. ... Most important of all, the will for peace on the part of peace-loving nations must express itself to the end that nations that may be tempted to violate their agreements and the rights of others will desist from such a course. There must be positive endeavors to preserve peace.

—Franklin D. Roosevelt, "Quarantine" Address, October 5, 1937

1. In the passage above, Franklin D. Roosevelt is expressing concern about which of the following?
   A. The economic consequences of the Great Depression
   B. The explosion of the U.S.S. *Maine*
   C. American interventions in Central America and the Caribbean
   D. Aggressive actions by Japan, Italy, and Germany

The correct answer is D. In the "Quarantine" Address, President Franklin D. Roosevelt was warning his fellow Americans about the dangers posed by the military actions taken by Japan in China, Italy in Ethiopia, and Germany in the Rhineland and Spain. Note that to correctly answer this, you have to understand what President Roosevelt is saying in the passage and put it into the historical context of the 1930s, a time when war clouds were gathering because of the aggressions of the totalitarian states.

Sometimes multiple-choice questions will ask you to make connections between the topic discussed by a source and another historical period. Here is an example:

2. The policy being proposed by Franklin D. Roosevelt in the passage above can *best* be compared to which of the following?
   A. The Monroe Doctrine
   B. The containment policy
   C. George Washington's policy of "no entangling foreign alliances"
   D. Isolationism

The correct answer is B. President Roosevelt was calling for a policy in which the "peace-loving nations" combined to "quarantine" the warlike states, dissuading them from further aggressive action. This is similar to the containment policy of the cold war, in which the United States and its allies attempted to halt or "contain" the expansion of communism. Note that the question asks you to compare policies from a wide range of U.S. history.

Useful Hints for the Multiple-Choice Section

- **Guessing:** On the multiple-choice portion of the test, no points are deducted for incorrect responses. Therefore it is to your advantage to guess on every question when you are not sure of the correct answer.
- **There may be more than one possible right answer.** The directions ask you to "select the one that is *best* in each case." Get rid of one or two responses that are obviously incorrect, and focus on the others. For example:

3. Which of the following would be most likely to support the perspective of Franklin D. Roosevelt in the passage above?
   A. A believer in Manifest Destiny
   B. An Isolationist
   C. A supporter of collective security
   D. A Democrat

Looking at the possible answers, let's eliminate those that are obviously incorrect. Manifest Destiny was an ideology of American continental expansionism that flourished in the mid-nineteenth century; it is inapplicable to the situation Roosevelt was describing. Isolationists opposed American interventionism abroad; this runs counter to what Roosevelt was proposing. This leaves C and D. Roosevelt was a Democrat and obviously could normally expect heavy support from members of his party. But a number of Democrats were Isolationists. Supporters of collective security, regardless of party affiliation, believed that the United States should act with other countries to preserve international peace. Therefore, though D is a plausible answer, C is the *best* response.

- **Memorizing the facts is *not* enough.** Although you do need to have a good knowledge of the facts of U.S. history, these questions place a heavy emphasis on analysis and a thematic understanding of the American past.
- **Don't overlook the obvious.** Questions on the AP U.S. History test emphasize major themes in U.S. history. Don't overthink the question. If you think an answer is so obvious that it has to be right, it probably is! The questions in this exam are not designed to test you on obscure trivia.
- **Use a good pencil with a good eraser.** We know that this may seem a little far-fetched, but we have a colleague who is convinced that this is an approach to be emphasized. He maintains that many students get marked off because they don't entirely fill in the bubbles or totally erase when they change their answers. He claims to have proof of this. Don't take this lightly; be sure you don't lower your score just because your eraser left a lot of smudges.

Short-Answer Questions

Short-answer questions require you to prepare brief responses to questions that ask you to address themes in U.S. history and utilize your historical analytical skills. Very important, short-answer questions do *not* require thesis statements. Short-answer questions may relate to prompts similar to those in the multiple-choice questions, or they may ask you to evaluate broad assertions about U.S. history. You will have 40 minutes to answer three short-answer questions. You must answer the first two short-answer questions. You may choose between the third and fourth questions. The first two questions will cover periods 3–8. The third question will cover periods 1–5, and the fourth will cover periods 6–9.

The following question is an example of the format of questions you may encounter on the exam.

1. Answer Parts A, B, and C.
   A. Briefly explain how ONE of the following reform movements transformed American life during the late nineteenth and early twentieth centuries.
      - Populism
      - Progressivism
      - Feminism
   B. Explain how your choice affected *one* of the other options.
   C. Provide an example of opposition in the late nineteenth and early twentieth centuries to *one* of the options.

Useful Hints for the Short-Answer Section
- **Don't waste time!** You should answer three of these in 40 minutes. Don't get bogged down with an elaborate response—remember that these are *short*-answer questions.
- **Just answer the question.** You don't have to develop a persuasive argument.
- **Be sure to provide supporting facts.** The directions may ask for ONE example or piece of evidence, but it would be to your advantage to provide a few more facts.

- **Write in full sentences.** To properly answer the question, responses need to be in the form of sentences. Fragments and phrases won't cut it.
- **Keep your response inside the box on the answer sheet.** Many short-answer questions are scanned and scored online. Readers scoring online cannot see any writing that is outside the box.

Document-Based Question (DBQ)

During this essay section of the exam, you are required to use a number of documents and previously learned knowledge to answer a question. This question tests your historical analytical skills, your ability to interpret a variety of sources, and your ability to synthesize what you know into an effective response. You will need to craft a thesis that addresses a historical theme or a significant period in U.S. history. *Not all of the information needed to earn a 5 is included in the documents.* You need to bring what you know about the subject of the question to the table as well. In a typical question, you might be presented with a political cartoon, a graph, extracts from speeches and letters, and part of an editorial from the 1850s and asked to discuss the causes of the Civil War. By the time of the AP exam, your teacher will have probably provided you with numerous document-based questions. For a specific example of a DBQ, refer to the DBQ in the diagnostic test in the previous chapter. On the exam, the DBQ will contain no more than seven documents. The document-based question will focus on topics from periods 3–8.

You'll be given a total of 100 minutes to complete both Parts A and B of Section II. It is recommended that you spend 60 of the 100 minutes completing Part A, which is the document-based question.

The detailed instructions concerning the DBQ that you will get when you take the AP U.S. History exam will remind you to address the points above in your essay. Note that all of these parts emphasize your mastery of historical practices and historical analytical skills. You can place your thesis in the introduction or the conclusion of your essay, though it is usually a good idea to place it in your introduction.

Useful Hints for the DBQ*

- **Be aware of the skills needed for the DBQ.** The DBQ will focus on one of the following historical analytical skills: identifying cause and effect, differentiating between change and continuity, comparing historical events, and connecting events to broader historical trends. Answering the DBQ will test your effectiveness with the following historical practices: evaluating and interpreting historical data and creating and assessing historical arguments.
- **Use the standard essay format.** This is the format that you have used for all historical essays. Start off with a thesis and then use analysis of individual documents to prove your thesis. If the documents are presented chronologically, then write about them in the same way.
- **You don't have to use all the documents, but it might be a good idea.** According to the DBQ instructions, you must use at least six of the seven documents. If possible, use all seven. This way, if you use one document inaccurately you won't lose a point. Also remember to provide information on the author's point of view or intention, the audience, or the historical context of at least four of the documents. Doing this for more than

---

* Please note this book was printed before rubrics for the 2018 DBQ and long essay question were posted at the AP U.S. History website.

four documents will help you avoid losing a point if you make a mistake "sourcing" one of the documents.

- **You don't need to keep writing on and on.** It is not necessary to spend every second of the 60 minutes writing the essay. Answer the question, including what the documents say and what you can say about them, and be done with it. Remember, some of what you already know has to be included in your answer. You might want to spend up to 15 minutes outlining your answer and 45 minutes writing.
- **There must be logic to your answer.** Organization as well as knowledge is important. Please remember that there is no "right answer" to the DBQ.
- **Spelling:** Many students ask whether spelling counts. The answer is generally, no. Scorers know that you are rushed on these essays; in all probability, if you think your handwriting is bad they have likely seen worse. Nevertheless, do what you can to make your presentation as readable as possible. Avoid writing with a pencil. Avoid messiness—lots of scratch-outs, arrows going off in different directions pointing to material you forgot to insert—as much as is possible under the circumstances. Don't write using extremely small script. We know from personal experience as instructors and scorers that it is hard to give a high score to a student if you can hardly read what the student wrote.
- **Don't waste time with direct quotes from the documents.** It will not help your score to spend time or space including direct quotes from the sources in your DBQ essay. If you are going to quote your sources, it is perfectly acceptable to paraphrase your quote. It is much more important to be sure to comment on any and all quotes that you include in your essay.
- **Answer the question.** This generally involves analysis and interpretation. Simply quoting the documents without analyzing them is not answering the question. You need to relate the documents to each other and their time period. You should craft a sophisticated argument that explains historical complexity and places the material covered by the question into a broader historical context.
- **Demonstrate your historical knowledge.** To excel on the DBQ you must bring in outside information—the more the better. Don't just mention nouns or proper nouns. This information must be put in context and used to support your argument.
- **Watch the time!** Don't get so wrapped up in the DBQ that you forget that you still have to do a long essay question.

Long Essay Question*

Immediately after writing the DBQ essay, you will have to answer a long essay question. You will get to choose which of three questions you will answer. The long essay question asks you to utilize higher-level thinking skills, which means you will be asked to analyze and interpret events and themes of the past rather than simply give some historical facts. It is recommended that you spend 40 of the 100 minutes you are given for Section II of the exam to answer the long essay question.

The following question is an example of the format of questions you may encounter on the exam:

1. Evaluate the extent to which the development of different economic systems in the North and South was a major cause of the Civil War.

---

* Please note this book was printed before rubrics for the 2018 DBQ and long essay question were posted at the AP U.S. History website.

The prompt for the question will indicate what historical analytical skills are being emphasized. Use of these historical analytical skills is just as important as the effective use of factual evidence. You will pick the long essay that you answer from three options, focusing on periods 1–3, 4–6, and 7–9.

Useful Hints for the Long Essay Question

Use the organizational approach that you have probably utilized in answering long essay questions all year. Specifically this means you should:

- **Create a thesis.** What will your essay say? Decide the position you will take and then clearly state that position.
- **Write an effective opening statement.** This is crucial. Your thesis should be part of your opening statement.
- **Support your opening statement with historical facts.** Don't include facts for the sake of including them: make sure you use the historical facts you mention to support your opening argument.
- **If you can, include a discussion of counterarguments.** This shows that you thoroughly understand the issue at hand. This is usually done after you have supported your opening statement with sufficient evidence. This section often begins with "However, some historians believe …" and discusses and evaluates evidence that contradicts your thesis.
- **Don't forget a conclusion.** An effective conclusion includes a restatement of your thesis.
- **Make a rough outline before you begin to write.** Make sure to answer the question. Don't just go around in circles with information you know about the topic in question.
- **Be sure to pick the question that you know the most about.** We have known students who said they chose a specific question because it "looked easier." Avoid that approach. You'll do your best on the question about which you have the most historical knowledge.
- **Watch your time!** Finally, don't spend too much time on your outline. If you decide to do the long essay before the DBQ, don't forget that you still have that task before you.

Using Primary Source Documents

As a student of AP U.S. History, you will undoubtedly be spending a lot of time this year analyzing primary source documents. Your teacher will probably give you a number of them to read during the year. The document-based question (DBQ) that is on every AP examination will most likely ask you to read and interpret a number of primary sources and then to make a historical argument based upon them.

Historical documents, accounts, and books can be either primary or secondary sources. A secondary source is an account written after the fact. A chapter in your textbook is a secondary source, as is a biography, for example, of Franklin D. Roosevelt written in 2005. However, when historians write secondary source accounts, their research should include a thorough study of the available primary sources. A primary source is a document from the era or person in question. A primary source relating to George Washington might be a letter that George Washington wrote when he was at Valley Forge, an account on Washington written by someone who knew him personally, or a portrait of Washington that was done when he was alive. Primary sources relating to the 1950s might be a speech made by Senator Joseph McCarthy, a recording of the song "Hound Dog" by Elvis Presley, or an episode of the television show "The Adventures of Ozzie and Harriet." (Note that primary source documents are not limited to written documents.) Secondary source accounts such as your textbook usually have excerpts from various primary source accounts scattered throughout the chapters.

Analyzing primary source documents allows you to study history as a historian does. When you are analyzing, for example, the actual text of a fireside chat given by Franklin D. Roosevelt in 1933, you are the one doing the historical analysis; no other historian or author is doing the work for you.

Types of Primary Source Documents

Types of primary source documents that you will be reading will likely include:

- **Documents published during the time period.** These will include magazine articles, newspaper accounts, official government documents, posters, Supreme Court decisions, novels written during the era, and countless other sources.
- **Resources published after the fact.** These will include letters and diaries written by historical (and nonhistorical) figures that were not originally meant for publication. These can be incredibly revealing; many politicians, for example, are much more honest in their diary entries than they are when they are giving speeches to the public. Oral histories are also very valuable and can be found at many local historical societies. A wonderful primary source, for example, would be the transcript (or audiotape) of a "common person" telling about the effects of the Great Depression on his or her family and community.
- **Visual documents.** Paintings and photographs can provide incredibly revealing details about any time period you may be studying. Recently, the photographs of people waiting for help after Hurricane Katrina told more about the suffering of New Orleans than a thousand-word article could have. In 1945, photographs from recently liberated Nazi concentration camps shocked the world. Newsreel and television footage of historical events can be invaluable.
- **Films.** Movies from any era can provide a fascinating window into the values and beliefs of that period. By watching a film from, for example, the 1980s, you can get an idea of how people talked, what they wore, and what they believed in that era. A 1967 movie, *Bonnie and Clyde,* glorified the lives of Bonnie Parker and Clyde Barrow, two small-time gangsters who continually flouted authority during the Great Depression. Although this film was about the 1930s, it perfectly reflected the disrespect for authority of many young people in the late 1960s.
- **Songs, recordings, etc.** Sources that one can listen to can also be valuable. As with films, songs are very valuable windows into the culture and values of a time period, whether it is "Fight the Power" by Public Enemy or "Masters of War" by Bob Dylan. Listening to speeches given by historical figures can also be a valuable historical tool.

Analyzing Primary Source Documents

It should be remembered that virtually every single primary source document contains some amount of bias. Memoirs written by many historical figures are generally self-serving and do not dwell on mistakes and problems from the writer's past. It is virtually impossible to write about anything without bias; therefore, it is critical to consider this when evaluating primary sources. A source in which an observer discusses the impact that Theodore Roosevelt had on people when he met them would be influenced by preexisting judgments and opinions the author already had about Theodore Roosevelt. As a result, it is necessary to use a number of primary sources when evaluating a historical figure, event, or era.

There are many methods that historians and students can utilize when studying primary source documents. When looking at a document, try to find some information about its producer. What was the relationship of the author to the person or event being described? Did the producer have preexisting biases toward the subject of the document? How far after the events being described was the document written? Another important question is the audience; the historian/student should identify the target group at which the document was aimed, and whether or not this might have influenced what was stated by the author.

Students wanting more specific information on analyzing primary source documents can go to the Teacher Resources page at the Library of Congress and the Primary Sources and Research Tools page at the Wisconsin Historical Society.

STEP **4**

Review the Knowledge You Need to Score High

CHAPTER 6

Settling of the Western Hemisphere (1491–1607)

IN THIS CHAPTER

Summary: There were several reasons why Europeans became interested in the Americas during this period. Economic and political factors were most important. The Spanish originally viewed the Americas as a barrier to a direct route to the Indies. However, soon they developed a large empire in South and Central America and viewed the region as a potential source of tremendous wealth. Some Native American tribes had developed complex civilizations in the years before the Europeans arrived. The ecosystem of the Americas was drastically altered by the arrival of the Europeans.

Key Concept

On the North American continent, contact among the peoples of Europe, the Americas, and West Africa created a new world.

Keyword

Columbian Exchange: exchange of crops, animals, diseases, and ideas between Europe and colonies of the Western Hemisphere that developed in the aftermath of the voyages of Columbus.

Native America

The Europeans did not encounter a cultural or political vacuum when they arrived in the Americas. North and South America were populated by a great number of peoples, ranging in social complexity from hunter-gatherer groups to city-based empires. In Mexico, the warlike Aztecs carved out an empire centered on their magnificent city of Tenochtitlan, crisscrossed with canals and adorned with great temples and palaces. Here flowed the tribute of their subject peoples, and also long lines of captives fated to be bloodily sacrificed to appease the Aztecs' gods. The Inca created the largest empire in the Americas; with its capital in Cusco, Peru, the Inca Empire stretched south to parts of what are now Chile and Argentina, and north to portions of modern Colombia. The Inca Empire was a highly organized state, held together by the most impressively developed road system in the Americas. Parts of this extensive network of roads still exist today.

In North America, the Mississippian culture arose in the Mississippi River Valley and then spread into what is now the Midwestern and southeastern United States. The Mississippian culture flourished from around A.D. 800 to 1600 and was notable for its urban development and the mounds it built, upon which temples and other buildings were erected. The great city of Cahokia, in Illinois, at its peak in the 1200s may have been home to 20,000 people. In the southwest, the Puebloans built villages and towns, sometimes in the faces of cliffs for greater protection. Many other North American peoples did not live in permanent settlements; instead they lived a nomadic existence, following the movement of fish and game. The first English settlers in North America encountered people collectively known as Woodland Indians. The tribes of Woodland Indians lived on the bounty of the eastern forests, hunting and gathering their food. Two of the major language groups among the Woodland Indians were Algonquian and Iroquoian.

The Europeans Arrive

In the late 1400s and early 1500s, Europe was going through a period of intense intellectual ferment. The Renaissance saw renewed interest in Europe's Classical Greek and Roman heritage; this rediscovery of the past stimulated new ideas and perspectives on the world. The Scientific Revolution encouraged an exciting new experimental approach to the acquisition of knowledge about the natural environment; with more knowledge came the power to begin to alter that environment. The Reformation and Catholic Counter-Reformation inaugurated a period of religious upheaval leading to a flowering of religious fervor but also to intense religious conflict that would dominate international relations in Europe for more than a century. This period saw the inventions of technologies crucial to exploration. The Portuguese developed the caravel, a sailing ship capable of long ocean voyages. Improved navigational aids, such as the **astrolabe** and compass, made such voyages more practicable. Ever since the **Crusades**, which reintroduced Europeans to the markets of the East, demand had escalated for spices and other Asian goods. European merchants, blocked from the sources of these goods by the Islamic powers of the Middle East, yearned for different routes to Asia. As the medieval period drew to a close, states were growing more powerful; kings had the resources to finance overseas expeditions. All the pieces were coming together for an explosion of European exploration around the world.

Columbus

In this period of expanding intellectual horizons, many Europeans were looking beyond their traditional boundaries to the wider world. Prince Henry the Navigator of Portugal sponsored voyages of discovery to the Azores in the Atlantic and along the coast of Africa in the mid-1400s. After Henry's death, Portuguese mariners continued their explorations along the African coastline, reaching the Cape of Good Hope at the southern tip of Africa in 1488. A decade later, the Portuguese explorer Vasco da Gama led an expedition around the Cape of Good Hope and sailed on to India. Da Gama was the first person to succeed in opening a direct link between Europe and the markets of Asia.

Christopher Columbus was a Genoese navigator with a dream. He believed that by sailing due west across the Atlantic Ocean, he would reach China and open a trade route that would allow the treasures of the East to flow into Europe. He was not the first person to think of this. No serious scholar or navigator in the 1400s thought that the Earth was flat. But most scholars correctly believed that the Earth was so big that any ship sailing west into the Atlantic would run out of provisions before it reached Asia. Columbus's enthusiasm for this voyage was based on a mistake; he believed that the globe was smaller than it actually is. Hoping to find a sponsor for his voyage, Columbus first approached the Portuguese. Confident in the prospects opening up as a result of their discovery of a sea route to India, the Portuguese turned him down. Columbus turned next to King Ferdinand and Queen Isabella of Spain, who had just unified their country. These monarchs decided to take a chance on this persuasive visionary and provided Columbus with the resources to outfit and crew three small ships. After a long voyage, Columbus sighted land on October 12, 1492. Columbus landed on an island in the Bahamas, which he named San Salvador. Believing that he had reached the East Indies, Columbus called the native people he met "Indians." To his dying day, Columbus believed that he had reached the outer regions of Asia. In fact, he had reached a New World and had launched a new epoch in human history.

Columbus was a man of his time, not a modern anthropologist or social worker. He claimed his discoveries for Spain and regarded himself as the governor of the lands he had found. He hoped to convert the native people to Christianity; he also expected them to accept their new lot as subjects of the King and Queen of Spain. Beginning with Columbus, the Spanish colonists forced Native Americans to work for them. The **encomienda** system forced Native Americans onto Spanish plantations in exchange for the dubious benefit of Spanish "protection." Those who refused were hunted down and often killed. However, many more Native Americans died of the diseases that the Europeans inadvertently brought with them. These diseases were the most lethal dimension of an immense transfer of plants and animals back and forth between the continents of Europe and North America. This flow of products across the Atlantic, known as the **Columbian Exchange**, permanently altered both continents. Another exchange was initiated in the 1500s. As new cash crops like sugar developed in the Americas, the European colonizers ran out of Native American labor. Beginning in the 1540s, African slaves were sold to colonists. This was the origin of the great African diaspora in the Americas.

Cortes in Mexico

The people whom Columbus first encountered lived in relatively simple societies. They possessed small amounts of gold, which greatly intrigued the Spanish, who wanted to find the source of this precious metal. The Spanish learned that on the mainland of Mexico, great Native American states existed, some possessing immeasurable wealth. In 1519, Hernan Cortes led a small army of 500 men from Cuba to Mexico. Here he encountered representatives of the great Aztec Empire. The Aztecs did not know what to make of Cortes; some thought that he was a god. Through a ruthless combination of force and diplomacy, Cortes made his way to the Aztec capital of Tenochtitlan. Here he was treated as a guest by the Aztec ruler, Montezuma. Relations soon deteriorated between the Spanish and the Aztecs. In the ensuing violence, Montezuma was killed, and Cortes and remnants of his army were forced from the city. Cortes rebuilt his forces and organized a coalition of tribes who hated their Aztec overlords. He besieged and overran Tenochtitlan in 1521, destroying the Aztec Empire. Cortes was one of the first and greatest of the Spanish conquistadors to overthrow the native states of Mexico, Central America, and Peru. The conquistadors incorporated the subjugated Native Americans into a vast new empire that was soon sending a glittering stream of gold and silver back home to Spain.

Chapter Review

Rapid Review

- Economic difficulties in Europe, the desire for geographic knowledge, the desire to acquire lands, riches, and raw materials, and the desire to spread Christianity all caused Europeans to become interested in the Americas.
- Cortes, Francisco Pizarro, and other Spanish conquistadors entered much of Central America, South America, the southeastern section of North America, and the area now known as Florida, conquering the Aztecs, the Incas, and other Native American tribes. Guns, horses, and diseases brought from Europe all aided the Spanish in their efforts to defeat the native tribes.
- The Columbian Exchange was the exchange of animals, plants, diseases, and ideas that took place between the Western Hemisphere and Europe as a result of initial Spanish and Portuguese exploration.

Time Line

2500 BCE: Migration of Asians to the Americas across the Bering Strait begins
1492: Voyage of Columbus to the Americas
1519: Cortes enters Mexico
1520–1530: Smallpox epidemic devastates Native American populations in many parts of South and Central America, virtually wiping out some tribes
1542: Spanish explorers travel through southwestern United States

❯ Review Questions

Multiple-Choice Questions

1. Which of the following was *not* an initial result of interaction between Spanish explorers and Native Americans?
   A. Diseases that killed many of the Native Americans
   B. Domestication by Native Americans of animals brought by Spanish explorers
   C. Spread of Catholicism among Native Americans
   D. Plants from South and Central America being sent back to Europe

2. Slave labor was brought to the Western Hemisphere by colonists because
   A. the region was lightly populated when the Spanish arrived.
   B. Native Americans were unfamiliar with the tools and methods necessary to harvest sugarcane.
   C. Aztec and Inca leaders had already begun to import slaves even before Spanish explorers arrived.
   D. there was a lack of manpower to do the labor-intensive work of harvesting sugarcane.

3. North American Native American tribes
   A. displayed a uniformity of lifestyle.
   B. modeled themselves after tribes from Central America and Mexico.
   C. were greatly varied in lifestyle and economic systems.
   D. formed alliances on numerous occasions to fight competing tribes.

4. One factor *not* responsible for European expansion into the Western Hemisphere was
   A. desire for economic expansion.
   B. desire to expand Christianity.
   C. democratization of European society.
   D. better shipbuilding and navigational tools.

5. The very first Americans
   A. were nomadic wanderers.
   B. lived in permanent sites.
   C. were subsistence farmers.
   D. predated Spain's arrival in the New World by only two centuries.

Short-Answer Question

6. Answer Parts A, B, and C.
   A. Briefly explain ONE example of how Christopher Columbus's 1492 voyage of discovery transformed life for Native Americans and Europeans.
   B. Briefly explain a SECOND example of how Christopher Columbus's 1492 voyage of discovery transformed life for Native Americans and Europeans.
   C. Briefly explain ONE example of another consequential European voyage of discovery in the period 1480 to 1600.

› Answers and Explanations

1. **B.** It would take a long time before these animals were used by Native Americans; Native Americans were terrified of them and the Spanish explorers who rode on them.

2. **D.** Harvesting sugar took a massive amount of manpower. Since the Spanish had killed off a large number of native laborers and many more died from European diseases, slaves were needed.

3. **C.** There was a tremendous variety in the lifestyles and economic systems of Native Americans living in North America.

4. **C.** European expansion into the Western Hemisphere was supported and financed by European monarchs; no democratization of society or government was taking place at this time.

5. **A.** Almost all early Native American tribes were nomadic in nature.

6. **Parts A and B**: Columbus's voyage opened up lands with vast resources to the Europeans. The Spanish found great supplies of silver and gold in Central and South America. The Europeans also found new crops such as potatoes, maize, and tobacco. For the Native Americans, Columbus's voyage brought dramatic and often disastrous change. European diseases ravaged Native American populations. Europeans began conquering Native American lands, sometimes enslaving conquered populations. European missionaries brought Christianity to the New World. The Europeans also introduced new animals such as horses, pigs, and cattle.

   Part C: The Portuguese explorer Bartolomeu Dias sailed around the Cape of Good Hope in Southern Africa in 1488. His countryman Vasco da Gama followed route and sailed on to India in 1497 to 1499. Ferdinand Magellan led a Spanish expedition that in 1519 to 1522 eventually circumnavigated the globe. In 1497, John Cabot led an English expedition that landed somewhere in modern Canada. The French explorer Jacques Cartier led expeditions that explored the Gulf of St. Lawrence and the St. Lawrence River in Canada.

CHAPTER 7

Colonial America (1607–1650)

IN THIS CHAPTER

Summary: The French settled in Canada and eventually turned to trapping and fur trading. Overcrowding in England and religious persecution were both factors in driving some Englishmen toward America. In the Jamestown colony indentured servants and the first slaves brought to the Americas made up a majority of the workforce. The Massachusetts Bay Colony was established in 1629 by the Puritans; Governor John Winthrop envisioned the colony as a "city upon a hill." Religious dissent led to the founding of several more New England colonies. The ecosystem of the Americas was drastically altered by the Europeans.

KEY IDEA

Keywords
Puritans: group of religious dissidents who came to the New World so they would have a location to establish a "purer" church than the one that existed in England.
Separatists: religious group that also opposed the Church of England; this group first went to Holland, and then some went on to the Americas.
Indentured servants: individuals who exchanged compulsory service for free passage to the American colonies.

New France

French explorer Jacques Cartier sailed up the St. Lawrence River in what is now Canada in the 1530s. Despite this early start, the French did little to colonize Canada until the arrival of Samuel de Champlain in the early 1600s. The "Father of New France," Champlain founded the settlement of Quebec in 1608. Canada never attracted many French colonists. The wintry climate was uncongenial, and the prospect of living in a wilderness amidst tribes of sometimes hostile Native Americans did not appeal to most inhabitants of Ancien Régime France. Some of those who might have been willing to move to New France, such as members of the dissident Protestant **Huguenot** minority, were forbidden to settle there by the king. As a result, although farming communities did develop along the St. Lawrence River, key roles in New France were played by Catholic missionaries, fur traders, and soldiers.

Sometimes these missionaries, fur traders, and soldiers did double duty as explorers, striking out deeply into the interior of the continent. The Jesuit priest Jacques Marquette teamed with Louis Jolliet to discover the upper reaches of the Mississippi River. Robert La Salle expanded on these discoveries in the Great Lakes region and along the Mississippi River, establishing a series of forts that laid claim to the Mississippi River Valley for France.

For the most part, the French got along better with the Native American peoples than did the English or Dutch. The French did not need large amounts of land for farming, thus avoiding disputes over land with their Native American neighbors. The French were mainly interested in converting the Native Americans to Christianity and trading for furs. Beyond that, they were generally more respectful of Native American customs and traditions; many French traders and explorers married Native American women. The sometimes heroically self-sacrificing **Jesuit** missionaries were often keen students of Native American culture. As a result, the Jesuit missions were great successes. The Jesuits did better than their **Franciscan** competitors in Spanish North America; the Franciscans' efforts were hurt by Spanish forced labor laws. With the important exception of the Iroquois Confederacy, most Native American tribes allied with the French in their wars with the British in the seventeenth and eighteenth centuries.

At the same time that Samuel de Champlain was pioneering New France, the commercially entrepreneurial Dutch were laying the foundations of their own colonial experiment in North America. Henry Hudson explored the river that would be named after him in 1609. He set up the first Dutch trading posts on Manhattan Island and the site that would eventually become Albany. Here the Dutch bartered for beaver pelts. The settlement of New Amsterdam was officially established on Manhattan in 1625. Though the Dutch prospered with the fur trade, the struggling colony of New Netherland never attracted many settlers and territorially was hemmed in by hostile Native American tribes. Ultimately it was the power of England's Royal Navy that doomed the Dutch colony. In 1664, New Amsterdam surrendered to an English fleet. From that time on, the bustling commercial center on Manhattan was known as New York.

English Interest in America

Population growth in England was spurred colonization. The government saw overseas settlements as a social safety valve, where jobless workers or landless farmers who might otherwise pose a threat to the established order might find new lives. Close to half the white immigrants to the British colonies before the American Revolution arrived as indentured servants, working for a set number of years in return for the price of their passage. A minority of these people were convicts, exported by the authorities to the colonies as a way of reducing the expense of confining them at home.

Another major impetus for English colonization was the quest of religious minorities to find a place where they could practice their faith undisturbed. During the English Reformation of the sixteenth century, the Church of England was established as the officially supported church of the kingdom. While the Church of England rejected the spiritual authority of the Pope in Rome and distanced itself from some Roman Catholic doctrines, it maintained an episcopal structure and liturgical practices rooted in the Catholic past. English **Puritans**, who adhered to the more radically Protestant doctrines of John Calvin intensely disliked what they saw as the Catholic tendencies of the Church of England. Under Queen Elizabeth I, the Puritans had been allowed to worship in their own way. Following the accession of James I to the English throne, the government began to crack down on the Puritan dissidents. By the 1620s and 1630s, many Puritans were looking to America as a refuge from the authorities.

Akin to the Puritans as religious dissenters were the **Separatists**. The Separatists were small groups of Calvinists who went beyond the practice of most Puritans by rejecting any association with the Church of England. One band of Separatists moved to the Netherlands hoping to find religious freedom but soon grew disillusioned as their children began to blend in with their Dutch neighbors.

Jamestown

In 1606, the **London Company** was given a charter by King James I to establish colonies in North America. The investors in this joint-stock company hoped to make a profit from the natural riches of the New World. In 1607, an expedition dispatched by the London Company founded Jamestown, the first permanent English settlement in North America. Unfortunately, the site of Jamestown was swampy and unhealthy; disease and the distaste for agriculture on the part of the adventurers who made up the bulk of the early settlers led to the Starving Time, a period of starvation resulting in the deaths of almost two-thirds of the population. Arguably, only the leadership of Captain John Smith saved the struggling colony.

Relations with the nearby Native American Powhatan Confederacy were difficult. At one point, Smith was captured by the Powhatans and later claimed that he had been saved from execution by Pocahontas, the daughter of the chief. Smith eventually established trade relations with the Powhatans, which helped sustain Jamestown. Pocahontas later married John Rolfe, one of the ablest English settlers. Rolfe played a decisive role in the history of what would become the colony of Virginia by systematizing the cultivation of tobacco. Despite the opposition of King James, who abhorred smoking, tobacco became a highly lucrative cash crop, and guaranteed the future prosperity of the colony.

Tobacco was a labor-intensive crop. Initially, **indentured servants** were sent to Virginia to work on tobacco plantations. In 1619, a passing Dutch ship paid for a load of supplies with 19 African slaves. Because these slaves had been baptized, they were treated as indentured servants and freed after a period of service. Later in the seventeenth century, more Africans were brought to English America, and slavery became a vital economic institution in the Southern colonies.

Massachusetts

While a desire for riches drove the colonization of Virginia, a search for religious freedom spurred the initial settlement of New England. The Separatists who had settled in the Netherlands and grown unhappy there received a charter from the London Company to settle in America. In 1620, a group of them, led by William Bradford, set sail in the *Mayflower*. Because they were looking for a place to practice their faith, the settlers saw this voyage as a pilgrimage and became known to history as the "Pilgrims."

After a stormy voyage, the Pilgrims made landfall at Cape Cod in Massachusetts. Before going ashore at a place they called Plymouth Rock, the men among the Pilgrims drew up and signed the Mayflower Compact, which established a representative government for the new colony. This is an early example of a social contract. Because the Pilgrims arrived late in the year and were unused to their new environment, they suffered many hardships and much loss of life. Eventually, with the help of Native Americans like Samoset and Squanto, the Pilgrims' colony of Plymouth became self-sustaining. Though Plymouth endured, it never became a great economic success, and, in 1691, it was absorbed into the larger Massachusetts Bay Colony.

Puritans anxious about the deteriorating political and religious situation in England founded the Massachusetts Bay Colony. In America, they hoped to create a truly godly commonwealth, what their leader John Winthrop called a "city upon a hill." In 1629, a large, well-financed, and well-organized expedition sailed to Massachusetts with more than 700 people. They suffered no "starving times" and soon were joined by thousands more settlers. By 1640, over 20,000 people had moved to Massachusetts, which had become a thriving colony with numerous chartered towns, such as Boston and Salem. In addition to farming, settlers engaged in lumbering, shipbuilding, and fishing. The Massachusetts Bay Colony was different from Virginia as most of its founders came over as members of family groups rather than as individual adventurers. Given its very different economy, slavery never took root in Massachusetts the way that it did in Virginia.

Most of the colonists were Puritans, and the only men who could vote were freemen who belonged to a Puritan congregation. The elected legislature was called the General Court. John Winthrop was elected governor in 1629 and would hold that office for 20 years. In some ways, Massachusetts was a democratically representative theocracy. While the Puritans were seeking religious freedom for themselves, they were not necessarily interested in it for others. They were creating a polity that reflected their vision of God's commandments; this did not leave room for dissent.

Anne Hutchinson believed that she and others could experience direct revelations from the Holy Spirit and challenged the teaching authority of most of the colony's ministers. This unorthodox position attracted the attention of Governor Winthrop. After a trial, Hutchinson was expelled from the colony. She and her family settled in what would become Rhode Island. Roger Williams criticized the religious establishment in Massachusetts and was forced to leave. He also settled in what would become the more theologically unconstrained colony of Rhode Island. Other offshoots of Massachusetts also sprang up. Thomas Hooker and John Davenport founded settlements that eventually merged in the colony of Connecticut.

New Southern Colonies

In the seventeenth century, English kings sometimes gave grants of land in America to individuals or groups of individuals. In 1632, King Charles I gave a charter to the Calvert family to found the colony that would become Maryland. The Calverts hoped that Maryland would become a refuge for Catholics, who were persecuted in England. Despite some difficulties with Puritan settlers, Maryland became a place where Catholics could worship in peace. Carolina, which later split into North and South Carolina, was a proprietary colony given by King Charles II to a group of aristocrats in the 1660s. Maryland and the Carolinas developed plantation-dominated economies dependent upon slave labor.

Effects of European Settlement

The advent of the Europeans had dramatic consequences for North America. The diseases inadvertently brought by the Europeans devastated the Native Americans. One reason that the Pilgrims were able to easily move into the lands that became Plymouth is that the previous inhabitants had been killed off by maladies brought by earlier visitors. The Europeans brought new plants and animals that reshaped the ecology of North America. The need for labor in the South contributed to an Atlantic slave trade primarily focused on the Caribbean and South America. In the English colonies, the growth of self-government and the gradual emergence of genuine freedom of religion created a society very different from Europe and the rest of the world.

Chapter Review

Rapid Review

To achieve the perfect 5, you should be able to explain the following:

- French settlers in Canada were less oppressive than the Spanish. Jesuit priests converted thousands of Native Americans to Christianity. French settlers became increasingly interested in fur trading.
- Puritans and other religious dissidents came to the Americas because they felt the Church of England was too close to Catholicism.
- The first English settlement in America was the Jamestown colony, founded in 1607. Tobacco became the main crop in Jamestown, and the first slaves arrived in 1619.
- A group of religious Separatists arrived in Plymouth, Massachusetts, in 1620. The first year of settlement was difficult for these Pilgrims, who had to rely on help from the Native Americans to survive.
- The Massachusetts Bay Colony was established in 1629 by the Puritans. This colony was established as a "city upon a hill," where the will of God could be manifested. A limited representative government was established. Religious dissent was not tolerated in this colony: Dissenters were thrown out, and they founded new colonies in Rhode Island, Connecticut, and Portsmouth.
- The ecosystem of the Americas was tremendously altered by European settlement.

Time Line

1534–1535: French adventurers explore the St. Lawrence River

1607: The English settle in Jamestown

1619: Virginia establishes House of Burgesses (first colonial legislature)

1620: Plymouth colony founded

1629: Massachusetts Bay Colony founded

1634: Maryland colony founded

1636: Roger Williams expelled from Massachusetts Bay Colony and settles in Providence, Rhode Island; Connecticut founded by John Hooker

1642: City of Montreal founded by the French

› Review Questions

Multiple-Choice Questions

1. Which colonists enjoyed the best relations with the Native Americans?
   A. The Spanish
   B. The French
   C. The Dutch
   D. The English

2. Who of the following was *not* a religious dissenter in Massachusetts Bay?
   A. William Bradford
   B. Roger Williams
   C. Anne Hutchinson
   D. Thomas Hooker

3. A colony designated as a refuge for English Catholics was
   A. Pennsylvania.
   B. South Carolina.
   C. Maryland.
   D. Virginia.

4. English people came to the New World because of
   A. their dislike for the Church of England.
   B. overcrowding in English cities.
   C. economic opportunity.
   D. All of the above

5. Most early English colonies were different from those of Spain and France because they
   A. were not directly ruled by the crown.
   B. granted rights to Indians.
   C. were economic failures.
   D. were more sparsely populated.

Short-Answer Question

6. Answer Parts A, B, and C.
   A. Briefly explain ONE reason why English colonies in the New World proved successful.
   B. Briefly explain a SECOND reason why English colonies in the New World proved successful.
   C. Briefly explain ONE advantage enjoyed by the rival French colonies.

› Answers and Explanations

1. **B**. The French were mainly interested in fur trading rather than farming, and so posed less of a threat to Native American lands. French missionaries and fur traders were more respectful of Native American culture.

2. **A**. Bradford was a governor of Massachusetts Bay for 20 years; all of the others left for religious reasons and founded colonies elsewhere.

3. **C**. George Calvert settled this colony in 1632 for exactly that purpose.

4. **D**. The overcrowding of cities was an additional factor in convincing some English people to "try their lot" in the New World.

5. **A**. Most of the early English colonies were governed by companies or proprietors granted charters by the King.

6. **Parts A and B**: The English colonies early on developed institutions of self-government, such as the Virginia House of Burgesses in 1619. The English colonists discovered and exploited valuable crops and natural resources such as tobacco, corn, fish, furs, and timber. The English colonies often provided refuges for religious dissenters back home—Puritans settled in Massachusetts and the New England colonies, Catholics in Maryland, and Quakers in Pennsylvania. Colonies such as Rhode Island and Pennsylvania were notable for their respect for religious freedom.

   Part C: The French were more interested in converting the Native Americans to Christianity and fur trading than taking land for agriculture. As a result the French generally got along better with the Native Americans than the English. This proved an advantage to the French in times of war with the English. The centralization of power in the hands of the governor of New France also often proved an advantage during wars with the English.

CHAPTER 8

British Empire in America: Growth and Conflict (1650–1750)

IN THIS CHAPTER

Summary: The economic theory of mercantilism, which held that a state should be as economically self-sufficient as possible, helped to motivate England and other European powers to discover and develop colonies, as colonies could provide raw materials. The triangular trade system tied together the economies of Europe, the Americas, and Africa and brought slaves to the Americas. The Salem Witch Trials in Massachusetts were a result of social unrest existing in the Massachusetts colony. Wars between the European powers spilled over into the Americas during this period, with Native American tribes cultivated as allies by either the English or the French.

Keywords

Mercantilism: economic system practiced by European powers in the late seventeenth century stating that economic self-sufficiency was crucial; as a result, colonial empires were important for raw materials.

Navigation Acts (1660): acts passed by the British Parliament increasing the dependence of the colonies on the English for trade; these acts caused great resentment in the American colonies but were not strictly enforced.

Triangular trade system: complex trading system that developed in this era between Europe, Africa, and the colonies; Europeans purchased slaves in Africa and sold them to the colonies, raw materials from the colonies went to Europe, while European finished products were sold in the colonies.

Middle Passage: voyage taken by African slaves on horribly overcrowded ships from Africa to the Americas.

Salem Witch Trials (1692): trials in Salem, Massachusetts, after which 19 people were executed as witches; historians note the class nature of these trials.

Salutary neglect: early eighteenth-century British policy relaxing the strict enforcement of trade policies in the American colonies.

Part of an Empire

European leaders in the seventeenth and eighteenth centuries expected colonies to generate wealth for the mother country. Most European statesmen subscribed to the economic theory of **mercantilism**. The proponents of mercantilism believed that a state's economic health depended upon a favorable balance of trade. Governments promoted this by regulating commerce, encouraging the export of goods while discouraging imports through high tariffs. Colonies served as the producers of cheap raw materials and staple products and as consumers of the mother country's finished goods. An operative assumption of mercantilists was that the wealth of the world was finite and that a state had to maximize its share of that wealth through governmental action. The American colonies played their part in this mercantilist scheme by supplying England with valuable commodities like tobacco, rice, fish, and lumber.

The first law regulating American trade was passed by Parliament in 1651. Under King Charles II, the **Navigation Acts** were passed in 1660 and 1663, with later revisions in the 1670s. These acts were designed to strengthen English trade, while hurting that of competitors like the Dutch. These acts required that English goods be transported only on English ships with majority-English crews. Colonial products such as tobacco, sugar, and rice intended for European markets had to be shipped to England first where they would be taxed. European goods intended for the American colonies also had to first be shipped to England and taxed.

The Navigation Acts increased the cost of living and the cost of doing business for the colonists. Many colonists colluded with the Dutch and other trading partners to evade these regulations. This led to some of the first conflicts between the colonies and the government in London. Disregard for English trade regulations was so extensive in New England that, in 1684, an English court convicted the Massachusetts Bay Colony of violating the Navigation Acts. This, along with Puritan resistance to the royal government, led to the revocation of the colony's charter. In 1686, King James II merged the New England colonies, New York, and New Jersey into the **Dominion of New England**. This new administrative structure increased royal authority under the King's hand-picked governor, Sir Edmund Andros.

Trouble also flared up in the south. When the price of tobacco began to fall in the 1660s, many planters blamed the unpopular Navigation Acts. This grievance was joined by others. Virginians living in the western part of the colony believed that the well-connected royal governor Sir William Berkeley was more concerned with the profits that he reaped from his office than protecting the colonists from raids by Native Americans. In 1676, a landowner named Nathaniel Bacon raised the standard of rebellion. He gathered an army of between 400 and 500 men to attack Native American settlements, some of which had been living at peace with the colonists, and to overawe the colonial government in what became known as Bacon's Rebellion. At one point, Bacon's men burned down Jamestown. Bacon died of dysentery shortly thereafter, and Governor Berkeley routed the remainder of the rebels, hanging 23 of them. In later years, some historians chose to interpret this discreditable episode as a rising of the "little man" against the colonial elite. Royal reinforcements arrived after Berkeley had crushed the rebellion. The governor was recalled to England.

In subsequent years, the power of the larger landowners grew relative to that of the royal governors. Believing that white indentured servants were more politically fractious, the landowners increased the proportion of powerless slaves in their workforces.

Growth of Slavery

African slavery became increasingly widespread and institutionalized in the Chesapeake colonies during the 1670s and 1680s. In 1662, a law was passed in Virginia declaring that the child of a slave mother was also a slave. This nullified the English common law practice that one's legal status came from that of the father and ensured that children born into slavery remained in that condition. The number of indentured servants decreased because of doubts of their political reliability after Bacon's Rebellion and because fewer were willing to endure the hardship of agricultural labor in the south when more attractive working conditions could be found in the northern colonies. The Dutch had dominated the slave trade for many years. The end of their monopoly in 1682 led to lower prices for slaves in the English colonies. A labor force of enslaved Africans became increasingly attractive to prosperous planters. So as the number of indentured servants in the south dwindled, the number of African slaves greatly increased.

Europeans began to participate in the African slave trade when Portuguese explorers and merchants developed business contacts along the west coast of Africa in the 1440s. Once the Americas were opened up to European settlement in the sixteenth century and labor-intensive cash crops like sugar became enormously lucrative, African slaves became a valuable commodity. The burgeoning slave trade of the seventeenth and eighteenth centuries was an essential component of the **triangular trade system**. This was an Atlantic-wide system of trade and economic interdependence that knitted together Africa, the Caribbean islands, both South and North America, and Europe. Finished goods from Europe were traded for slaves in Africa, who were sold in the Western Hemisphere, where they helped produce staple products that were in turn shipped to Europe. The transportation of slaves from Africa to the Americas was known as the **Middle Passage**. Conditions for the people chained in the holds of the relatively primitive sailing ships of the day were horrifying. Disease in these confined quarters made the voyages deadly for both the slaves and the ships' crews. The mortality rate among the imprisoned slaves often rose as high as 20 percent.

Only about 6 percent of the Africans shipped across the Atlantic arrived in the British colonies in North America. Most African slaves were sent to South America or the Caribbean. A healthier climate and a better balance between the sexes meant that slave populations in the British North American colonies grew through natural reproduction, unlike the situation in the Caribbean islands where high death rates demanded a continuous importation of new slaves. Until the rise of larger plantations in the south from the 1730s forward, most slaves worked on small farms in groups of two or three with their master. Over time, the slaves developed a unique culture that blended both African and European elements. Their religious beliefs also sometimes exhibited a syncretic merger of African traditions and Christianity.

Slaves sometimes rose up against their owners, and slave rebellions were a major fear for colonists in the south. The largest slave uprising in the British colonies was the **Stono**

Rebellion, which took place in South Carolina in 1739. A group of about 100 slaves rose up and began killing isolated planters. They lost a pitched battle against a force of militia-men, and eventually most of the rebels were killed in the fighting or were executed after being captured. In the aftermath of this rebellion, regulations concerning the control and treatment of slaves were tightened. Most slaves did not launch violent but futile revolts; instead they protested their treatment through work slow-downs, breaking tools, and other acts of minor sabotage. Although most slaves lived in the southern colonies, slavery existed in the north as well, where slaves worked as farmhands and servants.

Political Unrest in the Colonies

Massachusetts and the other New England colonies resented the loss of their authority to Sir Edmund Andros, the governor of the newly created Dominion of New England. King James II was overthrown during the **Glorious Revolution** of 1688 in England. The new English monarchs, William of Orange and Mary, the daughter of James II, gained power by agreeing to respect the prerogatives of Parliament. This was the beginning of constitutional monarchy in England. The Glorious Revolution inspired political upheaval in the colonies. In Massachusetts, Governor Andros was turned out of office and jailed. Protestant rebels overthrew the Catholic leaders of Maryland. In New York, a militia officer named Jacob Leisler took control of the colony.

The rebellious colonists declared their loyalty to William and Mary. The new monarchs abolished the Dominion of New England and restored most representative institutions in Massachusetts, though it became a royal colony with a royally appointed governor. Because William and Mary were Protestants, whereas James II had been a Catholic, the new English government supported the protestants in Maryland. Jacob Leisler ran afoul of the new regime and was hanged as a rebel. This was a sign that the royal government intended to continue to play an important role in colonial affairs.

Salem Witch Trials

Rapid political change was only one of the stresses the colony of Massachusetts underwent during the late seventeenth century. The dominance of traditional Puritanism began to break down. Economic tensions developed between small farmers and a flourishing class of merchants and business entrepreneurs. For many, John Winthrop's godly commonwealth seemed to be a thing of the past. Anxieties associated with this religious and social change probably played a key role in the still controversial **Salem Witch Trials** of 1692.

Accused witches had been prosecuted and executed before in the colonies, but never on the scale that exploded in Salem, Massachusetts. A group of girls began to experience inexplicable seizures and complained of attacks by invisible forces. The girls accused people of persecuting them through witchcraft, which began an expanding series of judicial investigations. Before the hysteria abated, over 100 people had been jailed and 20 executed. Nineteen men and women were hanged, and one man was pressed to death. Five other people, including an infant, died in prison. Eventually, the accusers began to lose their credibility, and people began to question the likelihood that so many people were engaged in witchcraft. A new governor put an official end to the proceedings. Historians have noted that social tensions may have fueled the accusations of witchcraft; the accusers came from economically marginal farming families, whereas the accused were members of the better-off "commercial" class.

Imperial Wars

Louis XIV, the "Sun King" of France, attempted to establish his nation as the dominant power in Europe in the late seventeenth and early eighteenth centuries. England, a growing maritime power, resisted this. Beginning in 1689, the English and French fought a long series of wars that would culminate in the Battle of Waterloo in 1815. Early on, the American colonies of England and France became involved in these wars. The War of the League of Augsburg was known as King William's War in America and lasted from 1689 to 1697. War parties of French and Native Americans raided the frontier and destroyed the town of Schenectady, New York. In turn, colonists assisted the Iroquois tribe in attacking Canada. A force largely recruited in Massachusetts captured the French base of Port Royal in Acadia. The war ended without any decisive results in America.

Just a few years later, England and France were at war again. The War of the Spanish Succession, called Queen Anne's War in America, was waged from 1702 to 1713. Because Spain was allied with France, an English force from South Carolina attacked and burned St. Augustine in Florida. They armed local Native Americans, who then attacked Spanish missions. In the north, it was the English who suffered from Native American raids on the frontier. The most spectacular of these raids occurred in 1704, when a force of French and Native Americans devastated the town of Deerfield, Massachusetts, killing 48 people and taking 112 into captivity. As in King William's War, no decisive battles took place in America. English victories in Europe, under the great general the Duke of Marlborough, compelled the French to surrender Newfoundland, Acadia, and other territories in America at the Treaty of Utrecht.

American Self-Government

England and Scotland were formally united with the Acts of Union of 1706 and 1707. From this point on, the united kingdoms were known as Great Britain. In the early eighteenth century, the British encountered some limits to their control of the North American colonies. Because of the various ways the colonies had been formed, there was no consistent method of governance across the colonies. While most colonies were royal colonies with governors appointed by the monarch, some, such as Connecticut and Rhode Island, elected their own governors; in **proprietorships**, such as the Carolinas, Maryland, and Pennsylvania, governors were appointed by the proprietors who held title to the colony.

Despite this, everywhere in British North America, the principle of self-government had taken hold. However governors were appointed, **colonial assemblies** were elected by the people. The "people" of this time were men who owned a certain amount of property. This electorate was broader than that back in Great Britain or in any other of the great European powers, however. Though the assemblies were usually composed of substantial landowners, to some degree they did reflect public opinion, especially in New England, with its vital institution of town meetings. The colonial assemblies, beginning with Massachusetts in the 1720s, resisted pressure from Great Britain to regularize the payment of salaries to royal governors. This gave the assemblies powerful financial leverage in disputes with their governors and familiarized the assemblies with "the power of the purse."

Salutary Neglect

During the reigns of George I (1714–1727) and George II (1727–1760), the British government was preoccupied with international relations and the balance of power in Europe. Having come from the Electorate of Hanover, these kings were especially concerned with affairs in Germany and central Europe. The British government's chief goal in dealing with its colonies was furthering Great Britain's economic interests. Pursuant to their mercantilist worldview, British officials attempted to prevent Americans from manufacturing their own textiles (1699), hats (1732), and iron goods (1750). Because the Navigation Acts allowed the colonists as Englishmen to own ships and carry on trade, a vibrant merchant class emerged in America. These merchants followed their own interests, evading the Navigation Acts by doing business with the French West Indies and other non-British colonies. The British government became so concerned about the American sugar trade with the French in the Caribbean that Parliament passed the **Molasses Act** of 1733, raising duties on foreign sugar. Many American shippers continued to ignore British regulations. By 1750, a new generation of British colonial administrators was anxious to tighten the government's control over its insubordinate American subjects.

First Great American Religious Revival

The **First Great Awakening** was a religious revival that profoundly influenced spiritual and intellectual values in America. Beginning in the 1720s and lasting through the 1740s, the First Great Awakening challenged the established religious authorities and called for a personal and more emotional approach to divine worship. Exponents of the Great Awakening criticized traditional, overly intellectual sermonizing by ministers. Jonathan Edwards reduced his congregation to tears by preaching on "Sinners in the Hands of an Angry God," vividly describing the yawning pit of hell and the horrors awaiting sinners there. The dynamic Anglican preacher George Whitefield attracted crowds of thousands to his sermons as he travelled through the colonies in the 1740s.

By scorning the "establishment" and emphasizing fervor over traditional ministerial learning, the Great Awakening encouraged a greater sense of personal equality in the American colonies. A growing number of people became accustomed to thinking for themselves rather than deferring to authority. A people willing to question religious leaders soon proved ready to challenge political figures as well.

Chapter Review

Rapid Review

To achieve the perfect 5, you should be able to explain the following:

- The dominant economic theory of the era was mercantilism; British mercantilist measures such as the Navigation Acts created resentment in the American colonies.
- The importation of African slaves became increasingly important for the continued economic growth of several southern colonies.
- The Salem Witch Trials demonstrated the social conflict present in the American colonies.
- Eighteenth-century European wars between the British and the French spilled over into the Americas, with British and French colonies becoming involved.

- In the early eighteenth century, colonial assemblies became increasingly powerful and independent in several colonies, including Massachusetts.
- Even during the era of "salutary neglect," the British attempted to increase their economic control over the colonies.
- The religious revival called the Great Awakening caused some colonists to question many of the religious, social, and political foundations on which colonial life was based.

Time Line

1651: First of several Navigation Acts approved by British parliament

1676: Bacon's Rebellion takes place in Virginia

1682: Dutch monopoly on slave trade ends, greatly reducing the price of slaves coming to the Americas

1686: Creation of Dominion of New England

1688: Glorious Revolution in England; James II removed from the throne

1689: Beginning of the War of the League of Augsburg

1692: Witchcraft trials take place in Salem, Massachusetts

1702: Beginning of the War of the Spanish Succession

1733: Enactment of the Molasses Act

1739: Stono (slave) Rebellion in South Carolina

1740: George Whitefield tours the American colonies—the high point of the Great Awakening

› Review Questions

Multiple-Choice Questions

1. The creation of the Dominion of New England
   A. increased democracy in the colonies.
   B. increased the power of the governor of the area.
   C. allowed New England colonies to discuss common grievances.
   D. guaranteed direct control of the king over affairs in the New England colonies.

2. A major effect of the Stono Rebellion was
   A. an increase in the number of slaves brought into the Southern colonies.
   B. increased fortifications around several southern cities.
   C. an attempt by slave owners to lessen the horrors of the Middle Passage.
   D. harsher treatment of slaves in many parts of the South.

3. The growth of colonial assemblies alarmed the British for all of the following reasons *except*
   A. assemblies holding the "power of the purse" could ultimately undermine British control.
   B. assemblies increased democratic tendencies in the colonies.
   C. assemblies occasionally ignored or resisted instructions from Great Britain.
   D. governors appointed in Britain had little control over these assemblies in most colonies.

4. For the British, the major economic role of the American colonies was
   A. to produce manufactured goods the English did not want to produce.
   B. to produce crops such as tobacco.
   C. to produce raw materials such as lumber.
   D. B and C above

5. What changes in the slave system of the south-ern colonies began in the 1730s?
   A. The Dutch lost the monopoly on slave trad-ing, thus increasing the number of slaves being brought into the Americas.
   B. Conditions during the Middle Passage began to slightly improve.
   C. More slaves began to live and work on larger plantations.
   D. A series of slave rebellions created much harsher treatment for slaves.

Short-Answer Question

6. Answer Parts A, B, and C.
   A. Briefly explain ONE way the British imperial system affected the colonies.
   B. Briefly explain a SECOND way the British imperial system affected the colonies.
   C. Briefly explain ONE way the colonies resisted greater British control.

❯ Answers and Explanations

1. **B**. This occurred after resistance in Massachusetts to the Navigation Acts, and it gave increased power to Sir Edmund Andros.

2. **D**. Many plantation owners were fearful of additional rebellions and felt that harsh treatment of slaves would prevent rebellious behavior.

3. **B**. These assemblies were in no way demo-cratic, as in every colony they were dominated by the landowning elite.

4. **D**. The role of the colonies under mercantil-ism was to provide England with crops and raw materials.

5. **C**. Before the 1730s, most slaves worked on small farms. The Dutch lost their monopoly on slave trading back in 1682. The Stono Rebellion was the first major slave rebellion and occurred in 1739.

6. **Parts A and B**: The American colonies were affected by the British government's mercan-tilist policies. In 1660 and 1663 Parliament passed Navigation Acts compelling colonists to ship tobacco, rice, sugar, and other crops to England. Goods bound to the colonies had to go through English ports. The British contin-ued to pass other financial regulations for the colonies, such as the 1733 Molasses Act. At times, the English attempted political reorgan-izations of the colonies, revoking their char-ters, as with Massachusetts in 1684. In 1686, the English government attempted to group New York, New Jersey, and the New England colonies into the Dominion of New England. This fell apart in 1689 after the overthrow of King James II. Another way the British impe-rial system affected the colonies was by involv-ing them in imperial wars with the French and Spanish. Americans were involved in King William's War (1689-1697) and Queen Anne's War (1702-1713).

   Part C: Colonists resisted greater British control by violating the Navigation Acts and later economic regulations. The colonists overthrew the Dominion of New England. In the period of "salutary neglect" colonial legislatures increased their independence and resisted efforts to strengthen the power of royal governors.

CHAPTER 9

Resistance, Rebellion, and Revolution (1750–1775)

IN THIS CHAPTER

Summary: Tensions between the British and the French intensified in the 1740s; a result of this tension was the Seven Years' War, in which colonial militias were involved. The French were defeated in this war, essentially ending their political influence on the Americas. During and after this war the British imposed a number of taxes and duties on their colonies, creating unrest. The Stamp Act created great resentment in the colonies. The results of this resentment included the Stamp Act Congress of 1765, the Boston Massacre of 1770, and the Boston Tea Party of 1773. The First Continental Congress met in 1774 and resolved that the colonies would resist efforts to tax them without their consent.

Keywords

French and Indian War (1756–1763): also known as the Seven Years' War, a conflict between the British and the French that also involved Native Americans and colonial militias. French defeat in this war greatly decreased their influence in the colonies.

Stamp Act (1765): imposed by the British, this act dictated that all legal documents in the colonies had to be issued on officially stamped paper. This act created strong resentment in the colonies and was later repealed.

Townshend Acts (1767): British legislation that forced colonies to pay duties on most goods coming from England; these duties were fiercely resisted and finally repealed in 1770.

Boston Massacre (1770): conflict between British soldiers and Boston civilians on March 5, 1770; five colonists were killed and six wounded.

Sons of Liberty: radical group that organized resistance against British policies in Boston in the 1760s and 1770s. This was the group that organized the Boston Tea Party.

Committees of Correspondence: created first in Massachusetts and then in other colonies, these groups circulated grievances against the British to towns within their colonies.

Boston Tea Party (1773): in response to British taxes on tea, Boston radicals disguised as Native Americans threw 350 chests of tea into Boston Harbor on December 16, 1773; important symbolic act of resistance to British economic control of the colonies.

First Continental Congress (1774): meeting in Philadelphia at which colonists vowed to resist further efforts to tax them without their consent.

War in the West

In 1750, the lands west of the Appalachian Mountains were inhabited by Native American tribes eager to trade with the Europeans but determined to maintain their independence. Both the British and French wanted to lay claim to this expansive territory. Ambitious speculators from Virginia began to purchase land in the Ohio Valley. The French, resolved to uphold their own interests in the area and to protect the tenuous lines of communication between Canada and Louisiana, responded by beginning construction on Fort Duquesne on the site of what is now Pittsburgh, Pennsylvania.

Now it was the turn of the British to be concerned about developments in the Ohio Valley. In 1754, Governor Robert Dinwiddie of Virginia dispatched a small force to the Ohio Territory to uphold British interests and persuade the French to leave. This detachment was commanded by a young militia officer named George Washington. After an initial success, Washington and his men were defeated and captured. The next year, the British responded by sending General Edward Braddock and a large force of British Regular troops to destroy Fort Duquesne. The French and Native American allies ambushed and destroyed Braddock's army near the fort. The frontier fighting of 1754 and 1755 began the French and Indian War, merging in 1756 with the much larger European Seven Years' War.

As fighting began with the French, the colonies and the British government found it difficult to coordinate their policies. In 1754, delegations from seven of the more northern colonies gathered for the **Albany Congress**. Benjamin Franklin and others hoped that the colonies and the British government could work out common measures for dealing with the Native Americans and the threat posed by the French. Franklin proposed a plan of union that would have created a colonial council with a president appointed by the king. Franklin's plan was rejected by both the colonial assemblies and the British government.

Defeat of New France

Despite the British and American advantages in numbers and sea power, the French won a series of impressive victories in North America from 1756 to 1758. The Native American allies of the French ravaged the western frontier. The turning point in the war came in 1757, when William Pitt rose to power in the British government. Pitt devised a strategy that focused on capturing French colonial possessions around the world. He poured resources into North America, including a fleet and 25,000 Redcoats. Willing to spend freely to get what he wanted, Pitt paid all expenses in raising colonial troops. Eventually 24,000 Americans fought with the British against the French. Faced with such overwhelming force, the French retreated back into Canada. The British followed them there in 1759, and at the Battle of the Plains of Abraham on September 13 defeated their main army and captured the city of Quebec. Montreal fell in 1760, completing the British conquest of Canada.

The war between Great Britain and France ended officially with the Treaty of Paris in 1763. The war made Britain the dominant power in North America. Britain retained Canada and had conquered Florida from Spain; thus, the British controlled the entire eastern seaboard. The war also eliminated France as a power in North America; driven from Canada, France gave Louisiana to its ally, Spain, as compensation for the loss of Florida.

The American colonists took pride in the important role that they had played in defeating the French. They were proud to be part of the victorious British Empire. At the same time, the French and Indian War had exposed differences between the colonists and the British. Many British soldiers and officials believed that the colonists could have done more to contribute to the war effort, both financially and in terms of fighting. In turn, many colonists resented what they believed was British condescension directed toward them. They disliked what they saw as the brutal and authoritarian behavior of the British military. They were outraged when British troops were quartered in their homes. The seeds had been planted for later divisions.

The British Need Money

Wars are expensive. War in the wilderness of America was especially expensive. William Pitt had focused on victory, not finances. Now his successors in office had to find the money to pay off an enormous government debt.

In 1763, King George III supported the rise of George Grenville to the position of prime minister. Grenville knew that one of his most important tasks as the head of the government would be to address the debt. He believed that the American colonies should pay a greater share of the cost of maintaining the empire. Like a growing number of British leaders, he was angered by American defiance of the Navigation Acts and wanted to bring an end to the period of salutary neglect in the British administration of the colonies.

Grenville began his campaign to bring the colonies to heel with the **Currency Act** of 1764. This act prohibited the colonies from issuing their own paper money. This forced the cash-strapped American colonists to pay British merchants in hard currency. Grenville followed this up with the **Sugar Act**, which lowered the duties on molasses imported to the colonies but strengthened the measures taken to ensure that the colonists would pay what they owed. Both laws added to the economic woes of the colonists, who were suffering from a post-war business slump. Many colonists criticized Grenville's acts, and some began to question the nature of the relationship between the colonies and their mother country.

Stamp Act Crisis

Grenville overplayed his hand with the **Stamp Act** of 1765. This was the first time that Parliament imposed a direct tax on the colonies, rather than a customs duty on imported goods. Colonists now had to purchase paper with a revenue stamp for such common documents and printed items as wills, newspapers, and playing cards. To pay this tax, the colonists had to use scarce hard currency rather than local issues of paper money. Not only was the British government raising money from the colonies, something Americans grudgingly accepted when it came to trade regulation, but the British revenue service was now reaching into the colonists' domestic affairs, taxing elements of their everyday lives. Americans across the colonies reacted to the Stamp Act with fury. They were being taxed without representation, in violation of more than a century of precedent during which they had managed their own internal finances. In July 1765, Samuel Adams played a leading role organizing the **Sons of Liberty** in Boston. Riots led by the Sons of Liberty intimidated the stamp agent for Massachusetts into surrendering his office. Branches of the Sons of Liberty sprang up in other colonies, and other stamp agents were compelled to resign. In the Virginia House of Burgesses, Patrick Henry made a name for himself denouncing the tyranny of George III.

Across the colonies, leaders looked for a constructive response to what they regarded as the overreaching of the British government. Since the colonies were being taxed without representation, James Otis in Massachusetts and Benjamin Franklin in Pennsylvania argued that Americans should be elected to Parliament. In October 1765, delegates from nine colonies gathered at the **Stamp Act Congress** held in New York City. The Congress issued a Declaration of Rights and Grievances affirming that, as Englishmen, the colonists could not be taxed by a body that did not represent them. Colonists began talking about economic boycotts against British goods as a way of protesting against the Stamp Act.

Adding to the anger of the colonists was the passage of the **Quartering Act** requiring that the colonies house and feed the British troops stationed in America. Supporting soldiers whose only role after the defeat of the French seemed to be as enforcers of unpopular laws struck Americans as the height of tyranny.

Grenville left office in July 1765 and was replaced by Lord Rockingham. The new prime minister was anxious to calm the uproar in the colonies. British business owners, worried about a loss of trade with the colonies, lobbied effectively against the Stamp Act. Rockingham persuaded Parliament to repeal the Stamp Act early in 1766. Repeal of the Stamp Act delighted Americans and led to celebrations in the colonies. This self-congratulatory mood ended, however, when word came that Parliament, as a face-saving measure, had also passed the **Declaratory Act**, which asserted its right to legislate for the colonies "in all cases whatsoever."

Townshend Acts

In 1766, an ailing William Pitt returned as prime minister. Charles Townshend, the **Chancellor of the Exchequer**, became the dominant figure in formulating policy toward the colonies. Like Grenville before him, Townshend was driven by the need to raise revenue. As the Americans had objected to the Stamp Act because it taxed transactions within the borders of the colonies, Townshend assumed that the colonists would not object to taxes on British goods that they imported. In 1767, the **Townshend Acts** placed new duties on lead, paper, glass, and tea, all goods that the colonists bought from British merchants. In order to strengthen the position of the British authorities in America, Townshend used some of the money raised by the taxes to pay the salaries of royal governors and other British office holders, which weakened the power of the colonial assemblies. Townshend also tightened up the enforcement of British tax collection and trade regulations with the creation of an American Customs Board and new admiralty courts whose purpose was to try smugglers.

Townshend soon learned that the distinction that he made between "internal" and "external" taxes did not wash with most American colonists. The Americans believed that Parliament could not tax them without their consent. Soon a number of American leaders eloquently expressed this point of view. In his *Letters from a Farmer in Pennsylvania* (1767), John Dickinson argued that Parliament could regulate the empire's trade but lacked the authority to raise revenue from colonists. When some defenders of the Townshend Acts pointed out that the taxes were low, Dickinson responded, "If they have a right to levy a tax of one penny upon us, they have a right to levy a *million* upon us; for where does their right stop?" In an article about American opposition to taxation without representation, Benjamin Franklin warned British readers that "this unhappy new system of politics tends to dissolve those bands of union and to sever us forever."

Samuel Adams organized opposition to the Townshend Acts in Massachusetts. Early in 1768, he wrote a letter urging other colonies to join Massachusetts in resisting Parliament. In the letter, he declared that "taxation without representation is tyranny." The Massachusetts Assembly endorsed this **Circular Letter** and forwarded it to the other colonial assemblies. The British authorities were outraged, and the colonial secretary urged royal governors to dissolve any assemblies that joined with Massachusetts. Despite this, five other colonies issued similar documents. Boycotts of British goods became widespread across the colonies. Once again, American economic power made itself felt in Britain. Lord North became prime minister in 1770. He led Parliament in repealing all Townshend duties except that on tea, which was left as a reminder that the British government maintained its power to tax the colonies.

Boston Massacre

Boston, Massachusetts, became a flashpoint for tensions between British officials and colonists. Boston merchants defied British trade regulations, much to the fury of customs officers. In 1768, the British seized a smuggling ship belonging to John Hancock. American mobs retaliated by assaulting British officials. The British responded to this by stationing two regiments of British soldiers in Boston. The Redcoats soon became very unpopular as a symbol of British repression. Many working-class Bostonians hated the soldiers because, in their spare time, they took on part-time jobs that had once gone to local workers. Harassing soldiers became a sport for some Bostonians. On March 5, 1770, a mob started throwing snowballs laced with ice and rocks at a group of soldiers standing guard. The infuriated soldiers fired a volley at their tormentors, killing five men and wounding eight others. Samuel Adams turned the **Boston Massacre** into a public relations disaster for the British, propagandizing the event as a demonstration of British brutality. Despite this, many Americans who opposed British policy also deplored mob violence. John Adams undertook the defense of the British soldiers when they went on trial; of the eight accused, six were acquitted and two received the relatively mild punishment of a brand on their thumbs.

Tensions between the colonies and Britain seemed to subside a bit between 1770 and 1773. Business appeared to go on as usual. But fundamental issues had not been resolved. Samuel Adams formed a **Committee of Correspondence** in Boston to share news and coordinate protests against the British. Committees of Correspondence quickly spread across Massachusetts and throughout the colonies. These committees provided an essential organizational framework for American resistance to British policy.

Boston Tea Party

One British tax still remained, that on tea. Some Americans expressed their opposition to the tax by boycotting British tea. The boycott had an effect, hurting the British East India Company, which was in dire financial straits because of troubles in India. In an effort to provide assistance to the East India Company, Lord North's government sponsored the **Tea Act** of 1773. This legislation allowed the East India Company to market its tea to the Americans without having to go through middlemen in England; the tea tax stayed the same, but the price of high-quality British tea went down.

Lord North thought that the Tea Act was a win for everyone; the East India Company would be saved and the Americans would get cheaper tea, despite the tax. The Americans saw things differently. They saw the Tea Act as an insidious way of reaffirming Parliament's power to tax the colonies. They distrusted the special privilege granted the well-connected East India Company. At several ports, popular gatherings ensured that the East India Company tea stayed aboard ship. Things went further in Boston. On the evening of December 16, 1773, men dressed as Mohawk Indians swarmed onto the East India Company's ships and tossed some 350 chests of tea into the dirty waters of the harbor. The **Boston Tea Party** was an act of defiance that quickly focused the wrath of the British government on the city.

Intolerable Acts

The **Intolerable Acts**, also known as the Coercive Acts, were passed by Parliament early in 1774. They were designed to punish Massachusetts for the Boston Tea Party. The British closed the port of Boston to all but military or officially approved traffic. The British took control of government in Massachusetts, giving the royal governor the authority to appoint most officials in the state and limiting town meetings to just once a year. Finally, the unpopular Quartering Act was reimposed on all colonies. Although Massachusetts was the focus of the Intolerable Acts, Americans living elsewhere recognized that the British could just as easily impose coercive laws in their own colonies. Spontaneously, legislators in different colonial legislatures began calling for a gathering of colonial representatives to address the crisis in Massachusetts.

The passage of the Quebec Act of 1774 was associated in the minds of American colonists with the Intolerable Acts. In many ways an enlightened approach to governing the French population of Canada, the Quebec Act angered Americans because it included the western territories in an expanded province of Quebec and guaranteed freedom of worship to French Catholics. To the American colonists, it seemed as if the British were cutting them off from the west and surrounding them with their hereditary enemies.

First Continental Congress

The Continental Congress convened in Philadelphia on September 5, 1774. Fifty-six delegates from every colony but Georgia took part. The delegates were undecided about what to do. Samuel Adams wanted a complete boycott of British trade, whereas others urged a diplomatic approach to Parliament. John Adams united Congress with his **Declaration of Rights and Grievances**, which reiterated the American position that Parliament could regulate the trade of the colonies but could not tax the colonies without representation.

Congress also adopted the **Suffolk Resolves**, a declaration that originated in Massachusetts. The Suffolk Resolves defied the Intolerable Acts by refusing to recognize the changes that the British had made to the Massachusetts government. They also imposed a boycott of British products. Recognizing the increasing seriousness of the political situation, the Suffolk Resolves called on the colonies to see to the readiness of their militias.

Before adjourning on October 26, 1774, Congress drew up a petition to George III requesting the repeal of the Intolerable Acts. Congress also set May 10, 1775, as the date for the convening of a Second Continental Congress. As 1774 drew to a close, Americans pondered what the British government would do next.

Chapter Review

KEY IDEA

Rapid Review

To achieve the perfect 5, you should be able to explain the following:

- Tensions between the British and the French intensified in the 1740s when land speculators from English colonies began to acquire land in the Ohio Valley.
- The Seven Years' War (the French and Indian War in American textbooks) was between the English and colonial militias and the French; Native Americans fought on both sides.
- The defeat of the French in this war largely ended their influence in the Americas; after the war, the British attempted to make the colonies pay their fair share for the war effort.
- Parliamentary efforts during this era to produce money for Great Britain by imposing various taxes and duties on the colonies resulted in great unrest in the colonies.
- The impact of the Stamp Act on the colonies was great; as a result, nine colonies met at the 1765 Stamp Act Congress and the Sons of Liberty formed in Boston.
- Boston remained a center of opposition to British policy; the Boston Massacre in 1770 and the Boston Tea Party in 1773 helped to create resistance to the Crown in other colonies as well.
- The 1774 Intolerable Acts that closed the port of Boston and curtailed freedom of speech in Massachusetts outraged many in the colonies.
- The 1774 First Continental Congress passed a resolution that firmly stated the colonies would firmly resist measures that taxed them without their consent. At this meeting it was also decided that individual colonies should start to raise and train state militias.

Time Line

1754: Representatives of colonies meet at Albany Congress to coordinate further Western settlement

1756: Beginning of Seven Years' War

1763: Signing of Treaty of Paris ending Seven Years' War

1764: Parliament approves Sugar Act, Currency Act

1765: Stamp Act approved by Parliament; Stamp Act Congress occurs and Sons of Liberty is formed, both in opposition to the Stamp Act

1766: Stamp Act repealed, but in Declaratory Act, Parliament affirms its right to tax the colonies

1767: Passage of the Townshend Acts

1770: Boston Massacre occurs

1773: Boston Tea Party takes place in December in opposition to the Tea Act

1774: Intolerable Acts adopted by Parliament
First Continental Congress held in Philadelphia

❯ Review Questions

Multiple-Choice Questions

1. William Pitt was able to convince the colonies to fight in the Seven Years' War by
   A. threatening military reprisals by the British army.
   B. threatening to make the colonists fight the French by themselves.
   C. putting the recruiting of troops in the colonies totally in the hands of the colonies themselves.
   D. paying colonial soldiers generous bonuses to fight against the French.

2. The Stamp Act created great fury in the colonies because
   A. it imposed massive duties on the colonies.
   B. it was the first time Parliament had imposed a duty on the colonies.
   C. it took badly needed revenue away from colonial legislatures.
   D. this was the first time that Parliament imposed a direct tax on the colonies.

3. The statement "taxation without representation is tyranny" was first proclaimed by
   A. Benjamin Franklin.
   B. John Hancock.
   C. Samuel Adams.
   D. Patrick Henry.

4. After the Seven Years' War, resentment between the British and the colonists existed for all of the following reasons *except*
   A. the British resented the fact that few colonists had actually helped them in the war against the French.
   B. British soldiers had been quartered in colonial homes.
   C. the British resented the fact that some colonists continued to trade with the French at the beginning of the war.
   D. colonial militiamen felt the British exhibited a patronizing attitude toward them.

5. Most delegates at the First Continental Congress of 1774
   A. felt that there should be a total boycott of British goods by the colonies.
   B. felt that the colonies should firmly resist measures to tax them without their consent.
   C. felt that it was time to seriously consider military measures against the British.
   D. wanted the British to totally refrain from regulating trade to the colonies.

Short-Answer Question

6. Answer Parts A, B, and C.
   A. Briefly explain ONE reason for conflict between the colonies and the British government in the 1760s and 1770s.
   B. Briefly explain a SECOND reason for conflict between the colonies and the British government in the 1760s and 1770s.
   C. Briefly explain ONE way the colonists expressed their opposition to the actions of the British government.

❯ Answers and Explanations

1. **C.** Pitt put the recruiting of colonial troops totally in local hands and agreed to reimburse the colonies for all their expenses during the war.

2. **D.** All previous taxation of the colonies had been self-imposed.

3. **C.** This statement was first made by Adams in 1768 in an article he wrote opposing the Townshend Acts.

4. **A.** The colonies contributed nearly 24,000 men to the war effort—while the British contributed 25,000.

5. **B.** Although some, including Sam Adams, wanted a boycott of all British goods, John Adams crafted a compromise that called for the colonies to oppose "taxation without representation."

6. **Parts A and B:** Victory in the French and Indian War eliminated the serious military threat posed by the French. The colonists now had much less need for the military security provided by Great Britain. The French and Indian War had been enormously expensive for the British government. The British attempted to meet a budget deficit by taxing the American colonies. This conflicted with the American opposition to taxation without representation; the Americans believed that they should be taxed only by their own elected representatives. Successive British taxes—the Sugar Act (1764), the Stamp Act (1765), the Townshend Acts (1767), the Tea Act (1773)—were opposed and resisted by the colonists. The Americans also resented the Quartering Act (1765), which forced them to find housing and provisions for British troops stationed in their colonies. Many Americans were outraged by the Intolerable Acts (1774), imposed on Massachusetts following the Boston Tea Party; the port of Boston was shut down, and British officials were given the power to appoint all officials in the colony, and citizens had to ask British permission to hold town meetings.

Part C: Americans expressed their opposition in a variety of ways. A Stamp Act Congress composed of representatives from nine colonies organized resistance to the Stamp Act. Sam Adams founded the Sons of Liberty in 1765. In 1768, Sam Adams issued the Circular Letter opposing the Townshend Acts. Other colonists published works criticizing British policy, such as John Dickinson's *Letters from a Farmer in Pennsylvania* (1767). Sam Adams set up a Committee of Correspondence in Boston; soon similar committees of correspondence appeared across the colonies to exchange ideas and information. The 1773 Boston Tea Party was a protest against the Tea Act; men dressed as Indians dumped British tea into Boston Harbor. Following the imposition of the Intolerable Acts on Massachusetts in 1774, the First Continental Congress met in Philadelphia to coordinate resistance to British policy. It issued the Declaration of Rights and Grievances. The Suffolk Resolves called for a boycott of British goods until the Intolerable Acts were repealed. Militia began training across the American colonies.

CHAPTER 10

American Revolution and the New Nation (1775–1787)

IN THIS CHAPTER

Summary: The Second Continental Congress, meeting in May 1775, began to prepare the American colonies for war. The impact of *Common Sense* by Thomas Paine and other documents continued to fan anti-British sentiment in the colonies, although there were still a number of Loyalists who supported British policies. As commander of the colonial army, George Washington practiced a defensive strategy, which, along with invaluable assistance from the French, helped to defeat the British army. The first government of the new nation was established by the Articles of Confederation, which created a weak national government.

Keywords

Second Continental Congress (May 1775): meeting that authorized the creation of a Continental army; many delegates still hoped that conflict could be avoided with the British.

***Common Sense* (1776):** pamphlet written by Thomas Paine attacking the system of government by monarchy; this document was very influential throughout the colonies.

Battle of Yorktown (1781): defeat of the British in Virginia, ending their hopes of winning the Revolutionary War.

Treaty of Paris (1783): treaty ending the Revolutionary War; by this treaty Great Britain recognized American independence and gave Americans the territory between the Appalachian Mountains and the Mississippi River.

Articles of Confederation (ratified 1781): document establishing the first government of the United States; the federal government was given limited power and the states much power.

Northwest Ordinances (1784, 1785, 1787): bills authorizing the sale of lands in the Northwest Territory to raise money for the federal government; bills also laid out procedures for these territories to eventually attain statehood.

Lexington and Concord

King George II and the British government headed by Lord North did not respond favorably to the petition of the First Continental Congress. The British government saw no reason to compromise with the American colonists. They failed to comprehend that events were moving out of their control. The Americans were rapidly establishing a unified front against the Intolerable Acts and British attempts to weaken colonial self-government. In Massachusetts, the assembly met in defiance of the orders of General Thomas Gage, the acting governor; it became in effect a shadow government, exerting its influence over most of the colony outside of Boston, where Gage sat with his small army of Redcoats.

Pursuant to the Suffolk Resolves' call for the colonies to upgrade their militias, the Massachusetts assembly created a militia system independent of General Gage's control. Arms and munitions for these men were stored at the town of Concord. In February 1775, the British government declared Massachusetts to be in a state of rebellion. On the night of April 18–19, Gage sent a force of 700 men to destroy the militia arsenal at Concord. Word of this expedition soon leaked to the Americans, and Paul Revere and William Dawes rode out of Boston to spread the word that the Redcoats were coming. As the sun rose on April 19, the British vanguard encountered a force of 80 militiamen gathered on the town common at **Lexington**. The British ordered the militia to disperse; the American militia commander ordered his men to fall back, but not everyone heard him. At this moment of uncertainty, someone fired a shot. More shots followed, and the British charged with bayonets. Within minutes, eight colonists were dead and ten wounded.

The British continued their advance to **Concord**. The Americans were ready for them; more and more militiamen were gathering. The British found and destroyed some military supplies but did little significant damage. A large group of militiamen advanced on the British troops guarding the North Bridge on the outskirts of the town and after an exchange of fire drove them away. The British began to march back to Boston; along the way, they were attacked by groups of angry militiamen. Only the timely arrival of reinforcements sent by Gage saved the column. In this fighting, the British lost 275 men; 93 Americans were killed.

In May, Ethan Allen and his Vermont Green Mountain Boys seized Fort Ticonderoga from its tiny British garrison. Almost a year later, in March 1776, cannon dragged through the snow from Ticonderoga would persuade the British to evacuate Boston.

Second Continental Congress

When the **Second Continental Congress** assembled in May, it faced unprecedented challenges; the colonies were in rebellion and engaged in a war with the greatest maritime empire in the world. As word of Lexington and Concord spread, British authority in the colonies rapidly collapsed. Colonial legislatures assumed local power, but the Second Continental Congress would have to guide the united destinies of the colonies in the coming conflict.

Congress acted with decisiveness. It created the Continental Army and appointed the experienced soldier George Washington of Virginia its commander. Congress created a committee to formulate and conduct foreign policy; it also began issuing paper money to finance the war.

Even as it prepared for military operations, Congress made a last effort at peace. Congress sent the "Olive Branch Petition" to George III, asking the king to mediate a "happy and permanent reconciliation" to the conflict between the colonies and the British government. George II was in no mood to offer concessions to the Americans. He and his government were determined to quell the rebellion in the colonies by force. British intransigence forced even political moderates in the colonies to consider the possibility of American independence.

Thomas Paine's *Common Sense*

Although Thomas Paine had only emigrated to America from England in 1774, he warmly embraced the cause of the colonists. In January 1776, he published ***Common Sense***, one of the most influential political works in American history. Paine's pamphlet struck a nerve and sold phenomenally. Within three months, over 100,000 copies were printed, and by the end of the Revolutionary War, some 500,000 copies had been distributed in a country with a population of around two million. Paine managed to reach almost everyone who was literate in America; it was an extraordinary mass media success for the eighteenth century.

Paine wanted the colonies to separate themselves from Great Britain. He argued that the colonies would prosper once freed from the political and economic shackles imposed by the British. He attacked the institution of the monarchy, to which many Americans were still attached. He declared that "monarchy and hereditary succession have laid the world in blood and ashes." Paine's *Common Sense* played an important role in persuading many Americans of the necessity of independence. The **Loyalist** minority recognized the power of Paine's pamphlet; one New Yorker observed that "the unthinking multitude are mad for it. . . ."

Declaration of Independence

On June 7, 1776, Richard Henry Lee of Virginia placed a motion before Congress resolving "that these United Colonies are, and of right ought to be, free and independent States. . . ." Lee also called for Congress to consider a governmental framework through which the states could address continental issues. While the congressional delegates discussed independence with each other and communicated with the legislatures in their home states, a committee including Benjamin Franklin, John Adams, and Thomas Jefferson was appointed to draft a declaration of independence. The committee gave Thomas Jefferson the task of producing a first draft. Jefferson had a reputation of being a gifted writer, and he was well read in the writings of the great political philosophers of the **Enlightenment**.

Jefferson's text evoked the natural rights theory of John Locke, asserting that men have "certain unalienable rights," and "that among these are life, liberty, and the pursuit of happiness." Jefferson also echoed Locke in arguing that when a government "becomes destructive of these ends it is the right of the people to alter or abolish it." Jefferson embraced the notion of government as a social contract, writing that governments derive "their just powers from the consent of the governed." The bulk of Jefferson's text was a long list of the wrongs that the colonies had suffered at the hands of the British. Jefferson attributed these to George III rather than Parliament, accentuating a tyrannical view of British rule. After some changes at the hands of the committee and in Congress, the Declaration of Independence was debated on July 1. The next day, July 2, Congress voted for independence. This decision was announced on July 4.

Reactions to Independence

The Declaration of Independence was greeted with celebrations throughout the newly minted states. While supporters of independence were in the ascendency and controlled the state governments, not all Americans wanted to renounce their allegiance to the mother country. Although sometimes caricatured as wealthy grandees with close economic and political ties to the British colonial administration, Loyalists in fact came from all economic strata. Many valued the economic and cultural connections to Great Britain; others doubted the legality and good sense of challenging Great Britain's power.

Many African Americans greeted the Declaration of Independence with hope. The strong affirmation of natural rights in the document seemed to challenge the institution of slavery. (In fact, Jefferson had blamed American slavery on the British in his first draft; this section of the text was removed by Congress.) In the short run, independence would not lead to emancipation for slaves. Some slaves fled to the British, and a few were recruited into special "Ethiopian" units fighting with the British Army. Some slaves in the northern states won their freedom by serving in the militia or the Continental Army. Free blacks saw the ideals of the American Revolution as supporting their attempts to claim their rights as citizens.

Native Americans saw nothing for themselves in the Declaration of Independence or a free United States. While some Native Americans fought with the Americans, most supported the British because they feared the land hunger of the new nation.

Balance of Forces

Great Britain possessed an overwhelming military advantage over the colonies. The British Navy controlled the seas. The British Army was a highly regarded professional force. The British supplemented their Redcoat Regulars with thousands of German troops, known collectively as **Hessians**. The British could also rely on the services of American Loyalists, many of whom joined the British army or formed their own military units. In contrast, the Americans had no navy at the outset of the war. The Continental Army was poorly paid and supplied by Congress and the states; it had to address an initial lack of discipline and training while engaging in military operations against the British. The Continental Army was supported in the field by units of inexperienced militiamen who often proved unreliable under fire.

Despite their military superiority, the British faced serious problems in combatting the American rebellion. British forces were a long way from home, at the end of a supply line that stretched across the Atlantic Ocean. Because it could take months to sail back and forth between America and Great Britain, it was very difficult for British commanders to communicate with the government in London. America was a vast place, much of it wilderness; the British could not hope to occupy it all with the troops that they had available, and they ended up occupying only a few cities along the coast. The new United States had no capital or decisive point at which capture would force an American surrender. British armies would march through the American countryside hoping to force a battle that would end the war; sometimes they would not return.

On the other hand, the Americans were fighting on their home ground. George Washington proved to be an able strategist, who realized that the United States would win the war if it simply avoided defeat; as a result, he made the survival of his army a priority, making it a rallying point for American resistance. American spirits were lifted early in the war when, in June 1775, American militiamen fought the British at **Bunker Hill** outside Boston. The Americans were forced from their position, but before this happened, they shot down almost 1,000 British soldiers. This gave the impression that American citizen soldiers could easily defeat British Regulars. However, subsequent experience would demonstrate that this was not the case.

The War in the North

The British were forced out of Boston in March 1776, when cannon dragged from Fort Ticonderoga threatened their ships in Boston Harbor. The British retreated to Halifax, Nova Scotia, to regroup. At the end of June, the British general William Howe arrived at New York City with a massively reinforced army. That summer, Howe defeated Washington's army and maneuvered it out of New York, chasing the Americans across New Jersey into Pennsylvania.

That winter, the prospects for the American cause seemed bleak. Washington's army suffered from low morale and was dwindling due to desertions and expiring enlistments. Washington retrieved the situation with a brilliant counterstroke. On the evening of December 25, he led his men across the Delaware River, surprising and capturing the Hessian garrison of Trenton, New Jersey. A few days later, Washington defeated a British detachment at Princeton. As a result, the British hastily evacuated their outposts in New Jersey, surrendering much of the gains of their summer campaign. Washington had reversed the momentum of the war and given American morale a much needed boost.

The Saratoga Campaign

The fighting of 1776 resulted in failure for the British. The following year, they attempted to cripple the rebellion with an ambitious strategy of cutting the colonies in two. British forces from Canada, New York City, and the Great Lakes would drive toward Albany, New York, and the Hudson River. With the Hudson River Valley under firm British control, the New England colonies would be divided from the colonies to the south. With different sections of the country isolated, the British believed that they could then suppress the rebellion.

Unfortunately for the British, difficulties in communication and the ambitions of generals upset the plan before it began. Instead of marching up the Hudson River to Albany, General Howe in New York City instead set sail for Philadelphia, hoping to capture the American capital and destroy Washington's army. Howe defeated Washington and captured Philadelphia, but as Washington demonstrated with an attack on British forces in the Philadelphia suburb of Germantown, his army was anything but destroyed. Howe's Philadelphia gambit not only failed to achieve any decisive results, but it deprived General John Burgoyne's army, advancing toward Albany from Canada, of desperately needed support.

Burgoyne's army bogged down in the New York wilderness and was surrounded at Saratoga by hard-fighting American forces. Burgoyne surrendered on October 17, 1777.

This defeat was disastrous for the British. Not only was an entire British army eliminated, but the American victory at Saratoga convinced the French to declare war on Great Britain in 1778. Until this point, the French had been assisting the Americans only with covert shipments of arms and military supplies. The French did this not because of any love for the Americans or their principles, but because they wanted to weaken their long-time enemy, Great Britain. Saratoga convinced the French government that the Americans could win and that the British were vulnerable. French intervention changed the nature of the war, which now became an international conflict with French and British forces clashing around the world. Later, the Spanish and Dutch would join the fight against Great Britain. French naval and military support would prove crucial for the Americans in the final campaign of the war.

While American men served in militias or Continental Army, American women also played a vital role in sustaining the war effort. They ran farms and businesses while men were away and provided many needed services for the Army. Some women hoped that revolutionary ideals would lead to an improvement in their legal status. In March 1776, Abigail Adams urged her husband, John Adams, to "Remember the ladies. . . . Do not put such unlimited power in the hands of the husbands."

The War in the South

Facing a new war after Saratoga and the American alliance with France, the British reassessed their strategy. A new British commander, General Henry Clinton, abandoned Philadelphia and marched overland to New York City. Along the way he encountered Washington's Continental Army. During the winter of 1777–1778, Washington's men suffered terribly from cold and famine at **Valley Forge**. Washington supported the efforts of a German officer, Baron von Steuben, to improve the training of his troops. Steuben's labors paid off when Washington's and Clinton's armies faced each other at the Battle of Monmouth in June 1778. Although Clinton was able to continue his retreat to New York, Washington's Continental troops more than held their own in very hard fighting.

The British now decided to focus their increasingly stretched military resources on the south, which they believed to be a hotbed of colonists with Loyalist sympathies. Initially, all went well for the British. They reoccupied Georgia, and Clinton forced the surrender of Charleston and a garrison of 5,000 men in May 1780. After General Charles Cornwallis defeated the remaining American army in the south a few months later, it appeared that the British southern strategy had succeeded.

The tide soon turned. George Washington sent General Nathanael Greene south to rally what was left of the Continental forces. Although he never won a battle, Greene waged a brilliant campaign that left British forces in the Carolinas confined to a few cities and outposts.

After winning a bloody battle with Greene, General Cornwallis marched his battered Redcoats into Virginia to rest and resupply. He stationed his army at **Yorktown**. Learning of this, Washington marched his army and a force of French troops, led by the Comte de Rochambeau, south. The British hoped to evacuate Cornwallis's army by sea, but a French fleet, under the Comte de Grasse, arrived in Chesapeake Bay before them. On September 5, 1781, the French fleet held off the British at the Battle of the Virginia Capes. This left Cornwallis trapped. Late in September, Washington began a formal siege of Yorktown.

His situation hopeless, Cornwallis surrendered on October 19. Yorktown was the last major battle of the war; with another army captured, the British realized that they had lost America.

The Treaty of Paris

Peace negotiations began in Paris in 1782. Benjamin Franklin, John Adams, and John Jay represented the United States in these talks. Negotiations were protracted because fighting was still going on between the British and the French and their allies. Finally, the American delegation signed a treaty with the British on September 3, 1783.

In the Treaty of Paris, Great Britain recognized the independence of the United States. The British retained Canada but ceded to the United States the lands between the Appalachian Mountains and the Mississippi River. For the new nation, the western boundary of the Mississippi River in part reflected the wartime victories of George Rogers Clark in the Ohio River Valley. The Americans won lucrative fishing rights off Newfoundland and Nova Scotia, while promising the British that prewar debts to British merchants would be paid and that Loyalists would have confiscated property returned.

New State Constitutions and the Articles of Confederation

Independence meant that old colonial charters had to be replaced by new state constitutions. Ten states had drawn up new constitutions by the end of 1777. These documents reflected a suspicion of executive power borne of the years of struggle with Great Britain, so most governors were given limited authority. All states but Pennsylvania and Vermont instituted **bicameral legislatures**. Many states ensured the freedoms of their citizens with bills of rights. Most states broadened their electorates by lowering the property qualification to vote.

The Continental Congress completed work on a constitution for a limited national government by the fall of 1777. The **Articles of Confederation** were sent to the state legislatures for ratification. As with the state constitutions, this constitution for the new nation was a reaction against the overly powerful government the Americans had rebelled against. The Articles of Confederation created a very weak continental government.

The centerpiece of the new government was a **unicameral legislature** in which each state would have one vote. Limited executive authority was vested in a Committee of Thirteen, in which each state would have a representative. There was no national judiciary. To ratify the Articles of Confederation or to amend them, all 13 state legislatures would have to vote affirmatively. This held up ratification for almost four years. Because of disputes over western lands, Maryland did not ratify the Articles of Confederation until 1781, finally allowing the new form of government to take hold.

As a governmental framework designed to avoid governmental tyranny, the Articles of Confederation gave Congress few powers. The national government could carry on foreign relations, manage the western territories, and make treaties with Native Americans. The national government could not regulate trade or interstate commerce or impose taxes; it remained financially dependent upon financial contributions from the states.

Financial Problems

During the Revolution, Congress never found a way to effectively finance the war effort. The government resorted to issuing large amounts of unsecured paper money. Rampant inflation soon ate away the value of these so-called **"Continentals."** Because of its financial embarrassment, Congress never paid many soldiers who had served in the Continental Army. Only loans from France and other European countries kept the government operating. Conditions did not improve for the government after the war; it had many debts and no way to raise enough money to pay them. Efforts to place tariffs on imports failed to get a unanimous vote in Congress. The nation's financial woes were multiplied by a postwar economic depression.

Northwest Ordinances

The government did have one potential source of income open to it, the sale of western lands. Settlers were pouring into the territories west of the Appalachian Mountains. By 1790, 110,000 Americans had moved into Kentucky and Tennessee. The **Northwest Ordinances** of 1784, 1785, and 1787 established regulations for the sale of land and territorial organization of the Northwest Territory, which would become the foundation for the government's policy toward all western lands that it acquired in the future.

The 1784 Ordinance determined that the western territories would be organized as new states. The Land Ordinance of 1785 established a system for selling western lands and also ensured that a section of land in every township would be reserved for the support of public education. The Ordinance of 1787 ceded all state claims to western lands to the national government; created the Northwest Territory, a jurisdiction expected to eventually be divided into three to five states; and established a procedure for a territory to apply for statehood. The Ordinance prohibited slavery in the Northwest Territory, making the Ohio River a dividing line between eventual slave and free states. Taken together, the Northwest Ordinances were the most consequential legislation passed during the period of the Articles of Confederation.

Shays' Rebellion

Farmers in western Massachusetts had suffered in the bad economic times that followed the Revolution. Many suffered from heavy loads of debt and the scarcity of hard currency that creditors demanded. Adding to their burdens were heavy taxes imposed by the Massachusetts legislature. In 1786, groups of protesters began to forcibly stop foreclosures on bankrupt farms and disrupt court proceedings. The rebellion was named for Daniel Shays, a veteran of the Continental Army who had experienced the financial hardships that drove the uprising.

At one point, it seemed as if a force led by Shays might seize the unguarded national armory at Springfield. However, a force of privately funded militia dispersed the rebels. A timely decrease in taxes helped pacify the situation. The most important result was that Shays' Rebellion highlighted for many people the need for a stronger central government in the United States.

Chapter Review

Rapid Review

To achieve the perfect 5, you should be able to explain the following:

- The first armed resistance to the British army occurred at Lexington and Concord.
- The Second Continental Congress began to prepare the American colonies for war against the British, but by passing the Olive Branch Petition, they tried to accommodate colonial interests with those of the Crown.
- The impact of the message presented in *Common Sense* by Thomas Paine was widespread throughout the colonies.
- Many Loyalists lived in the colonies at the outbreak of the Revolutionary War; many were members of the economic elite.
- Blacks and women played large roles in the war effort of the colonies.
- The defensive tactics of George Washington as leader of the Continental forces proved decisive, since a longer war was disadvantageous to the British army.
- French assistance to the Continental war effort proved invaluable; the French navy proved to be especially critical as the war progressed.
- The Treaty of Paris ended the Revolutionary War. In this treaty, American independence was recognized by the British and large amounts of territory west of the Appalachians became American territory.
- The Articles of Confederation created a weak national government, partially to avoid replicating the "tyranny" of the Crown in England.
- To many colonial observers, Shays' Rebellion demonstrated that a stronger national government was needed.

Time Line

1775: Battles of Lexington and Concord
      Meeting of Second Continental Congress
1776: *Common Sense* published by Thomas Paine
      Declaration of Independence approved
      Surrender of British forces of General Burgoyne at Saratoga
1777: State constitutions written in 10 former colonies
1777–1778: Continental army encamped for the winter at Valley Forge
           French begin to assist American war efforts
1781: Cornwallis surrenders at Yorktown
      Articles of Confederation ratified
1783: Signing of the Treaty of Paris
1786–1787: Shays' Rebellion in Massachusetts
1787: Northwest Ordinance establishes regulations for settlement of territories west
      of the Appalachian Mountains

› Review Questions

Multiple-Choice Questions

1. The purpose of the Olive Branch Petition was to
   A. rally colonial support for war against Great Britain.
   B. petition the king for redress of economic grievances suffered by the colonies.
   C. ask the king to craft a solution to end the tensions between Great Britain and the colonies.
   D. ask the king to grant independence to the colonies.

2. At the beginning of the Revolutionary War, the British were extremely confident of victory because all of the following reasons *except*
   A. they had outstanding generals that would be commanding British forces in the Americas.
   B. there were many Loyalists throughout the American colonies.
   C. the Continental army suffered from poor discipline.
   D. the British had an outstanding navy.

3. All of the following were contained in the Treaty of Paris of 1783 *except*
   A. territory west of the Appalachian Mountains was ceded to the Americans.
   B. American independence was recognized by Great Britain.
   C. Quebec and the area immediately surrounding it was ceded to the Americans.
   D. former Loyalists in the colonies could retrieve property seized from them during the Revolutionary War.

4. Women were important in the war effort because they
   A. provided much of the financial backing for the colonial cause.
   B. wrote influential articles in colonial newspapers urging the colonies to resist the British.
   C. provided clothing and blankets for the frozen troops at Valley Forge.
   D. maintained economic stability in the colonies by managing households across the colonies while men were off fighting the British.

5. The weakness of the national government created by the Articles of Confederation was demonstrated by the fact that it was *not given the power to*
   A. mediate disputes between states.
   B. raise an army.
   C. conduct foreign relations.
   D. print money.

Short-Answer Question

6. Answer Parts A, B, and C.
   A. Briefly explain ONE reason for American victory in the Revolutionary War.
   B. Briefly explain a SECOND reason for American victory in the Revolutionary War.
   C. Briefly explain ONE advantage that the British enjoyed in the Revolutionary War.

› Answers and Explanations

1. **C.** Although the Second Continental Congress began to prepare the colonies for war against Great Britain, the delegates also voted to send this petition to George III, asking him to create harmony between Great Britain and the colonies.

2. **A.** Several of the main generals commanding British troops in the Revolutionary War proved early on to be quite ordinary in tactical and leadership skills.

3. **C.** None of the British territory in Canada was taken from them as a result of the treaty.

4. **D.** Although women assisted the war effort in many ways, they made an important contribution by managing estates and farms while their husbands were serving in the colonial militias or in the Continental army.

5. **B.** The national government was not given the power to issue taxes, regulate commerce, or raise an army.

6. **Parts A and B**: America was a very big place, much of it wilderness, with few roads and major cities. This made it difficult for British armies to win decisive victories against the Americans. The United States under the Second Continental Congress and then the Articles of Confederation was able to create a government that maintained an impressive degree of unity among the states while waging the war. The United States brought forward skillful military commanders like George Washington and Nathanael Greene. Despite many hardships, thousands of Americans served bravely in the Continental Army and militias. Thanks to the training efforts of men like the Baron von Steuben, the Continental Army eventually became capable of meeting the British army on equal terms. The United States conducted an effective foreign policy, bringing France into the war in 1778. Spain and the Netherlands also joined in the war against Great Britain. French naval and military support helped George Washington win the decisive victory at Yorktown in 1781.

Part C: The British enjoyed the advantage of possessing a large professional military. To supplement these forces, the British were able to hire the services of thousands of German troops, known collectively as Hessians. The British were able to rally many Native American tribes to their side. They were also able to count on the loyalty of about a fifth of the American population, and many loyalists served in British military units. The royal navy gave the British the command of the sea.

CHAPTER 11

Establishment of New Political Systems (1787–1800)

IN THIS CHAPTER

Summary: In 1787 the Articles of Confederation were discarded and the Constitution of the United States was created, establishing a stronger federal government. The Constitution established a bicameral legislature, three branches of government, and the division of power between the states and the federal government. The Bill of Rights also established many basic freedoms central to the identity of the United States. During the presidency of George Washington, different visions of America were expressed by Thomas Jefferson and Alexander Hamilton.

Keywords

Virginia Plan: during debate over the Constitution, the plan proposing a bicameral legislature with representatives determined by proportional representation.

New Jersey Plan: during debate over the Constitution, the plan proposing one legislative body for the country, with each state having one vote.

Great Compromise: Connecticut plan that stated that one house of the Congress would be based on population (the House of Representatives) while in the other house all states would have equal representation (the Senate).

Electoral College: procedure for electing the president and vice-president of the United States as outlined in the Constitution; electors from each state, and not the popular vote, ultimately elect the president.

Three-Fifths Compromise: as the Constitution was being created, the plan that stated that slaves would be counted as three-fifths of a free person; this was used to determine eventual membership in the House of Representatives.

Federalists: party in the first years of the republic that favored a larger national government; was supported by commercial interests. Federalists were opposed by Jeffersonians, who wanted a smaller national government.
Alien and Sedition Acts: proposed by President John Adams, gave the president power to expel "dangerous" aliens and outlawed "scandalous" publications against the government.

The Constitutional Convention

The financial frustrations of the national government and episodes like Shays' Rebellion convinced a number of American leaders that a stronger national government was a necessity. They believed that the loose system of the Articles of Confederation was inadequate to the needs of a potentially powerful nation. Some of the advocates for changes, such as Alexander Hamilton, had served in the army during the Revolutionary War and had developed a "continental" perspective that transcended loyalties to particular states.

In the wake of Shays' Rebellion, the nationalists were able to persuade Congress to authorize a convention to explore revisions to the Articles of Confederation. On May 25, 1787, delegates from all 13 states gathered in Philadelphia. Among the delegates were George Washington, who was elected president of the convention; Benjamin Franklin; Alexander Hamilton; and James Madison. Two prominent leaders who missed the convention were John Adams and Thomas Jefferson, both of whom were serving as ambassadors in Europe. Early on, it was decided to abandon efforts to reform the Articles of Confederation and instead craft a new governing document.

A consensus emerged that the new government needed more powers, such as the ability to tax, regulate trade and interstate commerce, and create a military. Where the delegates disagreed was on just how powerful the central government should be. Although the current government was clearly too weak, the delegates did not want to lay the foundations of a tyranny, in which small cliques of men could wield influence at the expense of the majority.

A major division emerged between the large states and small states over representation in a prospective national legislature. Small states wanted to retain the practice of the Articles of Confederation, wherein each state received one vote in Congress. Large states wanted representation determined by population. Sectional divisions between north and south over issues such as slavery came to the fore. Also controversial was the proper balance of power between the central government and the states.

Contention and Compromise

The basis for much of the discussion at the Constitutional Convention was the **Virginia Plan** devised by James Madison. Madison's framework called for a federal government with three branches: legislative, executive, and judicial. He also proposed a bicameral congress, with its membership determine by **proportional representation**. Madison played a leading role at the Convention and is often called the "Father of the Constitution." Madison's notes on the debates at the Convention are a vital historical source for understanding the constitutional thinking of the founding fathers.

The delegates from smaller states opposed the Virginia Plan because they feared that the larger states would dominate the national government. Instead, they rallied behind the **New Jersey Plan**, which proposed a Congress similar to that of the Articles of Confederation: unicameral and with each state having one vote. Arguments between the advocates of the two competing plans continued until delegates from Connecticut outlined a third possibility that became known as the **Great Compromise**. The Connecticut proposal stipulated that each state would have two members in the upper house of the new legislature, while the members of the lower house would be chosen through proportional representation.

The delegates at the Constitutional Convention were not believers in pure democracy. They believed that an unchecked majority could be just as tyrannical as a king. To guard against this, they decided that the president would be elected by an **Electoral College**, the composition of which would be determined by the states. State legislatures elected senators; only the members of the House of Representatives would be directly elected by the people. The framers of the Constitution were intent on creating a government that would be strong enough to do the nation's business, but not so mighty that it could oppress the people. As a result of this, they crafted a government of checks and balances, carefully balancing the powers of the three branches of government.

Slavery

The issue of slavery was debated at the Constitutional Convention. Many Americans in the 1780s believed that, for economic reasons, the institution of slavery would gradually disappear. Many southerners, still heavily invested in slaves and dependent on them for their livelihood, defended slavery.

The delegates compromised on the slavery issue to ensure southern support for the Constitution. The ability of the federal government to regulate or outlaw the slave trade was postponed for 20 years, until 1808. Southerners wanted slaves to count toward congressional representation; northern delegates resisted this. In the end, the delegates agreed to the **Three-Fifths Compromise**, counting three-fifths of a state's slave population when allocating seats in the House of Representatives.

The Ratification Battle

The finished Constitution was signed on September 17, 1787. The delegates decided that the new Constitution would go into effect if **ratifying conventions** in nine states approved the document. Because the Constitution increased the strength of the national government, its supporters became known as **Federalists**. The Federalists were confident that the new federal structure of the government would meet the needs of the nation, while the balance of powers among the three branches of government would protect American liberties. **Anti-Federalists** were unwilling to trust a stronger central government. They remembered the tyrannical behavior of the British and believed that a powerful national government would inevitably diminish the authority of the states, which they saw as the best defenders of the people's rights.

The anti-Federalists highlighted the fact that the proposed Constitution lacked a bill of rights. The two sides were well matched, and the voting in some state conventions was quite close. To win in crucial states like Virginia and New York, Federalists signaled a willingness to accept amendments to the Constitution protecting the rights of American citizens.

When New York voted to ratify the Constitution on July 26, 1788, it was the eleventh state to throw its support behind the new governing document. On September 13, Congress certified the ratification of the Constitution. Rhode Island, the last state to ratify the Constitution, did so on May 29, 1790.

George Washington was the inevitable choice to be the first president. He was elected unanimously by the Electoral College. Washington established crucial precedents as chief executive, helping define the role of president in the new government. He upheld the dignity of his office and emphasized his duties as an administrator of government policies.

The Bill of Rights

While helping draft the Constitution, James Madison did not believe that it needed a bill of rights; he thought its outline of powers sufficiently protected people's liberties. During the ratification debates, however, he changed his mind. While running for a seat in the first Congress, he promised to sponsor a bill of rights as a series of amendments to the Constitution. This way, Madison could both address the fears of the anti-Federalists and protect his constitutional handiwork. Once in Congress, he submitted 12 amendments; by 1791, 10 of these had been ratified by the states.

The **Bill of Rights** reconciled anti-Federalists to the Constitution. Over time, the Bill of Rights has become a cherished guarantee of such fundamental American values as freedom of religion, freedom of speech, and freedom of assembly. The Bill of Rights ensured the right to bear arms and prohibited the quartering of soldiers in citizens' homes. It also ensured crucial protections to people caught up in the judicial system, such as trial by jury and a ban on "cruel and unusual punishments."

The last two amendments of the Bill of Rights offered broad support to the Revolutionary War principle that rights reside in the people and the vitality of federalism in the new governmental system. The Ninth Amendment states that the listing of rights in the Constitution does not "disparage" any others held by the people. The Tenth Amendment reserves all powers not given to the federal government by the Constitution, or forbidden to the states by it, for the states and the people. Taken together, the Amendments of the Bill of Rights reinforced the balance of powers so important to Madison and the other Founding Fathers.

The Birth of the Party System

Washington staffed his cabinet with brilliant men. Thomas Jefferson served as secretary of state and Alexander Hamilton as secretary of the treasury. These two men had competing visions of America's future. Out of their differences would come the first party system in the United States.

Alexander Hamilton wanted the United States to become a great commercial and manufacturing power. He wanted to emulate British economic practices, including **mercantilist policies** to support American trade. To do this, he supported a "loose" interpretation of the Constitution, which argued that the federal government had powers not specified in the document.

Thomas Jefferson favored an agrarian America, predominantly made up of independent yeoman farmers. He believed that manufacturing would be economically secondary in America, "a handmaid to agriculture." Instead of Hamilton's system of protective tariffs, he supported **free trade**, which would keep the price of manufactured goods low for farmers. Jefferson called for a "strict" interpretation of the Constitution, which held that the federal government had only the powers listed in its text. James Madison joined Jefferson in his opposition to Hamilton's program.

As Hamilton and Jefferson articulated their disagreements and gathered supporters, a two-party system emerged. Hamilton's followers called themselves Federalists. Jefferson's followers called themselves Democratic-Republicans, or simply Republicans. Federalists argued for an activist government that created a favorable economic climate for business. Commercially expansive cities and ports provided the strongest support for the Federalists. Republicans focused on agriculture and defended **laissez-faire economic principles**. Their appeal was especially strong in the rural areas of the south and west.

Hamilton's Economic Program

Hamilton realized that if the United States was going to become a great commercial and manufacturing power, the nation's chaotic finances had to be addressed. He laid out an ambitious program to put the United States on a sound financial footing in his **Report on the Public Credit**. Hamilton proposed that all notes issued by the national government under the Articles of Confederation be redeemed at face value. He also proposed that the federal government assume the outstanding debts of the states. He argued for the formation of a **national bank**; this would both facilitate financial transactions with the federal government and stimulate investment in American businesses. Hamilton wanted the federal government to actively support business expansion through its policies. He proposed a high tariff on foreign goods to pay for his economic program.

Jefferson and Madison were repelled by Hamilton's activist vision of government and disliked his partiality for business. They believed that Hamilton was sacrificing America's agrarian majority to commercial interests. They were able to block some of Hamilton's initiatives, but Hamilton was still able to set up his system of public credit with a national bank and tariffs.

Effects of the French Revolution

The French Revolution erupted in the summer of 1789, just a few months after George Washington took office as president. Americans watched the evolution of the French Revolution from a constitutional monarchy to the Reign of Terror with a mixture of fascination and horror. Jefferson and the Republicans tended to favor the progress of the revolutionaries because of their professions of support for democracy and their celebration of Enlightenment ideals. Hamilton and the Federalists disdained the Revolution's contempt for established authorities and its descent into mass violence. By 1793, revolutionary France was at war with most of Europe. Great Britain was once again France's most implacable foe. British and French naval forces fought each other at sea, endangering American shipping. President Washington issued a **Declaration of Neutrality**. He hoped that the United States could avoid entanglement in what had become a world war.

Washington also faced troubles at home. The easiest way for western farmers to get their grain to market in a period of poor roads and difficult transportation was to distill it into alcohol. Hamilton placed a tax on whiskey to help pay for his economic program. This angered the western farmers, who already sympathized with Jefferson's agrarian outlook. A group of farmers in western Pennsylvania rebelled, evoking the egalitarian principles of the French Revolution. Angered and alarmed, Washington gathered a large force of militia and easily suppressed the rebellion.

Washington's Foreign Policy

Professing neutrality, American merchants attempted to trade with both Great Britain and France; this angered both combatants. In 1794, the British began searching and seizing American ships trading with the French West Indies. The British were also plotting with Native Americans in the Northwest Territory.

Washington attempted to settle these problems by sending Chief Justice John Jay on a diplomatic mission to London. The British were not in the mood to make concessions on American trade; they refused to recognize the principle of the freedom of the seas and insisted on removing French products from American ships. The British did agree to withdraw from military posts that they held in the American west. These posts were soon rendered untenable anyway by General Anthony Wayne's defeat of a Native American coalition at the Battle of Fallen Timbers. **Jay's Treaty** proved to be widely unpopular in the United States. The Senate ratified the treaty after a protracted debate and much political maneuvering in its favor by Alexander Hamilton.

Thomas Pinckney negotiated a treaty with Spain that opened up the Mississippi River to American navigation. Pinckney's Treaty proved popular because it gave western and southern farmers a vital waterway to transport their crops to the markets of New Orleans.

Washington decided against running for a third term as president, establishing a long-lasting precedent. Before he left office, he released his Farewell Address. In it, he gave policy advice to his fellow citizens. Washington was dismayed by the intensifying acrimony between Federalists and Republicans and warned against the divisive dangers of political parties. He also urged the United States to avoid "foreign entanglements" and alliances with other nations. For 150 years, America would follow Washington's advice on foreign affairs.

The Presidency of John Adams

John Adams served two terms as Washington's vice-president. In the election of 1796, he ran as a Federalist. His opponent was Thomas Jefferson, the Republican candidate. Adams received the most votes in the Electoral College, but under the rules of the time, Thomas Jefferson, who came in second, became the vice-president. This created an awkward situation in which the president and vice-president belonged to different political parties.

Adams lacked Washington's public stature, but he proved to be an effective president who successfully managed a major crisis during his term of office. Adams spent many months of his presidency at his home in Quincy, Massachusetts, leading by letter. In 1800, he would be the first president to take up residence in the Executive Mansion.

Crisis with France

The French resented the fact that the United States did not maintain the 1778 alliance that had been signed with the royal government that was overthrown in the French Revolution. Jay's Treaty led the French government to believe that the Americans were tilting toward the British. The French responded by capturing American ships. In 1798, Adams sent three diplomats to France to attempt a negotiated settlement. The French foreign minister, Talleyrand, was notoriously corrupt. He sent three agents to the Americans demanding a bribe before he would talk with them. The Americans indignantly refused and were supported by public opinion back in the United States. This became known as the "XYZ Affair" after the code names of Talleyrand's emissaries.

The breakdown in diplomacy led to limited hostilities. The Washington administration had begun the construction of a small but efficient navy. From 1798 to 1800, the United States and France fought an undeclared naval war. American vessels won most of the war's ship-to-ship battles. By 1800, Napoleon Bonaparte had taken control of France, and diplomacy resumed. In the Convention of 1800, the French compensated the Americans for the merchant ships that they had seized, and the alliance of 1778 was officially terminated.

The Alien and Sedition Acts

Partisan politics continued unabated during the undeclared war with France. Some Republican journalists still sympathetic to the French Revolution published virulently worded attacks on the Adams administration. A few French immigrants joined in the verbal assault. Many Federalists saw the conflict with France as an opportunity to crush the Republican party. They reacted to the intemperate journalism of their opponents with two laws in 1798. The **Alien Act** gave the president the authority to imprison or deport any alien who was thought to be "dangerous to the peace and safety of the United States." The **Sedition Act** enabled the president to prosecute persons who published "malicious" criticisms of his administration.

These laws proved very controversial. The Sedition Act led to the prosecution and jailing of a number of journalists and other citizens. Republicans denounced the Alien and Sedition Acts. The state legislatures of Kentucky and Virginia passed the **Kentucky and Virginia Resolves**, which maintained that states had no obligation to respect unconstitutional laws. Thomas Jefferson authored the Kentucky Resolves, and James Madison wrote the Virginia Resolves. These resolves helped lay the foundation for the doctrines of nullification and states' rights that would play an important role in later American history. The Alien and Sedition Acts became an important issue in the election of 1800. Their unpopularity hurt the candidacy of John Adams.

Chapter Review

Rapid Review

To achieve the perfect 5, you should be able to explain the following:

- The 1787 meeting on amending the Articles of Confederation turned into a historical session when the Constitution of the United States was drafted.
- The importance of James Madison in the formulation of the Constitution cannot be overemphasized.
- The format of the bicameral legislature, the branches of power established at the federal level, and the division of powers between federal and state governments made the U.S. Constitution a unique document for its time.
- The division between Federalists and anti-Federalists demonstrated that very different visions of America and the scope of the federal government existed in the United States at this time.
- The Bill of Rights established the basic freedoms that Americans cherish today.
- During the Washington administration, very different visions of America were expressed by Alexander Hamilton and Thomas Jefferson. The ideas of Hamilton helped spur American economic growth during the Washington administration.
- The United States had a great deal of trouble convincing the British and the French that the United States was a major power during this era.

- Many critics viewed the Alien and Sedition Acts of John Adams as gross overextensions of the power given to the federal government by the Constitution.

Time Line

1787: Constitutional Convention ratifies U.S. Constitution

1788: U.S. Constitution ratified by states

1789: Washington sworn in as first president

1790: Hamilton issues plans proposing to protect infant U.S. industries

1791: Establishment of First National Bank
Ratification of the Bill of Rights

1793: Democratic-Republican clubs begin to meet

1794: Whiskey Rebellion begins

1795: Jay's Treaty with England/Pinckney's Treaty with Spain

1796: John Adams elected president, Thomas Jefferson, vice-president (each from a different political party)

1798: XYZ Affair
Sedition Act of John Adams issued
Kentucky and Virginia Resolves

1800: Convention of 1800
Thomas Jefferson elected president

› Review Questions

Multiple-Choice Questions

1. The Connecticut Plan presented to the Constitutional Convention of 1787a
   A. proposal for a two-house legislature based on proportional representation.
   B. proposal for a one-house legislature based on proportional representation.
   C. proposal for a two-house legislature, with one house based on proportional representation.
   D. proposal for a balance of power between executive, legislative, and judicial branches.

2. The Kentucky and Virginia Resolves
   A. expressed support for the new U.S. Constitution.
   B. stated that individual states do not have to enforce laws the states consider unconstitutional.
   C. were written to support John Adams's support of the Sedition Act.
   D. were written in opposition to the economic policies of Alexander Hamilton.

3. Many in America felt that the English and the French failed to treat the United States as a major power in this era. All of the following are evidence of that *except*
   A. the Convention of 1800.
   B. Jay's Treaty.
   C. the treatment of American ships by the British during the 1790s.
   D. the XYZ Affair.

4. Thomas Jefferson and Alexander Hamilton had different views on all of the following *except*
   A. the amount of power the federal government should have.
   B. the tariff policy of the United States.
   C. the importance of a national bank.
   D. their belief in the power of the U.S. Constitution.

5. Under the Electoral College system
   A. voters directly elect the president of the United States.
   B. voters approve electors, who elect the president of the United States.
   C. it is possible to win the popular vote and lose the election in the Electoral College.
   D. B and C above

Short-Answer Question

6. Answer Parts A, B, and C.
   A. Briefly explain ONE example of debate over constitutional principles in the United States in the period 1786 to 1800.
   B. Briefly explain a SECOND example of debate over constitutional principles in the United State in the period 1786 to 1800.
   C. Briefly explain ONE example of a political leader taking a policy stance based on constitutional principle.

> Answers and Explanations

1. **C.** The Connecticut Plan, also called the Great Compromise, was ratified by the delegates. Under this plan, representation in the House of Representatives would be by population, while all states would have equal representation in the Senate.

2. **B.** After the passage of the Sedition Act, legislatures in Kentucky and Virginia passed resolutions stating that states do not have to enforce laws they consider to be unconstitutional.

3. **A.** As a result of the Convention of 1800, the French agreed to compensate the United States for ships seized during the previous decade. Events mentioned in all of the other choices demonstrate that the French and English had little respect for American rights in diplomatic matters and on the high seas during this era.

4. **D.** Both believed in the power of the Constitution, although their interpretations of the Constitution were different. Jefferson believed in a strict interpretation of the Constitution, while Hamilton believed in a broad interpretation.

5. **D.** As demonstrated in the presidential election of 2016, it is possible to get the most number of votes nationwide but to lose the presidential election in the Electoral College. This also occurred in the presidential elections of 1876, 1888, and 2000.

6. **Parts A and B**: Delegates debated constitutional principles at the 1787 Constitutional Convention. Issues included the type of state representation in Congress; this was resolved by the Great Compromise, which provided for two senators for each state, while members of the House of Representatives were allocated by population. A debate over ratification ensued. *The Federalist Papers*, authored by James Madison, Alexander Hamilton, and John Jay, made a powerful case for ratifying the new Constitution. Once the new government was launched, there were debates over the powers of the new central government and about how to interpret the Constitution. The Bank of the United States became a centerpiece of this debate, with supporters of a limited government and strict interpretation of the Constitution opposing the Bank, and supporters of a stronger government and a looser interpretation of the Constitution in favor of it. In 1798, the Federalist-dominated federal government passed the Alien and Sedition Acts giving the president power to deport certain immigrants and to regulate the press. Democratic-Republican critics of these measures passed the Kentucky and Virginia Resolves, arguing that the states could nullify laws that they believed were unconstitutional.

Part C: George Washington staked his prestige in supporting the new Constitution. James Madison fulfilled promises made during the ratification debate by sponsoring the amendments that became the Bill of Rights. Secretary of the Treasury Alexander Hamilton built his economic program, including the Bank of the United States, around his vision of a strong central government. Thomas Jefferson led the opposition to Hamilton's plans. Thomas Jefferson wrote the Kentucky Resolves, and James Madison wrote the Virginia Resolves.

Jeffersonian Revolution (1800–1820)

IN THIS CHAPTER

Summary: The election of Thomas Jefferson in 1800 was a critical election in American history; Jefferson's view of America differed greatly from that of the Federalists. Alexander Hamilton and other Federalists envisioned America as a future industrial power. For Jefferson, the independence and pride of the yeoman farmer would guide America into the future. During the time when John Marshall was chief justice of the Supreme Court, the power of the federal courts increased. The overall size of America also increased in this era as a result of the Louisiana Purchase. The War of 1812 was fought over continued tensions between the Americans and the British. Many Americans in this era envisioned massive economic growth in the United States; this was the focus of Henry Clay's "American System."

Keywords

Marbury v. Madison **(1803):** critical Supreme Court decision that established the principle of judicial review, stating that the Supreme Court has the right to review all federal laws and decisions and declare whether or not they are constitutional.

Louisiana Purchase (1803): massive land purchase from Emperor Napoleon of France that virtually doubled the size of the United States.

Lewis and Clark Expedition (1804): expedition that discovered much about the western part of the North American continent and the economic possibilities there.

War of 1812: war between the British and the Americans over British seizure of American ships, connections between the British and Native American tribes, and other tensions. The British sacked Washington, DC, in 1814. The treaty ending the war merely restored diplomatic relations between the two countries.

American System: plan proposed by Senator Henry Clay and others to make America economically independent by increasing industrial production in the United States and by the creation of a Second National Bank.

Missouri Compromise (1820): political solution devised to keep the number of slave states and free states equal; Missouri entered the Union as a slave state and Maine entered as a free state. Potential states in the northern part of the Louisiana territory would also come in as free states in the future.

Election of 1800

John Adams decided to run for a second term as president in 1800. Charles Pinckney of South Carolina ran as the Federalist candidate for vice-president. Thomas Jefferson was again the Republican candidate for president. Aaron Burr of New York was the Republican running for the vice-presidency. Jefferson edged out Adams in the Electoral College with 73 votes to Adams's 65. However, because the Constitution made no distinction in the Electoral College between presidential and vice-presidential candidates, Aaron Burr also received 73 votes, throwing the election to the House of Representatives for a decision. Burr was an ambitious and unscrupulous politician and did not concede to Jefferson. Instead, he garnered substantial votes from Federalists who detested Jefferson. The election in the House of Representatives, where each state cast one vote, was a cliffhanger, with the voting going through 35 ballots without a victor. Ironically, Jefferson owed his victory on the thirty-sixth ballot to Alexander Hamilton, who told supporters that Burr was "the most unfit man in the United States for the office of president." This political crisis led to the adoption of the **Twelfth Amendment** in 1804, which allowed members of the Electoral College to cast separate ballots for the president and vice-president.

The election of 1800 was the first time that control of the presidency passed from one party to another. Because of this, it has sometimes been called the "Revolution of 1800." Thomas Jefferson brought remarkable abilities and a wealth of experience to the presidency. He was an Enlightenment man, fascinated by the latest scientific and political ideas, and a gifted writer. He was an able political leader who had built a successful party, yet as a former diplomat and secretary of state, he also had extensive experience in foreign affairs.

As a strict constitutional constructionist, Jefferson was determined to reverse the policies of the Federalists and scale back the reach of the federal government. Once in office, he and his secretary of the treasury, Albert Gallatin, cut taxes like that on whiskey. He allowed the hated Alien and Sedition Acts to lapse. Jefferson did not wipe out all the legislative achievements of the Washington and Adams administrations, however. At his inaugural, he had reached out to the political opposition by declaring, "We are all Republicans; we are all Federalists." Jefferson had opposed the creation of Hamilton's national bank; once in office, he accepted its economic usefulness and left it alone.

An Assertive Supreme Court

Until the 1930s, there was a long interval between presidential elections and the new president's inauguration in March of the following year. In 1801, the outgoing Federalists took advantage of this period to pass the **Judiciary Act**, creating many new federal circuit and district courts. Outgoing president Adams appointed Federalist judges to these courts. These were known as **"midnight appointments,"** because President Adams was erroneously believed to be signing these many commissions on his last night in office.

Jefferson and his partisans were outraged by this effort to pack the federal bench with Federalists. The new Republican Congress promptly repealed the Judiciary Act and launched the impeachment of a pair of Federalist judges. One of John Adams's last-minute judicial appointees was John Marshall, whom Adams nominated to be chief justice of the Supreme Court. Marshall was an able lawyer and Federalist politician who served as secretary of state in the last year of Adams's presidency. Marshall would become the longest-serving chief justice, heading the Court from 1801 to 1835. He would also be the most influential. His judicial rulings profoundly shaped American law. Federalist in principle, he asserted the supremacy of federal over state law. Marshall also elevated the stature and political significance of the Supreme Court.

One of Marshall's most important rulings came early, in the 1803 *Marbury v. Madison* decision. William Marbury was a Federalist whom John Adams appointed to be a justice of the peace in the District of Columbia. Marbury's letter of appointment was not delivered to him, and James Madison, secretary of state in the new Jefferson administration, refused to deliver it to him. Marbury sued for his letter. Marshall disliked Madison's action but ruled against Marbury anyway, arguing that the provision of the Judiciary Act of 1789 that enabled Marbury to sue was itself unconstitutional. This established the principle of **judicial review**, which gives the courts the ability to rule on the constitutionality of legislation. Marshall's assertion of judicial prerogative laid the foundation for the Supreme Court's later political influence.

A New Frontier

Thomas Jefferson envisioned a republic of independent farmers. He believed that only self-sufficient, property-owning citizens would be able to resist corruption and tyranny. To ensure such a future for the United States, Jefferson needed land. He became fascinated with the west. Settlers were already streaming into the lands west of the Appalachian Mountains. By 1800, one million Americans lived there. The Jefferson administration encouraged western settlement by easing the terms to purchase land; a down payment of $80 gave a purchaser rights to 160 acres of land. The movement west accelerated.

This massive influx of settlers inevitably led to conflict with the Native Americans who lived and hunted on these western lands. Jefferson believed that the Native American way of life must inevitably give way to the march of American civilization. He hoped that the Native Americans would eventually assimilate into American society and become farmers themselves, but he doubted that this would happen any time soon. As a result, Jefferson believed that the best thing for the Native Americans would be to remove them to a more distant territory, where, over time, they could adapt to American ways. Jefferson thus laid the foundation of the policy of Indian removal that would come to a head in the later presidencies of Andrew Jackson and Martin Van Buren. Unsurprisingly, many Native Americans resisted American expansionism, including the brilliant Shawnee diplomat and soldier Tecumseh and his brother Tenskwatawa, a religious visionary called the "Prophet" by the Americans.

The Louisiana Purchase

The French dictator Napoleon Bonaparte forced the Spanish government to secretly cede Louisiana to France in 1800. Napoleon was hoping to recreate a French empire in the Americas. The American government learned that the French intended to return to Louisiana in 1801. The prospect of a militarily powerful and aggressive neighbor bordering the United States worried President Jefferson. He decided to attempt a diplomatic resolution to the problem and sent William Livingstone to France with an offer to purchase New Orleans. Livingston was later joined by James Monroe. In the meantime, Napoleon's dreams of a North American empire faded as an army dispatched to recapture the Caribbean island of Haiti perished of disease. War also loomed between France and Great Britain, and Napoleon knew that any French possessions in North America would be cut off by the British Navy. In 1803, Napoleon startled Livingston and Monroe by offering to sell the entire Louisiana territory for $15 million. The **Louisiana Purchase** was a financial bargain for the United States. The Americans had been willing to offer $10 million for New Orleans alone; the purchase price for the entire territory worked out to roughly 3 cents an acre. The acquisition of the Louisiana Territory doubled the size of the United States.

Jefferson had some legal scruples about the federal government's ability to purchase such an expanse of territory since no such power is explicitly mentioned in the Constitution; he set these concerns aside because the Louisiana Purchase was so obviously in the interest of the United States and because the accession of so much new land in the west greatly strengthened his dream of an agrarian republic. Although some Federalists opposed the Louisiana Purchase because it reinforced Jefferson's political base in the west, the Senate ratified the treaty with France, and the House of Representatives quickly approved the expenditure of the purchase price.

Jefferson was anxious to know more about the interior of the North American continent, its flora and fauna, the peoples living there, and its economic potentialities. Even before the Louisiana Purchase, he had been contemplating sending mapping expeditions west. Once Louisiana was acquired, Jefferson sponsored the **Lewis and Clark Expedition** to explore the new lands that had been added to the United States. Meriwether Lewis and William Clark left St. Louis with a party of nearly 50 men in 1804. Over the course of a two-year journey, they made their way to the Pacific Ocean and back. The voluminous records of Lewis and Clark's trip provided Americans with a wealth of information about the lands that the pair had traversed and whetted the appetite for further western exploration and settlement.

Burr's Conspiracy

Political strife did not abate during Jefferson's presidency. The Federalists were declining but continued to oppose Jefferson's policies. The **Essex Junto**, a group of extreme Federalists based in New England, denounced what they saw as a "decline in public virtue" with Jefferson in office. Massachusetts senator Thomas Pickering believed that the president was a "Parisian revolutionary monster." In 1804, the Federalists nominated Charles

C. Pinckney to run against Jefferson, but the Federalist candidate was overwhelmed in the election, winning only 14 electoral votes.

More problematic for Jefferson than the Federalist opposition was the challenge posed by his vice-president. After demonstrating his disloyalty during the electoral crisis of 1800, Aaron Burr recognized that he had lost any hope of playing an influential role in the Jefferson administration. A wily schemer, Burr was accused of negotiating with secessionist Federalists. Alexander Hamilton believed the charge and criticized Burr in a letter. Learning of this, Burr challenged Hamilton to a duel. Hamilton agreed to the encounter, and on July 11, 1804, he was shot and killed by Burr.

Under indictment for murder in New York and New Jersey, Burr completed his term as vice-president and then traveled to the West. Here he launched a conspiracy with the equally unscrupulous general James Wilkinson and others to foment a rebellion against Spanish rule in Mexico. Burr hoped to restore his fortunes by conquering lands for himself in the southwest. Wilkinson betrayed Burr's scheme to both the Spanish and American governments. President Jefferson ordered Burr's arrest on a charge of treason. Jefferson hoped to see the conviction of his old rival, but Chief Justice John Marshall, who presided over the trial, was unsympathetic to the arguments of the prosecution, and Burr was acquitted.

Renewal of War in Europe

The resumption of war between France and Great Britain in 1803 had far-reaching effects on the United States. Once again, the United States attempted to maintain its neutrality while finding itself caught between the competing ambitions of two great powers. American merchants hoped to trade freely with all countries, but Great Britain imposed a blockade on all French-controlled Europe, seizing ships that did not have expensive British licenses. Napoleon created his Continental System, which placed an embargo on trade with Great Britain. As a result, the French Navy captured American ships doing business with the British. In addition to interfering with American commerce, the British Navy, short on manpower, instituted the practice of **impressment**. After stopping American ships on the high seas, British naval officers kidnapped American sailors and forced them to serve on their ships. The British claimed that the men they seized were British subjects; some probably were, but many were naturalized or American-born citizens. British warships ranged up and down the American seacoast, interfering with American shipping and impressing American sailors. The most notorious incident occurred in 1807, when a British warship fired on the unsuspecting U.S.S. *Chesapeake*, forcing it to strike its colors before taking off four members of its crew.

Most Americans were outraged by the *Chesapeake* incident. President Jefferson could have led a largely united nation to war. Instead, he decided to try a peaceful means of resolving the crisis. Jefferson believed that the United States could change British and French policy through an economic boycott. He persuaded the Republican-dominated Congress to pass the **Embargo Act of 1807**, which prohibited American exports. Unfortunately, the Embargo Act at first seemed to have a greater effect on the American economy than on the British and French. Seaborne trade largely dried up, hurting merchants and putting sailors out of work. Planters and farmers were hurt because they could not get their products to foreign markets. Economically disastrous, the Embargo Act became deeply unpopular, especially in the Federalist bastion of New England, where ocean-going commerce was especially important. Jefferson's economic policy failed to have its intended effect and divided the American people.

The Democratic-Republican Party was still strong enough to elect James Madison as president in 1808. Madison recognized that the Embargo Act had to be abandoned in order to restore American prosperity. As a replacement, he supported the **Non-Intercourse Act**, which allowed Americans to trade with all countries except Great Britain and France. Congress continued to pass bills through 1810, attempting to put enough economic pressure on Great Britain and France to compel them to stop interfering with American trade.

The War of 1812

Years of humiliation at the hands of the British led a group of young Republicans in Congress to call for war. Henry Clay of Kentucky was one of the leaders of these "War Hawks." He believed that if the United States did not resist British policies, it could not honorably call itself an independent nation. The War Hawks were also concerned about the situation in the west. Tecumseh and the Prophet were rallying the Native Americans of the trans-Appalachian region against further American settlement. Tecumseh hoped to organize a confederacy of tribes powerful enough to resist the American military. The Americans believed that Tecumseh was allied with the British in Canada. In 1811, the governor of Indiana, William Henry Harrison, led a force of 1,000 men against Prophetstown, which had been built by Tecumseh and his brother. Tecumseh was away, and the Prophet unwisely attacked the Americans and defeated at the Battle of Tippecanoe. Harrison's army burned Prophetstown and dispersed its inhabitants, dealing Tecumseh's cause a severe blow. The War Hawks believed that a war with Britain would enable the United States to break what was left of Tecumseh's power. They also hoped to conquer new lands in Canada.

President Madison asked for war in June 1812. The enthusiasm of the War Hawks was not matched by everyone in the country. Many Federalists loathed Napoleonic France and believed that it would be economically advantageous to reach a diplomatic accommodation with Great Britain. Federalist New England would show little support for the war, and many New Englanders traded with the British in Canada.

Despite their bellicosity, the War Hawks had done little to ready the United States for a war against Great Britain. The army was tiny and untried, and the navy possessed just 17 ships. The weaknesses in the American army were exposed as attempts to invade Canada ended in ignominious failure. The navy did better, winning a number of ship-to-ship combats, but the British soon bottled up most American warships in their harbors. In 1813, an American naval victory on Lake Erie paved the way for William Henry Harrison to defeat a force of British and Indians at the Battle of the Thames near Detroit. The most significant result of the battle was the death of Tecumseh. In the south, members of the Creek tribe, allied with the British, attacked American settlers. Andrew Jackson at the head of a force of Tennessee militiamen crushed the Creeks in a series of bloody battles.

The End of the War

Napoleon's enemies forced him to abdicate in 1814. This freed up large numbers of British troops who were then deployed to America. The United States had to withstand major British attacks. A British invasion from Canada was turned back by an American naval victory on Lake Champlain. Another British army landed in Chesapeake Bay and captured the city of Washington, burning the Presidential Mansion and the Capitol. A follow-up attack on Baltimore was repulsed, inspiring Francis Scott Key to write "The Star-Spangled Banner." Andrew Jackson became a national hero in January 1815, when he handily defeated a British army attempting to seize the city of New Orleans. Jackson's victory actually took place *after* a peace treaty had been signed between the United States and Great Britain, but that news hadn't yet reached New Orleans.

In late 1814, negotiators gathered in Ghent, in what is now Belgium. Both sides were tired of the war, and the defeat of Napoleon put an end to the British blockade and impressment. The **Treaty of Ghent** ended the war on the basis of the status quo ante, the situation before the war. Aside from breaking the power of the Native Americans living east of the Mississippi, the United States gained nothing tangible from the war. Militarily, the war had been at best a draw with the British. But the culminating victory at New Orleans and the fact that the United States held its own against Great Britain enabled Americans to see the war as a success, a veritable second war of American independence.

A Federalist Debacle and the Era of Good Feelings

During the war, many Federalists remained outspoken in their opposition to the conflict. While American diplomats were negotiating at Ghent, a number of New England Federalists gathered at the **Hartford Convention**. Here they denounced the war and debated topics including the **nullification** of laws, such as the embargo that they regarded as unconstitutional. Some delegates advocated the **secession** of New England from the union, although the convention as a whole never endorsed this.

The timing of these Federalists was bad. The end of the war and Jackson's victory at New Orleans left them looking both unwise and unpatriotic. The Federalist party never recovered from this embarrassment and faded away over the next few years. For a time, the triumphant Democratic-Republicans led a unified country in which they faced no significant political opposition. James Monroe was easily elected president in 1816 and served for two terms. The period from 1816 to 1823 became known as the **Era of Good Feelings**.

Henry Clay and the American System

Taking advantage of the confident post-war mood, Henry Clay publicized an economic program that he termed the **American System**. Clay expressed the reinvigorated nationalist spirit of the time by aiming to make the United States economically independent of Europe by encouraging American industry. President Madison and then President Monroe supported the plan. The failures of the War of 1812 had convinced many Republicans that the government should play a more vigorous role in the economy; in effect, they adopted important elements of Alexander Hamilton's economic vision.

In 1816, Congress created the **Second National Bank** to facilitate credit and financial transactions across the United States. The **Tariff of 1816** increased the tariff rate on foreign goods to 22 percent in order to encourage domestic manufacturers. The revenue from the tariff was earmarked for roads and other internal improvements to help American farmers, industrialists, and merchants get their products to markets. These policies helped spur a post-war economic boom that lasted until the onset of an economic depression in 1819.

Missouri Compromise

Slavery became a major political issue for the first time in 1819, when Missouri asked to enter the Union as a slave state. At this time, the number of free and slave states was equal at 11 each. In earlier years, slavery had seemed to be a declining institution. The Northwest Ordinance barred slavery from the Northwest Territory. In 1808, the importation of slaves from overseas was outlawed. But Eli Whitney's invention of the cotton gin had made cotton a lucrative cash crop. The demand for slave labor increased, making slaves much more valuable to their masters.

The expansion of slavery into the western territories suddenly became a heated issue. The balance of slave and free states gained new political urgency. The possibility of Missouri tipping this balance in favor of the slave states outraged many in the north. Acrimonious political debate ensued. Henry Clay, the speaker of the house, resolved the issue in 1820 with the **Missouri Compromise**. Clay paired the admission of Missouri to the Union with the admission of Maine as a free state. To prevent further disputes, he drew a line through the Louisiana Territory at 36 degrees, 30 minutes; states admitted south of that line would be slave states, whereas states admitted north of the line would be free states. Clay and many contemporaries hoped that the Missouri Compromise had put an end to the contentious issue of slavery.

Chapter Review

Rapid Review

To achieve the perfect 5, you should be able to explain the following:

- The election of Thomas Jefferson in 1800 is called the "Revolution of 1800," as the new president had a completely different vision of America from the Federalists whom he replaced.
- Thomas Jefferson was one of the most brilliant men ever to serve as president, and he instituted many "Republican" policies during his eight years in office.
- The role of the federal courts was greatly strengthened during the tenure of John Marshall as chief justice of the Supreme Court.
- The Louisiana Purchase more than doubled the size of the United States and allowed the "empire of liberty" to continue to expand.
- The case of Aaron Burr showed the deep political divisions that existed in the United States during this period.
- The Napoleonic Wars greatly impacted the relationship between the United States, England, and France.
- America entered the War of 1812 because President Madison convinced the nation that America's rights as a neutral power had been violated and because many in Congress felt that the British were encouraging the resistance by Native American tribes.
- The American System of Henry Clay and others was proposed after the War of 1812 and outlined a plan for broad economic growth for the United States.
- The Missouri Compromise temporarily solved the issue of the number of slave states versus the number of free states.

Time Line

1800: Thomas Jefferson elected president in "Revolution of 1800"

1801: John Marshall named chief justice of the Supreme Court

Alien and Sedition Acts not renewed

1803: Louisiana Purchase

Marbury v. Madison established federal judicial review

1804: Alexander Hamilton killed in duel with Aaron Burr

Thomas Jefferson reelected

Twelfth Amendment ratified (separate voting for president, vice president)

Beginning of Lewis and Clark expedition

1807: Embargo Act greatly harms foreign trade

1808: James Madison elected president

Further importation of slaves into the United States made illegal

1812: Beginning of the War of 1812

1814: British army sacks Washington

Treaty of Ghent formally ends the War of 1812

Indian removal from Southern territories begins in earnest

1814–1815: Hartford Convention (meeting of Federalists)

1815: Victory of Andrew Jackson at the Battle of New Orleans (after the War of 1812 was officially over)

Henry Clay proposes the American System

1816: James Monroe elected president

1816–1823: Era of Good Feelings

1820: Missouri Compromise

› Review Questions

Multiple-Choice Questions

1. The *Marbury v. Madison* decision
   A. gave powers to the president that the Republicans of Thomas Jefferson claimed he didn't have.
   B. gave broad judicial power to the state courts.
   C. declared that the Alien and Sedition Acts were constitutional.
   D. established the principle of judicial review.

2. As a result of the election of Thomas Jefferson in 1800,
   A. more assistance was given to the commercial sector.
   B. American foreign policy became more pro-British.
   C. the federal debt rose dramatically.
   D. federal excise taxes were eliminated.

3. All of the following are reasons why America entered the War of 1812 *except*
   A. the impressment of American naval crews.
   B. the existence of a strong American navy ready to demonstrate its capabilities.
   C. the relationship between the British and Native American tribes in the western territories of North America.
   D. the desire of American leaders to acquire additional western territories.

4. The Hartford Convention demonstrated that
   A. the Federalist party had remained a dominant party in American political life.
   B. the War of 1812 brought political union to the United States.
   C. the concept of nullification was not exclusively a Southern one.
   D. the Treaty of Ghent was a controversial treaty.

5. The American System of Henry Clay
   A. favored strong economic growth and a Second National Bank.
   B. wanted to make the United States the military equivalent of Great Britain or France.
   C. favored lowering tariffs so that more goods could be purchased from abroad.
   D. advocated the elimination of slavery.

Short-Answer Question

6. Answer Parts A, B, and C.
   A. Briefly explain ONE example of the influence of foreign wars on American policy during the period 1801 to 1812.
   B. Briefly explain a SECOND example of the influence of foreign wars on American policy during the period 1801 to 1812.
   C. Briefly explain ONE consequence of the War of 1812.

› Answers and Explanations

1. **D**. The decision stated that the Supreme Court had the right to decide on the constitutionality of federal rulings and laws.

2. **D**. All of the remaining answers would have been true if a Federalist had been elected president. Jefferson favored lessening the power of the federal government, and eliminating federal excise taxes was one way in which he did so.

3. **B**. The United States had an army of 6,000 men and 17 ships when war began. All the other choices are reasons why Americans supported the War of 1812.

4. **C**. Kentucky and Virginia spoke of nullification after the Sedition Act. New England Federalists saw the War of 1812 as a disaster and at the Hartford Convention also spoke of nullification.

5. **A**. The American System favored American economic growth, a National Bank, and increased tariffs to protect American businesses and finance new transportation systems within the United States.

6. **Parts A and B**: The 1803 Louisiana Purchase was made possible by the imminence of foreign war. Napoleon Bonaparte's hopes of reviving a French empire in America were foiled by the failure of a French army to subdue the slave rebellion in Haiti and by the prospect of renewed war in Europe. Napoleon knew that the British navy would cut Louisiana off from France, so he decided to sell the territory to the United States and acquire some funds for the coming war. Once the European war resumed in 1803, both the British and French interfered with American trade. The British sometimes stopped American ships and seized sailors, forcing them to serve in the British navy. This practice was known as impressment. In 1807, a British warship suddenly fired on the American warship the USS *Chesapeake,* before boarding it and taking away four sailors. President Thomas Jefferson responded with the Embargo Act of 1807, which cut off American trade with Europe. This effort at economic coercion failed to hurt the British and French, but badly hurt American shippers and traders. The Embargo Act was repealed in 1809 and was replaced by the Non-Intercourse Act, which prohibited trade just with Britain and France. Tired of British interference with American trade, the United States declared war in 1812.

Part C: Though essentially a military draw, the War of 1812 did have important consequences. The military power of the Native American tribes living east of the Mississippi River was broken. The great Shawnee military leader and orator Tecumseh was killed in the war. The remains of the Federalist party was discredited by the 1814 Hartford Convention, which had briefly discussed the secession of New England. Following the conclusion of the war and the great 1815 victory at the Battle of New Orleans, a renewed spirit of nationalism dominated the country. This period of political dominance by the Democratic-Republican party became known as the Era of Good Feelings. In 1816, the government created the Second Bank of the United States and passed the Tariff of 1816 to foster American business growth.

CHAPTER 13

Rise of Manufacturing and the Age of Jackson (1820–1845)

IN THIS CHAPTER

Summary: Large-scale textile production began in the United States during this era of factories in places like Lowell, Massachusetts. As America grew economically, it also began to assert its authority in the Western Hemisphere. The Monroe Doctrine boldly stated that the hemisphere was offlimits to European intervention. Beginning in 1824, the United States began the resettlement of Native American tribes east of the Mississippi. The era of "Jacksonian Democracy" was one where many say that the values of the "common man" reigned supreme. In the 1830s, the Whig party emerged as an opposition party to the Democratic party of Jackson. Several state legislatures began to claim that they could nullify federal laws that were not in the interests of their individual states.

Keywords

Monroe Doctrine (1823): proclamation that countries of the Western Hemisphere "are not to be considered as subjects for future colonization by any European powers."

Removal Act of 1830: Congressional act that authorized the removal of all Native American tribes east of the Mississippi to the west. The Trail of Tears and other forced migrations caused the deaths of thousands.

The Liberator: abolitionist newspaper began by William Lloyd Garrison in 1831.

Spoils system: system used heavily during the presidency of Andrew Jackson whereby political supporters of the winning candidate are given jobs in the government.

Nullification: in reaction to tariff legislation passed in 1828, the South Carolina legislature explored the possibility of nullification, by which individual states could rule on the constitutionality of federal laws. Other Southern legislatures later discussed the idea of nullifying federal laws in their own states.

Whig party: political party that emerged in the 1830s in opposition to the Democratic party; Whigs favored policies that promoted commercial and industrial growth.

The Rise of Manufacturing

The end of the War of 1812 saw efforts to boost American manufactures and stimulate the economy. Henry Clay's American System was a conspicuous manifestation of this. The Tariff of 1816 protected domestic industries by placing a 25 percent duty on imports. States took the lead in internal improvements to spur commerce. New York State constructed the Erie Canal between 1817 and 1825, providing a waterway to allow goods to be easily transported between New York City and the Great Lakes.

At the beginning of the nineteenth century, most manufacturing was done through the **putting-out system**. Merchants provided raw materials to families, who then did the manufacturing work in their homes. A merchant might have dozens or hundreds of families working for him, producing textiles or making shoe components, for example.

The factory system in the United States began in the 1790s. The beginning of the Industrial Revolution in Great Britain had seen the creation of power-driven machinery to produce textiles. Manufacturers in New England used this new technology to turn southern cotton into cloth. Eli Whitney's cotton gin made it possible for southern planters to greatly increase their production of cotton. This in turn spurred an acceleration of the Industrial Revolution in the United States and Great Britain. Over 75,000 workers, nearly half of whom were women, were employed in American textile mills by the early 1840s.

Lowell, Massachusetts, was a center of the American textile industry. Here mill owners developed the **"Lowell System."** They drew their workforce from young women in the surrounding areas. These young women worked in the mills for up to a few years, living in dormitories provided by the mill owners. Though the wages were poor, the employment gave these young women an income they might not otherwise have had. Some of them saw their time in the mills as an opportunity to build up a small nest egg before they returned home and married. The mill owners in turn benefitted from a low-cost and continually replenished supply of workers. In Lowell and other industrial towns, a new middle class of white-collar workers associated with the factories emerged. They joined the manufacturers and bankers in bringing a new commercial prosperity to these cities.

A **labor movement** among industrial workers was slow to develop. The Panic of 1819 was a financial crisis caused by changes in the international economy following the Napoleonic Wars and inflationary policies spurred by branches of the Second Bank of the United States speculating in land sales. Labor unrest emerged later, in the 1830s, with a call for state legislatures to limit working hours. In the 1840s, the textile industry saw increased demands by workers for better pay and working conditions.

The Monroe Doctrine

In the early 1820s, President James Monroe and Secretary of State John Quincy Adams became concerned that Spain and its ally France would attempt to reconquer the Latin American republics that had gained independence during the Napoleonic Wars. The British, worried about the loss of new markets in South America, shared this concern. The British proposed that they and the United States jointly guarantee the sovereignty of the new Latin American states. Reluctant to be seen acting in the shadow of the British, Monroe and Adams instead issued their own statement in 1823. The Monroe Doctrine declared that the United States would resist new European colonization in the Western Hemisphere. In turn, Monroe pledged that the United States would not interfere in European affairs. The Monroe Doctrine became a key tenet of American foreign policy for more than a century.

Native American Removal

Since the presidency of Thomas Jefferson, American political leaders had been convinced that the only solution to conflict with the Native Americans was to move all tribes to new lands west of the Mississippi. In 1824, the last year of his presidency, James Monroe called for the implementation of this removal policy. Monroe, like Jefferson before him, convinced himself that this exile to unfamiliar territory in the west would be good for Native Americans, giving them time to learn how to farm and adjust to the ways of the "white man" without interference by land-hungry settlers. Monroe ignored the fact that some Native Americans, such as the Cherokee, were already successfully adapting to a settled agricultural lifestyle.

The pressure to remove the Native Americans intensified during the presidency of Andrew Jackson. Congress passed and Jackson signed the **Removal Act of 1830**, which enabled the federal government to negotiate the removal of tribes living east of the Mississippi. Jackson had made his reputation as a military commander fighting Native Americans during the War of 1812, crushing the powerful Creek tribe and forcing the remaining Creeks to cede to the United States 60 percent of their land. Although professing to have no animus toward Native Americans, Jackson moved against them as efficiently and brutally as he had in the days when he had been a soldier.

The Cherokee fought removal in the courts. In 1831, in the Supreme Court case ***Cherokee Nation v. Georgia***, Chief Justice John Marshall raised questions about the legal standing of the Cherokee in American courts. A year later, in *Worcester v. Georgia*, Marshall nevertheless confirmed the right of the Cherokee to the land they held by treaty with the United States. President Jackson responded by refusing to implement Marshall's ruling. Jackson declared, "John Marshall has made his decision; let him enforce it."

Tribes began to be moved west in 1831. The Cherokee were compelled to leave their land in 1838, during the presidency of Jackson's chosen successor Martin Van Buren. The Cherokee were rounded up and escorted west by detachments of the Army. Along the way, the Cherokee suffered great privations from disease and inadequate provisions. About a third perished. In Florida, the Seminole resisted removal in a series of wars that lasted into the 1850s.

The Transportation Revolution and Religious Revival

Following the War of 1812, the American economy was transformed by rapid urbanization, the growth of industry, and the rapid settlement of the west. Facilitating this economic expansion was a transportation revolution. The federally constructed National Road connected the Potomac and Ohio Rivers. Steamboats traveled up and down America's great rivers. The construction of the Erie Canal inspired a spurt of canal building. Some states drove themselves into bankruptcy financing the construction of ill-conceived canals. Challenging the economic viability of canals in the 1840s was the rapid expansion of railroads. The transportation revolution stimulated American commercial development and ensured that more and more Americans were participants in a growing market economy.

While the economy of the United States expanded, a tremendous outpouring of religious feeling was shaping American culture. The **Second Great Awakening** stressed a personal, more emotional approach to traditional religion. The fervor that it stirred strengthened many existing Christian denominations, among them the Baptists and Methodists, and led to the creation of others such as the Adventist movement. Popular preachers such as Charles Grandison Finney and Timothy Dwight traveled the country spreading their evangelism to large gatherings. **Revival meetings** flourished throughout the country, where fervent sermonizing inspired some congregants to engage in public conversions, emotional outbursts, and speaking in tongues. The Second Great Awakening flourished in both the countryside and cities. Women played a growing role in their churches as volunteers in evangelical Christianity's "Benevolent Empire" of missionary organizations. The need to read and understand scripture stimulated efforts to provide women with education.

An Age of Reform

Economic and religious upheaval spurred an era of reform. Often motivated by religious ideas, reformers attempted to address a wide range of social problems. Dorothea Dix became famous in the 1830s and 1840s for her efforts to persuade states to provide better treatment for the mentally ill. Horace Mann campaigned for universal public education and improvements in teacher training. Other activists worked to improve prisons and conditions for the urban poor. One of the most influential reform causes was the **temperance movement** which attempted to combat the widespread problem of alcoholism. Temperance crusaders persuaded many localities to go "dry."

The evangelical Christian fervor that drove the temperance movement also empowered a growing opposition to the institution of slavery. The **Abolitionist movement** became a major social and political force in the 1820s and 1830s. One of the most conspicuously vocal abolitionists was William Lloyd Garrison, the founder and editor of the *Liberator*, an uncompromisingly abolitionist newspaper. Some abolitionists opposed slavery because they believed that it was sinful for people to own other human beings. Other abolitionists were motivated by concerns about the perceived dangers of racial mixing and conflict in the United States. The **American Colonization Society**, founded in 1817, encouraged the settlement of freed slaves in Africa.

African Americans played a leading role in abolitionism and the resistance to slavery. Frederick Douglass, a former slave from Maryland, became a powerful abolitionist speaker and in 1845 published his antislavery memoir *Narrative of the Life of Frederick Douglass*.

Very different was Nat Turner, a slave in Virginia who led a violent slave insurrection that killed 60 white men, women, and children. White citizens and state authorities responded by killing some 200 African Americans. Turner and 56 others were captured and executed. Frightened by the rebellion, slave owners imposed harsh **Black Codes** that further restricted the activities of their slaves.

Jacksonian Democracy

Politically, the 1820s inaugurated an era of the "common man." By the 1820s, property qualifications for voting had been eliminated or lowered in most states. In 1800, only five states allowed the selection of electors to the Electoral College by popular vote; in 1824, 18 of 24 states did so. By the end of the Era of Good Feelings in 1824, politics had become a popular pastime, complete with parades, buttons, and posters.

Alexis de Tocqueville, an aristocratic visitor from France, noted this egalitarian spirit and was inspired to write his classic *Democracy in America* (1835, 1840). Andrew Jackson dominated this period politically and encouraged the ascendency of the "common man." As a result, these years are often termed the era of "Jacksonian democracy."

The Election of 1824

Four **Democratic-Republican** leaders contended for the presidency in 1824. John Quincy Adams was secretary of state, William Crawford was secretary of the treasury, Henry Clay was speaker of the house, and Andrew Jackson was the leading military hero of the War of 1812. In the four-way race, Jackson won the most popular votes but failed to get a majority in the Electoral College. This threw the election to the House of Representatives. Henry Clay, effectively out of the race, instructed his supporters to vote for John Quincy Adams, who had come in second place to Jackson. This enabled Adams to edge out Jackson and win the presidency.

Adams promptly appointed Clay his secretary of state. Andrew Jackson was outraged at losing the election after having won the most popular and electoral votes. He denounced what he believed was a "corrupt bargain" between Adams and Clay. Jackson immediately began preparing the ground for a rematch in 1828, becoming a spokesman for the democratic assault on "privilege" in American politics.

The Election of 1828

John Quincy Adams was an able chief executive, but his presidency was blighted by the implacable opposition of the Jacksonians, who were coming to be known as the **Democratic Party**. The election of 1828 was bitterly contested, with defamation and mudslinging on both sides. The Jacksonians portrayed Adams as a thief who had stolen the election of 1824 and as an aristocrat with effete habits. Adams's supporters described Jackson, who had fought duels, as a violent killer. Because Jackson and his wife had unwittingly married before her divorce had become finalized, they were condemned as adulterers. Mrs. Jackson died soon after the election, and Jackson blamed her demise on the attacks on her character. Jackson decisively won the election, inaugurating a new political era.

President Jackson

Andrew Jackson had been born in a log cabin, but by the time he became president, he was a wealthy landowner and slaveholder in Tennessee. Although famous as a general, he had been active in politics for decades and had served as a congressman and senator from Tennessee. Positioning himself as the political champion of the people, Jackson cultivated an aura of stern democratic rectitude. He was affectionately called "Old Hickory" by his followers.

As both a Democrat and a democrat, Jackson believed that his supporters should take over federal offices held by the partisans of John Quincy Adams. He did not believe that any special expertise was necessary to hold a government job; he believed that any reasonably capable and well-informed citizen could perform these duties. Jackson consequently became a champion of the **spoils system**, appointing loyal Democrats to positions in the federal government. Jackson came to distrust his cabinet; instead he relied on the advice of his "**Kitchen Cabinet**," a group of his most trusted political cronies.

Jackson subscribed to the Jeffersonian ideal of a United States dominated by self-sufficient yeoman farmers. He was also a traditional Jeffersonian, believing in limited government and opposing federal involvement in the economy. He repeatedly vetoed bills calling for federal support for internal improvements. As a slave owner, Jackson opposed the abolitionist ferment in the country. Following the death in 1835 of John Marshall, Jackson appointed Roger B. Taney as chief justice of the Supreme Court. The Taney Court would become a stalwart defender of states' rights. Although Jackson advocated limited government, by sheer force of personality, he paradoxically strengthened the presidency. He would take actions that led his opponents to call him "King Andrew I."

The Nullification Controversy

The first crisis Jackson faced ironically forced him to assert the primacy of federal over state power. In 1828, during the waning days of the Adams administration, Congress passed a tariff bill designed to protect northern manufacturing interests. The increase in the cost of imported manufactured goods hurt southern and western farmers confronted with higher prices. Southern leaders termed the Tariff of 1828 the "Tariff of Abominations." The South Carolina legislature asserted the right of **nullification**, whereby states could refuse to enforce federal laws that they held to be unconstitutional. The chief theorist behind this new version of nullification was John C. Calhoun, a South Carolinian who had been elected Jackson's vice-president. Calhoun believed that the states needed a defense against the power of the federal government. He was worried that the more populous north would eventually force abolitionism on the south.

In 1830, a famous debate over nullification erupted in the U.S. Senate. In the **Webster-Hayne Debate**, Daniel Webster eloquently declared that if nullification were allowed, the consequence would be "states dissevered, discordant, belligerent; on a land rent with civil feuds, or drenched . . . in fraternal blood!"

President Jackson supported states' rights but resolutely opposed nullification. He took decisive action to demonstrate this. In 1832, after the passage of new tariffs, a convention in South Carolina voted to nullify this legislation. Jackson responded by preparing to send troops and federal marshals to South Carolina to enforce the law. Congress passed a **Force Act** supporting this action. Calhoun resigned as vice-president, while Jackson told confidantes that he would cheerfully send his former running mate to the gallows. The crisis was defused when Henry Clay helped engineer a bill that lowered the tariffs. Satisfied by this, the South Carolinians rescinded their act of nullification.

The Bank War

President Jackson's next great crisis involved the Second Bank of the United States, which had been chartered in 1816. The Bank was a vital component of Henry Clay's American System; it issued bank notes that served as a de facto national paper currency and played a key role in regulating credit and the activities of the state banks. The Bank was partly owned by the United States government and partly owned by private investors. Nicholas Biddle had managed the Bank since 1823. As a Jeffersonian, Jackson disliked the Bank on principle. He believed that the Bank had helped bring on the Panic of 1819. He was convinced that Biddle and the directors of the Bank enjoyed a power that was both unchecked and undemocratic.

Henry Clay ran against Jackson in the election of 1832. He used the Bank as an election issue, calling for it to be rechartered early. Clay saw to the passage of a rechartering bill, which Jackson promptly vetoed. Clay misjudged public opinion, believing that the electorate would support the Bank because of its obvious economic utility. Instead, Jackson portrayed the Bank as a sinister special interest. His attack on economic privilege resonated with voters, and he easily won reelection.

By now, Jackson regarded Biddle as a personal enemy and the Bank as a corrupt institution that had to be destroyed. In 1833, he withdrew federal money from the Bank and placed the funds in state banks, which were termed "pet banks" by his opponents. Biddle responded by calling in loans in an effort to keep his bank afloat. Jackson's **Bank War** and economic policies like the Specie Circular, which required gold or silver coins to purchase federal land, contributed to the onset of the **Panic of 1837**. This in turn led to an economic depression that carried into the 1840s.

The Whig Party and the Second Party System

In the 1830s, the opponents of Andrew Jackson gradually coalesced into the **Whig party**. The Whigs would form the primary opposition to the Democrats into the 1850s. This period of party politics is known as the Second Party System.

While the Democrats maintained the Jeffersonian tradition of standing by limited government, the Whigs believed in a more active government. The Whigs supported Henry Clay's vision of the American System and supported a national bank, tariffs, and internal improvements. The Whigs wanted a government that would foster commerce, industry, and better markets for farmers. Because of their belief in the efficacy of governmental action, Whigs were more likely to favor reform legislation than were the Democrats. More oriented to business and commerce, Whigs were less land hungry and expansionist than the Democrats, and the Whigs were more cautious about calls for America's Manifest Destiny. Many wealthy businessmen and planters supported the Whig party, but so too did many young men anxious to better themselves, such as Abraham Lincoln.

Andrew Jackson's chosen successor, Martin Van Buren, won the election of 1836. The Panic of 1837 undermined support for Democratic economic policy. In 1840, the Whigs nominated William Henry Harrison, another hero of the War of 1812, as their candidate for president. After a colorful campaign, which included the catchy slogan "Tippecanoe and Tyler Too," Harrison was elected. Harrison died a month after taking office, the victim of pneumonia contracted at his inauguration. John Tyler became the first vice-president to succeed to office after the death of a president.

Chapter Review

Rapid Review

To achieve the perfect 5, you should be able to explain the following:

- A new production system developed in textile mills such as those that existed in Lowell, Massachusetts, in the early nineteenth century.
- The Monroe Doctrine boldly proclaimed that the Western Hemisphere was off limits to European intrusion.
- Beginning in 1824, it was official American policy to move Native American tribes west of the Mississippi; the horrors of many of these relocations are well documented.
- The Second Great Awakening influenced many to become involved in reform movements, including the Abolitionist movement.
- The presidency of Andrew Jackson is celebrated as an era when the "common man" reigned supreme, although Jackson greatly expanded the powers of the presidency.
- The Democratic party of Andrew Jackson was the first real political party in American history.
- Jackson's tariff policy caused a renewal of interest in the policy of nullification in several Southern state legislatures.
- In the 1830s, the Whig party emerged as the major party opposing the Democratic party of Jackson.

Time Line

1790s: Beginning of Second Great Awakening

1816: Second bank of United States chartered
Tariff of 1816 imposes substantial import tariffs
Election of James Monroe

1819: Panic of 1819 (unemployment lasts until 1823)

1820: Missouri Compromise
Reelection of James Monroe

1820s: Growth of New England textile mills

1823: Monroe Doctrine

1824: Proposal by President Monroe to move Native Americans west of the
Mississippi River

1825: John Quincy Adams elected president by House of Representatives (no candidate
had won a majority in Electoral College)

1828: Andrew Jackson elected president

1830: Passage of Indian Removal Act in Congress
Webster-Hayne Debate

1830s: Growth of the Whig party

1831: Cherokee nation goes to court to defend tribal rights in
Cherokee Nation v. Georgia
First issue of William Lloyd Garrison's *The Liberator* published

1832: Andrew Jackson reelected
Nullification crisis after nullification of tariffs by South Carolina

1834: First strike of women textile workers in Lowell, Massachusetts

1836: Democrat Martin Van Buren elected president

1840: Whig William Henry Harrison elected president

› Review Questions

Multiple-Choice Questions

1. President Monroe claimed that westward relocation of Native Americans would be to the advantage of the Native Americans because
   A. they would not be bothered west of the Mississippi.
   B. the American military would protect them during the journey.
   C. they would be well compensated for the tribal lands that they were leaving.
   D. settlers west of the Mississippi were receptive to Native American settlement there.

2. The concept of nullification became an issue during this period when
   A. Georgia opposed congressional legislation concerning slavery.
   B. South Carolina nullified congressional legislation concerning the removal of Native Americans.
   C. South Carolina nullified congressional tariff bills.
   D. Southern representatives to the Electoral College switched their votes in the 1824 election.

3. Critics of Andrew Jackson would make all of the following claims *except* that
   A. he was a very common man and not fit to be president.
   B. he gave too much power to the presidency.
   C. he lacked experience in governmental affairs.
   D. he relied too much on his "Kitchen Cabinet."

4. The following are *true* about the textile mills of New England in the early nineteenth century *except*
   A. a large percentage of their workforce was made up of women.
   B. they depended on water for power.
   C. they used a system called the putting-out system.
   D. there was little labor unrest in the mills until the 1830s and 1840s.

5. Horace Mann is associated with
   A. abolitionism.
   B. the temperance movement.
   C. prison reform.
   D. educational reform.

Short-Answer Question

6. Answer Parts A, B, and C.
   A. Briefly explain ONE example of how Andrew Jackson fostered the growth of "Jacksonian democracy" in the United States.
   B. Briefly explain a SECOND example of how Andrew Jackson fostered the growth of "Jacksonian democracy" in the United States.
   C. Briefly explain ONE policy promoted by Andrew Jackson's political opponents.

› Answers and Explanations

1. **A.** Monroe stated that Native Americans could not avoid being continually harassed if they lived east of the Mississippi, but that this would not happen after they moved.

2. **C.** Because the tariff bills increased the prices of cloth and iron, the South Carolina legislature first nullified the Tariff of 1828.

3. **C.** All of the other criticisms were often made against Jackson. However, he did have an impressive background: before becoming president, he had served as a congressman and a senator from Tennessee and as the territorial governor of Florida.

4. **C.** It was the putting-out system that these mills replaced.

5. **D.** Horace Mann wrote and spoke about the need to improve schools and to improve teacher training methods.

6. **Parts A and B**: Andrew Jackson supported the lowering of property qualifications that allowed more men to vote. In 1824, Jackson won the popular vote and the largest number of electors, but not enough to claim the presidency; after the election was thrown into the House of Representatives, he was defeated by John Quincy Adams when Henry Clay gave his support to the former secretary of state.

Jackson denounced what he called a "corrupt bargain," and called for a more democratic and anti-elitist politics. As a Jeffersonian, he opposed government intervention in the economy, believing that "big" government would favor special interests. Once elected to the presidency in 1828, Jackson filled government jobs with his supporters. He defended this "spoils system" by arguing that any man should be able to carry out the duties of a government post. At his inauguration, Jackson invited the public to a reception at the White House, a gesture never made before. Jackson vetoed a bill re-chartering the Bank of the United States. He believed that the bank served the interests of the moneyed elite rather than the common man. Initially, Jackson's "Bank War" enhanced his image as a champion of the "common man."

Part C: President Jackson's opponents coalesced into the Whig party. Whigs tended to support a greater government role in the economy. Most opposed Jackson's "Bank War." Many subscribed to Henry Clay's "American System," which called for a national bank to facilitate commerce, internal improvements to help farmers and businessmen get their goods to markets, and a tariff to help protect American industry.

CHAPTER **14**

Union Expanded and Challenged (1835–1860)

IN THIS CHAPTER

Summary: Guided by the principle of "Manifest Destiny," Americans began to stream westward in the 1830s. By the mid-1840s settlers were entrenched in the Oregon and California territories. Adventurers also settled in Texas and helped the Texans defeat the Mexican army in 1836. The Mexican-American War took place between 1846 and 1847. By the terms of the treaty ending this war the United States paid Mexico $15 million dollars; in return the United States acquired the northern part of the Texas territory and New Mexico and California. The pivotal issue for Americans remained whether newly acquired territories would enter the Union as slave states or as free states. Under the Missouri Compromise a line was drawn westward to the Pacific Ocean; all territories north of the line would enter the Union as free states and all territories south of the line would come in as slave states. The issue of whether California would enter the Union as a free or slave state necessitated the Compromise of 1850. The Kansas-Nebraska Act of 1854 stated that settlers living in those territories could vote on whether they would become slave states or free states. The *Dred Scott* Supreme Court decision of 1857 stated that Congress had no right to prohibit slavery in the territories and that even though Scott, an ex-slave, had spent time in a free state and a free territory this did not make him a free man. Tensions between the North and the South remained high. In the 1860 presidential election, Illinois Congressman Abraham Lincoln campaigned on the need to contain slavery in the territories. After his election, representatives of seven Southern states met to create the Confederate States of America, with Jefferson Davis as the first president of the Confederacy.

Keywords

Manifest Destiny: concept that became popularized in the 1840s stating that it was the God-given mission of the United States to expand westward.

Mexican-American War: war fought over possession of Texas, which was claimed by both Mexico and the United States; the settlement ending this war gave the United States the northern part of the Texas territory and the territories of New Mexico and California.

Compromise of 1850: temporarily ending tensions between the North and the South, this measure allowed California to enter the Union as a free state but also strengthened the Fugitive Slave Law.

Fugitive Slave Act: part of the Compromise of 1850, legislation that set up special commissions in northern states to determine if accused runaway slaves were actually that. Commissioners were given more money if the accused was found to be a runaway than if he/she was not. Many northern state legislatures attempted to circumvent this law.

Kansas-Nebraska Act (1854): compromise that allowed settlers in Kansas and Nebraska to vote to decide if they would enter the Union as free states or slave states. Much violence and confusion took place in Kansas as various types of "settlers" moved into this territory in the months before the vote in an attempt to influence it.

***Dred Scott* case:** critical Supreme Court ruling that stated that slaves were property and not people; as a result they could not seek a ruling from any court. The ruling also stated that Congress had no legal right to ban slavery in any territory.

Manifest Destiny

Americans had always dreamed of expanding their settlements westward. The acquisition of new lands to the west had been a core component of Thomas Jefferson's vision of an agrarian republic. In the 1840s, the age-old American urge to push against the line of the frontier became a clearly articulated ideology. In 1845, the journalist John O'Sullivan coined the term **Manifest Destiny**. He called for the United States "to overspread the continent allotted by Providence for free development of our yearly multiplying millions."

In the 1830s Americans began taking the long and arduous **Oregon Trail** west to the Williamette Valley of the Oregon territory. Tales of rich soil, plentiful wildlife, and a salubrious climate attracted settlers from the east. In the early 1840s people talked of "Oregon Fever." More than 5,000 Americans had made their way to Oregon by 1845. Among them was the missionary Marcus Whitman. He, his family, and 12 others were murdered by Indians in 1847. Despite the dangers, Americans were determined to settle and control the Oregon territory. The United States shared sovereignty in Oregon with Great Britain. American expansionists demanded all of Oregon, making their rallying cry "Fifty-four Forty or Fight." President James K. Polk decided to pursue diplomacy rather than conflict with the British. The **Oregon Treaty** of 1846 awarded most, though not all of the Oregon territory to the United States. Proponents of Manifest Destiny also called for the United States to acquire California. American settlers began to arrive in California in the 1830s. Like with Oregon, expansion into California became a political issue in the 1840s.

The Alamo and Texas Independence

American expansionism helped spur conflict with Mexico. Mexico won its independence from Spain in 1821, but entered into a protracted period of political instability. Hoping to develop its underpopulated northern province of Texas, Mexican officials encouraged an influx of American settlers, who in return for accepting Mexican citizenship and adopting the Roman Catholic religion were provided with extensive grants of land. By 1836, there were 30,000 American settlers in Texas.

These American settlers soon found themselves at odds with the Mexican authorities. In the early 1830s they became caught up in Mexican political struggles between supporters of a federal system of government and those who wanted a stronger central government. The Texans favored the federalist cause. Centralizers won control of the Mexican government and began tightening their control over Texas. Most of the American settlers and many Mexicans in Texas responded by revolting. On March 2, 1836, the rebels proclaimed Texan independence. The Mexican president, General Antonio López de Santa Anna led an army into Texas. On March 6, his troops overwhelmed a garrison of 180 to 250 men, including Davey Crockett and Jim Bowie, at the Alamo in San Antonio. All the defenders of the Alamo died, but their heroic resistance inspired the Texan war-cry "Remember the Alamo!" The remaining Texan forces, aided by volunteers from the United States, rallied under General Sam Houston. On April 21, Houston's army surprised and routed Santa Anna's command at San Jacinto. Santa Anna was captured and forced to order all Mexican soldiers out of Texas.

The newly independent Texas became the Lone Star Republic, with Sam Houston as its president. Most Texans wanted their republic to be annexed by the United States. The politics of slavery prevented this. Many Northerners opposed the acquisition of a territory that would become another slave state. The admission of Texas into the Union would also lead to inevitable conflicts with Mexico, which refused to officially recognize the independence of Texas. President Andrew Jackson sympathized with the aspirations of the Texans, but was unwilling to risk the electoral prospects of his protégé Martin Van Buren in the presidential election that fall. He contented himself with extending diplomatic recognition to the Lone Star Republic.

The American annexation of Texas remained a political nonstarter until 1844. President John Tyler and his secretary of state, John C. Calhoun, both Southerners, worked to negotiate a treaty that would bring Texas into the Union as a slave state. Until the election of 1844, their efforts proved unavailing in the Senate.

Expansion and the Election of 1844

The election of 1844 proved to be the political high tide of Manifest Destiny. James K. Polk won the Democratic nomination for the presidency. He was the first American **dark horse candidate** to win a major party nomination; he was not put forward as a candidate until the Democratic nominating convention. Polk was hardly a political nonentity. A protégé of Andrew Jackson, he had served as Speaker of the House and as governor of Tennessee. Polk warmly embraced American expansionism. He called for the annexation of Texas and of all of the Oregon Territory. The nomination of Polk also demonstrated the growing dominance of the South in the Democratic Party. Polk would later sign the 1846 Walker Tariff that angered Northern manufacturing interests by lowering the tariff on imported products.

The Whig nominee in 1844 was Henry Clay, making his third run for the presidency. In an effort to conciliate all sectional interests, Clay refused to embrace expansionism. He hoped that his long experience in American politics and personal popularity would carry him through to victory. Clay's hopes would be frustrated by political abolitionism. The new anti-slavery Liberty party ran James Birney for the presidency in 1844. Though the Liberty party failed to attract widespread support (only 62,000 votes in total), its presence on the ballot probably cost Clay the electoral votes of New York and the election.

Polk's expansionism proved popular enough for him to win a close election. Before Polk's inauguration in March 1845, the outgoing president, John Tyler, secured the annexation of Texas through the unusual method of a joint resolution of Congress. Once in office, Polk began the diplomatic negotiations with Great Britain that resulted in the successful resolution of the Oregon boundary dispute. Polk's efforts to acquire more land from the Mexicans would not be resolved peacefully.

The Mexican War

Polk hoped to obtain all of his expansionist goals with Mexico through diplomacy. He wanted the Mexicans to accept the Rio Grande River as the southern boundary of Texas, rather than the more northerly Nueces River, which the Mexicans argued was the Texas border. Dreaming of trade on the Pacific Ocean, Polk wanted the superb harbor of San Francisco and all the California Territory around it. In October 1845, he sent the diplomat John Slidell to Mexico with a proposal to purchase the territory between the Nueces and Rio Grande rivers for $5 million, California for $25 million, and $5 million for the Mexican lands between Texas and California. The Mexican government refused to see Slidell. It took more emphatic action against an army led by General Zachary Taylor that Polk had provocatively posted along the Rio Grande River. In April 1846, Mexican troops attacked a patrol of American soldiers. This began hostilities between Mexico and the United States. Once Polk learned of the outbreak of fighting, he asked Congress for a declaration of war. The United States declared against Mexico on May 13, 1846.

The Mexican War was controversial, and opposed by many Americans. Many Whigs believed that Polk had forced the war on Mexico, without fully exploring a diplomatic solution. Many Northerners assumed that the war was a scheme by Southern Democrats to conquer new territories for the institution of slavery.

Although some contemporary observers predicted a Mexican victory because of the large number of men Mexico had under arms, the American army soon proved its military superiority. General Taylor defeated the Mexican forces confronting them along the Rio Grande and advanced into Northern Mexico. There he repulsed a Mexican counterattack at the hard-fought Battle of Buena Vista. In California, the United States fomented an uprising of American settlers. Supported by a small force of soldiers led by the explorer John C. Fremont, the rebels declared California independent on July 4, 1846, renaming the province as the **Bear Flag Republic**. Detachments of American troops conquered New Mexico and the rest of the Mexican lands Polk wanted for the United States. Territorially satisfied, Polk was ready to make peace. The Mexicans spurned his overtures, refusing to submit. To compel a Mexican surrender, Polk dispatched an army led by General Winfield Scott to the Mexican port of Vera Cruz. On March 8, 1847, Scott supervised the first major amphibious landing in American military history. Scott abandoned his lines of communication and supply and marched into the heart of Mexico. After winning several battles, Scott's army captured Mexico City on September 13, 1847. This effectively ended the war, though Mexican partisans continued to harass American troops.

Political Consequences of the Mexican War

The Mexican War was ended by the **Treaty of Guadalupe Hidalgo**, signed in Mexico on February 2, 1848. The United States paid Mexico $15 million for the territory in Texas north of the Rio Grande, New Mexico, and California. The United States also agreed to pay all the claims that American citizens had against the Mexican government. While some Americans criticized the treaty for being too lenient with the Mexicans and argued that even more Mexican territory should have been taken, the spoils of the Mexican War increased the territory of the United States by one-third. Much of the dream of Manifest Destiny had been realized. The United States now truly was a continental nation.

The expansion of American territory inevitably raised the question of the expansion of slavery. In the summer of 1846, David Wilmot, a Democratic representative from Pennsylvania ignited a political firestorm. He attached an amendment to a military appropriations bill that prohibited slavery in any territory taken from Mexico during the war. The **Wilmot Proviso** outraged Southerners. It was passed by the House four times, but was defeated in the Senate. Wilmot's amendment forced a political debate that further polarized sectional tensions over slavery. Northerners argued that slavery should not be introduced where it had been illegal under Mexican rule. John C. Calhoun eloquently articulated the Southern position that an institution that was legal in many American states could not be prohibited in federal territories held in common by all the states. President Polk attempted to forge a compromise settlement by extending the **Missouri Compromise** line to the Pacific Ocean.

Both major parties attempted to avoid the issue of slavery in the election of 1848. The Whigs attempted to replicate their previous winning strategy of running a war hero and nominated General Zachary Taylor. Lacking a suitably famous general, the Democrats nominated Lewis Cass, a senator from Michigan. Members of the Liberty party and dissident Whigs and Democrats coalesced into the Free-Soil party dedicated to opposing the extension of slavery into the western territories. Former president Martin Van Buren accepted the Free-Soil nomination and received 10 percent of the popular vote. Taylor's military charisma trumped all other considerations and he won the election.

The Political Crisis of 1850

The need to organize the territories won from Mexico would not allow the issue of slavery to be set aside or postponed. Americans had to make a decision about slavery in the West. Heightened passions over the morality of slavery made normal political compromises more difficult to achieve.

In January 1848, gold was discovered in California. Within a year, the ensuing California "gold rush" brought more than 80,000 "forty-niners" into the territory. By late 1849 there were enough settlers in California to apply for statehood. Settlers in New Mexico also petitioned for statehood. Gatherings in both territories drafted constitutions that prohibited slavery. President Taylor encouraged the Californians in their efforts and was willing to allow them to enter the Union as a free state. In doing this, he roused the anger of many Southerners. Much of California lay below the extended Missouri Compromise line. Both the western territories and the balance of power in the Senate seemed to be slipping away from the South. Calls were made for a convention in the South to discuss secession. John C. Calhoun spoke for many Southerners when he declared, "I trust we shall persist in our resistance until restoration of all our rights or disunion, one or the other, is the consequence."

Henry Clay criticized talk of Southern secession. Known as the "great pacificator" for having engineered the Compromise of 1820, the aging Clay hoped to fashion one more great compromise to hold the Union together. He packaged a series of resolutions designed to give both Northern and Southern legislators victories to take home to their constituents. The provisions of the **Compromise of 1850** included the admission of California as a free state, the freedom of the residents of New Mexico and Utah to decide if they wanted slavery in their territories, the ending of slave-trading in the District of Columbia, and a strengthened **Fugitive Slave Act**. Clay could not get his compromise passed as an omnibus bill because of the opposition of President Taylor and the unwillingness of congressmen to vote for elements of the bill that went against their sectional interests. Following Taylor's unexpected death, his successor Millard Fillmore expressed support for the compromise. Senator Stephen A. Douglas, a Democrat from Illinois, shepherded the compromise through Congress, passing each element separately with the crucial support of moderate Southern Whigs and Northern Democrats.

Aftermath of the Compromise of 1850

For a time the Compromise of 1850 brought a degree of sectional harmony. Beneath the surface profound differences between Northern and Southern interests simmered. The entrance of California into the Union tilted the balance of the Senate against the South. The admission of Minnesota and Oregon later in the decade made the South's dwindling legislative influence more worrisome to extremist defenders of slavery. The Fugitive Slave Act, which increased the federal role in apprehending runaway slaves, was deeply unpopular in the North. African Americans accused of being escaped slaves were denied normal judicial due process, making it obvious that the new federal system was stacked against anyone with a dark skin. Northerners who were caught helping escaped slaves were heavily fined. The Fugitive Slave Act proved counterproductive for Southern interests by inflaming abolitionist sentiment in the North. The most powerful expression of this was Harriet Beecher Stowe's novel *Uncle Tom's Cabin* (1852), which powerfully dramatized the evils of slavery. Stowe's novel helped crystallize antislavery feelings in the North, selling almost 275,000 copies within a year.

In the election of 1852, the major political parties hoped that the slavery issue had been laid to rest. The Whigs nominated yet another war hero, General Winfield Scott. The Democrats turned to another **dark horse candidate**, Franklin Pierce. The strength of the Democratic Party carried Pierce to victory.

Franklin Pierce in the White House

Pierce reverted to the expansionist policies of James K. Polk. His administration negotiated the **Gadsden Purchase** from Mexico, which gave the United States a strip of territory that would facilitate the construction of a transcontinental railroad routed through the South. Pierce sent a naval expedition commanded by Commodore Matthew C. Perry to open up trade and diplomatic relations with Japan. The president fostered Northern suspicions that he was Southern in his sympathies by attempting to buy Cuba from Spain. When this failed, members of his administration discussed a military occupation of the island. The main impetus behind talk of acquiring Cuba, and also behind privately run expeditions to seize territory in Central America, was a Southern desire to open up new lands to slavery.

Following its failure in 1852, the Whig party fell apart. Many Whigs drifted into the newly emergent American or **Know-Nothing party,** which capitalized on anti-immigrant feeling. Large numbers of Irish and German immigrants had flooded into the United States during the 1840s. This spurred a **nativist** reaction. The Know-Nothings were especially hostile to the Roman Catholicism practiced by many of the immigrants. During its brief moment of popularity the Know-Nothing party tried to restrict further immigration and prevent recent immigrants from voting. The Know-Nothing party faded away when slavery once again became the leading political issue.

The Kansas-Nebraska Act

Stephen A. Douglas reignited sectional conflict because of his dream of running a transcontinental railroad from Chicago to California. To do this, the territories of Kansas and Nebraska had to be politically organized. According to the terms of the Missouri Compromise, slavery was banned in these territories. Douglas needed Southern support to begin the process of organizing Kansas and Nebraska. The price for this support was abandoning the Missouri Compromise and allowing the people living in Kansa and Nebraska to decide whether they would allow the introduction of slavery. Douglas embraced the bargain and became a spokesman for popular sovereignty in the territories. In 1854, President Pierce signed Douglas's **Kansas-Nebraska Act** into law.

The immediate result was a political uproar in the North. Many Northerners regarded the bill as an outrageous attempt to spread slavery into free territory. Free-Soilers, former Whigs, and defecting Democrats joined in launching the **Republican party**. Drawing its strength from the North and West, the new party vehemently opposed the extension of slavery into the western territories. The Republican party swiftly replaced the Know-Nothings as the most significant political rival to the Democrats.

"Bleeding Kansas"

There was never any realistic prospect that Nebraska would become a slave state. Kansas, with its long border with Missouri, was another story. Elections in Kansas were scheduled for 1855. Knowing this, supporters and opponents of slavery worked to send settlers into the territory. When the election was held, illegal voting by Missourians who flocked across the border helped the proslavery side to victory. The resulting proslavery legislature crafted the "Lecompton Constitution" that legalized slavery in Kansas. Outraged antislavery settlers elected their own legislature and wrote a constitution that banned slavery. With two legislatures and two constitutions, Kansas was locked into conflict. The differences between the two sides escalated into bloodshed. In 1856, a band of proslavery gunmen shot up or burned much of Lawrence, Kansas, a community founded by abolitionists. In retaliation, the fiercely antislavery fanatic John Brown led a gang that butchered five proslavery settlers. The ongoing violence led newspapermen to term the stricken territory **"Bleeding Kansas."**

In the 1856 presidential election the Democrat, James Buchanan, won in a three-way race with John C. Fremont, the first Republican presidential candidate, and former president, Millard Fillmore, running as a Know-Nothing. Buchanan won 45 percent of the popular vote and only triumphed because of his support in the "Solid South."

The *Dred Scott* Decision

Dred Scott was a slave in Missouri who went to court and sued for his freedom. Scott's master had taken him to live for several years in the free state of Illinois and the free territory of Wisconsin. Scott argued that his residence for a time in free territory made him free. Scott's case made its way to the Supreme Court in 1856. In the **Dred Scott case**, the Supreme Court ruled that Scott was still a slave. The Court majority went beyond the specifics of the case and declared that African Americans were inherently inferior and could not be granted citizenship. It also ruled that Congress could not prohibit slavery in the territories because this violated constitutionally protected property rights.

The *Dred Scott* decision further inflamed sectional tensions. Southerners felt vindicated by the Supreme Court's ruling on slavery in the territories. Northerners were infuriated at the prospect of a panel of mostly Southern judges justifying the spread of slavery throughout the Union.

President Buchanan proved just as politically tone deaf as the Supreme Court. Ignoring the illegality surrounding the Lecompton Constitution, and a growing majority of free-soil settlers in Kansas, he urged Congress to recognize the territory as a slave state. Congress refused his recommendation. Kansas would enter the Union as a free state in 1861.

The Lincoln-Douglas Debates

Stephen A. Douglas ran for reelection to the Senate in 1858. He was opposed by Abraham Lincoln, the candidate of the Republican party. Lincoln had been an admirer of Henry Clay and a longtime Whig. He served a term in Congress in the 1840s and criticized the Mexican War. Lincoln was drawn back into politics by the Kansas-Nebraska Act and the *Dred Scott* decision. Because of Douglas's political prominence, his series of debates with Lincoln received national attention. These debates became a landmark of political oratory. They all centered on the issue of slavery and the territories. At the debate at Freeport, Illinois, Lincoln asked Douglas how he could continue to promote popular sovereignty after the *Dred Scott* decision. Douglas replied with what came to be known as the **Freeport Doctrine**. He argued that the people of a territory could keep out slavery by legislating rules and regulations that would make it too difficult to maintain slaves. Douglas's position satisfied enough voters in Illinois, ensuring the retention of his Senate seat in the fall, but it won him many enemies in the South. Lincoln's brilliant performance during the debates marked him as a rising leader of the Republican party.

John Brown and Harpers Ferry

John Brown left Kansas and returned to the East dreaming of leading a great slave insurrection. He persuaded a few wealthy Northern abolitionists to fund his scheme. On October 16, 1859, Brown and 18 followers attacked the federal arsenal at Harpers Ferry, Virginia. He hoped to use the rifles that he captured there to arm slaves. Brown's raid proved to be a fiasco. He and his men were quickly surrounded and then captured by federal troops led by Colonel Robert E. Lee. Brown was convicted of treason and publically hanged. Some Northerners saw Brown as a martyr. Henry David Thoreau called him "the bravest and humanest man in all the country." Southerners were appalled by this sympathy for a man they regarded as a terrorist.

The Election of 1860

As the presidential election of 1860 approached, the Democratic party divided along sectional lines. Stephen A. Douglas was the frontrunner for the nomination, but many Southern Democrats could not forgive him for the Freeport Doctrine. These Southerners walked out of the Democratic convention and nominated John Breckinridge. In the ensuing election campaign, Douglas defended the principle of popular sovereignty, while Breckinridge took the position that slavery should be allowed in all the territories. The Democratic split helped persuade John Bell, a former Whig from Tennessee, to run as the candidate of a new Constitutional Union party that appealed to sectional moderates. The divided political field opened up an electoral opportunity for the Republicans. Out of a crowded field of candidates, Abraham Lincoln emerged as the Republican nominee. He attempted to reassure Southerners that slavery would not be molested in the slave states, but adamantly opposed permitting the introduction of slavery into the western territories. When the final votes were tallied, Lincoln received 40 percent of the popular vote, but won decisively in the Electoral College, carrying all the Northern and Western states.

The election of Abraham Lincoln was a Southern nightmare come true. Lincoln had triumphed at the head of a party that received virtually no votes in much of the South. Southerners now faced the prospect of a party hostile to slavery controlling Congress and the presidency.

South Carolina led the way in seceding from the Union on December 20, 1860. Within six weeks Mississippi, Georgia, Florida, Alabama, Texas, and Louisiana followed. Representatives from the seceded states met at Montgomery, Alabama, in February 1861. They formed the **Confederate States of America**. The men gathered at Montgomery elected Jefferson Davis as the president of the new Confederacy. Davis's experience as a soldier and secretary of war were points in his favor. Few expected the Union to break up peacefully.

Chapter Review

Rapid Review

To achieve the perfect 5, you should be able to explain the following:

- The concept of Manifest Destiny spurred American expansion into Texas and the far West.
- American settlers much more loyal to the United States than to Mexico entered Texas in large numbers and encouraged Texas to break away from Mexico and eventually become an American state.
- The issue of slavery in the territories came to dominate American political debate more and more in the 1840s and 1850s.
- California entered the Union as a free state under the Missouri Compromise, upsetting the balance between free and slave states and intensifying the conflict between them.
- The Kansas-Nebraska Act created violence in these territories as they "decided" on whether they would be slave or free; both Abolitionists and proslavery forces shipped in supporters to help sway the elections in these territories.

- The *Dred Scott* decision only intensified tensions between the North and the South.
- The election of 1860 was seen as an insult to many in the South, and after its results were announced, the secession of Southern states from the Union was inevitable.

Time Line

1836: Texas territory rebels against Mexico; independent republic of Texas created

1841: Beginning of expansion into Oregon territory

1844: James K. Polk elected president

1845: Texas becomes a state of the United States

1846: Oregon Treaty with Britain gives most of Oregon to United States
War with Mexico begins
Wilmot Proviso passed

1848: Gold discovered in California; beginning of California gold rush
Treaty of Guadalupe Hidalgo
Formation of Free-Soil party
Zachary Taylor elected president

1850: Passage of Compromise of 1850

1852: Franklin Pierce elected president
Uncle Tom's Cabin by Harriet Beecher Stowe published

1854: Kansas-Nebraska Act passed
Formation of the Republican party

1856: Democrat James Buchanan elected president
"Bleeding Kansas"

1857: *Dred Scott* decision announced

1858: Lincoln-Douglas debates
Freeport Doctrine issued by Stephen Douglas

1859: Harper's Ferry raid of John Brown

1860: Abraham Lincoln elected president
South Carolina secedes from the Union (December)

› Review Questions

Multiple-Choice Questions

1. Northerners approved all of the provisions of the Compromise of 1850 *except*
   A. the section of the document concerning slavery in California.
   B. the section of the document concerning the Fugitive Slave Law.
   C. the section of the treaty on slave trading in Washington, DC.
   D. the section of the document concerning slavery in New Mexico.

2. During the presidential election of 1860
   A. the Democratic party had split and was running two candidates.
   B. the new president was someone whom almost no one in the South had voted for.
   C. the issue of the future of slavery in the territories was a major issue.
   D. all of the above

3. According to the concept of Manifest Destiny
   A. it was primarily economic factors that caused Americans to expand westward.
   B. it was primarily political factors that caused Americans to expand westward.
   C. westward expansion was the fulfillment of America's destiny.
   D. overpopulation on the eastern seaboard forced westward expansion.

4. American settlers first came to Mexico in the early 1830s
   A. to avenge the attack on the Alamo.
   B. for political reasons; most who came were disenchanted with American policy toward Native Americans.
   C. out of personal loyalty to Davey Crockett or Jim Bowie.
   D. because they could receive a large plot of land for next to nothing.

5. The political party of the era that supported nativist policies was the
   A. Free-Soil party.
   B. Democratic party.
   C. Know-Nothing party.
   D. Whig party.

Short-Answer Question

6. Answer Parts A, B, and C.
   A. Briefly explain ONE example of an issue leading to sectional hostility between the North and South in the period 1840 to 1860.
   B. Briefly explain a SECOND example of an issue leading to sectional hostility between the North and South in the period 1840 to 1860.
   C. Briefly explain ONE example of an effort to achieve compromise between the North and South in the period 1840 to 1860.

› Answers and Explanations

1. **B**. In the Compromise of 1850, provisions of the Fugitive Slave Law were made tougher. California was to enter the Union as a free state, the residents of New Mexico and Utah could decide if they wanted to be slave or free, and slave trading was outlawed in Washington, DC.

2. **D**. All of the factors mentioned concerning the 1860 election are true.

3. **C**. The concept of Manifest Destiny stated that social, political, and economic factors all came together to encourage western expansion, and that western expansion was actually "God's plan" for America.

4. **D**. Settlers who came and became Mexican citizens and Catholics could receive very large plots of land for almost nothing. The incident at the Alamo did not occur until 1836.

5. **C**. The Know-Nothing party, a popular party in the early 1850s, supported a number of anti-immigrant and anti-Catholic policies.

6. **Parts A and B**: The rise of abolitionism in the North angered many in the South. The House of Representatives imposed a gag rule on antislavery petitions that lasted from 1836 to 1844. Many opponents of slavery believed that the expansionism that resulted in the Mexican War of 1846 to 1848 was an attempt to create more slave states. The 1846 Wilmot Proviso in the House of Representatives calling for the prohibition of slavery in territory taken from Mexico angered many Southerners. The Fugitive Slave Act, part of the Compromise of 1850, offended Northerners who did not want

escaping slaves hunted in their states. Harriet Beecher Stowe's *Uncle Tom's Cabin* (1852) was a powerful literary indictment of slavery. The 1854 Kansas-Nebraska Act inflamed sectional tensions by overturning the Missouri Compromise and raising the prospect of slavery in these two territories. Kansas became known as "Bleeding Kansas" because of the violence between proslavery and antislavery settlers. The 1856 *Dred Scott v. Sandford* Supreme Court decision, which ruled that Congress could not prohibit slavery in the territories, outraged many in the North. John Brown's unsuccessful attempt to start a slave rebellion by attacking the Harpers Ferry federal arsenal in 1859 terrified many Southerners. The election of the Republican candidate Abraham Lincoln to the presidency in 1860 on a purely sectional vote convinced many Southerners that they had to secede from the Union.

Part C: President James K. Polk tried to ensure both Northern and Southern support for American expansionism by seeing to it that both sections benefitted. In his 1844 presidential campaign he called for the annexation of slaveholding Texas and all of the Oregon Territory. Henry Clay tried to solve sectional tensions with his Compromise of 1850, which, among other provisions, saw California enter the Union as a free state and imposed a strong Fugitive Slave Law. During the 1850s, Senator Stephen A. Douglas believed he could reconcile sectional disputes over the western territories with his doctrine of "popular sovereignty," which would allow the settlers of territories decide whether they wanted slavery or not.

CHAPTER 15

Union Divided: The Civil War (1861–1865)

IN THIS CHAPTER

Summary: The Civil War was the culmination of nearly 40 years of tensions between the North and the South. Northern Abolitionists looked forward to the war with great anticipation: victory over the South would finally allow the dreaded institution of slavery to be eliminated. Northern industrialists saw the war as an opportunity, at long last, to expand their control of American industry. The majority of Southerners rejoiced at the onset of war; they perceived that victory would allow the "Southern way of life" to continue without constant criticism from the North. As in many wars, politicians and generals on both sides predicted a quick victory. Newspapers in both the North and the South declared that the war would be over by Christmas of 1861.

To state that the Civil War was just about slavery is an oversimplification. Certainly, criticism by Northern Abolitionists of the "peculiar institution" of slavery, and Southern responses to that criticism, were important factors. However, other tensions between the North and the South also existed. The future of the American economy as seen by Northern industrialists differed drastically from the desires and needs of the leaders of Southern plantation societies. Most important, the Southern view of "states' rights" differed most dramatically from the view of the Union held in the North. By 1861, many political leaders in the South fervently espoused the views that John C. Calhoun had formulated decades earlier. It was up to the individual state to decide on the validity of any federal law or federal action for that state. This position was intolerable to President Lincoln and most political leaders in the North. If anything, it was debate over the state's rights issue that made the Civil War inevitable.

Other factors increased the animosity between the North and the South. By this point, slavery was synonymous with Southern identity; in Southern eyes, any attack on slavery was an attack on the South as a whole. The fact that this struggle between the North and the South had gone on for 40 years served to harden positions on both sides. In addition, by this point the population of the North was greater than the population of the South, and the number of free states was greater than the number of slave states. As a result, Southerners knew that Northern antislave interests would control the Congress (and the ability to influence Supreme Court appointments) and the Electoral College for the foreseeable future.

Keywords

First Battle of Bull Run (1861): early Civil War engagement ending in defeat for the Union army; this battle convinced many in the North that victory over the Confederacy would not be as easy as they first thought it would be.

Emancipation Proclamation: January 1, 1863, proclamation that freed slaves in Southern territories was controlled by the Union army; this executive proclamation by President Lincoln also committed the Union to the abolition of slavery.

Battle of Gettysburg (1863): bloodiest overall battle of the Civil War; many historians claim that the Southern defeat in this battle was the beginning of the end for the Confederacy.

Appomattox: Virginia courthouse where General Robert E. Lee surrendered Confederate forces on April 9, 1865.

North and South on the Brink of War

The North brought a number of advantages to a military struggle with the seceded states. Most of the nation's wealth was concentrated in the North. The North housed the largest banks and financial markets in great cities like New York and Chicago. The Northern states were far more industrialized and were connected together by an extensive network of railroads. The North was in a much better position to manufacture and transport weapons and other war supplies. The North also had an edge in manpower, with a population three times that of the South. Despite this, Southern supporters of the Confederacy still believed that they could win a war with the North. Many in the agrarian South overvalued the importance of cotton to international markets, believing that the great European powers of Great Britain and France would intervene to protect their textile industries. Southerners also saw themselves as enjoying a moral advantage; they would be fighting a defensive war to protect their homes and institutions. Southerners also realized that geography posed a problem for the North; the South was a huge territory that would require an enormous expenditure of resources to capture and hold.

Searching for Compromise

In the aftermath of the creation of the **Confederate States of America** in February 1861, there was no immediate rush of slave states in the upper South to secede. They had fewer slaves and were reluctant to leave the union. Leaders in these states attempted to formulate a compromise that would end the secession crisis. Congressional representatives from

Kentucky and Maryland urged the passage of legislation that would guarantee the continued existence of slavery in states and territories where it was already established. President James Buchanan, very much a lame duck, provided little leadership. In December 1860, he declared that secession was illegal, but he also believed that there were no constitutional grounds to compel states to remain in the Union.

The leaders of the Confederacy grew confident that they had nothing to fear from Buchanan. Confederates occupied most federal installations in the seceded states. In South Carolina, the new authorities demanded that federal troops evacuate **Fort Sumter**, a fortress situated on an island in Charleston harbor. In January 1861, Buchanan attempted to resupply the fort by sending south an unarmed merchant ship. When the Confederates drove the supply ship off with gunfire, Buchanan refused to use the navy to protect another supply run. This emboldened the Confederates in Charleston.

While Fort Sumter was the center of most Americans' attention, Senator John Crittenden of Kentucky proposed another compromise. The **Crittenden Plan** called for an assurance of federal protection of slavery where it already existed, and the formal extension of the Missouri Compromise line to the Pacific; territory to the south of the line would be open to slavery, while that north of the line would be free. Crittenden's compromise failed because Republicans refused to surrender their free-soil position on slavery in the territories that had just won them the national election.

Gunfire at Fort Sumter

Abraham Lincoln had to be politically circumspect in the long interval between his election in November 1860 and his inauguration in March 1861. Though all looked to him, he was not yet the president. He attempted to reassure Southerners that he would not interfere with slavery in the slave states, while holding firm to his position on slavery in the territories. He affirmed federal authority, while saying nothing to provoke a war. At his inauguration, Lincoln stated his desire for conciliation with the seceded states, but declared that if necessary he would use the military to restore the Union.

Lincoln knew that to rally opinion for a war against the secessionists he could not fire the first shots. He used the Fort Sumter crisis to maneuver the Confederates into doing that. In April 1861, Lincoln dispatched another supply ship toward Fort Sumter. Aware of the ship's impending arrival, Jefferson Davis and the Confederate authorities in Charleston decided to strike. The Confederates began a bombardment of the fort on April 12, and two days later the federal garrison surrendered.

Davis hoped that the attack on Fort Sumter would demonstrate Confederate strength and rally support for the secessionist cause. Once Lincoln issued a call for 75,000 volunteers to put down the rebellion, Virginia, North Carolina, Tennessee, and Arkansas did secede and join the Confederacy. But by various means Lincoln was able to keep the slave states of Maryland, Delaware, Kentucky, and Missouri in the Union; control of these states greatly improved the strategic position of the federal government.

Opening Strategies

Southerners sincerely claimed to be defending the principle of **states' rights**. What drove this concern was a resolute attachment to the institution of slavery, despite the fact that the great majority of Southerners owned no slaves. The centrality of slavery to secession undercut Confederate attempts to use cotton to win diplomatic support from Britain and France. These European powers were not particularly friendly to the U.S. government, and they wanted Southern cotton. But both Britain and France had long since outlawed slavery and were wary of being seen as supporting the "peculiar institution." Early in the war, a Confederate decision to embargo cotton exports to Europe backfired. President Davis and his advisors hoped that this would hurt Britain and France enough economically that their governments would be pressured into offering diplomatic recognition to the Confederacy. Instead, the Europeans discovered other sources of cotton, with disastrous long-term consequences for the South.

In 1861, great numbers of volunteers joined the Union and Confederate armies. In the first flush of enthusiasm, both sides predicted a quick and easy victory. President Lincoln rallied Northern public opinion for a war to preserve the Union; he argued that to allow the rebellion to succeed would be to undermine the foundations of representative government. The Confederate capital was moved to Richmond, Virginia, once that populous and prestigious state seceded. Northern newspapers editorialized "On to Richmond!" because they believed that the capture of this city within striking distance of Washington D.C. would end the war. The only important official who believed that the war would be long and hard was General Winfield Scott, the elderly commander of the U.S. Army. Lincoln urged the federal forces gathering outside Washington to attack. A half-trained army set off for Richmond. On July 21, 1861, this force was defeated by an equally green Confederate army at the **First Battle of Bull Run**. The Union troops retreated to Washington in disorder. The victorious Confederates were too disorganized to pursue them.

The Loss of Illusions

The heavy casualties at First Bull Run shocked both sides. President Lincoln began to realize that the war would be a hard one and studied the strategy proposed by General Scott. Termed the **Anaconda Plan** by uncomprehending journalists, Scott proposed a strict blockade of the southern coastline and the seizure of the Mississippi River; the Confederacy would be economically strangled before well-trained federal armies moved in to finish it off. Lincoln ordered the Navy to close off all Southern ports. This took time, but as the war went on, the blockade grew increasingly effective. By the end of the conflict, the South was economically crippled; it could not export cotton or import manufactured goods. The U.S. Navy captured New Orleans in April 1862, a vital first step in closing off the Mississippi River to the Confederacy.

Jefferson Davis also realized that he faced a long and difficult war. In April 1862, he persuaded the Confederate Congress to institute the first national draft in American history. Davis's efforts to bring more focus and efficiency to the war effort were hampered by the states' rights principles built into the Confederacy. Southern governors resisted the president's efforts to get more control over their states' troops and resources. Davis never solved the economic challenges facing the Confederacy. Repeating the mistake made by American leaders during the Revolutionary War, he printed paper money with no gold reserves to back the currency. The result was an inflation that eventually made Confederate money worthless.

Union Victories in the West

While often frustrated militarily in the East, the Union armies made steady progress in the West. In February 1862, a promising young federal general named Ulysses S. Grant captured Fort Henry and Fort Donelson in Tennessee, taking many prisoners and driving back Confederate forces in the Mississippi Valley. On April 6, the Confederates counterattacked Grant at Shiloh. The fighting was the bloodiest yet seen in the war, but in the end the Confederates were forced to retreat. Federal forces advanced further south after Shiloh, leaving them poised to attack Vicksburg, the last important Confederate bastion in the Mississippi River.

General George McClellan was appointed commander of the Union army in November 1861, displacing General Scott. McClellan was an able strategist, but proved extremely cautious; he always believed, erroneously, that the enemy outnumbered him. His job was to take Richmond, and he tried President Lincoln's patience with many delays. He finally moved in the spring of 1862, approaching Richmond from a different direction than Bull Run. Unfortunately for his army, he moved so slowly that the Confederates, under a new commander named Robert E. Lee, drove him back in a series of hard-fought battles. Lee proved his mastery of battle tactics by whipping another federal army at the **Second Battle of Bull Run**.

In an innovative attempt to frustrate the Union blockade, the Confederates constructed an **ironclad ship**, originally named the *Merrimack.* In March 1862, after sinking some federal ships, it fought an inconclusive battle with the *Monitor*, a hastily launched federal ironclad. The Confederates could not construct enough ironclads to make a difference in the war, but the new ships pointed the way to the future of all navies.

The Home Fronts

The states' rights ethos of the South posed challenges for the men charged with running the war. Many Southerners volunteered to serve for a year in 1861. By 1862, these men were looking forward to returning home. Concern about the effects of these departures upon the muster rolls of the Confederate armies led Jefferson Davis and Robert E. Lee to support the **conscription** law. This Confederate draft required three years of military service from all white men between the ages of 18 to 35. The ages were later extended from 17 to 50. The draft proved to be very unpopular. The exemptions granted to some large slave owners to keep a watch on their slaves led to cries that the conflict was "a rich man's war and a poor man's fight." Efforts to obstruct the law by state leaders meant that in parts of the Confederacy up to 60 percent of the military aged men did not serve in the army.

Southerners began to experience serious economic hardships in late 1862. Inflation drove up prices. Food shortages became common. Desertion from the army became a problem as men headed home to provide support for their families. In another measure that defied states' rights principles, the Confederate government imposed an income tax. This effort to bring in much-needed revenue met limited success in an increasingly poverty-stricken South; by the end of the war, the government was accepting payments in grain and livestock rather than money.

Unlike the South, the North prospered economically during the war. A positive balance sheet could not alleviate all the tensions resulting from the waging of a bloody and destructive war. Northern leaders were also worried about military manpower. In 1863, Congress passed a draft law that called up men between the ages of 20 and 45. The law was intended to stimulate voluntary enlistments, often accompanied by financial bounties. Relatively few men were drafted. Despite this, the law was widely condemned. Especially reviled was a provision that allowed wealthier citizens to avoid the draft by hiring a substitute or buying themselves out by paying the government a $300 fee. In July 1863, the law led to riots in New York City. Irish immigrants and others who felt threatened by the draft went on a rampage that destroyed property and resulted in 200 deaths; many of the victims were African Americans whom the rioters unfairly blamed for the war.

Though much more financially secure than the South, the North also faced challenges in funding an expensive war. The federal government passed an income tax law in 1861. The next year, the government issued **"greenbacks,"** paper money that was not backed by gold. Because of the superior credit of the United States, this paper money was accepted by the people and worked well through the end of the war.

President Lincoln expanded the power of the presidency during the war. He issued an executive order that put portions of Kentucky under **martial law**. He took vigorous action against Northern Democrats who publicly opposed the war. These antiwar Democrats were popularly known as **Copperheads**. During the war, 14,000 Copperheads were imprisoned without facing trial. Three men were deported into the Confederacy. Several times Lincoln suspended the **writ of habeas corpus** when Copperheads were arrested.

The Emancipation Proclamation

At the outset of the war, President Lincoln's only goal was to restore the Union. He resisted abolitionist appeals, fearing that talk of freeing slaves would cost the government support in the crucial border states. As the war dragged on, Lincoln realized that slavery was helping sustain the Southern war effort. He decided to free the slaves in the territories still controlled by the Confederacy as a war measure. He realized that he had to do this after a federal victory, to avoid it seeming an act of political desperation. Lincoln received his victory on September 17, 1862, where on the bloodiest single day of the Civil War, General McClellan's army turned back an invasion of Maryland by Robert E. Lee at the Battle of Antietam.

The **Emancipation Proclamation** went into effect on January 1, 1863. It changed the nature of the war. For the North the war was now about extending freedom as well as ending a rebellion. Initially, many Northerners were dubious about this, and the Democrats did well in the 1862 elections. Over time, the logic of ending slavery proved more compelling. This new moral purpose of liberating slaves ended any possibility of the European powers intervening to save the Confederacy. The problem of slaves living in Union territory remained to be settled at the end of the war. Southerners were outraged by the Emancipation Proclamation and vowed defiance.

The Turn of the Tide

The Confederacy remained formidable in late 1862 and early 1863. Robert E. Lee won impressive victories on December 13, 1862, at the **Battle of Fredericksburg**, and on May 1 to 3, 1863, at the **Battle of Chancellorsville**. For all his battlefield successes, Lee realized that Northern superiority in men and material could not be resisted forever. He convinced President Davis that the best way to end the war would be to crush the enemy's morale by winning a great victory on Northern soil.

In June 1863, Lee led his army north. A federal army commanded by General George Meade moved to intercept him. The two armies grappled with each other in a small town in Pennsylvania at the **Battle of Gettysburg**. From July 1 to July 3, Lee unsuccessfully attacked Meade's well-sited defenses. He was forced to retreat, having lost 28,000 men, a third of his army. The federal forces lost 24,000 men, and were too bloodied to quickly follow up on their victory. Lee was still a masterful tactician and his weakened army remained dangerous, but never again would he be able to take the initiative in the fighting. The war had reached a turning point.

That the balance of the war had shifted against the Confederacy was reinforced by important events in the West. Even as combat raged at Gettysburg, General Ulysses S. Grant was completing a long-drawn-out campaign to isolate and capture Vicksburg. The **Battle of Vicksburg** culminated in the surrender of the city on July 4, 1863. This gave Union forces control of the entire span of the Mississippi River, splitting the Confederacy. In November, President Lincoln gave his **Gettysburg Address** while dedicating a national cemetery at the battle site. On November 23 to 25, General Grant won the Battle of Chattanooga in southeastern Tennessee, opening up an invasion route into Georgia. Because of his outstanding successes, Grant was put in charge of the Union army in early 1864. He brought a new sense of energy and direction to federal military strategy. He devised a coordinated assault on the Confederacy. In May 1864, Grant traveled with Meade's army as it advanced toward Richmond, while General William Tecumseh Sherman aimed another army at the vital Southern railroad hub of Atlanta, Georgia.

War Weariness

Already by early 1864 some Confederate officials were calling for peace talks. Economic conditions continued to deteriorate. The Confederate army fought on, but under enormous strain. Once Grant's forces attacked in Virginia, they never broke contact with Lee's army. Showing his customary brilliance, and well-acquainted with the terrain, Lee inflicted heavy casualties on the invaders, but suffered irreplaceable losses as well. Grant knew that he could sustain an unequal exchange of casualties; he also knew that as he tied down and wore down Lee's army, other federal forces were knifing into the overstretched Confederacy. In Georgia, Sherman slowly maneuvered toward Atlanta, held back by a determined Confederate defense.

1864 was an election year. As the death toll mounted, President Lincoln's reelection prospects dimmed. The Democrats nominated General George McClellan, proclaiming their patriotism while hoping to capitalize on antiwar sentiment. By late summer, even Lincoln thought that he would be defeated. Battlefield victories changed the momentum of the campaign. Dissatisfied with the defense of Atlanta, Jefferson Davis appointed a more aggressive commander. The Confederates attacked Sherman and were badly defeated. Their losses were so great they had to evacuate Atlanta. The fall of Atlanta was a clear indication that the Confederacy was tottering. In Virginia, Grant forced Lee into a sustained defense of the town of Petersburg outside Richmond. Both sides settled down to trench warfare. Lee's devoted army was all but trapped. With victory in sight, Lincoln won reelection.

The End of the War

Determined to wreck what was left of Southern morale, General Sherman burned the militarily useful parts of Atlanta in November 1864. Then, living off the land, he marched an army across Georgia and captured the port of Savannah on the coast. Along the way, his men left a swathe of destruction. This made it clear that the Confederate army could no longer protect civilians in the Southern heartland. Desertions from Confederate forces mounted as men went home to protect their families. In early 1865, Sherman launched an equally devastating invasion of the Carolinas. In Virginia, Lee's position at Petersburg gradually grew worse. In early April, Grant threatened to encircle his army. Lee tried to escape but was cornered by Grant at **Appomattox**. On April 9, Lee surrendered his army. By the beginning of June, all other Confederate forces had laid down their arms.

President Lincoln hoped for a peace of reconciliation. On April 14, he was assassinated while attending a performance of *Our American Cousin* at Ford's Theater. The assassin was John Wilkes Booth, a failed actor and Southern fanatic who organized a conspiracy to kill Lincoln, the vice president, and the secretary of state. Booth was the only conspirator to succeed in his mission. He escaped, but was hunted down and killed a few days later by federal troops. Most of the other conspirators were captured, and after a trial by a military tribunal, several were hanged. For the 1864 election, Lincoln had chosen Andrew Johnson, a rough-hewn Unionist Democrat, to be his running mate. Now president, Johnson would have to lead the nation as it attempted to heal the wounds of a civil war.

› Review Questions

Multiple-Choice Questions

1. The North held many advantages at the beginning of the Civil War *except*
   A. the North occupied more territory than the South.
   B. the North had more railroad lines.
   C. the North had more factories.
   D. the North had a larger population.

2. European states did not aid the Confederacy in the Civil War because
   A. there were alternative sources of cotton and other crops that they could turn to.
   B. they opposed the Confederacy's position on slavery.
   C. they did not believe that the Confederacy could win.
   D. all of the above.

3. The military draft was unpopular to many in the North because
   A. the draft allowed blacks to enter the armed forces.
   B. the draft allowed Irish-American immigrants to enter the army.
   C. the draft allowed those drafted to hire "replacements."
   D. martial law was needed in many locations to enforce the draft provisions.

4. The Battle of Vicksburg was an important victory for the Union because
   A. it reversed several Union defeats in the same year.
   B. it gave the Union a pathway to Atlanta.
   C. it gave the Union virtual control of the Mississippi River.
   D. it demonstrated that General Lee could, in fact, be beaten.

5. Copperheads were
   A. Democrats in the North who opposed the war.
   B. Republicans in the North who suggested that Lincoln be replaced.
   C. Democrats in the North who switched alliance to Lincoln.
   D. Southern Democrats who wanted negotiations with the North as early as 1863.

Short-Answer Question

6. Answer Parts A, B, and C.
   A. Briefly explain ONE example of why the Civil War went on longer than people initially expected.
   B. Briefly explain a SECOND example of why the Civil War went on longer than people initially expected.
   C. Briefly explain ONE example of an important turning point in the Civil War.

› Answers and Explanations

1. **A**. All of the others were major advantages for the Union war effort.

2. **D**. All of the reasons given helped convince the Europeans not to assist the Confederacy. The Confederacy's position on slavery proved to be especially troublesome, since slavery had long been outlawed in Europe.

3. **C**. The fact that replacement soldiers, usually immigrants, could be hired or that a payment of $300 to the government could get a man out of the draft made the system very unpopular to many.

4. **C**. The six-week Battle of Vicksburg occurred in 1863 and helped turn the war in the Union's favor. As a result of Vicksburg, the Mississippi River was virtually in the hands of the Union. Lee did not command the Confederate forces at Vicksburg.

5. **A**. Copperheads were Democrats in the North who claimed that the war would bring economic ruin to the North, with freed slaves taking jobs that whites now had. Some were arrested and deported.

6. **Parts A and B**: Although the North had significant advantages going into the war, such as a larger population, more railroads and industry, and greater financial resources, the South also possessed advantages. The South was a very large territory with 3,500 miles of coastline. To effectively occupy this territory and blockade this coastline would require large Northern army and naval forces. Technology helped prolong the war. Weapons such as the rifled musket made close encounters between troops more deadly. The rifled musket, and later repeating rifles, gave the defense an advantage over the offense. Battles became longer range firefights and less decisive. Both sides developed excellent generals whose skill helped frustrate the strategies of their opponents. Great Southern generals included Robert E. Lee and Thomas "Stonewall" Jackson. Great Northern generals included Ulysses S. Grant, William Tecumseh Sherman, and Philip Sheridan. Another factor that prolonged the war was the political determination of citizens on both sides to support their cause; the Civil War was a conflict between two popularly supported governments.

   Part C: The Battle of Antietam on September 17, 1862, was enough of a Northern victory to enable President Abraham Lincoln to issue the Emancipation Proclamation, which made freeing slaves a federal war objective. General George Meade's defeat of General Lee at Gettysburg on July 1 to 3, 1863, ended the last major Southern offensive of the war. General Grant's victory at Vicksburg on July 4, 1863, gave the North control over the Mississippi River, splitting the Confederacy. General Sherman's capture of Atlanta on September 2, 1864, led Northerners to believe that the end of the war was in sight and ensured the reelection of President Lincoln. Sherman's subsequent "March to the Sea" from November 15 to December 21 demonstrated the inability of the Confederate government to prevent federal forces from operating in the heartland of the South.

CHAPTER 16

Era of Reconstruction (1865–1877)

IN THIS CHAPTER

Summary: Postwar plans for assimilating the South back into the Union provoked strong resentment among many white Southerners. In addition, the plans of President Abraham Lincoln, the Radical Republicans in the Congress, and President Andrew Johnson all contained significant differences. Policies enacted that improved the political and economic position of former slaves were opposed by many Southern whites. The impeachment of Andrew Johnson demonstrated the disagreements over Reconstruction policy between Johnson and the Radical Republicans. Congressional passage of the Thirteenth, Fourteenth, and Fifteenth Amendments outlawed slavery, established the rights of blacks, and defined the framework by which Southern states could rejoin the Union. Passage of these amendments, profits made by carpetbaggers and scalawags, and the increased economic and political power held by some Southern blacks all caused some elements of traditional Southern society to feel long-lasting anger and resentment. The Compromise of 1877 ended Reconstruction, bringing another reordering of the political, economic, and social structures of the South.

Keywords

Reconstruction Era (1865–1877): period after the Civil War during which Northern political leaders created plans for the governance of the South and a procedure for former Southern states to rejoin the Union; Southern resentment of this era lasted well into the twentieth century.

Radical Republicans: congressional group that wished to punish the South for its secession from the Union; pushed for measures that gave economic and political rights to newly freed blacks in the South and that made it difficult for former Confederate states to rejoin the Union.

Reconstruction Act (1867): act placing Southern states under military rule and barring former supporters of the Confederacy from voting.

Carpetbaggers: northerners who moved to the South during the Reconstruction Era; traditional elements of Southern society were deeply resentful of profits made by carpetbaggers during this period.

Scalawags: term of derision used in the South during the Reconstruction Era for white Southern Republicans.

Ku Klux Klan: this group was founded in Tennessee in 1866; its oftentimes violent actions during the Reconstruction Era represented the resentments felt by many Southern whites toward the changing political, social, and economic conditions of the Reconstruction Era.

Compromise of 1877: political compromise ending the disputed presidential election of 1876. By the terms of this compromise Republican candidate Rutherford B. Hayes was awarded the electoral votes of Florida, Louisiana, and South Carolina, thus giving him the presidency; in return, all federal troops were removed from the South and Congress promised to stop enforcing much Reconstruction Era legislation concerning the South.

"Some men are born great, some achieve greatness and others lived during the Reconstruction period"

—Paul Laurence Dunbar, 1903

Lincoln and Reconstruction

The end of the Civil War raised difficult questions about what to do with the defeated South. On what terms would the seceded states be reintegrated into the Union? What would be done with Confederate military and political leaders? What should be done for the newly liberated slaves? Issues such as these tested a federal government that up to the Civil War had played a limited role in most Americans' lives.

Adding to the difficulty of rehabilitating the South was wartime devastation. Virtually the entire Southern railway net had been destroyed. Countless farms and plantations had been ruined. Several cities had been sacked and burned. Almost one-third of adult white males had been killed or wounded. Southern landowners lacked the capital to restore their property. Freed slaves and poor whites needed employment. The white workers feared economic competition from the **freedmen**, the name given to the former slaves.

The murder of Abraham Lincoln further confused the situation. Lincoln had long pondered the problem of restoring the Union. He laid the foundations of the **Reconstruction Era**. In 1863, Lincoln formulated the **Ten Percent Plan**. This plan allowed Southerners who had not held important Confederate military or political positions to swear their allegiance to the United States. Once 10 percent of registered voters in a seceded state did this, they could form a new state government loyal to the Union.

Radical Republicans in Congress opposed this plan. When Tennessee, Louisiana, and Arkansas attempted to resume their participation in the government on Lincoln's terms, the politically powerful Radical Republicans turned them down. The Radical Republicans included congressmen and senators who had been ardent abolitionists. They were determined to protect the freed slaves and push for their social and political equality. The Radical Republicans did not believe that the Southern states could truly be reintegrated into the Union until the freedmen participated politically in Reconstruction. They were well aware that the freedmen offered an enormous pool of Republican votes in the South. The Radical Republicans also hated and distrusted the old Southern political elite, and thought that the South should be punished for its rebellion. They countered Lincoln's plan with their own. The **Wade-Davis Act** passed Congress in 1864. It required a majority of voters in the Southern states to take an "ironclad" oath proclaiming their current and past loyalty to the Union. The only way that a Southern state could reenter the Union on these terms would be by enfranchising large numbers of African American voters. President Lincoln contained this congressional challenge to his policy with a **pocket veto**.

The Southern legislatures later fed the Radical Republican's suspicions of them by passing **Black Codes,** which imposed such strict regulations of the freedmen that they appeared to be a step back toward slavery. The Black Codes denied African Americans free choice in employment, restricted their movements, and outlawed interracial marriage.

Andrew Johnson and Reconstruction

Andrew Johnson attempted to continue what he believed were the policies of his predecessor. He offered lenient terms to the South. Most Southerners would receive "amnesty and pardon" for swearing an oath to defend the Union and the Constitution. The exceptions would be former Confederate leaders and people whose property was valued over $20,000. As a man who had worked his way up from poverty, Johnson was hostile to the old planter elite and blamed them for secession. All that he demanded of states to resume their place in the Union was to acknowledge the illegality of secession, repudiate Confederate debt, and recognize the abolition of slavery. A Southerner himself, he turned a blind eye to the Black Codes that had emerged by 1866.

The Southern states had reorganized themselves on these terms by the end of 1865. The prospect of Southern representatives, many of them ex-Confederates, swiftly returning to Congress dismayed many in the North. The indifference of the Southern state legislatures to the rights of the freedmen outraged the Radical Republicans.

Efforts to Help the Freedmen

The Radical Republicans rejected President Johnson's Reconstruction program. Though they had many leaders, they were united by their desire to improve conditions for the freedmen in the South. In early 1865, Congress passed a bill establishing the Freedman's Bureau. This federal agency was responsible for assisting the freed slaves, helping them get an education and find employment. The Freedman's Bureau faced a daunting task. By 1866, most freed slaves were working on the plantations of their former masters as **tenant farmers**.

Opinions varied on the best way to help the freedmen. Senator Charles Sumner of Massachusetts believed that the surest guarantee of a better status for the freedmen would be the vote and political influence. Congressman Thaddeus Stevens argued that the freedmen needed economic independence, and advocated confiscating land from wealthy Confederates and distributing it to their former slaves. In late 1865, Congress created a Joint

Committee on Reconstruction to investigate conditions in the South and make recommendations on the reintegration of the Southern states.

The Joint Committee persuaded Congress to renew the authorization of the Freedman's Bureau. It also proposed a Civil Rights bill. Unhappy with Congressional interference with his Reconstruction policies, Johnson vetoed both these bills, declaring them unconstitutional. Johnson's sympathy for former Confederates and growing political combativeness began to alienate moderates in Congress and across the North. He did not help himself by giving a Washington's Birthday speech in which he denounced the Radical Republicans as traitors and charged that they wanted to murder him.

Moderate Republicans joined with their radical colleagues to override Johnson's vetoes. The life of the Freedman's Bureau was extended, and the **Civil Rights Act of 1866** granted the rights of citizenship to the freedmen. The freedmen could look to the federal courts and the U.S. military to enforce these rights. This act also provided support for the **Thirteenth Amendment**. Ratified in December 1865, this amendment to the Constitution outlawed slavery and involuntary servitude. The Thirteenth Amendment confirmed the effects of Lincoln's Emancipation Proclamation and freed all the slaves living in what had been Union territory.

Congress also passed the **Fourteenth Amendment**. This amendment defined national citizenship and gave the federal government the responsibility to protect equal rights for all Americans. It also contained measures aimed at the Southern states. Former Confederate leaders could not hold federal office, and states that denied freedmen the vote would have their congressional representation reduced. Anti-black riots in New Orleans and Memphis helped the amendment pass Congress. President Johnson spoke out against the Fourteenth Amendment. He was rebuked by Northern voters in the 1866 congressional elections, which returned a Radical Republican majority.

Radical Reconstruction

The Radical Republicans now had the political power to assert their Reconstruction agenda. They could override any presidential veto. In 1867, Congress passed a **Reconstruction Act** that put the former Confederacy under military rule. The South was divided into five regions, and army generals were placed in command of each. The Southern states had to hold new constitutional conventions. They were required to provide freedmen equal rights and the vote. Former Confederates lost their franchise. To be officially recognized, the Southern states had to ratify the Fourteenth Amendment. Congress also enacted two laws designed to weaken the recalcitrant President Johnson. The Army Act limited his ability to interfere with the army in the South. The **Tenure of Office Act** removed the power of the president to dismiss a cabinet secretary without the concurrence of the Senate. This measure was designed to protect the position of Secretary of War Edwin Stanton, an ally of the Radical Republicans.

The Impeachment of Andrew Johnson

President Johnson believed that the Tenure of Office Act was an unlawful infringement of his powers. In the fall of 1867, he attempted to fire Secretary Stanton. This precipitated a constitutional crisis. The Radical Republicans, anxious to be rid of Johnson, declared that he had violated the Constitution and launched an **impeachment** process. The House of

Representatives voted articles of impeachment on February 24, 1868. No president had been impeached before. In May, Johnson was tried in the Senate. A vote of two-thirds of the Senate was necessary to convict him and remove him from office. He escaped conviction and removal by a one vote margin.

Though Johnson remained as president, he had become politically irrelevant. (He would briefly return to Washington as a senator from Tennessee before his death in 1875.) In the presidential election of 1868, the Republicans nominated General Ulysses S. Grant, the preeminent Union hero of the Civil War, who swept to an easy victory.

Final Phase of Radical Reconstruction

President Grant supported the goals of Radical Reconstruction. He advocated for the passage of the **Fifteenth Amendment**, which was ratified in March 1870. The Fifteenth Amendment protected African American voting rights, stating that no American could be prevented from voting "on account of race, color, or previous condition of servitude." In the elections of 1870, many freedmen voted for the first time. They helped elect 630 African Americans to Southern state legislatures. Sixteen African Americans were elected to the House of Representatives, and one was elected to the Senate. P.B.S. Pinchback was elected governor of Louisiana.

Grant had to deploy federal troops to protect African American voters in this election. White Southerners profoundly resented a political milestone that challenged their deeply held beliefs. They regarded the Reconstruction authorities as an oppressive and illegitimate occupation. Many did not bother to vote because of their anger over the process. They called Northerners who had moved south to assist with Reconstruction **carpetbaggers**. They dismissed Southerners who cooperated with the Republicans as **scalawags**.

Some Southerners resisted Reconstruction through violence. The **Ku Klux Klan** was founded in Tennessee in 1866. The Klan terrorized freedmen and their white allies, intimidating voters and burning schools. Their vigilante actions included torture and murder. Congress passed "Force" acts to make the interference with voting a crime. President Grant sent soldiers and federal marshals to pursue the Klan, and in parts of the South a low-intensity guerilla war festered for years.

The End of Reconstruction

Grant was reelected in 1872. He continued to support the rights of the freedmen and signed the Civil Rights Act of 1875 that called for equal treatment for African Americans in public accommodations, public transportation, and on juries. Despite this Northern enthusiasm for Reconstruction waned in the face of obdurate Southern opposition. A major recession in 1873 focused most peoples' attention on economic concerns. Scandals in the Grant Administration further diverted attention away from the South. Federal troops were gradually withdrawn from the South, allowing Southern whites to begin recapturing control of state governments.

In the presidential election of 1876, the Democrats nominated Samuel Tilden, the governor of New York. Tilden had become famous for his opposition to the Tammany Hall political machine in New York City and its corrupt boss William M. Tweed. The Republican candidate was Rutherford B. Hayes, the governor of Ohio. Hayes had served as a Union general during the Civil War. The election was close. Tilden won the popular vote, and once voting concluded, he seemed just one vote short of an Electoral College majority. The electoral votes of Florida, Louisiana, and South Carolina remained in dispute. These Southern states were still controlled by Republican reconstruction administrations. If Hayes received these electoral votes, he would win the election by one vote. To resolve this situation, Congress created a special commission with an equal number of Democrats and Republicans, and one independent. When the independent resigned to run for office, he was replaced by a Republican. The commission duly awarded all the contested electoral votes to Hayes, making him the prospective president. Democrats in and out of Congress protested loudly. To ease the contention and smooth Hayes' path to power, Democratic and Republican leaders worked out the **Compromise of 1877**. The Democrats did not attempt to block Hayes from becoming president. In return, the Republicans pulled the last federal troops out of the South and withdrew support for the remaining Republican state governments. Democratic "redeemer" regimes took over across the South. African Americans were quickly deprived of hard-won social and political rights. Southerners would write an early and highly critical history of Reconstruction that portrayed it as a colossal and misguided failure. The "Solid South" would remain Democratic and starkly racially segregated for almost a century.

Chapter Review

Rapid Review

To achieve the perfect 5, you should be able to explain the following:

- Any plan to assimilate the Southern states back into the Union after the Civil War would have major difficulties; a problem was determining the appropriate postwar status of former supporters of the Confederacy.
- The plans for Reconstruction proposed by Abraham Lincoln, the Radical Republicans, and Andrew Johnson all varied dramatically.
- Radical Republicans instituted policies to improve the political and economic status of former slaves; this created great resentment in other segments of Southern society.
- The impeachment of Andrew Johnson went forward because of major disagreements over policy between Johnson and the Radical Republicans in Congress.
- The Thirteenth, Fourteenth, and Fifteenth Amendments outlawed slavery, established the rights of blacks, and established the framework by which Southern states could rejoin the union.
- Profits made by carpetbaggers and scalawags further angered the traditional elements of Southern society. Many in the South, including members of the Ku Klux Klan, felt great resentment toward the carpetbaggers and scalawags and toward the political and economic power now held by some Southern blacks.
- The Compromise of 1877 ended Reconstruction in the South; as Union troops left, blacks were again reduced to the status of second-class citizens.

Time Line

1865: Andrew Johnson institutes liberal Reconstruction plan

Whites in Southern legislatures pass Black Codes

Thirteenth Amendment ratified

1866: Civil Rights Act, Freedmen's Bureau Act approved by Congress (vetoed by Johnson)

Fourteenth Amendment passes Congress (fails to be ratified in Southern states)

Antiblack riots in New Orleans, Memphis

Republicans who favor Radical Reconstruction win congressional elections, in essence ending Johnson's Reconstruction plan

Ku Klux Klan founded

1867: Tenure of Office Act approved by Congress (Congress had to approve presidential appointments, dismissals)

Reconstruction Act approved by Congress (Southern states placed under military rule)

Constitutional conventions called by former Confederate states

Johnson tries to remove Edwin Stanton as secretary of war, leading to cries for his impeachment

1868: Impeachment of Andrew Johnson: Johnson impeached in the House of Representatives, not convicted in the Senate

Southern states return to Union under policies established by Radical Republicans

Final ratification of Fourteenth Amendment

Former Civil War General Ulysses S. Grant elected president

1870: Amendment ratified

Many blacks elected in Southern state legislatures

1872: Confederates allowed to hold office

Ulysses S. Grant reelected

1876: Disputed presidential election between Tilden, Hayes

1877: Compromise of 1877 awards election to Hayes, ends Reconstruction in the South

› Review Questions

Multiple-Choice Questions

1. Radical Republicans favored all of the following *except*
   A. the governing of the South by military generals.
   B. the impeachment of Andrew Johnson.
   C. the return of former Confederate leaders to positions of power in the South.
   D. the election of newly enfranchised blacks to positions in Southern state legislatures.

2. The official reason for impeachment proceedings against Andrew Johnson was
   A. he had violated the Tenure of Office Act.
   B. he had violated the Reconstruction Act.
   C. his Reconstruction policies were much too lenient to the South.
   D. he had failed to enforce the Civil Rights Act of 1866.

3. Black Codes were instituted to
   A. increase black participation in Southern politics during Reconstruction.
   B. increase the effectiveness of the Freedmen's Bureau.
   C. prevent blacks from having certain jobs.
   D. maintain slavery in some sections of the Deep South.

4. Reconstruction ended as a result of the Compromise of 1877 because
   A. a presidential mandate ordered that Reconstruction end.
   B. by the provisions of the compromise, the U.S. Army was removed from Southern states.
   C. the new president, Rutherford B. Hayes, was strongly against the existing Reconstruction policy.
   D. many blacks were now in positions of power in the South, and Reconstruction policies were no longer needed.

5. The Fifteenth Amendment
   A. allowed Southern states to reenter the Union.
   B. outlawed slavery.
   C. stated that a person could not be denied the vote because of his color.
   D. said that former Confederate officials could not hold public office.

Short-Answer Question

6. Answer Parts A, B, and C.
   A. Briefly explain ONE example of a way that the federal government attempted to assist African Americans in the South during Reconstruction.
   B. Briefly explain a SECOND example of a way that the federal government attempted to assist African Americans during Reconstruction.
   C. Briefly explain ONE example of a way white Southerners resisted the federal government's attempts to assist African Americans during Reconstruction.

› Answers and Explanations

1. **C.** All of the other choices were favored by Radical Republicans. The Reconstruction Act of 1867 placed the former Confederate states under military rule.

2. **A.** By attempting to remove Edwin Stanton as secretary of war, many in Congress stated that Johnson had knowingly violated the Tenure of Office Act, thus violating provisions of the U.S. Constitution.

3. **C.** Black Codes were adopted by Southern legislatures in 1866 and limited movement by blacks, prevented them from having certain jobs, and prohibited interracial marriage.

4. **B.** After Hayes was given the presidency by the Compromise of 1877, the U.S. Army left control of the South to the South. Without the army present to enforce Reconstruction policies, these policies ended. Blacks were soon second-class citizens again.

5. **C.** The Fifteenth Amendment stated that no American could be denied the right to vote "on account of race, color, or previous condition of servitude."

6. **Parts A and B**: Congress passed and the states ratified the Thirteenth Amendment in 1865, which ended slavery. In 1865, Congress also created the Freedmen's Bureau, which was charged with helping the freed slaves get employment and an education. The Fourteenth Amendment, ratified in 1868, guaranteed the citizenship rights of African Americans. The Radical Republicans in Congress passed the 1867 Reconstruction Act, putting the Southern states under military rule until they revised their state constitutions and recognized the Fourteenth Amendment. In 1870, the Fifteenth Amendment was ratified giving African American men the right to vote.

Part C: Many white Southerners resisted Reconstruction policies designed to help the freedmen. Shortly after the end of the Civil War, Southern legislatures passed Black Codes, which severely restricted the ability of African Americans to move about and freely contract for their labor. Interracial marriages were prohibited. In addition, Southerners elected many former Confederate officials and military leaders to high office, helping inspire Radical Reconstruction. Beginning in 1866, some Southerners joined the Ku Klux Klan and other secret organizations to terrorize African Americans and keep them from voting and asserting their rights. Once Reconstruction ended in 1877, Southerners gradually stripped African Americans of most of the rights that they had won after the Civil War.

CHAPTER 17

Western Expansion and Its Impact on the American Character (1860–1895)

IN THIS CHAPTER

Summary: Settlers were encouraged to move westward after the Civil War by federal legislation such as the Homestead Act, which gave 160 acres of land to American citizens who were committed to settling on the land and who could pay the $10 registration fee. However, farming on the plains proved much more difficult than many settlers thought it would be. Thousands of blacks moved west after the Civil War to escape life in the South; mining, ranching, and lumbering also attracted settlers to the West. This westward expansion greatly affected the lives of Native Americans, who were removed to Oklahoma and South Dakota. Farmers in the West began to organize; Farmers' Alliances and the Grange were established to protect farmers' rights. The 1893 Turner Thesis (a well-known theory promulgated by a distinguished historian) proposed the idea that settlers had to become more adaptable and innovative as they moved westward and that these characteristics would slowly become ingrained into the very fabric of American society.

Keywords

Homestead Act (1862): bill that did much to encourage settlers to move west; 160 acres of land were given to any settler who was an American citizen or who had applied for citizenship, who was committed to farming the land for six months of the year, and who could pay the $10 registration fee for the land.

Massacre at Wounded Knee (1890): battle that was the last large-scale attempt by Native Americans to resist American settlement in the Great Plains region. Federal soldiers opened fire on Native Americans, killing more than 200.

Dawes Act (1887): act designed to break up Native American tribes by offering individual Native Americans land to be used for either farming or grazing.

Farmers' Alliances: organization that united farmers at the statewide and regional levels; policy goals of this organization included more readily available farm credits and federal regulation of the railroads.

Populist party: formed in 1892 by members of the Farmers' Alliances, this party was designed to appeal to workers in all parts of the country. Populists favored a larger role of government in American society, a progressive income tax, and more direct methods of democracy.

Turner Thesis (1893): thesis by the historian Frederick Jackson Turner suggesting that the innovations practiced by western settlers gradually became ingrained into the fabric of American society; democracy and self-improvement were also central to western expansion, Turner claimed. In short, Turner suggested that many of the characteristics of the "American character" were created by westward expansion. Later historians questioned parts of this thesis.

Government Encouragement of Western Settlement

Americans were moving into the lands west of the Mississippi River well before the Civil War. Beginning in 1862, actions taken by the federal government spurred a surge of settlement that rapidly transformed the West.

The **Homestead Act** encouraged farmers to move west. This legislation provided a settler 160 acres of land; to be eligible for this land, the settler had to be an American citizen, or, if an immigrant, to have applied for American citizenship; the settler had to be the head of a family and at least 21 years old; the settler had to commit to improving the property, building a house or other structures there, and residing on the property for at least six months during the year; and the settler needed to be able to pay a $10 registration fee for the land. The farmer would receive the title to the 160 acres after working it for five years. Homesteaders flooded into the western lands. By 1900, 610,000 plots of land had been distributed to settlers; this resulted in the transfer of 85 million acres of public land into private hands. Also passed in 1862 was the **Morrill Land Grant Act**. This bill was intended to stimulate higher education in the states. The federal government gave hundreds of thousands of acres of public land to state governments; this land was sold to support the establishment of "land grant" colleges. This land was often sold to settlers and **land speculators** for 50 cents an acre or less.

The federal government strongly supported the expansion of railroads into the western territories. Congress passed bills in 1862 and 1864 to assist the Union Pacific and Central Pacific railways in constructing a transcontinental railroad. These companies received 10 square miles of land on either side of every mile of track that they laid down. The railroads often sold some of this land to settlers.

Challenges for Western Farmers

The yeoman farmer had long been celebrated by Thomas Jefferson and others as the backbone of the American nation. The farmer was seen as the paradigmatic citizen, self-sufficient and independent. This idealized vision of the farmer would be severely tested on the Great Plains.

Conditions on the western plains were harsh. Winters were bitterly cold, and in the summers temperatures frequently rose above 100 degrees. Because of the lack of trees and wood, many settlers had to build their homes out of sod. These sod houses were less comfortable than more traditionally constructed homes, both in the winter and summer. Water was often in short supply, and tainted sources of water spread diseases such as typhoid. The pleasantly bucolic image of western farming purveyed by Currier and Ives prints and other popular media sources in the East was very different from the experience of settlers battling hordes of locusts, dust storms, and deadly blizzards. Most homesteaders failed. By 1900, two-thirds had given up on their farms. Many former homesteaders headed to a new life in the cities or returned East.

The only way to survive the conditions farmers faced on the arid Great Plains was to cooperate with neighbors. Barn-raising and fencing were collective enterprises. Farm women helped each other with chores and children. Rugged individualism was not a recipe for success on this new agricultural frontier.

Agricultural Innovation

The farmers who thrived on the Great Plains relied on new technologies and business methods. The U.S. Department of Agriculture was established in 1862, and it distributed information on new agricultural developments to farmers. The 1860s and 1870s saw the introduction of new and better plows and threshers, some of them steam-powered.

In many places on the Great Plains, small family farms were displaced by much more extensive **bonanza farms**. These larger agricultural concerns grew only one or two cash crops. Genuine agribusinesses, bonanza farms benefited from economies of scale, and sold produce in bulk to Eastern or foreign markets. The owners of bonanza farms could afford the latest and best technologies to help maximize their yields.

The growing prevalence of bonanza farms by the 1870s reflected larger changes in the American economy. They were the agricultural equivalent of the big businesses that were beginning to dominate American industry. Bonanza farms operated more efficiently than smaller farms and helped account for a significant rise in agricultural production. Because of these larger farms, the number of farmers fell even as agricultural output rose. Between 1860 and 1900, the percentage of Americans working on farms fell from 60 percent to 37 percent.

The productivity of American agriculture led to problems for farmers, both big and small. An oversupply of grain at different points in the 1880s and 1890s led to sharp drops in price. Most farmers responded to this decrease in their income by increasing their crop production, which just exacerbated the problem. Many farmers fell into debt. Those who could not pay their mortgages had their farms foreclosed by banks. Distressed farmers looked for explanations of their difficulties and began to organize politically.

Women and Minorities on the Agricultural Frontier

Most farms on the Great Plains were worked by families. While the men labored in the fields, diaries and letters left by western women show that they were often beset by loneliness in a world where neighbors might be miles away. O. E. Rolvaag's novel *Giants of the Earth* (1927) describes how the bitter struggle for existence on the prairie drives the wife of an immigrant settler to insanity and death. Willa Cather's *O Pioneers!* (1913) provides a more positive picture of farming life in Nebraska. Though the immigrant protagonists of the novel suffer many hardships as they build up their farms, they eventually prosper and partake of the American dream. A female character holds the family together and guides them to their material success.

Perhaps because of the important role played by women on the farm, it was in the West that they first began to receive the right to vote. In 1887, two towns in Kansas allowed women to vote in local elections, and one elected a woman mayor. Wyoming led the way in giving women the right to vote in statewide elections.

Following the Civil War, many African Americans moved west to escape the oppressive life that they faced in the South. Few of these African American emigrants were able to start profitable farms; they often lacked financial reserves and still encountered racial discrimination. Some African Americans did become successful western farmers. The most famous group of African Americans to leave the South for the West were the **Exodusters**. These people modeled their journey on the exodus of the Israelites from Egypt to the Promised Land. Unfortunately the West did not prove to be a land of milk and honey for most of the Exodusters; fewer than 20 percent were able to establish themselves as farmers.

The Mining and Lumbering Frontier

Farmers were not the only people traveling west. People hoping to strike it rich flocked to the many places where gold and silver were reputed to have been discovered. Miners sought gold at Pike's Peak, Nevada, or the Black Hills of the Dakota Territory, and silver at Comstock, Nevada. A heterogeneous group of people, including Chinese laborers who had abandoned their jobs working on the railroads, crowded into mining towns that boomed for a time and often went bust. These towns had a deserved reputation for extravagance and lawlessness. Most prospectors never found anything of value. Those who did rarely had the means to fully exploit and profit from what they found. Eventually mining came to be dominated by large Eastern-based mining corporations like the **Anaconda Copper Company**. Like Anaconda, these firms discovered that they could profit just as much by mining copper and tin for industrial purposes as digging up precious metals.

Lumber companies moved into the Northwest in the 1870s. These companies reaped great rewards from the 1878 **Timber and Stone Act**, which allowed them to purchase government land that was unsuitable for farming at bargain rates. Lumber companies also hired front men to buy up woodlands inexpensively and then transfer the land titles to them. Fortunes were made providing lumber to a nation that was building at a frantic pace.

The Ranching Frontier

Western settlers inherited a cattle-ranching culture from the Mexicans. Following the Civil War, Texas ranchers had plenty of cattle, but no easy way of getting them to Eastern markets. In 1866, some Texas ranchers drove their herds of cattle overland to the nearest railroad in Kansas. This began the era of the "long drive" celebrated in countless westerns, as bands of cowboys, up to a third of whom may have been Mexican or African American, braved bandits, hostile Indians, stampedes, and bad weather, and moved vast numbers of cattle across the plains to an ever-growing number of rail depots. The cattle were then shipped by rail to Chicago or other cities where they were slaughtered and processed. The beef could then be sent on for marketing in cities further east because of newly invented refrigerated rail cars.

Cattlemen grazed their animals on the "open range," unsettled public lands. As homesteaders moved into these lands, conflicts arose between farmers and ranchers. Farmers were planting crops on land where ranchers wanted to drive their cattle. Joseph Glidden's invention of barbed wire in 1873 enabled farmers to protect their land. The weather dealt another blow to traditional "open range" ranching. The exceptionally severe winters of 1885 to 1887 killed up to 85 percent of the cattle grazing on the plains. The ranchers who survived this disaster turned to new methods, enclosing their land and utilizing scientific techniques of improving their stock.

The End of Native American Independence

The Native American tribes that lived west of the Mississippi River were overwhelmed in a very short period of time. Within two decades of the end of the Civil War the Plains tribes had lost their independence.

The completion of the transcontinental railroad in 1869 helped facilitate a massive wave of western settlement. Native American tribes could not pursue their traditional way of life as farmers, miners, and ranchers encroached on their lands. Whether tribes cooperated with the settlers or attacked them, the results were the same; they lost most of their lands and were relegated to reservations and government supervision. The federal government did not aim for the extermination of the Plains tribes, but it did not intend to allow them to stand in the way of settlement and economic development. The government hoped that a combination of missionaries and schools would "civilize" the Native Americans and integrate them into American society.

The tribe that most famously fought back against the tide of settlers was the **Sioux**. In 1865, the government declared that it was going to build a road through Sioux lands. This started a war that the Sioux waged very effectively. In one engagement in 1866, they killed 88 soldiers who fell into an ambush. The government began negotiations. In 1868, the Sioux accepted a reservation in the Black Hills of South Dakota. Unfortunately for them, gold was discovered in the Black Hills and miners poured into their lands. This led to a resumption of war. Chiefs including Sitting Bull and Crazy Horse led the Sioux off the reservation. The government dispatched columns of federal troops to round up the Sioux and their Cheyenne allies. One of these columns, a force of the Seventh Cavalry led by General George Custer, found the main Sioux encampment in June 1876. Not realizing how many Sioux warriors had gathered there, Custer attacked without waiting for reinforcements. He and more than 200 of his men were killed at the **Battle of the Little Bighorn**. This unusually decisive victory did not change the outcome of the war. More soldiers arrived, forcing the Sioux back onto their reservation. Other tribes such as the **Nez Perce** attempted to escape their reservations, but invariably were defeated and compelled to return.

Even had the Native Americans won more battlefield victories, they would have been forced to rely on government support because of the disappearance of the buffalo. The Plains tribes depended on the buffalo for food and much else; their lives were organized around the pursuit of buffalo herds. With government approval and support, settlers hunted the buffalo to near extinction. In doing so, they destroyed the foundation of Native American life on the Great Plains.

By the late 1880s, most Native Americans in the West lived on reservations, subsisting on rations provided by the government. Eastern humanitarians, hoping to improve the lot of these people and help them become self-sufficient, provided the impetus behind the passage of the 1887 **Dawes Act**. This legislation assumed that Native Americans would be better off if they emulated their white neighbors and became farmers. The Dawes Act broke up the reservations and divided the land among the individual members of the tribes. Ironically, this well-intentioned bill hurt the Native Americans. Few Native Americans became thriving farmers. Many sold their farms to settlers or land speculators. Much Native American land was permanently lost as a result.

The despair of the Plains Indians was reflected in a religious movement that emerged in 1890. Participants believed that **Ghost Dances** would lead to the disappearance of white settlers, the return of the buffalo, and the resurrection of dead warriors. The military authorities grew alarmed when Sitting Bull sponsored the Ghost Dance religion among the Sioux. Sitting Bull was killed when Indian Police attempted to arrest him. A band of Ghost Dancers fled the reservation. They were surrounded by troops of the Seventh Cavalry. As soldiers disarmed the Sioux camp, someone fired a shot. The troops unleashed a barrage of fire that killed over 200 men, women, and children in what came to be known as the **Massacre at Wounded Knee**.

On April 22, 1889, the "Indian territory" of Oklahoma was opened to settlement. A great land rush took place as "boomers" raced to place their stakes on unclaimed land. People who had entered Oklahoma a day early to grab land were called "sooners." The opening of Oklahoma was the last act in a process that saw settlers displace the Native Americans on the Great Plains.

Agrarian Anger and Populism

By the 1880s many Western farmers faced severe economic problems. Many Southern farmers were in a similar situation. These farmers blamed government policies for their troubles. Since the Civil War, the federal government had imposed high tariffs on imported goods to protect American industries. The farmers believed that these high tariffs hurt their ability to export their products abroad. Farmers were also angered by government fiscal policy and the state of the currency.

The Gold Standard

After the Civil War, the federal government took the wartime "greenbacks" out of circulation and pursued a **"tight money"** policy. The men driving government economic policy believed in a solid and stable currency, which they believed was best for business. They put the United States on the **gold standard**, where every dollar in circulation could in theory be exchanged for an equivalent value in gold held in reserve by the government. This restricted the amount of money available in the country and prevented inflation. In fact, as the country grew, the currency saw some deflation, as its limited supply made it more relatively valuable. Distressed farmers saw their debts grow more expensive because of deflation at the same time that the prices for their crops declined. They called for various measures to increase the money supply and drive up the price of their produce. Fiscally conservative presidents did little to expand the amount of currency.

The Grange and Farmers' Alliances

Western farmers founded the **Grange** in 1867. By 1875, over 800,000 farmers had joined the organization. Grangers formed farmer cooperatives to enable members to enjoy economies of scale by buying and marketing products. Members of the Grange also organized politically and sponsored state legislation to regulate railroads and grain elevators. In 1878, many of these farmers supported the **Greenback party**, which called for the printing of paper money to inflate the currency. The Greenback party elected some congressmen and local officials, but was unable to change American fiscal policy.

The Grange usually organized farmers on the local level. The **Farmers' Alliances** linked farmer associations on a statewide and regional level. In 1889, the Southern Alliance represented a million members. An African American association, the Colored Farmers National Alliance also had a million members. Two million farmers joined Farmers' Alliances in the Plains states. The Farmers' Alliances demanded federal regulation of the railroads, currency reform, easily accessible farm credits, and agriculture departments in every state. Another proposal called for federal warehouses where farmers could store grain for credit when prices were too low. In 1890, this program was summarized in the **Ocala Platform**, which was issued at an Alliance Convention held in Ocala, Florida.

By 1890, leaders of the Farmers' Alliances were exploring ways to exert their political power on the national level. In the South, the Alliance had helped elect four governors and forty-seven congressmen. In the West the Farmers' Alliances were flexing their political muscles as well. Women played an important role in the Farmers' Alliances. Mary Lease became a popular speaker, telling farmers to "raise less corn and more hell."

The federal government did respond to the unrest amongst farmers. The **Interstate Commerce Act** of 1887 created the Interstate Commerce Commission to regulate railroads, though initially, this did not prove effective. The **Sherman Antitrust Act** of 1890 outlawed any business that exercised a "restraint of trade." As with the Interstate Commerce Act, it would take some time for this legislation to produce results.

The Populist Revolt

On July 4, 1892, a convention of Farmers' Alliances launched the People's party. Supports of the party became known as Populists. Its founders hoped that the **Populist party** would unite all working people across the country. Breaking from a century of tradition, Populists argued that because of the powerful forces transforming the economy, the federal government had to play a more active role in American life. The Populist platform called for increasing the amount of currency, a progressive income tax aimed at the wealthy, the direct election of senators, government ownership of railroads, as well as the telegraph and telephone systems, the eight-hour day for workers, and restrictions on immigration. James Weaver, who had served as a Union general during the Civil War and long been involved in the currency issue, was nominated for president.

The Populists received a million popular and 22 electoral votes in the 1892 election. Most of these came from the West. The Populists could not make headway in the Northeast, and the Democrats still dominated the South.

Populism and the Election of 1896

The Populists remained a political force after 1892. They opposed President Grover Cleveland because he was a strong defender of the gold standard. The great depression that began in 1893 spread deep hardship across the country. The Populists responded by continuing their criticism of government fiscal policy and the influence of Eastern business interests.

In 1896, the Republicans nominated William McKinley, who aligned himself with the industrial economy, calling for the gold standard, a high tariff, and a "full dinner pail" for industrial workers. The Democratic candidate was William Jennings Bryan, who won the nomination after giving an eloquent speech at the convention when he declared, "You shall not crucify mankind upon a cross of gold!" Bryan's fervent support for coining more silver to expand the currency won him the Populist nomination as well. In a bellwether election, Bryan won the South and West but lost to McKinley, who carried the Northeast and Midwest. The new urban and industrial order had triumphed over the agrarian vision of Bryan and the Populists.

Prosperity returned in the late 1890s. The economic problems of the farmers eased. It became clear that American society was changing as the great cities grew in population. The Populist party faded away, but most planks of their 1892 platform were eventually enacted into law.

The Idea of the West

The settlement of the trans-Mississippi West coincided with the growth of the modern mass media. Inexpensive and popular dime novels made millions familiar with western figures such as trappers, miners, and cowboys. One of the most prolific dime novel authors was Edward L. Wheeler. In works such as *Deadwood Dick: The Prince of the Road*, Wheeler romanticized a Wild West of gamblers and gunmen. Traveling Wild West shows started touring the country in 1883. Buffalo Bill Cody, a former buffalo hunter and Army scout, became world famous as the impresario of a show that featured cowboys doing rodeo tricks, staged battles between Indians and cavalry, and trick shooting by stars like Annie Oakley. Cody even persuaded Sitting Bull to tour with his show for a season. The West that Cody and others dramatized would be immortalized in the movies and on TV.

Another influential interpretation of the West would be provided by the historian Frederick Jackson Turner. In an 1893 paper he asserted that the American national character was shaped by the move west. He argued that American democracy and self-reliance were products of the frontier experience. The **Turner Thesis** proved to be enormously influential. It also raised serious questions for Turner's contemporaries. The 1890 census had recently declared the frontier closed. How, wondered some, could Americans maintain their democratic traditions in an increasingly urban and industrial nation?

Neither Cody nor Turner fully captured the full range of the Western experience. They both left out important perspectives and voices as they strove to explain the West. Yet they were correct in highlighting the historical importance of what was passing away.

Chapter Review

Rapid Review

To achieve the perfect 5, you should be able to explain the following:

- The Homestead Act and the Morrill Land-Grant Act encouraged thousands to go westward to acquire land for farming.
- Farming on the Great Plains proved to be very difficult and was oftentimes accomplished by help from one's neighbor; many farmers were not successful on the Great Plains.
- Bonanza farms were part of a transformation of agriculture that began in the late 1860s.
- Western states were the first states where women received the vote.
- Mining and lumbering also attracted many settlers to the West.
- Native American tribes were gradually forced off their lands because of American expansion to the West; some resistance to this by Native Americans did take place, such as at the Battle of the Little Bighorn and through the Ghost Dances.
- The 1887 Dawes Act did much to break up the remaining Native American tribal lands.
- American farmers organized beginning in the late 1860s through the Grange, through the Farmers' Alliances, and eventually through the Populist party.
- Dime-store novels of the era and the Turner Thesis presented contrasting views of western settlement and its overall impact on American society.

Time Line

1848: California Gold Rush
1859: Silver discovered in Comstock, Nevada
1862: Homestead Act, Morrill Land-Grant Act
　　　　Department of Agriculture created by Congress
1867: Founding of the Grange
1869: Transcontinental Railroad completed
1870s: Popularity of *Deadwood Dick* stories by Edward L. Wheeler and other dime-store novels on the West
1874: Barbed wire invented by Joseph Glidden
1876: Battle of the Little Bighorn
1879: Exoduster movement leaves the South for the Great Plains
1880s: Large movement of immigrants westward
1883: "Buffalo Bill's Wild West Show" begins
1886: Beginnings of harsh weather that would help destroy the cattle industry
1887: Dawes Act
1889: Indian territories open for white settlement
1890: Massacre at Wounded Knee
　　　　Wyoming women get the vote
　　　　High point of political influence of the Farmers' Alliances
1893: Beginning of great depression of the 1890s
　　　　Publication of the Turner Thesis
1896: William Jennings Bryan's "Cross of Gold" speech

› Review Questions

Multiple-Choice Questions

1. Those farmers who were successful on the Great Plains
   A. came to the West as single men, without families.
   B. utilized many farming techniques they had learned in the East.
   C. personified the spirit of rugged individualism.
   D. relied on the assistance of other settlers around them.

2. Exodusters were
   A. newly arrived miners in Oregon.
   B. Southern blacks who went west to settle.
   C. those who "dusted" or cleaned crops on bonanza farms.
   D. immigrants who went west to farm.

3. The Dawes Act
   A. tried to turn Native Americans into farmers who would farm their own individual plots only.
   B. protected Native American land from further encroachment.
   C. broke up large Native American reservations into smaller ones.
   D. made Ghost Dances illegal.

4. The organization that expressed the views of farmers to the largest national audience was the
   A. Greenback party.
   B. Populist party.
   C. Grange.
   D. Farmers' Alliances.

5. The Turner Thesis
   A. agreed with accounts of the West in the dime-store novels of the 1870s concerning the character of western expansion.
   B. took into account the massacre of Native Americans.
   C. noted the impact of western expansion on the American character.
   D. emphasized the "hard living" that went on in many western settlements.

Short-Answer Question

6. Answer Parts A, B, and C.
   A. Briefly explain ONE example of a way that American settlement rapidly transformed the West in the 25 years following the Civil War.
   B. Briefly explain a SECOND example of a way that American settlement rapidly transformed the West in the 25 years following the Civil War.
   C. Briefly explain ONE example of a way that Native Americans attempted to resist American settlement in the West in the 25 years following the Civil War.

› Answers and Explanations

1. **D**. Almost every diary from individuals who lived on the plains noted that rugged individualism was not enough to be successful.

2. **B**. This group went west to farm in 1879 and modeled their journey after the journey of the Israelites fleeing Egypt to the Promised Land.

3. **A**. The Dawes Act tried to "civilize" Native Americans and destroy their tribal lands.

4. **B**. The Populist party platform was intended to appeal to all workers in society, including those in the city. The policies of the Populist party were heard nationwide in the 1892 presidential election; however, because of the power of the Democratic party in the South, the Populist presidential candidate received only 1 million votes in the election.

5. **C**. Turner himself would later revise his thesis based on some of the characteristics of western expansion noted in the other possible answers.

6. **Parts A and B**: The federal government provided support for western settlement by encouraging the building of a transcontinental railroad. The Union Pacific and Central Pacific Railroads finally met at Promontory Summit, Utah, on May 10, 1869. The rapid expansion of railroads in the west facilitated settlement. The federal government encouraged farmers to move west with the 1862 Homestead Act, which gave 160 acres to farm families that worked this land for five years. In addition to many family farms, large bonanza farms expanded through the west. Bonanza farms were an early form of agribusiness and grew only a few staple crops for the market. The lumber industry benefitted from the 1878 Timber and Stone Act, which offered land unsuitable for agriculture in the Northwest to "settlers." Miners followed strikes of gold at places like Pike's Peak Nevada and the Black Hills in the Dakota Territory, and silver at Comstock, Nevada. Individual prospectors were replaced by large corporations. The Anaconda Copper Company became powerful mining minerals other than gold and silver. In the postwar years ranching became a big business in the west, raising cattle to feed people in the Eastern cities. Beginning with a cattle drive from Texas to Sedalia, Kansas, in 1866, cowboys drove herds across the open range to towns with railroads that enabled the cattle to be shipped east. The era of the great cattle drives ended in the middle 1880s, as ranchers turned to new ways of raising and marketing their herds.

   Part C: Many Native American attempted to resist American settlement by waging war against the newcomers. The Battle of the Little Bighorn was a notable victory won by the Sioux against a force of U.S. Cavalry commanded by General George A. Custer on June 25 to 26, 1876. Ultimately the Native Americans could not prevail militarily against the U.S. government, and were forced onto reservations. Some Native Americans hoped for a miracle to restore their old way of life. In 1889, a Paiute prophet named Wovoka began preaching that if the Native Americans danced Ghost Dances they could bring back their dead ancestors, and the great herds of buffalo; the white men would also disappear from the West. The Ghost Dance phenomenon disturbed federal authorities. An attempt by U.S. Cavalry to round up Sioux Ghost Dancers leaving their reservation led to the tragic Wounded Knee Massacre on December 29, 1890.

CHAPTER 18

America Transformed into the Industrial Giant of the World (1870–1910)

IN THIS CHAPTER

Summary: During this era, there was massive industrial growth in the United States, making America the major industrial producer of the world. This growth was largely a product of the expansion of heavy industry; steel was an important component of this industrial growth. The development of the assembly line and Taylorism, which encouraged efficiency in the workplace, created a factory setting where skilled workmanship was de-emphasized. Horizontal and vertical integration allowed major American businesses such as Standard Oil and United States Steel to expand greatly. American workers began to unionize in this era through labor organizations such as the Knights of Labor, the American Federation of Labor, and the Industrial Workers of the World. "New" immigrants from eastern and southern Europe took unskilled jobs in many of the expanding factories but were not wanted by some labor organizations. The American city was also greatly transformed in this era. Political machines dominated many city governments, although efforts took place at the federal level to create a professional civil service system.

Keywords

Taylorism: following management practices of the industrial engineer Frederick Winslow Taylor, the belief that factories should be managed in a scientific manner, utilizing techniques that would increase the efficiency of the individual workers and the factory process as a whole.

Horizontal integration: strategy of gaining as much control over a single industry as possible, often by creating trusts and holding companies; this strategy was utilized by John D. Rockefeller and Standard Oil.

Vertical integration: strategy of gaining as much control over a single industry as possible by controlling the production, marketing, and distribution of the finished product. Andrew Carnegie and United States Steel are the best examples from the era of this approach.

"Gospel of Wealth": philosophy of Andrew Carnegie who believed that wealthy industrialists had an obligation to help local communities and philanthropic organizations.

Knights of Labor: established in the 1880s, this was the major union of that decade. It was made up of unions of many industries and accepted unskilled workers.

American Federation of Labor: national labor union formed by Samuel Gompers in 1886; original goal was to organize skilled workers by craft.

Industrial Workers of the World: more radical than the American Federation of Labor, this union was formed in 1905 and attempted to unionize unskilled workers not recruited by the AFL. Members of this union were called "Wobblies."

Gilded Age: depiction of late nineteenth-century America that emphasizes a surface of great prosperity hiding problems of social inequality and cultural shallowness.

Pendleton Civil Service Act (1883): federal act that established a civil service system at the federal level. For the first time, not all government jobs would be political appointments.

Tammany Hall: political machine that ran New York City Democratic and city politics beginning in 1870; became a model for other urban political machines in the late 1800s.

An Industrial Revolution

By the early 1890s the United States had supplanted Great Britain as the leading industrial nation in the world. American industrial growth after the Civil War was spectacular. In 1860, almost one out of four Americans worked in industry; by 1900, it was one out of two. The size of the factories in which these workers were employed changed dramatically; by the turn of the century some industrial plants were huge, with thousands of laborers. This rapid industrialization had profound effects on people's ordinary lives. Large numbers of Americans left their farms for the cities. They left behind rural rhythms of life and had to grow accustomed to time clocks and whistles indicating changing shifts. Instead of being able to wander from place to place and task to task, they had to stay put in a work station, engaged in the same repetitive motions for hours.

These Americans were part of the **Second Industrial Revolution**, which saw the emergence of new industries such as steel and chemicals, new sources of power such as electricity and petroleum, and new forms of business organization such as the trusts. Something that facilitated the early growth of American industry was a lack of involvement by the government. In the late nineteenth century, most American leaders believed in laissez-faire economics and left American business development to the "invisible hand" of the market.

Changes in American Industry

American industrial expansion was driven by the growth of **heavy industry**. Before the Civil War, American factories turned out consumer goods such as food products and textiles. These industries continued to be important, but in the post-war years industries emerged that produced goods for other industries, such as steel, petroleum products, and machinery. The steel industry thrived by supplying railroads, builders, and other industries. The oil industry provided fuel to factories as well as homes. High-grade machine products enabled businessmen to launch new industries.

In 1860, most American factories relied on water power. The opening of anthracite coal mines in Pennsylvania and West Virginia led to a drop in coal prices that made possible a speedy transition to steam power.

Industrial development occurred outside the Northeast and Midwest. Apostles of the **New South** promoted industrialization in their predominantly agrarian region. Steel production flourished around Birmingham, Alabama. Textile mills with modernized machinery took advantage of the proximity to raw materials and the availability of cheap labor in the South. The American Tobacco Company produced machine-made cigarettes, launching a new industry in the land of Dixie.

A Changing Workplace

As business became bigger in America, industrialists looked for ways to compete more efficiently and maximize profits. Consultants known as efficiency experts advised factory owners on the best ways to produce their goods. The most famous of these was Frederick W. Taylor, a mechanical engineer who pioneered a discipline that he called "scientific management." He timed the movements of workers and machines, and redesigned work spaces to eliminate unnecessary and time-consuming motions. He had no use for traditional ways of working that got in the way of speedy and efficient production. **Taylorism** could be hard on workers. Some jobs were lost as tasks were combined for efficiency. Taylor advocated paying workers "by the piece" so they would be incentivized to produce more.

One expression of the drive for efficiency was the development of the assembly line. The assembly line embodied the combination of new business organization and the application of new technologies that made the United States the world's industrial leader. Henry Ford founded the Ford Motor Company in 1903. In 1910, using a more traditional "craft" approach to manufacturing automobiles, his company turned out 12,000 vehicles. Ford introduced the assembly line to his factories in 1913; that year his company produced 250,000 cars. New manufacturing methods led to similar bursts of productivity in other industries.

The role of workers changed in this period. Most no longer needed to be skilled craftsmen. Instead, as critics of the new industrial order put it, they became "one more cog in the machine." Workers in Henry Ford's assembly line might spend their entire day repeating the same task, such as attaching a door or a lamp. Ford compensated his workers for the monotony of their labor by paying them the groundbreaking wage of five dollars a day. Few other assembly line workers did so well at that time.

Since most factory jobs came to involve the repetition of simple motions, they could be easily learned by unskilled workers. Immigrants became a major source of industrial labor in the late nineteenth century. In some industries such as textiles, women continued to make up a large part of the workforce. Many children were employed in factories, especially in shoe manufacturing and in textile mills. In 1900, 20 percent of children aged 10 to 15 worked. Some states attempted to regulate child labor, but with limited results.

Employers saw no reason to pay men and women the same wages. Men were paid more because they were often regarded as the heads of households, and were believed to be stronger and able to work harder. Unskilled male workers might make eight dollars a week, compared to five dollars a week for skilled female workers. Despite these inequities, many working class women regarded factory work as preferable to the even lower pay of maids and household servants. Some women with educational attainments found work in offices. Others worked as shop clerks. The difficulty of supporting themselves on low wages drove many women into prostitution.

The cultural expectation of the time was that women would leave their jobs once they married; they and their children would be supported by the husband. This was more an ideal than a reality for poor women. Some married women continued to work outside the home, or supplemented their family incomes by sewing or laundering for others.

Big Business

The period after the Civil War saw a period of intense creativity in business organization as new industries emerged and all industries grew larger. A dynamic generation of business tycoons built huge companies that required new corporate structures to be effectively managed. Some of these entrepreneurs became enormously wealthy and world famous. Andrew Carnegie embodied the classic American success story; arriving in the United States as a penniless eight-year old, he made his fortune manufacturing steel and retired one of the richest men in the world. John D. Rockefeller founded Standard Oil and at one time had a near monopoly of the American oil business.

Some of these industrialists could be quite ruthless in their pursuit of wealth. They saw themselves operating in a business climate where only the strong survived. Sometimes companies attempted to reduce this competition by agreeing to fix prices and production quotas. This collusion amongst businesses could hurt consumers and was outlawed by the **Interstate Commerce Act** of 1887. This act was primarily intended to regulate the railroads, but proved ineffective for many years because the Interstate Commerce Commission that it established was staffed by men sympathetic to business interests.

As businesses grew larger in the postwar years, they faced legal complications because state laws made it difficult to run interstate businesses or for corporations to own other corporations. An early legal response to this was the formations of **trusts**. This form of corporate organization was pioneered by John D. Rockefeller and Standard Oil. The creation of a trust allowed the stockholders of a subsidiary company to place control of their shares of that company "in trust" to the corporate board of Standard Oil. This organizational technique made it possible for Rockefeller to expand Standard Oil through **horizontal integration** by purchasing control of many smaller oil companies.

Trusts were eventually declared illegal. This led to the emergence of **holding companies**. In 1889, New Jersey became the first state to allow businesses incorporated there to own the stock of other corporations. This allowed the shareholders of Standard Oil to buy up the stock, and thus control of other oil companies. Rockefeller and his management team used the holding company model to merge 43 oil companies into Standard Oil of New Jersey. By the 1890s, Rockefeller produced 90 percent of the oil used in the United States. Rockefeller next aimed at **vertical integration** by buying up oil fields and moving from the refining and distribution of oil products into marketing them. He would then be able to control every phase of the oil business, from drilling for crude oil to selling refined oil products in stores and gas stations. Other practitioners of vertical integration were Gustavus Swift in meat-packing and Andrew Carnegie in steel.

The gap between rich and poor grew dramatically as great industrialists accumulated vast fortunes. The wealth of these businessmen was justified by the popular and influential ideology of **Social Darwinism**. Proponents of Social Darwinism, such as the philosopher William Graham Sumner, believed that human interactions reflected Charles Darwin's evolutionary principle of "natural selection." Those better suited to succeed because of intelligence, determination, and strength would thrive, while those less fit would fall behind. By this logic, the money and power accumulated by the rich was the just reward of their superiority and a manifestation of the working out of nature's plan. Andrew Carnegie softened some of the harder edges of Social Darwinism with his **"Gospel of Wealth."** He wrote that the great industrialists were the "guardians" of American wealth. He believed that the industrialists should not pass on all their fortunes to their children, but should devote much of it to improving the community. One manifestation of this on Carnegie's part was his enthusiasm for building libraries across the country so that able young people could improve themselves and rise in the world. Both Carnegie and Rockefeller created foundations that over the years have dispensed over $650 million to educational and artistic causes. Carnegie and Rockefeller were not alone. Many industrialists endowed universities and museums. Despite this record of charitable giving, many of the industrialists of this period have been criticized as "Robber Barons" because of their Social Darwinist attitude toward their workers.

The Emergence of Labor Unions

Craft unions existed before the Civil War. Because of the relatively small size of businesses, they did not have a major impact on society. As industry grew, so did the unions. Strife between workers and industrialists became a major issue in the postwar years. In July 1877, railroad workers launched the first nationwide strike. Because of hard economic times the railroads were cutting back at their workers' expense, and the strikers were protesting layoffs and reduced wages. Violence marred the strike. Railroad property was destroyed in various parts of the country. In Pittsburgh, Pennsylvania, 30 strikers were killed in clashes with militiamen. President Hayes eventually deployed federal troops to stop the violence and break the strike. Though he sided with the owners, the president did call on them to "remove the distress which afflicts laborers."

The most influential union to arise in the 1870s was the **Knights of Labor**. Instead of being a craft union that protected the interests of one type of worker, such as shoemakers, the Knights of Labor attempted to represent all workers, skilled and unskilled. They encouraged immigrants, African Americans, and women to join their union. At its height in the mid-1880s, the Knights of Labor had 750,000 members. The leaders of the Knights of Labor dreamed of a more cooperative society in which working people would more fully share in the fruits of their labor. Their peaceableness made them reluctant to call strikes; this, in turn, made them less effective in dealing with hard-nosed employers. The Knights of Labor faded away as more confrontational labor unions captured the loyalties of workers.

The Knights of Labor were also blamed for radical actions over which they had no control. In the spring of 1886, workers went on strike at the McCormick reaper plant in Chicago. On May 1, 100,000 people gathered at a rally to show their solidarity with the workers. The next day, a smaller demonstration was scheduled at **Haymarket Square**. A few of the people supporting the strike were radicals and anarchists influenced by violent social strife in Europe. When police arrived to break up the demonstration, someone set off a bomb. Seven policemen were killed. In the chaotic aftermath of the explosion, a gun battle erupted that left four civilians dead. Scores of police and citizens were injured by the bomb and bullets. Eight anarchists were arrested and convicted of the bombing. The Haymarket Square tragedy convinced many Americans that labor organizations like the Knights of Labor were breeding grounds for violent extremism. It fed antipathy toward immigrants and radical political beliefs.

The **American Federation of Labor (AFL)** proved more successful than the Knights of Labor. The AFL was an association of craft unions composed of skilled workers. For many years, the AFL was headed by Samuel Gompers, a tough and wily leader who carefully dissociated his unions from political or social radicalism. Instead, Gompers emphasized "bread and butter issues," and focused on achieving higher wages and shorter hours rather than remaking American society. The AFL was prepared to use strikes to attain its goals. A strike against the Carnegie Steel Company at Homestead, Pennsylvania, in 1892, and the American Railway Union's strike against the Pullman Palace Car Company in 1894 received national attention. The leader of the American Railway Union was Eugene V. Debs. The suppression of the Pullman strike convinced him to embrace socialism. Debs would run for president several times as head of the Socialist party. Despite the failure of some strikes, the AFL grew more powerful and influential; by 1917, the AFL claimed 2.5 million members.

A very different labor organization was the **Industrial Workers of the World (IWW)**. This union originated amongst industrial miners in the West, who faced very difficult working conditions. The IWW embraced a radical social vision; it called for revolutionary violence and the imposition of socialism. Members of the IWW were nicknamed "Wobblies." The leader of the IWW was Big Bill Haywood of the Western Federation of Miners. "Mother" Jones worked with coal miners. The IWW did not shy away from strikes and bloodshed. Because of its extremist reputation, the union was brutally quashed by the federal government during World War I.

Unions helped some workers raise their wages and improve their working conditions. Many workers were unable to effectively organize themselves. The most successful labor organization, the AFL, focused only on skilled workers. The AFL resisted organizing women, African Americans, and other unskilled workers, believing that the presence of these groups in the workforce undercut the bargaining power of its members. Some women formed their own unions. In 1909, the International Ladies Garment Workers Union launched a notable strike in New York City.

Organized labor faced other challenges. Most industrialists discouraged their workers from joining unions. Many people associated unionism with radicalism, while others thought that unions weakened American individualism and self-reliance. The government generally supported business owners during strikes and occasionally used the military to break up strikes. Businessmen could also usually rely on the support of state and local governments and their police forces. Factory owners could also hire Pinkerton detectives to guard their plants and intimidate strikers.

Uneven Affluence

Many Americans prospered in the new industrial economy. They were able to take part in the emergence of a **consumer society** in which ordinary Americans were able to buy goods such as tea and silk stockings that had earlier been luxury items for the rich. The proliferation of department stores symbolized the new possibilities for American consumers. Many middle-class Americans could buy what they wanted, not just what they needed. The average life expectancy increased by six years between 1900 and 1920. A growing number of middle-class homes now benefited from indoor plumbing and electricity.

Not all shared in this new affluence. Large numbers of Americans, from rural sharecroppers to immigrants living in overcrowded urban neighborhoods, could not afford to join in the new consumer society. A majority of working-class homes did not get flush toilets until the 1920s and 1930s. Higher wages were counterbalanced by increases in the cost of living that kept many consumer goods priced out of the reach of most workers.

The New Immigration

The late 1880s and early 1890s saw a significant change in the pattern of immigration to the United States. Prior to this period, most immigrants came from Northern Europe, usually from the British Isles and Germany. Assimilation was easier for the Irish and English because they shared a common language with Americans; Germans may have spoken a different language, but they came from a society with many cultural similarities to the United States. This was not the case with the **"new immigrants"** who began pouring into the United States in the late 1880s. These people came from Italy, Eastern Europe, and Russia. They did not speak English. Most were very poor, and looked and sounded very different from the Northern European immigrants Americans had grown used to. Many were Roman Catholic or Jewish, which made them seem even more alien in what was still a largely Protestant America.

This new immigration was alarming to some Americans because of the sheer numbers of arriving immigrants. Between 1870 and 1920, 28 million immigrants entered the United States. The high point of this immigration came between 1900 and 1910. The federal government opened Ellis Island in New York City harbor as a reception center in 1892. Here immigrants had to pass rudimentary health and security testing. Angel Island in San Francisco was opened as a similar reception center for the Pacific Coast.

14,000 Chinese workers were brought to the United States to help complete the construction of the transcontinental railroad. These Asian immigrants faced intense hostility from "native" workers who feared that they would depress wages by working for less. This anti-Chinese sentiment found political expression in the Chinese Exclusion Act of 1882, which restricted the entrance of Chinese laborers into the United States. To protect themselves from racial animosity, many Chinese moved to ethnically homogenous "Chinatowns" in large cities. The annexation of Hawaii in 1898 opened the way for Japanese living there to move to California and work on farms. This Japanese immigration reignited the same sorts of concerns and prejudices that the Chinese had encountered. In 1906, the San Francisco Board of Education segregated Asian students in separate schools. In 1913, the persistently anti-Japanese Californians passed the **Webb Alien Land Law** which prohibited Asians who were noncitizens from owning land in the state. Because Japan was a proud and powerful nation, these initiatives in California cause severe diplomatic trouble for the United States.

Most immigrants at first settled in the big coastal cities. Many of the Eastern and Southern European immigrants were fleeing religious persecution and economic hardship at home. They faced a wrenching process of acculturation in the United States as most of them transitioned from rural to urban life, and found work in large factories. Like the Chinese, many sought the comfort of living with their compatriots in ethnic neighborhoods in the cities, where they could speak their language and more easily practice their religion. There they were jammed into teeming tenement houses. At the end of the nineteenth century, the Lower East Side of New York City was the most densely populated place in the world.

Many immigrants planned to work in the United States for a period of years and then return to their homelands. Some did go home, but most remained and played a critical role in American economic expansion. Many of the new immigrants worked in factories on the East Coast and in the Midwest. A number of immigrants joined the movement west and farmed. Some became miners. The one region that did not see a significant influx of immigrants was the South, where its relatively depressed agrarian economy offered newcomers few opportunities.

The Rise of the Modern American City

American cities grew dramatically after the Civil War because of industrialization and immigration. The newcomers to the cities were not all from overseas. Many people were leaving their farms as mechanization encouraged consolidation in agriculture. The booming cities beckoned as sources of economic opportunity. Not everyone in the cities prospered, and the poor found themselves crowded into slums.

Before the Civil War, most American cities were small enough that people could walk to where they wanted to go. As the cities grew, new forms of transportation allowed people to traverse the growing urban landscape. New York City unveiled elevated trains in 1867, and Boston opened a subway in 1897. Many cities installed cable cars and electric trolleys. This public transportation made it possible for upper- and middle-class commuters to live farther away from their workplaces in the city. In the early nineteenth century, the well-to-do built their homes in the center of town; now they began a movement to **suburbia**. City centers became business districts, dominated by banks, department stores, and office buildings. Factories and warehouses were located just outside the central business district. Blocks of inexpensive housing clustered around the factories, so workers could easily get to their jobs. The rich and the poor were increasingly far apart, geographically as well as in their incomes.

Housing was often in short supply for the working class. Older middle-class apartment buildings were divided and subdivided to house more and more poor families. Tenement houses were specially constructed to provide rooms for large numbers of people. They afforded their residents few amenities. Bathrooms were located outdoors. Many rooms had no windows for ventilation, much less a view. There were no elevators. These buildings were dingy and dirty. Because of poor plumbing and inadequate sewers, disease was rampant. Poverty bred crime, and gangs often terrorized neighborhoods. Gradually conditions improved. Building codes helped clean up the worst tenements. Some buildings began to offer running water, gas, and electricity.

The skylines of American cities changed dramatically. Before the Civil War, buildings rarely rose above four of five stories. New construction materials and methods led to an architectural revolution. The production of strong and durable **Bessemer steel** girders allowed builders to construct taller buildings around a steel framework. The introduction of elevators in the early 1880s provided a practical means to move people up and down these taller buildings. Architects like Chicago's Louis Sullivan began designing the first "skyscrapers." The Home Insurance Company building in Chicago, completed in 1885, was an early example of the new style of office building. It was ten stories high and had four elevators conveying passengers up and down.

American cities in the late nineteenth and early twentieth centuries were ongoing construction sites. In addition to office buildings, factories, and apartments, public works such as schools, roads, sewers, and parks were being built or extended. City planners began to seek ways to bring some order to the frantic pace of development.

Gilded Age Politics

Mark Twain popularized the term **"Gilded Age,"** which refers to the period between 1875 and 1900. For Twain, it was an expression that satirized the political corruption and crude money-grubbing that he thought characterized contemporary American society. (Something that is gilded has only a thin layer of gold over a baser metal.) It was an era of striking contrasts, politically and economically, that left many observers bewildered.

Modern commentators often criticize the politics of the Gilded Age as being much ado about nothing much. They find debates over the tariff and the currency superficial, and condemn the politicians of the day for not intervening more actively as the country industrialized and urbanized. What these commentators forget is that nineteenth-century Americans had different ideas about politics and government. They believed that the role of government was strictly limited, and after the crisis of the Civil War and Reconstruction, they wanted to restore what they believed was a more normal political equilibrium. President Grover Cleveland was widely commended for saying that "the lesson should be constantly enforced that though the people support the Government the Government should not support the people."

Politics was a popular avocation for Americans in the Gilded Age. They took a deep interest in political issues and party identification was high. Often nearly 75 percent of registered voters participated in presidential elections, a far higher rate than today.

The Democratic and Republican parties were very evenly balanced. Elections were close and control of Congress regularly passed back and forth. This had a moderating effect on political positions because the parties feared alienating swing voters. The Republicans could usually count on the support of the industrial Northeast, while the Democrats relied on the "Solid South." Most elections hinged on the results in a few swing states like New York, Indiana, and Ohio.

In the postwar period, Congress grew more important as presidents took a more restrained view of their powers. An issue that came to the forefront was the **spoils system**. This practice dated back to the days of Andrew Jackson and held that after an election the victorious party should reward its supporters by giving them government jobs. This often meant turning members of the opposing party out of their government positions and became a major burden for presidents as heads of the office-rich executive branch.

President Rutherford B. Hayes tried to reform this patronage system. He attempted to appoint officials for their qualifications rather than their political connections. He angered his own party's political bosses in Congress by removing some men from office who had benefited from the spoils system, including Chester A. Arthur, the Collector of the Port of New York.

Hayes's actions led to divisions in the Republican Party and ensured that he would not be renominated for the presidency in 1880. The eventual Republican nominee, Congressman James Garfield of Ohio, also called for reform of the spoils system. Garfield won the election, but in July 1881, only a few months after taking office, he was assassinated by a deranged man who believed that he should have been given a government job.

Garfield's assassination convinced Congress that something had to be done about the spoils system. President Chester A. Arthur, ironically a man associated with the spoils system, threw his support behind reform. In 1883, Congress passed the **Pendleton Civil Service Act**, which took a number of government jobs out of political control. It established the **Civil Service Commission**, which administered these positions. Applicants for these jobs had to demonstrate their fitness by passing examinations. The Pendleton Act also prohibited government officials from contributing to political campaigns, a practice that had been routine when officeholders were openly political functionaries. These reforms were the beginning of a **professional bureaucracy** in the legislative and executive branches. Initially only a few jobs were covered by the new civil service regulations, but the number grew over time. Even today, there are many managerial positions in the federal bureaucracy that are filled by political appointees.

The election of 1884 was dominated by the personal issues of the candidates. The Republicans nominated Senator James Blaine of Maine. He was accused of taking gifts of stock in exchange for supporting bills favorable to railroads. The Democrats nominated Grover Cleveland, the governor of New York. As a younger man, Cleveland accepted responsibility for an illegitimate child. During the election, Republicans chanted, "Ma, Ma, where's my Pa!" Despite this scandal, Cleveland won a close election.

Along with concerns about the currency, tariffs were one of the most prominent political issues of the Gilded Age. Generally Republicans supported high tariffs to protect American industry and jobs. Most Democrats, with their party base in the agrarian South and West, wanted to lower tariffs. Complicating matters were Eastern Democrats and Western Republicans who voted with the economic interests of their region. President Cleveland wanted to lower tariffs and made this the central issue of the 1888 presidential campaign. The results showed how closely divided Americans were politically. Cleveland won the popular vote, but lost in the Electoral College. His Republican opponent Benjamin Harrison became president. Cleveland came back to defeat Harrison in 1892, becoming the only president elected to two nonconsecutive terms.

Soon after Cleveland's second inauguration, the United States fell into one of the worst depressions in its history. Many factories closed their doors and millions of workers lost their jobs. The economic downturn aggravated the problems facing farmers. The Populists took the lead in calling for governmental relief. A Populist leader in Ohio named Jacob Coxey led a column of unemployed workers to Washington. President Cleveland and Congress ignored **Coxey's Army**. Pressure intensified to loosen the currency supply by coining more silver. Cleveland, an economic conservative, held to the gold standard.

This currency debate framed the election of 1896. William McKinley's decisive victory ended the period of political parity between the Democrats and Republicans, and began an era of Republican electoral dominance. McKinley was an able president, who is seen by some historians as the first "modern" chief executive because of the way that he organized and concentrated authority in his office. McKinley's campaign manager, Mark Hanna, is credited with pioneering the modern presidential campaign.

The governments of many cities were controlled by **political machines**. These were highly structured organizations designed to keep a leader, the "boss," and his associates in political power. Machines often relied on immigrants for their electoral strength; they provided working class citizens jobs, loans, and other favors in exchange for their votes. Once in control of city hall, the machine generated funds by extorting kickbacks from contractors doing city business. Machine operatives who received city jobs often paid back a percentage of their salary to the organization. This cash helped provide the funds that kept the machine well-oiled and running smoothly. The most famous political machine was **Tammany Hall** in New York City. In the 1860s and 1870s, the Tammany boss William M. Tweed and an unscrupulous group of officials embezzled millions of dollars from City Hall. Tweed was mercilessly lampooned by the political cartoonist Thomas Nast and eventually was investigated and jailed for his crimes. Despite Tweed's incarceration, Tammany Hall lived on and dominated New York City politics for decades. Though corrupt, machines did provide rudimentary social relief for the poor. Some machine politicians supported reforms in education and social services.

Social Criticism in the Gilded Age

Beginning with Mark Twain, a number of writers criticized American society during the Gilded Age. Edward Bellamy achieved a surprising literary success with *Looking Backward* (1888), which envisioned a socialist future for the United States. The hero of the book finds himself transported to Boston in 2000 and learns that peaceful economic "nationalism" has replaced the unfettered capitalism of his day. The journalist Jacob Riis published a groundbreaking study of the poor in New York City entitled *How the Other Half Lives* (1890). Riis described the appalling conditions in the tenement houses of the Lower East Side and documented this with evocative photographs that pioneered modern photojournalism. Upton Sinclair created a sensation in 1906 with *The Jungle*, a searing indictment of conditions in Chicago's meatpacking industry. Sinclair hoped to make the case for socialism, but most readers focused on his graphic descriptions of unsanitary practices in the meatpacking plants.

Chapter Review

Rapid Review

To achieve the perfect 5, you should be able to explain the following:

- The industrial growth that occurred in the United States during this era made the United States the major industrial producer of the world.
- The industrial growth was largely based on the expansion of heavy industry; the availability of steel was critical to this expansion.
- Taylorism and the assembly line created major changes in the workplace for factory workers.
- Horizontal and vertical integration allowed businesses to expand dramatically during this era; Standard Oil (John D. Rockefeller) and United States Steel (Andrew Carnegie) are the best examples of this type of expansion.
- Andrew Carnegie's "Gospel of Wealth" proclaimed it was the duty of the wealthy to return large amounts of their wealth back to the community.
- American workers began to unionize in this era by joining the Knights of Labor, the American Federation of Labor, and the Industrial Workers of the World. Because of intimidation by company bosses and the publicity that came from several unsuccessful strikes, union membership remained low, even into the twentieth century.
- The impact of the "new immigrants" from eastern and southern Europe on American cities and in the workplace was immense.
- The American city became transformed in this era, with new methods of transportation allowing many from the middle and upper classes to move to suburbia and still work in the city.

- Political life at the state and city levels during this era was dominated by various political machines, although reforms were instituted at the federal level and in some states to create a professional civil service system.

Time Line

1869: Knights of Labor founded in Philadelphia

1870: Beginning of Tammany Hall's control over New York City politics

1879: Publication of *Progress and Poverty* by Henry George

1881: Assassination of President James Garfield

1882: Chinese Exclusion Act passed by Congress

1883: Pendleton Civil Service Act enacted

1885: Completion of Home Insurance Company building in Chicago, America's first skyscraper

1886: Haymarket Square demonstration and bombing in Chicago

1887: Interstate Commerce Act enacted
   Major strike of railroad workers; President Hayes sends in government troops to break up strike in Pittsburgh

1888: New Jersey passes legislation allowing holding companies
   Publication of *Looking Backward* by Edward Bellamy

1890: Publication of *How the Other Half Lives* by Jacob Riis

1892: Ellis Island opens to process immigrants on the East Coast

1893: Beginning of major depression in America

1894: March of Coxey's Army on Washington, DC
   United States becomes world's largest manufacturing producer

1896: Decisive victory of Republican William McKinley breaks decades-long deadlock between Democrats and Republicans
   America begins to recover from great depression of early 1890s

1897: America's first subway begins regular service in Boston

1901: Assassination of President William McKinley

1903: Ford Motor Company established

1905: Industrial Workers of the World formed

1906: Publication of *The Jungle* by Upton Sinclair

1909: Strike of International Ladies Garment Workers Union in New York City

1910: Angel Island opens to process immigrants on West Coast
   Number of American children attending school nears 60 percent

1913: Webb Alien Land Law enacted, prohibiting aliens from owning farmland in California
   Ford Motor Company begins to use assembly line techniques; 250,000 automobiles produced in one year

› Review Questions

Multiple-Choice Questions

1. The practices championed by Frederick W. Taylor that were championed by many factory owners of the era
   A. made it easier for immigrant workers to assimilate into the American working class.
   B. ensured that all workers would receive higher wages and conditions in the factories would improve.
   C. emphasized the need for greater efficiency in factory operations.
   D. reemphasized the need for extensive training before the worker could do almost any job in the factory.

2. Many citizens became involved in the political process by actively supporting the Republican and Democratic parties for all of the reasons listed *except*
   A. the parades, rallies, and campaigns of the era provided an exciting entry into the American political system.
   B. the strength of the two parties was roughly identical in this era, thus creating close and interesting races.
   C. the expansion and spread of newspapers in this era made more people aware of political developments.
   D. candidates for president from both parties in almost every race of this era were dynamic and very popular campaigners, thus energizing the forces of both parties.

3. An analysis of the march on Washington by Coxey's Army in 1894 demonstrates that
   A. large segments of the unemployed in America were willing to become involved politically to protest their situation.
   B. all classes in American society were deeply affected by the depression of the early 1890s.
   C. the policies of dealing with the depression in the 1890s were somewhat similar to policies championed by Herbert Hoover from 1929 to 1932.
   D. the march was extremely well covered by the press.

4. The following statements are true about the new industrial city of the late nineteenth century *except*
   A. the working class lived around the factories, usually somewhat near the center of the city.
   B. the factories of the city were almost always found near a source of water, since water power was common.
   C. the central area of the city usually consisted of offices, banks, and insurance buildings.
   D. many saloons existed in working-class neighborhoods.

5. Evidence that the standard of living for the working class improved in this era could be found by carefully analyzing all of the following *except*
   A. a comparison of increased wages with increased living costs for factory workers.
   B. an analysis of the increased diversity of foods available for purchase by factory workers.
   C. an analysis of the growth of amusement parks, sporting events, and movie theaters in the major cities.
   D. a comparison of the wages of most immigrant workers with the wages of workers who remained to work in the "old country."

Short-Answer Question

6. Answer Parts A, B, and C.
   A. Briefly explain ONE example of a way in which American political leaders responded to rapid industrial growth in the late nineteenth century.
   B. Briefly explain a SECOND example of a way in which American political leaders responded to rapid industrial growth in the late nineteenth century.
   C. Briefly explain ONE example of a way that American workers responded to rapid industrial growth in the late nineteenth century.

❯ Answers and Explanations

1. **C.** Taylorism made efficiency in the workplace a science and set the stage for assembly line production techniques.

2. **D.** Most of the presidential candidates—and presidential winners—of this era were nondescript men, thus allowing much power to go over to Congress.

3. **C.** The march had little effect on government policy. Coxey's Army was relatively small by the time it got to Washington. Official policy of the time was that it was not the job of the federal government to actively intervene during hard times, a policy similar to that supported by Herbert Hoover in the first years of the Great Depression.

4. **B.** By 1890, most American industry had converted to steam power.

5. **A.** Many diverse foods were available for purchase by factory workers, but few could afford them. For many workers, wages did go up in this period; however, increased living costs often outstripped higher wages.

6. **Parts A and B**: Most American political leaders did very little about the rapid industrial growth in the late nineteenth century. They believed in laissez-faire economics and did not believe in extensive government regulation of business. Popular concerns about the differences between what railroads charged individual consumers and big businesses led Congress to pass the Interstate Commerce Act in 1887. This created the Interstate Commerce Commission, which was charged with monitoring railroad rates. The emergence of "trusts," large businesses that owned more than one company, worried many people. Congress responded by passing the Sherman Antitrust Act in 1890, which outlawed trusts. Big business found a way around this. In 1888, the New Jersey legislature passed a law legalizing holding companies. A holding company owned a controlling interest in the stock of other companies. Soon many big corporations such as Standard Oil had reorganized themselves as holding companies.

Part C: One way that American workers responded to rapid industrial growth and the rise of large corporations was by organizing unions. The Knights of Labor was founded in 1869 and by the mid-1880s had a membership of 750,000 people. The Knights of Labor had both skilled and unskilled workers in its membership. It declined after being blamed for radical outrages like the 1886 Haymarket Square Bombing. The American Federation of Labor (AFL) was a grouping of unions that organized skilled workers. Under its longtime president Samuel Gompers, the AFL became the leading labor organization in the United States, with a membership of 2.5 million in 1917. The Industrial Workers of the World (IWW) was founded in 1905. The IWW was a radical union that emphasized class conflict. It organized skilled and unskilled workers.

Rise of American Imperialism (1890–1913)

IN THIS CHAPTER

Summary: Beginning in the 1890s, the United States began to practice some of the same imperialistic policies that it had previously criticized major European powers for. Spurred on by sugar planters, America expanded its influence in Hawaii and in 1896 annexed the islands. Americans also pushed for an "Open Door" trading policy with China. Efforts to expand American influence abroad were motivated by economic, political, religious, and social factors; the "white man's burden" argument was influential in both Europe and the United States. There were also opponents to imperialism who often based their opposition on moral grounds. American imperialistic impulses flourished during the Spanish-American War; newly created American naval power was one important factor in the defeat of Spain. After contentious debate within the United States, America finally decided to annex the Philippines; it took three years for American forces to defeat Filipino rebels, who instead of fighting the Spanish now resisted their new occupiers, the Americans. Americans finished building the Panama Canal in 1914; the Roosevelt Corollary to the Monroe Doctrine further increased American influence in Latin America.

Keywords

Open Door policy: policy supported by the United States beginning in 1899 that stated that all major powers, including the United States, should have an equal right to trade with China.

Social Darwinism: philosophy that emerged from the writings of Charles Darwin on the "survival of the fittest"; this was used to justify the vast differences between the rich and the poor in the late nineteenth century as well as American and European imperialistic ventures.

Spanish-American War: war that began in 1898 against the Spanish over treatment of Cubans by Spanish troops that controlled the island. As a result of this war, the United States annexed the Philippines, making America a major power in the Pacific.

Yellow journalism: method of journalism that utilized sensationalized accounts of the news to sell newspapers. This approach helped to whip up nationalistic impulses that led to the Spanish-American War.

U.S.S. *Maine*: U.S. naval ship that sank in Havana harbor in February 1898 following an explosion. The incident was used to increase calls for war against Spain. It was never definitively determined why or how the ship was sunk.

Panama Canal: canal across the Panama isthmus that was begun in 1904 and completed in 1914; its opening enabled America to expand its economic and military influence.

Roosevelt Corollary (1904): policy that warned Europeans against intervening in the affairs of Latin America and that claimed the right of the United States to intervene in the affairs of Latin American nations if "chronic wrongdoing" was taking place.

Dollar Diplomacy: foreign policy supported by President William Howard Taft and others that favored increased American investment in the world as a way of increasing American influence.

Postwar Diplomacy

Even before the Civil War, the U.S. government was interested in opening up new overseas markets for American goods and seeking sources of raw materials for American factories. These efforts continued in the postwar years. In 1867, Secretary of State William Henry Seward successfully orchestrated the purchase of Alaska from Russia. Initially termed "Seward's Folly," it soon became recognized that Alaska was rich in resources. Also in 1867, the United States acquired the Midway Islands in the Pacific Ocean. Midway could serve as a stopping point on the way to China and Japan. Changes in marine technology during this period saw ships shift from sails to coal-powered steam engines. The United States began seeking coaling stations in the Pacific, where American ships could refuel.

Initially, the United States did not join the great European powers in establishing colonies in Africa and Asia. Americans were still busy filling in the western frontier. Rapid industrialization and urbanization also absorbed much American energy. Only when the frontier was declared closed in the 1890s did a new generation of leaders like Theodore Roosevelt and Henry Cabot Lodge begin calling for American expansion overseas. These men were too young to have experienced the horrors of the Civil War and were willing to fight to secure the United States an empire of its own.

The United States was not prepared for imperial adventures. The State Department employed fewer than 100 people in the 1870s and early 1880s. The army was tiny by European standards; most of its troops were scattered across the West in small forts and engaged in patrolling the frontier. The navy had been allowed to deteriorate after the Civil War. Only during the presidency of Chester Arthur was there an effort to rebuild the navy, equipping it with modern all-steel ships.

Acquiring Hawaii

American missionaries arrived in Hawaii during the 1820s. The island chain was a port of call for American whalers and merchant ships. American entrepreneurs began cultivating sugar cane on the islands and their plantations became highly lucrative businesses. In 1887, Congress allowed the importation of Hawaiian sugar duty-free. This enhanced the influence of the sugar planters in Hawaii, and they pressured King Kalakaua into promulgating a constitution that gave them greater political power.

In 1891, Queen Liliuokalani ascended to the Hawaiian throne. She was determined to reassert royal control over Hawaii and resist the political encroachments of people she saw as outsiders, such as the American planters. For their part, the sugar magnates feared the queen's nationalist program and wanted to convert Hawaii into a protectorate of the United States. This embrace of the United States flag was also spurred by changes in American trade policy; only if Hawaii was an American colony could its sugar be considered domestic produce and compete effectively in American markets. In 1893, the planters staged a coup that overthrew the queen. They were assisted by a small detachment of Marines provided by an American diplomat. The planters proclaimed a Hawaiian republic and immediately asked to be annexed by the United States.

Despite the intervention of the diplomat, Washington was not a party to the coup. President Cleveland sent a commission to Hawaii to investigate the attitudes of the Hawaiian people toward the new regime. When the commission reported back that a majority still supported Queen Liliuokalani, Cleveland refused to annex the islands. The United States took no action to restore the queen and eventually extended diplomatic recognition to the Republic of Hawaii. William McKinley did not share Cleveland's qualms about acquiring Hawaii and in the 1896 election declared that it was America's **"Manifest Destiny"** to possess the islands. Congress finally approved the annexation of Hawaii in 1898, against the backdrop of the Spanish-American War. American policymakers realized that Pearl Harbor provided the Navy with a strategically valuable base on the Pacific Ocean.

The New Imperialism

In the 1890s, American attitudes toward imperialism began to change. Though industrialists and businessmen generally feared that war would disrupt markets, they did begin to worry that they would need to find places to sell their goods overseas. Some sought sources of raw materials, such as rubber, that were unavailable in the continental United States.

Strategists such as the naval officer Captain Alfred Thayer Mahan argued that the United States needed to expand in order to protect its international position as a major economic and political power. One of history's most influential military theorists, Mahan published *The Influence of Sea Power upon History* in 1890. In this work, Mahan persuasively made the case that naval power was necessary to acquire markets overseas and to protect continued access to them. Mahan's writings were studied by naval officers around the world. They inspired the naval enthusiasms of American leaders like Theodore Roosevelt and helped justify legislation like the **Naval Act of 1900** that rapidly expanded the United States Navy.

The idea of **Social Darwinism** that rationalized economic inequality in the United States was also used to justify imperialism. This view of international relations held that nations, like people, struggled for survival, and the strong would rule the weak. Social Darwinism was easily harmonized with contemporary racial ideas and convictions about the superiority of the Anglo-Saxon "race." In 1885, the well-known minister Josiah Strong asserted that God had made the Anglo-Saxons their "brother's keepers" in his book *Our Country*. This same vision was conveyed in Rudyard Kipling's poem **"White Man's Burden,"** in which he urged Americans to accept the mission of ruling and civilizing "inferior races." American missionaries embraced imperialism because it offered them an opportunity to convert "heathens" in Africa and Asia. Some intellectuals like the scholarly Senator Albert J. Beveridge of Indiana saw imperialism overseas as a way for Americans to open a new frontier and recapture the pioneer spirit of their forebears.

The Spanish-American War

The United States burst onto the world scene as an imperial power in the **Spanish-American War.** Short, and relatively bloodless, this "splendid little war" ended a century of American noninvolvement in overseas affairs. The issue that brought on the war began close to home. The island of Cuba lies 90 miles off the coast of Florida. In 1868, some Cuban colonists launched a revolt against the Spanish authorities that governed the island. Though the revolt failed, it began a long period of unrest in Cuba. In 1895, an economic depression caused by falling sugar prices led to another revolt. Many Americans owned sugar plantations or had other financial investments in Cuba; they did not support the revolutionaries.

The U.S. government was initially indifferent to the situation in Cuba. This began to change when the Spanish government used ruthless methods to quell the insurrection. The Spanish sent 150,000 troops to Cuba and began a policy of **reconcentration**, which attempted to deny the rebels support by rounding up rural civilians and placing them in government-controlled camps. The Spanish concentration camps bred disease, and 225,000 people died. Cuban exiles in the United States implored Presidents Cleveland and McKinley to intervene in the war and end Spanish rule. Neither president showed any enthusiasm for a war in Cuba. McKinley had fought in the Civil War and had vivid memories of the human cost of battle. The rebels began burning American-owned plantations and sugar mills to intensify interventionist pressure on the U.S. government.

An emerging mass media pushed public opinion in favor of war. Large circulation newspapers like Joseph Pulitzer's *New York World* and William Randolph Hearst's *New York Morning Journal* attracted readers with boldly headlined news stories that privileged sensationalism over accuracy. This new style of newspapering became known as **yellow journalism**. Both Pulitzer and Hearst sent teams of reporters to Cuba charged with getting stories that would sell newspapers. Soon these papers were publicizing lurid, and often fanciful, accounts of Spanish misdeeds. These stories were widely reprinted across the United States and outraged Americans who believed what they read. The yellow press encouraged **jingoism**, a belligerent patriotism that demanded war with Spain.

President McKinley recognized the political power of the anti-Spanish sentiment whipped up by the newspapers. War became inevitable after the **U.S.S. *Maine*** exploded and sank in Havana Harbor on February 15, 1898. The *Maine* had been sent to Cuba after riots in the capital seemed to threaten American lives and property. The *Maine* probably blew up because of a failure with its boilers; the yellow journalists loudly declared that the Spanish had sunk the ship and demanded that readers "Remember the *Maine*!" A subsequent naval investigation failed to conclusively explain the explosion; the naval authorities were reluctant to blame a technical fault with their own ship. A foolish gaffe by a Spanish diplomat further inflamed American public opinion. In a letter stolen by Cuban revolutionaries the diplomat called McKinley "weak."

Combat in the Philippines and Cuba

Theodore Roosevelt, the assistant secretary of the navy, was an ardent imperialist who assumed that the United States would go to war with Spain. On February 25, while the secretary of the navy was out for the day, Roosevelt cabled American commanders in the Pacific to be ready to strike against the Spanish. President McKinley and the navy secretary later confirmed that in the event of war, Commodore George Dewey should attack the Spanish fleet in the Philippines.

By April, both expansionists dreaming of empire and humanitarians shocked by newspaper reports of Cuban suffering were calling for war. McKinley attempted to defuse the crisis with diplomacy. The Spanish were prepared to meet most of McKinley's conditions for a settlement in Cuba. The Spanish concessions were not enough. McKinley decided that war had become a political necessity. He sent a message to Congress recommending an intervention in Cuba. The next day, Congress authorized the use of force to drive the Spanish from the island.

While the small but modern American navy was ready for war, the army was not. It took time to gather an invasion force at Tampa, Florida. The war would be over before the army's supply services fully organized themselves. Fortunately for the Americans, the Spanish in Cuba were equally disorganized and had become demoralized by years of guerilla warfare. A small American army landed in Cuba in June. The main fighting took place on July 1, when the Americans seized high ground outside the city of Santiago. Theodore Roosevelt, who had resigned his post in the Navy Department, became a national hero because of the courage he showed leading his regiment of volunteer "**Rough Riders**" up San Juan Hill. Two days later, the aged Spanish warships in Santiago harbor made a dash for the open sea and were annihilated by better-armed American warships. This ended the fighting in Cuba. The war cost 2,500 American lives, most of them to disease. Fewer than 400 Americans died in combat.

On the other side of the world, the U.S. Navy seemed to justify Mahan's theories about the importance of maritime power. Commodore Dewey sailed a small American squadron into Manila Harbor on May 1 and destroyed the decrepit Spanish fleet anchored there. This one-sided battle gave the United States a claim to the Philippines. The war officially ended with the **Treaty of Paris**. Spain granted Cuba independence and for $20 million ceded the Philippines, Guam, and Puerto Rico to the United States.

The Cuban Conundrum

Almost immediately after ensuring Cuban independence, some American policymakers began to have doubts about the ability of the Cubans to govern themselves and safeguard American interests. Concerns about imperial temptations had led a majority in Congress to insert the **Teller Amendment** in the April war resolution. This amendment declared that the United States had no intention of annexing Cuba. Postwar reconsiderations led Congress to soften its support for full Cuban autonomy.

Immediately following the defeat of the Spanish, President McKinley created a military government to rule Cuba. This regime lasted until 1901 and had some notable successes in improving public health and combating yellow fever. In the meantime the Cubans worked on a constitution. Reflecting the new imperial mood in Washington, the American government compelled the Cubans to integrate the **Platt Amendment** into their new constitution. This prohibited the Cubans from making treaties without American approval. It also gave the United States the power to intervene in Cuban politics "when necessary." The Platt Amendment limited full Cuban independence until the United States withdrew it in the 1930s.

The Debate over Empire

Cuba was next door to the United States. The acquisition of the Philippines, an extensive and heavily populated island chain thousands of miles away, spurred controversy. This debate was intensified as the Filipinos organized a government and demanded independence. Americans prided themselves on their revolutionary struggle for independence against Great Britain. Did traditional American political values sanction the United States becoming a colonial power?

The **Anti-Imperialist League** was founded in 1898 to oppose a colonial adventure in the Philippines. Eminent Americans such as Mark Twain, Andrew Carnegie, and William Jennings Bryan spoke out against imperialism. Arguments against empire ranged from the idealistic to the practical. Anti-imperialists condemned the hypocrisy of Americans forcing their rule on peoples overseas, while the United States still faced many social and economic challenges at home. Some opposed imperialism for racial reasons, fearing that it would facilitate a flood of "inferior races" into the United States.

The defenders of American policy in the Philippines had their own arguments. An empire was an extension of the American frontier, allowing modern-day Americans to maintain pioneer virtues. Control of the Philippines helped establish the United States in Asian markets. There was a strong likelihood that if the United States withdrew from the Philippines, the Germans or the Japanese would move in and colonize the islands. Finally, many ministers supported keeping the Philippines so missionaries could convert the people to Christianity, heedless of the fact that most Filipinos were already Catholic.

After wrestling with the issue himself, President McKinley decided that the United States had to rule the Philippines for practical and moral reasons. He believed that the Filipinos were "unfit for self-government." If left alone they would fall into civil war and some predatory imperial power would gobble them up. The Filipinos did not acquiesce to American control easily. The United States fought a war against Filipino rebels from 1899 to 1902. This war was much bloodier than the better-known Spanish-American War; around 4,500 Americans and 200,000 Filipinos were killed. The fighting in the Philippines was brutal, and both sides occasionally committed atrocities. The Americans eventually won the war because they employed the skills that they had learned fighting Indians against the Filipinos. They ensured their victory by combining military measures with an effort to win hearts and minds by building schools and encouraging local self-government.

One reason for American interest in the Philippines was a desire to trade in what they hoped would be a lucrative market in China. The weakness of the Chinese government made that nation vulnerable to partition by imperial powers. In 1899, to prevent this, Secretary of State John Hay promoted an **Open Door policy** that would allow all nations equal access to trade in China. The next year, the United States joined with the European powers and Japan to suppress the Boxer Rebellion in China. The Boxers resented foreign influence in China and attacked missionaries, merchants, and diplomats. An international army that included a contingent of American troops bloodily defeated the rebels.

The Panama Canal

The election of 1900 was a rematch of 1896. Once again McKinley defeated William Jennings Bryan, who this time unsuccessfully campaigned on a platform of anti-imperialism. McKinley's running mate was Theodore Roosevelt, who had parlayed his wartime heroism into the governorship of New York. When McKinley was assassinated in 1901, Roosevelt succeeded him. McKinley's friend Mark Hanna lamented "now that damned cowboy is president of the United States." Roosevelt was still determined to expand America's global influence. He strongly supported the construction of the **Panama Canal**, which would provide merchant ships and American warships an easier and more rapid connection between the Atlantic and Pacific Oceans. Control of this canal would help ensure American dominance of the Western Hemisphere.

A French company had attempted to construct a canal through Panama, but failed. The United States made arrangements to buy out the French and negotiated for rights to build a canal with Colombia, which owned the Panamanian isthmus. When the Colombian Senate rejected a treaty because it felt that the United States was not offering enough money, President Roosevelt lost patience with the Colombians. In 1903, agents of the French company organized a rebellion in Panama. The United States immediately recognized the new government and stationed warships off Panama to prevent the Colombians from sending troops to crush the rebellion. The 1904 Hay-Bunau-Varilla Treaty, signed with the new Panamanian regime, gave the United States permanent sovereignty over a 10-mile-wide strip of land across the country. For this, the Panamanians received $10 million.

Construction of the canal began immediately, and it was opened for business in 1914. The Panama Canal was a technological, economic, and strategic success. This sophisticated engineering project facilitated trade, and made it much easier to shift American naval vessels between the oceans. The United States did pay a diplomatic price for this success in Latin America. The American collusion in the dismemberment of Colombia convinced many Latin Americans that the United States was a bullying power. Further actions taken by Roosevelt reinforced this view.

The Roosevelt Corollary

President Roosevelt's belief that military power was the final arbiter of international affairs was reflected in his recommendation to "speak softly and carry a big stick." In 1904, the Dominican Republic defaulted on its debts to Europeans during an economic crisis. Angry European powers threatened to collect these debts through military force. This inspired Roosevelt to declare the **Roosevelt Corollary** to the Monroe Doctrine. This asserted the right of the American government to police any country in the Western Hemisphere that acted in ways "harmful to the United States" and risked the intervention of outside powers.

In the Dominican Republic, Roosevelt took over the Dominican customs service and arranged for the orderly payment of that nation's foreign debt. In the years to come, the United States intervened in other Central American and Caribbean countries. Though this promoted the political stability the American government desired, it also intensified anti-American feelings.

President Roosevelt played an important role on the world stage. In 1905, Roosevelt mediated a peace treaty that ended the Russo-Japanese War. For this, he received the Nobel Peace Prize in 1906. Also in 1906, the United States participated in the Algeciras Conference that addressed colonial disputes between France and Germany.

William Howard Taft, Roosevelt's hand-picked successor, shied away from the "big stick" and preferred "dollars over bullets." During his administration he pursued a policy of extending American influence abroad through investment and economic engagement. Taft's critics called this financial approach to foreign relations **"Dollar Diplomacy."**

Chapter Review

Rapid Review

To achieve a perfect 5, you should be able to explain the following:

- America became the economic and imperialistic equal of the major European powers by the beginning of the twentieth century.
- The United States acquired territory in the years immediately following the Civil War, but then entered a period where little foreign expansion took place.
- Americans and natives friendly to America increased the economic and political control of Hawaii by the United States, signaling a new trend in foreign policy.
- America desired trade in China; these desires were represented in John Hay's Open Door policy.
- Economic, political, and strategic motives pushed America to pursue imperialist goals in the 1890s.
- Many in this era also opposed imperialism, often on moral or humanitarian grounds.
- The Spanish-American War allowed American imperialistic impulses to flourish; religious figures also supported imperialism in this era.
- Spanish incompetence and the strength of the American navy were important factors in the American victory in the Spanish-American War.
- America was deeply conflicted but finally decided to annex the Philippines, with three years of fighting between Americans and Filipino rebels to follow.
- The Panama Canal was built by the United States for military, strategic, and economic reasons; its construction began in 1904 and was completed in 1914.
- The Roosevelt Corollary to the Monroe Doctrine increased American control over Latin America.

Time Line

1867: United States purchases Alaska from Russia
       United States annexes Midway Islands
1871: Beginning of European "Scramble for Africa"
1875: Trade agreement between United States and Hawaii signed

1885: Publication of *Our Country* by Josiah Strong; book discusses role of Anglo-Saxons in the world

1890: Captain Alfred T. Mahan's *The Influence of Sea Power upon History* published

1893: Pro-American sugar planters overthrow Queen Liliuokalani in Hawaii

1895: Revolt against Spanish in Cuba; harsh Spanish reaction angers many in United States

1898: Explosion of U.S.S. *Maine* in Havana harbor; beginning of Spanish-American War
Annexation of Hawaii receives final approval from Congress
Anti-Imperialist League formed

1899: Secretary of State John Hay asks European leaders for an Open Door policy in China
First fighting between American army forces and Filipino rebels in Manila

1900: Naval Act of 1900 authorizes construction of offensive warships requested by navy

1901: Assassination of President McKinley; Theodore Roosevelt becomes president

1904: Roosevelt Corollary to Monroe Doctrine announced
United States begins construction of Panama Canal

1905: Roosevelt mediates conflict between Japan, and Russia in Portsmouth, New Hampshire

1914: Completion of the Panama Canal

❯ Review Questions

Multiple-Choice Questions

1. The intent of the Roosevelt Corollary to the Monroe Doctrine was
   A. to prevent European powers from becoming directly involved in affairs of the Western Hemisphere.
   B. to allow the United States to "assist" countries in the area that demonstrated economic or political instability.
   C. to allow the United States to remove "unfriendly governments" in the Western Hemisphere.
   D. all of the above.

2. Many humanitarians in the United States initially supported the Spanish-American War because
   A. they were appalled at the Spanish policy of reconcentration in Cuba.
   B. they were able to ignore editorial comments found in most American newspapers.
   C. they desired to assist the Filipino natives.
   D. of American economic interests in Cuba.

3. The major criticism that some Americans had concerning the construction of the Panama Canal was that
   A. the canal would force America to have a navy in both the Pacific and the Atlantic.
   B. the canal would be outlandishly expensive to build.
   C. the tactics that the Americans used to get the rights to build the canal were unsavory at best.
   D. American forces would have to be stationed indefinitely in Panama to guard the canal.

4. The United States was able to annex Hawaii because
   A. Queen Liliuokalani desired increased American investment in Hawaii.
   B. pro-American planters engineered a revolt in Hawaii.
   C. public opinion in Hawaii strongly favored annexation.
   D. Hawaii felt threatened by other Pacific powers.

5. American missionary leaders supported imperialism in this era because
   A. they thought their involvement would temper the excess zeal of other imperialists.
   B. they admired the "pureness of spirit" found in the Filipinos and other native groups.
   C. religious leaders in Europe favored imperialism.
   D. they saw imperialism as an opportunity to convert the "heathens" of newly acquired territories.

Short-Answer Question

6. Answer Parts A, B, and C.
   A. Briefly explain ONE example of the United States asserting itself as a world power in the period 1890 to 1913.
   B. Briefly explain a SECOND example of the United States asserting itself as a world power in the period 1890 to 1913.
   C. Briefly explain ONE example of Americans rejecting the assertion of the United States as a world power in the period 1890 to 1913.

› Answers and Explanations

1. **D.** The Roosevelt Corollary allowed the United States to intervene in affairs of Latin American countries under several circumstances, but was also intended to keep the European powers out of Latin America.

2. **A.** The Spanish policy of placing civilians in camps horrified many Americans. Most American newspapers initially supported the war as well. Concern for the Filipinos only became an issue during the debate over whether or not the United States should annex the Philippines.

3. **C.** The United States acquired the rights to build the canal through the encouragement of a "revolt" by Panamanians against Colombia. The American navy wanted the canal.

4. **B.** The United States was able to annex Hawaii after pro-U.S. planters led a rebellion against Queen Liliuokalani, who had opposed U.S. influence.

5. **D.** Missionary leaders worked in conjunction with other imperialists in this era. Little admiration of the natives was demonstrated by missionary leaders; the possibility of conversions was the major reason for religious support for imperialism.

6. **Parts A and B**: In 1893, American sugar planters with the help of local U.S. officials overthrew the queen of Hawaii and declared the islands a republic. The United States officially annexed Hawaii in 1898. After a rebellion against Spanish rule in Cuba broke out in 1895, the American public grew increasingly sympathetic to the Cubans because of an exaggerated press campaign by "yellow journalists." The unexplained explosion of the USS *Maine* in Havana harbor intensified calls for war. The United States declared war on Spain in April 1898. In the brief Spanish-American War that ensued, the United States drove Spain out of Cuba and annexed Puerto Rico, Guam, and the Philippines. From 1899 to 1902, the United States fought a successful war to suppress a Filipino insurrection against American rule. In 1899, the U.S. secretary of state, John Hay, circulated an Open Door Note amongst the great powers calling for all countries to have equal access to Chinese markets. In 1900, American forces joined an international army in crushing the Boxer Rebellion, an anti-foreigner uprising in China. President Theodore Roosevelt supported a revolution that separated Panama from Colombia in 1904. That same year the United States signed the Hay-Bunau-Varilla Treaty with Panama, making possible the construction of the Panama Canal. Also in 1904, Roosevelt issued his Roosevelt Corollary to the Monroe Doctrine, stating that the United States had the right to intervene in Latin American countries if their actions threatened to precipitate European interventions in the Western Hemisphere. President William Howard Taft promoted "Dollar Diplomacy," which promoted American economic investment as a way of encouraging stability in foreign countries.

Part C: Following the overthrow of the Queen of Hawaii in 1893, President Grover Cleveland refused to annex the Hawaiian Islands because he believed that most Hawaiians still supported the monarchy. Many Americans opposed the annexation of the Philippines as a colony following the Spanish-American War. An Anti-Imperialist League was formed in 1898. Andrew Carnegie and Mark Twain were prominent anti-imperialists. After being re-nominated as a candidate for the presidency by the Democratic party in 1900, William Jennings Bryan made anti-imperialism a central part of his platform during the presidential campaign.

CHAPTER 20

Progressive Era (1895–1914)

IN THIS CHAPTER

Summary: Progressivism began in the 1890s as a movement that attacked the political, social, and political inequalities of the age. Many Progressives blamed capitalism for the evils of society. However, unlike the Socialists, who wanted to destroy the capitalist system, the Progressives wanted to fix that system. Many Progressives were tied to the Social Gospel movement of the Protestant church; others wanted to reform city governments, while still others desired to instill even more democracy in the electoral process (direct primaries, more use of the referendum, etc.). Many Progressives launched projects to aid the immigrant population that existed in America's cities. One example was Hull House, a settlement house that aided Chicago's poor. The high point of the Progressive movement was the "Square Deal" of the presidency of Theodore Roosevelt. Progressives did much to reform America's cities but were less effective in aiding America's farmers and minorities.

Keywords

Social Gospel movement: movement originating in the Protestant church that aimed to help the urban poor; many Progressives were influenced by this movement.

Muckrakers: writers who exposed unethical practices in both government and business during this era; newspaper editors discovered that these types of stories increased circulation.

Seventeenth Amendment (1913): U.S. Constitutional amendment that allowed voters instead of state legislatures to elect U.S. senators; this amendment had been championed by Progressives.

Initiative process: this Progressive-supported process allowed any citizen to propose a law. If enough supporters' signatures could be procured, the proposed law would appear on the next ballot.

Referendum process: this process allowed citizens (instead of legislatures) to vote on proposed laws.

Recall process: this process allowed voters to remove an elected official from office before his or her term expired.

Direct primary: this process allowed party members to vote for prospective candidates; previously most had been chosen by party bosses.

Hull House: Settlement house in Chicago founded by Jane Addams; Hull House became a model for settlement houses around the country.

National American Woman Suffrage Association: created in 1890 by a merger of two womens' suffrage organizations and led in its early years by Elizabeth Cady Stanton and Susan B. Anthony; was instrumental in demanding women's right to vote.

Triangle Shirtwaist Fire (1911): fire in New York City that killed 146 female factory workers. It was later found that the workers had been locked in the factory; as a result, many factory reforms were enacted.

The Jungle: Novel written by Upton Sinclair that highlighted numerous problems of the meatpacking industry and inspired the Pure Food and Drug Act and the Meat Inspection Act.

Roots of Progressivism

Progressivism was a complicated social and political phenomenon. There never was a unified Progressive movement. Progressives could be found in both major parties, and in both urban and rural settings; they often disagreed on the role of government and on the ideal size of American businesses. What all Progressives shared was a desire for reform.

Progressivism was rooted in many late-nineteenth century ideas and social causes. Many Progressives were influenced by books such as Henry George's *Progress and Poverty* (1879) and Edward Bellamy's *Looking Backward* (1888). **Taylorism** and the ideal of a "scientific" approach to work and social organization inspired some Progressives.

Progressives joined with Socialists in criticizing the excesses of big business. This did not mean that all Progressives wanted to overthrow the capitalist system as the Socialists did. Most Progressives believed in the economic benefits of capitalism; they intended to reform and regulate business and the markets to prevent the wealthy from abusing their power. Some Socialists played important roles in the Progressive movement. Upton Sinclair, the author of *The Jungle* (1906), believed that Progressive reforms could lay the foundation for a democratic socialism.

Many Progressives were influenced by religious convictions. The **Social Gospel movement** reflected a growing desire amongst some liberal Protestants to apply Christian principles in the quest for social justice. These church-based reformers worked to improve conditions for the working class poor. Proponents of the Social Gospel sometimes came into conflict with their coreligionists because they emphasized political and economic reforms over efforts to achieve personal salvation. Jane Addams was a reformer whose Progressivism was driven by her religious beliefs.

Progressivism derived much of its energy from the emerging mass media. Newspapers and magazines published many investigative reports on political corruption and the iniquities of business monopolies. These articles proved very popular, boosting circulation for the publishers of these exposés and disseminating Progressive ideas to a wide public. Theodore Roosevelt thought the writers of these investigations went too far in their criticisms; he called them **muckrakers**, and the term stuck. There were many well-known muckrakers. Upton Sinclair became famous for his indictment of the meatpacking industry. Ida Tarbell wrote a critical history of Standard Oil. Lincoln Steffens denounced machine politics in *The Shame of the Cities* (1904). Jacob Riis publicized the depth of urban poverty in *How the Other Half Lives* (1890). These muckraking works became calls to action for Progressives.

Progressive Objectives

Most Progressives came from the middle class. Many came from the upper class. Because of their social background, very few Progressives wanted revolutionary changes in the United States. They wanted to reform society, not blow it up. Some Progressives such as Theodore Roosevelt saw themselves as conservatives working to head off potential uprisings by correcting abuses and improving social and political efficiency. Progressives wanted to help the lower classes, but they wanted power to remain in the hands of the middle and upper classes. This would be achieved by creating a regulatory state, with power shifting into the hands of a highly educated and professional bureaucratic elite. Increasingly, Progressives saw a powerful government as the answer to many of the challenges facing Americans.

Not everyone embraced Progressive goals. Many poor people resented the paternalistic approach of Progressive reformers and new government agencies. In the name of democracy Progressives attacked political machines and worked to weaken the power of the political parties, yet these machines and the parties had fostered a vibrant political culture; ironically the robust voter participation rates of the Gilded Age began to decline during the Progressive Era.

Because of the multifaceted complexity of the Progressive movement, it has been difficult for historians to assign an overall goal to Progressivism. Some see Progressivism as an attempt to resist the social forces transforming American life. Others see Progressivism as a means of adapting Americans to conditions in the new urban and industrialized social system.

Urban Progressivism

Progressive reforms were launched at every level of American politics. In many American cities, Progressives challenged the power of the political machines. In some cases, reform politicians built their own machines. In a few instances, traditional machines sponsored reforms to protect their power. "Reform mayors" such as Tom Johnson in Cleveland received national attention for their efforts to clean up local government and improve city services. In Cleveland, the city took over municipal utilities, believing that this would make these services more efficient. Some reform mayors established relief programs for the poor. A number of cities dispensed with politics altogether in crucial areas, replacing elected mayors with city managers and making elected utility commissioners appointed positions. By taking these offices out of political contention, Progressives reduced the power of urban politicians, but also that of the working class voters who had elected them. Almost invariably, the "professionals" who filled these ostensibly depoliticized positions came from the same middle class background as the Progressive reformers.

State-Level Progressivism

Important Progressive initiatives were launched at the state level. Progressive governors such as Robert La Follette in Wisconsin and Hiram Johnson in California sponsored measures to constrain the power of political parties and their state legislatures. Progressive political measures that were adopted in many states included the following:

1. The **initiative process**. The initiative enabled a citizen to propose a law and get it on the ballot during the next election.
2. The **referendum process**. A referendum allowed citizens to vote for the adoption of a proposed law during an election.
3. The **recall process**. The recall made it possible for voters to remove an elected official from office.
4. The **direct primary**. Traditionally party nominees had been picked at political conventions dominated by the party leadership. The direct primary allowed rank and file party members to pick a nominee through a public vote.

A national measure that diminished the influence of state legislatures was the **Seventeenth Amendment**, which was adopted in 1913. The Seventeenth Amendment changed the method of electing U.S. senators from election by state legislatures to direct election by the voters.

Progressivism and Women

Women played important roles in the Progressive movement. Women enjoyed an influence in progressive organizations that they could not have in the political parties. Florence Kelley founded the **National Consumers League**, which promoted legislation protecting women and children in both the workplace and the home. Kelley's organization, run mostly by women, was a conspicuous voice calling for laws limiting child labor and establishing minimum wages for female workers. From 1911 on, such laws began to be passed in various states.

Women were leaders in starting **settlement houses** in the slums of American cities. In 1889, Jane Addams and Ellen Gates Starr began serving the poor at **Hull House** in Chicago. Hull House became a model that was imitated in other cities. Settlement houses helped immigrants acculturate to life in the United States. They provided space for classes aimed at both children and adults. Often settlement houses ran kindergartens to prepare children for school. Settlement houses also sponsored clubs and recreational activities. Assisting poor women was a special focus with programs on child care and family health.

Progressive women did not have a single approach to helping the poor. Some focused on improving conditions for working men and women so they could better support their families. Others tackled social problems such as prostitution and alcoholism. The **Anti-Saloon League** argued that alcoholism was a major contributor to poverty as working men spent their paychecks in bars. The prohibition movement became increasingly powerful during the Progressive Era. Many women believed that economic and social issues would be better addressed if women got the vote. Beginning with Idaho, western states began giving women the vote in local elections during the Gilded Age. Colorado and Utah did so in the 1890s. In 1890, two women's suffrage organizations merged to form the **National American Woman Suffrage Association**. At first, Elizabeth Cady Stanton and Susan B. Anthony led this influential women's group. In 1916, Alice Paul founded the **National Woman's Party**, a more aggressive organization that was influence by the radical British suffragette movement. Both groups played important roles in winning the vote for women in the aftermath of World War I.

Some women went beyond advocating the vote and began discussing **feminism**, which envisioned far-reaching changes in women's lives. The term *feminism* was first used by a group of women who gathered in New York City in 1914. Feminists no longer wanted to live with the restraints society placed upon women. A reality few women could avoid in the early twentieth century was the possibility of pregnancy. Margaret Sanger, who had worked with the poor of New York City as a nurse, became a well-known advocate of birth control. She scandalized many people by attempting to make such information readily available. Sanger was an enthusiast of eugenics and believed in fewer but better babies. She also thought birth control offered women greater personal freedom.

Laws designed to protect working women were passed during the Progressive Era. The Supreme Court provided sanction for this effort in *Muller v. Oregon*. This decision ruled that it was constitutional for states to limit the number of hours women could work. This reflected contemporary ideas about women. It was thought that working too long would overtax women's limited strength. It was also believed that overlong shifts would interfere with women's most important duty as mothers.

Workplace Reform

Industrial accidents were commonplace in the early twentieth century, leading to the death or injury of many workers. The tragic **Triangle Shirtwaist Fire**, where 146 workers were killed when a fire swept through a badly maintained factory, convinced many Progressives that safety regulations were needed in the workplace. Progressives also sought accident insurance programs for workers. Between 1910 and 1917, many states passed legislation to provide relief to the families of people killed or injured in workplace or mining accidents.

Progressives and labor unions had a complicated relationship. Progressives were not wholehearted supporters of union activity; some union members worried about Progressive interference in the workplace. One Progressive initiative that the unions endorsed was restricting immigration. It is a measure of the complexity of Progressivism that many of these middle-class reformers distrusted Southern and Eastern European immigrants who were "unlike ourselves" and tended to vote for machine politicians. Union members wanted to reduce immigration because recent immigrants avoided unions; unionists also believed that the influx of large numbers of immigrants drove down wages. Progressives laid the groundwork for the immigration restrictions of the 1920s.

Theodore Roosevelt's Square Deal

Theodore Roosevelt became president because of the assassination of William McKinley in 1901. Despite his unexpected ascent to power, Roosevelt aggressively used the powers of his office. He also was a master of public relations. This, and his exuberant personality, made him a larger-than-life figure on the American scene. Unlike the chief executives of the Gilded Age, Roosevelt believed that government should take the lead in reforming society. Roosevelt's activist approach to the presidency set a new standard for the presidents who would follow him.

In 1902, Roosevelt played an unprecedented role in negotiating an agreement between mine operators and the striking United Mine Workers union. He declared that the resulting contract was a "**Square Deal**" for both management and the workers. This term was later used to describe Roosevelt's policy of using the government to protect the interests of all members of society.

Roosevelt was easily elected president in 1904, defeating the Democratic candidate Judge Alton B. Parker. He used his victory as a mandate to press for Progressive legislation in Congress. 1906 was an active legislative year for him. The Hepburn Act strengthened the **Interstate Commerce Act**, giving the Interstate Commerce Commission more authority to regulate railroads. The **Pure Food and Drug Act** and the **Meat Inspection Act** gave the government power to regulate food products and medicine and addressed concerns raised by Upton Sinclair's *The Jungle*.

President Roosevelt reinvigorated the **Sherman Antitrust Act**. Though passed in 1890, little had been done to use the law to break up illegal **trusts** or monopolistic **holding companies**. Concern about the burgeoning power of big business was a driving force in the Progressive movement. Roosevelt decided to demonstrate that the people, through their government, still wielded final authority in the land. He ordered the Justice Department to use the Sherman Antitrust Act to sue for the breakup of the Northern Securities Company, a holding company that controlled most of the railroads in the northwest. The Supreme Court eventually upheld the Justice Department's suit. Roosevelt had the Justice Department sue to break up 45 corporations, including Standard Oil, and the American Tobacco Company. Roosevelt acquired the reputation of a "trustbuster," but, in fact, he was not anti-big-business. Roosevelt applied the Sherman Antitrust Act to corporations that he believed had used their size and power to exploit consumers.

Roosevelt made conservation of the nation's resources a major Progressive cause. An avid hunter and outdoorsman, as well as a gifted naturalist, he set aside 200 million acres of land for national forests and increased the national park system. In 1905, he established the **U.S. Forest Service** to protect the nation's woodlands.

Taft and Progressivism

William Howard Taft was Theodore Roosevelt's chosen successor. Originally a judge, he was Roosevelt's friend and a member of his cabinet. In 1908, Taft defeated William Jennings Bryan, running for the third time as the Democratic presidential candidate. Taft attempted to follow in Roosevelt's Progressive footsteps, in some ways even going beyond his mentor. Taft was a far more aggressive trustbuster than Roosevelt; in four years he brought suit against 95 corporations.

Unfortunately, Taft lacked Roosevelt's political and public relations skills. He also was much more deferential to Congress. This led him to support the Payne-Aldrich Tariff of 1909, which angered many Progressives because it kept tariffs unnecessarily high on many products, which hurt consumers. Taft found it impossible to reconcile the conservative and Progressive wings of the Republican party. Taft also ran afoul of Progressives in the **Ballinger-Pinchot Affair**. Richard A. Ballinger was Taft's secretary of the interior. He allowed businesses to purchase a million acres of public land in Alaska. This enraged

Gifford Pinchot, the head of the Forest Service. He publically accused Ballinger of corruption. Taft investigated and fired Pinchot. This episode began to alienate Taft from many Progressives who accepted Pinchot's allegations that Taft was undermining conservation. Pinchot, a good friend of Roosevelt's, complained about his treatment to the former president. Relations between Taft and Roosevelt began to cool.

By 1910, Taft was relying for support on the Republican "Old Guard." He opposed some of his Progressive critics in the 1910 primaries. Theodore Roosevelt was back in the United States after a much-publicized safari in Africa. He vigorously campaigned for some of the Progressives that Taft opposed. As he barnstormed across the country, Roosevelt proposed an ambitious series of reforms to protect workers and consumers that would be implemented by a bigger and stronger federal government. Roosevelt called his plan the **New Nationalism**. Progressive candidates made gains in the 1910 elections, reflecting a reformist mood in the country. This paved the way for the passage of the **Sixteenth Amendment**, which gave the federal government the power to collect income taxes. President Taft and a broad cross-section of the public supported this as a way to collect revenue and balance the fiscal cost of lowering tariffs. Initially it was thought that only the wealthy would pay an income tax. This amendment proved consequential for the future because it gave Congress the means to pay for expanded government and more government programs.

The Election of 1912

Many factors contributed to the breakdown of relations between President Taft and Theodore Roosevelt. Taft's decision to launch an antitrust suit against U.S. Steel over an acquisition that Roosevelt had approved in 1907 deeply angered the former president because it made it look as if he had colluded in an illegal action. Roosevelt also was frustrated on the political sidelines and wanted to be president again. He threw his "hat into the ring" in 1912. In the race for the Republican presidential nomination, Roosevelt won most of the primaries in states where these were held, but Taft controlled the party machinery and was supported by most of the delegates from nonprimary states. This allowed Taft to edge Roosevelt out for the Republican nomination.

Roosevelt believed that he had been robbed; his delegates withdrew from the Republican convention. Roosevelt and his supporters formed the Progressive party, popularly known as the **Bull Moose party**. The Progressives nominated Roosevelt for president and California governor Hiram Johnson for vice president. The new party called for the eight-hour day, women's suffrage, and the end of child labor. Many women were Bull Moose activists. The Progressives shied away from championing the cause of African Americans because Roosevelt hoped to win Southern support for the party.

The split in the Republican party was an electoral gift to the Democrats. Taking advantage of this opportunity, the Democrats turned to a fresh face and nominated Woodrow Wilson, a first-term governor of New Jersey. Wilson was a Progressive who had sponsored many reforms in his two years as governor. Wilson proposed the **New Freedom policy**, which reflected what had long been a traditional Democratic suspicion of a powerful federal government. Wilson was more hostile to the bigness of business than Roosevelt. Instead of government regulating business, he called for the dismantling of monopolistic corporations. With Taft and Roosevelt dividing the once-ascendant GOP, Wilson easily won the election, even though he won only 42 percent of the popular vote. Roosevelt came in second with 27 percent, and Taft received 23 percent. Eugene Debs, running as the head of the Socialist party, won 6 percent of the popular vote. Given the records of the candidates, 1912 was the electoral high-water mark of the Progressive Era.

Wilson and Progressivism

President Wilson immediately set to work to enact the New Freedom into legislation. He was just as much an activist president as Roosevelt and devoted much effort to marshalling his allies in Congress. The Underwood Tariff Act of 1913 imposed the greatest tariff reductions since the Civil War; the resulting loss of revenue was compensated for by the new income tax. The **Clayton Antitrust Act** of 1914 extended the prohibitions of the Sherman Antitrust Act by outlawing price discrimination and a list of other corporate abuses. The Clayton Act was a great victory for organized labor because it legalized strikes. In office, Wilson began to move from the New Freedom toward the New Nationalism. He decided to pursue a regulatory approach to government dealings with big business. The legislative manifestation of this new perspective was the Federal Trade Commission Act of 1914, which created the **Federal Trade Commission (FTC)**. The FTC was a bipartisan agency that regulated business activity by working closely with companies to help them avoid illegal activities. This began a relationship between business and government that would grow closer during the twentieth and twenty-first centuries. Wilson also addressed the perpetual problem of currency supply and financial panics with the Federal Reserve Act of 1913, which created the **Federal Reserve System**. This set up a system of twelve regional banks that could lend money to commercial banks in their districts. A Federal Reserve Board in Washington oversaw the system and controlled the issuing of a new form of paper money, the Federal Reserve notes that we use today. The authors of the Federal Reserve Act hoped that it would strengthen the American economy by establishing a decentralized support system for banks and by providing the country with a stable, yet flexible, currency.

Assessing Progressivism

Progressives could point to many achievements. On all levels of government a flood of legislation attempted to improve the efficiency of government and improve conditions for the disadvantaged. In the name of democracy, the Progressives attacked political machines and weakened political parties, though at the cost of shifting a growing amount of power to unelected bureaucrats and administrators. The enforcement of antitrust laws against some corporations had the important symbolic effect of affirming the people's authority to regulate big business. Progressivism ended the unfettered laissez faire of the Gilded Age.

Progressives were primarily interested in urban issues; they did little to address the problems of the rural poor. Predominantly members of the middle class, most Progressives were uninterested in aggressively championing social equality. Many distrusted recent immigrants. Few wanted to assist African Americans. Theodore Roosevelt invited Booker T. Washington to a meal at the White House, but received so much criticism from Southerners over this that he never did so again. Woodrow Wilson was born in the South. When he and the Democrats took over the executive branch in 1913, Wilson allowed members of his cabinet to resegregate the workers in their departments. D. W. Griffith's 1915 film ***Birth of a Nation*** was an epic tale of the Civil War and Reconstruction. Technically and artistically a landmark in the history of film, Griffith's movie reflected a Southern view of Reconstruction that had become dominant among historians, and celebrated the Ku Klux Klan's suppression of the freedmen. Woodrow Wilson had written a history that was referenced in the film, and he said that its portrayal of Reconstruction was "truthful." The Progressive movement did not promote progress for African Americans. As a result, African Americans organized to help themselves. In 1909, a group of African American and white reformers founded the **National Association for the Advancement of Colored People (NAACP)** to combat racism and advocate equal rights for all.

American intervention in World War I marked the beginning of the end of the Progressive Era. Supporters of reforms such as women's suffrage and prohibition would achieve important victories during the war. But the war would turn the attention of many leaders to foreign affairs. The way the government conducted the war would exhaust many people's patience for reform and government activism.

Chapter Review

Rapid Review

To achieve the perfect 5, you should be able to explain the following:

- Political, economic, and social inequities and problems existed in America in the late 1890s, and the Progressive movement developed to attempt to address some of those problems.
- The Progressive movement did not have a unifying set of goals or leaders.
- Progressives shared some of the same critiques of American society as the Socialists, but wished to reform and not attack the American system.
- Progressive reformers were closely tied to the Social Gospel movement of the Protestant church; progressivism and religious fervor often marched hand in hand.
- Muckraking magazines and newspapers of the era often created and published the Progressive agenda.
- Many Progressives were determined to reform city government and the services provided by city government.
- Progressive political reforms included the initiative, the referendum, and the recall processes, and the direct primary.
- Hull House was an example of a settlement house copied by reformers across the country.
- The presidency of Theodore Roosevelt was a high point of progressivism; Roosevelt's "Square Deal" included many progressive measures.
- Progressive policies were sometimes challenged by Roosevelt's successor, William Howard Taft; the advent of World War I blunted the Progressive reform impulse for many.
- Progressivism succeeded in achieving some of its goals but fell short in aiding farmers and minorities in America.

Time Line

1879: *Progress and Poverty* by Henry George published
1888: *Looking Backward* by Edward Bellamy published
1889: Formation of National Consumers League
1890: National American Woman Suffrage Association founded
1901: Theodore Roosevelt becomes president after the assassination of William McKinley
Progressive Robert La Follette elected as governor of Wisconsin
Progressive Tom Johnson elected as mayor of Cleveland, Ohio
1903: Founding of Women's Trade Union League
1904: *The Shame of the Cities* by Lincoln Steffens published

1905: IWW (Industrial Workers of the World) established
　　　Establishment of U.S. Forest Service
1906: *The Jungle* by Upton Sinclair published
　　　Meat Inspection Act enacted
　　　Pure Food and Drug Act enacted
1908: William Howard Taft elected president
1909: Foundation of the NAACP
1910: Ballinger-Pinchot controversy
1911: Triangle Shirtwaist Company fire
1912: Progressive party (Bull Moose party) founded by Theodore Roosevelt
　　　Woodrow Wilson elected president
　　　Establishment of Industrial Relations Committee
1913: Establishment of Federal Reserve System
　　　Ratification of Sixteenth Amendment, authorizing federal income tax
　　　Ratification of Seventeenth Amendment, authorizing direct election of senators
1914: Clayton Antitrust Act ratified
　　　Outbreak of World War I in Europe
1915: First showing of D. W. Griffith's film *Birth of a Nation*

❯ Review Questions

Multiple-Choice Questions

1. Successful reforms initiated by the Progressives included all but which of the following:
   A. Governments became more efficient in American cities such as Cleveland.
   B. Health and safety conditions improved in some large factories.
   C. The conditions of migrant farmers improved to some degree.
   D. The federal government began to collect a national income tax.

2. Theodore Roosevelt ran for president in 1912 because
   A. the policies of William Howard Taft's administration were almost exclusively antiprogressive.
   B. he desired to split the Republican party and give the election to the Democrats.
   C. he was appalled by the results of the Ballinger-Pinchot Affair.
   D. of the Taft administration's decision to apply the Sherman Antitrust Act to United States Steel.

3. American blacks were discouraged by their lack of racial progress during the Wilson administration. Which of the following is *not* true?
   A. The film *Birth of a Nation* presented a positive view of blacks in Reconstruction states after the Civil War.
   B. Black and Progressive leaders forged tight political bonds during the Wilson administration and battled for many of the same causes.
   C. Booker T. Washington and Theodore Roosevelt developed close political ties after their two meetings together.
   D. All of the above.

4. Many Progressives agreed with Socialists that
   A. capitalism had created massive inequality in America.
   B. the American factory system had to be fundamentally altered.
   C. labor unions were inherently evil.
   D. revolutionary tactics were needed to reform the economic and social systems.

5. Which of the following was *least* likely to be a Progressive in this era?
   A. A member of the Protestant Social Gospel movement
   B. A large stockholder in United States Steel
   C. A follower of Eugene Debs
   D. A member of the Bull Moose party

Short-Answer Question

6. Answer Parts A, B, and C.
   A. Briefly explain ONE example of Progressive actions aimed at reforming the American economy.
   B. Briefly explain a SECOND example of Progressive actions aimed at reforming the American economy.
   C. Briefly explain ONE example of Progressive actions aimed at reforming American politics.

› Answers and Explanations

1. **C**. Progressives did much less for workers in the agricultural sector than they did for factory workers.

2. **D**. The Taft administration enacted many important progressive measures. Roosevelt considered the actions against United States Steel to be a personal affront to him.

3. **D**. D. W. Griffith's film presented a very negative view of blacks during Reconstruction. Progressives and black leaders never worked closely together. Theodore Roosevelt met twice with Booker T. Washington but did little to help the conditions of blacks.

4. **A**. Progressives and Socialists were both critical of the effects of capitalism in the United States. Progressives, however, were intent on reforming that system.

5. **B**. Progressives were insistent that corporations like United States Steel be made to reform. Members of the Social Gospel movement and Socialist followers of Eugene Debs shared goals with the Progressives.

6. **Parts A and B**: Progressive mayors like Tom Johnson in Cleveland took over utilities in an attempt to provide better service to their constituents. Progressive governors like Robert La Follette in Wisconsin worked to regulate railroads and other businesses. President Theodore Roosevelt intervened to mediate the 1902 coal strike. That same year, Roosevelt also directed the Justice Department to launch an antitrust suit against the Northern Securities Company, a large railroad corporation. Roosevelt would follow this up with more "trust-busting" suits. The Elkins Act of 1903 and Hepburn Act of 1906 strengthened the Interstate Commerce Commission. The Pure Food and Drug and Meat Inspection Acts of 1906 provided for federal regulation of food and medicines. The Sixteenth Amendment, adopted in 1913, allowed Congress to levy income taxes. In 1913, President Woodrow Wilson signed into law the Federal Reserve System, which created the modern American central banking system. He also promoted the Clayton Antitrust Act of 1914, which was intended to strengthen antitrust laws. The Federal Trade Commission Act of 1914 created a new federal agency to regulate business and trade practices.

Part C: In an effort to combat political corruption and inefficiency, many cities replaced elected mayors with appointed city managers. Other Progressive reforms on the local and state level included the initiative, which allowed citizens to propose laws, the referendum, which allowed citizens to vote on proposed laws, the recall, which allowed citizens to remove elected officials, and the direct primary, which allowed party members rather than bosses to pick political candidate. The seventeenth Amendment, adopted in 1913, provided for the direct election of U.S. senators.

CHAPTER 21

United States and World War I (1914–1921)

IN THIS CHAPTER

Summary: The United States was officially neutral in the first two years of World War I. In 1916, one of President Woodrow Wilson's campaign slogans was "he kept us out of war." However, America was soon drawn into this conflict on the side of the British and French against the Germans (and the Austro-Hungarians). The 1915 sinking of the British passenger ship the *Lusitania* infuriated many Americans, as did the publication of the Zimmerman Note, in which Germany tried to entice Mexico to go to war against the United States. In January 1917, Germany announced a policy of unrestricted submarine warfare, and several American ships were sunk. These events caused President Wilson to call for a declaration of war against Germany. American entry into the war was a tremendous psychological lift for the British and the French. On the American home front, the government imposed unprecedented controls on the economy and on the spreading of news. The war ended with an armistice in November 1918. At the subsequent Paris Peace Conference, Wilson attempted to convince the Allies to accept his peace plan, called the "Fourteen Points." Britain and France were generally not enthusiastic about Wilson's proposals, but they did support the creation of a League of Nations. However, the League was opposed by isolationist members of the U.S. Senate, and the United States never became a member of the League. Instead, U.S. foreign policy became isolationist and remained largely so through the 1930s.

Keywords

American Expeditionary Force: American force of 14,500 men that landed in France in June 1917 under the command of General John J. Pershing. Both women and blacks served in the American army during the war, although black units were segregated and usually had white officers.

War Industries Board: board that regulated American industry during World War I; it attempted to stimulate war production by allocating raw materials to factories that aided the war effort.

Committee on Public Information: agency created during the war whose mission was to spread pro-Allied propaganda through the press and through newsreels; newspapers were asked to print only articles that were helpful to the war effort.

Fourteen Points: plan for the postwar world that Woodrow Wilson brought to the Paris Peace Conference; Wilson's plan proposed open peace treaties, freedom of the seas, arms reductions, and a League of Nations. Britain and France were openly suspicious of these plans, but they supported the creation of a League of Nations.

League of Nations: world body proposed by Woodrow Wilson as part of his 14-point peace plan. The League was created but without the participation of Germany, the Soviet Union, and the United States (isolationists in the Senate ensured that the treaty creating the League was never signed). As a result, the League remained a relatively ineffective body throughout its existence.

War and American Neutrality

Although few expected war in Europe in the summer of 1914, conditions were ripe for an explosion of violence. The growth of aggressive nationalisms set various countries against each other and threatened the stability of multinational states like the Austro-Hungarian Empire. Competition over colonial possessions and conflicts over spheres of influence in places like the Balkans further complicated relations between the great European powers. Most dangerous of all, the most important European states were grouped into two alliance systems. This meant that a conflict between two countries would likely entangle their allies and lead to a European-wide war. The assassination of the Austrian Archduke Franz Ferdinand by Serbian terrorists on June 28, 1914, sparked a diplomatic chain reaction that in August resulted in a war involving most of the European powers. Great Britain, France, and Russia comprised the Triple Entente, or **Allied Powers**, and Germany and Austria-Hungary made up the **Central Powers**. Turkey later joined the Central Powers, and Italy later became one of the Allied Powers.

Great numbers of Americans had emotional ties to the warring powers. In 1914, over one-third of the American population were first- or second-generation immigrants. Many Americans felt an affinity for Great Britain because of long-standing cultural connections. Most German-Americans sympathized with their former fatherland.

President Wilson deeply admired the British and their political system, and distrusted German militarism. Despite this, he officially proclaimed American neutrality on August 4, 1914. Whatever their individual sympathies, Americans overwhelmingly wanted to stay out of the war. Americans also wanted to maintain their trade relationships with both warring parties. The war consumed enormous amounts of resources, and the United States became a desirable source of raw materials and manufactured goods. European war orders helped pull the United States out of a recession that began in 1913. In the competition for American trade, Great Britain and France had the advantage, because their navies controlled the Atlantic. The British used their naval power to prevent American ships from carrying goods to Germany. The Germans retaliated by using a new weapon, the submarine, to sink Allied ships carrying American goods to Britain and France.

Growing Ties to the Allies

Increasing economic ties drew the United States closer to the Allies. By 1916, almost all trade with the Central Powers had ceased, while trade with the Allies had gone up 400 percent. When the Allies ran out of cash in 1915, the Wilson administration allowed Wall Street banks to lend the Allies the money they needed to continue purchasing American products. This meant that many in the United States were literally banking upon an Allied victory. Some interest groups called on the federal government to prepare for war with the Central Powers. Beginning in late 1914, the **National Security League** launched an information campaign to convince Americans that war was necessary. By 1915, Congress began to take steps to strengthen the army and navy. Countering this, organizations promoting peace sprang up across the United States. Many of these were headed by women.

What decisively turned the American people against the Central Powers was German submarine warfare. Given that Allied warships dominated the surface of the sea, the only way that the Germans could strike at ships carrying supplies to Britain and France was with undersea or U-boats. Initially U-boats followed international law and warned ships before sinking them. Then the Allies armed their merchant ships with guns that could sink the unarmored submarines. From that point on, U-boats torpedoed ships without warning; this inevitably led to loss of life among the crew and passengers. Unsympathetic to the difficulties facing submariners, Americans found this form of warfare barbarous, and many began referring to Germans as the **"Hun."**

American opposition to the German submarine campaign came to a head with the sinking of the *Lusitania* on May 7, 1915. The *Lusitania* was a passenger liner that carried munitions as well as people. The Germans had printed notices warning passengers against traveling on the ship. None of this mattered to American public opinion; Americans were horrified by the shocking casualties, with almost 1,200 men, women, and children dead, including 128 Americans. President Wilson lodged a strong diplomatic condemnation of the sinking, but resisted calls for war.

In August, the Germans struck again at a passenger liner, sinking the *Arabic*. President Wilson strongly protested this attack. Anxious to placate the Americans, the German government announced that their submariners would not sink passenger ships without warning if they were allowed to search these vessels for military contraband.

Relations between the United States and Germany continued to deteriorate. On March 24, 1916, a U-boat sank the *Sussex*, a French ship carrying passengers and supplies. Among the injured were seven Americans. President Wilson sent an ultimatum to the Germans declaring that the United States would sever diplomatic relations if they persisted in attacking nonmilitary ships. The German government was anxious to avoid a possible American entrance into the war. The Germans backed down and subscribed to the **Sussex Pledge**, declaring that they would not sink any more ships without warning. This was a perilous diplomatic victory for Wilson; if the Germans resumed full submarine warfare, he would have few options other than war.

The Breakdown of German-American Relations

For a time it looked as if President Wilson had secured peace. In the election of 1916, he ran as the peace candidate, and the Democrats popularized the slogan "He kept us out of war." This enabled Wilson to win a narrow reelection victory over the reunited Republicans and their candidate, former New York governor and Supreme Court Justice Charles Evans Hughes.

Ironically, Wilson would take the country to war soon after his second inauguration. The war in Europe was a bloody stalemate. In an effort to achieve victory, the Germans announced **unrestricted submarine warfare** on January 31, 1917. From that point on, they would sink any ship carrying supplies to the Allies. Neutral flags would be no protection. The Germans realized that this would likely lead to war with the United States. They calculated that they could starve Britain and France into submission before the Americans could intervene effectively. Wilson ended diplomatic relations with Germany on February 3. He urged Congress to legalize the arming of merchant ships. As war loomed between Germany and the United States, Arthur Zimmermann, the German foreign minister foolishly sent an inflammatory diplomatic note to the Mexican government. In the event of a German-American war, he encouraged the Mexicans to attack the United States and promised German support for a Mexican reconquest of the American Southwest. British intelligence intercepted the **Zimmermann Telegram** and passed it on to the Americans. Publication of the Zimmermann Telegram infuriated Americans and helped prepare them for war.

As they had promised, the Germans began sinking American ships headed to Britain and France. This violated the traditional American conviction that neutrals should have the freedom of the seas to sail wherever they wanted. On April 2, President Wilson made the short trip to Capitol Hill and in person asked Congress to declare war against Germany. The following day, Congress acceded to Wilson's request and voted for war. Though the overwhelming majority in Congress supported the war, six senators and 50 representatives voted against intervening in the conflict. Wilson had tried to preserve American neutrality, though by the time the United States entered the war it was effectively a supply depot for the Allies. The German submarine campaign proved unacceptable to many Americans; given the German conviction that it was essential for victory, war was hard to avoid. Once the United States became a combatant, Wilson looked forward to playing a major role in shaping the eventual peace.

America in the War

The war was not going well for the Allies in early 1917. Russia had been unable to effectively wage modern war. After a long series of defeats and growing domestic chaos, the tsar was overthrown in March 1917. The liberal government that succeeded the tsar hoped to stay in the war and sustain a relationship with the western Allies. The crumbling of Russian armies as soldiers deserted and went home put this in doubt. It appeared that the Germans might be able to transfer large numbers of troops from Russian to the western front. The British and French were strained to their limits. After a disastrous offensive that ended in bloody failure, large numbers of disgusted French soldiers mutinied, decrying callous leadership and calling for better treatment.

President Wilson decided to send American troops to fight in Europe. Their commander would be General John J. Pershing. The first contingent of the **American Expeditionary**

Force (AEF) arrived in France in June. Though numbering only 14,500 men, a paltry figure by World War I standards, this first detachment of the AEF helped revive Allied morale. In this handful of "doughboys" lay the promise of many more American soldiers to come.

One reason Pershing initially led so few men to France was the small size of the American army. To fight a modern total war, the American armed services would have to be massively increased. The most efficient way to do this was through a draft. Congress passed a Selective Service Act in May. All men between the ages of 21 and 30 could be drafted; the age limits were later extended to 17 and 46. Eventually 400,000 African Americans served in the military, though in segregated units with mostly white officers. 11,500 women wore a uniform; most served as nurses and office staff.

The U.S. Navy was better prepared to take immediate action than the army. In the Atlantic, German U-boats were sinking enough ships to cause the Allies real hardship. The Americans navy took a leading role in organizing a **convoy system** in May 1917. Ships traveling in convoys protected by the navy were much more secure from submarine attack. Only two American troop transports were sunk during the war. A combination of convoys and better patrolling greatly reduced shipping losses. By the end of the war, the German submarines had failed in their strategic mission.

The American Expeditionary Force in France

Thanks to volunteers and the draft, the size of the American army increased to 4 million men by the end of the war; 2 million of these men were in France. They were needed. The Bolshevik Revolution in November 1917 ended Russian participation in the war. The Germans were able to transfer large numbers of soldiers to France. Beginning in March 1918, they launched a series of offensives that battered the Allied lines; by June the Germans were 50 miles from Paris.

American troops played an important role in stopping the Germans. At the **Battle of Chateau-Thierry**, Americans blunted the German drive on Paris. The AEF launched a successful offensive of its own in September and erased a German salient at St. Mihiel. In late September, the Americans began the **Meuse-Argonne Offensive**, which lasted into November. This massive offensive involved a million American soldiers, cut a vital German supply line, and helped convince the enemy that they had lost the war.

The Germans signed an armistice that ended the fighting on November 11, 1918. Around 115,000 Americans died in the war; roughly half of these lost their lives in battle, and the rest perished of disease, including the great flu epidemic of 1918. These losses were light compared to the 8 million European dead. Americans who returned home as heroes included Eddie Rickenbacker, the leading American flying ace, and Alvin York, who during the Meuse-Argonne fighting killed 25 German soldiers and captured 132 more.

The Home Front

For Americans the war was a conflict fought far away "over there." The government looked for ways to give Americans a sense of personal involvement in the war. Ordinary citizens could help finance the war by buying **Liberty Bonds**. Celebrities like the movie star Charlie Chaplin demonstrated their patriotism by promoting the purchase of these bonds.

In a vast expansion of regulatory power, the federal government took over much of the economy. The **Lever Food and Fuel Control Act**, passed in August 1917, gave the government the power to regulate the production and consumption of food. Herbert Hoover, who had become famous for feeding European refugees, headed the Food Administration. Here he worked to increase food production, and encouraged Americans to conserve food with voluntary "Wheatless Mondays" and "Meatless Tuesdays." Daylight saving time was an innovation designed to give farmers more time to bring in their crops. A Fuel Administration was charged with conserving fuel supplies. It encouraged Americans to help with this through "Fuelless Mondays" and "Gasless Sundays." The **War Industries Board (WIB)** was given the power to support war production by allocating industrial resources. Under the leadership of the Wall Street tycoon Bernard Baruch, the WIB was beginning to harness the industrial might of the nation by the end of the war. The government also controlled the railroads, allowing it to set priorities in transportation.

This unprecedented control of the economy has led some historians to see World War I as the high-water mark of **progressivism**. The wartime emergency allowed the government to exercise powers that would have been unthinkable a few years before. Thanks to the skill of administrators like Baruch and Hoover, much of this was accomplished with the cooperation of business and farm leaders. The mobilization of the economy during World War I would become a model for the later New Deal and government agencies during World War II. But such an aggrandizement of governmental power also raised concerns about freedom. This triumph of Progressivism would lead to a reaction against it.

Regulating Thought

Nothing did more to eventually discredit the extension of governmental power than efforts to regulate what people could think and express publically. In 1917, the government established the **Committee on Public Information (CPI)**. Headed by the journalist George Creel, the CPI was tasked with providing information about the war to the American people. Explanation soon became propaganda. In lectures, books, posters, and films, the Germans were depicted as bestial barbarians. Creel encouraged newspapers to censor stories that did not follow the government's line on the war. Liberty Leagues were organized across the United States; their members were tasked with spying on their neighbors, and reporting any suspicious activity or disloyal talk to the authorities.

The war led to a heightened distrust of immigrants and "hyphenated-Americans," especially German Americans. The **National Security League** persuaded Congress to impose a literacy test on immigrants. In various communities anti-German hysteria led to the banning of German music and foods, and the teaching of the German language in high schools. Individual German Americans were often subject to harassment or worse. In a notorious incident that took place in April 1918, a German-American man was mobbed and lynched in St. Louis; the victim had just enlisted in the navy.

The federal government added legal muscle to the suppression of dissent. The 1917 **Espionage Act** outlawed interfering with the draft and gave postal authorities the power to seize any publications sent through the mail that they considered treasonous. The 1918 Sedition Act went further and outlawed criticism of the government, the Constitution, or the armed forces. Thousands of Americans were charged with violating these laws, and over 1,000 were convicted. The Socialist leader Eugene Debs was sent to prison for speaking against the war. Robert Goldstein, a movie producer, was sentenced to three years in prison for making a movie about the American Revolution in which the British were portrayed as the villains; this previously unexceptionable view of the struggle for American independence was deemed seditions because the British were currently allies in the war. The government used these laws to break up radical organizations such as the IWW.

Social Change

The war opened up economic possibilities for African Americans. With millions of men entering the military and wartime demands on their capacity, northern industries needed workers. African Americans living in the South moved north in the **Great Migration**. 600,000 African Americans made this journey during the war. The war also made it possible for women to step into jobs that had not been open to them before the war. Although most would leave these positions once the soldiers began returning home, their efforts during the war would help make the case for women's suffrage.

Wilson and the Peace

President Wilson was determined to play a leading role in shaping the new postwar international order. While the war was still in progress, he published his **Fourteen Points**, an idealistic program to lay the foundations for a peaceful world, which included open diplomacy (no more secret military treaties), freedom of the seas, national self-determination, and a league of nations. Defying presidential precedent, Wilson sailed to France to take part in the Paris Peace Conference, which began on January 12, 1919. The peacemaking would be driven by the leaders of the "Big Four" allies—Britain, France, Italy, and the United States. While the ordinary people of Europe greeted Wilson as a hero for his inspiring vision of a better future, the other allied leaders were less impressed by his ideas and were determined to press their national interests. Wilson wanted a peace based on the Fourteen Points, but the French in particular were set on punishing Germany.

During the hard negotiating that took place in Paris, Wilson had to make many concessions. Harsh terms were imposed on Germany, which had to accept guilt for starting the war and pay reparations to France and Britain. Germany also lost its colonies, 10 percent of its territory, and most of its military. German diplomats were not allowed to discuss the terms of the Treaty of Versailles; they had to sign the document or face an Allied invasion. German bitterness over this treatment planted the seeds of World War II. Though disappointed by aspects of the Treaty of Versailles, Wilson believed that its establishment of a **League of Nations** would make it possible to rectify the treaty's errors in the future.

Americans and the Middle East

Aside from Theodore Roosevelt's diplomatic involvement in the 1905–1906 Moroccan crisis, the United States had shown little interest in the Middle East. Great Power rivalries during and after World War I focused American attention on the region.

Prior to the war, much of the Middle East was controlled by Turkey, or the Ottoman Empire. The Turkish empire had been declining for over a century. The leaders of the empire hoped that they could arrest this decline by entering the war on the side of the Central Powers. This proved a grave mistake. Defeat in the war brought on the final collapse of the Ottoman Empire. Since the late nineteenth century, Jews inspired by the Zionist movement had been settling in Ottoman-ruled Palestine. In 1917, in an effort to weaken the Turks, the British issued the Balfour Declaration, which expressed support for an independent Jewish state in Palestine. President Wilson also favored the creation of a Jewish state. Many American Jews provided financial assistance to the Zionists.

As the war turned against them, the Turkish authorities grew suspicious of the Armenian minority who lived within the empire. In 1915, the Turks launched a bloody pogrom against the Christian Armenians, massacring thousands and killing many more by starvation and ill-treatment. American missionaries and diplomats helped get word of these atrocities to the outside world. In 1916 and 1917, thousands of Americans rallied to protest the slaughter of the Armenians and to support Armenian relief organizations. (To this day, the Turkish government refuses to acknowledge that the Armenian massacres took place.)

President Wilson made the breakup of the Ottoman Empire American policy. (He also wanted to dismantle the German and Austro-Hungarian empires.) He called for the peoples of all the territories ruled by the Central Powers to work towards "autonomous political development." At the Paris Peace Conference, the United States was authorized to form the **King-Crane Commission** to study the political aspirations of the people living in the Middle East.

What the King-Crane Commission found was that the Middle Easterners wanted to be free from foreign control. They deeply distrusted the intentions of the British and French who had defeated the Turks. If any of the Allies were to be given a mandate to control territory in the Middle East, the people there preferred it to be the Americans, who they believed had no long-term interests in the region. The findings of the King-Crane Commission ran counter to the imperial ambitions of Britain and France. These Allied powers saw to it that the commission's report was buried. The British and French divided up most of the Middle East. The British received mandates in Palestine, Transjordan, and Iraq, and the French accepted mandates in Lebanon and Syria. By the early 1920s, only Saudi Arabia was independent.

Woodrow Wilson's Defeat

According to the Constitution, all treaties must be ratified by a two-thirds vote of the Senate. President Wilson did not appoint a senator to the delegation that he brought with him to Paris. Compounding this error, he failed to bring with him a leading Republican politician, despite the fact that the Republicans had won control of both houses of Congress in 1918. Having given the Republicans no reason to rally to his support, Wilson faced predictable opposition to the Treaty of Versailles when he returned to the United States. The most controversial element of the treaty was the League of Nations; most Republican and some Democratic senators worried that the league's collective security provisions threatened to embroil the United States in more conflicts. Twelve senators declared themselves **"irreconcilables"** and refused outright to vote for the treaty and the League. Most of the Republicans followed the lead of Henry Cabot Lodge, the chairman of the Senate Foreign Relations Committee. Lodge wanted to incorporate a series of reservations about the League into the American ratification of the treaty. As a result of this, his supporters were known as **"reservationists."** Lodge wanted to ensure that the League of Nations would not invalidate the Monroe Doctrine; he also wanted assurance that only Congress would authorize American military actions on behalf of the League.

Lodge was willing to guarantee the Senate's ratification of the treaty with his reservations. Important European leaders made it clear that they preferred the passage of the treaty with reservations to the failure of the treaty in the Senate. Despite this, Woodrow Wilson refused to compromise. The president had invested too much of himself into the struggle for the League to concede anything to his critics. Wilson's health had been failing for some time. Disregarding this, in September 1919 he set off on a strenuous speaking tour, hoping to make his case about the League to the American people. On October 2, Wilson suffered an incapacitating stroke. The president eventually made a partial recovery, but the stroke left him less willing to compromise on anything, including the League. Wilson ordered loyal Democratic senators to vote against the League with reservations. Given the equally firm positions of the reservationists and the irreconcilables, the Treaty of Versailles and the League of Nations were rejected by the Senate in successive votes in 1919 and 1920. The United States never joined the League of Nations. This gravely weakened the League, which proved ineffectual in preventing a second world war. The rejection of the League did not mean an American turn to isolationism, and the United States would play an important role in world affairs during the 1920s.

In 1921, President Wilson left office a physically broken man. That year his successor, Warren G. Harding, officially ended America's participation in World War I by signing separate peace treaties with the former member countries of the Central Powers.

Chapter Review

Rapid Review

To achieve the perfect 5, you should be able to explain the following:

- World War I greatly impacted the American mind-set and America's role in world affairs; this was the first time that America became directly involved in affairs taking place on the European continent.
- Many Americans expressed support for the Allied Powers from the beginning of the war; German U-boat attacks solidified American support for Britain and France.
- The sinking of the *Lusitania* and the Zimmermann Telegram did much to intensify American anger against Germany.
- Germany's decision to utilize unrestricted submarine warfare caused President Wilson to call for war in 1917; Wilson claimed that this policy violated America's rights as a neutral power.
- The American Expeditionary Force did much to aid the Allied war effort, both militarily and psychologically.
- The federal government did much to mobilize the American population at home for the war effort; Liberty Bonds were sold, voluntary rationing took place, and propaganda was used to encourage Americans to oppose the "Hun" however possible.
- Many blacks moved to northern cities to work in factories during World War I; this migration would continue through the 1920s.
- Woodrow Wilson's Fourteen Points met with opposition from French and English leaders at the Paris Peace Conference; many of them had to be abandoned to secure the creation of the League of Nations.
- The Treaty of Versailles was opposed by U.S. senators who felt that America should pursue an isolationist policy after the war. As a result, the treaty was never signed by the United States and the United States never joined the League of Nations.
- Many European leaders expected America to be active as a leader in world affairs after World War I. Instead, America adopted neo-isolationist policies that lasted until America entered World War II.

Time Line

1914: Outbreak of World War I in Europe

Woodrow Wilson officially proclaims American neutrality in World War I

National Security League founded to prepare America for war

1915: Sinking of the *Lusitania* by German U-boat

1916: Germany torpedoes *Sussex*, then promises to warn merchants ships if they are to be attacked

Woodrow Wilson reelected with campaign slogan of "He kept us out of war"

1917: Zimmermann Telegram

Germany declares unrestricted submarine warfare

United States enters World War I, stating that U.S. rights as a neutral had been violated

Russian Revolution; Russian-German peace talks

Conscription begins in United States

War Industries Board formed to create a war economy

Espionage Act passed

American Expeditionary Force lands in France

1918: Military success by American Expeditionary Force at Chateau-Thierry

Sedition Act passed; free speech limited (illegal to criticize government or American military forces)

Wilson announces the Fourteen Points

Armistice ends World War I (November 11)

1919: Paris Peace Conference creates Treaty of Versailles

Race riots in Chicago

Wilson suffers stroke during speaking tour promoting Treaty of Versailles

Senate rejects Treaty of Versailles; United States does not join the League of Nations

› Review Questions

Multiple-Choice Questions

1. All of the following events prepared America for war against Germany *except*
   A. the Sussex Pledge.
   B. German policy concerning use of U-boats in 1917.
   C. the sinking of the *Lusitania*.
   D. the Zimmermann Telegram.

2. The French were opposed to many of Wilson's Fourteen Points because
   A. they were fundamentally opposed to the creation of a world body such as the League of Nations.
   B. they were angry that Wilson had insisted that the Germans not take part in the creation of the treaty.
   C. French diplomats had little respect for Wilson and his American counterparts.
   D. the Fourteen Points disagreed fundamentally with what the French felt should be contained in the Treaty of Versailles.

3. After America declared war in 1917
   A. ration cards were issued to all families.
   B. camps were set up to detain "troublesome" Americans of German background.
   C. drills took place in American cities to prepare Americans for a possible attack.
   D. movie stars and other celebrities helped sell Liberty Bonds to the American public.

4. Some critics maintained that the United States had no right to be outraged over the sinking of the *Lusitania* because
   A. the *Lusitania* was carrying contraband, which meant that it could legally be sunk.
   B. the Germans had sunk passenger ships before.
   C. the Germans had placed advertisements in American newspapers warning Americans not to travel on the *Lusitania*.
   D. all of the above.

5. Many senators were opposed to American entry into the League of Nations because
   A. they feared that the United States would end up financing the organization.
   B. they feared the U.S. Army would be sent into action on "League of Nations business" without congressional authorization.
   C. American opinion polls demonstrated that the American public was almost unanimously opposed to American entry into the League.
   D. they feared that the Germans and Russians would dominate the League.

Short-Answer Question

6. Answer Parts A, B, and C.
   A. Briefly explain ONE example of the steps the American government took to mobilize the American people during World War I.
   B. Briefly explain a SECOND example of the steps the American government took to mobilize the American people during World War I.
   C. Briefly explain ONE example of a military contribution that the United States made to Allied victory in World War I.

› Answers and Explanations

1. **A**. In the Sussex Pledge, the Germans actually promised not to sink American merchant ships without warning. All of the other choices deeply angered many in America.

2. **D**. While Wilson saw the treaty as a chance to create a democratic world free of old diplomatic entanglements, the French saw it as an opportunity to punish the Germans, as much of the fighting of the war had taken place on French territory.

3. **D**. Charlie Chaplin and others appeared at rallies and urged Americans to buy Liberty Bonds. Rationing during World War I was voluntary.

4. **D**. Many maintain that the advertisements the Germans put in American newspapers were strong enough warnings that the ship was going to be sunk.

5. **B**. A major fear was that U.S. entry into the League would cause Congress to lose its right to declare war and approve American military actions. Germany and the Soviet Union were not initially members of the League of Nations.

6. **Parts A and B**: The American government helped finance the war by encouraging citizens to purchase Liberty Bonds. The Lever Food and Fuel Control Act of 1917 gave the government regulatory authority over the production and consumption of food and fuel. Herbert Hoover headed the Food Administration, which promoted "Wheatless Mondays" and "Meatless Tuesdays." A Fuel Administration instituted similar attempts at rationing coal and gasoline. The government took control of the nation's railroads during the war. The War Industries Board, headed by Wall Street financier Bernard Baruch, controlled the allocation of raw materials and set production goals in industry. The government also moved to control the flow of ideas. Newspaperman George Creel headed the Committee on Public Information (CPI), which disseminated information about the war and worked to build American support for the war effort. The CPI employed thousands of "Four Minute Men," who gave brief pro-war addresses while reels were being changed in movie theaters. The Espionage Act of 1917 prohibited interference with military recruitment or operations. The 1919 Supreme Court decision *Schenck v. United States* upheld the constitutionality of the Espionage Act. The Sedition Act of 1918 outlawed criticisms of the government, the military, and the Constitution. Hundreds of people were charged with and convicted of violations of the Espionage Act and the Sedition Act.

Part C: The U.S. Navy played an important role in defeating the German submarine campaign. In addition to providing reinforcements to the British Navy, the American began organizing a convoy system that offered better protection to merchant ships. The U.S. Navy also mined the routes the German submarines followed when leaving their home ports. Losses from submarine attacks dropped dramatically. The U.S. Army organized the American Expeditionary Force (AEF) of American troops that fought in France. General John J. Pershing was appointed the commander of the AEF. He and the first soldiers of the AEF landed in France in June 1917. The presence of the American troops bolstered Allied morale and provided important reinforcements at a time when the Allied armies were worn down from years of fighting. The AEF was eventually built up to a force of 2,000,000 men. In June and July 1918, American troops help stop German offensives at the Battles of Belleau Wood and Chateau-Thierry. American forces erased the German salient at Saint-Mihiel in September. One million American soldiers participated in the Meuse-Argonne Offensive, which lasted from September 26 to November 11, 1918. This attack cut crucial German supply lines. American forces played a vital role in defeating Imperial Germany on the Western Front.

CHAPTER 22

Beginning of Modern America: The 1920s

IN THIS CHAPTER

Summary: During the 1920s, Americans created a consumer culture in which automobiles, home appliances, and other goods were purchased at an unprecedented rate. Advertising helped to fuel this desire to purchase, and the popularity of radio and motion pictures helped to create a more uniform national culture. However, many small-town and rural Americans never felt totally comfortable with the values of the consumer-oriented, more urban "modern" America that they saw threatening their way of life. The conflict between urban and small-town American values was manifested in numerous ways: many in small-town America supported the Prohibition amendment banning alcohol, while many in America's cities tried to get around it. Many in small-town America feared immigration, while many American cities contained immigrant enclaves. Many in small-town America still opposed the teaching of evolution, while many urban newspapers mocked their views. The flapper and a more relaxed sense of morality were symbols of the Jazz Age; generally, these symbols were harder to find in small-town America. All Americans did rally around the two heroes of the age: aviator Charles Lindbergh and home run hitter Babe Ruth.

Keywords

Teapot Dome Scandal: major scandal in the scandal-ridden administration of President Warren Harding; Secretary of the Interior Albert Fall had two oil deposits put under the jurisdiction of the Department of the Interior and leased them to private companies in return for large sums of money.

Red Scare: after World War I, the fear of the spread of communism in the United States.

Palmer Raids: as part of the Red Scare, in these 1919 to 1920 raids thousands of Americans not born in the United States were arrested, and hundreds were sent back to their countries of origin. Today many view the raids as a gross violation of the constitutional rights of American citizens.

National Origins Act (1924): anti-immigration federal legislation that took the number of immigrants from each country in 1890 and stated that immigration from those countries could now be no more than 2 percent of that. In addition, immigration from Asia was halted. The act also severely limited further immigration from eastern and southern Europe.

Scopes Trial (1925): trial of teacher John Scopes of Dayton, Tennessee, for the teaching of evolution. During this trial, lawyers Clarence Darrow and William Jennings Bryan squared off on the teachings of Darwin versus the teachings of the Bible.

Jazz Age: image of the 1920s that emphasized the more relaxed social attitudes of the decade; F. Scott Fitzgerald's *The Great Gatsby* is seen by many as the novel that best depicts this view.

Flapper: "new woman" of the 1920s, who was pictured as having bobbed hair, a shorter skirt, makeup, a cigarette in her hand, and somewhat liberated sexual attitudes. Flappers would have been somewhat hard to find in small-town and rural America.

"Lost Generation": group of post–World War I writers who in their works expressed deep dissatisfaction with mainstream American culture. *A Farewell to Arms* by Ernest Hemingway is a novel that is representative of the works of these writers.

Harlem Renaissance: 1920s black literary and cultural movement that produced many works depicting the role of blacks in contemporary American society; Zora Neale Hurston and Langston Hughes were key members of this movement.

The Prosperous Twenties

Following the end of World War I, the American economy experienced some difficulties as it transitioned back from a wartime to a peacetime footing. It suffered a major downturn in 1920–1921. Then the economy took off. The 1920s were one of the most prosperous decades in American history. Not everyone shared equally in this prosperity. Many farmers did not do as well as some urban dwellers. The wealthy benefitted more than the working class. Nevertheless, a remarkably broad swathe of Americans saw their living conditions improve. A 1924 study showed that industrial workers had almost doubled their 1914 wages. Good times reduced industrial strife and the number of strikes declined. Though businessmen still generally opposed unions, many were increasingly open to heading off labor organization by providing their workers better pay and benefits.

Business, which had been demonized in the Progressive Era, was celebrated in the 1920s. American industry became an increasingly dominant force in the world economy. At the forefront of this phenomenon was the American automobile industry. Competition left Ford, General Motors, and Chrysler dominating the car-making business; between them, these three corporations controlled 85 percent of the American market. Improved assembly line techniques make affordable cars readily available. In 1925, a Ford **Model T** was rolling off the factory floor every 24 seconds.

American industrialists had embraced Frederick W. Taylor's program of "scientific management." Efficiencies in production were bringing down the costs of consumer goods. This made it possible for growing numbers of Americans to purchase radios, refrigerators, vacuum cleaners, and a range of new electric appliances. What had once been luxuries were now readily available on the "installment plan," a marketing innovation that enabled consumers to buy goods over the course of 36 to 48 monthly payments. By 1928, 65 percent of all cars were being bought this way. Eventually this marketing reliance on credit would cause problems, but these were difficult to anticipate in the boom years of the twenties.

This decade saw the exuberant dawning of the **advertising age**. The inventive promoters of Madison Avenue worked to convince consumers that the "good life" was only possible with a particular model of car or refrigerator. Advertising became a common cultural bond for all Americans, whether they lived in the city or the country. Everyone was being sold the same commercial dreams in print and radio ads.

The Republican "New Era"

The Republicans dominated the national government during the 1920s, controlling both houses of Congress and the presidency. Even the Supreme Court was headed by a Republican, Chief Justice William Howard Taft, who had served as president from 1909–1913. The Republicans of the "New Era" believed in limited government and supported free enterprise. In their hands the regulatory state became an exercise in government and business partnership. This was best exemplified by the creative statesmanship of Herbert Hoover, who as secretary of commerce under Presidents Warren G. Harding and Calvin Coolidge, helped organize a national radio system and encouraged industries to standardize parts and procedures.

Warren G. Harding as President

Warren G. Harding was not a frontrunner for the Republican presidential nomination in 1920. A U.S. senator from Ohio, he ran a clever dark horse campaign in which he attempted to make himself the second choice of most convention delegates. When the leading candidates deadlocked, he became an easy compromise choice as the nominee.

The Democrats nominated Governor James Cox as their presidential candidate. Cox's young running mate was Franklin D. Roosevelt, Woodrow Wilson's assistant secretary of the navy. Cox had to defend the Wilson administration and supported American entry into the League of Nations. Harding realized that Americans were tired of the stress and tumult associated with the war and Wilson. He waged an old-fashioned front-porch electoral campaign that evoked memories of the days of William McKinley. He promoted a traditional Republican platform of higher tariffs and lower taxes. Above all, Harding called for a "return to normalcy," a sentiment that resonated with millions of voters. On the first national election in which women could cast ballots, Harding won in a landslide, getting 61 percent of the popular vote. Harding saw his victory as a repudiation of Wilsonian idealism and the "social experiments" of Progressivism.

Harding's first order of business upon taking office was addressing the economy. He encouraged Congress to authorize a Bureau of the Budget to better manage the government's revenues and expenditures; he named Charles Dawes as the bureau's first head. Harding cut federal spending and persuaded Congress to cut taxes. Within a year, the

United States had recovered from the postwar depression. Unemployment fell from 12 percent in 1921 to a little over 3 percent for most of the decade. The economic boom economy of the twenties had been launched.

Harding wanted to surround himself with the "best minds" that he could find for his cabinet. Some of his cabinet appointees proved particularly distinguished. Former Supreme Court Justice and presidential candidate Charles Evans Hughes served as secretary of state. Hughes played a leading role in the 1921 **Washington Conference,** which was intended to head off a naval arms race. The United States invited diplomatic and military representatives from Great Britain, France, Japan, Italy, the Netherlands, Belgium, Portugal, and China to Washington. Here Hughes proposed the scrapping of many tons of battleships and a 10-year freeze on further construction of these expensive warships. The Five Power Agreement among the United States, Great Britain, Japan, France, and Italy acceded to this and set ratios for relative sizes of their navies. All the invited powers agreed to recognize Chinese sovereignty and uphold the Open Door in China. In the early 1920s, these agreements seemed to herald a period of peace and international cooperation. In the longer term, they failed to prevent the outbreak of World War II. Another notable American diplomatic success was the 1924 Dawes Plan. Charles Dawes persuaded the Allies to reduce the amount of German reparations. American banks provided loans to the Germans, which facilitated their reparations payments. This in turn gave the Allies funds to repay some of their war debts to the United States. This injection of American capital into the European economy helped spur an economic recovery there in the second half of the 1920s.

Harding chose Andrew Mellon as his secretary of the treasury. Mellon would serve in this position all through the rest of the 1920s. Mellon had headed the aluminum company Alcoa and was one of the richest men in America. Mellon believed in traditional Republican economics; he argued that limiting the size of government and cutting taxes would free up money for investment in business, which would then lead to more jobs. Over the course of the decade, Mellon worked to reduce tax rates. The immediate beneficiaries of his policies were the rich and corporations that paid the highest taxes. During the prosperous 1920s, Mellon's financial policies were regarded as successful, and he was hailed as a great secretary of the treasury.

Mellon also wanted to protect American industries and jobs with high tariffs. The 1922 **Fordney-McCumber Tariff** raised tariff rates on manufactured goods. Agricultural interests were still formidable in Congress, and a farm bloc composed of both Democrats and Republicans could not be ignored. To reconcile the farmers to the new tariff, rates also went up on imported agricultural products. The business-friendly Harding administration did not see a need to promote organized labor. The twenties were a period of doldrums for unions. The courts generally ruled in favor of employers and even sometimes ruled in favor of child labor.

President Harding struck some blows for civil liberties and civil rights. He freed Eugene Debs and other political dissidents imprisoned during World War I by the Wilson administration for violations of the Espionage and Sedition Acts. In October 1921, Harding made an unprecedented trip to Birmingham, Alabama, and gave a speech calling for political equality between the races.

Scandal and the Ruin of Harding's Reputation

Along with the "best minds," Harding also appointed to office men who betrayed his trust. Some of them were men that he had met during his rise in Ohio politics. Harding himself was not involved in their wrongdoing. The discovery of their corruption probably contributed to his death.

One of the worst of these malefactors was Charles Forbes, who as head of the Veteran's Bureau misappropriated $250 million dollars. Harding fired Forbes when he learned what he had done, but let him flee abroad for a time, before he returned home to a prison sentence. Attorney General Harry Daugherty, Harding's former campaign manager, was accused of taking bribes from bootleggers and others wanting government favors; a hung jury saved him from conviction and imprisonment.

The **Teapot Dome Scandal** became the best known malfeasance of the Harding administration. Prior to being appointed Harding's secretary of the interior, Albert Fall had been a well-regarded U.S. senator from New Mexico. Once in office, Fall experienced financial difficulties; in exchange for bribes, he leased the federal oil reserve in Teapot Dome, Wyoming, and other oil lands to private companies. Fall would become the first cabinet secretary to be convicted of a felony and was ordered to prison in 1929.

Harding was just beginning to become aware of the corruption in his administration in 1923. This knowledge greatly distressed him, and he was pondering what steps to take. He already suffered from bad health, and this stress aggravated his condition. On August 2, 1923, Harding died while on a political trip through the western states.

President Calvin Coolidge

Harding was succeeded by Vice President Calvin Coolidge. The new president had grown up in New England and was a man of simple tastes. He had come to national prominence in 1919, when as governor of Massachusetts he had quelled a strike by Boston policemen, declaring, "There can be no right to strike against the public safety by anybody, anywhere, anytime." At the time Coolidge assumed the presidency, little was known of the scandals afflicting the administration. Once they became public, Coolidge cleaned up the mess so thoroughly and efficiently that in 1924 he easily won the presidential election.

Coolidge was a more articulate advocate of limited government than Harding. He was an eloquent defender of free enterprise and became famous for the phrase "the business of the United States is business." As president, Coolidge worked with treasury secretary Mellon to reduce federal spending, the national debt, and taxes.

The Coolidge years were peaceful and prosperous. It ran against Coolidge's philosophy of government to launch major government programs or initiatives. During World War I, the federal government had built a dam on the Tennessee River at Muscle Shoals, Alabama; Coolidge proposed privatizing this public facility, but Congress rejected his plan. Coolidge and Mellon did convince Congress to pass the Revenue Act of 1926, which further reduced taxes. The president was willing to take unpopular stands in defense of his principles. Coolidge vetoed a bill providing a bonus to World War I veterans because he believed that it would cost too much; Congress overrode his veto.

The Election of 1928

Coolidge was popular enough to have run for another term as president. He chose not to and distributed a statement to the press stating, "I do not choose to run." This left the Republican field clear for Herbert Hoover. The Republican nominee was the embodiment of his party's economic philosophy. Orphaned and rendered penniless at an early age, Hoover worked his way through Stanford University and then made a fortune as a mining engineer. During World War I, he acquired an international reputation as an effective philanthropist for organizing relief for starving European civilians. He ran the Food Administration for President Wilson and was present at the peacemaking in Paris. He was a remarkably dynamic secretary of commerce for Harding and Coolidge, pioneering new levels of government cooperation with private industry. During the 1928 election campaign, Hoover defended the Republican economic record and extolled "American individualism."

During the 1920s, the Democrats had been divided between Northern urban politicians and Southerners, often heavily influenced by the Ku Klux Klan. In 1928, the Northerners were able to nominate New York Governor Al Smith. A product of New York City's Tammany Hall machine, Smith seemed to embody the spirit of America's bustling metropolis. This did not endear him to the many Americans who distrusted urban values. For these rural voters, his opposition to Prohibition and his Roman Catholicism disqualified him for the presidency. As a result, Smith lost to Hoover in a landslide; the popular vote margin was almost 60 to 40 percent, and Smith won only eight states in New England and the Deep South.

The City Versus the Country in the 1920s

Though Smith was heavily defeated in 1928, he did carry the 12 largest cities in the country. The rural and urban divide that brought him electoral disaster reflected a larger cultural divide of the 1920s. According to the census, the United States became a predominantly urban country at the beginning of the decade. This did not mean that most Americans lived in big cities, but the momentum was moving in that direction. More important, with the rise of the modern mass media, urban values were being disseminated across the country. Many rural and small-town Americans resented this influx of unfamiliar and unpalatable manners and mores.

Race Relations

One manifestation of a resistance to social and cultural change came in race relations. During the war years, many African Americans had moved to the North looking for work; they took jobs in urban factories. Once the war ended, these African Americans were seen as an economic threat by many returning soldiers who feared that they would prevent them from returning to their prewar positions. Other Northern workers did not want to compete for jobs with these migrants. In 1919 bloody race riots erupted in Washington, D.C.; Tulsa, Oklahoma; Omaha, Nebraska; and other cities. In Chicago, the rioting went on for two weeks. Thousands of African Americans saw their homes go up in flames; 15 whites and 23 African Americans were killed.

Southern repression of African Americans intensified, perhaps in reaction to the return home of black veterans. In 1919, 70 African Americans were lynched. Against this backdrop of renewed racial violence, Marcus Garvey started the **Universal Negro Improvement Association** in 1920. Garvey wanted to lead African Americans back to Africa, where he would found a new state. Eventually a half million people joined his association. Garvey's dream eventually fell apart. He was convicted of mail fraud in 1925. Few African Americans were actually prepared to embrace racial separatism, and Garvey's projected migration to Africa never took place. Garvey himself was deported to Jamaica in 1927.

In part inspired by the cinematic heroics of *The Birth of a Nation*, in part the beneficiary of modern marketing techniques, the **Ku Klux Klan** became a political and cultural phenomenon in the early 1920s; by 1925, it boasted a membership of over 5 million. This modern Klan was not an exclusively Southern organization. It gained recruits from across the country and was especially popular in small-town America. The Klan briefly controlled the politics of Indiana in the mid-1920s. This latter-day Klan opposed any concessions to African Americans, but it was equally driven by an animus against immigrants and Catholics, who were associated with the big cities. For a time, the Klan was a political force to be reckoned with.

The decline of the Klan was almost as rapid as its rise. In the Hoosier state, the head of the Indiana Klan was convicted of rape and second-degree murder. Other Klan leaders were credibly accused of sexual and financial corruption. Amidst this atmosphere of scandal, support for the Klan ebbed away. The prejudices it had championed remained.

Immigration and the Red Scare

Since the 1886 Haymarket Square bombing, many Americans had associated immigrants with political radicalism. Following the Bolshevik Revolution that imposed communism on Russia, there were concerns that agitators would try to import communism to the United States. These fears were intensified by a series of anonymous terrorist bombings in 1919. These outrages convinced many people that a communist revolution was coming and led to the **Red Scare**.

One of the bombs went off at the house of Woodrow Wilson's attorney general, A. Mitchell Palmer, and destroyed his front porch. Palmer responded by launching a roundup of suspected radicals. The **Palmer Raids** led to the arrest of thousands of people, most of them immigrants. In what was still a wartime atmosphere, little attention was paid to the civil rights of the people Palmer incarcerated. Hundreds of the accused were summarily deported. Palmer genuinely believed that the nation was threatened by a communist conspiracy. He also hoped his vigorous actions would further his political career. The Red Scare began to recede after Palmer erroneously predicted a radical uprising on May 1, 1920. When a bombing on Wall Street killed 33 people and wounded over 200 in September, most Americans attributed the atrocity to deranged zealots rather than a widespread communist plot. The Red Scare was over.

Suspicions about foreigners and radicals remained. This played a part in the 1921 trial of Sacco and Vanzetti, two immigrant Italian anarchists who were convicted of robbing a shoe factory and murdering two employees. Although some observers questioned the fairness of their trial, the men were executed in 1927.

Following the war, the massive flow of immigrants into the United States resumed. Many Americans worried that this influx would lower wages. The Red Scare had left a sense that immigrants could bring with them subversive and dangerous political ideas. Eugenicists like Madison Grant published works that warned of the dangers of Americans mixing with "lesser breeds." Small-town Americans continued to associate immigrants with the urban culture that threatened their values. The result of all this was legislation restricting immigration.

In 1921, Congress passed the **Emergency Quota Act,** which restricted new immigration to 3 percent of the population of a given nationality living in the United States in 1910. The effect of these quotas was to reduce the number of immigrants coming from Southern and Eastern Europe. In 1922, this cut the number of immigrants by 60 percent. The **National Origins Act** of 1924 imposed even stricter limits on immigration. This law set the immigration quota for every nationality at 2 percent of the population from that country living in the United States in 1890. A cap of 150,000 was set on all immigrants coming from outside the Americas. Immigration from Asia was prohibited. This act achieved the goal of the lawmakers to end the flow of immigrants from places like Italy, the Balkans, Poland, and Russia. The National Origins Act created a pause in mass immigration to the United States that would last for over forty years.

Prohibition

Another major flashpoint in the confrontation between rural and urban America was Prohibition. Rural America largely supported Prohibition. In 1924 it was estimated that 95 percent of the people in Kansas were respecting Prohibition, as opposed to only 5 percent in New York State. Many rural Americans associated liquor consumption with the big cities, with their immigrants, political machines, and gangsters. They saw alcohol as the "instrument of the devil," and the cities were the devil's playground. Prohibition certainly did unleash monsters in urban America. The high-minded attempt to ban alcohol consumption was a gift to organized crime.

When the government passed Prohibition in 1919, it did very little to ensure enforcement of the law. In cities like New York where few people supported full compliance with the law, efforts to enforce Prohibition failed. Illegal bars known as **speakeasies** proliferated in the cities. Often speakeasies were covertly protected by the local authorities, who would collect a cut of the profits. Sometimes speakeasies would sell "bathtub gin," liquor so bad it tasted like what an enterprising individual might distill in a bathroom. A demand for better liquor was met by bootleggers, criminals who organized the production and distribution of alcohol. This became a very big and profitable business, and bootleggers like Al Capone in Chicago became notorious. Capone controlled hundreds of gunmen and fought bloody turf wars with other gangsters. This street warfare culminated with the St. Valentine's Day Massacre in 1929, when some of Capone's men executed rival gangsters in a garage.

Religion and the Theory of Evolution

Rural and urban sensibilities also clashed over religion and the theory of evolution. Many fundamentalist Christians rejected Darwinian evolution, which contradicted the Bible. Other Christians worried about the implications of the theory of evolution for the traditional understanding of human beings as a special creation of God. These predominantly small-town Americans found a leader in William Jennings Bryan, who three times had been the Democratic presidential candidate. Bryan helped Tennessee legislators pass a law outlawing the teaching of evolution in the state's schools. In 1925, the American Civil Liberties Union (ACLU) announced that it would support any teacher who defied the law. John Scopes, a high school teacher in Dayton, Tennessee, took them up on their offer. The resulting **Scopes Trial**, popularly known as the "Monkey Trial," attracted national attention.

Clarence Darrow, one of the nation's most famous defense attorneys represented Scopes. William Jennings Bryan assisted the prosecution. Scopes was found guilty, though his conviction was later overturned on a technicality. The real point of the trial was a debate over the conflicting claims of science and religion, and the ability of rural Americans to resist ideas they found objectionable. The dramatic highpoint of the trial came when Bryan took the stand as an "expert on the Bible" and was cross-examined by Darrow. To the dismay of his supporters, Bryan revealed that he was not a full adherent of **creationism** and the literal accuracy of everything in the Bible, when he admitted that the world was not created in six days. The ailing Bryan died shortly after the conclusion of the trial.

Popular Culture in the 1920s

The mass media came of age in the 1920s. Americans in both the city and country were exposed to a glittering roster of heroes whose exploits were vigorously publicized in newspapers and magazines. It took an effort for Americans in the new media environment to be ignorant of athletes like the baseball home run king Babe Ruth, college football star Red Grange, or boxing champion Jack Dempsey. The faces of movie stars like Charlie Chaplin, Mary Pickford, Clara Bow, and Rudolph Valentino became familiar to millions. Favored actors and actresses enjoyed large followings of devoted fans. The most dramatic media event of the decade was the reaction to Charles Lindbergh's 1927 solo flight across the Atlantic Ocean in his plane *The Spirit of St. Louis*. The undeniably brave, handsome, and modest aviator was lionized as the quintessential American hero, a modern exemplar of the pioneer spirit. To his great regret, Lindbergh became an international celebrity.

The mass media promoted ideas and attitudes as well as individuals. In the 1920s the media embraced the business culture at the center of the New Era. It affirmed the pursuit of wealth and spread the message that with smarts and hard work anyone could become a millionaire. The media even contributed to financial boondoggles, most notably in booming a Florida real estate bubble that burst with disastrous results for many investors. The popular culture of the day did nothing to put a damper on Wall Street speculations.

Jazz Age Experimentation and Rebellion

In the postwar years many Americans were ready to reject traditional attitudes toward personal expression and sexuality. They believed that the manners and morals of the previous generation had been discredited by the war and become out of date in the more fast-paced modern America. Younger Americans in particular enthusiastically danced to jazz music. Doing so was pleasingly rebellious because this form of music had originated among African Americans and lower class whites, and was associated with uninhibited sexuality. The more traditionalists denounced jazz as "the devil's music," the more popular it became, much like rock and roll three decades later. Jazz music became the soundtrack of the decade, giving it its nickname as the **Jazz Age**.

Young women placed themselves on the cutting edge of social change in the 1920s. They shed the long hair and voluminous skirts that had been associated with prewar femininity. The **flapper** emerged—a girl with bobbed hair, short dress, de-emphasized bustline, and a powder case, cigarette, or drink in hand, an emancipated companion for equally carefree young men. Having won the vote with the Nineteenth Amendment in 1919, young most women pursued personal self-expression rather than political influence. Compared to later years, the sexual revolution of the 1920s was fairly tame, but it shocked defenders of tradition at the time. Thanks to the efforts of Margaret Sanger and other advocates, birth control was more readily available. Automobiles revolutionized dating and courtship, enabling young people to escape the supervision of their elders. Drinking and premarital sex increased in the 1920s, but most young people were far from the giddy "flaming youth" who fascinated and appalled contemporary social critics.

Although women did not move into politics en masse and failed to vote as a bloc, they did continue the gradual movement away from the cult of domesticity. More women entered the workforce, though most of these were single; married women were still expected to focus on the home. Though the numbers of working women rose, their labor was concentrated in traditionally female categories such as teachers, nurses, clerks, and, increasingly, secretaries.

Women's wages typically remained lower, and women rarely ascended to the managerial rank. A rise in the number of divorces was a measure of the growing personal freedom of women and the weakening of traditional social structures.

The Growth of the Mass Media

Undergirding the influence of the mass media in the 1920s was a massive growth in the number of people exposed to the press and popular entertainment. Newspaper reading was ubiquitous in this prosperous decade as most families could afford to subscribe to one or more newspapers. Movie attendance skyrocketed as the movie industry took shape and Hollywood became the center of American filmmaking. In 1922, 35 million people went to the movies every week; by 1929, the number had increased to 90 million. Films were silent for most of the 1920s. In 1927 moviemaking was altered forever by *The Jazz Singer*, a "talking" feature starring the popular entertainer Al Jolson. Silent movies, and along with them many famous silent stars, were quickly superseded by sound technology.

Possibly even more pervasive than movies in the 1920s was the new medium of radio. The commercial development of radio was explosive. In 1920, Station KDKA was the first radio station to get a license. Secretary of Commerce Herbert Hoover helped establish regulations for the new industry. In 1926, the National Broadcasting Company (NBC) organized the first radio network. By the end of the decade, listeners across the country had access to a wide range of news, entertainment, and sports programming.

A Lost Generation?

Many books celebrated the dominant business culture of the 1920s. One of the most popular, and to some egregious, was advertising executive Bruce Barton's *The Man Nobody Knows* (1925). Here Barton envisioned Jesus Christ as a dynamic businessman, whose leadership skills and gift for promotion enabled Him to build the most successful organization in history. Very different in spirit were the writers Gertrude Stein termed the **"Lost Generation."** Several of these writers had been heavily influenced by the disorienting experience of World War I. Most scorned the business, political, and cultural values of Republican "New Era" America. Some joined Stein in Paris, which became a rallying point for expatriate American writers. Others headed for the big cities, especially New York.

Sinclair Lewis achieved fame and financial success attacking what he perceived as the crass materialism and cultural philistinism of middle America. In *Main Street* (1920) and *Babbit* (1922) he produced devastating satires of small town life and the people who lived by small town values. Sherwood Anderson's *Winesburg, Ohio* (1919) was a similarly bleak portrayal of desperate people trapped in the social prison of a remote Midwestern community.

F. Scott Fitzgerald was critical of but also fascinated by Jazz Age materialism. In *The Great Gatsby* (1925) he brilliantly depicted the spiritual emptiness of upper-class characters living a life of decadent self-indulgence in the environs of New York City. Ernest Hemingway painted a similar picture of expatriate writers and artists journeying between France and Spain in *The Sun Also Rises* (1926). Hemingway was especially eloquent about the disillusioning impact of World War I. His *A Farewell to Arms* (1929) centers on a character who rejects the false idealism and brutal hypocrisy of the conflict and attempts to walk away from the war with the woman that he loves. At the time, the most influential critic of American society was the journalist H. L. Mencken. Gifted with a brilliant literary style and a taste for invective, Mencken heaped scorn on ordinary Americans, terming them the "ignorant mob" and the "booboisie." Mencken was a favorite with college students hoping to be fashionable in their opinions.

The 1920s saw a flowering of African American artistic expression in the **Harlem Renaissance**. Centered on, but not limited to, the Harlem neighborhood of New York City, African American intellectuals wrestled with the challenges of their American identity in a land where they were still second-class citizens. Many members of the Harlem Renaissance immersed themselves in African American folk art and Negro spirituals, looking for an authentic form of expression to convey the black experience. Leading writers of the Harlem Renaissance were the poet Langston Hughes and the novelist Zora Neale Hurston. The popularity of jazz music opened up opportunities for African American musicians. Amongst many others, musicians like Louis Armstrong and Duke Ellington achieved great success; through performances in clubs and in recordings they reached a mainstream audience.

As the decade of the 1920s neared its end, many believed the era of prosperity would continue indefinitely. Early in 1929, the stock market reached an all-time high. Herbert Hoover, inaugurated as president in March, spoke of ending poverty. Given his stellar record as a philanthropist and administrator, this did not seem to be empty posturing. For a moment, all the promise of the American dream seemed possible. The contrast between the hopes of early 1929 and what followed the events of October intensified the inexplicable cruelty of the ensuing Great Depression.

Chapter Review

Rapid Review

To achieve the perfect 5, you should be able to explain the following:

- A consumer economy was created in the 1920s on a level unprecedented in American history.
- Advertising, newspapers, radio, and motion pictures provided new forms of entertainment in the 1920s and helped create a uniform national culture.
- The changes of the 1920s were resisted by many in small-town/rural America, creating many of the cultural conflicts of the decade.
- Assembly line techniques and the ideas of scientific management of Frederick W. Taylor helped make industrial production in the 1920s quicker and more efficient, ultimately creating cheaper goods.
- Installment buying helped fuel consumer buying in the 1920s.
- The Republican party controlled the White House, Congress, and the Supreme Court in the 1920s, generally sponsoring government policies friendly to big business.
- The scandals of the Harding administration were among the worst in history.
- Resentment against blacks existed in both the American South and North in the years after World War I, resulting in race riots in the North and lynchings and the rebirth of the Ku Klux Klan in the South.
- The Red Scare of 1919 and 1920 resulted in the suspension of civil liberties and deportation of hundreds of immigrants, the vast majority of whom had committed no crime.
- Nativist fears also resulted in restrictive quota legislation passed in the early 1920s.

- Cultural conflicts between urban and rural America also developed over the issues of Prohibition and the teaching of evolution in schools (resulting in the Scopes Trial).
- During the Jazz Age, many Americans rejected the prominent business values of the decade and turned to jazz, alcohol, and looser sexual mores for personal fulfillment.
- The flapper was the single most prominent image of the Jazz Age.
- Writers of the Lost Generation expressed extreme disillusionment with American society of the era; writers of the Harlem Renaissance expressed the opinions of American blacks concerning American culture.

Time Line

1917: Race riots in East St. Louis, Missouri

1918: Armistice ending World War I

1919: Race riots in Chicago
Major strikes in Seattle and Boston
Palmer Raids

1920: Warren Harding elected president
First broadcast of radio station KDKA in Pittsburgh
Publication of *Main Street* by Sinclair Lewis
Arrest of Sacco and Vanzetti
Prohibition takes effect

1921: Immigration Quota Law passed
Disarmament conference held

1922: Fordney-McCumber Tariff enacted
Publication of *Babbitt* by Sinclair Lewis

1923: Teapot Dome scandal
Death of Harding; Calvin Coolidge becomes president
Duke Ellington first performs in New York City

1924: Election of Calvin Coolidge
Immigration Quota Law enacted
Ku Klux Klan reaches highest membership in history
Women governors elected in Wyoming and Texas

1925: Publication of *The Man Nobody Knows* by Bruce Barton
Publication of *The Great Gatsby* by F. Scott Fitzgerald
Scopes Trial held in Dayton, Tennessee

1926: Publication of *The Sun Also Rises* by Ernest Hemingway

1927: *The Jazz Singer*, first movie with sound, released
Charles Lindbergh makes New York to Paris flight
Execution of Sacco and Vanzetti
15 millionth car produced by Ford Motor Company
$1.5 billion spent on advertising in United States
Babe Ruth hits 60 home runs

1928: Election of Herbert Hoover

1929: Nearly 30 million Americans have cars
Stock market crash

› Review Questions

Multiple-Choice Questions

1. Many in rural/small-town America would support legislation that
   A. increased immigration from Eastern Europe.
   B. mandated the teaching of creationism in schools.
   C. lessened the penalties for those who sold illegal alcohol.
   D. made it harder to deport immigrants who might have "Red" ties.

2. The novel that supported the business philosophy of the 1920s most definitively was
   A. *Main Street.*
   B. *The Great Gatsby.*
   C. *The Man Nobody Knows.*
   D. *Babbitt.*

3. In 1928, in most Eastern cities, one could find
   A. a speakeasy.
   B. a continual flow of immigrants from Northern, Southern, and Eastern Europe.
   C. large numbers of supporters of the Ku Klux Klan.
   D. the first bread lines.

4. Republican leaders of the 1920s believed all of the following *except*
   A. "the business of government is business."
   B. the government should do as little as possible.
   C. labor unions should be strengthened through legislation.
   D. immigration should continue to be restricted.

5. The election of Herbert Hoover in 1928 demonstrated all of the following *except*
   A. most Americans believed that Republican policies had been responsible for the prosperity of the 1920s.
   B. fewer divisions existed between the urban and rural populations than had existed at the beginning of the decade.
   C. Prohibition was still a "hot-button issue" for many Americans.
   D. America was not ready for a Catholic president.

Short-Answer Question

6. Answer Parts A, B, and C.
   A. Briefly explain ONE example of social and cultural change in the 1920s.
   B. Briefly explain a SECOND example of social and cultural change in the 1920s.
   C. Briefly explain ONE example of resistance to social and cultural change in the 1920s.

› Answers and Explanations

1. **B**. All of the other "causes"—more immigration, the lessening of Prohibition, and the lessening of methods to deport potential Communists—were vehemently opposed by most in small-town America. They would, however, support the elimination of the teaching of evolution, and the continued teaching of creationism in American schools.

2. **C**. All of the other novels are unsympathetic to the world of business—both A and D are by Sinclair Lewis. In *The Man Nobody Knows,* Jesus Christ is portrayed as a businessman.

3. **A**. The influx of immigrants had been greatly reduced by immigration legislation passed in the first half of the decade. Supporters of the KKK were largely not city dwellers; the KKK had also lessened in importance by 1928. Bread lines were not found until the beginning of the Great Depression.

4. **C**. All of the other answers are solid beliefs of Republican leaders of the 1920s. Republicans did very little for labor unions in the decade.

5. **B**. Hoover's overwhelming election demonstrated the appeal of his business background and the fact that many Americans credited the Republicans for prosperity. The fact that Al Smith was defeated in this election demonstrated that his anti-Prohibition statements definitely hurt him. However, many in urban centers voted for him; this demonstrated that the divisions between urban and rural America were still wide at the end of the decade.

6. **Parts A and B**: The 1920s was a decade of prosperity for most Americans. Consumer goods such as refrigerators and radios became readily available; they could be purchased on installment plans. Sales were encouraged by a proliferation of the new advertising industry. Automobile ownership became widespread, with most Americans owning cars made by Ford, General Motors, and Chrysler. The United States experimented with Prohibition during the 1920s. The mass media helped drive a flourishing popular culture in the 1920s. Sports and movie stars became widely known celebrities. Many people in the 1920s began to reject traditional values. They embraced the rebellious spirit of the Jazz Age, with a soundtrack of raucous jazz music often associated with African Americans. Many young women shed the inhibitions of the past, wearing short dresses, smoking and drinking with their male friends, and bobbing their hair. The "Lost Generation" of American writers wrote critically of American society in the postwar years.

Part C: Many American resisted social change. Concern about mass immigration and the possibility of imported political radicalism helped spur the Red Scare. The Emergency Quota Act of 1921 and the National Origins Act of 1924 greatly restricted immigration, especially from Southern and Eastern Europe. The Ku Klux Klan grew influential in the early 1920s by agitating against immigrants and Catholics, as well as maintaining hostility toward African Americans. Many rural people rejected ideas that they associated with the Jazz Age. A law in Tennessee outlawing the teaching of evolution in public schools led to the Scopes Trial in 1925, and a famous forensic duel between the well-known lawyer Clarence Darrow criticizing the law and William Jennings Bryan defending it. Many Americans refused to adhere to Prohibition. The illicit sale of liquor led to the rise of organized crime and famous gangsters like Al Capone in Chicago. People patronized "speakeasies," where illegal alcohol could be found in great supply.

CHAPTER 23

Great Depression and the New Deal (1929–1939)

IN THIS CHAPTER

Summary: The Great Depression had a monumental effect on American society, and its effects are still felt today. Franklin Roosevelt, the architect of the New Deal, is considered by many to be one of America's greatest presidents, and he was the model for activist presidents who desired to utilize the power of the federal government to assist those in need. The origins of the Great Depression can be found in economic problems in America in the late 1920s: "installment buying" and buying stocks "on the margin" would come back to haunt many homeowners and investors. The stock market crash of 1929 was followed by bank failures, factory closings, and widespread unemployment. President Herbert Hoover believed that voluntary action by business and labor interest could pull America out of its economic doldrums. Franklin Roosevelt was elected president in 1932 with the promise of a "New Deal" for the American people. During his first hundred days in office, Roosevelt acted forcefully to restore confidence in the banks, stabilize prices, and give many young people work through the establishment of the Civilian Conservation Corps. During the Second New Deal later in the 1930s, measures such as the Social Security Act were enacted to provide a safety net for Americans in need. Some critics of the New Deal branded it socialism; others said it didn't go far enough to fight poverty in America. New Deal policies never ended the Great Depression; America's entry into World War II did.

Keywords

Hoovervilles: settlements of shacks found on the outskirts of many American cities beginning in the early 1930s.

Dust Bowl: name given in the 1930s to regions of Oklahoma, Kansas, Nebraska, Colorado, and Texas, where severe drought and poor farming practices caused massive dust storms. By the end of the decade, nearly 60 percent of all farms there were either ruined or abandoned. Many from the Dust Bowl ended up moving westward in search of jobs.

Hawley-Smoot Tariff (1930): tariff act that imposed severe tariffs on all incoming goods; European countries responded with their own high tariffs. Most historians say this tariff did little to help the American economy.

Federal Deposit Insurance Corporation (FDIC): federal agency established during the "First Hundred Days" of the New Deal in 1933 in an effort to halt panic over bank closings. The FDIC insures the bank deposits of individual citizens.

Civilian Conservation Corps (CCC): also established in 1933, the CCC eventually provided jobs for 2.5 million young Americans in forest and conservation programs.

National Industry Recovery Act: New Deal legislation requiring owners and labor unions in various industries to agree upon hours, wages, and prices; as a result, wages did go up for many workers but so did prices.

Tennessee Valley Authority: agency created in the New Deal to oversee the construction of dams, providing electricity and flood control for many in the Tennessee River Valley; for many in the region, this was the first time their homes had electricity.

Works Progress Administration (WPA): New Deal program that employed nearly 8 million Americans; WPA projects included the construction of schools and roads. Unemployed artists and musicians were also employed by the WPA.

Wagner Act: critical piece of New Deal legislation that protected the right of workers to form unions and utilize collective bargaining.

Social Security Act (1935): New Deal legislation providing pensions for workers reaching retirement age. Both workers and employers pay into the fund that provides this benefit. Initially, farm workers and domestic workers were not covered by Social Security.

New Deal Coalition: The political coalition created by Franklin Roosevelt that, by and large, kept the Democratic Party in power from the 1930s through the 1960s. This coalition consisted of workers in American cities, voters in the South, labor unions, and blacks.

Scottsboro Boys: nine black defendants in a famous 1931 case; they were accused of raping two white women on a train, and despite the lack of evidence, eight were sentenced to death. The American Communist party organized their defense.

American Economy of the 1920s:
Roots of the Great Depression

The vast majority of Americans in 1929 foresaw a continuation of the dizzying economic growth that had taken place in most of the decade. In his inauguration speech, newly elected president Herbert Hoover reemphasized his campaign promise that it was the goal of the Republican party to permanently wipe out poverty in America. In early September 1929, the average share of stock on the New York Stock Exchange stood near 350, a gain of nearly 200 points in a little over a year.

However, careful observers of the American economy noticed several disturbing trends that only seemed to be increasing. These included the following:

1. *Agricultural problems.* Farm prices were at a record high during World War I, dropped after the war, and never recovered. Many farmers were unable to pay back bank loans they had acquired to purchase land, tractors, and other equipment; many farms were foreclosed, and, in farm states, over 6,200 banks were forced to close. Legislation to help farmers had been passed by Congress, but bills to help the farmers were vetoed by President Coolidge on two occasions.

2. *Installment buying.* As stated in the previous chapter, large numbers of Americans purchased automobiles, refrigerators, vacuum cleaners, and similar household products on credit. Many Americans simply did not have anywhere near enough cash to pay for all they had purchased. The money of many families was tied up making installment payments for three or four big-ticket items; this prevented them from purchasing many other items available for sale. In 1928 and 1929, new goods continued to be produced, but many people simply could not afford to buy them. As a result, layoffs began occurring in some industries as early as 1928.

3. *Uneven division of wealth.* America was wealthy in the 1920s, but this wealth did not extend to all segments of society. The gains made by wealthy Americans in the 1920s far outstripped gains made by the working class. By the time of the stock market crash, the upper 0.2 percent of the population controlled over 40 percent of the nation's savings. On the other hand, over three-quarters of American families made less than $3,000 a year. Problems that could develop from this situation were obvious. The bottom three-quarters of families were too poor to purchase much to help the economy to continue to flourish. Furthermore, at the early signs of economic trouble, many of the wealthiest Americans, fearing the worst, curtailed their spending.

4. *The stock market.* There were cases in the late 1920s of ordinary citizens becoming very wealthy by purchasing stock. Some of these people were engaged in **speculation**, meaning that they would invest in something (like the previously mentioned Florida lands) that was very risky, but that they could potentially "make a killing" on. Another common practice in the late 1920s was buying shares of stock "**on the margin**." A stockbroker might allow a buyer to purchase stock for only a percentage of what it was worth (commonly as low as 10 percent); the rest could be borrowed from the broker. As long as stock prices continued to rise, investors would have no trouble paying brokers back for these loans. After the stock market crash, brokers wanted payment for these loans. Countless numbers of investors had no way to make these payments.

Stock Market Crash

The prices of stock crested in early September 1929. The price of stock fell very gradually during most of September and early October. Some investors noted that some factories were beginning to lay workers off; whispers were heard around Wall Street that perhaps the price of stock *was* too high, and that it might be good to sell before prices began to fall.

The first signs of panic occurred on Wednesday, October 23, when in the last hour of trading, the value of a share of stock dropped, on average, 20 points. On October 24 a massive amount of stock was sold, and prices again fell dramatically. Stockbrokers told nervous investors not to worry; Herbert Hoover announced that the stock market and the economy "is on a sound and prosperous basis."

A group of influential bankers and brokers pooled resources to buy stock, but this was unable to stop the downward trend. Prices fell again on Monday, October 28, and on the following day, Black Tuesday, the bottom fell out of the market. Prices fell by 40 points that day; it is estimated that total losses to investors for the day was over $20 million. Stockbrokers and banks frantically attempted to call in their loans; few investors had the money to pay even a fraction of what they owed.

How the Stock Market Crash Caused the Great Depression

In the weeks immediately following the crash, important figures from the banking world and President Hoover all assured the American people that America was still economically sound, and that the crash was no worse than other stock downturns that had had little long-term effect on the economy. In retrospect, it can be seen that through both direct and indirect means, the stock market crash was a fundamental cause of the Great Depression. As a result of the crash:

1. *Bank closings increased.* As stated previously, many banks in rural America had to close when farmers couldn't repay loans. The exact same thing happened to many city banks after 1929 when investors could not repay their loans. In addition, the news of even a single bank closing had a snowball effect; thousands of people went to banks across the country to withdraw their life savings. Banks did not have this kind of money (it had been given out to investors as loans); soon urban banks began to fail as well. It is estimated that by 1932 approximately 5,000 banks fell, with the life savings of over 5 million Americans gone forever

2. *Income fell for industrialists.* Many large industrialists invested heavily in the stock market. They had less available cash, and some started to close or reduce the scale of their factory operations. Workers were laid off or made much less money; as a result, they were able to buy fewer products made in other industrial plants, causing layoffs there as well. By 1933, nearly 25 percent of the labor force was out of work.

3. *Effect on the world.* Many European countries, especially Germany, utilized loans from American banks and investment houses in the 1920s and 1930s to remain viable. When American financial institutions were unable to supply these loans, instability occurred in these countries. Some historians make the argument that, perhaps indirectly, the American stock market crash opened the door for Hitler to come to power in Germany.

Social Impact of the Great Depression

Many Americans felt a huge sense of uprootedness in the 1930s. By late 1932, virtually all sectors of American society were affected in some way by the depression. Both professional men and common laborers lost their jobs. It was not uncommon during the depression for two people to share a job, or for a man who had lost his job to continue to put his suit on every morning and pretend to go to work, somehow averting the shame he felt for being unemployed. Women and minorities were often the first to lose their jobs, although women in certain "female" occupations (such as domestic work) were almost never uprooted by men. "Respectable" white men were willing to take jobs that had been previously seen as fit only for minorities. Many behaviors of the 1920s, such as buying on credit, were forgotten practices by 1932.

Many private agencies established soup kitchens and emergency shelters in the early 1930s, but many more were needed. Many couples postponed marriage and having children. Those with nowhere to live in cities often ended up in **Hoovervilles**, which were settlements of shacks (made from scrap metal or lumber) usually located on the outskirts of cities. Many unemployed young people, both men and women, took to the road in the 1930s, often traveling in empty railroad cars.

The greatest human suffering of the depression era might have existed in the **Dust Bowl**. For most of the decade, massive dust storms plagued the residents of Oklahoma, Kansas, Nebraska, Colorado, and Texas; farm production in this area fell drastically for much of the decade. A severe drought was the major cause of the dust storms, although poor farming practices (stripping the soil of any topsoil) also contributed to them. By the decade's end, nearly 60 percent of all farms in the Dust Bowl were either ruined or abandoned. Many Dust Bowlers traveled to California to get agricultural jobs there, and discovered that if an entire family picked grapes from sunup to sundown, it might barely scrape by. (John Steinbeck's book *The Grapes of Wrath*, as well as the film version, are highly recommended for further study of Dust Bowlers and their move to California, as are the recordings of Woody Guthrie entitled "Dust Bowl Ballads" and the depression-era photos taken by Dorothea Lange.)

The behavior and attitudes of many who lived through the depression changed forever. Many would *never* in their lives buy anything on credit; there are countless stories of depression-era families who insisted on paying for everything, including automobiles, with cash. Depression-era shortages led many in later life to be almost compulsive "savers" of everything and anything imaginable. Many who lived through the depression and had children in the 1950s were determined to given their kids all that they had been deprived of in the 1930s.

Hoover Administration and the Depression

To state that Herbert Hoover did nothing to stem the effects of the Great Depression is not entirely accurate. Nevertheless, he did believe that this crisis could be solved through **voluntarism**. Hoover urged Americans to donate all they could to charities, and held several conferences with business leaders where he urged them not to reduce wages or lay off workers. When it became obvious that these measures were not enough, public opinion quickly turned against Hoover.

The Hoover administration did take several specific measures to offset the effects of the depression. Even before the stock market crash, the **Agricultural Marketing Act** created a Federal Farm Board that had the ability to give loans to the agricultural community and buy crops to keep farm prices up. By 1932, there was not enough money to keep this program afloat. In 1930, Congress enacted the **Hawley-Smoot Tariff**, which to this day is the highest import tax in the history of the United States. In response, European countries drastically increased their own tariffs as well; some historians maintain that this legislation did little to improve the economy of the United States, but that its effects did much to ensure that the American Depression would be a worldwide one.

Hoover did authorize more money for public works programs, and, in 1932, he authorized the creation of the **Reconstruction Finance Corporation**. This agency gave money to banks, who were then authorized to loan this money to businesses and railroads. Another bill authorized loans to banks to prevent them from failing. To many in America, these bills were merely signs that Hoover was only interested in helping those at the top of society and that he cared little about the common person. Hoover vetoed legislation authorizing a federal relief program, although in 1932 he did sign legislation authorizing federal loans to the states; states could then administer relief programs with this money.

Those Americans who felt that Hoover was unconcerned about the plight of the common man had their views seemingly confirmed by federal actions against the **Bonus Army** that appeared in Washington in the summer of 1932. This group of nearly 17,000 unemployed World War I vets came to ask the federal government to give them the bonuses that they were supposed to get in 1945 immediately. At Hoover's urging, the Senate rejected legislation authorizing this. Most of the Bonus Army then went home, but a few thousand stayed, living in shacks along the Anacostia River. Hoover ordered them removed; military forces led by Douglas MacArthur used tear gas and cleared the remaining bonus marchers from their camp and burned down the shacks they had been living in.

1932 Presidential Election

The two candidates in the 1932 presidential election could not have been more different in both content and style. In a joyless convention, the Republicans renominated Herbert Hoover. In newsreels seen by Americans across the country, Hoover came across as unsmiling and utterly lacking in warmth. He insisted that his policies would eventually lead America out of the depression, stating that history demonstrated that lulls in the American economy are always followed by upturns. Hoover warned against "mindless experimentation" in the creation of government policies. It should be noted that Hoover was echoing the standard economic and political theory of the era.

Hoover's opponent in the election was the governor of New York, Franklin Delano Roosevelt. Roosevelt was a man of wealth. After serving as assistant secretary of the navy under Woodrow Wilson, Roosevelt unsuccessfully tried to get the vice presidential nomination in 1920. During the summer of 1921, he came down with polio, which left him unable to walk for the rest of his life. Several of Roosevelt's biographers maintain that the mental and physical anguish caused by his polio made Roosevelt much more sensitive to the sufferings of others.

Franklin Roosevelt married a distant cousin, Eleanor Roosevelt, in 1905. While Franklin spent much of the 1920s attempting to recover from polio in Warm Springs, Georgia, Eleanor became a tireless worker in New York state politics, pushing for governmental reform and better conditions for working women. The role that Eleanor Roosevelt played during the presidency of Franklin Roosevelt cannot be overestimated. FDR (this shortening of his name was done by a reporter in 1932) often stated that Eleanor served as his "legs," visiting miners, schools, and countless other groups. Eleanor also discussed policy with Roosevelt and continually urged him to do more to offset the effects of the depression.

As governor of New York during the first years of the Great Depression, Roosevelt instituted relief programs that became models for others across the country. During his campaign Roosevelt promised the "**New Deal**" for the American people; unlike Hoover, he also promised to experiment to find solutions to America's problems. Roosevelt's broad smile and personal demeanor contrasted drastically with the public image of Herbert Hoover; Americans were convinced that Roosevelt cared (this would be demonstrated during his presidency by the hundreds of letters that both Roosevelt and his wife received during the presidency, asking for things such as small loans, money to pay doctors, and old clothes; it should also be noted that many Americans had a picture of Franklin Roosevelt on display somewhere in their living quarters during the depression).

The 1932 presidential election was easily won by Roosevelt, who won by over 7 million votes. Hoover's only strength was in the Northeastern states. In addition, the Democrats won control of both houses of Congress. Some had feared (or hoped) that the depression would radicalize the American working class, yet the Socialist candidate for president, Norman Thomas, received considerably less than 1 million votes.

First Hundred Days

Franklin Roosevelt's inauguration speech in 1933 was one of optimism; the most quoted line of this speech is ". . . so first of all let me assert my firm belief that the only thing we have to fear is fear itself." Within a week of taking office, Roosevelt gave the first of his many **fireside chats**. During these radio addresses, Roosevelt spoke to the listening audience as if they were part of his family; Roosevelt would usually explain the immediate problems facing the country in these speeches and outline the reasons for his decided solutions.

Roosevelt surrounded himself with an able cabinet, as well as a group of unofficial advisors called Roosevelt's "brain trust." In dealing with the problems of the depression, Roosevelt urged his advisors to experiment. Some programs thus failed, some were continually reformed, and several conflicted with each other. The key, insisted Roosevelt, was to "do something."

During the first **Hundred Days** of the Roosevelt administration, countless programs were proposed by the administration and passed by Congress that attempted to stimulate the American economy and provide relief and jobs. A very popular act, for psychological reasons if nothing else, was the repeal of Prohibition, which was actually voted on by Congress in February 1933.

Roosevelt's economic advisor told him that his first priority should be the banking system. On March 5, 1933, he officially closed all banks for four days and had the federal government oversee the inspection of all banks. By March 15, most banks were reopened; this cooling-off period gave people a renewed confidence in the banks, and slowly people started putting back into banks instead of taking out. The Banking Act of 1933 created the **Federal Deposit Insurance Corporation (FDIC)**, which insured the bank deposits of individual citizens.

During the hundred days, large amounts of federal money were handed down to local relief agencies, and a Federal Emergency Relief Administration (led by Harry Hopkins) was also established. Efforts were also made to help people find work. Thousands were hired from funds distributed to states by the Public Works Administration; many schools, highways, and hospitals were built under this program.

The **Civilian Conservation Corps (CCC)** was founded during this period and would eventually employ over 2.5 million young men. Under this program, forest and conservation programs were undertaken. CCC workers were only paid a small amount (this money was actually sent to their families), but in a period where little work was available, many veterans of CCC programs later perceived the program as a godsend.

Roosevelt considered the bolstering of the industrial sector of the American economy to be a top priority. Falling prices had caused layoffs and the failure of many businesses. The **National Industrial Recovery Act (NIRA)** was established to try to stop falling prices in industry. Under this act, committees of both owners and union leaders in each industry would meet to set commonly agreed-on prices, wages, working hours, and working expectations. Unions and collective bargaining were accepted in industry as a result of the NIRA. Wages in many industries rose as a result of this; the thinking in the creation of the NIRA was that as wages rose, workers would then buy more, stimulating the economy and stopping the fall of industrial prices. The goals of this program were not largely met; as wages rose so did prices. As a result, many workers did not buy more, negating any benefit that rising wages were supposed to have.

Another body created by the NIRA was the National Recovery Administration (NRA), which was supposed to enforce the decisions of the NIRA. The entire process of the NIRA was declared unconstitutional in the 1935 Supreme Court case *Schechter v. United States*, although the agency had largely lost its effectiveness by then.

Two other important programs developed during the first hundred days. The **Agricultural Adjustment Administration (AAA)** attempted to stop the sharp decline in farm prices by paying farmers *not* to produce certain crops and livestock. It was hoped that this would cause the prices of these goods to rise. The **Tennessee Valley Authority** authorized the construction of a series of dams that would ultimately provide electricity and flood control to those living in the Tennessee River Valley. Thousands who had not had electricity in their homes now did.

The hundred days and the months that followed it provided some relief to those affected by the depression, but by no means solved the basic economic problems facing the United States. The 1934 midterm congressional elections showed that most Americans favored FDRs policies, yet even in 1935 some 20 percent of all Americans were still out of work.

Second New Deal

Many wealthy members of American society were appalled by the actions that Roosevelt took during his first year in office; he was called a traitor to his class, a Communist, and far worse. Other elements of Roosevelt's brain trust (as well as his wife Eleanor) were advising Roosevelt to do even more to help the unemployed of America. As a result, the **Second New Deal**, beginning in 1935, included another flurry of legislation.

It was obvious that even more dramatic measures were needed to help farmers; many farms were still being foreclosed on because farmers could not make necessary payments on their lands. The **Resettlement Administration**, established in May 1935, offered loans to small farmers who faced foreclosure. In addition, migrant farmers had not been affected by previous New Deal measures dealing with agriculture; funds to help them find work were included under the Resettlement Administration.

One of the outstanding achievements of the Second New Deal was the creation of the **Works Progress Administration (WPA)**. The WPA took people who were on relief and employed them for 30 or 35 hours a week. On average, 2 million people per month were employed by the WPA. By 1941, well over 8 million people had worked for the WPA. WPA workers were usually engaged in construction projects, building schools, hospitals, and roads across the country. In addition, unemployed musicians, artists, and actors were all employed by the WPA. WPA artists painted many of the murals found in public buildings, concerts were given for both urban and rural audiences, and plays were performed for audiences who had never seen one before.

Another important piece of legislation from this period was the **Wagner Act**, which reaffirmed the right of workers to organize and to utilize collective bargaining. These rights had been guaranteed by provision 7a of the NIRA guidelines, but when the NIRA was declared to be unconstitutional, additional legislation protecting workers was needed. The Wagner Act also listed unfair labor practices that were outlawed and established the **National Labor Relations Board (NLRB)** to enforce its provisions.

The most important legislation passed during the Second New Deal was the 1935 **Social Security Act**. The critical provision of this act was the creation of a retirement plan for workers over 65 years old. Both workers and employers paid into this retirement fund; the first payments were scheduled to be made in January 1942. It should be noted that the initial social security legislation did not cover agricultural and domestic workers.

Other provisions of this act established a program that provided unemployment insurance for workers who had lost their jobs; this was paid for by a payroll tax that was imposed on all employers with more than eight workers. The federal government also provided financial support to programs at the state level that provided unemployment insurance. The federal government also gave money to the states to provide aid programs for dependent children, for the blind, and for the physically challenged.

As stated previously, some Americans were exempt from the provisions of the Social Security Act. Nevertheless, this act fundamentally changed the relationship of the federal government with American citizens. At the root of the Social Security Act was the concept that it was the job of the federal government to take care of those who couldn't take care of themselves. This was a fundamentally new role for the federal government to have, and it justified the worst fears of many opponents of the Roosevelt administration.

Presidential Election of 1936

The 1936 election was the first true national referendum of the presidency of Franklin Roosevelt. In his campaign speeches, Roosevelt often railed against the business class; according to Roosevelt, they opposed many of his policies only so they could continue to get rich. The Republicans nominated Governor Alfred Landon of Kansas as their presidential candidate. Landon never actually repudiated the programs of the New Deal, but he stated that a balanced budget and less expensive government programs should be top priorities.

The election was one of the most one-sided in American history. Roosevelt won the electoral college 523 to 8, with Landon only winning the states of Maine and Vermont. Roosevelt was able to craft a **New Deal Coalition**, which made the Democrats the majority party in America throughout the rest of the 1930s and all the way into the 1980s. The fact that white urban dwellers supported the Democrats in large numbers was noted during the 1928 defeat of Smith; whites in the Solid South had largely voted Democratic since the nineteenth century. The two groups that joined the Democratic coalition in this era were labor unions and blacks (this was a dramatic shift, as most blacks had voted Republican since the period of Emancipation). Roosevelt enjoyed support in the agricultural community as well.

Opponents of Franklin Roosevelt and the New Deal

Despite the overwhelming electoral success of Franklin Roosevelt, many Americans vehemently disagreed with his programs. Some wealthy Americans called him a traitor to his class, while some businessmen called him a Socialist or a Communist. To others, the programs of Roosevelt were perceived as being designed to benefit the business interests of America and never truly addressed the human suffering of the country. Some of these Americans felt that neither the Democratic nor the Republican parties were really concerned with helping the average American, and perceived socialism as the only viable solution. Many idealistic Americans dabbled with socialism in the 1930s; for some the one- or two-party meetings they attended became career-threatening during the McCarthy era of the 1950s.

One group that thought the New Deal had gone too far was the **American Liberty League**. This group was led by former presidential candidate Al Smith and several very influential business figures, including prominent members of the Du Pont family. The membership of this organization was largely relatively wealthy Republicans; they were particularly incensed by the **Revenue Act of 1935**, which considerably increased the tax rate for those making over $50,000. The American Liberty League equated the New Deal with "bolshevism" in much of their literature.

The majority of those opposing the New Deal felt that it didn't go far enough. Dr. Francis Townsend of California proposed an **Old Age Revolving Pension Plan**; under this plan, a national sales tax would pay for a pension of $200 per month for all retired Americans. Townsend maintained that the benefit would be that more and more money would be put into circulation. In 1934, Upton Sinclair, author of *The Jungle*, ran for governor of California on the Democratic ticket and announced his "End Poverty in California" (EPIC) plan. Under this plan, California factories and farms would be under state control. Sinclair was defeated by the Republican candidate and was also sabotaged by members of his own party; the Democratic smear campaign against Sinclair was approved of by Franklin Roosevelt.

The two most vicious opponents of the New Deal were Father Charles Coughlin and Louisiana senator Huey Long. Millions of people listened to Coughlin on the radio. Originally a supporter of Roosevelt, by the mid-1930s he told his listeners that Roosevelt was a "liar" and "the great betrayer." By the late 1930s, Coughlin was praising Mussolini and Hitler on his broadcasts, and making increasingly anti-Semitic statements. By order of the church, Coughlin was pulled off the air during World War II.

As governor and later senator from Louisiana, Huey Long instituted many New-Deal-type programs in Louisiana, and also developed the most effective and ruthless political machine in the entire South. By 1934, Long felt that Franklin Roosevelt was not committed to doing enough to end the depression. Long called for a true redistribution of wealth in his "Share the Wealth" program, which would have allowed no American to make over a million dollars a year (the rest would be taken in taxes). From these taxes, Long proposed to give every American family $5,000 immediately and an annual income of $2,000. Long talked of running against Roosevelt in 1936, but was assassinated by the relative of a Louisiana political enemy in 1935.

Last Years of the New Deal

Franklin Roosevelt was frustrated that the United States Supreme Court had struck down several New Deal programs. In early 1937, he proposed the **Justice Reorganization Bill**, which would have allowed him to appoint an additional Supreme Court justice for every justice over 70 years old (nothing in the Constitution stated that there had to be only nine Supreme Court justices). Roosevelt would have been able to appoint six new judges under this scheme. Roosevelt claimed that the purpose of this plan was to help the older judges with their workload, but many Republicans and Democrats in Congress believed that Roosevelt was altering the balance of power between branches of government just to get his ideas enacted into law. Newspaper editorial writers and cartoonists compared Roosevelt to the dictators of Europe, Hitler and Mussolini. Many Southern Democrats joined with the Republicans to defeat this bill; the aftereffects seriously damaged Roosevelt's relationship with Congress. Ironically, without the bill, several justices retired in the next two years, allowing Roosevelt to appoint justices who would approve his programs anyway.

Any hopes that the New Deal was actually ending the depression were dashed by a fairly large recession that occurred in mid-1937. Once again, factories began major layoffs. Critics of the New Deal blamed Roosevelt's programs for this recession. Many in the administration were worried that the national debt was too high, and urged Roosevelt to cut programs. The WPA was drastically scaled back, putting some that had worked for it out of work. In addition, a part of every worker's salary was now deducted to be put into the Social Security fund; critics charged that this money would have been better utilized if it was actually being spent on goods and services. By 1940, the administration restored some of the cutbacks made to government programs, slightly improving the economy again.

Effects of the New Deal

The Wagner Act and other New Deal legislation permanently legitimized labor unions and collective bargaining. Some unions became emboldened by the Wagner Act, and several **sit-down strikes** occurred in the late 1930s. The most famous occurred at the General Motors plant in Flint, Michigan, in December 1936. Workers refused to leave the plant; by February, management had to give in to the worker's demands. Other strikes of the era turned bloody; in a 1937 strike at Republic Steel in Chicago, 10 strikers were killed. Nevertheless, union membership rose dramatically in the 1930s.

Another development was the creation of the **Congress of Industrial Organizations (CIO)**. The American Federation of Labor, founded in the 1880s, was made up mostly of skilled workers. The first president of the CIO was John L. Lewis; the goal of this union was to organize and represent unskilled factory and textile workers. By 1938, this organization represented over 4 million workers. CIO members were on the front lines of the strikes mentioned in the previous paragraph.

The burden on women and blacks was great during the New Deal. As men lost their jobs, more and more women were forced to take meager jobs to support their families (despite the fact that women workers were often criticized for "stealing" the jobs of men). It should be noted that Frances Perkins was the secretary of labor during the 1930s; Roosevelt employed a number of women in influential roles during his presidency.

Blacks were especially oppressed during the New Deal. Often, they were the first to be fired from a factory or business; relief programs in Southern states sometimes excluded blacks from receiving benefits. Lynchings continued in the South throughout the 1930s;

Roosevelt never supported an antilynching bill for fear of alienating Southern Democrats. The **Scottsboro Boys** trial received national attention. In 1931, nine black young men were accused of raping two white women on a train. Without any real evidence, eight of the nine were sentenced to die. It is ironic that the American Communist party organized the appeals of the Scottsboro Boys; in the end, some of their convictions were overturned.

Nevertheless, blacks did support Franklin Roosevelt, as they felt that he was generally supportive of their cause. Roosevelt did hire blacks for several policy posts in his New Deal administration. Mary McLeod Bethune, founder of the National Council of Negro Women, was appointed in 1936 as director of the Division of Negro Affairs of the National Youth Administration. Bethune lobbied Roosevelt on the concerns of blacks, and also worked to increase the support of influential black leaders for the New Deal.

New Deal Culture

Many authors attempted to capture the human suffering that was so pronounced in the 1930s. Zora Neale Hurston wrote *Their Eyes Were Watching God* about growing up black in a small Florida town. *Studs Lonigan* by James T. Farrell depicted the lives of the Irish in Chicago. The previously mentioned *The Grapes of Wrath* by John Steinbeck tells the story of Dust Bowlers moving to California for survival, while Erskine Caldwell's *Tobacco Road* describes the suffering of sharecroppers in Georgia. *Gone with the Wind* by Margaret Mitchell offered a romanticized tale of survival from another period of crisis, the Civil War.

Most Americans of the 1930s got their entertainment through radio. Radio in the 1930s offered soap operas, comedies, and dramas. Americans were also offered "high culture" on most radio stations, as symphonic music and operas were standard fare. The response to H. G. Well's dramatization of "War of the Worlds" demonstrated the power of radio in American life.

Going to the movies provided a way for Americans to escape the sufferings of their daily lives; by 1939, nearly 70 percent of all adults went to the movies at least once a week. Lavish sets and dancing in movies such as *Gold Diggers of 1933* allowed people to leave their cares behind, at least for a couple of hours. Shirley Temple charmed millions, and movies such as *Mr. Smith Goes to Washington* showed audiences that in the end, justice would prevail. Promoters attempted to make movie-going itself a special event in the 1930s; theaters were designed to look like palaces, air conditioning was installed, and dishes and other utensils were often given away as theater promotions.

Chapter Review

Rapid Review

To achieve the perfect 5, you should be able to explain the following:

- The Great Depression had numerous long-lasting effects on American society.
- Franklin Roosevelt was the first activist president of the twentieth century who used the power of the federal government to help those who could not help themselves.
- The Great Depression's origins lay in economic problems of the late 1920s.
- The 1929 stock market crash was caused by, among other things, speculation on the part of investors and buying stocks "on the margin."

- The stock market crash began to affect the economy almost immediately, and its effects were felt by almost all by 1931.
- Herbert Hoover did act to end the depression, but believed that voluntary actions by both business and labor would lead America out of its economic difficulties.
- Franklin Roosevelt won the 1932 election by promising the New Deal to the American people and by promising to act in a decisive manner.
- Suffering was felt across American society; many in the Dust Bowl were forced to leave their farms.
- During the first hundred days, Roosevelt restored confidence in the banks, established the Civilian Conservation Corps, stabilized farm prices, and attempted to stabilize industry through the National Industrial Recovery Act.
- During the Second New Deal, the WPA was created and the Social Security Act was enacted; this was the most long-lasting piece of legislation from the New Deal.
- Roosevelt was able to craft a political coalition of urban whites, Southerners, union members, and blacks that kept the Democratic party in power through the 1980s.
- The New Deal had opponents from the left who said it didn't do enough to alleviate the effects of the depression and opponents from the right who said that the New Deal was Socialist in nature.
- Roosevelt's 1937 plan to pack the Supreme Court and the recession of 1937 demonstrated that New Deal programs were not entirely successful in ending the Great Depression.
- Many Americans turned to radio and the movies for relief during the depression.

Time Line

1929: Stock market crash
1930: Hawley-Smoot Tariff enacted
1931: Ford plants in Detroit shut down
      Initial trial of the Scottsboro Boys
1932: Glass-Steagall Banking Act enacted
      Bonus marchers routed from Washington
      Franklin D. Roosevelt elected president
      Huey Long announces "Share Our Wealth" movement
1933: Emergency Banking Relief Act enacted
      Prohibition ends
      Agricultural Adjustment Act enacted
      National Industrial Recovery Act enacted
      Civilian Conservation Corps established
      Tennessee Valley Authority formed
      Public Works Administration established
1934: American unemployment reaches highest point
1935: Beginning of the Second New Deal
      Works Progress Administration established
      Social Security Act enacted
      Wagner Act enacted
      Formation of Committee for Industrial Organization (CIO)
1936: Franklin Roosevelt reelected
      Sit-down strike against GM begins
1937: Recession of 1937 begins
      Roosevelt's plan to expand the Supreme Court defeated
1939: *Gone with the Wind* published
      The Grapes of Wrath published

› Review Questions

Multiple-Choice Questions

1. Which of the following was *not* a cause of the stock market crash?
   A. Excessive American loans to European countries
   B. Uneven division of wealth
   C. Installment buying
   D. Purchasing of stocks "on the margin"

2. Wealthy businessmen who objected to the New Deal programs of Franklin Roosevelt claimed that
   A. they unfairly aided the many who did not deserve it.
   B. New Deal programs smacked of "bolshevism."
   C. New Deal programs unfairly regulated businesses.
   D. all of the above.

3. The purpose of the Federal Deposit Insurance Corporation (FDIC) was to
   A. ensure that poor Americans had something to fall back on when they retired.
   B. inspect the financial transactions of important businesses.
   C. insure bank deposits of individual citizens.
   D. increase governmental control over the economy.

4. One group of women who were able to keep their jobs during the Great Depression were
   A. schoolteachers.
   B. clerical workers.
   C. domestic workers.
   D. government employees.

5. The popularity of Huey Long and Father Coughlin in the mid-1930s demonstrated that
   A. most Americans felt that the New Deal had gone too far in undermining traditional American values.
   B. more Americans were turning to religion in the 1930s.
   C. most Americans favored truly radical solutions to America's problems.
   D. many Americans felt that the government should do more to end the problems associated with the depression.

Short-Answer Question

6. Answer Parts A, B, and C.
   A. Briefly explain ONE example of a way that government was expanded to combat the effects of the Great Depression in the 1930s.
   B. Briefly explain a SECOND example of a way that government was expanded to combat the effects of the Great Depression in the 1930s.
   C. Briefly explain ONE example of resistance to the expansion of government in the 1930s.

❯ Answers and Explanations

1. **A.** All of the others were major underlying reasons for the crash. American loans to Europe benefited both European countries and American banking houses until the crash.

2. **D.** All of the criticisms listed were heard throughout the 1930s.

3. **C.** The FDIC was established after the bank holiday to insure individual accounts in certified banks and to increase confidence in the banking system. Americans began to put money back into banks after its institution.

4. **C.** In the other occupations, women were often fired before men, or had their hours drastically reduced. Those women who were employed as domestic workers were relatively safe, as this was one occupation that men, as a whole, rejected.

5. **D.** Many Americans wanted more New Deal–style programs and felt that Roosevelt should have gone even further in his proposed legislation. Many may have listened to Long and Coughlin, but when the time to vote came, cast their ballots for Roosevelt—thus negating answer C. The idea that the New Deal went too far in destroying American capitalism was popular in the business community, but was not widely shared in mainstream America.

6. **Parts A and B:** President Herbert Hoover took vigorous measures to combat the Great Depression. He urged business leaders to avoid wage reductions and employee layoffs. He organized charitable giving to help the unemployed. In 1932, he supported the establishment of the Reconstruction Finance Corporation (RFC) to lend money to banks and businesses. President Franklin Roosevelt launched his First New Deal to combat the Depression. Among the many programs authorized by Congress in 1933 were the Civilian Conservation Corps (CCC), which employed young men in conservation work, and the Tennessee Valley Authority (TVA), which constructed a series of dams to provide electricity to people living in the Tennessee River Valley. The National Industrial Recovery Act (NIRA) created the Public Works Administration (PWA), which provided jobs constructing public works, and the National Recovery Administration (NRA), which encouraged industries to set standards for prices and wages. The Agricultural Adjustment Administration (AAA) attempted to revive agricultural prices by compensating farmers for limiting production. Roosevelt's Second New Deal in 1935 created more government agencies. The Resettlement Administration helped farmers facing foreclosure. The Works Progress Administration (WPA) provided jobs to people who were on relief. The Wagner Act protected workers' right to organize unions and bargain collectively. It created the National Labor Relations Board (NLRB) to ensure that collective bargaining rights were enforced. The Social Security Act created a pension program for workers over 65 years old. It also set up a system to fund unemployment insurance. The Social Security Act is seen as a landmark in the development of the welfare state in the United States.

Part C: Herbert Hoover became a leading critic of the New Deal's expansion of the government. Former New York governor and Democratic presidential candidate Al Smith led the American Liberty League, which opposed the New Deal, especially its increases in taxation on people making more than $50,000. In 1937, following the Supreme Court's striking down of some parts of the First New Deal, President Roosevelt attempted to "pack" the Supreme Court with supporters through his proposed Justice Reorganization Bill. This effort to expand the Supreme Court generated much opposition from both Republicans and conservative Democrats. From this point on, a coalition of Republicans and conservative, mostly Southern, Democrats blocked further New Deal legislation.

World War II (1933–1945)

IN THIS CHAPTER

Summary: Throughout the 1930s the United States followed a foreign policy based on isolationism, which emphasized noninvolvement in European affairs. After Adolph Hitler became the Nazi dictator of Germany, some Americans believed that he was a reasonable man who could serve as a European bulwark against Stalin and the Soviet Union. After World War II began in Europe, President Roosevelt sensed that America would eventually be drawn into it and began Lend-Lease and other measures to help the British. The December 7, 1941, Japanese attack on Pearl Harbor mobilized American public opinion for war. Americans fought on two fronts during the war: against the Germans and the Italians in Europe and against the Japanese in the Pacific. In Europe, U.S. forces and their British and Soviet Allies eventually invaded Germany and crushed the Nazis. In the Pacific, superior American air and sea power led to the defeat of the Japanese. The decision to drop the atomic bomb on two Japanese cities is still considered controversial by some historians today. At the time, President Truman decided to drop the bomb based on calculations of the human cost of an American invasion of Japan. Americans contributed greatly to the war effort at home through rationing, working extra shifts, and the purchase of war bonds. As a result of World War II, the United States and the Soviet Union emerged as the two major world powers.

Keywords

Isolationism: American foreign policy of the 1920s and 1930s based on the belief that it was in the best interest of the United States not to become involved in foreign conflicts that did not directly threaten American interests.

Yalta Conference: meeting held at Yalta in the Soviet Union between President Roosevelt, British Prime Minister Winston Churchill, and Soviet leader Joseph Stalin in February 1945; at this meeting critical decisions on the future of postwar Europe were made. At Yalta it was agreed that Germany would be divided into four zones, that free elections would take place after the war in Eastern Europe, and that the Soviet Union would join the war against Japan.

Bataan Death March: after the Japanese landed in the Philippines in May 1942, nearly 75,000 American and Filipino prisoners were forced to endure a 60-mile march; during this ordeal, 10,000 prisoners died or were killed.

Manhattan Project: secret project to build an atomic bomb that began in Los Alamos, New Mexico, in August 1942; the first successful test of a bomb took place on July 16, 1945.

Rosie the Riveter: figure that symbolized American working women during World War II. After the war, women were expected to return to more traditional roles.

Double V campaign: campaign popularized by American black leaders during World War II emphasizing the need for a double victory: over Germany and Japan and also over racial prejudice in the United States. Many blacks who fought in World War II were disappointed that the America they returned to still harbored racial hatreds.

Internment camps: mandatory resettlement camps for Japanese Americans from America's West Coast, created in February 1942 during World War II by executive order of President Franklin Roosevelt. In 1944, the Supreme Court ruled that the camps were legal.

American Foreign Policy in the 1930s

As Italy, Germany, and Japan all expanded their empires in the 1930s, most Americans favored a continuation of the policy of **isolationism**. An isolationist group, the **America First Committee**, attracted nearly 820,000 members by 1940. Isolationists believed that it was in America's best interests to stay out of foreign conflicts that did not directly threaten American interests. A congressional committee led by Senator Gerald Nye investigated the origins of America's entry into World War I and found that bankers and arms manufacturers did much to influence America's entry into the war. On a practical level, Americans were consumed with the problems of the Great Depression and were generally unable to focus on overseas problems.

Congressional legislation passed in the period attempted to keep America out of future wars between other powers. The **Neutrality Act of 1935** stated that if countries went to war, the United States would not trade arms or weapons with them for six months; in addition, any nonmilitary goods sold to nations at war would have to be paid for up front and would have to be transported in non-American ships (this was called "cash-and-carry").

German expansionism in Europe convinced Franklin Roosevelt that the United States, at some point, would *have* to enter the war on the side of Great Britain (even though public opinion strongly opposed this). On September 1, 1939, Germany invaded Poland, and two days later England and France declared war on Germany. Within three weeks, Roosevelt asked Congress to pass the **Neutrality Act of 1939**, which would allow the cash-and-carry sale of arms to countries at war (this legislation was designed to facilitate the sale of American arms to Britain and France). The bill passed on a party-line vote.

News of rapid German advances in Europe began to change American attitudes, with more and more people agreeing with Roosevelt that the best course of action would be to prepare for eventual war. The rapid defeat of France at the hands of the Nazis was stunning to many Americans. In September of 1940, Roosevelt gave Great Britain 50 older American destroyers in return for the rights to build military bases in Bermuda and Newfoundland.

United States and the Middle East in the Interwar Era

In the 1920s, the United States rejected Woodrow Wilson's vision of the United States as an active leader on the world stage and instead turned to a twenty-year period of isolationism. As a result, American political involvement in the Middle East became minimal, leaving France and Great Britain to exert tremendous influence in the region. As previously noted, France had a mandate to control Syria and Lebanon, while the British controlled Iraq, Transjordan, and Palestine. In 1932, the British granted Iraq independence, although the British continued to have major influence on government officials and their actions in Iraq.

In the 1920s, the Middle East remained a romantic and idealized region of the world to most Americans. They became fascinated with the adventures of T. E. Lawrence ("Lawrence of Arabia") leading and uniting Arab tribesmen against the Turks in World War I and went in droves to see romantic movies set in the deserts of the region, starring Rudolph Valentino. The appeal of Zionism for many American Jews waned in the post–World War I years as stories of the sufferings of Jews that were so widespread in the World War I era declined.

However, the concern among Jews in the United States for the plight of European Jews increased with the ascension of Adolf Hitler to power in Germany in 1933. With the increased persecution of the German Jews in the mid-1930s, pressure began to be exerted on European countries as well as on the United States to allow more German Jews to immigrate. In the 1930s, there was increased hope that a Jewish homeland could be established in Palestine, but this hope was dashed by a White Paper issued by the British government in 1939, which seriously limited the number of Jews who could immigrate to Palestine.

There are historians who are very critical of the conscious decision of the United States in the 1930s not to allow more Jewish refugees into the country. These critics state that if the United States had opened its shores to more Jews in the 1930s, their lives could have been saved. Provisions of the National Origins Act of 1924 limited the number of Germans who could enter the country to slightly over 25,000 per year. In addition, immigrants from all countries were refused admission if they could not prove that they could support themselves once they arrived in the United States, thus further limiting the number of Jewish immigrants who could settle in the United States. As a result, an average of fewer than 9,000 Jews from Germany entered the United States annually during the 1930s.

It should be noted that American public opinion in the decade was decidedly against allowing more immigrants to enter the country, especially immigrants who were Jewish. America was in the midst of the Great Depression; editorial page writers, politicians, and many average citizens stated that under these circumstances the last thing America needed was immigrants competing for precious jobs that existed there. Unfortunately, anti-Semitism did not exist only in Germany; anti-Semitic sentiment in the United States strongly opposed allowing any more Jewish immigrants into the country.

The one resource from the Middle East that attracted great interest from American investors in the 1920s and 1930s was oil. As more and more Americans began to drive automobiles in the 1920s, reliable sources of petroleum products were needed outside of the United States. In 1928, British, French, Dutch, and American oil companies agreed to the Red Line Agreement, in which they agreed to act together to export oil from the region; as a result, America began to export oil from Iraq in late 1928.

In 1933, the King of Saudi Arabia granted Standard Oil of California the right to export Saudi Arabian oil. Five years later, geologists working for Standard Oil of California discovered major oil reserves in Saudi Arabia.

During World War II, the United States would have to move to actively protect its oil reserves in Saudi Arabia from attack by the Axis powers. Thus began the trend, which has lasted into the twenty-first century, of the United States depending on the Middle East region for oil and using its military to protect its oil interests there.

Presidential Election of 1940 and Its Aftermath

No president in American history had ever served more than two consecutive terms. Just before the Democratic National Convention, Roosevelt quietly stated that if he was nominated, he would accept. Roosevelt was quickly nominated; his Republican opponent was Wendell Wilkie, an ex-Democrat. Roosevelt emerged victorious, but by a smaller margin than in his two previous victories. A number of those who voted against Roosevelt did so as a protest against the widerspread poverty and unemployment that still existed in America.

Roosevelt interpreted his victory as a mandate to continue preparations for the eventual U.S. entry into World War II. By early 1941, Roosevelt proposed giving the British aid for the war effort without getting cash in return (it was stated that payment could be made after the war). By the terms of the **Lend-Lease Act**, Congress gave the president the ability to send immediate aid to Britain; Roosevelt immediately authorized nearly $7 billion in aid. As Roosevelt had stated in a 1940 speech, the United States had become an "Arsenal of Democracy."

In August 1941, Roosevelt secretly met with British Prime Minister Winston Churchill off the coast of Newfoundland. The two agreed that America would, in all probability, soon be in the war and that the war should be fought for the principles of democracy. Roosevelt and Churchill authorized the publication of their commonly held beliefs in a document called the **Atlantic Charter**. In this document, the two leaders proclaimed that they were opposed to territorial expansion for either country, and they were for free trade and self-determination. They also agreed that another world organization would have to be created to replace the League of Nations and that this new world body would have the power to guarantee the "security" of the world. Roosevelt also agreed that the United States would ship lend-lease materials bound for Britain as far as Iceland; this brought the United States one step closer to full support for the Allied cause.

Attack on Pearl Harbor

The Japanese desire to create an Asian empire was the prime motivation behind their invasion of Manchuria in 1931, attacks on eastern China in 1937, and the occupation of much of French Indochina in 1941. As a result of Japanese actions in Southeast Asia, Roosevelt froze all Japanese assets in the United States, cut off the sale of oil to Japan, and closed the Panama Canal to Japanese ships.

From July 1941 until the beginning of December, near-constant negotiations took place between diplomats of Japan and the United States. The Japanese desperately wanted to regain normal trade relations with the United States, but American diplomats insisted that the Japanese leave China first, which the Japanese were unwilling to do. Most Japanese military and civilian leaders were convinced that the Japanese could never achieve their goal of a Pacific empire as long as the United States was militarily active in the region. By December 1, the planning was complete for the Japanese attack on Pearl Harbor.

A few revisionist historians believe that Franklin Roosevelt knew of the impending attack on Pearl Harbor. These historians maintain that Roosevelt was acutely aware that many Americans were still opposed to American entry into war, but that an event such as Pearl Harbor would put the entire country squarely behind the war effort. The vast majority of historians believe that American intelligence knew the Japanese were going to attack somewhere, but didn't know that the attack would be at Pearl Harbor; many in American military intelligence believed the Dutch East Indies would be the next target of the Japanese. The "Roosevelt Knew" thesis might be good for a documentary film or two but little else.

On Sunday morning, December 7, 1941, 190 Japanese warplanes attacked the American Pacific fleet anchored at Pearl Harbor. When the attack was done, 150 American airplanes were destroyed (most of them never left the ground), six battleships were sunk, as were a number of smaller ships, and nearly 2,400 Americans were killed. Luckily for the American navy, the aircraft carriers based at Pearl Harbor were out at sea on the morning of the attack.

The next day Roosevelt asked Congress for a declaration of war, stating that December 7 was "a date which will live in infamy." On December 11, Germany and Italy (who had signed a Tripartite Pact with Japan in 1940) declared war on the United States.

America Enters the War

In September of 1940, the President had authorized the creation of a system for the **conscription** of men into the armed forces; in the months immediately after Pearl Harbor, thousands were drafted and countless others volunteered for service. Soldiers in World War II called themselves "**GIs**"; this referred to the "Government Issued" stamp that appeared on the uniforms, tools, weapons, and everything else the government issued to them. A Council for National Defense had also been created in 1940; this body worked rapidly to convert factories over to war production. Additional legislation was also needed to prepare the country for war. In early 1942, the General Maximum Price Regulation Act immediately froze prices and established the rationing system that was in place for most of the war. The **Revenue Act of 1942** greatly expanded the number of Americans who had to pay federal income tax, thus increasing the amount of federal revenue.

America was forced to fight a war in Europe and a war in the Pacific. In the European theater of war, American naval forces first engaged the Germans as they attempted to protect convoys of ships taking critical food and supplies to Great Britain. These convoys were often attacked by German submarines. In this **Battle of the Atlantic**, German torpedoes were dreadfully accurate (even though sonar was being used by the Americans). Between January and August 1942, over 500 ships were sunk by German submarines.

American infantrymen were first involved in actual fighting in North Africa. American and British forces joined to defeat French North Africa in late 1942. American troops also played a role in the battles that eventually forced General Rommel's Africa Korps to surrender in May 1943. American and British soldiers also began a difficult offensive into Sicily and Italy two months later; by June 1944, Rome had surrendered.

Ever since 1941, the Soviet Union had been the only power to consistently engage the Nazi army (the Soviet Union lost 20 million people in World War II). Stalin had asked on several occasions that a second front be opened in Western Europe; by early 1944, an invasion of France by water was being planned by Dwight D. Eisenhower, commander of all Allied forces (who would become president in 1953).

The D-Day invasion took place on the morning of June 6, 1944. The initial Allied losses on Omaha Beach were staggering, yet the D-Day invasion was the beginning of the end for Nazi Germany. By the end of July, over 2 million Allied soldiers were on the ground in France, and the final squeeze of Nazi Germany began. American and British forces liberated French cities and towns as they moved eastward; at the same time, Russian troops were rolling westward. By August, Paris had been liberated.

The last major German offensive of the war was the **Battle of the Bulge**. Nearly 85,000 American soldiers were killed, wounded, or captured in this battle. The German attack moved the Allied lines back into Belgium, but reinforcement led by General George S. Patton again forced the Germans to retreat. When the German general staff learned that they had not been victorious at the Battle of the Bulge, most admitted that Germany would soon be defeated. American and British bombings did much to destroy several German cities.

Advancing American, British, and Russian troops were horrified to find concentration camps or the remnants of them. These camps were integral parts of Nazi Germany's **Final Solution** to the "Jewish problem." Between 1941 and 1945, over 6 million Jews were killed in the event now referred to as the **Holocaust**. Historians maintain that if the war continued for another two years, all of European Jewry might have been eliminated. Advancing troops were outraged at what they saw in these camps, and on several occasions shot all of the Nazi guards on the spot. Why the Holocaust occurred, and why it was endorsed by so many Germans, is the subject of hundreds of books and articles in scholarly journals.

Some historians are critical of the diplomatic and military actions of the United States both before and during the Holocaust. During the mid- to late 1930s, the State Department made it very difficult for European Jews to immigrate to the United States; with alarming unemployment figures in the United States because of the Great Depression, American decision makers felt it unwise to admit large numbers of immigrants to the country. Franklin Roosevelt knew of the existence of the concentration camps as early as late 1943, yet chose not to bomb them (which many in the camps say they would have welcomed). Roosevelt maintained that the number one priority of America had to be winning the war. Nevertheless, historians note that concern for the plight of the Jews caused a number of world leaders to support the creation of the state of Israel in the years immediately following the war.

In March 1945, Allied troops crossed the Rhine River, and met up with advancing Russian troops at the Elbe River on April 25. After a fierce battle, the Russians took Berlin. Deep in his bunker, Hitler committed suicide on May 1, and Germany unconditionally surrendered one week later. Celebrations for V-E Day (Victory in Europe Day) were jubilant in London and Paris, but were more restrained in American cities, as the United States still had to deal with the Japanese.

In February 1945, Roosevelt, Stalin, and Churchill met at the **Yalta Conference**. Franklin Roosevelt had been elected to a fourth term in 1944, but photos revealed him to be very ill at Yalta (he would live only another two months). At Yalta, the three leaders made major decisions concerning the structure of postwar Europe. It was agreed that Germany would be split into four zones of occupation (administered by England, France, the United States, and the Soviet Union), and that Berlin, located in the Soviet zone, would also be partitioned. Stalin promised to allow free elections in the Eastern European nations he had freed from Nazi control, and said that the Soviets would join the war against Japan after the surrender of Germany. Many historians consider the decisions made at the Yalta Conference (and the failure of the Soviet Union to totally adhere to them) to be major reasons for the beginning of the cold war.

Some historians are critical of Franklin Roosevelt for "giving in" to Stalin at Yalta. It should be remembered that, at the time of this meeting, Roosevelt had only two months to live. In addition, in February 1945, the atomic bomb was not yet a working weapon. American planning for the defeat of Japan was for a full attack on the Japanese mainland; in Roosevelt's eyes, Soviet participation in this attack was absolutely crucial (in return for this support, Roosevelt made concessions to Stalin on Eastern Europe and supported the Soviet acquisition of ports and territories in Korea, Manchuria, and Outer Mongolia). Winston Churchill had strong reservations about the ultimate goals and conduct of Stalin and the Soviet Union at Yalta; these reservations would later intensify, and were articulated by Churchill in his "iron curtain" speech of March 1946.

Role of the Middle East in World War II

The Middle East played an important strategic role in Allied military planning during World War II. Some historians argue that this is the first time American political leaders appreciated the true significance of the region in world affairs. The Americans and the British both thought it absolutely crucial that oil resources in the region not fall into German hands, and that these resources continue to be available for the Allied war effort. In addition, there were fears that the Germans and the Japanese might link up and cut off British access to India; control of the Middle East would be central to this plan.

Many of the efforts to maintain control of the Middle East for the strategic interests of the Allies fell on the Americans. The United States established diplomatic relations with Saudi Arabia and gave the Saudis large amounts of economic aid to ensure the continued flow of Saudi oil supplies. American diplomats in both Washington and Turkey worked to convince the Turks to stay neutral in the war, which would allow the Allies continued access to the Mediterranean Sea. In addition, American and British forces landed in Morocco and Algeria in 1942. Military planners placed Allied troops in the region to prepare for an eventual invasion of Italy. In 1943, British and American forces occupied Tunisia (which was controlled by the Germans), and from there began their assault on Sicily and eventually Italy itself.

American Lend-Lease efforts extended aid to both Great Britain and the Soviet Union by late 1941, and American efforts to assist the Soviet war effort also went through the Middle East. The Americans established large port facilities in Iran, where the parts for trucks, airplanes, weapons, and other war material were landed, assembled, and then sent by train to the Soviet armies fighting the Germans on the Eastern front. History of the war between Germany and the Soviet Union points to this assistance being absolutely indispensable for the eventual Soviet victory over the Nazis. The thousands of Iranians employed by the Americans in this effort were thankful for the additional income these jobs provided them, but sometimes complained about the arrogance and total disregard for local manners and customs exhibited by their employers and the majority of American soldiers stationed in Iran.

War Against Japan

In the aftermath of the attack on Pearl Harbor, Japan advanced against British controlled islands and territories in the Pacific. By April 1942, Hong Kong and Singapore were both in Japanese hands. General Douglas MacArthur controlled a large American and Filipino force in the Philippines. A large Japanese force landed there, and in March MacArthur was forced to abandon his troops and go to Australia. On May 6, 1942, Americans holding out on the Bataan Peninsula were finally forced to surrender. About 75,000 American and Filipino prisoners were forced to endure the 60-mile **Bataan Death March**, during which over 10,000 prisoners were executed or died from weakness (it was several years before Washington became aware of this march).

Just two days later, the Americans won their first decisive victory at the **Battle of the Coral Sea**. American airplanes launched from aircraft carriers were able to stop the advance of several large Japanese troop transports. Troops on these ships were to be used for an attack on Australia. After this defeat, the Japanese could never again mount a planned attack there. American airplanes also played a crucial role in the **Battle of Midway**. This battle took place in early June 1942; in it, the Japanese lost 4 aircraft carriers and over 200 planes. Many military historians consider the battle to be the turning point of the Pacific War; after this, Japan was never able to launch a major offensive. By mid-1942, American industrial might became more and more of a factor; the Americans could simply produce more airplanes than the Japanese could.

The Japanese were again halted at the **Battle of Guadalcanal**, which began in August 1942 and continued into the following year. American marines engaged in jungle warfare and even hand-to-hand combat. On many occasions Japanese units would fight nearly until the last man. Beginning in 1943, the Allies instituted a policy of **island-hopping**; by this policy, key Japanese strongholds would be attacked by air and sea power as American marines would push on around these strongholds. By late 1944, American bombers were able to reach major Japanese cities, and unleashed massive bombing attacks on them.

By 1944, the war had clearly turned against the Japanese. In late October, General MacArthur returned to the Philippine island of Leyte (although the city of Manila was not totally liberated until the following March). The Japanese began to use **kamikaze pilots** in a desperate attempt to destroy Allied ships. Several more bloody battles waited ahead for American forces. America suffered 25,000 casualties at the Battle of Iwo Jima, and another 50,000 at the Battle of Okinawa. After these battles, however, nothing was left to stop an Allied invasion of Japan.

Decision to Drop the Atomic Bomb

The incredibly bloody battles described in the preceding section greatly concerned military officials who were planning for an invasion of Japan. Japanese resistance to such an attack would have been fanatical. Franklin Roosevelt had suddenly died in April 1945; the new president, Harry Truman, was then informed about the atomic bomb. The actual planning for this bomb was the purpose of the **Manhattan Project**, begun in August 1942. Construction of this bomb took place in Los Alamos, New Mexico, under the direction of J. Robert Oppenheimer. The bomb was successfully tested in the New Mexico desert on July 16, 1945.

Much debate had taken place over the American decision to drop the atomic bomb on Japanese cities. For Harry Truman, this was not a difficult decision. Losses in an invasion of Japan would have been large; Truman later admitted that what had happened at Pearl Harbor and on the Bataan Death March also influenced his decision. Some historians also claim that some in both the State Department and the War Department saw the Soviet Union as the next potential enemy of the United States and wanted to use the atomic bomb to "show them what we had." After the atomic bombs were dropped, American public opinion was incredibly supportive of Truman's decision. It should be noted that movies, newsreels, and even comic books made the eventual decision to drop the bomb easier by turning the war against the Japanese into a race war. The Japanese, referred to as "Japs," were portrayed with crude racial stereotypes, and were seen as sneaky and certainly not to be trusted (it is interesting to note that the war against Germany was usually portrayed as a war against "Hitler" or against "the Nazis" and almost never as a war against the German people).

On August 6, 1945, the airplane **Enola Gay** dropped a bomb on the city of Hiroshima. Over 75,000 were killed in the attack. Three days later another bomb was dropped on Nagasaki. Some historians are especially critical of the dropping of the second bomb; there is evidence that the Japanese were pursuing a surrender through diplomatic circles on the day of the attack. Japan surrendered one day later, and V-J celebrations took place in many American cities the following day.

Home Front During the War

As previously stated, the federal government took action even before the war began, to prepare the American economy for war. Thousands of American businessmen also went to Washington to take on jobs relating to the war effort. These were called "dollar-a-year" men, as almost all still received their regular salary from wherever they worked.

The demand for workers increased dramatically during the war years, thus increasing wages for workers as well. Union membership increased during the war; unions generally honored "no-strike" agreements that were made in the weeks after Pearl Harbor. Beginning in 1943, some strikes did occur, especially in the coal mines.

The government needed money to finance the war effort. As stated previously, more money was raised by expanding greatly the number of Americans who had to pay income taxes. In addition, America followed a policy begun in World War I and sold **war bonds**.

During both wars, various celebrities made public appearances to encourage the public to buy these bonds.

Average Americans were asked to sacrifice much during the war. Goods such as gasoline, rubber, meat, sugar, and butter were rationed during the war; American families kept **ration cards** to determine which of these goods they could still buy during any given period. Recycling was commonplace during the war, and many had to simply do without the goods they desired. Women, for example, were desperate for silk stockings; some took to drawing a line up the back of their legs to make it appear that they had stockings on.

City dwellers had to take part in "blackouts," where they would have to lower all shades to make any enemy airplane attacks more difficult. Men and boys both took turns at lookout stations, where the skies were constantly scanned for enemy bombers. Many high schools across the country eliminated vacations during the year; by doing this, school could end early and students could go off and do essential work. Many workers stayed for extra shifts at work, called "victory shifts."

Popular culture also reflected the necessities of war. Many movies during the war were light comedies, designed to keep people's minds off the war. Other movies, such as *Casablanca,* emphasized self-sacrifice and helping the war effort. "White Christmas" (sung by Bing Crosby) was a favorite during the war, evoking nostalgia in both soldiers abroad and those on the home front. Professional baseball continued during the war, but rosters were made up of players who had been classified 4-F by local draft boards (unfit for military service). The All-American Girls' Baseball League was founded in 1943 and also provided a wartime diversion for thousands of fans.

Women also entered the American workforce in large numbers during the war. Many women working in "traditional women's jobs" moved to factory jobs vacated when men went off to fight. The figure of **Rosie the Riveter** symbolized American working women during the war. In the 1930s, women were discouraged from working (the argument was that they would be taking jobs from men); during World War II, many posters informed women that it was their patriotic duty to work. Problems remained for women in the workplace, however. For many jobs, even in the defense industry, they were paid less than men. It is also ironic that when the war ended, women were encouraged that it was now their "patriotic duty" to return home and become housewives.

Discrimination During the War

Many blacks also took important factory jobs and eagerly signed up for military service. However, discrimination against blacks continued during the war. Black military units were strictly segregated and were often used for menial chores instead of combat. Some American blacks at home began the **Double V campaign**. This pushed for the defeat of Germany and Japan but also the defeat of racial prejudice. CORE (the Congress for Racial Equality) was founded in 1942, and organized the very first sit-ins and boycotts; these actions would become standard tactics of the civil rights movement in the 1950s and 1960s.

Many on the West Coast feared that the Japanese who lived there were sympathizers or even spies for the Japanese cause (even though many had been born and brought up in the United States). On February 19, 1942, Franklin Roosevelt signed Executive Order 9066, which ordered Japanese Americans to **internment camps**. American public officials told the Japanese that this was being done for their own protection; however, many Japanese noted when they got to their camps that the guns guarding these relocation centers were pointed inward and never outward. Many businesses and homes were lost by Japanese citizens.

Influential Japanese Americans were outraged by these actions, and a legal challenge was mounted against the internment camps. In a 1944 decision, *Korematsu v. United States,* the Supreme Court ruled that the internment camps were legal, since they were based "on military necessity." In 1988, the United States government formally apologized to those who had been placed in camps and gave each survivor $20,000. It should be noted that

American units of soldiers of Japanese descent were created during the war, and that they fought with great bravery in the campaign against Hitler.

Chapter Review

Rapid Review

To achieve the perfect 5, you should be able to explain the following:

- War production for World War II pulled America out of the Great Depression.
- World War II turned America into one of the two major world powers.
- America continued to pursue a foreign policy of isolationism throughout the 1930s.
- Lend-Lease and other measures by Franklin Roosevelt brought America into the war on the side of England one year before America actually entered the war.
- The Pearl Harbor attack was part of an overall Japanese strategy, and it mobilized American public opinion for war.
- Battles fought by American GIs in Africa, Italy, and Western Europe were crucial in creating a "second front" and important in the eventual defeat of Hitler.
- Decision made at the Yalta Conference did much to influence the postwar world.
- Superior American air and sea power ultimately led to the defeat of the Japanese in the Pacific.
- The decision to drop the atomic bomb was based on the calculations of the human cost of an American invasion of Japan and as retaliation for Japanese actions during the war.
- Americans sacrificed greatly during the war and contributed to the Allied victory through rationing, extra work, and the purchase of war bonds.
- American women contributed greatly to the war effort, especially by taking industrial jobs that had been held by departed soldiers.
- Blacks continued to meet with discrimination both in and out of the armed services, as did the Japanese. Japanese citizens from the West Coast were forced to move to internment camps. The American government in 1988 issued a formal apology for these actions.

Time Line

1933: Hitler comes to power in Germany
1935: Neutrality Act of 1935
1938: Hitler annexes Austria, Sudetenland
1939: Nazi-Soviet Pact
      Germany invades Poland/beginning of World War II
1940: Roosevelt reelected for third term
      American Selective Service plan instituted
1941: Lend-Lease assistance begins for England
      Japanese attack on Pearl Harbor/United States officially enters World War II
      Germany declares war on United States
1942: American troops engage in combat in Africa
      Japanese interment camps opened
      Battle of Coral Sea, Battle of Midway
      Casablanca released

1943: Allied armies invade Sicily
United Mine Workers strike
1944: D-Day Invasion
Roosevelt defeats Thomas Dewey, elected for fourth term
Beginning of Battle of the Bulge
1945: Yalta Conference
Concentration camps discovered by Allied forces
FDR dies in Warm Springs, Georgia; Harry Truman becomes president
Germany surrenders unconditionally
Atomic bombs dropped on Hiroshima and Nagasaki
Japan surrenders unconditionally

› Review Questions

Multiple-Choice Questions

1. The internment of Japanese Americans began for all of the reasons listed *except*
   A. it was felt that Japanese living in California had divided loyalties when war began.
   B. newspapers on the West Coast reported incidents of Japanese Americans aiding the Japanese military effort.
   C. Japanese Americans needed protection, and the camps would provide it for them.
   D. the portrayal of the Japanese in American films and magazines.

2. Which was *not* a reason for the hatred many felt toward the Japanese during the war?
   A. The bombing of Pearl Harbor
   B. The fact that they were physically different in appearance from most Americans
   C. The outrage over the Bataan Death March as soon as Americans first learned of it in late 1941
   D. The portrayal of the Japanese in American films, magazines, and newspapers

3. Many observers would later be critical of the Yalta Conference for all of the following *except*
   A. at the conference the Soviet Union was given control over more of Germany than the other Allied powers.
   B. the Soviet Union did not promise to join the war against Japan immediately.
   C. Franklin Roosevelt was near death at the time of the conference.
   D. all of the countries liberated by the Soviet Union would remain at least temporarily under Soviet control.

4. The United States did little to stop the spread of Hitler and Nazi Germany in the 1930s because
   A. the United States was much more concerned with diplomatic and political affairs in the Pacific than in Europe in the 1930s.
   B. the United States was more interested in solving domestic problems in the 1930s.
   C. the findings of the Nye commission did much to sour Americans on future military involvement.
   D. B and C

5. Americans continued to crave diversions during World War II and went in large numbers to see all of the following *except*
   A. auto racing.
   B. professional baseball.
   C. movies.
   D. big band concerts.

Short-Answer Question

6. Answer Parts A, B, and C.
   A. Briefly explain ONE example of an American military contribution to Allied victory in World War II.
   B. Briefly explain a SECOND example of an American military contribution to Allied victory in World War II.
   C. Briefly explain ONE example of an effect of World War II on the American home front.

› Answers and Explanations

1. **C**. Although this was the official reason given at the time, the other reasons listed were the actual reasons. California newspapers reported fabricated stories of Japanese Americans assisting the Japanese war effort.

2. **C**. The Bataan Death March did not occur until 1942, and most Americans did not know about it until 1945.

3. **A**. At the conference, the Soviet Union, England, France, and the United States were all to administer parts of Germany; the Soviets did not get more than anyone else. Criticism existed because by the decisions made at Yalta, the Soviet Union joined the war against Japan only days before Japan was defeated. In addition, "temporary" Soviet control over Eastern Europe allowed Communist governments to be set up there. Other historians question the decisions Franklin Roosevelt made at Yalta; many wonder if his physical and mental condition were adequate for such a conference.

4. **D**. American policies in the 1930s were largely concerned with solving the problems of the Depression, and the Nye commission reported that arms manufacturers, looking for profits, were largely responsible for pushing America into World War I.

5. **A**. Because of shortages of gasoline and rubber for tires, auto racing was almost totally eliminated for much of the war.

6. **Parts A and B**: Because of its industrial might, the United States became the "Arsenal of Democracy." The United States provided tanks, trucks, and other military supplies to its allies through the Lend-Lease program that began in 1941. American military forces played an important role in defeating the Axis powers. In the Battle of Midway, fought on June 4 to 7, 1942, the U.S. Navy turned the tide of the war in the Pacific, decisively defeating the Japanese fleet, sinking four Japanese aircraft carriers. In August, the American troops landed on the island of Guadalcanal, beginning a campaign of island-hopping toward Japan that culminated in the bloody battles of Iwo Jima and Okinawa in 1945. In the European theater of war, the U.S. Navy helped defeat the German submarine threat. Bombers of the Army Air Force weakened German industrial production. American and British forces landed in North Africa in 1942, and Sicily and Italy in 1943. On June 6, 1944, the Allies invaded France, landing at beaches in Normandy. In December, American forces turned back a desperate German counterattack in the Battle of the Bulge. American forces helped force Germany to surrender on May 8, 1945. The Japanese Empire was still fighting on. The United States had been working on an atomic bomb since August 1942, in a top-secret program code-named the Manhattan Project. An atomic bomb was successfully tested at Alamogordo, New Mexico, on July 16, 1945. On August 6 an atomic bomb was dropped on the Japanese city of Hiroshima. Another bomb was dropped on the city of Nagasaki three days later. The Japanese surrendered soon afterward.

   Part C: The Revenue Act of 1942 greatly increased the number of Americans who paid income tax. The government raised more money selling Americans war bonds. Goods such as gasoline, meat, and sugar were rationed during the war. Families received ration cards that indicated what they could purchase at any given time. Many women replaced male workers who had joined the military. "Rosie the Riveter" symbolized the important contributions that women made to war industries. Most Americans supported the war effort following the Japanese attack on Pearl Harbor. Many songs and movies expressed patriotic themes.

CHAPTER **25**

Origins of the Cold War (1945–1960)

IN THIS CHAPTER

Summary: Even before the end of World War II, strains began to develop in the wartime alliance between Great Britain, the United States, and the Soviet Union. At the Yalta conference, Soviet leader Joseph Stalin had promised free elections in eastern European countries the Soviet Union liberated from nazism; in the months after the war it became obvious that these elections would not take place. British Prime Minister Winston Churchill warned that the Soviet Union was creating an "iron curtain" between Eastern and Western Europe; the United States began to follow a policy of containment to stop the spread of communism. Through the Marshall Plan, the United States spent millions to rebuild Western Europe after the war. Stalin tested Western will by enforcing a blockade of Berlin in 1948. Western anxieties increased in 1949 when the Soviets announced that they had an atomic bomb and when Communist forces led by Mao Zedong took power over mainland China. The cold war had a major impact at home; the House Un-American Activities Committee (HUAC) began to search for Communists in the entertainment industry, State Department official Alger Hiss was accused of being a Communist spy, and Julius and Ethel Rosenberg were executed for giving atomic secrets to the Soviet Union. During the Korean War, United Nations and American forces were severely tested as they attempted to "contain communism" in Korea. Senator Joseph McCarthy claimed knowledge of Communists in the State Department, the army, and in other branches of government. Both the United States and the Soviet Union built up their military arsenals in the 1950s; by the end of the decade, President Eisenhower warned of the spreading "military-industrial complex."

KEY IDEA

Keywords

Satellite countries: Eastern European countries that came under the control of the Soviet Union after World War II; the Soviets argued that they had liberated these countries from the Nazis and thus they had a right to continue to influence developments there.

Iron Curtain: Term coined by British Prime Minister Winston Churchill in a March 1946 speech in Fulton, Missouri; Churchill forcefully proclaimed that the Soviet Union was establishing an "iron curtain" between the free countries of Western Europe and the Communist-controlled countries of Eastern Europe.

Containment Policy: policy devised by American diplomat George F. Kennan; Kennan believed that the United States needed to implement long-term military, economic, and diplomatic strategies in order to "contain" the spread of communism. Kennan's ideas became official U.S. government policy in the late 1940s.

Truman Doctrine: articulated in 1947, this policy stated that the United States would support any democratic nation that resisted communism.

Marshall Plan: American plan that spent $12 billion for the rebuilding of Western Europe after World War II; the plan produced an economic revival and helped stave off the growth of Communist influence.

Berlin Airlift: American effort that flew in supplies to West Berlin after the Soviet Union and the East German governments blocked the roads to that city beginning in June 1948; American airplanes flew in supplies for 15 months, causing the Soviet Union to call off the blockade.

NATO: North Atlantic Treaty Organization, a military alliance between the United States and Western European countries that was formed in April 1949.

Warsaw Pact: military pact formed in 1955 between the Soviet Union and its Eastern European satellite countries.

HUAC: House Un-American Activities Committee; in 1947 this committee began to investigate the entertainment industry for Communist influences.

Blacklist: list created by HUAC and various private agencies indicating individuals in the entertainment industry who might be Communists or who might have been influenced by Communists in the past; many individuals named in the blacklist could not find work in the industry until the 1960s.

McCarthyism: term used to describe the accusations by Wisconsin Senator Joseph McCarthy and his supporters in the early 1950s that certain people in government, academia, and the arts were secret Communists. McCarthy's charges were largely unsubstantiated.

Domino theory: theory that if one country in a region fell under Communist rule, then other countries in the region would follow; this theory would be used to justify American involvement in Vietnam.

Sputnik: first artificial satellite, launched in 1957 by the Soviet Union; the fact that the Soviets launched a satellite before the United States shocked many in the American scientific community.

Winning the **cold war** was the central goal of the United States from 1945 all the way until the fall of communism in 1990 to 1991. Almost all domestic and foreign policy decisions made in this era related in some way to American efforts to defeat the Soviet Union and their Allies. A large part of the success of many sectors of the American economy in the post–World War II era was related to defense and defense-related contracts. Some politicians lost their careers in this era if they were perceived to be "soft on communism."

Exactly whose fault was the cold war? Hundreds of books and articles have been written about that very subject. American historians assigned blame to the Soviet Union for aggressive actions on their part in the period immediately following the end of World War II. "**Revisionist**" American historians have claimed that the Soviets were forced into these actions by the perceived aggressiveness of the United States and its Allies. What actually happened in those years immediately following World War II is the subject of this chapter.

First Cracks in the Alliance: 1945

The alliance that proved victorious in World War II began to show strains even before the end of the war. In the preceding chapter, it was mentioned that tough decisions were made at the **Yalta Conference**, including allowing elections in Eastern European nations. Stalin was especially reluctant to allow free elections in Poland; as Hitler demonstrated, it provided a perfect invasion route into Soviet territory.

The United States would be somewhat handicapped diplomatically by the death of Franklin Roosevelt in April 1945. Roosevelt had excellent personal relations with Winston Churchill and felt that he could at least "understand" Stalin. When Harry Truman took over the presidency, he had little experience in foreign affairs, and Roosevelt had met with him only a few times, sharing little about the appropriate way to deal with America's wartime allies.

Truman met Soviet diplomats for the first time at the initial session of the United Nations, which was held in San Francisco two weeks after he took over as president. His first face-to-face meeting with Stalin took place at the **Potsdam Conference**, held at the end of July 1945. Truman, Stalin, and Clement Atlee (who had just replaced Churchill as prime minster) represented the United States, the Soviet Union, and Great Britain, respectively, at this meeting. Again, the future of Eastern Europe was discussed. It was also decided to hold war-crimes trials for top Nazi leaders (the most famous of these would be known as the Nuremberg Trials). At this meeting, Truman announced to Stalin the existence of the atomic bomb (ironically, Stalin had learned of it some two weeks earlier from Soviet spies in the United States).

Great philosophical differences between the two sides were apparent at this meeting. Truman expressed the view that free elections should be held in all Eastern European countries. Stalin, on the other hand, expressed the desire to have Eastern European **satellite countries** that would act as buffers to potential future invasions of the Soviet Union.

The Iron Curtain

During 1946 and 1947, the Soviet Union tightened its hold on Eastern Europe (Romania, Hungary, Bulgaria, Poland, Czechoslovakia, and East Germany). Promised elections in Europe did not actually take place for two years. In some cases, Communists backed by Stalin forced non-Communists, who had been freely elected, out of office.

In March 1946, Winston Churchill made a speech at a college in Fulton, Missouri, where he noted that the Soviet Union had established an **iron curtain** that divided the Soviet Union and its Eastern European satellites from the independent countries of Europe. This speech is often viewed as the symbolic beginning of the cold war.

Another key document from this era was written by American diplomat and expert in Soviet affairs, George F. Kennan. Kennan wrote an anonymous article in *Foreign Affairs* magazine in July 1947 (the author was only identified as "Mr. X"), stating his opinion that Soviet policymakers were deeply committed to the destruction of America and the American way of life. The article maintained that the USSR felt threatened by the United States and felt that it had to expand for self-preservation. Kennan stated that a long-range and long-term **containment policy** to stop communism was needed. According to Kennan, if communism could be contained, it would eventually crumble under its own weight. The policy of containment was central to most American policy toward the Soviet Union for the next 45 years.

If President Truman was looking for an opportunity to apply the containment policy, opportunities soon presented themselves in Turkey and Greece. The Soviets desperately desired to control the Dardanelles Strait; this Turkish-controlled area would allow Soviet ships to go from the Black Sea into the Mediterranean. In addition, Communists were threatening the existing government in Greece. In February 1947, the British (still suffering severe economic aftershocks from World War II) stated that they could no longer financially assist the Turkish and Greek governments, and suggested that the United States step in (some historians maintain that this symbolically ended Great Britain's great power status and demonstrated that now the United States was one of the two major players on the world stage). In March 1947, the president announced the **Truman Doctrine**, which stated that it would become the stated duty of the United States to assist all democratic nations of the world who resisted communism. Congress authorized $400 million in aid for Greece and Turkey. The policies outlined in the Truman Doctrine and in George Kennan's article can be found embedded in American foreign policy all the way through the 1980s.

Marshall Plan

Most Americans applauded Truman's decision to help countries resisting communism. Others wanted to see a much larger American role in Europe in the postwar era. Several observers stated that Hitler was able to rise to power because of the lack of stability in both the German government and economy in the era following World War I, and that such a situation should never be allowed to develop again.

Many felt that it was the duty of the United States to rebuild the devastated countries of Europe after World War II; it was felt that, in the long run, this would bring both political and economic benefits to the Western world.

By the terms of the **Marshall Plan**, the United States provided nearly $12 billion in economic aid to help rebuild Europe. This assistance was of a strictly nonmilitary nature, and was designed, in large measure, to prevent Western Europe from falling into economic collapse. Seventeen Western European nations received aid under the Marshall Plan; several of them became valuable trading partners of the United States by the early part of the 1950s. The Soviet Union was invited to apply for aid from the Marshall Plan. Stalin refused and ordered the Soviet satellite countries to do the same.

Berlin: The First Cold War Crisis

In 1948, the Americans, French, and British announced that they were to combine their areas of occupation in Germany and create the Federal Republic of Germany. West Berlin (located within the eastern zone of Germany) was supposed to join this Federal Republic. Berlin was already a "problem city" for Communist authorities. Many residents of East Berlin (and other residents of Eastern Europe) escaped communism by passing from East Berlin to West Berlin.

In June 1948, Soviet and East German military units blocked off transportation by road into West Berlin. Historians of Soviet foreign policy note that this was the first real test by Stalin of Western cold war resolve. Truman authorized the institution of the **Berlin Airlift**; for nearly 15 months, American and British pilots flew in enough food and supplies for West Berlin to survive. The Americans and British achieved at least a public relations victory when Stalin ordered the lifting of the blockade in May 1949. Shortly afterward, the French, English, and American zones of occupation were joined together into "West Germany," and the Americans stationed troops there to guard against further Soviet actions.

One month earlier, the United States, Canada, and 10 Western European countries had announced the formation of **NATO (North Atlantic Treaty Organization)**. The main provision of the NATO treaty was that an attack on one signatory nation would be considered an attack on all of them. The NATO treaty placed America squarely in the middle of European affairs for the foreseeable future. NATO would expand in the early 1950s, and, as a response to NATO, the Soviet Union and its satellite countries created the **Warsaw Pact** in 1955.

1949: A Pivotal Year in the Cold War

In 1949, two events occurred that rocked American postwar confidence. In September, the Soviets announced that they had exploded an atomic bomb. The potential threat of nuclear annihilation was an underlying fear for many Americans throughout the 1950s. Truman quickly gave authorization for American scientists to begin work on the **hydrogen bomb**, a bomb much more powerful than the atomic bombs dropped on Hiroshima and Nagasaki.

An equally horrifying event occurred shortly after the successful Soviet atomic test. Since 1945, the United States had been a major financial backer of Nationalist China, led by Chiang Kai-shek. Communist guerrilla forces under Mao Zedong were able to capture much of the Chinese countryside. In 1949, Mao's forces captured Peking, the capital city. The People's Republic of China was established by Mao. Nationalist forces were forced to flee to Formosa (now Taiwan). From Formosa, Chiang Kai-shek and the Nationalists maintained that they were the "true" government of China, and continued to receive a very sizable aid package from the United States. The question of "who lost China" would be repeatedly asked over the next 10 years in the United States, usually to attack the president, Harry Truman, and the Democratic party, who were in power when Nationalist China fell.

Middle East in the Early Years of the Cold War

In the years immediately after World War II, the United States continued to take a back seat to the British in terms of influencing leaders and events in the Middle East. It was the 1947 decision by the British to stop assisting the Turks and Greeks (followed by the articulation of the Truman Doctrine by the president) that drastically increased the role of the United States in the region.

Since the 1920s, a major reason for American interest in the region was oil: this certainly did not decline in the cold war era. It should be noted that in the late 1940s and early 1950s, the United States itself was not dependent on oil from the region; however, two regions that the United States was trying to rebuild, Western Europe and Japan, desperately needed Middle Eastern oil. In the late 1940s, the Truman administration cemented relations with Saudi Arabia, America's major trading partner for oil since the 1930s. Tax policies encouraged American oil companies to do business with the Saudis, and the Americans pledged to assist Saudi Arabia if it was attacked by the Soviets. The fact that the United States was establishing a seemingly close relationship with a completely undemocratic regime was largely unnoticed by American commentators at the time; observers today note that in their quest for oil, Americans have developed these same "close relationships" with countless despotic kings and other authoritarian rulers in the region.

In addition, sections of the Middle East were very close to the U.S. new enemy, the Soviet Union. American planners and decision makers wanted to: (1) ensure that the region would not be vulnerable to potential attacks by the Soviets and (2) utilize the region as a staging point for potential military advances against the Soviet Union (American missiles placed in Turkey were as close to some of their targets as Soviet missiles in Cuba were to their targets in the 1962 Cuban Missile Crisis).

Role of the United States in the Creation of Israel

The entire dynamic of the Middle East was changed by the establishment of the state of Israel in 1948. The United States played a key role in this pivotal event. The pressure for the creation of a Jewish state in Palestine increased enormously as a result of the Holocaust in Europe. Great Britain had governed Palestine by mandate since the 1920s, but stated in 1947 that the United Nations should decide the future of the region. The UN announced its support for a plan that would divide Palestine into Jewish and Arab sections.

The Arab states unanimously rejected this plan, noting that countless non-Jewish residents of Palestine would be uprooted if it were implemented. The U.S. State Department opposed the partition plan, noting that it went against long-standing American support of the principle of "self-determination" in regions such as this. Nevertheless, President Truman announced his support of the plan and instructed American diplomats to "twist some arms" to get other countries to support it.

After the United Nations narrowly supported the plan, fighting began between Jews and Arabs living in Palestine. Countless Arabs were forced to flee the Jewish-controlled regions. Throughout the Arab world, the United States began to be blamed for the bloodshed in Palestine; President Truman and others in the American government were perceived as the ones who had forced this "solution" through the United Nations. In 1948, the independent state of Israel was proclaimed and was immediately recognized by the United States (some historians maintain that the main reason for this was to recognize Israel before the Soviets could). The Arab states surrounding Palestine immediately attacked the new state of Israel, but were defeated.

Conflict between Israel and its neighbors has remained a constant ever since, with Israel winning two more major wars with its neighbors. Another constant is the "special relationship" that will continue to exist between the United States and Israel. Israel's strongest backer in virtually every crisis has been the United States. Americans have given millions of dollars of military aid to the Israelis. There have been situations where virtually the entire world has condemned the Israelis for its actions against its neighbors; in almost every case, the United States has continued to back Israel. There are countless reasons why the United States and Israel have developed this special relationship. However, this relationship is also the reason for the animosity that exists in much of the Arab world toward the United States.

United States and the Shah of Iran

When Dwight Eisenhower became president in 1953, he faced a new and potentially more volatile force in the Middle East: Arab nationalism. In an early press conference, Eisenhower stated that he favored political independence for the peoples of the region. Nevertheless, he stated, this could not be done "too quickly," as a power vacuum might develop that would allow the Soviets an opportunity to expand into the region.

In 1951, Prime Minister Mohammed Mossadeq of Iran announced a plan to nationalize the British oil facilities in the country. Many in Iran viewed him as a hero for opposing British imperialism in the region. The British imposed an oil embargo on Iranian oil and proposed military action against Mossadeq (which was opposed by the United States). The Shah of Iran, who was actually in charge of the government, was a favorite of American officials; Washington became increasingly concerned when Mossadeq began to quietly question the Shah's relationship with the United States.

With Eisenhower's approval, the CIA went to Iran and financed anti-Mossadeq demonstrations, which eventually led to his downfall. Mossadeq was replaced by a prime minister who was loyal to the Shah (and not opposed to American influence in the country). In the long run, the American role in the removal of Mossadeq from power would prove detrimental to the image of the United States in the region. After the events of 1953, the Shah ruled as a brutal autocrat; the perception was that the Shah's actions were sanctioned by the United States. When the American embassy in Tehran was occupied by Islamic militants in 1979, the actions by the CIA in Iran in 1953 were long-forgotten by virtually everyone in the United States; to many Iranians, the effects of American actions in Iran in 1953 were still very much alive.

As this section demonstrates, anti-American sentiment in the Middle East did not begin with the Iranian hostage crisis or with Saddam Hussein. In reality, resentment of the United States began to brew in the early years of the cold war and intensified over the years as countless American officials have been pictured smiling and shaking hands with rulers in the region who have little or no regard for the people whom they govern.

Cold War at Home

During 1949 and 1950, many Americans felt a sense that the tides of the cold war were somehow shifting over in favor of the Soviet Union. Many felt that the Soviet Union could never do this alone, and that they *had* to have a large number of spies within the United States helping them. Thus, under President Truman and later under President Eisenhower, there was a tremendous effort made to rid the United States of a perceived internal "Communist menace."

As stated in Chapter 21, on the depression, many idealists had dabbled in communism in the 1930s; this "dabbling" would now come back to haunt them.

The Truman administration began by jailing the leaders of the American Communist party under the provisions of the 1940 Smith Act. This document stated that it was illegal to advocate the overthrow by force of the American government. When some Republicans claimed that the Truman administration was "soft on communism," Truman ordered the creation of a **Loyalty Review Board**, which eventually had the legal jurisdiction to investigate both new and experienced federal workers. Three or four million federal workers were examined by the board; as a result of these investigations, slightly over 100 workers were removed from their jobs. Investigations revealed that some of those investigated were homosexuals, who were often hounded out of office as well.

While the Truman administration was investigating the executive branch of government, Congress decided to investigate Communists in the government and in the entertainment industry. The congressional committee overseeing these investigations was the **HUAC (House Un-American Activities Committee)**. In 1947, the HUAC began to investigate the movie industry in earnest. Committee investigators relentlessly pursued actors, directors, and writers who had attended Communist party meetings in the past. Directors of movies made during World War II who cast the Soviet Union in a favorable light (such as *Mission to Moscow* and *North Star*) were brought in for questioning. Dozens of writers, actors, and directors were called in to testify about their political orientation. The Hollywood Ten was an influential group of writers and directors who refused to answer questions posed to them by members of the HUAC in an open congressional session. Members of the Hollywood Ten were all sentenced to jail time.

The effects on Hollywood were major. Some Hollywood movies of the late 1940s dealt directly with the problems of society (such as *The Best Years of their Lives*). As a result of pressure from the HUAC, Hollywood movies became much more tame. In addition, a **blacklist** was made of actors, directors, and writers who were potentially Communist and whom the major studios should *not* hire. Many Hollywood careers were ruined by the blacklist; some writers wrote under false names or had "fronts" turn in their screenplays for them. Some of those blacklisted were unable to get work until the early 1960s.

On the Senate side, Senator Pat McCarran sponsored several bills to "stop the spread of communism" in the United States. The **McCarran Internal Security Act** was enacted in 1950; under this bill, all Communist or Communist-front organizations had to register with the government, and members of these organizations could not work in any job related to the national defense. The **McCarran-Walter Act** of 1952 greatly limited immigration from Asia and Eastern Europe; this would hopefully limit the "influx of communism" into the United States. President Truman vetoed both these bills, but Congress passed both of them over the president's veto.

Were There Spies in America?

The trials of Alger Hiss and the Rosenbergs indicated to many Americans that there just might be Communist spies infiltrating America. In 1948, the HUAC began an investigation of Hiss, a former official in the State Department and an advisor to Franklin Roosevelt at the Yalta Conference. An editor of *Time* magazine, Whitaker Chambers, had previously been a Communist and testified to the HUAC that Hiss had been a Communist too. After several trials, Hiss was finally convicted for perjury and spent four years in jail. To this day, the guilt or innocence of Alger Hiss is still debated.

In 1950, Julius and Ethel Rosenberg were charged with passing atomic secrets to the Soviet Union. The government had much more evidence on Julius than on his wife, but they were both found guilty of espionage in 1952 and executed. Considerable debate has also taken place on the guilt of the Rosenbergs, although materials released from the Soviet archives after the fall of communism strongly implicated Ethel. Material from these archives demonstrated that some Communists in the United States had closer ties to Moscow than was previously believed.

Heating of the Cold War: Korea

After World War II, Korea was divided into a Communist North Korea and a non-Communist and pro-American South Korea, divided along the **38th parallel**. In late June 1950, North Korea invaded the south. The Security Council of the United Nations voted to send in a peacekeeping force (the Soviet Union was protesting the UN's decision not to allow Communist China in as a member and failed to attend the Security Council session when this was discussed). Douglas MacArthur was appointed to lead the UN forces, and the **Korean War** began.

UN forces under MacArthur drove northward into North Korea. In late November, forces from Communist China forced MacArthur's troops to retreat, yet by March 1951, his troops were on the offensive again. MacArthur was very critical of President Truman's handling of the war, demanding a greatly intensified bombing campaign and suggesting that Truman order the Nationalist Chinese to attack the Chinese mainland. In April 1951, Truman finally fired MacArthur for insubordination. Armistice talks to end the war dragged on for nearly two years; in the end, it was decided to divide North and South Korea along the 38th parallel (along virtually the same line that divided them before the war!). More than 57,000 Americans died in this "forgotten war."

Rise of McCarthyism

The seeming inability of America to decisively defeat communism both abroad and at home led to the meteoric rise of Senator Joseph McCarthy of Wisconsin. In a speech in Wheeling, West Virginia, on February 9, 1950, McCarthy announced that he had a list of 205 known Communists who were working in the State Department. McCarthy's list was sometimes longer and sometimes smaller, and often also included prominent diplomats, scholars, and Defense Department and military figures. **McCarthyism** was the ruthless searching out of Communists in the government that took place in this period, largely without any real evidence.

For four years, McCarthy reigned supreme in Washington, with few in power or in the news media being willing to challenge him. McCarthy offered a simple reason why the United States was not conclusively winning the cold war: because of Communists in the government. The Republican party was a semireluctant supporter of McCarthy in this era; a number of Republicans were skeptical of many of McCarthy's charges, but realized that anticommunism was a "winner" for Republicans politically. McCarthy even accused Harry Truman and former Secretary of State Marshall of being "unconscious" agents of the Communist conspiracy.

In March 1954, McCarthy claimed in a lengthy speech that the U.S. Army was full of Communists as well. It was at this point that McCarthy began to run into major opposition; Republican President Eisenhower (a former general) stated privately that it was definitely time for McCarthy to be stopped. Tensions between the army and McCarthy increased when it was announced that McCarthy had asked for special privileges for an aide of his that had been drafted.

The **Army-McCarthy Hearings** appeared on network television, and thousands found themselves riveted to them on a daily basis. Over the course of the hearings, it was discovered that McCarthy *had* asked for special favors for his aide, had doctored photographs, and had used bullying tactics on a regular basis. The end was clearly in sight for McCarthy when Joseph Welch, attorney for the army, received loud applause when he asked McCarthy if he had any "sense of decency" and when reporter Edwin R. Murrow went on CBS News with a negative report about McCarthy and his tactics. In late 1954, McCarthy was formally censured by the Senate. His power gone, McCarthy died only three years later. The McCarthy era is now remembered as one in which attack by innuendo was common and where, during the investigations to "get at the truth" about communism, the civil rights of many were violated. It should be noted that several biographies have been published in the last few years exonerating McCarthy and his tactics.

Cold War Policies of President Eisenhower

Foreign policy decisions of the Eisenhower administration were often crafted by the Secretary of State, John Foster Dulles. Dulles felt that the policy of containment was not nearly aggressive enough; instead of merely containment, Dulles often spoke of "**massive retaliation**" against Communist advances anywhere in the world. Dulles also spoke of the need to use nuclear weapons if necessary. At one press conference, Dulles stated that instead of containing communism, the goal of the United States should be to "make communism retreat" whenever and wherever possible.

Eisenhower hoped that the death of Stalin in 1953 would allow a "new understanding" between the United States and the Soviet Union. In some ways, Nikita Khrushchev was different from Stalin, speaking about the possibilities of "peaceful coexistence" with the United States. However, when Hungary revolted in 1956, Khrushchev ordered this to be brutally stopped by the Soviet army.

The fate of the Hungarian leader Irme Nagy was sealed when the United States failed to assist the anti-Soviet rebellion of his government. Despite the tough talk of John Foster Dulles, who had boldly proclaimed that the United States would come to the aid of any in Eastern Europe who wanted to "liberate" themselves from communism, it was determined that U.S. forces could not be used to help the Hungarian rebels (despite the fact that the CIA operatives in Hungary had promised Nagy this aid), because this might provoke war with the Soviets. Eisenhower was also reluctant to get militarily involved in Southeast Asia, even though he believed in the **domino theory**, which proclaimed that if one country in Southeast Asia fell to the Communists, others would follow. In 1954, French forces in Vietnam were being overrun by nationalist forces under the control of Ho Chi Minh. The French desperately asked for aid. Despite segments of the American military who pushed for assisting the French, Eisenhower ultimately refused.

As a result, the French were finally defeated at the **Battle of Dien Bien Phu**. After they left, an international conference took place and the **Geneva Accords** established a North Vietnam under the control of Ho Chi Minh and a South Vietnam under the control of the Emperor, Bao Dai. From the beginning, the United States supplied military aid to South Vietnam. By the terms of the Geneva Accords, a national election was scheduled for 1956 on the potential unification of the entire country. However, a coup in South Vietnam overthrew the emperor and sabotaged the election plans. Nevertheless, the United States continued to support South Vietnam.

The major Middle Eastern crisis during the era was the Suez Canal crisis. The United States had helped Egyptian leader Colonel Gamal Abdul Nasser build the Aswan Dam. The Egyptians wanted to purchase arms from the United States as well. When the Americans refused, the Egyptians went to the Soviets with the same request. When the United States (and Great Britain), in response, totally cut off all loans to Egypt, Nasser nationalized the British-owned Suez Canal. The British and the French attacked Egypt. In response to Soviet threats that they might join the conflict on the side of the Egyptians, the Americans got the British and French to retreat from Egypt.

Eisenhower and Dulles desperately wanted to prevent the spread of communism in the Middle East. In January 1957, the **Eisenhower Doctrine** was formally unveiled, which stated that Americans arms would be used in the region to prevent Communist aggression. The Americans invoked the Eisenhower Doctrine when they landed troops in Beirut, Lebanon, in mid-1958 to put down a rebellion against the government.

The Americans were equally concerned with the spread of communism in Latin America, where America had numerous economic interests. A defensive alliance of most nations of the Western Hemisphere was signed as the **Rio Pact** in 1947. Critics would argue that the United States was never shy about throwing its weight around in the region. In 1954, the CIA helped orchestrate the overthrow of the president of Guatemala on the grounds that his administration was too friendly with the Soviet Union; during this coup, property that had been seized from American businesses was restored to American hands.

In 1959, Fidel Castro orchestrated the removal of dictator Fulgencio Batista from power. Castro soon seized American businesses located in Cuba and began trade negotiations with the Soviet Union. Thus, beginning in late 1960, the United States cut off trade with Cuba, and eventually cut off diplomatic relations with the island (a situation that still exists today).

Dangerous Arms Buildup

During the Eisenhower administration, both the United States and the Soviet Union built up their nuclear arsenals to dangerously high levels. By August 1953 both countries had exploded hydrogen bombs, which made the bomb used at Hiroshima look primitive in comparison. Both countries carried out nuclear tests, although in 1958 Eisenhower and Khrushchev both agreed to suspend further atomic tests in the atmosphere.

The Soviets concentrated on building up their missile capabilities in this period, causing some Americans to fear that they were falling behind, and that a "missile gap" was developing. The startling fact that the Soviets might be ahead in technology was demonstrated by their 1957 launching of *Sputnik*, the first man-made satellite that could orbit the earth. Americans were shocked as they could look up in the sky and see the satellite whiz by (in the next two years, many American high schools and colleges increased the number of math and science courses students had to take so that Americans could "keep up" with the Soviets). Even more troubling was the fact that American tests to create a man-made satellite had failed.

A final humiliation for the United States came in May 1960, when the Russians shot down an American **U-2** spy plane. The pilot, Francis Gary Powers, was captured and taken prisoner by Soviet forces. For several days, the Americans refused to admit that an American plane had even been shot down; Eisenhower eventually took full responsibility for the incident.

Toward the end of his term in office, Eisenhower warned of the extreme challenge to peace posed by the massive "military-industrial complex" that existed in America in the 1950s. The size of the military-industrial complex would certainly not decline in the 1960s.

Chapter Review

Rapid Review

To achieve the perfect 5, you should be able to explain the following:

- Winning the cold war was the central goal of American policy for 45 years.
- Economic impact of the cold war on American industry was enormous; many plants continued making military hardware throughout the cold war era.
- Debate over who "started" the cold war has occupied the minds of historians since 1945.
- Decisions made at the Yalta and Potsdam conferences ushered in cold war tensions between the World War II victors.
- Concept of the "iron curtain" was first articulated by Winston Churchill in 1946.
- American strategy of containment motivated many foreign policy decisions in the cold war era.
- The Truman Doctrine, the Marshall Plan, and NATO united America and Western Europe both militarily and economically against the Soviet Union and its satellites.
- America's resolve to oppose communism was tested during the Berlin Crisis and the Korean War.
- 1949 was a critical year in the cold war, as the Soviet Union got the atomic bomb and mainland China turned Communist.
- Some Americans feared that Communists had infiltrated the American government and the entertainment industry; investigations by the House Un-American Activities Committee and Senator Joseph McCarthy were dedicated to "rooting out" Communists in America.
- Under President Dwight Eisenhower, Secretary of State John Foster Dulles formulated an aggressive foreign policy that would not just contain communism but also attempt to roll communism back whenever possible.
- During the Eisenhower administration, crises in Southeast Asia, the Middle East, and Latin America further tested American resolve.
- Both the Soviet Union and the United States built up their nuclear arsenals to dangerous levels in this era.

Time Line

1945: Yalta Conference
   Harry Truman becomes president
   Potsdam Conference
1946: Winston Churchill gives "iron curtain" speech
   Article by George Kennan on containment
1947: HUAC begins probe into movie industry
   Introduction of Federal Employee Loyalty program
   President Truman articulates Truman Doctrine

1948: Berlin Airlift
Implementation of Marshall Plan
Creation of nation of Israel
Alger Hiss implicated as a Communist
1949: NATO established
Soviet Union successfully tests atomic bomb
Mainland China turns Communist
1950: Joseph McCarthy gives speech on Communists in the State Department
Alger Hiss convicted of perjury
McCarran Internal Security Act enacted
Beginning of Korean War
1952: Dwight Eisenhower elected president
1953: CIA orchestrates return of Shah of Iran to power
Death of Joseph Stalin
Execution of the Rosenbergs
1954: Army-McCarthy hearings
Government in Guatemala overthrown
French defeated at Dien Bien Phu
Geneva Conference
1955: Creation of the Warsaw Pact
1956: Hungarian Revolt suppressed by Soviet Union
Suez crisis
1957: *Sputnik* launched by Soviet Union
1959: Castro comes to power in Cuba; United States halts trade with Cuba
1960: U-2 incident
John Kennedy elected president

› Review Questions

Multiple-Choice Questions

1. The Army-McCarthy hearings proved
   A. that Americans were largely uninterested in the issue of communism.
   B. that Eisenhower would support McCarthy at any cost.
   C. that McCarthy had little proof for his claims.
   D. the massive popularity of Joseph McCarthy.

2. The policy of containment stated that
   A. America should go out and attempt to dislodge Communist leaders wherever possible.
   B. America should hold firm against Communist encroachment in all parts of the world.
   C. America should not hesitate to use atomic weapons against the Soviet Union.
   D. the United States should depend on its Western European Allies for help against the Soviet Union.

3. America was especially interested in stopping Communist expansion in Latin America because
   A. the United States had many economic interests in the region.
   B. both presidents Truman and Eisenhower were close to many of the Latin American leaders.
   C. the Soviet Union expressed a special interest in expanding in this region.
   D. the CIA had repeatedly failed in operations in Latin America in the past.

4. When the HUAC began their investigation of the movie industry, they looked with suspicion at writers, actors, and directors who
   A. attended Communist party meetings in the 1930s.
   B. wrote or appeared in World War II–era films that were sympathetic to the Soviet Union.
   C. invoked the Fifth Amendment when testifying before the HUAC.
   D. all of the above

5. Republicans claimed that the Democrats were "soft on communism" for all of the following reasons *except*
   A. during the Truman administration mainland China had gone Communist.
   B. Alger Hiss was an advisor to Franklin Roosevelt at Yalta.
   C. the Truman administration failed to establish a system to check on the possibility of Communists working for the federal government.
   D. decisions made by Roosevelt and Truman at the end of World War II made it easier for the Soviet Union to control Eastern Europe.

Short-Answer Question

6. Answer Parts A, B, and C.
   A. Briefly explain ONE example of an American effort to contain communism overseas during the period 1945 to 1960.
   B. Briefly explain a SECOND example of an American effort to contain communism overseas during the period 1945 to 1960.
   C. Briefly explain ONE example of an effort to combat communism within the United States during the period 1945 to 1960.

› Answers and Explanations

1. **C**. The hearings did much to discredit McCarthy. By this point, Eisenhower had broken from McCarthy, and many Americans watched these hearings from beginning to end.

2. **B**. Containment emphasized stopping communism whenever it attempted to expand; containment did not emphasize attacking communism where it already existed.

3. **A**. The United States had factories in and active trade relationships with many Latin American countries, and feared that communism would destroy American economic interests in the region. The CIA had actually been quite successful in their operations in the region in the past—witness their role in Guatemala.

4. **D**. As a result of the HUAC hearings, the American movie industry changed dramatically.

5. **C**. All of the other three were used by Republicans to say that the Democrats were indeed "soft on communism." Truman instituted a Loyalty Review Board to verify that nearly 4 million federal workers were "true Americans."

6. **Parts A and B**: Inspired by the writings of the American diplomat George Kennan, the U.S. government began to develop a containment policy to limit the expansion of communism in 1947. President Harry Truman formulated the Truman Doctrine, which stated that the United States would assist any country threatened by Communist aggression or internal Communist subversion. In an effort to prevent the spread of communism in Europe, the United States launched the Marshall Plan, a program of economic assistance to Western Europe designed to help the European democracies recover economically from World War II. In 1948, when the Soviet Union cut off access to West Berlin, the United States and Great Britain supplied the city through the Berlin Airlift. In 1949, the United States, Canada, and 10 Western European countries formed the North Atlantic Treaty Organization (NATO); this military alliance confronted the Soviet Union and its allies for the next 40 years. In 1950, the United States came to the assistance of South Korea after it was invaded by Communist North Korea. The Korean War lasted until 1953. Following the defeat of French forces in Vietnam at the Battle of Dien Bien Phu in 1954, President Dwight D. Eisenhower provided support to the new country of South Vietnam. Eisenhower believed in the domino theory, arguing that if one country in Southeast Asia fell to communism, others would soon follow. In 1957, the president announced the Eisenhower Doctrine, which stated that the United States would provide support to any Middle Eastern country being threatened by other Middle Eastern countries associated with the Soviet Union. The United States engaged in an arms race with the Soviet Union, building atomic bombs, hydrogen bombs, and nuclear-armed guided missiles. The United States used U-2 spy planes to monitor nuclear missile sites in the Soviet Union; in 1960, the Soviets shot down a U-2 plane and captured its pilot, embarrassing the American government.

Part C: The revelation that Communist spies had penetrated the U.S. government and even acquired information about the atomic bomb contributed to the Second Red Scare. President Truman created a Loyalty Review Board to remove security risks from the federal workforce. The House Un-American Activities Committee (HUAC) launched investigations into the infiltration of communists into the government and the entertainment industry. This contributed to a growing hysteria about communist activities in the United States. Many Hollywood and Broadway actors, writers, and directors were blacklisted because of their supposed Communist sympathies. The McCarran Internal Security Act of 1950 compelled Communist and Communist associated organizations to register with the government; the act also provided for the investigation of people suspected of subversive activities. In 1950, Senator Joseph McCarthy of Wisconsin accused the State Department of harboring large numbers of Communists. Following this, McCarthy launched a number of investigations of supposed Communists in the U.S. government. McCarthy became very popular. He was finally censured by the Senate in 1954 after he was deemed to have gone too far in an investigation of the U.S. Army.

CHAPTER 26

Prosperity and Anxiety: The 1950s

IN THIS CHAPTER

Summary: In the 1950s, many middle-class, white American families experienced a prosperity they had never known before. Many young couples moved to the suburbs and purchased their first home (for veterans, this could be partially financed by the GI Bill). Observers noted that Dwight Eisenhower was the perfect president for the seemingly placid 1950s. Many commentators wrote on the conformity of American suburban life in the period. However, there were also many Americans pushing for change. Proponents of civil rights for black Americans were heartened by the 1954 *Brown v. Board of Education* Supreme Court decision outlawing segregation in public schools, yet found that their struggles would continue throughout this decade and all through the next. Many women felt frustrated in the role of housewife that they were expected to play in suburban America. Many teenagers rebelled in the decade as well, by emulating the "rebellious" movie star James Dean, by dabbling in Beat poetry, or by listening to the new rock 'n' roll music.

Keywords

Brown v. Board of Education **(1954):** Supreme Court decision stating that "separate but equal" schools for white and black students were unconstitutional and that school districts across America must desegregate with "all deliberate speed"; controversy over enforcement of this decision was to last for more than a decade.

Montgomery bus boycott (1955): effort by blacks in Montgomery, Alabama, to have the local bus company end discriminatory seating and hiring policies. The movement started with the arrest of Rosa Parks for refusing to give up her bus seat to a white man; the boycott was later led by the Rev. Martin Luther King, Jr.

Baby boom: from 1947 to 1962 Americans married and had children at a record pace; the "high point" of the baby boom was 1957.

The Feminine Mystique: book written by Betty Friedan describing the frustration felt by suburban women in the 1950s; this book was a landmark for feminists of the 1960s and 1970s.

James Dean: young actor whose character in the film *Rebel Without a Cause* inspired many rebellious young people of the 1950s.

Beat Generation: literary movement of the 1950s; writers of this movement rejected the materialistic American culture of the decade. Jack Kerouac, Allen Ginsberg, and William Burroughs were key writers of this movement.

Economic Growth and Prosperity

Some economists feared that the ending of World War II would lead to economic recession. Instead, the American economy enjoyed tremendous growth in the period between 1945 and 1960. In 1945, the American gross national product (GNP) stood at just over $200 billion; by 1960, the GNP had grown to over $500 billion.

A significant reason for this growth was the ever-growing spending on defense during the cold war era. The "military-industrial complex" (a term coined by Dwight D. Eisenhower) was responsible for billions of dollars of new spending during the 1950s (and far beyond). Millions were spent on technological research throughout the era.

Other significant factors were responsible for the economic growth of the era. Consumers had accumulated significant amounts of cash during World War II, but had little to spend it on, as the production of consumer goods was not emphasized in the war era. With the war over, consumers wanted to spend. Credit cards were available to consumers for the first time; Diner's Club cards were issued for the first time in 1950. Two industries that benefited from this were the automobile industry and the housing industry.

Many American households had never owned a new automobile since the 1920s, and in the postwar era, demand for cars was at a record high. If consumers needed assistance in deciding on which automobile to buy, they could receive assistance from the advertisers who were working for the various automobile companies (advertising reached levels in the 1950s equal to the 1920s). As the 1950s wore on, consumers could buy cars with bigger and bigger fins and fancier and fancier interiors. President Eisenhower and Congress encouraged America's reliance on the automobile when they enacted legislation authorizing the massive buildup of the interstate highway system (at the expense of the construction of an effective mass transit system). The highway system was a by-product of national defense plans of the cold war; planners thought they would be ideal for troop movements and that airplanes could easily land on the straight sections of them.

The other industry that experienced significant growth in the postwar era was the housing construction business. There was a dire shortage of available housing in the immediate postwar era; in many cities, two families living in an apartment designed for one was commonplace. Housing was rapidly built in the postwar era, and the demand was insatiable. The **GI Bill** of 1944 authorized low-interest mortgage loans for ex-servicemen (as well as subsidies for education).

William Levitt helped ease the housing crises when he built his initial group of dwellings in Levittown, New York. Several other **Levittowns** were constructed; homes were prefabricated, were built using virtual assembly line practices, and all looked remarkably the same. Nevertheless, William Levitt and developers like him began the move to the suburbs, the most significant population shift of the postwar era.

The economy was also spurred by the mass of appliances desired by consumers for their new homes in the suburbs. Refrigerators, televisions, washing machines, and countless other appliances were found in suburban households; advertising helped ensure that the same refrigerator and television would be found in homes across the nation. Economist John Kenneth Galbraith noted that, by the 1950s, America had become an "**affluent society.**" It should be noted, however, that even though the economy of the era enjoyed tremendous growth, the wages of many workers lagged behind spiraling prices. For many workers, real income declined; this led to labor unrest in the postwar era.

Political Developments of the Postwar Era

It would have been difficult for anyone to follow Franklin Roosevelt as president, and Harry Truman, in the opinion of many, definitely suffered in comparison. Although Truman stated that "the buck stops here" when decisions were made, many critics felt that he had no consistent set of beliefs to guide him as he decided policy. Truman was considered antiunion by much of organized labor, yet he vetoed a key piece of legislation designed to take power away from labor unions. There were many strikes in 1946 and 1947, and the **Taft-Hartley Act** was passed by Congress in 1947 over the president's veto (several biographers claim that Truman's veto was primarily symbolic and was done for political reasons). This bill stated that if any strike affected the health and safety of the country, the president could call for an 80-day cooling off period, during which negotiations could take place and workers would go back to work, that the union contributions of individuals could not be used in federal elections, and that union leaders had to officially declare they were not Communists. Unions were furious at these and other restrictions the bill imposed on them.

Truman declared a **Fair Deal** policy, in which he tried to expand the principles of the New Deal. Included in Truman's Fair Deal were plans for national health care and civil rights legislation; Truman also wanted to repeal the Taft-Hartley Act and increase government spending for public housing and education. In early 1948, he sent a civil rights bill to Congress (the first civil rights bill sent to Congress by a president since the Reconstruction). Nevertheless, Truman's popularity in early 1948 was low. Republicans rallied behind second-time candidate Thomas Dewey (who had been defeated by Franklin Roosevelt in 1944) and felt that victory would be theirs. Truman's chances seemed especially dim when Strom Thurmond also ran as a Dixiecrat candidate (in opposition to a civil rights plank in the 1948 Democratic platform) and Henry Wallace, Truman's secretary of commerce, ran as a Progressive. The highlight of Truman's political career was his eventual victory over Dewey; Truman's success is attributed to the fact that he campaigned more against the "do-nothing" Republican Congress than he did against Dewey. Truman could never capitalize on his 1948 victory; in the years after this victory, charges of being "soft on communism" plagued the administration.

Truman decided not to seek reelection in 1952, and former general Dwight D. Eisenhower defeated Adlai Stevenson in the general election. As president, Eisenhower saw his role as a crafter of compromise, and not as a creator of new policies. He tried to oversee a scaling back of government shift of power to the courts and to Congress. Eisenhower also shifted much of the power traditionally held by the president to his cabinet and other advisors. He was similar to the Republican presidents of the 1920s in that he was extremely friendly to business interests; most members of his cabinet were businessmen. At many levels, Dwight Eisenhower was the perfect president for the 1950s.

Eisenhower's vice president was Richard Nixon, a former member of the House of Representatives and U.S. Senate from California. Nixon had first made a political name for himself in the Alger Hiss case, and his role in the 1952 campaign was largely as an anti-Communist hatchet man. Midway through the campaign, it was charged that supporters had set up an illegal campaign fund for his personal use. Candidate Eisenhower gave Nixon the opportunity to give a public speech to try to save himself. During the **Checkers Speech**, Nixon declared that he had done nothing wrong, that his wife Pat wore a "very respectable Republican cloth coat," and the only thing given to him had been a dog, Checkers. Nixon remained on the ticket, thus saving a political career that would make him one of the most dominant figures in American politics for the next 25 years.

Civil Rights Struggles of the Postwar Period

Many black veterans who had gone overseas to fight for democracy were appalled to find that conditions for blacks had remained largely unchanged during the war years. After speaking to many leaders from NAACP and CORE in early 1948, Truman outlawed discrimination in the hiring of federal employees and ordered the end to segregation in the armed forces. Change in both the federal government and the armed forces was slow.

Black athletes had often been heroes for large segments of the black population. In the 1930s and early 1940s, it had been Joe Louis; starting in 1947, Jackie Robinson became the first black to play major league baseball, wearing the uniform of the Brooklyn Dodgers. Robinson had to endure threats and racial slurs throughout his first season. Nevertheless, Robinson maintained his dignity and was named National League Rookie of the Year in 1947.

Black leaders had long wanted to strike down the 1896 *Plessy v. Feguson* case, which stated that as long as black and white schools or facilities were "equal," it was not unconstitutional that they were separate. In reality, schools in many districts were separate, but they were in no way equal; white schools would get 80 or 85 percent of the financial allocations in some Southern cities and towns. The case that challenged the 1896 law came from Oliver Brown from Topeka, Kansas, who sued the Topeka school district because his daughter had to walk by an all-white school to get to the bus that took her to an all-black school on the other side of town.

The case made it all the way to the Supreme Court and was argued there by NAACP lawyer Thurgood Marshall (later a U.S. Supreme Court justice). The case was heard by a court presided over by Earl Warren, former governor of California and appointed chief justice by Eisenhower in 1953. By a unanimous decision, the 1954 ***Brown v. Board of Education*** decision stated that "separate but equal" was unconstitutional, and that local districts should desegregate with "all deliberate speed." Parents, government officials, and students in many districts in the South responded: "2, 4, 6, 8. We don't want to integrate!" Earl Warren was chief justice from 1953 to 1969, during which the Court practiced "judicial activism," making important decisions on topics such as the rights of the accused and prayer in schools.

The main battlefield for civil rights in 1955 was in Montgomery, Alabama. Rosa Parks, a secretary for the Montgomery NAACP, refused to give up her seat for a white man to sit in, and was arrested. Civil rights leaders in Montgomery began the **Montgomery bus**

boycott, during which blacks in the city refused to ride the city buses; instead, they carpooled or walked. The bus company refused to change its policies; finally, the Supreme Court stepped in again and stated that segregation on city buses (like in schools) was unconstitutional. A 27-year-old minister by the name of Martin Luther King, Jr., became the main spokesperson for the blacks of the city.

Another major battle for civil rights took place in Little Rock, Arkansas, in 1957. A small number of black students were set to enroll in Central High School in Little Rock in the fall of 1957. The governor of Arkansas, Orval Faubus, sent the National Guard to Central High School to keep the black students out. President Eisenhower had personally been opposed to the *Brown v. Board of Education* decision, but saw this as a direct challenge to a Supreme Court decision and to the authority of the federal government. Eisenhower sent in federal troops and federalized the National Guard; under armed guard, the black students attended Central High School in Little Rock, Arkansas, that year. Decisions by the federal courts outlawing various forms of segregation, and federal troops in Southern states enforcing these federal court orders, would become an increasingly common sight in the early 1960s.

Conformity of the Suburbs

Many young people who had grown up during the Great Depression and had come of age during World War II decided in the postwar era to move to the suburbs and to have families. It was decided by many that **domesticity** would be the avenue to happiness in the postwar world. As a result, the **baby boom** ensued, during which the birthrate soared beyond all expectations. The baby boom lasted from 1945 until 1962; during the peak of the baby boom, 1957, nearly 4.5 million babies were born.

The perfect place for large numbers of newly married couples to have these families was, as stated previously, in the suburbs. Many critics of the time noted the conformity of the suburbs: the houses looked much the same, everyone watched the same shows on TV, and because of TV advertising, everyone pretty much used the same appliances and wore the same clothes. Life (especially for women) was centered around their children, as there were endless rounds of PTA meetings, Littl League practices, and Boy Scout meetings to get to. Social historians state that young people were using the comfort of the family and home as a buttress against any return to the disruptions they had felt earlier in their lives. William H. Whyte's *The Organization Man*, written in 1956, analyzed the conformity and conservatism of suburban life.

Many men felt dissatisfaction with their lives in the postwar years. Many who had served in the "good war," World War II, found it difficult to return to civilian life. Many felt civilian jobs to be largely unrewarding. As the book and film ***The Man in the Gray Flannel Suit*** emphasized, a man who had fought in combat in World War II might find a 9-to-5 job in an office utterly unrewarding. Many men took on hunting and fishing as hobbies; here, they could at least symbolically duplicate the war experience. For men, the most popular magazines of the 1950s were *Field and Stream* and Hugh Hefner's *Playboy*.

Women felt equal frustration during this era. Many continued to work; yet women's magazines and other publications carried the clear message that now it was the woman's patriotic duty to return to the home and remain a housewife. Doris Day was the star of many films of the decade; she had a "girl-next-door" type of appeal, which was attractive to many women and men of the period. Women saw college as an avenue to meet potential husbands; many dropped out immediately after finding one. Many women *did* find fulfillment as mothers and by doing volunteer work in the community. Yet, to others, family life was terribly unsatisfying. Women who felt dissatisfaction with their role in suburban life were routinely told by their doctors that they were neurotics; the sale of tranquilizers to women skyrocketed. Many, many suburban women experienced discontent with their lives in the 1950s and early 1960s. Betty Friedan in *The Feminine Mystique* maintained that the lack of fulfillment experienced by many housewives was the genesis of the feminist revolution of the 1960s. Friedan would found NOW (National Organization for Women) in 1966.

Stereotypically, 1950s teenagers were seen as the "silent generation," interested in only hot rod cars, school mixers, and panty raids. There is a great deal of truth to this characterization. Teenagers in this era were the first teen generation to be targeted by advertisers; many teens wore the same styles and had similar tastes, as a result. Adults spent a great deal of time in ensuring that teenagers did nothing in any way rebellious. Educational films in schools taught students to obey authority, to fit in with the group, to control one's emotions, and to not even think about sex. Popular television shows of the era such as *Ozzie and Harriet* showed young people who acted in exactly that manner.

However, there was a youth rebellion in the 1950s. A few brave students would show it in their attitude and attire, using the main character played by James Dean in *Rebel Without a Cause* or Marlon Brando in *The Wild One* as models. Jackson Pollock and other artists were also at the vanguard of another form of cultural rebellion; the significance of their giant "abstract expressionist" painting moved the center of the art world to New York City. Other young people would attempt to copy the writings and attitudes of the **Beat Generation**, a group of writers and artists who rejected an American society obsessed with the atomic bomb and with material culture. In rejecting conventional society, many Beats and their followers enjoyed jazz and drugs, and studied Eastern religious thought. Key works of the Beats include Jack Kerouac's *On the Road,* in which the main characters travel simply for the joy of traveling, and *Howl,* a poem by Allen Ginsberg that outlines in graphic detail the evils of modern society and what that society does to those attempting to live decent lives in it. It should be emphasized that few young people were actual members of the Beat Generation; a larger number went to coffeehouses, dabbled in writing poetry, and sympathized with the plight of Holden Caufield in *The Catcher in the Rye.*

The main form of 1950s rebellion for young people was through rock 'n' roll. To many adults, rock 'n' roll was immoral, was the "devil's music," and caused juvenile delinquency; a few even charged that it was sent to America by the Communists as part of their plot to conquer the United States. Nevertheless, those who listened and danced to rock 'n' roll were, at some level, rejecting the core values of 1950s America. Young people were told to "control their emotions"; it was very hard to do that while listening to "Good Golly Miss Molly" sung by Little Richard.

The connection in the minds of many adults between rock 'n' roll blackness accounts for the reaction of many to Elvis Presley. To many, Elvis was very, very dangerous. He covered many black songs, and exuded sex during his live and television performances. For many who feared rock 'n' roll, the best thing that could have possibly happened was when Elvis went into the army in 1958. By the end of the decade, rock had lost much of the ferocity it possessed in 1956 to 1957.

The legacy of the cultural rebels of the 1950s would certainly have tremendous influence in the 1960s. The behavior of members of the Beat Generation would be copied by the hippies. In addition, the rules that were so carefully taught to 1950s teenagers would be very intentionally broken by many teens in the 1960s.

Chapter Review

Rapid Review

To achieve the perfect 5, you should be able to explain the following:

- The 1950s is viewed by some as a decade of complacency and by others as a decade of growing ferment.
- Large-scale economic growth continued throughout the 1950s, spurred by cold war defense needs, automobile sales, housing sales, and the sale of appliances.
- The advertising industry did much to shape consumer desires in the 1950s.
- The GI Bill gave many veterans low-income mortgages and the possibility of a college education after World War II.
- Many families moved to suburbia in the 1950s; critics maintain that this increased the conformity of American society.
- During the baby boom, the birthrate drastically increased; the baby boom lasted from 1945 to 1962.
- Presidents Truman and Eisenhower were both dwarfed by the memory of the personality and the policies of Franklin Roosevelt.
- Jackie Robinson did much to advance the cause of rights in the postwar era.
- *Brown v. Board of Education* was a tremendous victory for those pushing for school integration in the 1950s.
- The Montgomery bus boycott and the events at Central High School in Little Rock, Arkansas, demonstrated the techniques that would prove to be successful in defeating segregation.
- Many men and many women felt great frustration with suburban family life of the 1950s.
- 1950s teenagers are often called the "silent generation," although James Dean, the Beat Generation writers, and Elvis Presley attracted followers among young people who did rebel in the 1950s.

Time Line

1944: GI Bill enacted
1947: Taft-Hartley Act enacted
      Jackie Robinson first plays for Brooklyn Dodgers
1948: Truman elected president in stunning upset
      Truman orders desegregation of armed forces
1950: Diner's Club credit card offered
1951: Publication of *The Catcher in the Rye* by J. D. Salinger
1952: Dwight D. Eisenhower elected president
1953: Defense budget at $47 billion
      Alan Freed begins to play rock 'n' roll on the radio in Cleveland, Ohio
1954: *Brown v. Board of Education* Supreme Court decision
1955: First McDonald's opens
      Rebel Without a Cause released
      Bus boycott in Montgomery, Alabama

1956: Interstate Highway Act enacted
      Majority of U.S. workers hold white-collar jobs
      Howl by Allen Ginsberg first read
1957: Baby boom peaks
      Publication of *On the Road* by Jack Kerouac
      Resistance to school integration in Little Rock, Arkansas
1960: Three-quarters of all American homes have a TV set

❯ Review Questions

Multiple-Choice Questions

1. Consumer spending increased in the 1950s because of all of the following *except*
   A. many Americans were once again purchasing stock.
   B. many families were buying automobiles.
   C. many Americans were buying homes.
   D. advertising had a major impact on the American consumer.

2. The policies of the presidency of Dwight D. Eisenhower are most similar to the policies of the presidency of
   A. Franklin Roosevelt.
   B. William Howard Taft.
   C. Calvin Coolidge.
   D. Theodore Roosevelt.

3. How did their experiences in the Great Depression and World War II affect the generation who began to raise families in the postwar era?
   A. They turned inward to family for comfort.
   B. They were likely to want to give their children many of the things they had not been able to have.
   C. Interested in consumer goods, they would be likely to buy many things on credit.
   D. A and B above.

4. The most important impact of television on viewers of the early 1950s was that
   A. it provided them with comedies that allowed them to forget the difficult years of the 1950s.
   B. it allowed them to receive the latest news of the day.
   C. it imposed a sense of conformity on American society.
   D. it fostered a growing youth culture.

5. Many Americans were especially fearful of rock, 'n' roll in the 1950s because
   A. many of the musicians who played it were black.
   B. Elvis Presley and many of the early performers of rock 'n' roll came from a decidedly lower-class background.
   C. Elvis Presley and many other early rock 'n' roll performers came from the American South.
   D. the messages found in early rock 'n' roll supported communism.

Short-Answer Question

6. Answer Parts A, B, and C.
   A. Briefly explain ONE example of a social phenomenon reflecting American prosperity in the 1950s.
   B. Briefly explain a SECOND example of a social phenomenon reflecting American prosperity in the 1950s.
   C. Briefly explain ONE example of a critique of the prosperous American society of the 1950s.

› Answers and Explanations

1. **A**. Americans were buying consumer goods in the postwar era. Many had money but not goods to buy in World War II. The purchase of stock would become pronounced only after this post–World War II buying spree ended.

2. **C**. Although each was somewhat different in style, Coolidge and Eisenhower were both friends of big business, believed in a balanced budget, and believed in a smaller role for the federal government and the presidency.

3. **D**. Many of those who lived through the depression were never comfortable with the idea of buying on credit; some never got credit cards at any point in their lives. Some historians say that this generation of parents spoiled their children, forming the expectations that some of these children would have as young adults in the 1960s.

4. **C**. TV viewers could get comedies and news on the radio. There was little on television in the early 1950s that specifically appealed to youth.

5. **A**. Elvis, Carl Perkins, Jerry Lee Lewis, and others were of lower-class backgrounds and were from the South, but the main objection to rock 'n' roll was its connection to black culture—for instance, Fats Domino, Chuck Berry, and Little Richard. No known early rock 'n' roll song supported communism.

6. **Parts A and B**: The postwar prosperity increased demand for American-made consumer goods. The economist John Kenneth Galbraith wrote that America had become an "affluent society." The American automobile industry boomed. The American love affair with cars encouraged the launching of the interstate highway system in 1956. The mobility provided by automobiles also contributed to the growth of suburbs. Many Americans in the postwar years wanted to own their own homes. Veterans could use the GI Bill of 1944 to get low-interest mortgage loans. The homebuilder William Levitt used assembly line techniques to construct several Levittowns filled with affordable, but nearly identical suburban homes. Also helping fuel the rush to the suburbs was the postwar baby boom. Many Americans wanted to raise their growing families in a safe and comfortable suburban environment.

Part C: African Americans wanted to share fully in the prosperity of the 1950s, but they were held back by racial segregation. The 1954 Supreme Court decision *Brown v. Board of Education* ruled that "separate but equal" was unconstitutional, and ordered the desegregation of public schools. In 1955, Rosa Parks refused to surrender her seat to a white man on a Montgomery, Alabama, bus. Her arrest led to the Montgomery bus boycott. Victory in this struggle to desegregate public transportation in Montgomery brought Rev. Martin Luther King, Jr., to national prominence. In 1957, President Dwight D. Eisenhower used federal troops to protect African American students desegregating Central High School in Little Rock, Arkansas. Feminists rejected the role of housewife for women. Betty Friedan began collecting material for her book *The Feminine Mystique* (1963). A variety of writers criticized what they perceived as the conformity of the 1950s. William H. Whyte's *The Organization Man* (1956) condemned the conformity of modern corporate culture. The countercultural writer Jack Kerouac, a leader of the Beat Generation, described a free and highly individualistic lifestyle in *On the Road* (1957). For some young people, rock 'n' roll music became a way of expressing rebellion against the values of their parents.

CHAPTER 27

America in an Era of Turmoil (1960–1975)

IN THIS CHAPTER

Summary: The events and consequences of the 1960s still have the ability to provoke contentious debate. Many claim the changes that came out of the decade have had a positive long-term effect on American society; for example, women's rights and protection of the environment became popular causes during this period. Others point to destructive consequences of the decade, including the loosening of morality and excessive drug use, as more emblematic of the 1960s. The election of John Kennedy as president in 1960 caused many in America to feel optimistic about the future. But for some, Kennedy's assassination in 1963 was a sign of the violence that would consume America later in the decade. The construction of the Berlin Wall, the Cuban Missile Crisis, and the Vietnam War were the major foreign policy issues of the decade; opposition to the Vietnam War eventually drove President Lyndon Johnson from the White House. Blacks made many civil rights gains during the decade, but a number of younger blacks now called for "black power" rather than integration into white society. College and high school students became increasingly empowered in the decade; hundreds of thousands protested against the Vietnam War. While a number of students were increasingly involved in political affairs, other young people supported cultural instead of political revolution and became members of a widespread counterculture.

KEY IDEA

Keywords

New Frontier: group of domestic policies proposed by John Kennedy that included Medicare and aid to education and urban renewal; many of these policies were not enacted until the presidency of Lyndon Johnson.

Great Society: overarching plan by President Lyndon Johnson to assist the underprivileged in American society; it included the creation of the Department of Housing and Urban Affairs and the Head Start and Medicare programs. Some Great Society programs were later reduced because of the cost of the Vietnam War.

Civil Rights Act of 1964: major civil rights legislation that outlawed racial discrimination in public facilities, in employment, and in voter registration.

Black power: philosophy of some younger blacks in the 1960s who were impatient with the slow pace of desegregation; its advocates believed that blacks should create and control their own political and cultural institutions rather than seeking integration into white-dominated society.

Roe v. Wade **(1973):** Supreme Court decision that made abortion legal (with some restrictions).

Gulf of Tonkin Resolution: congressional resolution passed in August 1964 following reports that U.S. Navy ships had been fired on by North Vietnamese gunboats off the Vietnam coast; in essence it gave the president the power to fight the Vietnam War without approval from Congress. Many historians doubt if any attack on U.S. ships actually took place.

Students for a Democratic Society (SDS): radical, activist student organization created in 1960 that advocated a more democratic, participatory society. SDS was one of the major student organizations opposing the Vietnam War.

Counterculture: movement by young people in the 1960s who rejected political involvement and emphasized the need for personal instead of political revolution. Many members of the counterculture wore long hair and experimented with various drugs, with sex, and with unconventional living arrangements.

Kent State University: campus in Ohio where four students who were part of a 1970 protest against U.S. involvement in Cambodia were shot and killed by National Guardsmen.

1960 Presidential Election

Many Americans perceived the election of John Kennedy over Richard Nixon in 1960 as the beginning of a new age for America. His statement during his inauguration speech "Ask not what your country can do for you—ask what you can do for your country" is remembered by millions today. At age 43, Kennedy appeared young and vigorous (especially when flanked by his wife, Jacqueline). Kennedy was the son of a former ambassador to Britain and had served as a congressman and senator from Massachusetts. He was also a Roman Catholic.

Some voters considered Richard Nixon to be "too tied to the past"; as previously mentioned, he was the vice president under Dwight D. Eisenhower. Historians note that this was the first election greatly affected by television; in four presidential debates, Nixon appeared nervous and tired. Ironically, those who heard the debates on the radio didn't feel that Nixon lost them. Some historians argue that the television image projected by Nixon actually cost him the election. The 1960 popular vote was one of the closest in history; Nixon lost by only 120,000 votes (out of nearly 34 million votes cast).

Domestic Policies under Kennedy and Johnson

Early in his administration, John Kennedy stated that America was on the brink of entering into a **New Frontier**. The press from this point on dubbed his domestic policies "New Frontier" policies. Kennedy had plans to stimulate the economy and to seriously attack poverty in America (*The Other America* by Michael Harrington was published in 1962; this book outlined the plight of America's poor and had a great effect on Kennedy and his circle). Kennedy supported several important domestic programs, including a Medicare program (later approved during the administration of Lyndon Johnson) and substantial federal aid to education and to urban renewal.

Very little of Kennedy's domestic agenda was adopted by Congress. His plans to cut taxes and to increase spending on education never even got out of the congressional committee. One of Kennedy's domestic successes was to convince Congress to raise the minimum wage from $1.00 per hour to $1.25. Kennedy also established a Peace Corps program, in which young men and women volunteered to help residents in developing countries around the world.

One program that was considered a top priority by both Kennedy and Congress was the space program. Kennedy was barely in office when Soviet cosmonaut Yuri Gagarin became the first human to travel in space. In early May 1961, America put its first man in space (Alan Shepard), and in February 1962 John Glenn (later a U.S. senator) became the first American astronaut to orbit the earth. During this era, Kennedy also made the bold promise that America would land a man on the moon by the end of the 1960s.

The New Frontier programs ended permanently when John Kennedy was assassinated in Dallas, Texas, on November 22, 1963. Kennedy was in Texas to heal wounds in the local Democratic party and to rally support for the 1964 presidential election. Kennedy was riding in a motorcade through downtown Dallas when he was killed. An ex-marine named Lee Harvey Oswald was arrested and charged with Kennedy's death. Oswald never went to trial because he was shot and killed by a Dallas nightclub owner, Jack Ruby, two days later. The **Warren Commission** was formed to investigate the assassination; the report of this committee firmly supported those who said that Oswald acted alone. To this day, there are those who maintain that a conspiracy was responsible for Kennedy's death.

Vice President Lyndon Johnson was sworn into office shortly after Kennedy's assassination. In the year after Kennedy's death, Johnson was able to get much of Kennedy's domestic policy plans through Congress. Johnson had been the Senate majority leader before becoming vice president, and in early 1964 was easily able to maneuver the previously rejected Kennedy tax cut through Congress.

Johnson ran for reelection against Senator Barry Goldwater in the 1964 presidential election. Goldwater was a conservative from Arizona who was too far to the right for mainstream America to accept. He spoke of using nuclear weapons in Vietnam and famously stated that "extremism in the defense of liberty is no vice." Lyndon Johnson won nearly 62 percent of the popular vote and was able to institute his own economic plans in 1965; in a speech early in that year, Johnson stated that his goal was to create a **Great Society** in America.

In speech after speech, Johnson stated that it would be possible to truly end poverty in America. The Department of Housing and Urban Affairs was created as a cabinet-level department. In 1964, Johnson had begun the **VISTA (Volunteer in Service to America)** program, which organized volunteers who worked in the poorest communities of the United States. In 1965, Congress passed Johnson's Housing and Urban Development Act, which organized the building of nearly 250,000 new housing units in America's cities and authorized over $3 billion for further urban development. Johnson's major initiatives in education authorized grants to help schools in the poorest sections of America and established **Head Start**, a program to help disadvantaged preschool students. In 1965, Johnson established a **Medicare** system, which provided hospital insurance and medical coverage for America's senior citizens, and Medicaid, which assisted Americans of any age who could not afford health insurance.

The Great Society programs of Lyndon Johnson positively impacted the lives of thousands of Americans, but frustration set in when it appeared that, despite massive government efforts, a large number of Americans still lived in poverty. In addition, the cost of Great Society programs put a strain on American taxpayers. However, it should be noted that the number of those living in poverty was cut by at least 40 percent by Great Society programs. Many of these programs ended up being reduced or eliminated because of the expense of America's war in Vietnam.

Struggle of Black Americans: From Nonviolence to Black Power

As was noted in the previous chapter, Martin Luther King, Jr., emerged as a key leader of the civil rights movement during the Montgomery, Alabama, bus boycott. King and other Southern clergymen founded the Southern Christian Leadership Conference (SCLC), which taught that civil rights could be achieved through nonviolent protest. SCLC leaders taught that violence could never be utilized to achieve their goals, no matter what the circumstance.

Many younger blacks were eager for the fight for civil rights to develop at a quicker pace. In 1960, the Student Nonviolent Coordinating Committee (SNCC) was formed; its leaders were not ministers, and they demanded immediate, not gradual, change. During the first years of its existence, SNCC attracted both black and white members; many of the whites were college students from Northern universities.

An effective technique utilized by the civil rights movement in the early 1960s was the **sit-in**. Blacks were not allowed to eat at the lunch counters of many Southern stores, even though blacks could buy merchandise at these stores. Black and white civil rights workers would sit down at these lunch counters; when they were denied service, they continued to sit there (preventing other paying customers from taking their spaces). Picketers would often march outside the store in question. Those participating in sit-ins received tremendous verbal and physical harassment from other whites, yet the tactic of the sit-in helped to integrate dozens of Southern establishments in the first several years of the 1960s.

In May 1961, the Congress for Racial Equality sponsored the **Freedom Rides**. During the previous year, the Supreme Court had ruled that bus stations and waiting rooms in these stations had to be integrated. On the Freedom Rides, both black and white volunteers started in Washington and were determined to ride through the South to see if cities had complied with the Supreme Court legislation. In Anniston, Alabama, a white mob greeted the bus, beating many of the Freedom Riders and burning the bus. Freedom Rides continued throughout the summer; almost all riders experienced some violence or were arrested.

The Freedom Rides introduced an important influence into the civil rights struggle in the South: the public opinion of the rest of the country. Many Americans were horrified at the violence they witnessed; many called their representatives in Congress to urge that the federal government do more to support the Freedom Riders. By the end of the summer, marshals from the Justice Department were in every city the Freedom Ride buses passed through to ensure a lack of violence.

Under Attorney General Robert Kennedy, the federal government became much more involved in enforcing federal civil rights guidelines and court rulings. In September 1962, President Kennedy nationalized the Alabama National Guard and sent in federal marshals to suppress protesters and allow James Meredith to be the first black to take classes at the University of Mississippi. In Birmingham, Alabama, city officials turned fire hoses and trained dogs on civil rights protesters; the broadcast of these events to the entire nation again created a widespread outrage against those in the South who were opposing court-ordered integration.

President Kennedy went very slowly on civil rights issues, but in the summer of 1963, he presented to Congress a wide-ranging civil rights bill that would have withheld large amounts of federal funding from states that continued to practice segregation. To muster support for this bill, civil rights leaders organized the August 28, 1963, **March on Washington**. More than 200,000 people showed up to protest for civil rights legislation; it was at this rally that Martin Luther King, Jr., made his very famous "I have a dream" speech.

In 1964, Lyndon Johnson presented to Congress the most wide-ranging civil rights bill since Reconstruction. The **Civil Rights Act of 1964** stated that the same standards had to be used to register white and black voters, that racial discrimination could not be used by employers to hire workers, that discrimination was illegal in all public locations, and that an Equal Employment Opportunity Commission would be created. The Voting Rights Act of 1965 outlawed measures such as literacy tests, which had been used to prevent blacks from voting. Passage of this bill was aided by the public sentiment that followed the revelation that three civil rights workers had been killed the previous summer while attempting to register voters in Mississippi. Television reports of violence against civil rights workers, such as was seen during Martin Luther King's march in Selma, Alabama, in 1965, convinced many Americans that additional civil rights legislation was necessary.

Many blacks who lived in poverty in Northern cities believed that the civil rights movement was doing little or nothing for them. In August 1965, riots broke out in the Watts section of Los Angeles; Chicago, Newark, and Detroit soon experienced similar riots. The **Kerner Commission** was authorized to investigate the cause of these riots, and stated that black poverty and the lack of hope in the black urban communities were the major causes of these disturbances. The Kerner Commission reported that two societies existed in America, one white and rich, and the other poor and black.

One group that preached opposition to integration was the **Nation of Islam**. This organization (also called the Black Muslims) preached that it was to the benefit of white society to keep blacks poor and in ghettoes, and that for blacks to improve their position they would have to do it themselves. Malcolm X would become the most famous representative of this group, preaching **black nationalism**. Eventually, Malcolm X rejected the more extreme concepts of the Nation of Islam, and he was killed in February 1965.

The ideas of black nationalism exerted a great deal of influence on many of the younger members of SNCC. One, Stokely Carmichael, began to urge blacks to take up arms to defend themselves against whites; Carmichael also orchestrated the removal of all whites from SNCC. In addition, Carmichael began to urge SNCC members to support **black power**; this concept stated that blacks should have pride in their history and their heritage, and that blacks should create their own society apart from the all-controlling white society.

The most visible group supporting black power were the **Black Panthers**. This San Francisco group, founded by Bobby Seale and Huey Newton, had a militarist image. Several members died after vicious gun battles with police. At the same time, the Black Panthers set up programs that gave food to the poorest members of San Francisco's black population and established schools to teach black history and culture to the children in the community. However, the image of this organization was greatly damaged by its violent reputation.

Rise of Feminism

Another group that fought for additional freedoms in the 1960s were women. As discussed in the previous chapter, many women felt extreme frustration with their lives in the 1950s. Some college-aged women were active in the civil rights movement in the early 1960s, but often felt frustrated when they were always the ones asked to make the coffee or do the typing.

In the mid-1960s, even women in suburbia began to notice that the frustrations they had were shared by many of the women living around them. Women's support groups became common on both college campuses and in suburban communities. A pivotal book that helped bolster this growing **feminist movement** was *The Feminine Mystique* by Betty Friedan.

In 1966, **NOW (National Organization for Women)** was founded by Friedan. NOW was a decidedly middle-class organization and was dedicated to getting equal pay for women at work and to ending images in the media that objectified women. In 1972, Gloria Steinem founded the feminist magazine *Ms.* The key Supreme Court decision of the era concerning women was the 1973 *Roe v. Wade* ruling, which, with some restrictions, legalized abortion. Many feminists pushed for the passage of an Equal Rights Amendment, but this amendment was never ratified by enough states to become part of the Constitution. Some opponents to the amendment stated that its passage would eventually lead to other "unacceptable" actions, such as gay marriage.

Other groups protested for equal rights during this period. The **American Indian Movement (AIM)** wanted Native Americans to be knowledgeable about their heritage, and also influenced various tribes to mount legal battles to get back land that had been illegally taken from them. A standoff between AIM members and government authorities took place at Wounded Knee, South Dakota, in 1973; as a result, legislation passed in the 1970s gave Native Americans more autonomy in tribal matters.

Latino groups also began to protest for rights in this era. A large number of Latinos were employed as migrant farm workers in California; Cesar Chavez organized the **United Farm Workers** against farmers (especially grape growers) in California. Environmental groups also became active in this era. *Silent Spring* by Rachel Carson came out in 1962 and warned about the dangers of DDT. Many also protested throughout the decade against the dangers of nuclear power.

Cold War in the 1960s

Cold war tensions and fears continued to dominate in the early 1960s. The fear of the bomb continued unabated; movies such as *Fail-Safe* and *Dr. Strangelove* explored a world in which an "accident" with the bomb might occur. Both the United States and the Soviet Union openly tested nuclear weapons during 1961 and 1962.

A plan to liberate Cuba from Castro had actually been formulated during the Eisenhower administration; by this plan, the CIA would train Cubans living in America to invade Cuba, and the United States would provide air cover. This operation, called the **Bay of Pigs**, took place in April 1961 and was a complete fiasco, with virtually the entire invasion force killed or captured by Castro's forces. The Bay of Pigs was a major embarrassment for the Kennedy administration in its first months in office.

In Berlin, refugees from the East continued to try to escape to West Berlin on a daily basis; in August 1961, the East Germans and the Soviets constructed the concrete **Berlin Wall**, dividing the two halves of the city. The issue that almost brought the world to World War III was not in Europe, however; it was in Cuba. In mid-October 1962, American reconnaissance flights over Cuba indicated Soviet-made missile sights under construction. In the **Cuban Missile Crisis**, President Kennedy established a naval blockade of Cuba and told Soviet leader Nikita Khrushchev to remove the missiles from Cuba. Khrushchev backed down and removed the missiles, averting the potential of world war. It is known now that if American forces had landed in Cuba, Soviet authorities were seriously contemplating the use of tactical nuclear weapons against them. Luckily, effective diplomacy prevented the outbreak of a potentially catastrophic crisis. Shortly afterward, the United States and the Soviet Union signed a Limited Test Ban Treaty, and a "hot line" was installed, connecting the White House and the Kremlin so that future crises could be dealt with quickly.

Vietnam War and Its Impact on American Society

Since the 1950s, the United States had supported non-Communist South Vietnam against the North, led by Communist and nationalist Ho Chi Minh. The South Vietnamese government also had to fight the **Vietcong**, Communist guerrillas who lived in South Vietnam but supported the North. During the Kennedy administration, the number of American advisors in Vietnam increased. American officials became increasingly suspicious of the effectiveness of South Vietnamese president Diem; in the fall of 1963, these officials supported (or orchestrated, depending on which historian you read) the assassination of Diem.

Shortly after becoming president, Lyndon Johnson decided that to achieve victory, the war in Vietnam had to be intensified. In August 1964, Johnson announced to the nation that light North Vietnamese gunboats had fired on American destroyers in the Gulf of Tonkin, which is in international waters. Some historians are skeptical that these events ever took place. Nevertheless, Congress passed the **Gulf of Tonkin Resolution,** which gave the president the power to "prevent further aggression" in Vietnam; this resolution allowed the president to control the war without the necessity of consulting Congress.

Throughout 1965, 1966, and 1967, America continued to increase its commitment in Vietnam; by early 1968 nearly 540,000 American soldiers were stationed in Vietnam. Beginning in 1965, bombing campaigns against North Vietnam became commonplace. American soldiers in Vietnam became increasingly frustrated by the jungle tactics used by their enemies, by the fact that one's friend by day might be one's enemy by night, and by the seeming lack of effectiveness of the South Vietnamese army.

A key battle of the war was the **Tet Offensive**, which began on January 30, 1968. During the first day of the Vietnamese new year, the Vietcong initiated major offensives in cities across South Vietnam. Even Saigon, the capital, was attacked, and the Vietcong held the American embassy for several hours. In the end, the Vietcong and North Vietnamese suffered major losses as a result of the Tet Offensive. Nevertheless, this was the battle that began to conclusively turn American public opinion against the war. The sights on television of American forces trying to recapture their own embassy certainly made many question the idea that "victory was just around the corner," which is what was being told to the American people by military and civilian officials.

The Vietnam War drove Lyndon Johnson from the White House. Diaries of several in Johnson's inner circle show that he was consumed by the war. In February 1968, Johnson began his reelection bid by taking on Senator Eugene McCarthy of Minnesota, who was running on a peace ticket, in the New Hampshire presidential primary. Johnson won, but got only 48 percent of the total votes to 42 percent for McCarthy. Johnson considered this a humiliation, and one month later pulled out of the presidential race. Johnson endorsed Vice President Hubert Humphrey for president. By this point, Robert Kennedy had also announced his candidacy.

Throughout 1968, support for the Vietnam War continued to fade in America. The Republican candidate for president, Richard Nixon, gained support when he proclaimed that he had a "secret plan" to end the war. Reports of the brutality of the war also shocked many Americans. Many were disturbed to find that Americans were using **napalm**, a substance that sticks to the skin and burns, on civilian villages. The story of the 1968 **My Lai Massacre**, in which more than 300 Vietnamese women, children, and elderly men were murdered by American soldiers, horrified many Americans. Some Americans began to wonder what the United States was doing in Vietnam, and what the war was doing to the United States.

The student protest movement also began to furiously campaign against the war. Student activists had previously been active in the civil rights movement. In 1960, the **Students for a Democratic Society (SDS)** organization was formed. The *Port Huron Statement* was the founding document of this organization, and called for a less materialistic society that encouraged "participatory democracy." SDS would become one of the major student organizations opposing the war.

The **Free Speech Movement** had grown at the University of California at Berkeley in 1964 when school officials refused to allow political materials to be distributed on campus. Campus buildings were occupied, as students demanded college courses more relevant to their lives. Tactics used by Berkeley students were copied by students at colleges across the country.

The Vietnam War greatly expanded the student protest movement in America. Many students were passionately opposed to the war on moral grounds; to be fair, others were part of the movement because they didn't want to be drafted. Television pictures of young men burning their draft cards were commonplace. Antiwar demonstrations that had attracted a few hundred people in 1964 were now attracting thousands; a 1967 antiwar rally drew 500,000 people to Central Park in New York.

The year 1968 saw the protests grow, both in number and in intensity. Events of 1968 convinced many young people that getting involved in mainstream politics (as Eugene McCarthy had tried to get them to do) was fruitless. Martin Luther King and Robert Kennedy were killed in the spring of that year; to many, that left the presidential race between two representatives of the old guard, Richard Nixon and Hubert Humphrey. What, many students asked, was the point of even getting involved in politics if the candidates that they could choose from all ended up being traditional politicians? In the spring of 1968, major protests broke out at Columbia University; in August, as protesters chanted "the whole world is watching," Chicago police officers brutally beat students and others who had shown up to protest at the Democratic National Convention. By 1969, disputes over how much violence is acceptable began to tear SDS apart as well.

Another group of revolutionaries in the 1960s rejected political involvement and supported cultural revolution instead. Members of the **counterculture** rejected America and its values as much as antiwar protesters did, but believed that personal revolution was most vital. These "hippies," or countercultural rebels, often had little to do with members of SDS; the revolution of the hippies consisted of growing one's hair long, listening to the "right" music, and partaking of psychedelic drugs. Timothy Leary and other proponents of LSD implored young people to "tune in, turn on, and drop out." Sexual freedom was also commonplace in the counterculture. A birth control pill had been approved by the federal government in 1960; a button worn by many in the 1960s stated "If It Feels Good, Do It!" The Mecca for many of these rebels in 1967 was San Francisco, where the music and lifestyle of groups such as the Grateful Dead personified the counterculture of the 1960s. The **Woodstock Music Festival** of 1969 was the most outward manifestation of the "peace and love" rebels of the 1960s. For members of the counterculture, personal rebellion was a much more valid form of rebellion than political rebellion; it should be remembered that Pete Townshend of The Who threw radical political organizer Abbie Hoffman off the stage at Woodstock.

Richard Nixon was elected in November 1968, and soon announced his policy of **Vietnamization** of the war, which consisted of training the South Vietnamese army and gradually pulling American forces out. By 1972, American forces in Vietnam only numbered 24,000 (as the numbers of soldiers in Vietnam decreased, so did the antiwar protests). In April 1970, however, Nixon announced that to support the South Vietnamese government, massive bombing of the North was needed and that the war needed to be extended into Cambodia to wipe out Communist bases there. College campuses across the country, for one last time, joined together in massive protest. At **Kent State University** four students were killed by National Guardsmen who opened fire on the protesters; two students were killed at Jackson State University in Mississippi. American public opinion at this point was deeply divided on the war; two days after Kent State, nearly 100,000 construction workers marched in New York City for the war.

In 1971, the **Pentagon Papers** were leaked by a former Department of Defense employee, Daniel Ellsburg. The Pentagon Papers revealed that the government had deceived the American public and Congress about Vietnam as early as 1964. By this point, most Americans awaited the end of American involvement in the war.

America was involved in negotiations with the North Vietnamese in Paris. Negotiations intensified in December 1972 when President Nixon ordered the heaviest bombing of the war against North Vietnam. In January 1973, it was announced that American forces would leave Vietnam in 60 days, that all American prisoners would be returned, and that the boundary between North and South Vietnam would be respected. On March 29, 1973, the last American soldiers left Vietnam; 60,000 Americans had died there. On April 30, 1975, the North Vietnamese captured Saigon, the capital of South Vietnam, ending the Vietnam War. The last Americans had left the country one day earlier.

Chapter Review

Rapid Review

To achieve the perfect 5, you should be able to explain the following:

- The events that dramatically altered America including protests and cultural rebellion in the 1960s are seen by some in a positive light and others in a negative light.
- John Kennedy projected a new image of presidential leadership, although few of his domestic programs were actually passed by Congress.
- The Cuban Missile Crisis was the critical foreign policy crisis of the Kennedy administration, and may have brought the world close to world war.
- After Kennedy's death, Lyndon Johnson was able to get Congress to pass his Great Society domestic programs, which included Head Start and Medicare.
- Nonviolence remained the major tactic of the civil rights movement throughout the 1960s, although some black leaders began to advocate "black power."
- Women strove to achieve equal rights in the 1960s through the National Organization for Women (NOW) and consciousness-raising groups.
- Lyndon Johnson determined early in his presidency that an escalation of the war in Vietnam would be necessary, and more materials and men went to Vietnam from 1965 to 1968.
- The military in Vietnam was frustrated by the military tactics of the enemy and by faltering support at home.
- The Tet Offensive did much to turn American public opinion against the war.
- Student protesters held increasingly large demonstrations against the war; SDS was the main organization of student activists.
- Members of the counterculture advocated a personal and not a political rebellion in this era.
- Richard Nixon removed American troops from Vietnam through the policy of Vietnamization; the South Vietnamese government fell two years after American troops departed.

Time Line

1960: John Kennedy elected president
   Sit-ins began
   Students for a Democratic Society (SDS) formed
   Student Nonviolent Coordinating Committee (SNCC) formed

1961: Freedom Rides
   Bay of Pigs invasion
   Construction of Berlin Wall
   First American travels in space

1962: James Meredith enters University of Mississippi
   SDS issues *Port Huron Statement*
   Silent Spring by Rachel Carson published
   Cuban Missile Crisis
   The Other America by Michael Harrington published

1963: John Kennedy assassinated; Lyndon Johnson becomes president
   Civil rights march on Washington
   The Feminine Mystique by Betty Friedan published
   President Diem assassinated in South Vietnam

1964: Beginning of Johnson's War on Poverty programs
Civil Rights Act enacted
Free Speech Movement at Berkeley begins
Tonkin Gulf Resolution
Johnson reelected

1965: Elementary and Secondary Education Act passed
Johnson sends more troops to Vietnam
Voting Rights Act passed
Murder of Malcolm X
Watts riots burn sections of Los Angeles

1966: Stokely Carmichael calls for "black power"
Formation of Black Panther party
Formation of National Organization for Women (NOW)

1967: Riots in many American cities
Antiwar demonstrations intensify

1968: Martin Luther King assassinated
Robert Kennedy assassinated
Student protests at Columbia University
Battle between police and protesters at Democratic National Convention
Richard Nixon elected president
American Indian Movement (AIM) founded
Tet Offensive
My Lai Massacre

1969: Woodstock Music Festival

1970: United States invades Cambodia
Killings at Kent State, Jackson State

1971: *Pentagon Papers* published by the *New York Times*

1972: Nixon reelected

1973: Vietnam cease-fire announced; American troops leave Vietnam
Roe v. Wade decision

1975: South Vietnam falls to North Vietnam, ending the Vietnam War

› Review Questions

Multiple-Choice Questions

1. The initial fate of the Freedom Riders demonstrated that
   A. Southerners had largely accepted Northern orders to integrate bus stations and other public facilities.
   B. state governments were at the forefront in the enforcement of civil rights laws.
   C. television news broadcasts had a powerful hold on the American public.
   D. by 1961 the federal government was committed to vigorously protecting the civil rights of all citizens.

2. The Tet Offensive demonstrated that
   A. American forces were fairly close to a decisive victory in Vietnam.
   B. military and civilian officials had been less than candid with the American people on the progress of the war.
   C. the Vietcong could defeat American soldiers in the battlefield.
   D. cooperation between Americans and the South Vietnamese army was improving.

3. The membership rolls of Students for a Democratic Society were at an all-time high when
   A. the struggles of the civil rights movement in the South were shown on national television.
   B. Nixon invaded Cambodia.
   C. Nixon intensified the bombing to its highest levels of the war in 1972.
   D. more young men were being sent to Vietnam between 1965 and 1967.

4. Some Northern blacks were attracted to the call for "black power" for all of the following reasons *except*
   A. Martin Luther King and others in the civil rights movement seemed more interested in improving the position of Southern blacks.
   B. ghetto sections of Northern cities remained poor, and many residents there felt little hope.
   C. Malcolm X and Stokely Carmichael evoked powerful images of black pride.
   D. vast numbers of Northern blacks had joined the Nation of Islam.

5. Highlights for feminist leaders of this era included all of the following *except*
   A. the founding of *Ms.*
   B. the formation of NOW
   C. the drive for passage of the Equal Rights Amendment
   D. the increased awareness of "women's issues" in society

Short-Answer Question

6. Answer Parts A, B, and C.
   A. Briefly explain ONE example of a movement calling for more rights in the 1960s.
   B. Briefly explain a SECOND example of a movement calling for more rights in the 1960s.
   C. Briefly explain ONE example of a response by the government to these movements.

❯ Answers and Explanations

1. **C**. The images of burned buses and beaten Freedom Riders horrified many Americans. At this point, neither the federal nor state governments protected the rights of Freedom Riders.

2. **B**. The Tet Offensive was a military defeat for the Vietcong. However, it did prove that victory was not "around the corner," which is what many military officials were publicly claiming.

3. **D**. By the time of the invasion of Cambodia and the massive bombing at the end of the war, SDS had split into factions. The civil rights movement attracted a relatively small number of new members to SDS.

4. **D**. All of the other reasons caused some Northern blacks to abandon Martin Luther King's call for integration. Only a small proportion of blacks ever joined the Nation of Islam.

5. **C**. After a long struggle, the drive to get the ERA into the Constitution was finally abandoned when it became obvious that not enough state legislatures would ever pass it.

6. **Parts A and B**: African Americans continued to work for full civil rights in the 1960s. African American students staged sit-ins at Southern lunch counters that refused them service. Black and white civil rights workers took Freedom Rides on buses to desegregate interstate transportation. Dr. Martin Luther King, Jr., and other civil rights leaders led marches the South, including the August 28, 1963, March on Washington. The later 1960s saw a growing movement of black nationalism, inspired by leaders like Malcolm X. This led to calls for black power, and a celebration of the African heritage of African Americans. Feminists agitated for more opportunities for women and specific objectives like equal pay for equal work. In 1966, Betty Friedan founded the National Organization for Women (NOW). In 1972, Gloria Steinem launched *Ms* magazine. The American Indian Movement (AIM) protested the treatment of Native Americans. In 1973, AIM activists occupied Wounded Knee, South Dakota, and for a time defied federal authorities. Cesar Chavez started the United Farm Workers to organize Latino farm workers. In 1960, leftist students established the Students for a Democratic Society (SDS). The *Port Huron Statement* (1962), with its demand for "participatory democracy," launched the "New Left." In 1964, students at the University of California at Berkeley began the Free Speech Movement as a protest against the efforts of school administrators to limit the distribution of political materials on campus. Many students took the lead in organizing protests against the Vietnam War. Other students joined the counterculture, preferring to "tune in, turn on, and drop out."

Part C: Presidents John F. Kennedy and Lyndon B. Johnson expressed support for the civil rights movement. Johnson played a key role in passing the Civil Rights Act of 1964, which outlawed discrimination in public places, and the Voting Rights Act of 1965 that abolished practices such as literacy tests, which had been used to prevent African Americans from voting. The Supreme Court gave feminists a controversial victory with its 1972 *Roe v. Wade* decision legalizing abortion in the first two trimesters of a pregnancy. Following the Wounded Knee incident, the federal government passed laws giving Native American tribes more autonomy. In 1971, in response to student protests and the dispatch of many young men to the Vietnam War before they could vote, Congress and the states passed the Twenty-sixth Amendment giving the vote to citizens 18 years of age.

CHAPTER 28

Decline and Rebirth (1968–1988)

IN THIS CHAPTER

Summary: Some historians claim that the accomplishments of the presidency of Richard Nixon are often overlooked. Nixon opened diplomatic relations with China, improved relations with the Soviet Union, and began to break the Democratic stranglehold on politics in the South that had existed since the New Deal. Despite these developments, Richard Nixon will always be associated with the Watergate scandal. Watergate began a period when faith in the national government sharply declined; this lasted through the presidencies of Gerald Ford and Jimmy Carter. With the election of Ronald Reagan, many Americans began to "have faith in America again." Just as Nixon began a new relationship with China, under Reagan, America entered into a more positive relationship with its formal rival, the Soviet Union.

Keywords

Southern Strategy: political strategy implemented by President Richard Nixon to win over Southern whites to the Republican party; the strategy succeeded through administration policies such as delaying school desegregation plans.

Détente: foreign policy of decreasing tensions with the Soviet Union; began in the first term of the Nixon administration.

Watergate: series of events beginning with the break-in at the Democratic party headquarters in the Watergate complex in Washington, DC, that led to the downfall of President Richard Nixon; Nixon resigned as the House of Representatives was preparing for an impeachment hearing.

OPEC: Organization of Petroleum Exporting Countries; the group of twelve countries that produce most of the world's oil and, by determining production quantities, influence worldwide oil prices.

Camp David Accords (1978): peace agreement between Israel and Egypt that was mediated by President Jimmy Carter; many consider this the highlight of the Carter presidency.

Iranian Hostage Crisis: diplomatic crisis triggered on November 4, 1979, when Iranian protesters seized the U.S. embassy in Tehran and held 66 American diplomats hostage for 444 days. President Carter was unable to free the hostages despite several attempts; to many this event symbolized the paralysis of American power in the late 1970s.

Religious right: right-leaning evangelical Christians who increasingly supported Republican candidates beginning with Ronald Reagan.

Iran-Contra Affair: scandal that erupted during the Reagan administration when it was revealed that U.S. government agents had secretly sold arms to Iran in order to raise money to fund anti-Communist "Contra" forces in Nicaragua. Those acts directly contravened an ongoing U.S. trade embargo with Iran as well as federal legislation limiting aid to the Contras. Several Reagan administration officials were convicted of federal crimes as a result.

Presidency of Richard Nixon

Richard Nixon's election to the presidency in 1968 capped one of the greatest comeback stories in American political history. Nixon's political obituary had been written after successive defeats in 1960 (when he was defeated by John Kennedy for the presidency) and in 1962 (after being defeated by Pat Brown for governor of California; he informed the press on election night that "you won't have Nixon to kick around anymore," as he was resigning from politics).

Nixon was one of the most interesting men to be elected to the presidency in the twentieth century. He was never comfortable with large groups of people, and even in staged photo events sometimes appeared uncomfortable and out of place (such as the time he was pictured walking "informally" along the beach in dress shoes). Nixon was convinced that large numbers of the news media and many members of Congress were his enemies. He relied on a small group of close-knit advisors, including H. R. Haldeman, his chief of staff, and John Ehrlichman, his advisor for domestic affairs.

Nixon's Domestic Policies

As mentioned in the previous chapter, the Vietnam War took up large amounts of Nixon's time and energies. However, other potentially crucial crises also existed. As Nixon entered office in 1969, inflation was growing rapidly, unemployment was rising, the gross national product was exhibiting a lack of growth, and the United States had a rather substantial trade deficit. Some of these economic problems can be attributed to the administration of Lyndon Johnson; paying for Great Society programs and the Vietnam War at the same time created serious strains on the federal budget.

At first, Nixon tried to raise taxes and cut government spending; this policy only worsened the economy. The president then imposed a 90-day freeze on prices and wages; after these measures, he also established mandatory guidelines for wage and price increases. By 1971, Nixon also directed that a program of **deficit spending** begin. This was somewhat similar to the approach utilized by Franklin Roosevelt in attacking the economic problems of the Great Depression.

"Southern Strategy" of Richard Nixon

Southern whites had voted firmly Democratic since the Reconstruction Era. In the 1968 presidential election, cracks in this relationship between the Democratic party and the South began to show. George Wallace, former governor of Alabama, broke from the party and ran for president as a candidate of the American Independence Party in 1968. He picked up 13.5 percent of the popular vote (a large percentage of these from the South); this aided Richard Nixon in his victory over Hubert Humphrey.

Richard Nixon decided to take decisive measures to appeal to these Southern whites and win them over to the Republican party. Nixon's "**Southern Strategy**" included delaying school desegregation plans (that had been ordered by a federal court) in Mississippi and attempting to block an extension of the Voting Rights Act of 1965. Nixon also attempted to block school integration by busing after the Supreme Court had endorsed busing as a method to achieve integration. Under Nixon, the Supreme Court also became much more conservative, especially with Warren Burger as the new chief justice (nevertheless, it should be remembered that in *Roe v. Wade* this court outlawed state legislation opposing abortion).

Nixon's Foreign Policy

The greatest achievements of the Nixon presidency were undoubtedly in the area of foreign affairs. In formulating foreign policy, Nixon was aided by former Harvard professor Henry Kissinger, his national security advisor and, beginning in 1973, his secretary of state. Kissinger had conducted many of the negotiations with the North Vietnamese that allowed American troops to leave Vietnam in 1973. Nixon greatly trusted the judgment of Kissinger on foreign policy affairs.

Nixon's greatest accomplishments included better relationships with both the Soviet Union and China. Nixon had been a fierce anti-Communist in the 1950s, but during his first term in office, he instituted a policy of "**détente**" with the Soviet Union. The reduced tensions that this policy created were a welcome relief from the fierce anti-Communist rhetoric that had existed through most of the Kennedy and Johnson administrations.

In addition, Nixon realized the foolishness of continued **nuclear proliferation**. He visited the Soviet Union in 1972 and, during discussions with Soviet Premier Leonid Brezhnev, agreed to halt the continued buildup of nuclear weapons. The **SALT I** treaty (Strategic Arms Limitation Talks) was historic, since this was the first time the two superpowers agreed not to produce any more nuclear ballistic missiles and to reduce their arsenals of antiballistic missiles to 200 per side.

A journey that Nixon took earlier in 1972 was even more significant. During much of the 1950s and 1960s, Nixon spoke about the need to support Nationalist China (the non-Communist state established on the island of Taiwan) and the need to be vigilant against the expansion of "Red" China (the Communist state on the Chinese mainland). Henry Kissinger was an admirer of **realpolitik** and convinced Nixon that a new approach to Communist China was necessary. Kissinger maintained that it was foolish to think that the Communist Chinese would ever be overthrown, and that it would be to America's advantage to recognize that fact. In addition, Nixon felt that a friendlier China could be used as a wedge to get future concessions from the Soviet Union.

In February 1972, Nixon and Kissinger made a historic trip to Communist China. Meetings were held with Chinese leader Mao Zedong and other officials. At these meetings, it was decided that trade talks between the two countries would begin, and that cultural exchanges would start almost immediately. Most importantly, Nixon agreed to support the admission of Communist China to the United Nations (going against what had been traditional U.S. policy for the entire cold war period).

Watergate Affair

As a result of his foreign policy successes, Nixon's ratings in public opinion polls were extremely high as the presidential election of 1972 approached. Nixon's opponent was Democrat George McGovern, who campaigned for a faster pullout from Vietnam. Nixon's victory in 1972 was truly staggering; in the Electoral College he won 521 to 17.

The one-sided nature of the 1972 election makes the desires of Richard Nixon and his campaign associates for the events leading up to the **Watergate Affair** difficult to understand. Nixon's paranoid view of the American political system colored the decisions that he and his aides made in the months leading up to the 1972 campaign. In 1971, Nixon created an "enemies list" and suggested various forms of harassment that could be used on everyone on the list (wiretaps, investigating income tax records, etc.). On this list were politicians (Senator Edward Kennedy), newsmen (Daniel Schorr of CBS News), and even sports personalities (New York Jets quarterback Joe Namath).

After the Pentagon Papers were released in the spring of 1971 by Daniel Ellsberg, a former employee of the State Department, a special unit to "plug" leaks was formed by the White House. This unit was known as the **Plumbers**, and included Howard Hunt, a former member of the CIA, and Gordon Liddy, a former agent of the FBI. One of the first actions of the Plumbers was to break into Daniel Ellsberg's psychiatrist's office to try to find incriminating information about Ellsberg. Other aides working for CREEP (the Committee to Reelect the President) performed various "dirty tricks" on political opponents. In the 1972 Democratic primaries, CREEP operatives on two occasions ordered 200 pizzas delivered to an opposing campaign office unannounced, "canceled" political rallies for opponents without the opponents knowing it, and, with no basis whatsoever, charged that Democratic Senator Edmund Muskie had made negative remarks about French Canadians living in New Hampshire.

On the night of June 16, 1972, James McCord, an assistant in the office of security of CREEP, led four other men into Democratic National Committee headquarters at the Watergate Hotel in Washington, DC. The goal of this group was to photocopy important files and to install electronic surveillance devices in the Democratic offices. The five were caught and arrested; money they had on their person could be traced back to CREEP. This was the beginning of the chain of events that came to be called Watergate or the Watergate scandal.

Five days later, Nixon became part of the illegal cover-up of the Watergate break-in. On that day, he publicly announced that the White House had absolutely nothing to do with the break-in. More importantly, on the same day Nixon contacted friendly CIA officials and tried to convince them to call the FBI and tell the FBI to cease its investigation of Watergate. This was the first illegal action taken by Nixon in the Watergate Affair.

In the months before the 1972 presidential election, "hush money" was paid to the Watergate burglars, and several officials of CREEP committed perjury by denying under oath that Nixon had any knowledge of the break-in.

The Watergate story most assuredly would have died if not for the efforts of reporters Carl Bernstein and Bob Woodward of the *Washington Post*. Despite threats from the White House and other political operatives, the two reporters continued to follow the story. They were aided by a secret source named "Deep Throat," who provided them with valuable background information about the case. It was revealed in 2005 that "Deep Throat" was Mark Felt, former associate director of the FBI.

James McCord and the other Watergate burglars were found guilty in their January 1973 trial; no mention of White House involvement was made by any of the defendants. It later became known that Nixon personally approved the payment of hush money to one of the defendants during the trial. In February, the Senate Select Committee on Presidential Campaign Activities began to investigate the Watergate Affair. During these hearings, White House attorney John Dean testified that Nixon was involved in the cover-up and another aide revealed the existence of a taping system in the Oval Office that recorded all conversations held by the president. H. R. Haldeman, John Ehrlichman, and Attorney General Richard Kleindienst all resigned in an attempt to save the presidency of Richard Nixon. Nixon's public approval ratings began to fall.

In an effort to quell the firestorm building around him, Nixon appointed a **special prosecutor** to investigate the Watergate Affair. Almost immediately after being appointed, Archibald Cox demanded that the White House hand over the tapes of all taped conversations.

After losing a court argument that the tapes should be exclusive property of the president, Nixon ordered the new Attorney General, Elliot Richardson, to fire Cox. Richardson refused, as did his assistant, William Ruckelshaus, and both resigned. Solicitor General Robert Bork (who would later be an unsuccessful Supreme Court nominee) finally fired Cox. All of these events took place on October 20, 1973, and are referred to as the "**Saturday Night Massacre**."

After these events, the president's approval rating dipped dramatically. The Judiciary Committee of the House of Representatives began to discuss the formal procedures for impeaching a president. Nixon turned over heavily edited transcripts of most of the tapes to Leon Jaworski, Cox's replacement; many of the vulgar comments made by Nixon on the tapes shocked both opponents and supporters. Also, during this period, it was revealed that Spiro Agnew, Nixon's vice president, had taken bribes as an elected official in Maryland before he was vice president. Agnew resigned in October 1973, and it was two months before his appointed successor, Congressman Gerald Ford of Michigan, was approved as the new vice president.

During the following months, the calls for Nixon's resignation increased. In April 1974, Nixon released more, but not all, of the tapes requested by the special prosecutor. In July, the House Judiciary Committee formally approved three articles of impeachment, stating that the president had ignored their subpoenas, had misused presidential power, and had obstructed justice. Debate was to begin in the full House on impeachment; Nixon's supporters admitted that Nixon would have been impeached.

Before House hearings could begin, the White House finally complied with a Supreme Court order to release all remaining tapes. One had an 18½-minute gap on it; another was the "smoking gun" that Nixon's opponents had been looking for. Nixon had always denied that he had known about the cover-up, yet a tape made one week after the break-in demonstrated that Nixon was actually participating in the cover-up at that point.

With no support left, Nixon finally resigned on August 9, 1974. Gerald Ford took over as president and announced that "our long national nightmare is over." In retrospect, the Watergate Affair was one of the low points of American political history in the twentieth century, rivaled only by the scandals of the presidency of Warren G. Harding.

Presidency of Gerald Ford

As described previously, Gerald Ford came to the presidency under the worst of circumstances. To his advantage, he was incredibly well liked in Washington and totally free of any hint of scandal. However, during his time in office, Ford seemed to lack a grand "plan" for what he wanted to accomplish. Several historians note that Ford's presidency was doomed from September 8, 1974, when he pardoned Richard Nixon for any crimes that he might have committed. This soured many Americans on Ford; his later explanation was that up until that point virtually his entire time in office was spent dealing with Watergate-related affairs, and that the only way to move past that was to pardon the former president. The public expressed their opinion in the fall congressional elections, when many Democrats were swept into office.

Ford became the second American president to visit China, and the first to visit Japan. It should be remembered it was during the Ford administration that South Vietnam fell to the North Vietnamese and the Vietcong. The last American troops had left in 1973; by 1975, the North Vietnamese army began to occupy several major South Vietnamese cities. Ford toyed with the idea of sending in troops to aid the South Vietnamese, but ended up asking Congress for a major aid package for South Vietnam. By this point, the vast majority of Americans wanted nothing to do with the situation in Southeast Asia, and Congress defeated Ford's request. In late April, the North Vietnamese were closing in on Saigon; some of the most gripping photographs of the era were photos of American helicopters evacuating Americans and Vietnamese who had worked for them from the roof of the American embassy in Saigon one day before the city was captured by the North Vietnamese.

The major problem that Ford's presidency faced was the economy. During the Ford administration, the economy suffered from both unemployment and inflation. This economic situation was termed **stagflation**. Critics of Ford claimed that his tactics were no different from those of Herbert Hoover, as he tried to restore confidence in the economy by asking people to wear "WIN" buttons ("Whip Inflation Now") and to voluntarily spend less to lessen the effects of inflation. Ford pushed for tax cuts and for less government spending; despite these various approaches, by 1975, unemployment in America stood near 10 percent and inflation remained a problem. On several occasions, Ford fell or tripped in public settings, which did not improve the image of the presidency.

In the race for the Republican presidential nomination, in 1976, President Ford was able to fend off the campaign of former governor of California and actor Ronald Reagan. In the election, Ford faced the former governor of Georgia, Jimmy Carter. During the campaign, Carter continually stressed that he would be an outsider in Washington, and not tied to any of the messes that had gone on in Washington since 1968; to many in a post-Watergate America, this message sold perfectly. In addition, Ford did not help himself in the campaign by making several misstatements, such as claiming in one debate that Eastern Europe was not controlled by the Soviet Union. Carter won the presidency by a fairly narrow margin by keeping the New Deal Democratic coalition together. Some Southerners who had voted for Nixon in 1968 and 1972 returned to vote Democrat in 1976 because of Carter's Southern roots.

Presidency of Jimmy Carter

Jimmy Carter discovered that coming into the presidency as an outsider had some advantages but also some definite drawbacks. One of the weaknesses of the Carter presidency was his inability to find "insiders" in Congress with whom he could successfully work to get legislation passed. Carter hired many women and minorities for his White House staff and did away with some of the pomp and circumstance traditionally associated with the presidency (he sometimes wore sweaters when giving addresses to the nation). To Carter's critics, these were signs that he was not really up to the responsibilities of the presidency.

Domestic problems continued to exist in the Carter presidency. Unemployment and inflation remained as major problems. As Ford had done, Carter asked the American people to voluntarily refrain from spending and excessive energy use to bring down inflation. He then tried to cut government spending to cool the economy, and angered many liberal Democrats by cutting social programs. Another approach tried by the administration was to have the Federal Reserve Board tighten the money supply, hoping this would stop inflation; the resulting high interest rates served to depress the economy. Unfortunately, none of these policies worked, and confidence in Carter's abilities to solve economic problems began to wane; by the end of his term, unemployment still stood near 8 percent, with inflation over 12 percent.

Other domestic measures undertaken by Carter included the granting of amnesty to those who had left America to avoid the draft during the Vietnam era and measures for the federal cleanup of chemical waste dumps. Pressures from **OPEC** drove the price of gasoline higher during the Carter presidency; in 1978, the National Energy Act was passed, which taxed cars that were not energy efficient and deregulated the prices of domestic oil and gasoline. During the Carter administration, a cabinet-level Department of Energy was created.

On foreign policy, Carter's early speeches stated that the goal of America should be the spreading of basic human rights around the world. Critics maintained that Carter's idealism blinded him to the real interests of America at the time. Conservatives were very critical of his treaty that gave the Panama Canal back to Panama (this would not actually take place until 1999). Critics also attacked his decision to officially recognize the People's Republic of China as the government of China (thus reducing America's support of Taiwan) and his continued negotiations with the Soviets to limit nuclear weapons (critics stated that America's military might should not be limited). Conservatives were cheered by his response to the 1979 Soviet invasion of Afghanistan. Carter cut aid programs to the Soviet Union and refused to allow the athletes to compete in the 1980 Moscow Summer Olympics.

One of the high points of the Carter presidency was the September 1978 negotiations between Menachem Begin of Israel and Anwar Sadat of Egypt, which produced the **Camp David Accords**. These negotiations were mediated by Carter; as a result of these talks, Israel promised to return occupied land to Egypt in return for official recognition of Israel's right to exist by Egypt. Carter was unable to negotiate a solution to the problem of Palestinian refugees (a problem that still exists today).

The nadir of the Carter presidency was the **Iranian Hostage Crisis**. Iran had been governed by the repressive Shah of Iran, who was propped up by arms and economic aid from the United States. In 1978, a revolution of Fundamentalist Muslims forced the Shah to leave the country; the Ayatollah Khomeini, a Fundamentalist Muslim leader, became leader of Iran. In October 1979, the exiled Shah was suffering from cancer, and Carter allowed him into the United States for treatment. This outraged the Iranians; on November 4, protesters stoned and then seized the American embassy in Tehran, Iran, taking 66 Americans who worked there hostage.

The Americans were kept hostage for 444 days. Some were kept in solitary confinement, while others were not; most were moved around on a regular basis to discourage rescue attempts. Carter tried various attempts to win the release of the hostages, including freezing Iranian assets in America, stopping trade with Iran, and negotiating through third parties. A 1980 attempt to rescue the hostages ended in a military embarrassment when helicopters sent to rescue them either crashed or could not fly because of heavy sand. Carter had been criticized for being ineffectual on domestic programs; as the hostage crisis wore on, he increasingly was seen as ineffectual in the diplomatic sphere as well. The hostages were finally released in January 1981, but only after Carter had left office and Ronald Reagan was sworn in as president.

Election of 1980

Carter was able to win the 1980 Democratic nomination for president despite a challenge from Edward Kennedy. Ronald Reagan, portraying himself as the spokesperson for the conservatives of America, won the Republican nomination. Carter was forced to campaign on his record, which was a very difficult thing to do. Reagan promised while campaigning to build up the military; at the same time, he promised to cut taxes. He promised strong leadership from Washington and also pledged to take power from Washington and give it to the states. Reagan also pledged support for a renewed emphasis on family and patriotism. Reagan won the election by a decisive margin.

The 1980 election was the first totally successful assault on the New Deal Democratic coalition. Social issues of the era, such as the increasing rights of women, sexual freedom, and **affirmative action**, drew many blue-collar workers away from the Democrats and into the Republican camp. (Conservatives successfully convinced many Americans that the Democrats were the cause of the declining image of America abroad and the reason for the decline in traditional morality at home.) Members of the **religious right** supported the Republicans in large numbers (and would continue this pattern in elections that followed). Many Southerners saw the Republicans and Reagan representing their interests more than Jimmy Carter; others perceived Carter to be "soft on communism." As a result of these factors, the **New Right** had become a major force in American politics; besides electing Reagan, they had also pushed the Republicans to the majority in the Senate in 1980.

Presidency of Ronald Reagan

Admirers and detractors of Ronald Reagan both agree that he was a true master of politics (Bill Clinton studied the techniques Reagan used to achieve political success). Reagan used his previously honed skills as an actor to set the right tone and present the right messages at meetings and speeches throughout his presidency. Reagan also used his staff well; on many occasions, he would set the general policy and allow staff people to set up the details.

Upon becoming president, Reagan instituted traditional conservative economic practices. In 1981, federal taxes were cut by 5 percent, and then cut by another 10 percent in 1982 and 1983. Reagan and his economic staff believed in "**supply-side economics**," which stated that if more money was put in the hands of wealthy Americans by cutting taxes, they would invest it in the economy, thus creating more jobs and additional growth (and eventually additional tax revenue). Capital gains taxes were reduced, also with the intent of encouraging investment.

Political battle lines were drawn early in the Reagan administration. As a result of the tax cuts, the government was taking in less money, causing many domestic programs to be cut, including aid to education, to urban housing programs, and to the arts and the humanities. Liberals were outraged over the fact that, at the same time that social programs were being cut, Reagan increased the defense budget by nearly $13 billion. Reagan also pushed for funding for a Strategic Defense Initiative (SDI; nicknamed "Star Wars") program. As envisioned, this system could shoot down enemy missiles from outer space. Reagan also pushed to give more power back to the states at the expense of the federal government. Reagan called this plan the **New Federalism**. Under this program, how federal money was spent by states was determined by the states and not by the federal government. During the Reagan administration, the policy of deregulation was intensified; industries such as the energy industry and the transportation industry were freed from "cumbersome" regulations imposed by previous administrations (supporters of these regulations would maintain that they were in the interest of the consumers). In addition, funding for the Environmental Protection Agency was greatly reduced during the Reagan presidency. Many perceived the Reagan administration to be antiunion as well; in 1981, the government actively destroyed the union for the air traffic controllers, and striking controllers were fired.

In response to the perceived foreign policy weakness of America in the Carter years, Reagan worked hard to build up America's image in the world. On a small scale, the American army successfully invaded the island of Grenada in 1983. On a much larger scale, Reagan ended the friendlier relations between the United States and the Soviet Union of the détente era. He put new cruise missiles in Europe and referred to the Soviet Union as the "evil empire." Reagan's harsh rhetoric won him much support in the United States. Reagan's popularity also had gone up after the attempt on his life by John Hinckley in 1981.

Reagan ran for reelection in 1984 against Walter Mondale (Mondale's running mate was Geraldine Ferraro, a congresswoman from New York). Mondale criticized Reagan on economic issues; the supply-side approach had not produced as much growth, and as much income from taxes, as its proponents had said it would. However, Reagan's tough cold war rhetoric and support of conservative social issues allowed him to continue to break up the Democratic New Deal coalition; Reagan got nearly 60 percent of the popular vote in 1984. Critics who said that the major beneficiaries of Reagan's economic policies who were the very rich were still very much in the minority.

Reagan continued to practice conservative policies during his second term. The **Tax Reform Act of 1986** dramatically reduced federal tax rates; the tax the wealthiest Americans had to pay on their income, for example, was reduced from 50 percent to 28 percent. In 1986 and 1987, both unemployment and inflation declined. Under Reagan, the Supreme Court also became more conservative, as William Rehnquist became chief justice and Antonin Scalia was one of the new justices on the court. Reagan also nominated Sandra Day O'Connor to be the first woman to serve on the Supreme Court. Most women's groups, however, strongly disapproved of the Reagan administration, citing actions such as efforts during Reagan's second term to cut food stamps and the federal school lunch program.

During Reagan's second term, serious economic problems also developed. On October 19, 1987, known as "Black Monday," the average price for a share of stock fell nearly 20 percent. During Reagan's second term, federal government deficits grew drastically; this occurred because less income was coming into the government because of the previously enacted tax cuts and because of a large increase in defense spending. In addition, for the first time since World War I the United States began to import more than it exported.

Nevertheless, Reagan's foreign policy remained incredibly popular. In April 1986, the United States bombed Libyan air bases after Muammar Gaddafi, the leader of Libya, ordered Libyan gunboats to challenge American ships sailing close to Libya. Reagan and the new leader of the Soviet Union, Mikhail Gorbachev, established a close personal relationship and held meaningful negotiations on the reduction of nuclear weapons. Reagan also supported anti-Communist forces fighting in Nicaragua and El Salvador.

Many critics of Reagan had claimed since 1980 that he was unaware of what was being done by others working for him. This view seemed to be validated by the **Iran-Contra Affair** of 1986 and 1987. Apparently without the knowledge of the president, National Security Advisor John Poindexter, Lieutenant Colonel Oliver North, and several others devised an "arms for hostages plan." By this plan, the United States sold arms to Iran, hoping that it could use Irani influence to help free American hostages held in Lebanon. The problem with this plan was that at this point America had an official trade embargo with Iran and had persuaded several European countries to support this. The money for this sale was to be used to fund anti-Communist fighters in Nicaragua, called the "Contras." Again, a problem existed: Congress had passed legislation carefully regulating how much funding could go to the Contras. Congressional and legal hearings were held on the Iran-Contra Affair; as a result, nearly a dozen officials of the Reagan administration were forced to resign.

Many Americans felt (and continue to feel) that the political hero of the modern era was Ronald Reagan. Many supporters felt he restored pride to America, stood up to our enemies abroad, restored the economy of America, and reasserted "traditional" American values. Critics of Reagan maintain that the economic policies of the Reagan administration only benefited the wealthiest Americans; they point out that the gap between the richest Americans and the poorest Americans dramatically increased under Reagan, with the real income of middle- and lower-class Americans actually receding. Critics stated that the Iran-Contra Affair proved the fact that Reagan was dangerously out of touch on many policy decisions. Nevertheless, Reagan's vice president, George H. Bush, would certainly have a tough act to follow as he ran for president on his own in 1988.

Chapter Review

Rapid Review

To achieve the perfect 5, you should be able to explain the following:

- One of the low points of American political life in the twentieth century was the Watergate Affair.
- Richard Nixon's greatest accomplishments were in the field of foreign policy, as he crafted new relationships with both China and the Soviet Union.
- The Watergate Affair developed from the paranoid view of American politics held by Richard Nixon and several of his top aides.
- Gerald Ford's presidency was tainted from the beginning by his pardoning of Richard Nixon.
- Ford faced huge economic problems as president; during his presidency, America suffered from both inflation and unemployment.
- Jimmy Carter and many politicians of the post-Watergate era emerged victorious by campaigning as outsiders.

- President Carter's outsider status hurt him, especially in terms of getting legislation passed in Congress.
- Carter demonstrated his diplomatic skills by helping Egypt and Israel bridge their differences through the Camp David Accords; he was unable to negotiate a release of the American hostages in Iran, and this may have cost him the presidency.
- Ronald Reagan was elected as a conservative and restored the pride of many Americans in America.
- Reagan practiced "supply-side" economics, which benefited the American economy but which also helped create large deficits.
- Under Reagan, the gap between the wealthiest Americans and the poorest Americans increased.
- Reagan reinstituted cold war rhetoric, but later created cordial relations with leaders of the Soviet Union.
- Reagan's lack of direct control over the implementation of presidential policies was demonstrated by the Iran-Contra Affair.

Time Line

1968: Richard Nixon elected president

1971: Nixon imposes wage and price controls
Pentagon Papers released

1972: Nixon visits China and Soviet Union
Nixon reelected
SALT I signed
Watergate break-in

1973: Watergate hearings in Congress
Spiro Agnew resigns as vice president
"Saturday Night Massacre"

1974: Inflation peaks at 11 percent
Nixon resigns; Gerald Ford becomes president
Ford pardons Richard Nixon
WIN economic program introduced

1975: South Vietnam falls to North Vietnam, ending Vietnam War

1976: Jimmy Carter elected president

1977: Carter signs Panama Canal treaty
Carter issues Vietnam-era draft amnesty

1978: Camp David Accords

1979: Americans taken hostage in Iran

1980: Ronald Reagan elected president

1981–1982: Major recession
Assassination attempt on Reagan

1981–1983: Major tax cuts instituted

1983: Reagan proposes "Star Wars"
Americans victorious in Grenada

1984: Reagan reelected

1985: Gorbachev assumes power in Soviet Union

1986: Additional tax reform measures passed
Iran-Contra Affair

1987: "Black Monday"

1988: George Bush elected president

› Review Questions

Multiple-Choice Questions

1. What tactic was *not* used by supporters of Richard Nixon in the 1972 presidential campaign?
   A. Breaking into private offices
   B. Reviewing income tax records of suspected "enemies"
   C. Falsifying war records of opposing presidential candidates
   D. Attempting to halt official investigations of actions of campaign officials

2. According to supply-side economics, when wealthy Americans received tax cuts, they would proceed to do all but which of the following?
   A. Invest heavily in the economy.
   B. Open new factories.
   C. Purchase stocks.
   D. Increase their savings dramatically.

3. Which of the following did *not* help create the deficits of the second term of the Reagan years?
   A. Reduction of federal tax rates
   B. Desperately needed increases in funding for education
   C. Increases in military spending
   D. Changes in the tax code that favored wealthier Americans

4. Critics of Ronald Reagan would most emphasize
   A. the effects of the 1981–1983 tax cuts.
   B. the U.S. response to threats from Libya.
   C. the effects of Reagan's economic policies on the middle and lower classes.
   D. his public image and political skills.

5. Gerald Ford's WIN program demonstrated to many Americans that Ford
   A. had no real grasp of economic issues.
   B. had the uncanny knack of knowing how to inspire the American public.
   C. was still under the shadow of Richard Nixon.
   D. understood sophisticated foreign policy issues.

Short-Answer Question

6. Answer Parts A, B, and C.
   A. Briefly explain ONE example illustrating the conservative direction of the nation in the 1970s and 1980s.
   B. Briefly explain a SECOND example illustrating the conservative direction of the nation in the 1970s and 1980s.
   C. Briefly explain ONE example of an approach taken to the Cold War by a president of the 1970s and 1980s.

› Answers and Explanations

1. **C.** Of all of the "dirty tricks" practiced by the Republicans in 1972, this was not one of them.

2. **D.** The key to supply-side economics is that when tax cuts give individuals large amounts of money, they will reinvest that money in the economy.

3. **B.** Even though education advocates were saying that funding had to be drastically increased in many urban school districts, funding for education declined during the Reagan era.

4. **C.** The 1981 to 1983 tax cuts did help bring down inflation; at this same time, employment possibilities increased. Compared to the wealthiest Americans, the middle and lower classes experienced little benefit from Reagan's economic policies, especially from the tax cuts of the second term.

5. **A**. Many Americans saw the WIN program as a public relations gimmick, demonstrating that Ford did not truly understand the economic problems of America; many equated WIN to some of the public pronouncements of Herbert Hoover in 1930 and 1931.

6. **Parts A and B**: During the 1970s and 1980s there was only one Democratic president, who served for one term. In 1968, the victorious Republican presidential candidate Richard Nixon campaigned on a platform calling for "law and order," appealing to voters disturbed by the rioting and social upheaval caused by racial unrest and the Vietnam War. In office, Nixon advocated a "New Federalism," hoping to transfer some governmental functions back to state and local governments. In 1972, he signed into law a revenue sharing bill that sent some federal income tax money to local governments. Nixon also worked to build his political base by taking a conservative stance on cultural and social issues like abortion and busing. He claimed to speak for the "silent majority" of Americans. Nixon's successor, Gerald Ford, attempted to combat the economic stagflation of the 1970s through the conservative remedies of tax cuts and lower government spending. President Jimmy Carter, though a liberal Democrat, also wrestled unsuccessfully with stagflation. He encouraged the deregulation of the transportation industry. During the Carter years, voter dissatisfaction with high taxes became a political issue. In 1978, businessman Howard Jarvis successfully lobbied for Proposition 13, which slashed property taxes in California. Also during the late 1970s, the religious right emerged as a political force, with ministers like Jerry Falwell, head of the Moral Majority, becoming prominent figures. President Ronald Reagan came into office in 1981 advocating "supply-side economics," which argued that tax cuts would lead to greater consumer spending, a revitalized economy, and ultimately, because of renewed prosperity, greater tax revenues. Reagan secured significant tax cuts during his presidency. He also called for a New Federalism, sending more powers and money back to the states. Under Reagan, deregulation intensified, spreading from transportation to energy and other industries.

Part C: Richard Nixon and his National Security Advisor Henry Kissinger believed in realpolitik, or power politics in foreign policy. They also recognized that the world was becoming multipolar with more nations than just the United States and the Soviet Union exercising power. Nixon and Kissinger orchestrated a diplomatic opening to Communist China, while simultaneously pursuing a policy of détente, or improved relations, with the Soviet Union; they hoped to be able to play the two communist powers against each other. Presidents Gerald Ford and Jimmy Carter continued détente with both the Soviet Union and China for most of the 1970s. The Soviet invasion of Afghanistan in 1979 led Carter to cool relations with Moscow and to begin a rebuilding of the American military. President Reagan was a committed anticommunist who believed that the United States could win the Cold War. He responded vigorously to the Soviet placement of short-range nuclear missiles in Eastern Europe, placing equivalent American missiles in Western Europe. He denounced the Soviet Union as an "evil empire." He increased the defense budget by $13 billion, putting enormous strain on the ailing Soviet Union. Late in Reagan's second term, as the Soviets attempted to improve relations with the United States, Cold War tensions began to recede. In 1987, Reagan signed the INF Treaty with the Soviet Union, eliminating intermediate range nuclear missiles.

CHAPTER 29

Prosperity and a New World Order (1988–2000)

IN THIS CHAPTER

Summary: For much of the post–World War II era, the popularity of a president was largely determined by his success in foreign policy and in handling foreign crises. With the ending of the cold war at the end of the 1980s, skills in handling domestic issues became equally important for presidents and their staffs. Presidents Bush (I) and Clinton are perfect examples of this: Bush's popularity was sky-high after his Desert Storm victory, yet he ended up being defeated by Bill Clinton largely because of economic problems that developed in the closing years of his term. Despite a mountain of personal and ethical issues that surrounded him, President Clinton was able to keep high approval ratings because of a continuing successful economy.

Keywords

New Right: conservative movement that began in the 1960s and supported Republican candidates into the twenty-first century; many voters from the South and from the middle class were attracted by the New Right's emphasis on patriotism and strict moral values.

Operation Desert Storm (1991): military action by the United States and a coalition of Allied nations against Iraq and its leader Saddam Hussein after Iraq had invaded Kuwait; this operation was a resounding success, although the decision was made not to force Saddam Hussein from power.

Whitewater: series of real estate dealings in Arkansas involving Bill Clinton long before he became president; Republicans accused Clinton of associated financial improprieties, but no charges were ever proven. The Whitewater affair was one of several accusations that eventually led to Clinton being impeached by the House of Representatives but acquitted by the Senate.

Contract with America: list of conservative measures proposed by Republicans after winning control of the House of Representatives in 1994; it included term limits and promises to balance the federal budget and to reduce the size of the federal government. Republican supporters of the Contract were led by Speaker of the House Newt Gingrich.

1988 Election

Republican advertisements in 1988 touted George H. Bush as "the most qualified man of our times" to be president. Bush had served as a congressman, as the American ambassador to the United Nations, and as the director of the CIA. The **New Right** had never been entirely comfortable with Bush during his eight years as Reagan's vice president; to appease them, he nominated Senator Dan Quayle, a staunch Conservative, as his vice presidential nominee.

The Democrats nominated Massachusetts Governor Michael Dukakis as their candidate. Dukakis campaigned on his experience as a governor, touting the "Massachusetts miracle" that had pulled the state out of its economic doldrums. Televisions during the 1988 campaign were glutted with negative advertisements, the most notable being one that linked Dukakis to Willie Horton, a black man who had raped a woman while taking advantage of a furlough program established in Massachusetts by the governor. Bush won the election rather handily, despite being behind Dukakis in early polls.

Presidency of George H. Bush

Conservative suspicions of Bush increased during the first months of this presidency. Many considered his stated desires for a "kinder, gentler America" as a heretical attempt to distance himself from the social policies of former president Reagan. Bush's major domestic problem was an ever-growing federal deficit. To broker a deal with Congress to lower the deficit, Bush broke his campaign promise of "no new taxes" and, in 1990, signed a bill authorizing tax increases. Many Conservatives never forgave him for this decision. During Bush's term, few substantive domestic programs were instituted; some commentators complained of the **gridlock** created by a Republican president and a Democratic congress.

During the presidency of George Bush, the 45-year-old cold war ended. In late 1988, Soviet leader Mikhail Gorbachev admitted to Communist party leaders that the vast portion of the Soviet economy that was devoted to military spending and to "protecting" the satellite countries was preventing economic growth of any type from taking place. In 1989, the Soviets began to withdraw support from the satellite states; many in Moscow naively believed that Communist leaders in the satellite states could remain in power without being propped up by the Soviet Union. In Poland, Solidarity, the non-Communist labor party, removed the Communist government from power; throughout late 1989, Communists were removed from power in all of the satellite nations. Many of the republics of the Soviet Union also desired independence. In December 1991, Russian President Boris Yeltsin announced the abolition of the Soviet Union and the creation of 11 independent republics.

A large amount of American aid was pumped into Russia and the other Eastern European states. American academics rushed to Moscow and other major centers in the region, explaining to leaders how capitalism could be introduced in the shortest period of time.

American aid was also sent to help several of the former Soviet republics dismantle the nuclear missiles that had been placed there in the cold war era. The meaning of the cold war is still being debated by academics; whether the United States won the cold war or whether the Soviet Union lost is still a topic of numerous books and historical papers.

The central crisis of the Bush presidency began on August 2, 1990, when the army of Iraq invaded Kuwait. Fears that Saddam Hussein's next target would be Saudi Arabia, the largest exporter of oil to the United States, pushed the United States into action. Almost immediately, in **Operation Desert Shield**, large numbers of American troops were sent to protect Saudi Arabia.

Encouraged by the United States, member states of the United Nations condemned the Iraqi aggression and authorized the creation of a multinational military force to remove Saddam Hussein from Kuwait. The high point of the Bush presidency was the personal diplomacy undertaken by the presidency to get almost all of the states of the Middle East to support military action against Iraq. On February 24, 1991, a ground offensive, termed **Operation Desert Storm**, was mounted against Iraq. Iraqi casualties were over 40,000, while the Americans (who made up most of the troops of the UN international force) lost 150 soldiers in battle. Iraqi soldiers surrendered by the hundreds as they retreated from Kuwait. In a decision that would later be questioned, American forces did not move into Iraq and force Saddam Hussein from power. It should be noted that this was *not* part of the United Nations mandate, and that such an action would have definitely created division in the Middle Eastern coalition so carefully crafted by Bush.

Bush's popularity was at an all-time high after Desert Storm. However, problems soon arose that his administration seemed incapable of solving. A recession and continued economic difficulties hit the United States in early 1992. In addition, the end of the cold war brought new difficulties in several states formerly controlled by the Soviet Union. In former Yugoslavia, Serbs began to practice "ethnic cleansing" against Bosnian Muslims. Critics of Bush claimed that he lacked any "vision" of what the role of the United States should be in a post–cold war world.

1992 Election

George Bush and Bill Clinton ran against each other in 1992. The buzzword of politics in 1992 was "change," and both candidates claimed they were prepared to offer it. At the 1992 Republican National Convention, speakers of the New Right spoke about the need for "family values" and that a "religious war" against the Democrats was needed.

The former governor of Arkansas, Bill Clinton, had the political sense to realize that Americans in the early 1990s were interested in economic rather than social issues, and pledged that as president he would overhaul the health care system and work for the preservation of the Social Security system. Clinton campaigned as a "**New Democrat**," stating that he was not another typical big-spending advocate of big government. During his presidency, Clinton on occasion took Republican concepts and claimed them as his own; right-wing critics such as Rush Limbaugh maintained that he would say or do anything if it meant his position would be improved in the polls.

A third candidate in the 1992 race was Texas multibillionaire Ross Perot. Perot spent a lot of money on campaign ads, complaining in these ads about how the politicians in Washington were beholden only to special interests, and that if elected he would bring "common sense" back to the White House. However, the charts depicting the American economy that he used on his advertisements were understood by few people.

Clinton won the 1992 election fairly easily. Many from the New Deal Democratic coalition that had deserted the Democrats for Reagan came back to vote for Clinton in 1992. Bush appeared oddly out of touch at several points during the campaign; at one point, he was caught looking at his watch in the middle of a presidential debate. Nearly 19 million Americans supported Perot; analysts maintain that the support for Perot hurt Bush more than it did Clinton.

Presidency of Bill Clinton

From the beginning, Clinton strove to create an administration different from the one that had preceded it. He appointed minorities and women to his cabinet. During his first term, there were several legislative successes, such as the Brady bill, which created a waiting period for handgun purchases, and the anticrime bill (officially known as the Violent Crime Control and Law Enforcement Act of 1994), which provided federal funds to hire more police officials. However, several issues that Clinton attempted to tackle during his first term drew the ire of many. His attempt to legislate the proper status of gays in the military caused many in all branches of the military service to distrust him. His attempt to legislate a national health insurance plan was defeated by a combination of effective lobbying by the American Medical Association and intense advertising paid for by the healthcare industry. In addition, the fact that Hillary Rodham Clinton was actively involved in the formulation of healthcare policy caused debate over the proper role of a First Lady.

Many also began to question the Clintons concerning their financial dealings. Investments in a failed savings and loan company and in a land development called **Whitewater** caused much controversy; in August 1994, Kenneth Starr became the independent counsel in charge of investigating the Whitewater Affair. Many Clinton supporters felt that Starr moved too vigorously and was out to "get" the Clintons.

The 1994 Congressional elections appeared to be a sweeping rejection of the presidency of Bill Clinton. Republicans, led by new Speaker of the House Newt Gingrich, supported the **Contract with America**, and promised to get rid of many social programs long supported by liberals. Republicans soon learned that the political skills of Bill Clinton were formidable, however. In an attempt to lessen the size of the federal government, there were brief shutdowns of the federal government in 1995 and 1996; on each occasion, public opinion polls stated that the American public strongly sided with the president in his argument that all of this was the fault of the Republicans.

Clinton's popularity rose further as the economy improved steadily in 1995 and 1996. The values of stocks rose, economic growth continued at a steady rate, and inflation remained low (many credited Alan Greenspan, chairman of the Federal Reserve, for his ability to skillfully maneuver interest rates to keep inflation low and growth high).

Clinton's role as a "New Democrat" was again demonstrated when he supported passage of the Personal Responsibility and Work Opportunity Reconciliation Act of 1996. This legislation more carefully regulated the welfare system, cut the food stamp program, and gave power to the states to organize their own "welfare-to-work" programs. This program, which ended "welfare as we know it," was hailed by Clinton supporters as a sign of his pragmatism; many liberals were appalled that he so easily "sold them out."

In foreign policy, Clinton faced some of the same criticisms as Bush. Many claimed that the United States still did not have a post–cold war foreign policy "focus." Many debated the appropriate role of the U.S. military. A humanitarian mission to Somalia led to the death of 18 American soldiers in 1992. The U.S. military was sent in to restore the government of Jean-Bertrand Aristide in Haiti; Clinton also supported NATO air and military efforts to protect Muslims from the "ethnic cleansing" policies of President Slobodan Milosevic of Serbia. Americans remain as peacekeepers in Bosnia to this day.

President Clinton also favored the continued **globalization** of the economy, which included the lowering of tariffs and the expansion of global markets. Clinton worked with many Republicans to secure the passage of **NAFTA (North American Free Trade Agreement)** in Congress. The goal of NAFTA was to gradually remove all trade barriers between the United States, Canada, and Mexico. As with welfare reform, a segment of the traditional Democratic base was infuriated by one of Clinton's policies. In this case, it was the labor unions who felt betrayed.

In 2000, Clinton unsuccessfully attempted to broker peace between the Palestinians and Israel. He increasingly became aware of the threats of Fundamentalist Muslims against the United States. In 1993, bombings took place at the World Trade Center in New York City; American embassies were bombed in Tanzania and Kenya in 1998; and a United States naval ship docked in Yemen was bombed in 2000. Clinton attempted several bombing missions in response to these terrorist attacks, and in one instance came fairly close to killing Osama bin Laden, leader of the Al Qaeda terrorist network.

Campaigning on the continued strength of the American economy, Clinton became the first Democrat since Franklin Roosevelt to win back-to-back terms when he defeated long-time Senator Robert Dole of Kansas in the 1996 presidential election. Early in Clinton's second term, the era of gridlock appeared to be over, as both parties joined in passing legislation to reduce the federal budget. Yet, it was the Whitewater Affair that consumed the most political energy in Washington during the last years of Clinton's second term.

As was stated previously, Kenneth Starr and the Whitewater investigation was originally charged with analyzing the financial dealings of the Clintons in Arkansas. However, the investigation soon delved into other areas of the president's life. It was revealed that he had an affair with a White House intern, Monica Lewinsky. Clinton boldly proclaimed on television that he had never had "sexual relations with that woman." In a lawsuit brought against the president by Paula Jones (for alleged sexual harassment when Clinton was governor of Arkansas), Clinton denied, under oath, having an affair with Lewinsky. Physical evidence obtained from Lewinsky seemed to prove otherwise. Talk show hosts and other opponents stated that the case had long gone beyond merely the matter of the president having an affair; he had actually lied under oath about it.

Clinton's approval ratings remained high throughout his second term; his approval was especially strong in black districts across the country. In the 1996 congressional elections, the Republicans lost five seats in the House of Representatives. Congressional calls for impeachment began; others wondered whether the actions of the president were actually the "high crimes and misdemeanors" that the Constitution stated were grounds for impeachment. On December 19, 1998, the House of Representatives passed two articles of impeachment (obstruction of justice and perjury), thus preparing the way for a trial in the Senate. Two-thirds of the Senators had to vote for an article of impeachment in order to remove him from office. Senate voting took place on February 12, 1999; neither article of impeachment received the necessary two-thirds vote. Many Clinton supporters that spoke during the congressional proceedings noted that despite millions of dollars being spent and years of investigation, the special prosecutor was unable to uncover any illegal actions by the president or his wife. Popular support for the president remained high, and economic prosperity and expansion continued.

2000 Presidential Election

Excitement for the candidates in the 2000 presidential election was very low. The Democrats nominated Al Gore, Clinton's vice president, who often appeared wooden when giving speeches and stirred little emotion, even among longtime Democrats. George W. Bush, son of the former president, was the Republican nominee; in several early interviews, he appeared to lack the knowledge of critical issues that might be expected of a presidential candidate. Ralph Nader ran as a candidate of the Green Party.

When the final results were tabulated, Al Gore actually received some 500,000 votes more than Bush (Nader received less than 3 million votes). However, Gore surprisingly lost his home state of Tennessee, and the winner in the Electoral College would be the winner of the popular vote in Florida. Several recounts were held there, with Bush holding on to a tiny lead. Blacks in several parts of Florida (who voted heavily for Gore) complained that in parts of the state they had been prevented from voting. Further recounts were planned in contested counties. By a 5-to-4 vote on December 9, 2000, the Supreme Court of the United States temporarily halted all recounts. On December 12, the court ruled, again by a 5-to-4 margin, that recounts in contested counties only was a violation of the constitution, thus securing the election of George W. Bush. In the first months of his presidency, Bush concentrated much of his effort on domestic affairs; the events of September 11, 2001, would dramatically change the course of his presidency.

Chapter Review

Rapid Review

To achieve the perfect 5, you should be able to explain the following:

- The ability to manage domestic issues were critical for a president's political success in the post–cold war era.
- George Bush alienated many conservatives, especially when he broke his "no new taxes" pledge.
- The end of the cold war can be attributed to American policy decisions and to weaknesses in the infrastructure of the Soviet Union.
- George Bush skillfully managed the Desert Storm operation against Iraq.
- Bill Clinton presented himself as a "New Democrat" and focused on economic issues in the 1992 presidential campaign; these were important factors in his victory.
- Clinton's failure on national health insurance helped pave the way for large Republican gains in the 1994 congressional elections.
- Clinton and Newt Gingrich were formidable opponents in the budget battles of the mid-1990s.
- The Whitewater scandal and investigations of the personal life of Bill Clinton were the defining political events of the second term of Clinton's presidency.
- George W. Bush's election demonstrated the difficulties of arriving at a "final tally" in any election and was finally secured by the intervention of the U.S. Supreme Court.

Time Line

1988: George Bush elected president
Solidarity replaces Communist government in Poland
1989: Berlin Wall opened, Communist governments fall in Eastern Europe
1991: Persian Gulf War
Breakup of the Soviet Union
Beginnings of economic recession
1992: Election of Bill Clinton
American troops killed in Somalia
1993: NAFTA ratified by Senate
Terrorist bombings at World Trade Center
1994: Republicans sweep congressional elections
U.S. military enters Haiti
Kenneth Starr becomes Whitewater independent counsel
1996: Clinton reelected
1998: Federal budget surplus announced
Articles of impeachment passed in House of Representatives
1999: Clinton acquitted in impeachment trial in U.S. Senate
2000: George W. Bush elected president

› Review Questions

Multiple-Choice Questions

1. A defining characteristic of the Clinton presidency was his
   A. strict adherence to traditional Democratic values.
   B. pragmatic policy making.
   C. close alliance with liberals in the Democratic party.
   D. unprecedented alliance with labor unions.

2. George H. Bush alienated many conservative Republicans by
   A. appointing the relatively inexperienced Dan Quayle as vice president.
   B. continuing to urge the tearing down of the Berlin Wall.
   C. signing the 1990 agreement with the Democrats to reduce the deficit.
   D. pursuing policies against Iraq.

3. Critics accused Bush of lacking "vision" because
   A. he failed to articulate a successful policy to end the economic deficit.
   B. he failed to remove Saddam Hussein from power.
   C. he failed to sign an arms treaty with Mikhail Gorbachev.
   D. he failed to explain his perception of America's role in the post–cold war world.

4. All of the following were reasons for the end of the cold war *except*
   A. the U.S. military buildup under Ronald Reagan.
   B. the fact that many producers of military weaponry in the United States did not want to continue to produce this weaponry.
   C. the weaknesses of the Soviet economy.
   D. the cold war rhetoric of both Ronald Reagan and George Bush.

5. Bill Clinton was a formidable political opponent for the Republicans for all of the following reasons *except*
   A. his ability to eventually win over former Republicans of the New Right.
   B. his support in the black community.
   C. his ability to take Republican positions and make them appear to be his own.
   D. his ability to withstand political scandal.

Short-Answer Question

6. Answer Parts A, B, and C.
   A. Briefly explain ONE example of an effect of the end of the Cold War on American foreign policy or domestic politics.
   B. Briefly explain a SECOND example of an effect of the end of the Cold War on American foreign policy or domestic politics.
   C. Briefly explain ONE example of the "centrist" political policies pursued by President Bill Clinton during the 1990s.

› Answers and Explanations

1. **B**. In claiming to be a "New Democrat," Clinton sometimes adopted traditional Republican ideas as his own. To many critics, the pragmatism of the Clinton White House masked the fact that President Clinton had few principles that he actually believed in.

2. **C**. This was the agreement where Bush broke his "no new taxes" pledge and broke with traditional Republican policy.

3. **D**. Several historians state that a weakness of both Bush and Clinton was that they were unable to articulate a coherent post–cold war foreign policy.

4. **B**. Most manufacturers had no desire to stop producing weaponry for the cold war. When the cold war finally ended, many of these companies were forced to lay off workers, and some that could not diversify were forced to close.

5. **A**. The New Right was the group that came to despise Bill Clinton the most. Members of the New Right interested in social issues were among Clinton's most passionate detractors during the Whitewater scandal.

6. **Parts A and B**: President George H. W. Bush skillfully handled the diplomacy of ending the Cold War. The Berlin Wall fell in 1989, and Bush helped with the reunification of Germany the following year. At the same time, the Communist regimes in Eastern Europe were replaced by noncommunist governments. Good relations with the Soviet Union enabled Bush to build an international coalition to respond to Iraqi dictator Saddam Hussein's 1990 invasion of Kuwait. In February 1991, Kuwait was liberated in Operation Desert Storm. Once the Soviet Union collapsed in late 1991, Bush began talking about a "peace dividend," arguing that with the end of the Cold War the United States and other Western powers could reduce defense spending. With the world seemingly peaceful after the end of the Cold War and the successful resolution of the Gulf War, Americans began to focus on domestic economic problems. President Bush, an old Cold Warrior, seemed increasingly out of touch. In the 1992 presidential election, Americans turned to Bill Clinton, the first baby boomer president. President Clinton was primarily interested in domestic policy. Clinton favored the growth of economic globalization. In 1993, he secured ratification of the North American Free Trade Agreement (NAFTA), which had been negotiated by President Bush. Clinton also addressed some of the aftershocks in the Balkans that followed the end of the Cold War, launching brief bombing campaigns in Bosnia in 1995 and Kosovo in 1999. In each case, these bombing campaigns led to peace agreements.

Part C: Bill Clinton campaigned for the presidency as a "New Democrat," claiming to be a more centrist and economically conservative Democratic leader. In his first term, Clinton pushed some liberal policies such as health care reform and higher taxes, but he also took some more conservative positions. He supported NAFTA despite the opposition of many Democrats who worried about the treaty's effects on organized labor. He also signed the 1994 Omnibus Crime Bill, which increased the number of federal crimes for which the death penalty could be imposed. After the Republicans won control of Congress in the 1994 elections, Clinton signed a number of laws that reflected political compromises with the new Congressional majority. These included the 1996 Defense of Marriage Act (DOMA), which recognized only marriages between one man and one woman; the 1996 Personal Responsibility and Work Opportunity Act, which put some limits on welfare and imposed some work requirements on recipients; and the 1997 Balanced Budget Act, designed to cut federal spending and balance the federal budget by 2002.

CHAPTER 30

Threat of Terrorism, Increase of Presidential Power, and Economic Crisis (2001–2014)

IN THIS CHAPTER

Summary: The threat of terrorism following the September 11, 2001, attack on the World Trade Center in New York City revived the historic conflict between the need for a strong central authority during wartime and the need to maintain civil liberties. President Bush and Congress enacted the Patriot Act, giving the federal government wide powers to investigate terrorists in the United States. The administration argued that policies such as wiretapping the telephones of suspected terrorists without warrants were necessary for security. Civil libertarians stated that the president's actions were unauthorized and probably illegal.

U.S. forces attacked terrorist strongholds in Afghanistan in late 2001. In 2003, U.S. and Allied forces invaded Iraq and toppled the regime of Saddam Hussein. The Bush administration claimed that Iraq was a military threat and a potential terrorist ally. Critics disputed these claims.

At home, America remained politically divided. When sectarian violence broke out in Iraq, public opinion questioned the rationale for the invasion and the continued American military presence there. Social issues such as abortion and gay marriage also caused huge divides in American society.

In the 2006 congressional elections, Democrats regained control of both the Senate and the House of Representatives. National debate continued over the war in Iraq and decisions made by the Bush administration. The presidential election of 2008 took place just as the U.S. economy entered a severe downturn. In the voting, Democratic Senator Barack Obama defeated Senator John McCain for the presidency, and Democrats solidified their control over Congress.

Continued foreign policy debates and severe economic problems challenged the Obama administration from day one. Efforts to revive the economy and to lower the unemployment rate had only mixed results. In Iraq, U.S. military efforts brought some stability, and in 2010, U.S. troops were withdrawn from that country. However, ongoing combat against guerrilla fighters in Afghanistan proved frustrating. At home, there were battles over immigration issues and an effort by the administration to expand health care insurance. There was also a rise in antigovernment sentiment led by the so-called "Tea Party" movement. The result was Democratic losses in the 2010 congressional elections.

In the 2012 presidential elections, President Obama won a second term, defeating the Republican candidate, former governor Mitt Romney. Obama was supported by a diverse coalition that included large numbers of younger voters, women, minorities, and working class Americans.

Keyword

Neoconservatism: modern American political philosophy that opposes big-government approaches to domestic issues yet favors an interventionist and aggressive foreign policy; most neoconservatives advocated American intervention in Iraq in 2003.

9/11 and Its Aftermath

On September 11, 2001, Saudi Arabian terrorists hijacked four American commercial airliners. Two slammed into the World Trade Center, one crashed into the Pentagon, and the fourth slammed into a field near Pittsburgh (after passengers attempted to seize control of the plane from the terrorists). World opinion stood firmly on the side of the United States in the immediate aftermath of 9/11. It soon became known that Osama bin Laden, living in Afghanistan and protected by the Taliban government there, had helped mastermind the terrorist attack. On September 20, President Bush addressed a joint session of Congress, stating that the United States would prevail in this conflict and that Osama bin Laden would be brought to justice.

The United States and its allies began a military assault on Afghanistan in November 2001; within two weeks, resistance to the American and allied attacks ended, with many members of the Taliban and their supporters fleeing to the mountains between Afghanistan and Pakistan. It was later reported that Secretary of Defense Donald Rumsfeld began to plan for a military invasion of Iraq during this same period. Secretary Rumsfeld and others in the administration followed the policies advocated by an influential group of American thinkers called **neoconservatives** (or neocons), who wanted to use American might to remake the Middle Eastern region into a democracy. Neocons firmly believed that, to accomplish this, Sadaam Hussein had to be removed from power in Iraq.

Events Leading Up to the American Invasion of Iraq

During his State of the Union address in January 2002, President George W. Bush stated that Iraq, Iran, and North Korea were all part of an "Axis of Evil," and that Iraq possessed weapons of mass destruction (and was close to developing a nuclear weapon). Vice President Dick Cheney urged the president to act quickly and forcefully against Iraq during this period, while

Secretary of State Colin Powell suggested a more cautious approach. It was also revealed that, during the months before the attack, both the CIA and FBI had information on the activities of the Al Qaeda terrorists who flew the airplanes on 9/11, but that some of it was not acted upon. President Bush announced the creation of the new Department of Homeland Security, which would attempt to reorganize America's intelligence-gathering organizations as a result of the **Homeland Security Act of 2002** being signed into law.

In his 2003 State of the Union address, President Bush stated that a war against Iraq was not inevitable, and that Saddam Hussein should reveal his weapons programs to United Nations inspectors. At the same time, plans were being developed in the United States military establishment for the invasion of Iraq. During Operation Desert Storm, President Bush's father was successful in creating a strong coalition of nations (including several in the Middle Eastern region) that supported the invasion of Iraq; fewer nations enthusiastically supported American claims that Iraq might have to be invaded again. In his State of the Union address, President Bush stated that he had learned from the British that Iraq had attempted to obtain uranium from Niger, an African country. (Uranium is necessary for nuclear development.) This claim would later become controversial when it would become known that the CIA had already discredited it. The fact that North Korea might possess a nuclear weapon was another very thorny international issue facing the Bush administration.

Operation Iraqi Freedom

On March 18, 2003, American and British forces invaded Iraq and faced only minor resistance as they moved toward Baghdad. (By April 11, most of the city was occupied by American and British army units.) Many Americans viewed with pride the televised scene of Iraqis cheering the pulling down of a statue of Saddam Hussein. Secretary of Defense Rumsfeld had led the move in the Defense Department toward an emphasis on smaller, more mobile military units; initial successes in Iraq seemed to vindicate this new approach.

Looting and violence took place in Baghdad and other Iraqi cities in the aftermath of the fall of Saddam Hussein and continued unabated for several weeks. American efforts to bring running water and electricity to citizens in Baghdad and other cities were a very slow process; some Iraqis began to resent the Americans because of this. From the very beginning, Americans attempted to rebuild schools and the basic infrastructure of Iraq; news broadcasts around the world emphasized the violence that became a daily feature of Iraqi life as Kurds, Shiites, and Sunnis (the three major groups in Iraq) began to attack each other. These attacks would only intensify in the ensuing years. In addition, Americans were unable to locate the weapons of mass destruction in Iraq that had been the major justification for the invasion in the first place, and connections between Al Qaeda and Saddam Hussein remained elusive.

Effects of the War at Home

After the initial euphoria of victory in Iraq wore off, an intense debate developed in the United States over the justification and purpose of American efforts in Iraq. President Bush and others in the administration portrayed the war in Iraq as a crucial part of America's worldwide attack on terrorism; critics of the administration said the war had sidetracked America from its mission of fighting terrorism. Additionally, in July, unnamed officials in the administration were accused of illegally revealing the identity of CIA agent Valerie Plame in order to discredit her husband Joseph Wilson; Wilson had cast doubt on the administration's account of Iraq purchasing uranium from Niger. Eventually, I. Lewis

"Scooter" Libby, Vice President Cheney's chief of staff, was indicted on charges related to this case, and, by 2006, it was suggested that the president himself had authorized the release of this information.

Continued violence in Iraq, the cost of the war, and claims by several former administration officials that President Bush was preparing for war against Iraq even as he was taking office dominated the presidential elections of 2004. Supporters of American efforts in Iraq were cheered by the fact that an interim Iraqi government took power on June 28, 2004; however, the authority of this government remained uncertain.

Democrats chose Senator John Kerry of Massachusetts to oppose President Bush in November. Many Democrats felt that Kerry was the perfect choice as a candidate, since he was a decorated veteran of the Vietnam War and could thus credibly attack the war policies of the president. As the campaign wore on, however, many were unable to comprehend the nature of Senator Kerry's opposition to the war in Iraq, since he had voted to support the resolutions authorizing American efforts in Iraq. (Kerry responded that he opposed the war that was being conducted.) In addition, what each candidate had done during the Vietnam conflict (some 35 years earlier) became a focus of the campaign. Charges that had been lodged against President Bush in 2000 questioning his service in the National Guard resurfaced. A group of "swift boat veterans," several of whom had served with Senator Kerry in Vietnam, questioned the nature of the medals he had won and the nature of the wounds he had received in Vietnam; in addition, they were deeply critical of Kerry's attack on American efforts in Vietnam when he returned home after the war. President Bush also emphasized moral values in his campaign, thus winning the strong support of the "**religious right**" in America. As a result, President Bush was victorious in the 2004 presidential election; Republican majorities in both the House and the Senate also increased as a result of this election.

Victory of Conservatism in the Bush Era

Many policy initiatives that Conservatives had long desired were either discussed or enacted by the Bush administration and Congress during this era. Gay marriage was a campaign issue in 2004, and, in many states where the president was victorious in the November election, ballot initiatives to allow gay marriage were convincingly defeated. (At the same time, the state of Massachusetts was making gay marriage legal.) In 2004, the president supported and signed legislation expanding the legal rights of human fetuses; prochoice supporters saw this as part of the Conservative agenda to slowly chip away at abortion rights. In 2005, President Bush nominated two new justices to the Supreme Court, John Roberts and Samuel Alito, who were both considered Conservative; those opposing abortion were hopeful that the Supreme Court might be in a position to overturn the *Roe v. Wade* case in the near future. In the 2005 Terri Schiavo case, many Conservatives stated that the feeding tube should not be removed from this seemingly brain-dead woman, even though she had reportedly expressed the desire not to be kept alive in such a condition some 10 years earlier (well before she had gone into a coma). In an extraordinary development, Congress passed, and the president signed, a bill authorizing the federal courts to review her case. (Federal courts had previously refused to order the feeding tube be reinserted, as did this federal court.)

Conservatives had long desired a decrease in the size of the federal budget and a decrease in taxes; under the Bush administration, these goals were partially achieved. A 2004 bill authorized a sweeping reform of corporate tax law, giving businesses tax breaks that the president stated were necessary to ensure economic prosperity. Taxes on income were also decreased during the Bush administration; the administration stated that all Americans would benefit from this, although critics stated that these tax cuts largely benefited the wealthy.

Congress and the Bush administration were unable to find significant ways to decrease government spending; as a result, federal deficits skyrocketed. The administration argued that the war in Iraq and the war on terrorism created a necessary increase in spending on the military and on items related to internal security. Those cuts that were enacted included reductions in farm subsidies, benefits for veterans, and spending on education and the environment. Large-scale reform of the Social Security system, which President Bush had stated to be a top priority on several occasions, was not enacted during his presidency.

Another difficult problem facing the United States during this period was the balance between environmental concerns and the needs of the American economy. President Bush stated in his 2006 State of the Union address that "America is addicted to oil" and that this issue had to be addressed. But proposals to drill for oil in Alaska worried many **environmentalists**, who were concerned with the impact on presently pristine land, and American car manufacturers were slow in developing hybrid automobiles. President Bush was attacked by environmentalists for a number of his policies, which they claimed served American business interests at the expense of the environment. Ironically, some suggested that after the United States "won" in Iraq, we could import a substantial amount of oil from that country. However, Iraqi oil production remained far below what it had been before the American invasion.

The ultimate success or failure of America's decision to invade Iraq remained uncertain. Certainly, the goal of the neoconservatives to have Iraq serve as a model of democracy in the Middle East was far from being achieved. Public attitudes toward the president were at an all-time low in mid-2006. Much of this concerned the war in Iraq, but it also came from the perceived failure of the administration to deal effectively with the level of devastation caused in 2005 by Hurricane Katrina. Many Americans recall viewing the utter destruction caused by the hurricane in New Orleans and the perception that the administration was horribly slow to respond to the crisis.

Several influential Republicans in Congress were also damaged by their alleged ties with influential lobbyists in Washington; at least two members of Congress resigned as a result of investigations into the influence of such lobbyists, the most famous being Tom DeLay from Texas, the former majority leader of the House of Representatives. By 2006, Republicans controlled the presidency, both branches of Congress, and the Supreme Court. In the fall of 2006 congressional elections, Democrats won control of both the House of Representatives and the Senate for the first time since 1994.

United States in Transition: 2007–2008

Democratic gains in the 2006 congressional elections demonstrated the dissatisfaction felt by many with the policies of the Bush administration and the Republican Congress that supported the vast majority of those policies. One day after the election, President Bush announced the resignation of Defense Secretary Donald Rumsfeld, the major architect of American policy in Iraq. In the new Congress, California Democratic Representative Nancy Pelosi became the first female Speaker of the House of Representatives.

At the same time, President Bush announced a new policy in Iraq: a "surge" of an additional 20,000 troops were sent to Baghdad to reduce sectarian fighting between Sunnis and Shiites. On a military level, this policy was a success: from 2007 to 2009 violence was dramatically reduced in Iraq, as were American casualties.

Other problems continued to damage the credibility of the Bush administration in 2007. It was found that returning veterans were receiving inadequate military care at the Walter Reed Army Medical Center. Lewis "Scooter" Libby, former chief of staff to Vice President Dick Cheney, was found guilty of lying to a grand jury over the issue of who leaked the name of a covert CIA agent to the press; the agent, Valerie Plame, was married to former ambassador Joseph Wilson, who had questioned President Bush's claim that Saddam Hussein was developing a nuclear weapons program in Iraq. In congressional hearings, it was charged that seven U.S. attorneys had been fired in late 2006 for purely political reasons; ultimately, Attorney General Alberto Gonzales was forced to resign over this issue. In January 2008, it was reported that CIA videotapes of the use of "harsh interrogation techniques" on Al Qaeda suspects had been inappropriately destroyed.

Primary elections for the 2008 presidential election began in February 2008. Senator John McCain of Arizona emerged as the Republican candidate, but many Conservative Republicans remained unconvinced that McCain was "Conservative enough" to truly represent the party. Senators Barack Obama and Hillary Clinton battled for the Democratic nomination. Signs of economic distress intensified. In January 2008, the economy lost jobs for the first time in 52 months, and in February, General Motors announced the largest ever loss for one of the major automakers in a single quarter.

Barack Obama won the Democratic nomination for president, making him the first African American to be selected to be the nominee for president of a major party. Obama chose Senator Joseph Biden as his vice-presidential nominee. At the Republican National Convention, John McCain officially became the nominee of his party. McCain surprised many by choosing Governor Sarah Palin from Alaska as his choice for vice president; Palin had little exposure at the national level.

As the American economy continued to deteriorate, financial and economic issues began to dominate the American presidential campaign. Barack Obama claimed that a major cause of the economic downturn was the deregulation of business championed by many Republicans during the Bush administration; McCain countered that Obama favored much more government spending and an increase in taxes. A huge financial crisis broke in September, leading Congress to pass a major bailout package for financial institutions; the crisis may have influenced the outcome of the election. Obama eventually won the presidential election, with Democrats increasing their control over both houses of Congress. Severe economic woes continued: the stock market continued to fall, unemployment continued to increase, and additional bailout plans for various financial institutions were discussed. By the end of the year many economic commentators began making comparisons with the Great Depression of the 1930s.

Obama Presidency

President Obama and his administration found that many of the issues confronting them were incredibly difficult to tackle. The economy, ongoing wars in Iraq and Afghanistan, healthcare, and immigration were all complicated ones. In Iraq, a civilian government had taken office in 2006, and despite ongoing incidents of sectarian violence, by 2010 the situation was stable enough to permit the withdrawal of U.S. troops. However, in Afghanistan, U.S. forces were engaged in continuing military operations against Taliban guerrilla fighters who were attempting to topple the U.S.-backed civilian government. After much debate, the president authorized a troop buildup in Afghanistan, although many inside and outside the administration questioned whether it would really be possible to "win" in Afghanistan. The administration enacted economic bailout plans that saved many jobs—and saved banks, the auto industry, and AIG (a large insurance and financial services company) from bankruptcy—while Republican opponents criticized the cost of these measures and the lack of progress in bringing down the unemployment rate, which remained near 10 percent. The issue of jobs was on the minds of most Americans; when it appeared that the president's policies didn't appear to be creating enough of them, his approval ratings fell. President Obama pressed hard to have Congress pass comprehensive healthcare legislation but some supporters of reform said that the bill didn't go far enough, while others believed that the bill was unconstitutional and resulted in "socialized medicine."

Other issues created political controversy during the period. A British Petroleum (BP) oil well in the Gulf of Mexico exploded and spilled huge amounts of oil into the sea, and for several months it appeared that neither private industry nor the government could contain the human and environmental damage. Some compared Obama's reaction to the oil spill to President Bush's inadequate response to Hurricane Katrina. A fear of illegal immigration grew in the southwestern United States and spread to other parts of the nation, with increased calls to place a fence or wall on the border with Mexico and to increase penalties on undocumented immigrants. There were also signs of an increase in anti-Islamic sentiment in the United States; a proposal to construct an Islamic center in the vicinity of the World Trade Center site in New York City generated loud debate. A number of Americans continued to state in opinion polls that they believed that President Obama was either a Muslim or was born outside the United States.

In this climate the so-called "Tea Party" movement developed. There was no unified set of beliefs that members of the Tea Party movement followed but, as a whole, Tea Party members favored a scaling down of the size of government and a reduction in taxes; some also favored the elimination or reduction of government "entitlement" programs. To many in the movement, President Obama and "political insiders" in Washington were the embodiment of all that was wrong with America. Tea Party members were also critical of "establishment" members of the Republican Party; in primaries leading up to the 2010 congressional elections a number of candidates supported by the Tea Party defeated "mainstream" Republicans.

On election day 2010, the Republican Party was able to win control of the House of Representatives and gain seats in the Senate. A number of Republican candidates supported by the Tea Party were victorious (although several prominent Republican Party candidates supported by the Tea Party were not).

The last two years of President Obama's first term were contentious ones. Republicans and Democrats fiercely battled on issues surrounding the budget and on the legitimacy of "Obamacare," President Obama's plan for many more American citizens to have healthcare insurance. Critics of Republicans argued that Republicans in Washington (especially those in the House of Representatives) refused to cooperate with the president on budgetary issues for purely political reasons. Republican Senate President Mitch McConnell stated that Republicans' main agenda during this period should be the defeat of president Obama. Critics of the president argued that he never legitimately attempted to achieve compromise with the Republicans on a multitude of issues, and that he lacked the political skills to do so. Many Americans were surprised when in the spring of 2012 the Supreme Court, by a 5-to-4 vote, validated most of the president's healthcare initiative.

Election of 2012

The 2012 presidential election pitted President Obama against Mitt Romney, former governor of Massachusetts. Both candidates agreed that the nation faced serious economic issues. President Obama emphasized his desire to increase taxes on the wealthiest Americans and to protect the middle class. Mitt Romney and his vice-presidential nominee, Congressman Paul Ryan, emphasized the need for fiscal responsibility and the need to reform "entitlement programs" (Social Security, Medicare, and Medicaid). The candidates generally focused on domestic affairs during the course of the campaign.

On election day 2012, President Obama was returned to office, defeating former Governor Romney in the Electoral College by a sizable 322 to 206 majority; Democrats also (surprisingly) increased their majority in the United States Senate and slightly increased their numbers in the House of Representatives. President Obama won all but one of the important "swing states" in the election; his winning coalition included many younger voters, women, Hispanic Americans, African Americans, and, especially in the Midwest, working class Americans. Governor Romney won the majority of white Americans and senior citizens.

There were numerous reasons for the Democratic victory in this election. Governor Romney was perceived as being supportive of wealthy Americans at the expense of the rest of American citizens; the Democratic campaign message was that the Romney/Ryan ticket favored the upper "1 percent" of Americans. Republicans were also perceived as being out of touch with mainstream America on social issues, especially those relating to women's rights. Remarks made by several Republican senatorial candidates on the issue of abortion alarmed a number of Americans. During the Republican primaries, Governor Romney took a very harsh stance on immigration issues; during the election this caused many Hispanic Americans to vote for President Obama.

President Obama's Second Term

Domestic Policy

In domestic policy, President Obama would find most of his legislative initiatives frustrated by Republicans in Congress. An attempt to strengthen gun control legislation after the shocking massacre of 26 schoolchildren and teachers at Sandy Hook Elementary School in Connecticut by a deranged gunman went nowhere. President Obama continued to spar with Congressional Republicans over the budget and economic policy. In October 2013, an effort by conservative Republicans to defund the Affordable Care Act led to a government shutdown for 16 days. This proved a public relations fiasco for the Republicans and resulted in a political victory for the president. The political advantage that President Obama won here was quickly dissipated by the disastrous rollout of the Healthcare.gov website through which citizens were supposed to enroll in new insurance plans under the Affordable Care Act. Numerous glitches caused consumers many problems. The failure of the Obama administration to create a fully functioning website fed popular perceptions of government incompetence. Although the problems with the website were eventually worked out, the Affordable Care Act remained unpopular with many Americans. This contributed to the sweeping Republican victory in the elections of 2014. The Republicans won control of the Senate, gaining nine seats, and increased their majority in the House of Representatives. With victories in gubernatorial and state legislative elections, the Republicans were in their strongest national position since 1928. President Obama turned to pursuing his goals on immigration and the environment through executive orders and administrative regulations issued by government departments. The president still had the power of the veto, vetoing Republican bills to repeal the Affordable Care Act and authorize the Keystone XL pipeline.

President Obama exercised the "bully pulpit" on social issues. He became a vocal supporter of gay marriage. In 2013, the Supreme Court struck down the 1996 Defense of Marriage Act, which had limited federal recognition to marriages between one man and one woman. In the wake of this decision, some states recognized gay marriage and others rejected it. In 2015, the Supreme Court's *Obergefell v. Hodges* decision legalized gay marriages across the country. In 2014, a young African American man named Michael Brown was fatally shot by a white police officer in Ferguson, Missouri. Although the Justice Department later ruled that the shooting was justifiable, this incident revealed pent-up African American frustration with policing methods. Protests spread from Ferguson across the country. The Black Lives Matter movement attained national prominence. Police shootings of African American men received greater scrutiny. A number of police officers were assassinated by gunmen. President Obama acknowledged the difficult job facing police but expressed sympathy for African American anger.

Domestic security became an issue in President Obama's second term. In 2013, Edward Snowden, a former National Security Agency contractor, leaked important information about American surveillance programs. His revelations dealt a severe blow to American intelligence operations. The U.S. government regarded Snowden as a traitor, but some saw him as a hero revealing the workings of an overly intrusive government. Concern also rose about foreign cyber attacks on the United States, including a 2014 data breach at the U.S. Office of Personnel Management that resulted in the compromising of the records of millions of government employees. In 2013, two Chechen brothers motivated by radical Islamist ideology bombed the Boston Marathon. Other Islamic terror attacks followed in Chattanooga, Tennessee, and San Bernardino, California, in 2015 and Orlando, Florida, in 2016. These incidents led to a growing debate about immigration and domestic terrorism.

Foreign Policy

The Syrian civil war that began in 2011 continued throughout President Obama's second term, destabilizing its neighbors and sending waves of refugees into Europe and elsewhere. President Obama condemned the government of Syrian President Bashar al-Assad and declared that the Syrian dictator had to leave office. The president eventually authorized some ineffective programs to train pro-Western rebel forces, but resolutely opposed military intervention. He declared that President Assad's use of chemical weapons would cross a "red line," inviting American retaliation. In August 2013, Syrian government forces used chemical weapons, killing nearly 300 people. President Obama declined to attack the Syrian government, instead agreeing to a Russian proposal to have President Assad surrender his chemical weapons to them. This began a strong revival of Russian influence in the Middle East. In 2015, Russian President Vladimir Putin intervened militarily in Syria. Russian air support helped turn the war in President Assad's favor; by the end of 2016, brutal Russian bombing attacks had enabled the Syrian government reclaim the important city of Aleppo.

The collapse of Syria into civil war offered an opportunity for formerly al-Qaeda-linked Islamic extremists in Iraq to expand their influence. They began to carve out a territory for themselves in Syria, and began styling themselves the Islamic State of Iraq and the Levant (ISIL). Initially, President Obama was dismissive of ISIL. Following the withdrawal of American troops from Iraq in 2011, the Iraqi government fell into sectarian dissension between the majority Shiite and minority Sunni Muslims. Government officials and military officers were advanced for political loyalty rather than competence. In 2014, ISIL took advantage of this governmental disarray to launch a devastating military offensive into Iraq, which captured a great swathe of territory and the large city of Mosul. President Obama was forced to send several thousand troops back to Iraq to help the Iraqi army fight ISIL. American Air Force and Navy pilots flew thousands of bombing sorties against the terrorists. American forces began bombing ISIL in Syria as well.

A centerpiece of President Obama's Middle Eastern policy was an effort to work out a deal with Iran to contain its nuclear weapons program. In 2015, the Obama administration and diplomats from the other permanent member states of the UN Security Council negotiated an agreement with the Iranians that ended economic sanctions against Iran, and returned funds that had been sequestered since the 1970s in exchange for concessions that would likely delay the development of an Iranian nuclear bomb for a decade or more. President Obama believed that this agreement would help preserve peace and begin a process of integrating the Iranian regime into the international community. Republican critics of the deal believed that it strengthened an enemy of the United States while failing to ensure that the Iranians would not acquire nuclear weapons. Because of opposition in the Senate, President Obama did not put forward the deal as a treaty, and it remains an executive agreement.

The Israeli government of Prime Minister Benjamin Netanyahu vehemently opposed the Iran nuclear agreement because of past Iranian threats to attack Israel with nuclear weapons. This helped worsen relations with the Obama administration, which had already become strained over disagreements on the peace process with the Palestinians. In December 2016, the United States refrained from vetoing a UN resolution condemning Israeli settlements on the West Bank and East Jerusalem.

The Russians posed challenges to the United States in other places than in Syria. In 2014, President Putin seized Crimea from the Ukraine and sponsored a bloody rebellion in the eastern part of that country. Russian forces made threatening gestures toward the Baltic states, and the United States and its NATO allies were compelled to bolster the region's defenses. In late 2016, the Obama administration accused the Russian government of attempting to influence the American presidential election by hacking into and leaking documents from the Democratic National Committee; the administration responded to this by expelling a number of Russian diplomats.

President Obama made another controversial decision in normalizing diplomatic relations with Cuba in 2015. Many Republicans denounced this overture to the Communist dictatorship of Fidel and Raul Castro. President Obama believed that the previous American policy of isolating Cuba had failed. In 2016, he became the first president to visit Cuba since 1928.

The Election of 2016

Sixteen Republican candidates ran for the Republican presidential nomination in what looked to be a good year for the opposition party. Unexpectedly, well-known candidates such as former Florida governor Jeb Bush and senators Marco Rubio and Ted Cruz were defeated by the New York real estate developer and reality television show host Donald Trump. Confounding the expectations of most political prognosticators, Trump won the Republican nomination by positioning himself as an opponent of the Republican establishment and championing such populist causes as building a wall along the border with Mexico to halt illegal immigration.

Former Secretary of State Hillary Clinton was the clear Democratic frontrunner. Before clinching the Democratic nomination, she had to fend off a challenge from Bernie Sanders, the socialist senator from Vermont. This pulled Clinton to the left. The 2016 Democratic party platform would be one of the most liberal in history.

Both candidates had high unfavorability ratings. Donald Trump had been a celebrity for decades. He was prone to making outrageous comments. A tape surfaced of him making lewd comments about women. Many questioned whether he had the temperament to be a president.

Hillary Clinton had also been in the public eye for years. Many believed that she and her husband, former President Bill Clinton, were ethically challenged and had used their Clinton Foundation to enrich themselves. As secretary of state, Clinton had avoided using secure government computer systems and instead had set up an insecure private computer server that raised a real possibility that foreign intelligence services had read classified e-mails. Clinton compounded her fault by initially lying about the contents of the server. FBI director James Comey eventually criticized her handling of her communications, but concluded that she had not intentionally broken government security regulations. A late and brief revival of Comey's investigation because of the discovery of more Clinton e-mails on another computer helped weaken the momentum of her campaign.

Donald Trump chose Indiana governor Mike Pence as his running mate. Pence had solid conservative credentials and appealed to traditional Republican voters. Clinton chose Virginia senator Tim Kaine as her vice presidential candidate. Kaine had served as governor of Virginia before entering the Senate, and was seen as an experienced and reliable choice.

During the presidential campaign Clinton spent much of her time questioning the fitness of Donald Trump to be president. She also touted the historic nature of her candidacy and the very real possibility that she would become the first woman to become the president of the United States. Trump continued to promote himself as an outsider who would clean up Washington. He defied political correctness, claimed that he would bring back American jobs from overseas, and called on his supporters to "make America great again."

In an historic political upset, Trump defeated Clinton by demolishing the Democratic "Blue Wall" of midwestern industrial states, capturing the electoral votes of Pennsylvania, Ohio, Michigan, and Wisconsin. Trump ended up winning the electoral vote 306 to 232. Clinton won the popular vote by almost 3 million votes, most of these coming from California. Trump won the election by gaining the votes of white working-class voters who had fallen behind economically during the years of slow economic growth under President Obama. These voters also resented the politically correct attitudes of those they termed the elites and associated with the Democratic party. Trump also did better with African American and Hispanic voters than Mitt Romney had done in 2012. Following his victory, Trump set about selecting a cabinet that appeared notable for its conservatism.

Chapter Review

Rapid Review

To achieve the perfect 5, you should be able to explain the following:

- The 9/11 attacks on the World Trade Center had a huge impact on America and its perceived role in the world, and affected policy decisions.
- The need for unity and strength in time of war versus the desire for individual liberty has created major divisions in public opinion during the period of the Iraqi war.
- The overall agenda of the neoconservatives greatly influenced the decision of the administration to go to war in Iraq.
- "Winning" the war in Iraq proved to be much more difficult than many of the supporters of the war initially imagined.
- Failure to find weapons of mass destruction and failure to establish a link between Al Qaeda and Iraq caused many in the United States to question the overall purpose of American efforts in Iraq.

- An effective emphasis on social issues and the failure of John Kerry to truly distance himself from President Bush on Iraq were factors in President Bush's victory in the 2004 presidential elections.
- Several Conservative policy positions concerning social issues and taxation were enacted during the presidency of George Bush.
- Public attitudes toward George Bush, his policies, and the war in Iraq were sharply divided during his presidency.
- The efforts of the Bush administration in countering the devastation of Hurricane Katrina caused many to doubt the effectiveness of that administration in confronting serious disasters.
- Continued dissatisfaction with Republican policies and a desire for new leadership helped lead to the election of Barack Obama in 2008.

Time Line

2001: Terrorist attack on World Trade Center and the Pentagon
American and British troops invade Afghanistan
Planning for military operations against Iraq begins

2002: President Bush terms Iran, Iraq, and North Korea the "Axis of Evil"
Creation of Department of Homeland Security
Homeland Security Act signed into law

2003: President Bush warns of possible war with Iraq in State of the Union address
Operation Iraqi Freedom: U.S. and British invasion of Iraq
"Outing" of CIA agent Valerie Plame
Violence in Iraq between Kurdish, Shiite, and Sunni factions
Controversy develops as weapons of mass destruction are not found in Iraq

2004: President Bush proposes budget with $521 billion deficit
Photographs show American soldiers torturing Iraqi prisoners at the Abu Ghraib prison
Provisional government with limited authority comes into power in Iraq
George Bush defeats John Kerry in presidential elections; Republicans increase their control of the House and the Senate

2005: Presidential budget proposes deep cuts in social programs
Violence between Sunnis and Shiites in Iraq increases dramatically
John Roberts becomes Supreme Court chief justice
Hurricane Katrina devastates New Orleans
I. Lewis "Scooter" Libby, Vice President Cheney's chief of staff, indicted on obstruction of justice concerning the Valerie Plame case
Samuel Alito becomes Supreme Court justice

2006: In an effort to deal with federal deficit, President Bush proposes reduction of many government programs
Controversy develops over secret wiretapping program by the federal government
Under investigation regarding his connections with a lobbyist, Tom DeLay, Republican majority leader of the House of Representatives, resigns

2007: Nancy Pelosi of California becomes first female Speaker of the House

2008: Barack Obama becomes first African American elected to the U.S. presidency
Severe economic downturn affects U.S. financial institutions

2009: Unemployment in the United States remains near 10 percent
President Obama announces "troop surge" in Afghanistan

2010: BP oil spill clogs Gulf of Mexico

Healthcare legislation passes

Tea Party candidates win some seats in midterm elections

2012: President Obama elected to a second term

Gunman murders 20 children and 6 staff members at Sandy Hook Elementary School in Connecticut

Supreme Court upholds the legality of most provisions of the Affordable Care Act

2013: Former National Security Agency contractor Edward Snowden leaks information about NSA surveillance practices

Supreme Court strikes down the Defense of Marriage Act, which limited federal benefits to marriages between a man and a woman

Two Islamic terrorist brothers bomb the Boston Marathon

Budget dispute between Congressional Republicans and President Obama leads to a partial shutdown of government for 16 days

Healthcare.gov website for purchasing Affordable Care Act health plans starts up but suffers many glitches

2014: U.S.-Russia relations deteriorate because of Russian takeover of Crimea

Supreme Court strikes down limits on biennial donations to politicians by individuals

Islamic State of Iraq and Syria (ISIS) makes great gains in the Middle East

Riots take place in Ferguson, Missouri, after a white police officer shoots and kills an African American teen during a confrontation on a street

Republicans take control of the Senate in the 2014 elections

2015: The Obama administration negotiates a controversial nuclear deal with Iran

Supreme Court upholds Affordable Care Act subsidies

Islamic terror attacks take place in Chattanooga, Tennessee, and San Bernardino, California

The Supreme Court upholds the constitutionality of gay marriage

The United States resumes diplomatic relations with Cuba

2016: Islamic terrorist attack at a gay nightclub in Orlando, Florida

Hillary Clinton becomes the first female presidential nominee of a major political party

Donald Trump wins the presidential election

› Review Questions

Multiple-Choice Questions

1. Major reasons stated by President Bush for the war in Iraq included all but which of the following?
   A. Iraq possessed weapons of mass destruction.
   B. Saddam Hussein had tried to assassinate the president's father.
   C. Iraq had links to terrorism.
   D. Saddam Hussein had killed his own people in the past.

2. Which of the following was not a major policy goal of the religious right?
   A. Have a constitutional amendment banning gay marriage
   B. Limit abortions in the United States
   C. Cut the income tax of wealthy Americans
   D. Take steps to save the life of Terri Schiavo

3. Which of the following developments that occurred during the Bush administration will potentially have the longest-lasting impact on American society?
   A. The creation of the Department of Homeland Security
   B. The passage of the Patriot Act
   C. The president's opposition to gay marriage
   D. The appointment of John Roberts and Samuel Alito to the Supreme Court

4. All of the following hurt John Kerry in his bid for the presidency in 2004 *except*
   A. his statements on the Vietnam War when he returned home after the war.
   B. his voting record on the Iraqi war.
   C. his performance in the 2004 debates.
   D. the fact that questions on social issues (gay marriage, etc.) appeared on the ballots in many states.

5. In his expressed desire to expand democracy to the Middle East, President Bush can be equated with which twentieth century president who wanted to expand American concepts of freedom and democracy to Europe and other parts of the world?
   A. Woodrow Wilson
   B. Franklin Roosevelt
   C. Dwight Eisenhower
   D. Lyndon Johnson

Short-Answer Question

6. Answer Parts A, B, and C.
   A. Briefly explain ONE example of a response of the American government to the 9/11 attacks.
   B. Briefly explain a SECOND example of a response of the American government to the 9/11 attacks.
   C. Briefly explain ONE example a way that President Barack Obama attempted to move the country in a new direction following his election in 2008.

› Answers and Explanations

1. **B**. All of the other three were given by administration officials as reasons for war. The president noted in several speeches that Saddam Hussein had tried to kill his father, but this was not used by the administration as a major reason for war.

2. **C**. Many fiscal Conservatives supported the reduction of income taxes in the United States. This was not an issue that was important to the socially Conservative members of the religious right.

3. **D**. The appointments of two Conservative justices to the Supreme Court caused the entire court to swing to the Conservative side; rulings from such a court on issues such as abortion might fundamentally alter American society.

4. **C**. Many Vietnam War veterans were deeply offended by Senator Kerry's statements when he returned home after the war. Many voters were never sure where Kerry actually stood on the issue of the Iraqi war. President Bush portrayed himself as the "moral" candidate; questions on any ballot dealing with morality served to help him. In reality, Senator Kerry did quite well in the 2004 debates.

5. **A.** Several observers have noted the similarity between President Bush's desire to spread democracy in the Middle East with Woodrow Wilson's Fourteen Points, which proposed the creation of a more democratic and freer Europe, and world, after World War I.

6. **Parts A and B**: The government of the United States quickly mobilized to defeat the al-Qaeda sponsors of the 9/11 attacks. President George W. Bush spoke of a "War on Terror" in a speech on September 20, 2001. In November, the United States launched an attack on the Taliban government of Afghanistan, which provided refuge and support for Osama bin Laden, the founder of al-Qaeda. The Taliban government was quickly overthrown, but the United States would become embroiled in a long and difficult struggle to pacify Afghanistan. In 2002, the Bush administration established a detention center for captured terrorism suspects at Guantanamo Bay Naval Base in Cuba. The detainees at Guantanamo were extensively interrogated for intelligence information. The CIA admitted waterboarding three prisoners, including Khalid Sheikh Mohammed, the mastermind of the 9/11 attacks. In October 2001, Congress passed the USA PATRIOT Act, which gave the government more powers to investigate and surveille suspected terrorists. President Bush created an Office of Homeland Security in October 2001. In November 2002, Congress created the Department of Homeland Security, which controls a number of agencies charged with protecting the United States from domestic threats. A new agency in the department was the Transportation Security Administration (TSA), which handles security at airports.

The Iraqi dictator Saddam Hussein expressed support for the 9/11 attacks. President Bush charged that Iraq, along with Iran and North Korea, was part of an "Axis of Evil" because of their support for terrorism and efforts to acquire nuclear weapons. The CIA and other Western intelligence agencies believed that Saddam Hussein was working to build up Iraq's supply of weapons of mass destruction. Saddam Hussein had used poison gas against his own people in the past. The Iraqi regime was also evading full compliance with United Nations Security Council Resolutions. Bush and his advisors decided that post-9/11 the United

States could take no chances with Saddam Hussein. On March 20, 2003, the United States and its allies invaded Iraq. The Iraqi government was soon overthrown and Saddam Hussein captured, but the United States found itself fighting a long and controversial war against Iraqi and al-Qaeda insurgents. In 2007, Bush ordered a "surge" of 20,000 more troops into Iraq; in conjunction with effective anti-insurgency techniques and cooperation with local militias, this initiative dramatically lowered the level of violence in Iraq, and for a time crippled al-Qaeda cadres in the country. Following years of patient intelligence work, President Barack Obama was able to order a commando raid that killed Osama bin Laden in Abbottabad, Pakistan, on May 2, 2011.

Part C: President Barack Obama came into office in 2009 promising "hope and change" to a nation unsettled by the frustrating war in Iraq and a recent banking crisis. Although he increased American forces for a time in Afghanistan, President Obama attempted to reduce the American military footprint in the Middle East. He withdrew American forces from Iraq in 2011, though he had to return some troops to that country in 2014 following the capture of Mosul by fighters of the Islamic State of Iraq and Syria (ISIS). Obama preferred to kill terrorists through drone strikes rather than through conventional military operations. His support for the overthrow of the Libyan dictator Muammar Gaddafi had equivocal results, with Libya descending into civil war and becoming a haven for terrorists. The Obama administration exerted little influence over the disastrous civil war in Syria. President Obama focused most of his attention on domestic policy. In 2009, he signed a $800 billion stimulus bill, which he hoped would spur economic recovery. His most important legislative achievement was the 2010 Affordable Care Act (ACA), which was intended to provide reasonably priced health care to most Americans. This highly ambitious reworking of the American health care system was controversial and passed with no Republican votes. Following the election of a Republican majority in the House of Representatives in 2010, President Obama was unable to pass any more major bills through Congress. He used his "bully pulpit" to encourage liberal causes such as gun control and gay marriage.

CHAPTER 31

Contemporary America: Evaluating the "Big Themes"

IN THIS CHAPTER

Summary: The current events and debates of today become the history of tomorrow. People's actions and opinions are affected by their knowledge and memories of the past. As students of history, you should remember to look at the connections running back and forth in time as we examine some important current issues.

Keywords
Economic crisis
United States and the world
Big vs. small government
Individual rights in "wartime"
Presidential power
Religion and government
Immigration

Americans in every period in U.S. history have evaluated the past in comparison to the time in which they lived. Many Americans in the 1980s viewed the 1960s in a negative light and maintained that a "better" America existed back in the 1950s. Many American writers in the 1920s noted that they were in a new era that was decidedly different from the America that existed before World War I. Indeed, as this is being written, many central questions about American identity and the American experience are under scrutiny. What are the big themes of American history that have relevance today, and what central characteristics of the American identity are being questioned during the first years of the Obama presidency?

To help you study, think of the following both in terms of present-day events and historical context. "History is in the past, period," a professor of mine once told me. However, one can sometimes get a richer interpretation of the past by viewing prior events through the lens of the present. Major themes to evaluate in this manner might include:

(1) What should the role of the government be in the economic affairs of the nation? This was a question that was being asked at the beginning of the Obama administration. Many commentators maintained there was very little regulation of big business and the banking industry as a result of Republican policies during the Bush administration; to offset this, the Obama administration authorized a stimulus package worth billions of dollars. In supporting this program, government officials emphasized that with big business and the banking industry in poor shape the only institution left to "prime the pump" of the economy was the federal government. When those in Congress voted on the stimulus package, only three Republican senators voted for the legislation; every other Republican in Congress voted against it.

This debate about whether government should be a "pump-primer" of the economy was a replica of economic debates that have gone on in the past about the role of government in the economy. "Free market" Conservatives (in recent decades, mainly Republicans) are generally opposed to government intervention in the economy (although some argued that the 2009 economic crisis was so severe that government intervention was necessary). Many would argue that the appropriate government response to economic downturns should be to cut taxes: Conservatives believe this will put money in the pockets of millions of consumers, who will do all the "pump-priming" that is necessary. Others would argue that, when they are left to their own devices, business interests are only interested in profits; supporters of this view would state that the sheer greed of business and banking interests led to the banking and housing crises besetting the country in 2009. These critics would argue that it is the job of government to regulate the economy and to have an active role in economic affairs, despite the uncertainty of success of the actual stimulus package that was passed by Congress.

During the first years of the Great Depression, Herbert Hoover did exactly what many "sensible" economists of the time said he should do: wait out the downturn and rely on state, local, and voluntary agencies to deal with the impact of the stock market crash and subsequent business failures. To many economists of the time, active government intervention in the economy would be nothing short of "socialism" (a charge that some made when discussing the policies of Barack Obama). Franklin Roosevelt responded with the New Deal, which turned the federal government into a major engine of economic growth.

The controversy over the role of the federal government in economic affairs goes back to the differing views of America held by Thomas Jefferson and Alexander Hamilton. It appears that the federal government will continue to be a major player in the economic affairs of the nation for the foreseeable future, although members of the "Tea Party" and other critics claim that government's role in the economy must be sharply curtailed.

(2) What should the role of the United States be in world affairs? Americans have asked this central question since the foundation of the republic. George Washington warned the nation to stay out of world affairs that are not of immediate concern to us. Many in the 1920s and 1930s agreed, pushing the United States to a position of severe isolationism. However, if America is to call itself a world leader, do we not have the responsibility to truly lead the world? If we are utterly convinced that democracy is the best form of government on the face of the earth, don't we have a responsibility to spread that form of government abroad?

This was the view of Woodrow Wilson as he tried to get Americans to support the Versailles Treaty after World War I, and it was the view of George Bush and the neoconservatives leading up to the latest invasion of Iraq. Those who support this view are forced to ponder the thorny possibility that parts of the world that we may want to transform may be opposed to some of the changes that we are proposing for their country or region. Which is more important: promoting self-determination (another stated American goal) or promoting the American way? These are fundamental issues that Americans have wrestled with in the past and are still concerned with today.

(3) **What should be the impact of the federal government be on the lives of American citizens?** This is another question that Americans have wrestled with, especially in the last 80 years. It is connected to the issue of the role of the federal government in the economy. Before the New Deal policies of Franklin Roosevelt, the role of the federal government in the lives of citizens was minimal. However, the New Deal created a radically new role for the federal government: it was now the responsibility of the federal government to take care of those who could not take care of themselves. The Social Security Act is perhaps the most famous example of a New Deal policy exemplifying this new thinking. The Great Society programs sponsored by Lyndon Johnson in the 1960s followed the New Deal spirit of assisting those who are unable to assist themselves.

During the past 30 years, there has been an effort by Conservative Republicans to roll back some of these "liberal policies"; a famous statement of this "end big government" philosophy was the 1992 Republican Contract with America. Many conservatives maintain that Americans act most nobly when they stand up and act independently and are not burdened with regulations, rules, and excessive taxation handed down by the federal government. However, it would be extremely hard to credibly argue that there was anything noble about the way that American business interests acted during the Bush years when concerted efforts *were* made to "get the government off the backs of the people."

A "New Deal liberal" would say that we need government to take care of those who can't take care of themselves, while many Conservatives would say that we need government to help people take care of themselves. However, during the economic crises of late 2008 and 2009 most public opinion polls stated that the majority of Americans felt that we needed a government that was strong enough to successfully handle domestic crises such as Hurricane Katrina or economic turmoil. Now some members of the Tea Party and others call for a reduction or elimination of Social Security benefits and the elimination of some government agencies such as the Department of Education and the Office of Environmental Protection.

(4) **How many of our individual rights should we be willing to give up when fighting a foreign enemy?** This is another difficult issue that Americans have debated since the founding of the nation. John Adams passed the Alien and Sedition Acts, Abraham Lincoln promoted censorship of the press during the Civil War, and dissidents who spoke against military intervention were jailed during World War I. Historians today still debate whether these actions were justified.

Debate on this issue flared again during the War on Terror: many Americans wondered how invasive the government should be when "protecting us" during major crises? Many maintained that if government officials wanted to look through their phone logs and e-mail messages to help defeat terrorism, so be it; others wondered about the impact of government actions such as these on individual freedoms. Also, how much freedom should the press have in times of crises? Many maintained that the freedom of the press should also be curtailed during times of crisis, while others argued that such restrictions were overly likely to be abused, whether from good intentions or to deliberately protect or benefit those in power.

(5) **Should the power of the three branches remain equal, or should the power of the executive branch expand in times of crisis?** This is another question that commentators and politicians have discussed over time. Critics complained that Abraham Lincoln, Franklin Roosevelt, George Bush, and even Barack Obama have acted as if the other branches of government didn't exist. But isn't there a need for a strong executive branch in times of crisis? During the latest Bush administration, the president and his supporters justified the expansion of the executive branch as being essential in the battle against terrorism; critics maintained that President Bush and Vice President Cheney used terrorism as an excuse to increase the power of the executive branch (at the expense of congressional power). In the past, there has been an ebb and flow of power between the executive and the legislative branches. Critics fear that some of the measures of recent years will make the increase in power of the executive branch permanent.

(6) **What connections should exist between religion and government?** This is another question that has been a topic of discussion since the earliest days of the republic. Historians point out that religion has always been an issue in American politics. Many voted against presidential candidate Al Smith in 1928 because he was a Catholic. John Kennedy faced many questions concerning his Catholicism when he ran for president in 1960; Joseph Lieberman had to state what he could do and not do on the Sabbath (he is an Orthodox Jew) when he ran for vice president in 2000. Since the 1980s some critics have voiced concern over the increasing role of the religious right in the Republican party. Ministers from the religious right urged congregations to support President Bush's reelection in 2004 because he was a "man of God" and the war in Iraq because it had "God's blessing." Yet in recent years, other diverse voices, even from within the religious right, have been heard. The religious right had always been keenly interested in issues such as abortion and homosexuality; some members of that community have recently maintained that the environment and helping America's homeless are equally important issues. Several Christian ministers have recently noted that Christianity can be liberal as well, reminding followers that Christian ministers were among the first supporters of the civil rights movement in the South in the 1960s.

(7) **What should American policy toward immigration be?** Recent American debates on illegal immigration mirror debates that have occurred on numerous occasions in American history. The words of those who wish to severely restrict immigration today somewhat match the pronouncements of nineteenth-century "Know-Nothings" or nativists of the 1920s; in each case, the work ethic, educational background, and moral character of those attempting to enter the United States has been questioned. Recent plans to build fences on the Mexican border were matched by demands in the 1920s to send immigrants back to Eastern and Southern Europe. Congressional debates in the early 1920s produced legislation that reduced immigration to a trickle. Passions concerning this issue are just as high in the early twenty-first century.

There are other major issues that have been continually redebated and reanalyzed throughout American history, including the question of the nature of the American dream. When studying American history and studying for this exam, I would encourage you to compare how key issues such as these were seen in the past compared to how they are perceived today. If you do this, past historical trends will make more sense to you; this approach will also help you write historical essays, and it certainly makes the historical material that you are studying much more interesting!

STEP 5

Build Your
Test-Taking Confidence

AP U.S. History Practice Exam 1
AP U.S. History Practice Exam 2

PRACTICE EXAM 1

Answer Sheet For Multiple-Choice Questions

1 Ⓐ Ⓑ Ⓒ Ⓓ	16 Ⓐ Ⓑ Ⓒ Ⓓ	31 Ⓐ Ⓑ Ⓒ Ⓓ	46 Ⓐ Ⓑ Ⓒ Ⓓ
2 Ⓐ Ⓑ Ⓒ Ⓓ	17 Ⓐ Ⓑ Ⓒ Ⓓ	32 Ⓐ Ⓑ Ⓒ Ⓓ	47 Ⓐ Ⓑ Ⓒ Ⓓ
3 Ⓐ Ⓑ Ⓒ Ⓓ	18 Ⓐ Ⓑ Ⓒ Ⓓ	33 Ⓐ Ⓑ Ⓒ Ⓓ	48 Ⓐ Ⓑ Ⓒ Ⓓ
4 Ⓐ Ⓑ Ⓒ Ⓓ	19 Ⓐ Ⓑ Ⓒ Ⓓ	34 Ⓐ Ⓑ Ⓒ Ⓓ	49 Ⓐ Ⓑ Ⓒ Ⓓ
5 Ⓐ Ⓑ Ⓒ Ⓓ	20 Ⓐ Ⓑ Ⓒ Ⓓ	35 Ⓐ Ⓑ Ⓒ Ⓓ	50 Ⓐ Ⓑ Ⓒ Ⓓ
6 Ⓐ Ⓑ Ⓒ Ⓓ	21 Ⓐ Ⓑ Ⓒ Ⓓ	36 Ⓐ Ⓑ Ⓒ Ⓓ	51 Ⓐ Ⓑ Ⓒ Ⓓ
7 Ⓐ Ⓑ Ⓒ Ⓓ	22 Ⓐ Ⓑ Ⓒ Ⓓ	37 Ⓐ Ⓑ Ⓒ Ⓓ	52 Ⓐ Ⓑ Ⓒ Ⓓ
8 Ⓐ Ⓑ Ⓒ Ⓓ	23 Ⓐ Ⓑ Ⓒ Ⓓ	38 Ⓐ Ⓑ Ⓒ Ⓓ	53 Ⓐ Ⓑ Ⓒ Ⓓ
9 Ⓐ Ⓑ Ⓒ Ⓓ	24 Ⓐ Ⓑ Ⓒ Ⓓ	39 Ⓐ Ⓑ Ⓒ Ⓓ	54 Ⓐ Ⓑ Ⓒ Ⓓ
10 Ⓐ Ⓑ Ⓒ Ⓓ	25 Ⓐ Ⓑ Ⓒ Ⓓ	40 Ⓐ Ⓑ Ⓒ Ⓓ	55 Ⓐ Ⓑ Ⓒ Ⓓ
11 Ⓐ Ⓑ Ⓒ Ⓓ	26 Ⓐ Ⓑ Ⓒ Ⓓ	41 Ⓐ Ⓑ Ⓒ Ⓓ	
12 Ⓐ Ⓑ Ⓒ Ⓓ	27 Ⓐ Ⓑ Ⓒ Ⓓ	42 Ⓐ Ⓑ Ⓒ Ⓓ	
13 Ⓐ Ⓑ Ⓒ Ⓓ	28 Ⓐ Ⓑ Ⓒ Ⓓ	43 Ⓐ Ⓑ Ⓒ Ⓓ	
14 Ⓐ Ⓑ Ⓒ Ⓓ	29 Ⓐ Ⓑ Ⓒ Ⓓ	44 Ⓐ Ⓑ Ⓒ Ⓓ	
15 Ⓐ Ⓑ Ⓒ Ⓓ	30 Ⓐ Ⓑ Ⓒ Ⓓ	45 Ⓐ Ⓑ Ⓒ Ⓓ	

AP U.S. HISTORY
PRACTICE EXAM 1

Section I

Time: 95 minutes

Part A (Multiple Choice)

Part A recommended time: 55 minutes

Directions: Each of the following questions refers to a historical source. These questions will test your knowledge about the historical source and require you to make use of your historical analytical skills and your familiarity with historical themes. For each question select the *best* response and fill in the corresponding oval on your answer sheet.

Questions 1–4 refer to the following quotation.

At a meeting of working girls held at Hull House during a strike in a large shoe factory, the discussions made it clear that the strikers who had been most easily frightened, and therefore the first to capitulate, were naturally those girls who were paying board and were afraid of being put out if they fell too far behind. After a recital of a case of peculiar hardship one of them exclaimed: "Wouldn't it be fine if we had a boarding club of our own, and then we could stand behind each other in a time like this?" After that events moved quickly. We ... discussed all the difficulties and fascinations of such an undertaking, and on the first of May, 1891, two comfortable apartments near Hull House were rented and furnished. The Settlement was responsible for the furniture and paid the first month's rent, but beyond that the members managed the club themselves. ... At the end of the third year the club occupied all of the six apartments which the original building contained, and numbered fifty members.

—Jane Addams, *Twenty Years at Hull House*, 1912

1. Which of the following *best* reflects the perspective of Jane Addams in the passage above?
   A. Poor people need the leadership of reformers like herself.
   B. Poor people need support in helping themselves.
   C. Poor people don't need outside help.
   D. Poor people don't deserve help.

2. Settlement houses like Hull House expressed a desire of reformers to do which of the following?
   A. Convert immigrants to Christianity
   B. Prevent political radicalism
   C. Provide cheap labor for industry
   D. Improve conditions in urban neighborhoods

3. A settlement house worker was most likely to be motivated by which of the following?
   A. The Social Gospel
   B. Social Darwinism
   C. Communism
   D. The support of an urban political machine

4. The perspective of the passage above would most directly support which of the following political goals?
   A. Women's suffrage
   B. Trust-busting
   C. Greater rights for unions
   D. Weakening political machines

Questions 5–8 refer to the following image.

Advertisement, Charleston, South Carolina, 1780s

5. Which of the following *best* reflects the perspective of the above image?
   A. Slaves represent a public health threat.
   B. The importation of slaves is a legitimate enterprise.
   C. The importation of slaves needs to be halted.
   D. Smallpox is a major danger to Charleston.

6. During the 1780s, which of the following was the most widespread crop cultivated by slaves in North America?
   A. Wheat
   B. Sugar
   C. Tobacco
   D. Cotton

7. Following the American Revolution, many Founding Fathers believed which of the following?
   A. Slavery would gradually disappear in the United States.
   B. The freeing of slaves should be outlawed.
   C. Slavery would be the foundation of the American economy.
   D. Freed slaves deserved government reparations for their suffering.

8. Which of the following was a reference to slavery in the Constitution?
   A. The banning of slavery in the Northwest Territory.
   B. Slavery was outlawed above the Mason-Dixon Line.
   C. Slavery could not be outlawed.
   D. No Federal law could ban the importation of slaves for 20 years.

Questions 9–12 refer to the following quotation.

Those who came before us made certain that this country rode the first waves of the industrial revolutions, the first waves of modern invention, and the first wave of nuclear power, and this generation does not intend to flounder in the backwash of the coming age of space. We mean to be a part of it—we mean to lead it. For the eyes of the world now look into space, to the moon, and the planets beyond, and we have vowed that we shall not see it governed by a hostile flag of conquest, but by a banner of freedom and peace. We have vowed that we shall not see space filled with weapons of mass destruction, but with instruments of knowledge and understanding. … We choose to go to the moon. We choose to go to the moon in this decade and do the other things, not because they are easy, but because they are hard, because that goal will serve to organize and measure the best of our energies and skills, because that challenge is one that we are willing to accept, one we are unwilling to postpone, and one which we intend to win, and the others, too.

—John F. Kennedy, September 12, 1962

9. John F. Kennedy in this passage is urging his fellow Americans to emulate which of the following?
   A. The pioneers
   B. Progressive reformers
   C. Captains of industry
   D. The Green Berets

10. Kennedy's statement *best* reflects which of the following?
    A. American unease in a time of troubles
    B. American confidence in a time of prosperity
    C. A liberal concern for social justice
    D. A conservative fear of big government

11. Kennedy's speech can *best* be compared to which of the following?
    A. Dwight Eisenhower's speech on the "military-industrial complex"
    B. George Washington's Farewell Address
    C. Abraham Lincoln's Gettysburg Address
    D. Franklin D. Roosevelt's "Arsenal of Democracy" speech

12. Kennedy's speech most directly led to which of the following?
    A. The Vietnam War
    B. The Mutually Assured Destruction (MAD) nuclear strategy
    C. The Apollo space program
    D. The Great Society social programs

Questions 13–16 refer to the following quotation.

I appeal to any white man to say, if ever he entered Logan's cabin hungry, and he gave him not meat: if ever he came cold and naked, and he clothed him not? During the course of the last long and bloody war, Logan remained idle in his cabin, an advocate for peace. Such was my love for the whites, that my countrymen pointed as they passed, and said, "Logan is the friend of the white man." I had even thought to have lived with you but for the injuries of one man. Colonel Cresap, the last spring, in cold blood and unprovoked; murdered all the relations of Logan, not even sparing my women and children. There runs not a drop of my blood in the veins of any living creature. This called on me for revenge. I have sought it: I have killed many; I have fully glutted my vengeance. For my country, I rejoice at the beams of peace. But do not harbor a thought that mine is the joy of fear. Logan never felt fear. He will not turn on his heel to save his life. Who is there to mourn for Logan? Not one.

—Address attributed to Logan, an Indian leader, 1774

13. Which of the following *best* expresses the perspective of Logan in the passage above?
    A. Logan believes the expansion of British settlements must be stopped.
    B. Logan laments the loss of his family.
    C. Logan opposes a new peace treaty.
    D. Logan believes that Indians need to find strength in unity.

14. Which of the following most directly expresses why Logan's Address became very popular in the early United States?
    A. Many Americans believed that the Indians had been treated badly.
    B. Many Americans believed that the only good Indian was a dead Indian.
    C. Many Americans believed that Indians were a noble people who were disappearing.
    D. Many Americans believed that Indians should abandon their way of life.

15. Which of the following in later years would be most likely to see themselves in Logan's position?
    A. An opponent of big government in the 1930s
    B. An opponent of consumerism in the 1950s
    C. A supporter of liberalism in the 1960s
    D. A supporter of feminism in the 1970s

16. A sympathetic reader of Logan's Address in the early years of the United States would be most likely to support which of the following Indian policies?
    A. Exterminating all Indians
    B. Respecting Indian territory and sovereignty
    C. Encouraging Indians to migrate to Canada and Mexico
    D. Building reservations and encouraging Indians to change their ways

Questions 17–20 refer to the following cartoon.

BORN TO COMMAND.

OF VETO MEMORY.

HAD I BEEN CONSULTED.

KING ANDREW THE FIRST.

Political cartoon, 1832

17. Which of the following groups would be most likely to support the perspective of the cartoon?
    A. Democrat supporters of Andrew Jackson
    B. Whig opponents of Andrew Jackson
    C. Know-Nothing opponents of immigration
    D. Anti-Masonic opponents of special privilege

18. The cartoon most likely refers to which of the following policies of Andrew Jackson?
    A. The "war" against the Bank of the United States
    B. Opposition to nullification threats in South Carolina
    C. Indian removal
    D. Support for the spoils system

19. Though a supporter of "strict construction" of the Constitution, Jackson was notable for which of the following?
    A. Weakening the presidency
    B. Spending on internal improvements
    C. Strengthening the presidency
    D. Weakening the party system

20. Andrew Jackson saw himself as a champion of which of the following continuities in United States history?
    A. The struggle for civil rights for all
    B. Government assistance for the underprivileged
    C. The cooperation of government and big business
    D. The democratization of American life

Questions 21–24 refer to the following quotation.

The 1980s have been born in turmoil, strife, and change. This is a time of challenge to our interests and our values and it's a time that tests our wisdom and skills.

At this time in Iran, 50 Americans are still held captive, innocent victims of terrorism and anarchy. Also at this moment, massive Soviet troops are attempting to subjugate the fiercely independent and deeply religious people of Afghanistan. These two acts—one of international terrorism and one of military aggression—present a serious challenge to the United States of America and indeed to all the nations of the world. Together we will meet these threats to peace. . . .

Three basic developments have helped to shape our challenges: the steady growth and increased projection of Soviet military power beyond its own borders; the overwhelming dependence of the Western democracies on oil supplies from the Middle East; and the press of social and religious and economic and political change in the many nations of the developing world, exemplified by the revolution in Iran.

Each of these factors is important in its own right. Each interacts with the others. All must be faced together, squarely and courageously. We will face these challenges, and we will meet them with the best that is in us. And we will not fail.

—Jimmy Carter, State of the Union Address, January 23, 1980

21. Which of the following has some of its roots in the conditions discussed by Jimmy Carter in this passage?
    A. The War on Terror
    B. High unemployment
    C. Tensions with China
    D. High budget deficits

22. The problems that Carter faced in 1980 can *best* be compared to those of which of the following?
    A. Abraham Lincoln in the 1860s
    B. Theodore Roosevelt in the 1900s
    C. Warren Harding in the 1920s
    D. Franklin D. Roosevelt in the 1930s

23. The situation Carter described led most directly to which of the following?
    A. The creation of the North Atlantic Treaty Organization (NATO)
    B. Carter's defeat in the next presidential election
    C. An American invasion in the Middle East
    D. Carter's victory in the next presidential election

24. Which of the following *best* expresses Carter's approach to foreign policy in the passage above?
    A. Isolationism
    B. Appeasement
    C. Containment
    D. A call for war

Questions 25–28 refer to the following advertisement.

Ford advertisement, 1952
Used with permission of Ford Motor company.

25. Which of the following *best* expresses the message of the advertisement?
    A. Ford cars are for the well-off
    B. Ford cars are great work vehicles
    C. Ford cars are for the whole family
    D. Ford cars are for the lower classes

26. The advertisement most directly reflects which of the following?
    A. The growing prosperity and leisure of Americans in the 1950s
    B. The materialistic excesses of the rich in the 1950s
    C. A push for social conformity in the 1950s
    D. The recreational limits imposed by a poor economy in the 1950s

27. The American embrace of the automobile in the twentieth century most directly reflects which continuity in U.S. history?
    A. A desire for social justice
    B. A desire for economic equality
    C. A desire for higher social status
    D. A desire for more personal freedom

28. In the 1950s the widespread availability of the automobile most directly helped make possible which of the following?
    A. The rise of international corporations
    B. The rapid growth of suburbs
    C. The prevalence of stay-at-home moms
    D. The baby boom generation

Questions 29–32 refer to the following quotation.

Let us not, I beseech you sir, deceive ourselves. Sir, we have done everything that could be done, to avert the storm which is now coming on. We have petitioned; we have remonstrated; we have supplicated; we have prostrated ourselves before the throne, and have implored its interposition to arrest the tyrannical hands of the ministry and Parliament. Our petitions have been slighted; our remonstrances have produced additional violence and insult; our supplications have been disregarded; and we have been spurned, with contempt, from the foot of the throne. In vain, after these things, may we indulge the fond hope of peace and reconciliation. There is no longer any room for hope. ... It is in vain, sir, to extenuate the matter. Gentlemen may cry, Peace, Peace, but there is no peace. The war is actually begun! The next gale that sweeps from the north will bring to our ears the clash of resounding arms! Our brethren are already in the field! Why stand we here idle? What is it that gentlemen wish? What would they have? Is life so dear, or peace so sweet, as to be purchased at the price of chains and slavery? Forbid it, Almighty God! I know not what course others may take; but as for me, give me liberty or give me death!

—Patrick Henry, March 23, 1775

29. The sentiments expressed by Patrick Henry led most directly to which of the following?
    A. The Declaration of Independence
    B. The Albany Plan
    C. The Boston Tea Party
    D. The Constitution of the United States

30. In this passage, Henry expresses an abiding American concern about which of the following?
    A. No entangling alliances with foreign countries
    B. The dangers of standing armies
    C. Self-government
    D. The separation of church and state

31. Which of the following nineteenth-century groups most directly saw themselves as following in the tradition of Patrick Henry?
    A. Supporters of Manifest Destiny
    B. Members of the Republican Party
    C. Abolitionists
    D. Southern secessionists

32. The "storm" that Henry refers to was most directly the result of which of the following?
    A. American efforts to trade with Spain and France
    B. British efforts to shrink a budget deficit after the French and Indian War
    C. British unwillingness to fight Indian tribes on the frontier
    D. British impressments of American sailors and interference with American trade

Questions 33–36 refer to the following quotation.

Of all the band of adventurous cavaliers, whom Spain, in the sixteenth century, sent forth on the career of discovery and conquest, there was none more deeply filled with the spirit of romantic enterprise than Hernando Cortes. Dangers and difficulties, instead of deterring, seemed to have a charm in his eyes. ... He conceived, at the first moment of his landing in Mexico, the design of its conquest. When he saw the strength of its civilization, he was not turned from his purpose. ... This spirit of knight-errantry might lead us to undervalue his talents as a general, and to regard him merely in the light of a lucky adventurer. But this would be doing him injustice; for Cortes was certainly a great general, if that man be one, who performs great achievements with the resources which his own genius has created. There is probably no instance in history, where so vast an enterprise has been achieved by means apparently so inadequate. ... He brought together the most miscellaneous collection of mercenaries who ever fought under one standard: adventurers from Cuba and the Isles, craving for gold; hidalgos, who came from the old country to win laurels; ... wild tribes of the natives from all parts of the country, who had been sworn enemies from their cradles, and who had met only to cut one another's throats, and to procure victims for sacrifice; men, in short, differing in race, in language, and in interests, with scarcely anything in common among them. Yet this motley congregation was assembled in one camp, compelled to bend to the will of one man, to consort together in harmony, to breathe, as it were, one spirit, and to move on a common principle of action!

—William Hickling Prescott, *History of the Conquest of Mexico*, 1843

33. Given the perspective of the passage above, William Hickling Prescott believed which of the following about the conquest of the Aztec Empire?
    A. The actions of Hernando Cortes were irrational.
    B. The conquest of Mexico was a racist atrocity.
    C. Cortes was chiefly motivated by a desire for wealth.
    D. The Aztec Empire had to give way to the superior civilization of Spain.

34. As Prescott makes clear in the passage above, an important reason for Cortes's military success was which of the following?
    A. The advantage of superior numbers
    B. The superior military skill of mercenaries
    C. Taking advantage of divisions among the Indians
    D. Effective use of European artillery

35. The Spanish in America were interested in which of the following?
    A. Escaping oppression at home
    B. Expanding territories under Spanish control
    C. Seeking religious freedom for themselves
    D. Creating independent principalities for themselves

36. Prescott's interpretation of the conquest of Mexico resembles which contemporary nineteenth-century American political movement?
    A. Support for Manifest Destiny
    B. Support for Southern secessionism
    C. Support for abolitionism
    D. Support for Know-Nothingism

Questions 37–40 refer to the following quotation.

I come not to urge personal claims, nor to seek individual benefits; I appear as the advocate of those who cannot plead their own cause; I come as the friend of those who are deserted, oppressed, and desolate. In the Providence of God, I am the voice of the maniac whose piercing cries from the dreary dungeons of your jails penetrate not your Halls of Legislation. I am the Hope of the poor crazed beings who pine in the cells, and stalls, and cages, and waste rooms of your poor-houses. I am the Revelation of hundreds of wailing, suffering creatures, hidden in your private dwellings, and in pens and cabins—shut out, cut off from all healing influences, from all mind-restoring cares. . . . Could their melancholy histories be spread before you as revealed to my grieved spirit during the last three months, how promptly, how earnestly would you search out the most approved means of relief; how trifling, how insignificant, by comparison, would appear the sacrifices you are asked to make; how would a few dimes and dollars, gathered from each citizen, diminish in value as a possession, compared with the certain benefits and vast good to be secured for the suffering insane . . . by the consecration and application of a sufficient fund to the construction of a suitable hospital. . . .

—Dorothea Dix, Memorial Soliciting a State Hospital for the Protection and Cure of the Insane,
Submitted to the General Assembly of North Carolina, November 1848

37. Which of the following best reflects the perspective of Dorothea Dix in the passage above?
A. The care of the mentally ill is a state concern.
B. The mentally ill are best left to the care of their families.
C. The federal government should regulate the treatment of the mentally ill.
D. More democracy will help the mentally ill.

38. Which of the following was a popular reform movement of the 1840s?
A. The free coinage of silver
B. Regulation of big business
C. The gay rights movement
D. The temperance movement

39. A key motivating factor for many reformers of the 1840s was
A. Marxism.
B. Evangelical Christianity.
C. distrust of big government.
D. laissez-faire economics.

40. Dorothea Dix can best be compared to whom?
A. Abigail Adams
B. Clara Barton
C. Shirley Temple
D. Hillary Clinton

Questions 41–44 refer to the following quotation.

Now, we have organized a society, and we call it "Share Our Wealth Society," a society with the motto "Every Man a King." . . .

We propose to limit the wealth of big men in the country. There is an average of $15,000 in wealth to every family in America. That is right here today.

We do not propose to divide it up equally. We do not propose a division of wealth, but we do propose to limit poverty that we will allow to be inflicted on any man's family. We will not say we are going to try to guarantee any equality . . . but we do say that one third of the average is low enough for any one family to hold, that there should be a guarantee of a family wealth of around $5,000; enough for a home, an automobile, a radio, and the ordinary conveniences, and the opportunity to educate their children. . . .

We will have to limit fortunes. Our present plan is that we will allow no man to own more than $50,000,000. We think that with that limit we will be able to carry out the balance of the program.

—Senator Huey P. Long of Louisiana, Radio Address, February 23, 1934

41. Senator Huey P. Long's "Share the Wealth Society" was a political program intended to
A. demonstrate Senator Long's commitment to fighting communism.
B. return the United States to the economic ideas of the late nineteenth century.
C. persuade voters that Senator Long had a plan to combat the Great Depression.
D. showcase Senator Long's understanding of the constitutional ideas of the Founding Fathers.

42. Senator Long ran a political machine that made him the virtual dictator of Louisiana. As a political boss, he can best be compared to whom?
A. George Washington
B. Theodore Roosevelt
C. William M. Tweed
D. Barack Obama

43. Senator Long's "Share the Wealth Society" attracted many followers in 1934 because
A. the New Deal had not ended the Great Depression.
B. a flourishing economy and a baby boom had led people to desire greater incomes.
C. the Second World War encouraged an egalitarian ethos.
D. Socialistic ideas were becoming popular in the United States.

44. President Franklin D. Roosevelt responded to political challenges like that of Senator Long by doing which of the following?
A. Announcing that he would not run for re-election
B. Launching the Second New Deal, a series of legislative acts including Social Security
C. Diverting people's attention by allowing the Japanese to bomb Pearl Harbor
D. Urging Congress to cut taxes and deregulate the economy

Questions 45–48 refer to the following quotation.

All this while the Indians came skulking about them, and would sometimes show themselves aloof off, but when any approached near them, they would run away; and once they stole away their tools where they had been at work and were gone to dinner. But about the 16th of March, a certain Indian came boldly amongst them and spoke to them in broken English, which they could well understand but marveled at it. At length they understood by discourse with him, that he was not of these parts, but belonged to the eastern parts where some English ships came to fish, with whom he was acquainted and could name sundry of them by their names, amongst whom he had got his language. He became profitable to them in acquainting them with many things concerning the state of the country in the east parts where he lived, which was afterwards profitable unto them; as also of the people here, of their names, number and strength, of their situation and distance from the place, and who was chief amongst them. His name was Samoset. He told them also of another Indian whose name was Squanto, a native of this place, who had been in England and could speak better English than himself.

—William Bradford, *History of Plymouth Plantation*

45. Which of the following best expresses the perspective of William Bradford in the passage above?
A. The only good Indian is a dead Indian.
B. The native peoples of America need to be converted to Christianity.
C. Native Americans need to be incorporated into their new colony.
D. Surprise that Native Americans could learn English and serve as cultural intermediaries.

46. The Pilgrims traveled to America and settled at Plymouth because
A. they were hoping to escape crushing debts in England.
B. they hoped to find gold or establish a lucrative trade in furs.
C. they were religious Separatists looking for a place to freely practice their faith.
D. they were ordered to establish an outpost to watch the French in Canada.

47. As the passage above makes clear, the Pilgrims were not the only Europeans in what would become Massachusetts during the 1620s. The area was already becoming important because of its
A. fishing.
B. farming.
C. mining.
D. shipbuilding.

48. Samoset and Squanto can most directly be compared to whom?
A. Tecumseh
B. Crazy Horse
C. Sacagawea
D. Geronimo

Questions 49–52 refer to the following poster.

—Poster advertising Buffalo Bill Cody's Wild West Show

49. William "Buffalo Bill" Cody won his nickname because of his skills as a frontier scout and buffalo hunter. The disappearance of the great buffalo herds led to which of the following?
A. The Dust Bowl
B. Global warming
C. Dietary changes in American cities
D. The destruction of the Plains Indians' way of life

50. The economic significance of the cowboys that Cody celebrated in his show was
A. driving herds of cattle to railroad depots where they were shipped to meatpackers in the east.
B. clearing land for farmers by driving Indian tribes onto reservations.
C. founding new towns in the west.
D. opening up rich minefields to fuel growing industries.

51. Buffalo Bill's Wild West Show celebrated a growing nostalgia for which of the following?
A. The horses that were being replaced by automobiles
B. The rapidly disappearing frontier
C. America's wilderness uncorrupted by development
D. The loss of America's role as a great power in the world

52. Buffalo Bill's Wild West Show was a popular example of which of the following?
A. The populist critique of Wall Street and big business
B. New forms of entertainment for the urban masses
C. The concern about Native Americans that led to the Dawes Severalty Act in 1887
D. A growing demand for classical drama and the fine arts

Questions 53–55 refer to the following quotation.

Clearly, no longer can a dictator count on East–West confrontation to stymie concerted United Nations action against aggression. A new partnership of nations has begun. And we stand today at a unique and extraordinary moment. The crisis in the Persian Gulf, as grave as it is, also offers a rare opportunity to move toward an historic period of cooperation. Out of these troubled times, our fifth objective—a new world order—can emerge; a new era, freer from the threat of terror, stronger in the pursuit of justice, and more secure in the quest for peace. An era in which the nations of the world, east and west, north and south, can prosper and live in harmony.

—President George Herbert Walker Bush, Speech to a Joint Session of Congress, September 11, 1990

53. President George Herbert Walker Bush's vision of a "new world order" was most directly made possible by
A. American economic prosperity.
B. President Ronald Reagan's Strategic Defense Initiative.
C. the Iranian Hostage Crisis.
D. the end of the Cold War.

54. President Bush was responding to which of the following?
A. Iraqi dictator Saddam Hussein's conquest of Kuwait
B. The fall of the Berlin Wall
C. Terror attacks by Al-Qaeda
D. The break-up of Yugoslavia and the start of the Bosnian War

55. President Bush's "new world order" most directly resembles which of the following?
A. The Monroe Doctrine
B. Theodore Roosevelt's "Big Stick"
C. Woodrow Wilson's Fourteen Points
D. Containment policy toward the Soviet Union

Go on to Part B. ➜

Part B (Short Answer)

Part B recommended time: 40 minutes

Directions: Answer three questions. You must answer questions 1 and 2, and you can choose to answer either 3 or 4. Carefully read and follow the directions for each question. Some will refer to historical sources. These questions will require you to make use of your historical analytical skills and your familiarity with historical themes. These questions do *not* require you to develop a thesis in your responses.

Question 1 is based on the following passage:

Each side had advantages. But neither section understood the other. If the South had known that secession must result in war and that the foe would be a united North, it is doubtful if she would have proceeded to the last extremity. It is still more doubtful if the North would have fought, had she known that she must contend with a united Southern people. ... But now the North confronted five and a half million earnest and brave people, supported by three and a half million servants, who grew the food and took care of the women and children at home while the men fought in the field. The North was contending for the Union on the theory that a strong and unscrupulous minority had overridden the majority of Southerners who had no desire for secession, loathed the idea of civil war, and if protected and encouraged, would make themselves felt in a movement looking towards allegiance to the national government. Lincoln comprehended the sentiment of the North and he never gave public expression to any opinion that he did not sincerely hold. In his Fourth of July message to the special session of Congress he said: "It may well be questioned whether there is today a majority of the legally qualified voters of any State, except perhaps South Carolina, in favor of disunion. There is much reason to believe that the Union men are the majority in many, if not every other one, of the so-called seceded states."

—James Ford Rhodes, *History of the Civil War*, 1917

1. Using the excerpt, answer A, B, and C.
   A. Briefly explain Rhodes's perspective on Southern and Northern attitudes at the beginning of the Civil War.
   B. Briefly explain ONE historical event or development that supports Rhodes's argument.
   C. Briefly explain ONE historical event or development that illustrates an unwillingness on the part of many Americans to embrace war in 1861.

Question 2 is based on the following passages:

The problem lay buried, unspoken for many years in the minds of American women. It was a strange stirring, a sense of dissatisfaction, a yearning that women suffered in the middle of the twentieth century in the United States. Each suburban wife struggled with it alone. As she made the beds, shopped for groceries, matched slipcover material, ate peanut butter sandwiches with her children, chauffeured Cub Scouts and Brownies, lay beside her husband at night—she was afraid to ask even of herself the silent question—'Is this all?'

—Betty Friedan

It is my belief, based on working with this movement for quite a number of years, that the movement is having an adverse effect on family life, that it is a major cause of divorce today, and that it is highly detrimental to our country and to our families. … Motherhood must be a self-sacrificing role. The mother must be able to subordinate her self-fulfillment and her desire for a career to the well being of her children so she can answer her child's call any hour of the day or night. This is what marriage and motherhood are all about.

—Phyllis Schlafly

2. Using the excerpts, answer A, B, and C.
   A. Briefly explain ONE example of a political or social position supported by Betty Friedan.
   B. Briefly explain ONE example of a political or social position supported by Phyllis Schlafly.
   C. Briefly explain ONE example of a way one of these perspectives influenced American politics in the 1960s and 1970s.

3. Answer A, B, and C.
   A. Briefly explain how ONE of the following reflected American expansionism.
      The French and Indian War
      The Louisiana Purchase
      The Mexican War
   B. Briefly explain how a SECOND of these options reflected American expansionism.
   C. Briefly explain the perspective of someone opposed to ONE of the examples that you chose.

4. Answer A, B, and C.
   A. Briefly explain how ONE of the following reflected American concerns about internal subversion.
      Haymarket Square Riot
      First Red Scare
      Second Red Scare
   B. Briefly explain how a SECOND of these options reflected American concerns about internal subversion.
   C. Briefly explain ONE example of a way one of these events affected American politics.

STOP. End of Section I.

Section II

Time: 100 minutes

Part A (Document-Based Question)

Part A recommended time: 60 minutes

Directions: Use the documents to answer the question. You may want to spend up to 15 minutes outlining your response and 40 minutes writing the essay that answers the question.

Be sure to provide a thesis that addresses all elements of the question.

Be sure to support your argument with evidence from at least six of the seven documents.

Be sure to support your argument by recognizing and explaining historical complexity, connecting different kinds of historical evidence in a coherent way.

Be sure to base your analysis of no less than four documents on at least one of the following: the point of view of the author, the purpose of the author, the intended audience of the document, the historical context of the document.

Be sure to support your argument by analyzing historical evidence that comes from outside the documents.

Be sure to connect historical evidence supporting your argument to broader historical events or processes.

Be sure to synthesize all the tasks above into a persuasive history essay.

1. Analyze the effects of American foreign policy in Latin America during the period 1899 to 1917.

Document A
Source: Platt Amendment, May 22, 1903

> *Article III. The Government of Cuba consents that the United States may exercise the right to intervene for the preservation of Cuban independence, the maintenance of a government adequate for the protection of life property, and individual liberty, and for discharging the obligations with respect to Cuba imposed by the Treaty of Paris on the United States, now to be assumed and undertaken by the Government of Cuba.*

Document B
Source: Hay-Bunau-Varilla Treaty, November 18, 1903

> *The Republic of Panama grants to the United States in perpetuity, the use, occupation and control of a zone of land and land under water for the construction . . . of said canal. . . . The Republic of Panama further grants to the United States in perpetuity, the use, occupation and control of any other lands and waters outside the zone . . . which may be necessary and convenient for the construction . . . and protection of the said Canal.*

Document C
Source: Theodore Roosevelt, Annual Message to Congress, December 6, 1904

> *If a nation shows that it knows how to act with reasonable efficiency and decency in social and political matters, if it keeps order and pays its obligations, it need fear no interference from the United States. Chronic wrongdoing, or an impotence which results in a general loosening of the ties of civilized society, may . . . ultimately require intervention by some civilized nation, and in the Western Hemisphere the adherence of the United States to the Monroe Doctrine may lead the United States, . . . in flagrant cases of such wrongdoing or impotence, to exercise an international police power.*

Document D

Source: W. A. Rogers, "The Full Dinner Pail," *Harper's Weekly,* April 13, 1907; courtesy of Theodore-Roosevelt.com.

Document E

Source: William Howard Taft, Fourth Annual Message to Congress, December 3, 1912

The diplomacy of the present administration has sought to respond to modern ideas of commercial intercourse. This policy has been characterized by substituting dollars for bullets. . . . It is an effort frankly directed to the increase of American trade upon the axiomatic principle that the government of the United States shall extend all proper support to every legitimate and beneficial American enterprise abroad.

Document F

Source: Erving Winslow, "Aggression in South America," excerpt from Report of the Thirteenth Annual Meeting of the Anti-Imperialist League, 1912

It is proposed that in the Honduras and Nicaragua . . . the United States government should be authorized to secure the collection and disbursement of the revenue in the interest of American capitalists who contemplate making loans to those countries. This involves serious risk of complications which may lead to further interferences and ultimate control.

The delicacy of these and other foreign relations of the United States is such as should put our citizens upon their guard and confirm their determination to treat with justice all their neighbors and to recognize generally their independent right to govern (or misgovern) their own countries.

Document G

Source: Woodrow Wilson, Address to Congress, April 20, 1914

> *A series of incidents have recently occurred which cannot but create the impression that the representatives of General Huerta were willing to go out of their way to show disregard for the dignity and rights of this government, . . . making free to show in many ways their irritation and contempt.*
>
> *I, therefore, come to ask your approval that I should use the armed forces of the United States in such ways . . . as may be necessary to obtain from General Huerta and his adherents the fullest recognition of the rights and dignity of the United States, even amidst the distressing conditions now unhappily obtaining in Mexico.*

Go on to Part B. ➜

Part B (Long Essay)

Part B recommended time: 40 minutes

Directions: Answer *one* of the following questions. State a thesis that addresses all aspects of the question. This thesis of one or more sentences must be in the introduction or conclusion.

Make use of your historical analytical skills and familiarity with historical themes as you develop your answer.

Support your thesis and substantiate your essay by citing examples of historical evidence.

Relate the topic of the question to broader historical trends or events.

2. Evaluate the extent to which differing economies shaped differing social structures in the English colonies in North America.

3. Evaluate the extent to which late nineteenth century urbanization affected politics, immigration, and popular culture.

4. Evaluate the extent to which mobilization for total war during World War I and World War II influenced American political and social development in the twentieth century.

STOP. End of Section II.

ANSWERS TO PRACTICE EXAM 1

Multiple Choice

1. B	15. A	29. A	43. A
2. D	16. D	30. C	44. B
3. A	17. B	31. D	45. D
4. C	18. A	32. B	46. C
5. B	19. C	33. D	47. A
6. C	20. D	34. C	48. C
7. A	21. A	35. B	49. D
8. D	22. D	36. A	50. A
9. A	23. B	37. A	51. B
10. B	24. C	38. D	52. B
11. D	25. C	39. B	53. D
12. C	26. A	40. B	54. A
13. B	27. D	41. C	55. C
14. C	28. B	42. C	

Explanations for the Multiple-Choice Questions

1. **B.** Poor people need support in helping themselves *best* reflects the perspective of Jane Addams in the passage. Jane Addams was a pioneering social worker who became famous for her work with the poor. She was a leader in the settlement house movement, which established social centers in disadvantaged urban neighborhoods. Addams founded Hull House in Chicago.

2. **D.** Settlement houses like Hull House expressed a desire of reformers to improve conditions in urban neighborhoods. Settlement houses provided a variety of social services such as childcare for working mothers and English language classes. Settlement house workers also helped the people in their neighborhoods lobby government for better living conditions and city services.

3. **A.** A settlement house worker was most likely to be motivated by the Social Gospel. The Social Gospel was a liberal strain of American Protestantism that called on the church to battle injustices in society and to work for social betterment as a way of saving souls.

4. **C.** The perspective of the passage would most directly support greater rights for unions. In the passage, Jane Addams helps young women workers find secure communal housing so they can safely strike for better working conditions. Settlement house workers often helped immigrants and the poor organize to protect their rights in their working places and elsewhere.

5. **B.** The image reflects the perspective that the importation of slaves is a legitimate enterprise. The image is a notice for a slave auction in Charleston, South Carolina, in the 1780s. Slavery was believed to be crucial to South Carolina's plantation economy.

6. **C.** During the 1780s, the most widespread crop cultivated by slaves in North America was tobacco. Cotton did not become the chief cash crop in the South until after Eli Whitney's invention of the cotton gin in the 1790s.

7. **A.** Following the American Revolution, many Founding Fathers believed that slavery would gradually disappear in the United States. Economically, tobacco was losing some of its importance as new sources appeared elsewhere in the world. Also the human rights ideals of the Revolution seemed to be at odds with the institution of slavery. The 1787 Northwest Ordinance banned slavery in the Northwest Territory. The Constitution, while recognizing the existence of slavery for representation purposes, ended the importation of slaves from Africa after 1807. What the Founding Fathers did not anticipate was the cotton gin, the cotton boom, and the renewed economic importance of slavery.

8. **D.** The Federal government could not ban the importation of slaves for 20 years, or until 1808. In 1807, Congress passed legislation that made the importation of slaves illegal from January 1, 1808. This was part of the growing consensus in the years after the Revolution that slavery was a weakening institution, for both economic and ideological reasons. Slavery was gradually outlawed in the Northern states. George Washington and others freed their slaves upon their deaths. Then the invention of the cotton gin made slavery highly profitable again in the South.

9. **A.** President John F. Kennedy in this passage is urging his fellow Americans to emulate the pioneers. Kennedy ran for the presidency on a program that he termed the New Frontier. He wanted Americans to emulate their pioneer forebears and surmount a number of challenges, from domestic problems to the cold war. Taking the lead in the space race with the Soviets and landing the first men on the moon would be a dramatic way of demonstrating this pioneering spirit.

10. **B.** Kennedy's statement best reflects American confidence in a time of prosperity. The early 1960s were a time of prosperity that had endured since the end of World War II. Kennedy and his successor, Lyndon B. Johnson, believed that the United States could achieve any task it set out to accomplish, whether it was landing a man on the moon, ending poverty in the United States, or winning a war in Vietnam.

11. **D.** Kennedy's speech can *best* be compared to Franklin D. Roosevelt's "Arsenal of Democracy" speech. In the "Arsenal of Democracy" speech, Roosevelt also set a challenge for the American people, producing weapons and supplies for the nations resisting Axis aggression during World War II.

12. **C.** Kennedy's speech most directly led to the Apollo space program. The Apollo space missions focused on landing men on the moon. *Apollo 8* circled the moon in December 1968. The *Apollo 11* mission set a lunar module down on the moon. Neil Armstrong and Edwin "Buzz" Aldrin became the first and second men to walk on the moon.

13. **B.** In the passage, Logan laments the loss of his family. Logan was an Indian war chief. After members of his family were murdered by settlers, Logan led a series of retaliatory raids. This began Lord Dunmore's War in 1774, named after the Governor of Virginia. Logan refused to attend the talks that led to a peace treaty but sent the message in the passage instead.

14. **C.** Logan's Address became very popular in the early United States because many Americans believed that Indians were a noble people that were disappearing. As Indians became perceived as a minor and fading threat, many Americans expressed sympathy for their plight. They were sometimes portrayed as "noble savages" free of the corruptions of society. A good example of this is the character of Uncas in James Fenimore Cooper's novel *The Last of the Mohicans* (1825).

15. **A.** In later years, an opponent of big government in the 1930s would be most likely to sympathize with Logan. Like Logan, an opponent of big government during the years of the New Deal and the rapid expansion of the welfare state would feel as if events were moving in the wrong direction.

16. **D.** A reader of Logan's Address in the early years of the United States would most likely support building reservations and encouraging Indians to change their ways. Thomas Jefferson believed that the only hope for Indians was for them to adopt American culture. Until they did so, he thought that they should be moved away from the settlements, giving them time to "civilize" themselves. The consensus of American policymakers during the nineteenth century was that the key to Indian survival was a combination of reservations and eventual assimilation into American society.

17. **B.** Whig opponents of Andrew Jackson would be most likely to support the perspective of the cartoon. The Whigs saw Jackson as an overbearing and tyrannical chief executive, most notably for his veto of the rechartering of the Bank of the United States. Hence, the portrayal of Jackson in the cartoon as "King Andrew."

18. **A.** The cartoon most likely refers to the "war" against the Bank of the United States. President Jackson believed that the privately run Bank of the United States had too much power over the nation's finances. He thought its power was undemocratic. When Henry Clay and Bank supporters passed a rechartering bill through Congress, Jackson vetoed it. He also pulled federal funds from the Bank of the United States, depositing the money in state banks that came to be known as "pet banks." These banks soon began issuing large amounts of paper money. Hoping to rein in inflation, Jackson issued the Specie Circular, requiring gold or silver coins in payment for public lands. This spurred a financial panic and depression in 1837.

19. **C.** Though a supporter of "strict construction" of the Constitution, Jackson was notable for strengthening the presidency. While philosophically a believer in limited government, temperamentally, Jackson could not resist vigorously using the powers of his office in instances as varied as his defiance of the Supreme Court over Indian removal or taking a strong stand against advocates of nullification in South Carolina. Jackson's veto of the recharter of the Bank of the United States because he thought this would be bad policy was unprecedented. Previous presidential vetoes had been based on the perceived unconstitutionality of bills. Jackson here expanded the range of presidential prerogative.

20. **D.** Andrew Jackson saw himself as the champion of the democratization of American life. Jackson portrayed himself as the representative of the common man. During the period of his political ascendency in the 1820s and 1830s most property qualifications for voting disappeared. The emergence of a vigorous two-party political system encouraged politicians to court and celebrate ordinary Americans.

Historians use the term "Jacksonian Democracy" to describe this new era.

21. **A.** The War on Terror has some of its roots in the conditions discussed by President Jimmy Carter in this passage. The difficulties with revolutionary Iran and the Iranian hostage crisis, as well as concerns about the free flow of Middle Eastern oil, spurred increased American involvement in the region. Resentment of this American role played a part in motivating the Al Qaeda attacks on September 11, 2001.

22. **D.** The problems that Carter faced in 1980 can *best* be compared to Franklin D. Roosevelt in the 1930s. Roosevelt also had to deal with great powers, such as Japan, Italy, and Germany launching wars of aggression, and the resulting international instability. Carter was responding to the Soviet Union's invasion of Afghanistan and the problems caused by the new revolutionary regime in Iran. Within a few months, Saddam Hussein's Iraq would start a long and bloody war with Iran.

23. **B.** The situation Carter described led most directly to his defeat in the next presidential election. Carter's inability to secure the release of the Americans held hostage in Iran and the perception that American foreign policy was ineffective contributed to his defeat by Ronald Reagan in the 1980 election.

24. **C.** Containment *best* expresses Carter's approach to foreign policy in the passage. The containment of the Soviet Union and the spread of communism had been a centerpiece of American foreign policy since the late 1940s. Carter's determination to confront the Soviet Union over the invasion of Afghanistan was consistent with the policy of containment.

25. **C.** Ford cars are for the whole family *best* expresses the message of the advertisement. The 1950s were a time of general prosperity. The baby boom was underway, and popular culture celebrated family togetherness. The Ford ad addresses this by showing a family vacationing in their new Ford convertible.

26. **A.** The advertisement most directly reflects the growing prosperity and leisure of Americans in the 1950s. The United States was enjoying a postwar economic boom. This prosperity and government programs such as the G.I. Bill facilitated the movement of many Americans to new levels of affluence. Family vacations such as that pictured in the advertisement became an attainable reality for millions of Americans.

27. **D.** The American embrace of the automobile in the twentieth century most directly reflects a desire for more personal freedom. From the beginning, Americans desired the easy and affordable mobility provided by automobiles. As early as 1929, there was one automobile for every five Americans, more cars than in all the rest of the world. By the 1950s, cars symbolized the prosperity and openness of American society.

28. **B.** In the 1950s, the widespread availability of the automobile most directly helped make possible the rapid growth of suburbs. The rapid spread of new roads, facilitated in part by the 1956 Interstate Highway Act, encouraged developers like the Levitt brothers to create extensive suburban housing developments outside cities. Suburbanites could enjoy the amenities of single family dwellings in attractive surroundings while using their automobiles to commute to work in the cities.

29. **A.** The sentiments expressed by Patrick Henry led most directly to the Declaration of Independence. Speaking in March 1775, shortly before the outbreak of the Revolutionary War in April, Henry pointed out the unwillingness of the British authorities to compromise with the American colonists. Once fighting began, the British continued to show little inclination to address American concerns. This led more and more Americans to contemplate independence. On June 7, 1776, Richard Henry Lee of Virginia submitted a resolution to the Second Continental Congress calling for independence.

30. **C.** In this passage, Henry expresses an abiding American concern for self-government. Unlike the Spanish and French colonies, the English colonies had been largely self-governing from the time of their founding. The Virginia House of Burgesses dated back to 1619. That meant that by the 1770s some of the American colonies had been governing themselves for close to 150 years. This tradition of self-governance led the American colonists to resent new British taxation after 1763

and to stand up for what they believed were their rights as Englishmen.

31. **D.** The nineteenth-century group of Americans that most directly saw themselves in the tradition of Patrick Henry were Southern secessionists. The secessionists of 1860–1861 saw themselves as people whose states' rights were being threatened by a federal government headed by a man that they regarded as a "radical" Republican. They saw their secession from the Union as equivalent to the American colonies withdrawing from the British Empire.

32. **B.** The "storm" that Henry refers to was most directly the result of British efforts to shrink a budget deficit after the French and Indian War. Faced with enormous debts after the expensive war with the French, the British government looked to the American colonies as a new revenue source, leading Parliament to pass a series of taxes on the Americans. The American colonists resented this "taxation without representation," provoking a series of political crises that ended with a war.

33. **D.** Given the perspective of the passage, William Hickling Prescott believed that the Aztec Empire had to give way to the superior civilization of Spain. Prescott, like most nineteenth-century Americans, was convinced that the European conquest of America was part of the upward march of human progress. He saw Hernando Cortes as a hero whose actions were justified by history.

34. **C.** As Prescott makes clear in the passage, an important reason for Cortes's military success was taking advantage of divisions among the Indians. Cortes never had enough Spanish troops to overthrow the Aztec Empire. He built a coalition with other Indian peoples who resented the rule of the Aztecs. This provided him with the manpower to achieve victory.

35. **B.** The Spanish in America were interested in expanding territories under Spanish control. This was a major goal of Cortes and other conquistadors. They were also anxious to spread the Christian religion and win riches for themselves. But whatever they conquered became part of the Spanish Empire, under the rule of the Spanish king.

36. **A.** Prescott's interpretation of the conquest of Mexico resembles the contemporary nineteenth-century support for Manifest Destiny. Just as Prescott believed that the Spanish conquest of Mexico represented human progress and demonstrated the superiority of European civilization, the supporters of Manifest Destiny argued that the inevitable spreading of American settlement to the Pacific Ocean and beyond was a measure of the glorious role that the United States would play in the future.

37. **A.** "The care of the mentally ill is a state concern" best reflects the perspective of Dorothea Dix. Before the early nineteenth century, the mentally ill were often treated with great cruelty by people who did not understand their affliction. Dorothea Dix argued persuasively for the humane treatment of the mentally ill. She convinced the legislators of several states to create new hospitals for the mentally ill.

38. **D.** The temperance movement was a popular reform movement of the 1840s. Heavy drinking was a serious problem in early-nineteenth-century America, sometimes aggravated by a lack of safe drinking water. The American Temperance Society was founded in 1826. Soon the push for temperance and the prohibition of the manufacture and sale of intoxicating liquor became widespread. Neal S. Dow became one of the most prominent leaders of the temperance movement. As the mayor of Portland, Maine, Dow sponsored the Maine Law of 1851, which established prohibition in the state.

39. **B.** A key motivating factor for many reformers of the 1840s was Evangelical Christianity. In the early nineteenth century, the Second Great Awakening stimulated a wave of religious enthusiasm in the United States. A "Benevolent Empire" of missionary and reform organizations was established by various Protestant denominations. Fueled by religious fervor, many reformers worked to create what they felt was a more godly and perfect society.

40. **B.** Dorothea Dix can best be compared to Clara Barton. Like Dix, Barton was a reformer who worked to help the suffering. After seeing the travails of wounded Union soldiers during the Civil War, Barton became a nurse. She later ran military hospitals and became famous as the "Angel of the Battlefields." After the war, Barton founded the American branch of the Red Cross.

41. **C.** Senator Huey P. Long's "Share the Wealth Society" was a political program intended to persuade voters that Senator Long had a plan to combat the Great Depression. Although initially a supporter of President Franklin D. Roosevelt, the ambitious Long broke with him and was laying the foundations of a presidential run of his own. He allied with other populist critics of Roosevelt such as Gerald L. K. Smith and Father Charles Coughlin. Long was assassinated by a Louisiana physician outraged by Long's policies in September 1935, a month after announcing that he was planning to run for the presidency.

42. **C.** As a political boss, Long can best be compared to William M. Tweed. Tweed was the leader of Tammany Hall, the Democratic political machine of New York City during the 1860s. While Tweed was the dominant figure in city politics, many millions of dollars were appropriated by his political cronies in bribes and graft.

43. **A.** Senator Long's "Share the Wealth Society" attracted many followers in 1934 because the New Deal had not ended the Great Depression. Although conditions had improved since the worst of the Depression in 1932 and 1933, unemployment remained high, and many families continued to suffer.

44. **B.** President Franklin D. Roosevelt responded to political challenges like that of Senator Long by launching the Second New Deal, a series of legislative acts including Social Security. The Second New Deal of 1935–1936 provided more support and benefits for ordinary Americans, while increasing taxes on the wealthy and heightening rhetorical attacks on big business. In addition to the Social Security Act of 1935, other important pieces of legislation enacted during this period included the National Labor Relations Act (the Wagner Act), which provided support to unions, and the Emergency Relief Appropriation Act of 1935, which created the Works Progress Administration (WPA), which provided work to unemployed people.

45. **D.** "Surprise that Native Americans could learn English and serve as cultural intermediaries" best expresses the perspective of William Bradford in the passage. Bradford and the Pilgrims did not have a lot of experience dealing with Native Americans. As the passage makes clear, most of their prior experience with the locals had highlighted incomprehension and distrust between the two peoples. Samoset and Squanto were very important in helping the Pilgrims adjust to the new land and get to know their neighbors.

46. **C.** The Pilgrims traveled to America and settled at Plymouth because they were religious Separatists looking for a place to freely practice their faith. As Separatists, the Pilgrims rejected the practices of the Church of England. They moved to Holland in 1608 hoping to find religious sanctuary. They were not persecuted there but feared that their children were "becoming Dutch." So, in 1620, the Pilgrims sailed to America on the *Mayflower*, hoping for a new beginning and a place where they could live the lives they desired.

47. **A.** The area where the Pilgrims settled was already growing important because of its fishing. European fishing off North America was a very big business by the seventeenth century. Fishermen caught and salted cod, which they sold to Catholic countries in Europe where people did not eat meat on Fridays. As the passage makes clear, fishermen were already engaged in many interactions with the Native Americans of New England. Samoset was introduced to English by fishermen.

48. **C.** Samoset and Squanto can most directly be compared to Sacagawea. A young Shoshone woman married to a French fur trader, Sacagawea also served as a cultural intermediary. She acted as a translator for the Lewis and Clark Expedition of 1804 to 1806.

49. **D.** The disappearance of the great buffalo herds led to the destruction of the Plains Indians' way of life. The Plains Indians were

dependent on the buffalo, using them for food and their skins for clothes and shelter. American expansion west put great pressure on the buffalo. Working for a railroad, William "Buffalo Bill" Cody killed over 4,000 buffalo to feed construction crews. Military leaders like General Philip Sheridan also encouraged the killing of the buffalo as a means of weakening the Indians. In 1868, some 15 million buffalo were roaming the western plains; by 1885, this immense herd had been reduced to a few thousand. The Plains Indians were forced onto reservations and into economic dependence on the government.

50. **A.** The economic significance of the cowboys that Cody celebrated in his show was driving herds of cattle to depots where they were shipped to meatpackers in the east. The growing cities of the east needed new sources of meat. Western ranchers stepped up to satisfy this demand. In 1866, Texas cattlemen drove a herd of cattle to the railhead at Sedalia, Missouri. Over the next 20 years, the heyday of the "Long Drive," cowboys drove millions of cattle to places like Abilene, Kansas; Dodge City, Kansas; and Cheyenne, Wyoming.

51. **B.** Buffalo Bill's Wild West Show celebrated a growing nostalgia for the rapidly disappearing frontier. Following the 1890 census, the Census Bureau announced that the frontier had come to an end. In 1893, the historian Frederick Jackson Turner promulgated his "Frontier Thesis" of American history, arguing that the frontier experience had shaped the American character and American institutions. Influential writers like Owen Wister and Theodore Roosevelt and artists like Frederic Remington favorably evoked the disappearing world of the cowboy. Roosevelt saw imperialism in the Philippines and elsewhere as a new frontier in which Americans could test themselves.

52. **B.** Buffalo Bill's Wild West Show was a popular example of new forms of entertainment for the urban masses. New forms of entertainment arose for the inhabitants of America's burgeoning cities. In addition to Buffalo Bill's show, which brought the West to city dwellers, the late nineteenth century saw the development of circuses like that of Barnum and Bailey, professional baseball, college football,

and by the very end of the period, the early beginnings of the motion picture.

53. **D.** President George Herbert Walker Bush's vision of a "new world order" was most directly made possible by the end of the Cold War. With the end of four decades of dangerous confrontation between the United States and its allies and the communist bloc, many people looked forward to a peaceful future. Some commentators talked of "the end of history." Bush's skillful organization of a broad international coalition to expel Saddam Hussein from Kuwait seemed to some to be an example of this new and better path to the future. Even the Soviet Union provided some assistance to the coalition. The triumphant defeat of Saddam Hussein's forces in Kuwait appeared to confirm the "new world order."

54. **A.** President Bush was responding to Iraqi dictator Saddam Hussein's conquest of Kuwait. Following Saddam Hussein's August 2, 1990, invasion of neighboring and oil-rich Kuwait, Bush launched Operation Desert Shield, placing American forces on the border of Kuwait and Saudi Arabia to ensure that Saddam Hussein did not attack that important oil-producing country. After securing United Nations Security Council resolutions denouncing the invasion and demanding Iraqi withdrawal, Bush organized a broad international coalition of forces to liberate Kuwait. On January 16, 1991, the coalition unleashed Operation Desert Storm with an air campaign to soften Iraqi defenses. On February 23, ground forces attacked Kuwait, and by February 27, when combat operations ended, Kuwait had been liberated.

55. **C.** President Bush's "new world order" most directly resembles Woodrow Wilson's Fourteen Points. The Fourteen Points were President Woodrow Wilson's plan for a new liberal world order following the end of World War I and included a League of Nations. Wilson believed that in a world where national self-determination existed in Europe, there would be no secret treaties, freedom of trade would prevail, international disputes would be regulated by the League of Nations, and the world would enter a period of unprecedented peace and prosperity.

Explanations for the Short-Answer Questions

1. A. James Ford Rhodes is arguing that both sides underestimated and misunderstood the other at the beginning of the Civil War. He believes that if the North and South had been better informed, they would have avoided war. He says that the South did not realize that the North would unite to suppress the rebellion. He also makes the case that the North dramatically overestimated the number of pro-government loyalists in the South. Most Northerners, including President Abraham Lincoln, at first thought that most Southerners at heart remained loyal to the Union.

B. Both sides believed at first that the war would be short, perhaps decided by a single battle. At the start, President Lincoln only called up 75,000 volunteers to serve for three months. The Confederates were a bit more realistic, setting enlistments at one year or the duration of the war. The Federal general Winfield Scott was ridiculed in the press because he believed that the war would be a long struggle. His plan to gradually build up federal forces and stifle the Southern economy with a blockade was derided as the "anaconda plan."

C. In late 1860 and early 1861, legislators in Congress attempted to find a political compromise to the secession crisis. Senator John Crittenden of Kentucky proposed his "Crittenden Plan," which would have guaranteed the institution of slavery in states where it already existed, and which would have revived the Missouri Compromise line and extended it to the Pacific Ocean. Virginia, Tennessee, Arkansas, and North Carolina did not secede from the Union until after the surrender of Fort Sumter, and they faced the prospect of being called upon to fight fellow Southern slave-owning states. Kentucky attempted to remain neutral in the war, and did not declare for the Union until Confederate forces crossed its border in September 1861.

2. A. This is a passage from Betty Friedan's *The Feminine Mystique* (1963), a major work of the "Second Wave" feminism that emerged in the 1960s. Friedan argued that women were facing an existential crisis in the "comfortable concentration camp" of their homes, and could not find personal fulfillment in their role as housewives. She believed women needed to express themselves outside the home. Inspired by the African American civil rights movement of the 1960s, "Second Wave" feminists (to distinguish them from the "First Wave" feminists who fought for the vote) worked to ensure equality for women in all fields of life, from the workplace to politics. Inspired by these ideas and changing economic circumstances, millions of women entered the workforce in the 1960s and 1970s.

B. Phyllis Schlafly was a woman who headed the conservative Eagle Forum. She defended the importance of the traditional role of women as mothers and housewives. She argued that modern feminists were "bitter women" who were inflicting their personal maladjustment on everyone else. She believed that feminism was hurting children and weakening the family. Schlafly led the successful opposition to the Equal Rights Amendment.

C. Betty Friedan helped found the National Organization of Women (NOW) in 1966. NOW became a major political force lobbying for feminist issues. In 1972, Title IX of the Educational Amendments prohibited discrimination by sex in any educational institution that received federal funding. This revolutionized women's athletics, opening up unprecedented options for female athletes. The 1973 Supreme Court decision *Roe v. Wade* guaranteed women the right to an abortion. Abortion became a polarizing political issue for decades to come. Congress passed an Equal Rights Amendment (ERA) to the Constitution in 1972. This amendment would have mandated that equality of rights could not be limited by sex. Within a short time, 28 states ratified the ERA. At the same time, opposition to the ERA grew in strength. Conservative critics of the ERA argued that such a sweeping amendment would lead to such things as the drafting of women into the military and same-sex bathrooms. As the momentum of the ERA stalled, Congress in 1979 extended the deadline for ratification.

The opponents of the ERA, led by Phyllis Schlafly, redoubled their efforts, and by 1982 the campaign to ratify the ERA had failed.

3. A, B. The French and Indian War began because of British and colonial concerns about French activity in the Ohio Valley, and in particular, the construction of Fort Duquense on the site of what is now Pittsburgh, Pennsylvania. The British claimed this territory, and many American colonists wanted to develop lands there. Once the French and Indian War was underway, the British leader William Pitt decided to commit resources to the eradication once and for all of French claims in North America. The French in Canada were decisively defeated outside Quebec at the Battle of the Plains of Abraham, on September 13, 1759. At the 1763 Treaty of Paris, France signed away all its North American lands. The British took control of Canada and all the lands east of the Mississippi River. The British also acquired Florida from Spain. The French and Indian War opened up vast lands for possible American settlement, and removed the major military obstacle to moving westward. The Louisiana Purchase of 1803 greatly expanded the United States. President Thomas Jefferson was very interested in western lands. He envisioned a great republic of independent yeoman farmers. To make this possible, he needed land. When Jefferson learned that the weak government of Spain had transferred the Louisiana Territory to the control of Napoleon's France, Jefferson grew concerned that the French might try to reconstitute a strong empire in America. This disquietude was intensified when Spanish officials closed New Orleans to American trade, threatening the economic well-being of Americans living in the west. Jefferson sent James Monroe to join the American minister in France, Robert Livingston. They were to negotiate the purchase of New Orleans. By this time, Napoleon had decided that Louisiana was a liability. He had lost an army to disease trying to reconquer Haiti, and he assumed that he would be cut off from Louisiana by the British navy once war resumed with Great Britain. Napoleon offered to sell the whole Louisiana Territory to the startled American diplomats. For a purchase price of $15 million dollars, the size of the United States was doubled. Jefferson had some constitutional scruples about the purchase because there was nothing in the Constitution about acquiring territory. He swallowed his scruples, and the Senate quickly ratified the purchase. The Mexican War took place at a time when many Americans were embracing the ideology of Manifest Destiny, and arguing that it was inevitable that American settlements and free institutions would spread throughout North America. President James Polk was elected in 1844 on a platform of American expansionism in Texas and Oregon.

Polk negotiated with the British on the Oregon border. Texas was annexed to the United States just before he became president. Mexico broke off diplomatic relations in protest. Polk sent the diplomat John Slidell to Mexico to resolve issues with the Mexicans. He also sent troops under General Zachary Taylor to the disputed border between Texas and Mexico along the Rio Grande. On April 24, 1846, Mexican forces attacked a troop of American soldiers. This began fighting between the United States and Mexico. Congress declared war on May 13. During the Mexican War, the United States won a series of victories that culminated in General Winfield Scott's occupation of Mexico City. In the 1848 Treaty of Guadalupe Hidalgo, Mexico ceded over 500,000 square miles of territory to the United States in return for a payment of $15 million dollars. This included California, Utah, Nevada, New Mexico, Arizona, and set the border of Texas at the Rio Grande.

C. In the French and Indian War, the expansionism of American colonists was obviously opposed by the French. Many Indians also opposed this expansionism, which came at their expense. Many Indians allied with the French realized that the defeat of the French would eliminate one of the great restraints on western settlement by the Americans. Following the conclusion of the French and Indian War, the Ottawa leader Pontiac led a brief war against the British, driving them from a number of western outposts. Some opposition to the Louisiana Purchase came from

Federalist politicians, unenthusiastic about acquiring more western lands likely disposed to return Democratic Republicans to Congress. Some people, including for a time Jefferson himself, had doubts about the Louisiana Purchase for constitutional reasons, seeing it as an example of federal overreach. The American acquisition of Mexican territory was opposed by the Mexicans, including many settlers in places like California, who did not like seeing their lands overrun by American invaders. There was strong opposition to the Mexican War in the United States. Many Americans believed that the war was unjust and was an excuse to acquire territories for the expansion of slavery. Among the opponents of the war were Congressman Abraham Lincoln and the writer Henry David Thoreau, who refused to pay his poll tax, was briefly arrested, and then wrote an essay on "Civil Disobedience."

4. **A, B.** In early May 1886, labor disturbances rocked Chicago, Illinois. Two strikers were killed by police at the McCormick Harvester Company. On May 4, a meeting was called at Haymarket Square to protest police brutality. When a phalanx of police arrived to disperse the gathering, someone threw a bomb into their ranks. The police responded by shooting into the crowd. Members of the crowd fired back. In this violent episode seven policemen were killed and 70 others were wounded. Four other people died, and many more injured. The Haymarket Square bombing was blamed on anarchists. These anarchists were radicals who called for the violent overthrow of government. Many were foreign-born. Eight anarchists were arrested and charged with the crime. All were convicted. Five were sentenced to death; one of these committed suicide in prison, and the other four were hanged. The Haymarket Square Riot and its legal aftermath convinced many people that bloody-minded anarchists threatened American institutions. During World War I, the federal government took action to stifle dissent with the Espionage Act of 1917 and the Sedition Act of 1918. The government also worked to suppress political radicalism, with federal agents rounding up activists of the International Workers of the World (IWW). Eugene Debs, the head of the Socialist Party,

was sent to prison for criticizing the war. Concerns about radical subversion intensified after the Bolshevik Revolution in Russia late in 1917. In 1919, rapid demobilization led to labor unrest and fears of "Bolshevik" uprisings. A series of terrorist bombings in the spring and early summer, including the explosion of a bomb at the home of Attorney General A. Mitchell Palmer, heightened fears of radicals unleashing a systematic campaign of revolutionary violence. Attorney General Palmer launched a series of raids in November 1919 that arrested hundreds of political radicals. In December, 249 detained aliens, including the famous anarchist writer Emma Goldman, were put on a ship bound for the Soviet Union. More raids followed in 1920. Altogether, around 6000 people were arrested. The First Red Scare began to die down after a predicted May 1, 1920 Communist outbreak failed to materialize. A terrorist bomb exploded on September 16 on Wall Street, killing 33 people and wounding over one hundred. Hostility towards political radicals, especially if they were foreign-born continued into the 1920s, playing a role in the Sacco and Vanzetti Case. The Second Red Scare emerged with the Cold War following World War II. Former Communists like Elizabeth Bentley declared that Soviet spy-rings were operating in the United States government. The writer Whitaker Chambers accused Alger Hiss, a distinguished former government official, of having spied for the Soviet Union. Congressman Richard Nixon of the House Committee on Un-American Activities (HUAC) pursued the case, and Hiss was eventually convicted of perjury. It was learned that Soviet agents had stolen atomic bomb secrets. For participating in this, Julius and Ethel Rosenberg were convicted of espionage in 1951, and executed in 1953. To address the security issue in the federal government, President Harry Truman created the Loyalty Review Board to screen federal employees. Anyone who belonged to a politically suspect organization, or who was thought to be a security risk because of behaviors such as alcoholism or homosexuality was removed from public service. Altogether about 3000 federal employees were fired or resigned.

C. The Haymarket Square Riot decisively weakened the Knights of Labor, the leading labor union in the United States, and the group that had sponsored the strikes in Chicago. Many people assumed that the Knights of Labor were associated with the anarchists. Unfairly labeled a radical organization, the Knights of Labor rapidly lost members. John P. Altgeld, the Democratic Governor of Illinois, investigated the Haymarket bombing, and was troubled enough by the way the trial of the anarchists was conducted to pardon the three remaining defendants. Public opinion was outraged by this decision and Altgeld's political career was ruined. The First Red Scare led to a deep and long-standing hostility to political radicalism in the United States during the 1920s. Attorney General A. Mitchell Palmer hoped to use his crusade against radicalism as a platform to launch a presidential campaign. His overselling the threat led to the frustration of his political hopes. Weariness with the upheaval associated with the First Red Scare played a role in the election of Republican Warren G. Harding in the 1920 presidential election, with his promise of a "return to normalcy." The popular identification of political radicalism with immigrants contributed to the postwar restriction of immigration. In 1921, immigration was limited to 350,000 a year. The 1924 National Origins Act cut this number to 150,000, and set national quotas based on the 1890 census, which reduced the number of people who could enter the United States from southern and eastern Europe. The Second Red Scare became a major political issue as fears grew of Communist infiltration of the federal government and other American institutions. Both parties worked to burnish their ant-communist credentials. HUAC not only worried about Communists in the government, but conducted investigations of Hollywood because of concerns that Communist messages might be inserted into movies and other forms of entertainment. Ten Hollywood writers and directors with Communist ties refused to cooperate in the investigation and went to jail. Leftists in Hollywood and the entertainment industry were blackballed, and saw their careers derailed. In 1950, Congress passed the McCarran Act, which forced Communists to register with the government, and gave authorities new powers to detain suspect aliens. In 1950, Senator Joseph McCarthy of Wisconsin claimed to have a list of Communists in the federal government. For the next four years, McCarthy launched a series of high-profile investigations in the Senate that made him a popular anti-Communist hero. He rarely could substantiate his accusations, but that did not matter to his supporters, and Senators who publically criticized him suffered politically. Finally, in 1954, after holding televised hearings on Communism in the Army, during which he appeared to be a bully, McCarthy was censured by the Senate. Though McCarthy's power waned, anti-Communism continued to be a force in the United States.

Explanation for the Document-Based Question

The thesis should focus on a historical analytical skill, in this case **Identifying cause and effect**. Support your thesis with evidence drawn from at least six of the seven documents. Analyze more fully at least four of the documents, discussing one or more of the following: the point of view of the author, the purpose of the author, the intended audience of the document, the historical context of the document. As you construct your argument, make connections between the documents. Note differences and agreements between them that help you strengthen your analysis. Be sure to bring in outside knowledge that you can relate to your analysis of the documents and that contributes to your argument. Simply dropping names is not enough. Demonstrate an understanding of the wider context of the subject of the question. With this question such context could include debates over isolationism and internationalism in American foreign policy, debates over realism and idealism in American foreign policy, and the influence of economic growth on American foreign policy in the late nineteenth and twentieth centuries.

Students might begin the essay with a brief discussion of the Treaty of Paris (1898) and its impact on Cuba. American military occupation under General Leonard Wood followed ratification of the treaty. Wood oversaw the construction of infrastructure, revamped Cuba's political administration, and pioneered health reforms. However, the United States violated the Teller Amendment by not affording Cuba complete independence. Congress retained the right to intervene in Cuban affairs and curbed Cuban autonomy in the Platt Amendment (Document A). Students may note that the United States sent troops into Cuba in 1906 and 1912 to quell rebellions and maintained a naval base at Guantanamo. Students may also refer to "dollar diplomacy" by discussing how American corporations came to dominate the oil, railroad, and, most importantly, sugar industries. Some might compare American involvement in Cuba to a different policy toward Puerto Rico (Foraker Act of 1900, Jones Act of 1917). Students should identify the policies of Theodore Roosevelt, William H. Taft, and Woodrow Wilson. They should examine how the Venezuela crisis (1902) precipitated the announcement of the "Roosevelt Corollary" to the Monroe Doctrine (Document C). Students will apply their knowledge of this policy to American intervention in the Dominican Republic in 1905. Some might note that U.S. control of Dominican customs undermined the nation's independence. Students might speculate on the results of involvement in the internal affairs of nations. A discussion of American interests in constructing an isthmian canal should include Secretary of State John Hay and overtures to Colombia. Students may discuss Philippe Bunau-Varilla, the USS *Nashville,* and Panamanian Revolution. Students will note how Panama reacted to the Hay-Bunau-Varilla Treaty (Document B). They might argue that the Hay-Bunau-Varilla Treaty enabled the United States to direct Panamanian affairs. An examination of "dollar diplomacy" under Taft (Document E) may touch upon his Secretary of State Philander C. Knox. Students will note how the growing influence of American mining companies in Nicaragua resulted in military intervention in 1909. Others might note that American banks financed and owned Nicaraguan railroads. American troops returned in 1912 to help maintain the government of Adolfo Diaz. Students might state that Document D reflects the belief that the United States used its military to open or preserve economic opportunities. Some might point to future problems with the Sandinistas or Contras. Students may use Document F to indicate that American imperialism did not enjoy universal support in the United States. Students could observe how the United States continued its involvement in the Dominican Republic and Nicaragua (Bryan-Chamorro Treaty, 1914) under Wilson. They may also touch upon how intervention in Haiti in 1915 paralleled involvement with its neighbor. Most students will discuss Wilson's relationship with Mexico. Some might begin with the transfer of power from Porfirio Diaz to Francisco Madero to General Victoriano Huerta and Wilson's refusal to recognize the Huerta regime. Students might observe that American businesses wanted to promote stability in Mexico in order to establish favorable trade. Students should examine the instability related to conflicts between Huerta and Venustiano Carranza. Students should discuss the effects of the Tampico affair (Document G) and seizure of Veracruz. Students should also refer to the tenuous relationship between Wilson and Carranza and the issue of recognition. Some may touch upon Pancho Villa and raids in the American Southwest that caused Wilson to send General John Pershing and an expeditionary force across the border. Students will note that the United States and Mexico approached war and should speculate about the long-term effects of American policy.

Explanations for the Long Essay Questions

2. The student can construct an argument making use of information that can include the following. The English colonies in the south were dominated by a plantation economy sustained through the production of staple crops for the market. In the Chesapeake Bay colonies of Virginia and Maryland, the chief cash crop was tobacco. In South Carolina, it was rice. These crops were labor intensive, and early on, plantations required more labor than could be supplied by the planter and his family. Virginia and Maryland encouraged the importation of indentured servants from Britain through the "headright" system. Planters received 50 acres of land for every laborer they brought into the colony. By 1700, over 100,000 indentured servants were brought into the Chesapeake Bay colonies. Indentured servants worked for their masters for a given term of years, then were released from service and provided with supplies, and possibly a piece of land. Indentured servants could not meet the labor needs in the southern colonies, where the hot and humid climate took a high toll on the new arrivals. Planters looked for other sources of workers. There were efforts to enslave Indians, but the susceptibility of Native Americans to European diseases, and the relative ease of escape to the frontier made them an unreliable labor source. The first African slaves arrived in Virginia aboard a Dutch ship in 1619. At first, African slaves were too expensive to be bought in large numbers. Over time, their numbers grew. Coming from a tropical climate, Africans were believed to more adaptable to the southern climate. At the end of the seventeenth century, greater competition in the slave trade led to a larger supply of slaves. At the same time, improving economic conditions in Britain limited the number of potential indentured servants. By the early eighteenth century, African slaves were becoming the major source of labor on southern plantations. Within 50 years, African slaves outnumbered white settlers in South Carolina, and comprised almost half the population of Virginia. At the same time that African slavery was establishing itself, a small number of large landowners were coming to dominate an increasingly hierarchical Southern society. These planters played a disproportionate role in politics and the economy. In Virginia, leading families like the Lees and Fitzhughs formed an informal landed aristocracy. Most white settlers were small farmers who owned few if any slaves. The plantation economy precluded the settlement and growth of many towns. The South was rapidly developing the agrarian model centered on slave-worked plantations that it would carry into the nineteenth century. In the northern colonies, the climate discouraged the growth of a plantation economy. Instead, the North was dominated by small farms and a more mixed economy. Although indentured servants and slaves were found in the North, farms were more likely to be worked by the members of a family. The temperate climate in New England and elsewhere proved healthier for immigrants from Britain, and the population grew rapidly. Towns and cities played an important role in the more densely populated North. A thriving commercial economy developed, with merchants in Boston, New York, Philadelphia, and elsewhere trading with Europe and the other colonies. American merchants played a key role in the triangular trade between the American colonies, Africa, and the West Indies. The wealth of American seaports supported prosperous artisans and businessmen. Benjamin Franklin's print shop in Philadelphia and Paul Revere's silversmith shop in Boston are examples of the businesses that flourished in the rich northern towns. Many Northerners made their living at sea, either working the large numbers of merchantmen sailing across the Atlantic, or as fisherman, catching and then drying fish for the European market. Abundant sources of timber provided lumber for export and for an extensive shipbuilding industry. An upper class of wealthy merchants and landowners were very influential in the North, but their power was checked to a degree by a larger middle class than existed in the South. A more dynamic economy made for a more egalitarian society.

3. The student can begin by talking about the rapidity of industrialization and urbanization in late nineteenth-century America. In 1865, the United States produced virtually no steel; by 1890, it was the largest steel producer in the world. Commensurate growth was seen in the cities. In 1860, no American city could boast a million inhabitants; in 1890, New York, Chicago, and Philadelphia all had more than a million inhabitants. Such rapid growth led to many problems, and American cities struggled to keep up with the paving and plumbing necessary to serve such masses of people. During the late nineteenth century, many cities were run by political "machines," highly organized operations that at their best ran with mechanical efficiency. At the top of the machine was the "boss." The boss often was not the mayor, preferring to exercise power behind the scenes. Political bosses took a very pragmatic, workmanlike attitude to politics. Richard Croker, leader of New York City's Tammany Hall, told a reporter that, "Politics is business." Machine politics could be very big business indeed, leading to famous examples of corruption. An earlier Tammany Hall boss, William Tweed, and his associates may have pocketed over $200,000,000 in city money. Machines more normally brought in money through their control of city contracts, taking payoffs from businessmen wanting to do work for the city. Much of this money went into paying for the army of sub-bosses and ward-heelers, who kept track of voters on the local level. Another way of supporting a machine operative was to get him a job on the city payroll. Often, machine loyalists might have more than one job. Reformers frequently attacked the machines for their corruption, but they proved quite resilient, in large part because they retained the loyalties of voters. In an era before social security or a social safety net, the operatives of the machines often provided assistance to voters in a time of trouble, their reward being a vote at election time. The machines also helped acculturate immigrants, providing assistance to them when many Americans were denouncing them as a threat to American society. The flow of immigrants increased in the late nineteenth century. In the 1850s through the 1870s two million immigrants arrived each decade. In the 1880s five million arrived. The 1880s also saw a shift in the national origins of immigrants. Previously, most immigrants had come from western and northern Europe. Now they began to come from eastern and southern Europe, from places like Russia and Italy. Many were Catholic and Jewish, and in their clothing and culture, seemed more alien than previous immigrants. Anti-immigrant feeling was nothing new in the United States. The Know-Nothings had flourished in the 1850s, opposing the arrival of Irish and German immigrants. The American Protective Association was launched in 1887, and carried on the tradition of anti-immigrant and anti-Catholic agitation. Over 80 percent of the new immigrants settled in the cities of the North and Midwest. In 1890, one third of the population of Boston and Chicago, and one fourth of Philadelphia were foreign-born. Many of these immigrants lived in crowded ethnic enclaves such as the Lower East Side of New York. Machine politicians were not the only people to provide assistance to immigrants as they adjusted to their new country. The Roman Catholic Church grew dramatically with the influx of immigrants. By 1900, Catholics had become the largest denomination in America, with ten million congregants. The Church oversaw an extensive network of schools, hospitals, and homes for the indigent or aged. Similar developments occurred in the Jewish community. Protestants stepped into the urban mix with evangelists like

Dwight Moody, and the liberal ministers of the Social Gospel movement. Idealistic reformers like Jane Addams established settlement houses in urban neighborhoods to assist immigrants. The immigrants joined with Americans moving into the city from the farm to create a vibrant popular culture that laid the groundwork for the mass media and mass entertainments of the twentieth century. People could get their news from the "Yellow Journals" that provided sensationalized headlines and stories, as well as popular features such as comic strips. Mass entertainments included professional sports. Baseball was becoming the national pastime. League play began in the 1870s, and fans could follow the fortunes of their favorite teams in the newspapers if they could not make it to the ballpark. Boxing was also a popular sport, and champions like John L. Sullivan and "Gentleman Jim" Corbett became famous. Also attracting patrons were spectacles such as circuses. In 1881, P.T. Barnum joined with James A. Bailey to put on the "Greatest Show on Earth," William "Buffalo Bill" Cody reached millions with his Wild West Show, featuring attractions like Annie Oakley, "Little Sure-Shot." Cody's vision of the west, with its dramatic displays of cowboys, Indians, and cavalry became the basis of the westerns that exerted such a popular hold for much of the next century. These and more highbrow intellectual attractions made the city an exciting and desirable destination, despite the many problems of urban America.

4. The student can construct an argument making use of information that can include the following. The First World War saw the culmination of the Progressive Era's movement towards greater government regulation of the economy. The federal government took unprecedented steps as it mobilized the American people and the American economy for total war against Imperial Germany. The administration of President Woodrow Wilson and Congress financed the war through the sale of "Liberty Bonds" to the American people, and through steep rises in income taxes and taxes on corporate profits. A War Industries Board (WIB) coordinated the production of war materials, setting prices and allocating resources. A series of "war boards" supervised different aspects of the economy, such as fuel and railroads, which had come under federal control. Herbert Hoover headed the food board, encouraging Americans to conserve different types of foodstuffs. This organization of the economy had mixed results. Initially there was some confusion and missteps as the government sorted out its programs. The United States was still not producing all the military supplies and weapons that it needed when the war ended in November 1918, but during the brief period of the war the United States had made impressive gains in organizing its enormous economic potential. Very important for the future, businessmen and government officials had learned the advantages of working together, establishing a longstanding cooperative relationship between big business and government. In addition to organizing the economy, President Wilson attempted to mobilize public opinion during the war. He created the Committee on Public Information (CPI), headed by the journalist George Creel. The CPI worked to educate American about the war through books, pamphlets, posters, and movies. Although the original intent was to provide largely factual material, the CPI ended up producing a lot of overt propaganda. The government also acted to repress dissent. The Espionage Act of 1917 and the Sedition Act of 1918 essentially criminalized public opposition to the war. The Socialist leader Eugene Debs was one of many who went to prison for criticizing the war. The government fomented an atmosphere of hysteria that stigmatized all things German, leading to such phenomena as the renaming of sauerkraut as "liberty cabbage," and also promoted the suppression of radical groups like the International Workers of the World (IWW). This search for internal enemies

eventually branched into the postwar First Red Scare. In large part because of the excesses of this attempt to regiment American opinion, there was a reaction against the wartime policies of Woodrow Wilson which resulted in the election of Warren G. Harding to the presidency in 1920, with his promise of a return to "Normalcy." Despite this reaction, elements of the wartime mobilization persisted, especially in the relationship between government and business, fostered in the 1920s by Commerce Secretary Herbert Hoover. The New Deal was influenced by the example of World War I. Once again the federal government intervened heavily in the economy. President Franklin Roosevelt and a number of his subordinates, such as General Hugh Johnson, the Head of the National Recovery Administration (NRA), were veterans of the First World War mobilization. The NRA, with its attempt to set up industry codes, echoed aspects of the WIB. The mobilization of the United States for total war again in World War II unsurprisingly echoed that of World War I. The war was financed through a combination of loans and high taxes. The Office of Price Administration (OPA) worked to prevent inflation by controlling prices and wages. It also supervised an elaborate system of rationing resources and goods important to the war effort such as sugar, meat, rubber, and gasoline. A succession of federal agencies worked to coordinate industrial production. The War Production Board (WPB) was eventually replaced by the Office of War Mobilization (OWM). Despite this bureaucratic experimentation, the government successfully organized the American industrial base to produce massive amounts of war material, becoming the "arsenal of democracy" during the war. Though Roosevelt created the Office of War Information (OWI) to coordinate war information and propaganda, it never took on the importance of Creel's CPI, and the Roosevelt Administration studiously avoided launching the sort of political repression seen during World War I. The Roosevelt Administration did make one notorious concession to wartime hysteria. In 1942, it rounded up Japanese and Japanese-Americans living on the West Coast, and sent them to internment camps. By the end of World War II, after years of expanding federal power, Americans had become used to the government playing an important role in their lives and in the economy. The overall success of the American war effort in World War I would foster a confidence in the abilities of government to meet challenges that would undergird the policies of later presidents such as John F. Kennedy and his New Frontier and Lyndon B. Johnson and his Great Society.

PRACTICE EXAM 2

Answer Sheet for Multiple-Choice Questions

1 Ⓐ Ⓑ Ⓒ Ⓓ	16 Ⓐ Ⓑ Ⓒ Ⓓ	31 Ⓐ Ⓑ Ⓒ Ⓓ	46 Ⓐ Ⓑ Ⓒ Ⓓ
2 Ⓐ Ⓑ Ⓒ Ⓓ	17 Ⓐ Ⓑ Ⓒ Ⓓ	32 Ⓐ Ⓑ Ⓒ Ⓓ	47 Ⓐ Ⓑ Ⓒ Ⓓ
3 Ⓐ Ⓑ Ⓒ Ⓓ	18 Ⓐ Ⓑ Ⓒ Ⓓ	33 Ⓐ Ⓑ Ⓒ Ⓓ	48 Ⓐ Ⓑ Ⓒ Ⓓ
4 Ⓐ Ⓑ Ⓒ Ⓓ	19 Ⓐ Ⓑ Ⓒ Ⓓ	34 Ⓐ Ⓑ Ⓒ Ⓓ	49 Ⓐ Ⓑ Ⓒ Ⓓ
5 Ⓐ Ⓑ Ⓒ Ⓓ	20 Ⓐ Ⓑ Ⓒ Ⓓ	35 Ⓐ Ⓑ Ⓒ Ⓓ	50 Ⓐ Ⓑ Ⓒ Ⓓ
6 Ⓐ Ⓑ Ⓒ Ⓓ	21 Ⓐ Ⓑ Ⓒ Ⓓ	36 Ⓐ Ⓑ Ⓒ Ⓓ	51 Ⓐ Ⓑ Ⓒ Ⓓ
7 Ⓐ Ⓑ Ⓒ Ⓓ	22 Ⓐ Ⓑ Ⓒ Ⓓ	37 Ⓐ Ⓑ Ⓒ Ⓓ	52 Ⓐ Ⓑ Ⓒ Ⓓ
8 Ⓐ Ⓑ Ⓒ Ⓓ	23 Ⓐ Ⓑ Ⓒ Ⓓ	38 Ⓐ Ⓑ Ⓒ Ⓓ	53 Ⓐ Ⓑ Ⓒ Ⓓ
9 Ⓐ Ⓑ Ⓒ Ⓓ	24 Ⓐ Ⓑ Ⓒ Ⓓ	39 Ⓐ Ⓑ Ⓒ Ⓓ	54 Ⓐ Ⓑ Ⓒ Ⓓ
10 Ⓐ Ⓑ Ⓒ Ⓓ	25 Ⓐ Ⓑ Ⓒ Ⓓ	40 Ⓐ Ⓑ Ⓒ Ⓓ	55 Ⓐ Ⓑ Ⓒ Ⓓ
11 Ⓐ Ⓑ Ⓒ Ⓓ	26 Ⓐ Ⓑ Ⓒ Ⓓ	41 Ⓐ Ⓑ Ⓒ Ⓓ	
12 Ⓐ Ⓑ Ⓒ Ⓓ	27 Ⓐ Ⓑ Ⓒ Ⓓ	42 Ⓐ Ⓑ Ⓒ Ⓓ	
13 Ⓐ Ⓑ Ⓒ Ⓓ	28 Ⓐ Ⓑ Ⓒ Ⓓ	43 Ⓐ Ⓑ Ⓒ Ⓓ	
14 Ⓐ Ⓑ Ⓒ Ⓓ	29 Ⓐ Ⓑ Ⓒ Ⓓ	44 Ⓐ Ⓑ Ⓒ Ⓓ	
15 Ⓐ Ⓑ Ⓒ Ⓓ	30 Ⓐ Ⓑ Ⓒ Ⓓ	45 Ⓐ Ⓑ Ⓒ Ⓓ	

AP U.S. HISTORY
PRACTICE EXAM 2

Section I

Time: 95 minutes

Part A (Multiple Choice)

Part A recommended time: 55 minutes

Directions: Each of the following questions refers to a historical source. These questions will test your knowledge about the historical source and require you to make use of your historical analytical skills and your familiarity with historical themes. For each question select the *best* response and fill in the corresponding oval on your answer sheet.

Questions 1–4 refer to the following quotation.

One of the rights which the freeman has always guarded with most jealous care is that of enjoying the rewards of his own industry. Realizing that the power to tax is the power to destroy and that the power to take a certain amount of property or of income is only another way of saying that for a certain proportion of his time a citizen must work for the government, the authority to impose a tax on the people has been most carefully guarded. ... A government which lays taxes on the people not required by urgent necessity and sound public policy is not a protector of liberty, but an instrument of tyranny. It condemns the citizen to tyranny. One of the first signs of the breaking down of free government is a disregard by the taxing power of the right of the people to their own property. ... Unless the people can enjoy that reasonable security in the possession of their property, which is guaranteed by the Constitution, against unreasonable taxation, freedom is at an end. ... With us economy is imperative. It is a full test of our national character. ... It is always the people who toil that pay.

—Calvin Coolidge, "Economy in the Interest of All," June 30, 1924

1. Which of the following political ideas *best* reflects the perspective of Calvin Coolidge in the passage above?
   A. Taxation is an effective means of redistributing wealth.
   B. Government should be limited.
   C. A bigger government can ensure social justice.
   D. Government has the final say on what people do with their property.

2. Which of the following presidents would be most likely to share Coolidge's sentiments?
   A. Franklin D. Roosevelt
   B. Lyndon B. Johnson
   C. Ronald Reagan
   D. Barack Obama

3. The ideas expressed above were influenced by which of the following?
   A. Widespread prosperity in the 1920s
   B. Widespread economic hardship in the 1920s
   C. The rapid growth of the welfare state in the 1920s
   D. Highly publicized antitrust prosecutions

4. In the passage above Coolidge is reacting against which of the following?
   A. The economic policies of his predecessor Warren G. Harding
   B. The growing strength of radical politics in America following the Russian Revolution
   C. Populist agitation in the West
   D. The governmental policies of the Progressive Era

Questions 5–8 refer to the following image.

Theodor de Bry, "The Natives of Florida Worship the Column Erected by the Commander on His First Voyage," *Grand Voyages*, 1591

5. Which of the following most directly reflects the perspective of de Bry in the image above?
   A. The natives of Florida are primitive and superstitious.
   B. The natives of Florida are highly religious.
   C. The Europeans are unjustly exploiting the natives of Florida.
   D. Conflict is inevitable between the natives of Florida and the Europeans.

6. The image above is an expression of which of the following?
   A. European fear of native peoples
   B. European religious fervor
   C. European doubts about the value of exploration
   D. European curiosity about the wider world

7. The column erected by the commander signified which of the following?
   A. European intentions to convert the Indians to Christianity
   B. European desires for trade and new products
   C. European desires to establish political control over new territories
   D. European interest in sharing the culture of the Indians

8. European rivalries would lead to the French depicted above being driven from Florida by which of the following?
   A. The natives of Florida
   B. The Spanish
   C. The English
   D. The Dutch

Questions 9–12 refer to the following quotation.

Here is the case of a woman employed in the manufacturing department of a Broadway house. It stands for a hundred like her own. She averages three dollars a week. Pay is $1.50 for her room; for breakfast she has a cup of coffee; lunch she cannot afford. One meal a day is her allowance. This woman is young, she is pretty. She has "the world before her." Is it anything less than a miracle if she is guilty of nothing less than the "early and improvident marriage," against which moralists exclaim as one of the prolific causes of the distresses of the poor? Almost any door might seem to offer a welcome escape from such slavery as this. "I feel so much healthier since I got three square meals a day," said a lodger in one of the Girls' Homes. Two young sewing-girls came in seeking domestic service, so that they might get enough to eat. They had been only half-fed for some time, and starvation had driven them to the one door at which the pride of the American-born girl will not permit her to knock, though poverty be the price of her independence.

—Jacob Riis, *How the Other Half Lives*, 1890

9. Which of the following would be *most* likely to support the perspective expressed by Riis in the passage above?
   A. A supporter of Social Darwinism
   B. A Progressive
   C. A businessman
   D. An opponent of immigration

10. The situation faced by the young women in the passage above is *most* directly comparable to which of the following?
    A. American revolutionaries in the 1770s
    B. Slaves in the antebellum South
    C. Populist farmers in the 1890s
    D. Detroit autoworkers in the 1930s

11. Concerns like those expressed by Riis in the passage above led *most* directly to which of the following?
    A. Laws regulating the working conditions of women
    B. Restrictions on immigration
    C. Women's suffrage
    D. Antitrust legislation

12. Riis's work as an investigator of the lives of the poor can *most* directly be associated with which of the following?
    A. Yellow Journalism
    B. Abolitionism
    C. The muckrakers
    D. Socialism

Questions 13–16 refer to the following quotation.

It is natural, it is a privilege, I will go farther, it is a right, which all free men claim, that they are entitled to complain when they are hurt. They have a right publicly to remonstrate against the abuses of power in the strongest terms, to put their neighbors upon their guard against the craft or open violence of men in authority, and to assert with courage the sense they have of the blessings of liberty, the value they put upon it, and their resolution at all hazards to preserve it as one of the greatest blessings heaven can bestow. ... But to conclude: The question before the Court and you, Gentlemen of the jury, is not of small or private concern. It is not the cause of one poor printer, nor of New York alone, which you are now trying. No! It may in its consequence affect every free man that lives under a British government on the main of America. It is the best cause. It is the cause of liberty. And I make no doubt but your upright conduct this day will not only entitle you to the love and esteem of your fellow citizens, but every man who prefers freedom to a life of slavery will bless and honor you as men who have baffled the attempt of tyranny, and by an impartial and uncorrupt verdict have laid a noble foundation for securing to ourselves, our posterity, and our neighbors, that to which nature and the laws of our country have given us a right to liberty of both exposing and opposing arbitrary power (in these parts of the world at least) by speaking and writing truth.

—Andrew Hamilton, concluding argument, libel trial of newspaper editor
John Peter Zenger, August 4, 1735

13. Which of the following *best* describes the significance of the Zenger Trial?
   A. An important incident in opposing British taxation policy
   B. An early attack on the institution of slavery
   C. A landmark case concerning voting rights
   D. A landmark case concerning freedom of expression

14. Andrew Hamilton assumes which of the following?
   A. Americans have more freedoms than people in other countries.
   B. People in other countries have more rights than Americans.
   C. Natural rights are merely ideas that don't really exist.
   D. Rights are granted by the government.

15. The Zenger Case can *best* be compared to which of the following?
   A. Abraham Lincoln's suspension of habeas corpus during the Civil War
   B. Government efforts to prevent the publication of the Pentagon Papers in 1971
   C. The trial of the accused Haymarket Square bombers in 1886
   D. The *Brown v. Board of Education* Supreme Court decision of 1954

16. Hamilton's success in the Zenger case *most* directly reflects which of the following?
   A. American desires for independence from Great Britain
   B. American rejection of Enlightenment ideals
   C. A long tradition of self-rule in the American colonies
   D. The weakening of economic ties between America and Great Britain

Questions 17–20 refer to the following cartoon.

Thomas Nast, "The Union as It Was / The Lost Cause, Worse
Than Slavery," *Harper's Weekly*, October 24, 1874

17. Which of the following *best* expresses the perspective of Thomas Nast in the cartoon above?
   A. The Reconstruction of the South is going well.
   B. The government is not adequately protecting freed slaves.
   C. White people in the South need to stand together.
   D. The Reconstruction of Southern society was a bad idea.

18. The situation described in the cartoon above *most* directly resulted in which of the following?
   A. The passage of the Fifteenth Amendment
   B. The passage of the Homestead Act offering settlers free land in the West
   C. Efforts to create an industrialized New South
   D. The *Plessy v. Ferguson* Supreme Court decision

19. The Southerners in the cartoon above wanted a "Union" characterized by which of the following?
   A. Sovereignty centered in the federal government.
   B. An "American System" of internal improvements.
   C. Sovereignty centered in the states.
   D. The anti-nullification nationalism of Andrew Jackson.

20. The ideas in the cartoon above *most* directly reflect which of the following continuities in U.S. history?
   A. Debates about civil rights
   B. Debates about the use of military power
   C. Debates about gun control
   D. Debates about the role of political parties

Questions 21–24 refer to the following quotation.

Tonight, the daughter of a woman whose highest goal was a future for her children talks to our nation's oldest political party about a future for us all. Tonight, the daughter of working Americans tells all Americans that the future is within our reach, if we're willing to reach for it. Tonight, the daughter of an immigrant from Italy has been chosen to run for (vice) president in the new land my father came to love. . . . Americans want to live by the same set of rules. But under this administration, the rules are rigged against too many of our people. It isn't right that every year the share of taxes paid by individual citizens is going up, while the share paid by large corporations is getting smaller and smaller. . . . It isn't right that young couples question whether to bring children into a world of 50,000 nuclear warheads. That isn't the vision for which Americans have struggled for more than two centuries. . . . Tonight, we reclaim our dream. We're going to make the rules of American life work for all Americans again. . . . The issue is not what America can do for women, but what women can do for America.

—Geraldine Ferraro, Vice Presidential Nomination Acceptance Address, July 19, 1984

21. The nomination of Geraldine Ferraro for vice president was most directly a continuation of which of the following?
   A. The successful assimilation of immigrants to the United States
   B. The struggle for civil rights for ethnic minorities
   C. Increased economic and political opportunities for women
   D. The increasing democratization of the political nomination process

22. The political ideas expressed by Ferraro in the passage above *most* directly reflect those of which of the following?
   A. Colonial opponents of British taxation in the 1760s and 1770s
   B. Abolitionists of the antebellum period
   C. Republicans of the 1920s
   D. New Dealers of the 1930s

23. The ideas expressed in the passage above would *most* directly have strengthened which of the following during the 1980s?
   A. Opposition to the administration's arms buildup
   B. Efforts to deregulate many industries
   C. Efforts to reform the welfare system
   D. Support for the administration's cold war policies

24. Geraldine Ferraro can be most directly compared to which of the following women?
   A. Abigail Adams
   B. Sandra Day O'Connor
   C. Jane Addams
   D. Rosa Parks

Questions 25–28 refer to the following quotation.

These were the first emigrants that we had overtaken, although we had found abundant and melancholy traces of their progress throughout the whole course of the journey. Sometimes we passed the grave of one who had sickened and died on the way. The earth was usually torn up and covered thickly with wolf-tracks. Some had escaped this violation. One morning a piece of plank, standing upright on the summit of a grassy hill, attracted our notice, and riding up to it we found the following words very roughly traced upon it, apparently by a red-hot piece of iron:

MARY ELLIS DIED MAY 7th, 1845
Aged two months.

Such tokens were of common occurrence, nothing could speak more for the hardihood, or rather infatuation, of the adventurers, or the sufferings that await them upon their journey. … We were late in breaking up our camp on the following morning, and scarcely had we ridden a mile when we saw, far in advance of us, drawn against the horizon, a line of objects stretching at regular intervals along the level edge of the prairie. An intervening swell soon hid them from sight, until, ascending it a quarter of an hour after, we saw close before us the emigrant caravan, with its heavy white wagons creeping on in their slow procession, and a large drove of cattle following behind. … Many were murmuring against the leader they had chosen, and wished to depose him. … The women were divided between regrets for the homes they had left and apprehension of the deserts and savages before them. … As we left the ground, I saw a tall slouching fellow with the nasal accent of "down east," contemplating the contents of his tin cup, which he had just filled with water.

"Look here, you," he said: "it's chock full of animals!"

The cup, as he held it out, exhibited in fact an extraordinary variety and profusion of animal and vegetable life.

—Francis Parkman, *The Oregon Trail: Sketches of Prairie and Rocky-Mountain Life*, 1849

25. The situation described in the passage above led *most* directly to which of the following?
    A. Passage of the Homestead Act
    B. Passage of the Northwest Ordinance
    C. The *Dred Scott* Supreme Court decision
    D. Passage of the Indian Removal Act

26. The actions of the people in the passage above *most* directly reflect the influence of which of the following political ideals?
    A. Popular sovereignty
    B. Jacksonian Democracy
    C. Manifest Destiny
    D. Progressivism

27. The experiences of the people encountered by Francis Parkman can be *most* directly compared to those of which of the following?
    A. The Spanish conquistadors
    B. The Pilgrims
    C. The Apollo astronauts
    D. Cowboys on the first cattle drives of the 1860s

28. Which of the following had *most* directly anticipated and desired the movement described by Parkman?
    A. Benjamin Franklin
    B. James Madison
    C. Alexander Hamilton
    D. Thomas Jefferson

Questions 29–32 refer to the following quotation.

Our leaders talk about stopping aggression from the north, but this was a struggle among groups of Vietnamese until we intervened. We seem bent upon saving the Vietnamese from Ho Chi Minh even if we have to kill them and demolish their country to do it. As the native people survey bombed-out villages, women and children burned by napalm, rice crops destroyed and cities overrun with our military personnel, they are doubtless saying secretly of the Vietcong guerillas and of the American forces, "A plague on both your houses." . . . Stop the bombing, north and south, end search and destroy offensive sweeps, and confine our military action to holding operations on the ground. Bombing the north has failed to halt or seriously check the flow of troops to the south and may, in fact, have prompted a much greater war effort by Hanoi.

—Senator George McGovern, "The Lessons of Vietnam," April 25, 1967

29. Which of the following opinions from the 1960s *most* directly reflects the perspective of George McGovern's speech?
    A. Americans must maximize their technological edge in Vietnam.
    B. American bombing in Vietnam is step by step leading to progress in the war.
    C. American bombing in Vietnam is a failure.
    D. America must not give in to defeatism about the war in Vietnam.

30. The sentiments expressed in the speech above *most* directly influenced which of the following?
    A. The passage of the War Powers Act of 1973
    B. The Tet Offensive of 1968
    C. The resignation of Richard Nixon in 1974
    D. The emergence of a youth counterculture

31. The sentiments expressed in the speech *most* directly reflect which popular attitude that became widespread in the 1960s?
    A. The United States should embrace isolationism.
    B. The United States should use force to spread American ideals abroad.
    C. American commanders were not being given enough weapons in Vietnam.
    D. Government statements about Vietnam could not be trusted.

32. Political discord during the Vietnam War most closely resembled the political dissensions during which of the following?
    A. The Spanish-American War
    B. The Mexican War
    C. World War I
    D. World War II

Questions 33–36 refer to the following quotation.

On Being Brought from Africa to America

'Twas mercy brought me from my Pagan land,
Taught my benighted soul to understand
That there's a God, that there's a Saviour too;
Once I redemption neither sought nor knew.
Some view our sable race with scornful eye,
"Their colour is a diabolic die."
Remember, Christians, Negroes, black as Cain,
May be refin'd, and join th' angelic train.

—Phillis Wheatley, *Poems on Various Subjects, Religious and Moral,* 1773

33. The ideas expressed in Phillis Wheatley's poem *most* directly reveal the influence of which of the following?
    A. The First Great Awakening
    B. The natural rights theory of John Locke
    C. British ideas about social hierarchy
    D. Eighteenth century scientific racism

34. The sentiments expressed in Wheatley's poem *most* directly reflect which of the following continuities in U.S. history?
    A. Debates over religious freedom
    B. Debates over social justice
    C. Debates over immigration
    D. Debates over freedom of expression

35. The literary success of Phillis Wheatley led *most* directly to questions about which of the following?
    A. The granting of political rights to women
    B. The harsh treatment of pro-British Loyalists
    C. The moral justification of slavery
    D. The legitimacy of established churches in the states

36. The point of Wheatley's poem can *best* be compared to which of the following?
    A. The Declaration of Independence
    B. Jonathan Edwards's sermon "Sinners in the Hands of an Angry God"
    C. The Seneca Falls Declaration of Rights and Sentiments
    D. Martin Luther King, Jr.'s "I Have a Dream" speech

Questions 37–40 refer to the following quotation.

Wrong as we think slavery is, we can yet afford to leave it alone where it is, because that much is due to the necessity arising from its actual presence in the nation; but can we, while our votes will prevent it, allow it to spread into the National Territories, and to overrun us here in these Free States? If our sense of duty forbids this, then let us stand by our duty, fearlessly and effectively. Let us be diverted by none of those sophistical contrivances wherewith we are so industriously plied and belabored—contrivances such as groping for some middle ground between the right and the wrong, vain as the search for a man who should be neither a living man nor a dead man—such a policy of "don't care" on a question about which all true men do care—such as Union appeals beseeching true Union men to yield to Disunionists, reversing the divine rule, and calling not the sinners, but the righteous to repentance. . . . Neither let us be slandered from our duty by false accusations against us, nor frightened from it by menaces of destruction to the Government nor of dungeons to ourselves. LET US HAVE FAITH THAT RIGHT MAKES MIGHT, AND IN THAT FAITH, LET US, TO THE END, DARE TO DO OUR DUTY AS WE UNDERSTAND IT.

—Abraham Lincoln, Cooper Union Address, February 27, 1860

37. In his Cooper Union Address, Abraham Lincoln called for which of the following?
    A. Northern voters to resist the demands of pro-slavery advocates
    B. The seceded Southern states to return to the Union
    C. More support for the war effort
    D. Compromise with pro-slavery advocates

38. A member of which of the following political parties would have been most likely to support Lincoln's position?
    A. Democrat
    B. Republican
    C. Progressive
    D. Federalist

39. Lincoln and his supporters called for which of the following in 1860?
    A. The abolition of slavery
    B. Preventing the expansion of slavery into the western territories
    C. Military action against the South
    D. Strict enforcement of the Fugitive Slave Act

40. Lincoln's Cooper Union Address can best be compared to
    A. the Declaration of Independence.
    B. the Northwest Ordinance.
    C. Franklin Roosevelt's "Arsenal of Democracy" speech in 1940.
    D. William Jennings Bryan's "Cross of Gold" speech in 1896.

Questions 41–44 refer to the following quotation.

They ask us how we shall govern these new possessions. I answer: Out of local conditions and the necessities of the case methods of government will grow. If England can govern foreign lands, so can America. If Germany can govern foreign lands, so can America. If they can supervise protectorates, so can America. Why is it more difficult to administer Hawaii than New Mexico or California? Both had a savage and an alien population; both were more remote from the seat of government when they came under our dominion than the Philippines are to-day.

   Will you say by your vote that American ability to govern has decayed; that a century's experience in self-rule has failed of a result? Will you affirm by your vote that you are an infidel to American power and practical sense? Or will you say that ours is the blood of government; ours the heart of dominion; ours the brain and genius of administration? Will you remember that we do but what our fathers did—we but pitch the tents of liberty farther westward, farther southward—we only continue the march of the flag?

—Albert Beveridge, "The March of the Flag," Indianapolis, September 16, 1898

41. In "The March of the Flag," Albert Beveridge supported which of the following?
   A. Populism
   B. War with Great Britain
   C. Constitutional reform in the United States
   D. The creation of an American overseas empire

42. Beveridge's speech was a response to which of the following?
   A. The purchase of Alaska
   B. The Mexican War
   C. The Spanish-American War
   D. World War I

43. The theme of Beveridge's speech can most directly be compared to which of the following?
   A. The Monroe Doctrine
   B. Containment
   C. Manifest Destiny
   D. The ideology of states' rights

44. The policy advocated by Beveridge foreshadowed which of the following?
   A. The rise of the United States to the status of a great power
   B. A period of growing isolationism
   C. A period of laissez-faire economics
   D. Growing support for constitutional strict constructionism

Questions 45–48 refer to the following quotation.

BECAUSE no People can be truly happy, though under the greatest Enjoyment of Civil Liberties, if abridged of the Freedom of their Consciences, as to their Religious Profession and Worship: And Almighty God being the only Lord of Conscience, Father of Lights and Spirits; and the Author as well as Object of all divine Knowledge, Faith and Worship, who only doth enlighten the Minds, and persuade and convince the Understanding of People, I do hereby grant and declare, That no Person or Persons, inhabiting in this Province or Territories, who shall confess and acknowledge One almighty God, the Creator, Upholder and Ruler of the World; and profess him or themselves obliged to live quietly under the Civil Government, shall be in any Case molested or prejudiced, in his or their Person or Estate, because of his or their conscientious Persuasion or Practice, nor be compelled to frequent or maintain any religious Worship, Place or Ministry, contrary to his or their Mind. . . .

—William Penn, *Charter of Privileges Granted by William Penn, esq. to the Inhabitants of Pennsylvania and Territories*, October 28, 1701

45. Which of the following best describes the colony of Pennsylvania?
   A. A charter colony in which the King granted a charter to a group of businessmen or colonists
   B. A proprietary colony in which the King entrusted government to a proprietor and his family
   C. A royal colony in which the King appointed the governor
   D. An independent colony governed outside the authority of the King

46. William Penn was a member of which of the following persecuted religious groups?
   A. Roman Catholics
   B. Puritans
   C. Quakers
   D. Anglicans

47. Because of Penn's Charter of Privileges, Pennsylvania became
   A. one of the most religiously diverse colonies in British America.
   B. one of the least religiously diverse colonies in America.
   C. notorious for witch hunting and popular superstition.
   D. known for its hostility to traditional religious practices.

48. Penn's Charter of Privileges can be seen as a forerunner to which of the following?
   A. The Declaration of Independence
   B. The Fourteen Points
   C. The Gettysburg Address
   D. The First Amendment to the Constitution

Questions 49–52 refer to the following quotation.

The man who mounted the steps of the Capitol, March 4, 1801, to claim the place of an equal between Pitt and Bonaparte, possessed a character which showed itself in acts; but person and manner can be known only by contemporaries, and the liveliest description was worth less than a moment of personal contact. Jefferson was very tall, six feet two-and-a-half inches in height; sandy-complexioned; shy in manner, seeming cold; awkward in attitude, and with little in his bearing that suggested command. . . . His skin was thin, peeling from his face on exposure to the sun, giving it a tettered appearance. This sandy face, with hazel eyes and sunny aspect; this loose, shackling person; this rambling and often brilliant conversation, belonged to the controlling influences of American history, more necessary to the story than three-fourths of the official papers, which only hid the truth. Jefferson's personality during these eight years appeared to be the government, and impressed itself, like that of Bonaparte, although by a different process, on the mind of the nation. In the village simplicity of Washington, he was more than a king, for he was alone in social as well as in political pre-eminence. Except the British Legation, no house in Washington was open to general society; the whole mass of politicians, even the Federalists, were dependent on Jefferson and "The Palace" for amusement; and if they refused to go there, they "lived like bears, brutalized and stupefied."

—Henry Adams, *History of the United States During the Administration of Thomas Jefferson*, 1889

49. As the great-grandson of President John Adams, the historian Henry Adams might have been expected to be which of the following?
A. Critical of the policies of Thomas Jefferson
B. Supportive of the policies of Thomas Jefferson
C. Critical of the Constitutional Convention
D. More interested in the French and Indian War

50. Thomas Jefferson's victory in the election of 1800 was important because
A. he was the first southerner to become president.
B. it was the first time the presidency shifted from one political party to another.
C. he believed it was necessary to go to war with Great Britain.
D. he encouraged the rapid industrialization of the United States.

51. Although Jefferson believed that government should be small and limited, once in office he
A. created a spoils system that bloated the size of the bureaucracy.
B. laid the foundations of the welfare state.
C. called for an ambitious program of road building and public works.
D. vigorously exercised federal power in foreign affairs.

52. According to Henry Adams, the city of Washington in 1801 was
A. the hub of American economic power.
B. rapidly turning into the "Paris" of North America.
C. still an underdeveloped cultural backwater.
D. still under the control of the British.

Questions 53–55 refer to the following quotation.

Perhaps, however, I am more conscious of the importance of civil liberties in this particular moment of our history than anyone else, because I travel through the country and meet people and see things that have happened to little people, I realize what it means to democracy to preserve our civil liberties.

All through the years we have had to fight for civil liberty, and we know that there are times when the light grows rather dim, and every time that happens democracy is in danger. Now, largely because of the troubled state of the world as a whole, civil liberties have disappeared in many other countries.

It is impossible, of course, to be at war and keep freedom of the press and freedom of speech and freedom of assembly. They disappear automatically. And so in many countries where ordinarily they were safe, today they have gone. In other countries, even before war came, not only freedom of the press and freedom of assembly, and freedom of speech disappeared, but freedom of religion disappeared.

And so we know here in this country, we have a grave responsibility. We are at peace. We have no reason for the fears which govern so many other peoples throughout the world; therefore, we have to guard the freedoms of democracy.

—Eleanor Roosevelt, Address to the American Civil Liberties Union, Chicago, Illinois, March 14, 1940

53. In her speech, Eleanor Roosevelt alluded to the earlier threat to civil liberties created by which of the following?
A. World War I
B. The New Deal
C. The Cold War
D. The Great Depression

54. An example of the threat to civil liberties that concerned Roosevelt was which of the following?
A. The Social Security Act
B. Executive Order 9066 interning Japanese Americans
C. The G.I. Bill
D. The Baby Boom

55. Roosevelt's concerns can most directly be compared to those of the people who debated which of the following?
A. The Gulf of Tonkin Resolution of 1964
B. The Voting Rights Act of 1965
C. The USA Patriot Act of 2001
D. The Affordable Care Act of 2010

Go on to Part B. ➡

Part B (Short Answer)

Part B recommended time: 40 minutes

Directions: Answer three questions. You must answer questions 1 and 2, and you can choose to answer either 3 or 4. Carefully read and follow the directions for each question. Some will refer to historical sources. These questions will require you to make use of your historical analytical skills and your familiarity with historical themes. These questions do *not* require you to develop a thesis in your responses.

Question 1 is based on the following passage:

Behold, then, the unlettered man of the West, the nursling of the wilds, the farmer of the Hermitage, little versed in books, unconnected by science with the tradition of the past, raised by the people to the highest pinnacle of honor, to the central post in the civilization of republican freedom, to the station where all the nations of the earth would watch his actions—where his words would vibrate through the civilized world, and his spirit be the moving star to guide the nations. ... The man of the West came as the inspired prophet of the West: he came as one free from the bonds of hereditary or established custom; he came with no superior but conscience, nor oracle but his native judgment; and, true to his origin and his education—true to the conditions and circumstances of his advancement, he valued right more than usage; he reverted from the pressure of established interests to the energy of first principles.

—George Bancroft, Eulogy on Andrew Jackson, 1845

1. Using the excerpt, answer A, B, and C.
   A. Briefly describe the historian and politician George Bancroft's assessment of Andrew Jackson.
   B. Briefly explain ONE historical event or development that supports Bancroft's assessment of Andrew Jackson.
   C. Briefly explain the perspective of someone opposed to Bancroft's assessment of Andrew Jackson.

Question 2 is based on the following passages:

It makes very little difference, however, where one opens the record of the history of the Indians; every page and every year has its dark stain. The story of one tribe is the story of all, varied only by differences of time and place; but neither time nor place makes any difference in the main facts. Colorado is as greedy and unjust in 1880 as was Georgia in 1830 and Ohio in 1795; and the United States Government breaks promises now as deftly as then, and with an added ingenuity from long practice.

—Helen Hunt Jackson, *A Century of Dishonor*, 1881

The settler and pioneer have at bottom had justice on their side; this great continent could not have been kept as nothing but a game preserve for squalid savages. Moreover, to the most oppressed Indian nations the whites often acted as a protection, or, at least, they deferred instead of hastening their fate.

—Theodore Roosevelt, *The Winning of the West*, 1889

2. Using the excerpts, answer A, B, and C.
   A. Briefly explain the perspective of Helen Hunt Jackson.
   B. Briefly explain the perspective of Theodore Roosevelt.
   C. Briefly explain ONE example of a development that supports the argument of one of the excerpts.

3. Answer A, B, and C.
   A. Briefly explain how ONE of the following was important in the formation of a distinctly American identity in the colonies.
      The Great Awakening
      The French and Indian War
      Resistance to the Stamp Act and other examples of British taxation
   B. Briefly explain how a SECOND of these options was important in the formation of a distinctly American identity in the colonies.
   C. Briefly explain how ONE of these events influenced the American Revolution.

4. Answer A, B, and C.
   A. Briefly explain how ONE of the following groups gained in rights and status during the twentieth century.
      Women
      African Americans
      Mexican Americans
   B. Briefly explain how a SECOND of these options gained in rights and status during the twentieth century.
   C. Briefly explain ONE example of how the experience of one of these groups was influenced by one of the others.

STOP. End of Section I, Part B.

Section II

Time: 100 minutes

Part A (Document–Based Question)*

Part A recommended time: 60 minutes

Directions: Use the documents to answer the question. You may want to spend up to 15 minutes outlining your response and 40 minutes writing the essay that answers the question.

Be sure to provide a thesis that addresses all elements of the question.

Be sure to support your argument with evidence from at least six of the seven documents.

Be sure to support your argument by recognizing and explaining historical complexity, connecting different kinds of historical evidence in a coherent way.

Be sure to base your analysis of no less than four documents on at least one of the following: the point of view of the author, the purpose of the author, the intended audience of the document, the historical context of the document.

Be sure to support your argument by analyzing historical evidence that comes from outside the documents.

Be sure to connect historical evidence supporting your argument to broader historical events or processes.

Be sure to synthesize all the tasks above into a persuasive history essay.

1. To what extent did the Supreme Court advance or inhibit Progressive regulation of corporations in the period 1885 to 1920?

Document A
Source: U.S. v. Debs, et al., 1894 (response to the Pullman Strike)

> *That the original design [of the Sherman Antitrust Act] to suppress trusts and monopolies . . . is clear; but it is equally clear that further and more comprehensive purpose came to be entertained. . . . Combinations are condemned, not only when they take the form of trusts, but in whatever form found, if they be in restraint of trade.*

Document B
Source: U.S. v. E. C. Knight Company, 1895

> *Congress did not attempt . . . to make criminal the acts of persons in the acquisition and control of property which the states of their residence or creation sanctioned or permitted.*

> *The contracts and acts of the defendants related exclusively to the acquisition of the Philadelphia refineries and the business of sugar refining in Pennsylvania, and bore no direct relation to commerce between states or with foreign countries. The object was manifestly private gain in the manufacture of the commodity, but not through the control of interstate or foreign commerce.*

Document C
Source: Smyth v. Ames, 1898

> *By the 14th Amendment it is provided that no state shall deprive any person of property without the due process of law nor deny to any person within its jurisdiction the equal protection of laws. That corporations are persons within this amendment is now settled.*

---

* Please note this book was printed before rubrics for the 2018 DBQ and long essay question were posted at the AP U.S. History website.

[The Court] adjudged that the enforcement of the schedules of rates established by the [Nebraska law reducing railroad rates] . . . would deprive the railroad companies of the compensation they were legally entitled to receive.

Document D
Source: Lochner v. New York, 1905

The act [state law limiting maximum hours of bakers] is not . . . a health law, but is an illegal interference with the rights of individuals, both employers and employees, to make contracts regarding labor upon such terms as they may think best. . . . Statutes of the nature of that under review, limiting the hours in which grown and intelligent men may labor to earn their living, are meddlesome interferences with the rights of the individual, and they are not saved from condemnation by the claim that they are passed upon the subject of the health of the individual whose rights are interfered with.

Document E
Source: Muller v. Oregon, 1908

The two sexes differ in structure of body, . . . in the amount of physical strength in the capacity for long-continued labor, . . . the influence of vigorous health upon the future well-being of the race, . . . and in the capacity to maintain the struggle for subsistence. This difference justifies a difference in legislation.

For these reasons, and without questioning in any respect the decision in Lochner v. New York, *we are of the opinion that it cannot be adjudged that the [state law limiting the hours women may work] is in conflict with the Federal Constitution, so far as it respects the work of a female in a laundry.*

Document F
Source: Standard Oil Company of New Jersey v. United States, 1911

The public policy has been to prohibit . . . contracts or acts entered into with the intent to wrong the public and which unreasonably restrict competitive conditions, limit the rights of individuals, restrain the free flow of commerce, or bring about public evils such as the enhancement of prices.

The combination of the defendants in this case is an unreasonable and undue restraint of trade in petroleum and its products moving in interstate commerce, and falls within the prohibitions of the [Sherman Antitrust Act].

Document G
Source: Wilson v. New, 1917

The effect of the [Adamson Act] is not only to establish permanently an eight-hour standard for work and wages as between the [railroad] carrier and employees affected, but also to fix a scale of minimum wages for the eight-hour day and proportionately for overtime.

Viewed as an act establishing an eight-hour day as the standard of service by employees, the statute is clearly within the power of Congress under the commerce clause.

Viewed as an act fixing wages, the statute merely illustrates the character of regulation essential, and hence permissible, for the protection of the public right.

Go on to Part B. ➔

Part B (Long Essay)

Part B recommended time: 40 minutes

Directions: Answer *one* of the following questions. State a thesis that addresses all aspects of the question. This thesis of one or more sentences must be in the introduction or conclusion.

Make use of your historical analytical skills and familiarity with historical themes as you develop your answer.

Support your thesis and substantiate your essay by citing examples of historical evidence.

Relate the topic of the question to broader historical trends or events.

2. Evaluate the extent to which differing ideas about the nature of government shaped the emergence of political parties in the 1780s and 1790s.

3. Evaluate the extent to which reform movements played an important role in shaping American society from 1820-1860.

4. Evaluate the extent of social and political changes in the lives of women during the period 1900–1930.

STOP. End of Section II.

ANSWERS TO PRACTICE EXAM 2

Multiple Choice

1. B	15. B	29. C	43. C
2. C	16. C	30. A	44. A
3. A	17. B	31. D	45. B
4. D	18. D	32. B	46. C
5. A	19. C	33. A	47. A
6. D	20. A	34. B	48. D
7. C	21. C	35. C	49. A
8. B	22. D	36. D	50. B
9. B	23. A	37. A	51. D
10. D	24. B	38. B	52. C
11. A	25. A	39. B	53. A
12. C	26. C	40. D	54. B
13. D	27. B	41. D	55. C
14. A	28. D	42. C	

Explanations for the Multiple-Choice Questions

1. **B.** The political idea that *best* reflects the perspective of President Calvin Coolidge in the passage is that government should be limited. A limited government would be an inexpensive government. Hence Coolidge opposed heavy taxes on citizens. He believed overtaxation hurt taxpayers, took money out of the private economy, and encouraged wasteful government spending.

2. **C.** The president most likely to share Coolidge's sentiments would be Ronald Reagan. President Reagan also worked to limit the size of government and cut taxes. Reagan admired Coolidge and prominently displayed a portrait of him in the White House.

3. **A.** The ideas expressed by Coolidge were influenced by the widespread prosperity in the 1920s. Coolidge believed that the growing prosperity of most Americans was the result of keeping government out of the way of business and allowing people to keep more of their money by reducing taxes. His ideas proved popular with voters. Taking office after the death of President Warren Harding in 1923, he won election to the presidency in his own right in 1924. His Republican party kept control of Congress throughout the 1920s.

4. **D.** In the passage, Coolidge is reacting against the governmental policies of the Progressive Era. The Progressives greatly expanded the role of the government in the economy and in American life. This culminated in the policies of President Woodrow Wilson during World War I, when the government coordinated much of the economy and monitored what people said about the war. Following the war, there was a reaction against such control. Warren Harding successfully appealed to this sentiment with his call for a "return to normalcy" in 1920. Coolidge was Harding's vice president and continued his policies.

5. **A.** de Bry in the image reflects the perspective that the natives of Florida are primitive and superstitious. The image shows the Indians worshipping a column erected by the French explorers, indicating that they thought the Europeans possessed special powers. The Europeans tended to regard the natives of America as heathens who had to be Christianized and subjected to the tutelage of their more advanced civilization.

6. **D.** The image is an expression of European curiosity about the wider world. This illustration is one of many that de Bry made picturing the peoples of the New World. In addition to looking for lands to conquer and new sources of trade, Europeans were interested in learning more about the world. This desire for learning was inspired by the Renaissance and the Scientific Revolution.

7. **C.** The column erected by the French commander signified European desires to establish political control over new territories. The European powers competed to acquire new territories in the New World, which they hoped would be rich sources of valuable goods and trade.

8. **B.** European rivalries would lead to the French being driven from Florida by the Spanish. In 1564, French Protestants, called Huguenots, built Fort Caroline, near modern-day Jacksonville. The following year Spanish forces from St. Augustine destroyed the settlement. The French retaliated with an attack of their own but were never able to reestablish themselves in Florida.

9. **B.** A Progressive would be most likely to support the perspective expressed by Riis in the passage. The Progressives were middle-class reformers interested in addressing the problems created by the rapid industrialization and urbanization of the United States during the first two decades of the twentieth century. Many Progressives worked to ameliorate labor conditions for workers.

10. **D.** The situation faced by the young women in the passage is most directly comparable to that of Detroit autoworkers in the 1930s. The autoworkers also needed better wages and working conditions. They staged famous sit-down strikes in 1936 and 1937 to win recognition of the United Auto Workers (UAW) union.

11. **A.** Concerns like those expressed by Riis in the passage led most directly to laws regulating the working conditions of women. During the Progressive Era, laws were passed

to protect women in the workplace. The great lawyer Louis Brandeis persuaded the Supreme Court to uphold a law mandating an eight-hour workday for women in *Muller v. Oregon* (1908).

12. **C.** Riis's work as an investigator of the lives of the poor can most directly be associated with the muckrakers. Muckrakers were Progressive Era journalists who exposed corruption and social injustice in American life. Examples of muckrakers were Lincoln Steffens, who wrote about urban political machines, Ida Tarbell, who documented the history of John Rockefeller's Standard Oil, and Ray Stannard Baker, who explored the living conditions of African Americans.

13. **D.** The Zenger Trial was a landmark case concerning freedom of expression. Zenger was a newspaper editor who had published criticisms of the royal governor of New York. Brought to trial for seditious libel, the judge instructed the jury that the truth or falsity of what Zenger wrote was immaterial; the law held that printing unflattering commentary on a royal governor was enough to declare the defendant guilty. The defense lawyer Andrew Hamilton appealed to the jurors' love of liberty and asked them to oppose governmental tyranny. The jury voted to acquit Zenger. This case helped ensure freedom of the press and freedom of speech in colonial America.

14. **A.** Andrew Hamilton assumes that Americans have more freedoms than people in other countries. Hamilton appeals to the natural rights enjoyed by free men and to the liberties accorded to British subjects. He urges the jurors to vindicate these rights against arbitrary power "in these parts of the world at least," indicating a sense that Americans are freer than people living elsewhere.

15. **B.** The Zenger case can best be compared to government efforts to prevent the publication of the Pentagon Papers in 1971. Daniel Ellsberg, a former Defense Department official, leaked a secret Pentagon study of the origins of the Vietnam War to the *New York Times*. The Nixon administration went to court to stop the newspaper from publishing these documents. Ultimately, the Supreme Court upheld the right of the newspaper to publish the Pentagon Papers in *New York Times Co. v. United States* (1971). This decision was a strong affirmation of First Amendment protections for a free press.

16. **C.** Hamilton's success in the Zenger case most directly reflects a long tradition of self-rule in the colonies. Hamilton's argument to the jury assumed a lack of deference on the part of the jurors toward established authority. This reflected a century during which the colonies had been largely self-governing. Hamilton correctly expected that the jurors knew that they had rights and would feel free to defend them. This tradition of self-government would be very important during the political crisis leading to American independence.

17. **B.** The perspective of Thomas Nast's cartoon is that the government is not adequately protecting freed slaves. Nast was worried that Southern whites working through organizations like the Ku Klux Klan were returning the South to places where African Americans were oppressed. He notes that in some ways the situation is worse than it was under slavery, with the terroristic Klan lynching freedmen and burning schools.

18. **D.** The situation described in the cartoon most directly resulted in the *Plessy v. Ferguson* Supreme Court decision. *Plessy v. Ferguson* (1896) ruled that separate but equal facilities for whites and African Americans were constitutional. This court case reflected a retreat on the part of the government in protecting African American rights in the South that began with the end of Reconstruction in 1877. Many in the North grew tired of trying to force Southern whites to accept African American rights. While *Plessy v. Ferguson* paid lip service to equality, in reality Southern whites were able to impose Jim Crow laws on African Americans.

19. **C.** The Southerners in the cartoon wanted a "Union" characterized by sovereignty centered in the states. The doctrine of states' rights had been used before the Civil War to protect the institution of slavery. Following the end of Reconstruction, Southerners would invoke states' rights to justify the enforcement of Jim Crow laws.

20. **A.** The ideas in the cartoon reflect continuities in debates about civil rights. Thomas Nast, at a late stage in Reconstruction, was worried about African American rights. His cartoon was a plea for the enforcement of laws passed to protect African Americans, including the Thirteenth, Fourteenth, and Fifteenth Amendments to the Constitution.

21. **C.** The nomination of Geraldine Ferraro for vice president was most directly a continuation of increased economic and political opportunities for women. The women's movement of the 1960s was remarkably successful in altering people's expectations for women. Large numbers of women entered the workforce in the 1970s and 1980s and flourished in fields that had previously been largely closed to them. Ferraro's nomination was an emblematic first for women in politics.

22. **D.** The political ideas expressed by Ferraro in the passage most directly reflect those of New Dealers of the 1930s. Ferraro was a liberal Democrat. Like the New Dealers of Franklin Roosevelt's day, she believed that government could be used to help the ordinary in a country dominated by the wealthy and big business. She opposed President Ronald Reagan's efforts to limit the size of government and deregulate business.

23. **A.** The ideas expressed by Ferraro would have most directly strengthened opposition to the administration's arms buildup. During the 1980s, President Ronald Reagan increased the size of the American military to carry on the cold war with the Soviet Union from a position of strength. Like many liberal Democrats, Ferraro opposed the size of this increase in military spending, preferring to spend money on domestic social programs.

24. **B.** Geraldine Ferraro can most directly be compared to Sandra Day O'Connor. In 1981, O'Connor became the first woman to serve on the Supreme Court, after being nominated by President Ronald Reagan. Like O'Connor, Ferraro was blazing new trails for women in the 1980s.

25. **A.** The situation described in the passage led most directly to the Homestead Act. Like the people Parkman met on the Oregon Trail, many Americans regarded the West as a land of opportunity. In 1862, Congress passed the Homestead Act. This law encouraged western settlement, giving people title to 160 acres of land if they lived on it for five years and made improvements.

26. **C.** The actions of the people in the passage most directly reflect the influence of Manifest Destiny. During the 1840s publicists popularized the idea of Manifest Destiny, that Americans would spread their democratic institutions across the North American continent. This idea helped justify the Mexican War. It also helped inspire American settlement in the Oregon Territory, where the United States disputed a boundary line with Great Britain. Thousands of settlers followed the Oregon Trail to the Oregon Territory.

27. **B.** The experiences of the people encountered by Francis Parkman can most directly be compared to the Pilgrims. The people Parkman met suffered many hardships as they traveled west. The Pilgrims also suffered a great deal, including a starving time, before their colony began to prosper.

28. **D.** Thomas Jefferson had most directly anticipated and desired the movement described by Parkman. Jefferson wanted to see a United States dominated by independent farmers. Land was necessary to fulfill this vision, so Jefferson was intensely interested in the West. Jefferson swallowed his constitutional scruples to purchase the Louisiana Territory in 1803 and then sent Lewis and Clark on an epic journey to explore it.

29. **C.** The perspective of Senator George McGovern's speech reflects the opinion that American bombing in Vietnam was a failure. Operation Rolling Thunder began in 1965 as a carefully calibrated bombing campaign designed to pressure the North Vietnamese regime to halt its support for its war against the South Vietnamese government. By 1967, it was becoming increasingly clear that bombing would not dissuade the North Vietnamese from carrying on the war. The American intervention into the war with a growing number of troops on the ground led the North Vietnamese to match this with a buildup of their own forces in South Vietnam.

30. A. The sentiments expressed in the speech most directly influenced the passage of the War Powers Act of 1973. Congress passed this law over the veto of President Richard Nixon. Hoping to prevent another situation like Vietnam where presidents involved the United States in a war without direct approval by Congress, this act required the president to notify Congress within two days of sending troops into combat. Unless Congress authorized the action, these troops would have to be withdrawn after 60 days.

31. D. The sentiments expressed in the speech most directly reflected the widespread popular attitude of the 1960s that government statements about Vietnam could not be trusted. As the war ground on without resolution, despite optimistic statements coming from the administration of President Lyndon Johnson, some commentators began to talk about a "credibility gap." Evoking memories of John F. Kennedy's political campaigning about a perceived "missile gap" with the Soviet Union, some now pointed to a gap between what the administration said and the truth.

32. B. Political discord during the Vietnam War most closely resembled the political dissensions during the Mexican War. Just as with Vietnam, there was significant opposition to the Mexican War. Many Americans thought it was an unjust war of aggression, and some thought it was intended to open up new territories to slavery. Prominent Americans who opposed the Mexican War included Congressman Abraham Lincoln and writer Henry David Thoreau.

33. A. The ideas expressed in Phillis Wheatley's poem most directly reflect the influence of the First Great Awakening. The First Great Awakening was a revival of religious fervor in the American colonies during the middle of the eighteenth century. It emphasized the need for salvation and a direct personal relationship with God. This religious movement spread to many slaves. Wheatley in her poem expresses her gratitude for her conversion to Christianity.

34. B. The continuity in American history most directly reflected in Wheatley's poem is debates over social justice. Wheatley makes a gentle case for human rights in her poem. She reminds her readers, almost exclusively white, that Africans can become Christians. The equality of all races in Christ could be a radical message in the 1770s.

35. C. The literary success of Phillis Wheatley led most directly to questions about the moral justification of slavery. Wheatley's critically acclaimed poetry contradicted racist assumptions that Africans were intellectually inferior. Wheatley, a slave who benefitted from an education, and who wrote poetry modeled on the best English forms, demonstrated that Africans, even slaves, possessed the same potential as white Europeans.

36. D. The point of Wheatley's poem can best be compared to Martin Luther King, Jr.'s "I Have a Dream" speech. Like King's speech, Wheatley's poem emphasizes the essential equality of all people and reminds readers that skin color should not be a barrier to unity. Just as King wanted all Americans to join together in equal enjoyment of their constitutional rights, so Wheatley urged all people to come together in Christian harmony.

37. A. In his Cooper Union Address, Abraham Lincoln called for northern voters to resist the demands of pro-slavery advocates. The Cooper Union Address was a long speech that enabled Lincoln to summarize his views in the wake of the Dred Scott case, his Senate race, and the John Brown affair. The success of this speech made Lincoln a leading contender for the Republican nomination for president.

38. B. A member of the Republican Party would have been most likely to support Lincoln's position. The Republican Party was created in 1854 in response to the passage of the Kansas-Nebraska Act, which repealed the Missouri Compromise and opened the possibility of slavery being established in territories where it previously had been barred. The Republican slogan was "Free labor, free land, free men."

39. B. In 1860, Lincoln and his supporters called for preventing the expansion of slavery into the western territories. Lincoln and the Republicans assured the South that, while they did not want slavery in the territories, they would leave it alone where it already existed. This did not reassure southerners who believed that the institution of slavery would collapse if it did not expand.

40. **D.** Lincoln's Cooper Union Address can best be compared to William Jennings Bryan's "Cross of Gold" speech in 1896. Lincoln's success in clearly articulating the antislavery argument in the Cooper Union Address helped him win the Republican presidential nomination. William Jennings Bryan's fiery pro-silver "Cross of Gold" speech at the 1896 Democratic National Convention helped him win the Democratic presidential nomination by capturing the concerns of western and southern farmers who were being economically hurt by the "hard money" gold standard.

41. **D.** In "The March of the Flag," Albert Beveridge supported the creation of an American overseas empire. Beveridge, at the time in the midst of what would be a successful campaign for the U.S. Senate in Indiana, was one of a number of American political figures, such as Theodore Roosevelt and Henry Cabot Lodge, who believed that the acquisition of an empire in the Caribbean and in Asia would increase American economic and political influence in the world. They also believed that an empire would offer Americans a new frontier to replace the one rapidly disappearing in the west.

42. **C.** Beveridge's speech was a response to the Spanish-American War of 1898. In this war, the United States rapidly defeated the Spanish and acquired control of Cuba, Puerto Rico, Guam, and the Philippines. While there was general agreement that the Cubans would be given their independence, at the time of Beveridge's speech, there was an ongoing debate about what to do with the Philippines. Some argued that the Filipinos, who had risen against their Spanish rulers, should be given independence. Beveridge believed that the United States should govern the Philippines as a colonial possession. His view prevailed, and the United States purchased the Philippines from Spain; the American Army then fought a war against Filipino forces from 1899 to 1902 before securely establishing the authority of the United States in the island chain.

43. **C.** The theme of Beveridge's speech can most directly be compared to Manifest Destiny. In the 1840s, many Americans believed that it was the destiny of Americans to carry the American flag and American institutions to the Pacific Ocean. Beveridge believed that it was the destiny of the United States as a rising power to plant its flag at outposts around the world.

44. **A.** The policy advocated by Beveridge foreshadowed the rise of the United States to the status of a great power. Victory in the Spanish-American War and the acquisition of a colonial empire made the United States a force to be reckoned with beyond the North American continent. Under Presidents William McKinley and Theodore Roosevelt, the United States exerted growing influence around the world. Under McKinley, the United States launched the Open Door Policy in China. Under Roosevelt, the United States mediated an end to the Russo-Japanese War of 1904–1905 and took part in the Algeciras Conference of 1906, settling a dispute between Germany and France over Morocco. Under President Woodrow Wilson, the United States would play a pivotal role in the First World War.

45. **B.** A proprietary colony in which the King entrusted government to a proprietor and his family best describes the colony of Pennsylvania. The English King Charles II owed a large sum of money to William Penn's father. To satisfy the debt, in 1681, the King granted Penn a charter to a vast area of 45,000 square miles, which became the province of Pennsylvania. Penn and his descendants owned the colony until the American Revolution.

46. **C.** The persecuted religious group to which William Penn belonged was the Quakers. The Quakers were a group of Christians that emphasized the individual's direct experience of God. This brought them into conflict with the established Church of England. William Penn was imprisoned for his religious writings. He envisioned his province of Pennsylvania as a refuge for Quakers, where they could practice their religion in freedom. As proprietor, Penn would extend this religious freedom to all Christian groups.

47. **A.** Because of Penn's Charter of Privileges, Pennsylvania became one of the most religiously diverse colonies in British America.

In addition to people from England, groups of Germans settled in Pennsylvania seeking religious freedom. German Mennonites arrived in the 1680s, and the Amish settled in Pennsylvania during the eighteenth century.

48. **D.** Penn's Charter of Privileges can be seen as a forerunner to the First Amendment of the Constitution. The First Amendment prohibited the creation of an established, or official government, Church in the United States and guaranteed freedom of religion.

49. **A.** As the great-grandson of President John Adams, the historian Henry Adams might have been expected to be critical of the policies of Thomas Jefferson. John Adams was a Federalist, and Thomas Jefferson was a Democratic-Republican. The two men were bitter rivals in the election of 1800. Following his defeat, Adams declined to attend the inauguration of Thomas Jefferson. In later years, the two men reconciled and resumed their earlier friendship. Both former presidents famously died on the same day, July 4, 1826.

50. **B.** Thomas Jefferson's victory in the election of 1800 was important because it was the first time the presidency shifted from one political party to another. President George Washington had warned against political parties in his Farewell Address. Despite that, political strife between the emerging Federalist and Democratic-Republican parties grew fierce. At his inauguration, Jefferson made a plea for unity, saying, "We are all republicans, we are all federalists."

51. **D.** Although Jefferson believed that government should be small and limited, once in office, he vigorously exercised federal power in foreign affairs. Jefferson fought a naval war against the Barbary Coast pirate state of Tripoli from 1801 to 1805. He recommended the Louisiana Purchase despite his fears that such a purchase might be unconstitutional. Jefferson used troops to enforce his unpopular Embargo Act, which was passed by Congress in December 1807.

52. **C.** According to Henry Adams, the city of Washington in 1801 was still an underdeveloped cultural backwater. Washington was founded as a city in 1791. Congress met for the first time in Washington in 1800. That same year, President John Adams moved into the Executive Mansion, later named the White House. The District of Columbia was officially organized as a territory under the control of the federal government with the Organic Act of 1801. In its early days, Washington was a very small place with few amenities, leading to Henry Adams's description of it as an "underdeveloped cultural backwater."

53. **A.** In her speech, Eleanor Roosevelt alluded to the threat to civil liberties created by World War I. During World War I, the federal government encouraged restrictions on civil liberties. The Espionage Act of 1917 set prison sentences for people who encouraged military insubordination or disloyalty. It also gave the postmaster general the power to confiscate publications that he deemed to violate the law. The Sedition Act of 1918 outlawed the use of "disloyal, profane, scurrilous, or abusive language" about the U.S. flag, government, and military. During the war, many people were imprisoned for violating these laws. The Socialist Party leader Eugene V. Debs was imprisoned for criticizing the war.

54. **B.** An example of the threat to civil liberties that concerned Roosevelt was Executive Order 9066 interning Japanese Americans. In the aftermath of Pearl Harbor, anti-Japanese feeling in California and fears that people of Japanese extraction might commit acts of sabotage led President Franklin D. Roosevelt to sign Executive Order 9066 calling for the forced relocation of 120,000 Japanese Americans living on the West Coast to camps elsewhere in the United States. Although the Supreme Court upheld the constitutionality of the relocation in *Korematsu v. U.S.* (1944), the United States government officially apologized in 1988 and paid each survivor $20,000.

55. **C.** Roosevelt's concerns can most directly be compared to those of the people who debated the USA Patriot Act of 2001. Following the Al-Qaeda terrorist attacks of September 11, 2001, Congress felt the need to strike a balance between imposing security and surveillance measures sufficient to protect the American public from further terrorist attacks while not sacrificing essential privacy rights and civil liberties. This led to a longstanding debate about the extent to which government electronic surveillance compromised the rights of American citizens.

Explanations for the Short-Answer Questions

1. A. The historian and politician George Bancroft sees Andrew Jackson as an embodiment of the West. Bancroft sees the West as untouched by the corruption of the more long-established, settled, and Europeanized East. As a product of the West, Bancroft regards Jackson as a child of nature, reflecting the virtues of an environment that produces people free from the stultifying manners and conventions of society. Bancroft's view of Jackson is heavily influenced by contemporary Romanticism. Similar ideas about the virtues of the "natural" man living on the frontier can be seen in James Fenimore Cooper's novel *The Last of the Mohicans*, 1826. Jackson's association with the West was also reflected in his reputation as a champion of democracy and the common man.

B. Much of Jackson's early years were spent on the frontier in the Carolinas and Tennessee. As a man who lived through some of the wilder aspects of life on the frontier, Jackson became a notable duelist and Indian-fighter. Jackson's military activities as a commander against the Creeks, British, and Spanish during and after the War of 1812 helped secure the Western territories in the South, and acquired new lands for settlement. As president, Jackson would champion Indian Removal to open up more land to settlers. A Jeffersonian in political philosophy, Jackson put himself at the head of the movement for an expanded franchise that became known as "Jacksonian Democracy." Jackson was the first president to come from the West. He promoted the "spoils system" in politics, which opened up government offices to ordinary men who were politically loyal. Jackson opposed any political or economic combination that struck him as representing illicit privilege, most notably the Second Bank of the United States which he ruined in his "Bank War."

C. Members of the Whig party, which coalesced in opposition to Jackson's policies, would not have seen him as a champion of opportunity for the average man. The Whigs, led by men like Henry Clay, were more open to using the government to spur economic activity. Clay's "American System" called for tariffs to protect American industries, internal improvements to provide roads to help farmers get crops to markets, and a national bank to facilitate financial transactions. Whigs would have seen Jackson's opposition to internal improvements and the Second Bank of the United States as obstacles to ambitious and hardworking men getting ahead.

2. A. Helen Hunt Jackson was a novelist and reformer who publicized the injustices done to Native Americans. In this passage, she argues that the United States government has a long record of breaking treaties with Indian nations, furthering the interests of settlers greedy for land. She believed that the United States had always behaved dishonorably toward Native Americans.

B. Theodore Roosevelt, at the time that he wrote this, was a historian and politician. He spent a few years as a rancher in the Dakota Territory. There he absorbed the attitudes of westerners concerning Indians. In his multivolume history *The Winning of the West* he dismissed criticisms of American Indian policy, arguing that the Native American peoples were savages with no legitimate claim to lands that they lived on but had not improved through extensive farming and permanent settlement. A believer in Social Darwinism and contemporary theories of racial hierarchy, Roosevelt assumed that the Indians would inevitably disappear as they came into contact with America's Anglo-Saxon civilization. Their only hope of survival came from the efforts of the American government to protect them.

C. There are many examples of broken treaties between the United States government and Indian tribes. In 1868 the Treaty of Fort Laramie created a great reservation in the Dakotas for the Sioux. In 1874, George Armstrong Cuter led an expedition into the Black Hills that discovered gold. A gold rush ensued, bringing many miners into the Sioux lands. The Sioux responded by going to war. This led to the 1876 Battle of the Little Big Horn in which Custer and the members of the Seventh Cavalry with him were killed. Despite this victory, the Sioux were soon defeated and lost more of their lands. Roosevelt would argue that the policy of placing Indian tribes on reservations, where they were often supported by the government, was evidence of the benign intentions of the United States, and that this offered the Indians the hope of a future as the continent was settled. Sometimes the best efforts of reformers hoping to help the Indians had unfortunate consequences. Legislators sympathetic to Native Americans passed the Dawes Severalty Act in 1887. The law was intended to help Indians assimilate into American society. Reservations were divided up, with heads of household receiving 160 acres of land to farm. Surplus reservation land was sold to fund schools intended to transform Indian children into Americans. This law intentionally weakened tribal society, but failed to effectively replace it. Many Indians ended up selling their land. By 1900, 50 percent of tribal lands had been sold. Conditions would not improve for Native Americans until the New Deal of the 1930s which attempted to restore tribal government.

3. **A, B.** The Great Awakening that began in the 1730s set off several decades of religious revivals in the American colonies. The preachers of the Great Awakening, such as Jonathan Edwards, George Whitefield, and Gilbert Tennant emphasized the dependence of individuals upon God's grace, and the need for the individual to develop a personal relationship with God. Many religious congregations split between the "New Lights" who embraced the revival, and "old Lights" who preferred the traditional religious authorities. The Great Awakening was a phenomenon that united all the colonies. Many Americans contrasted the new religious fervor around them with the less Godly state of affairs back in Britain. The French and Indian War saw the American colonies mobilize large forces to assist the British in the war effort. By the end of the war, 20,000 Americans had served in the military. The Americans cooperated in a joint effort that gave many young men like George Washington a more continental sense of American affairs. Following the conflict, Americans saw themselves as an important part of the growing British Empire. The resistance to the Stamp Act and other examples of British taxation was widespread throughout the American colonies.

Opposition to the Stamp Act and other actions by Parliament forced the colonies to cooperate as never before. The 1765 Stamp Act Congress saw representatives from nine colonies meet to coordinate measures against the Stamp Act. Over time, organizations like the Sons of Liberty and Committees of Correspondence appeared across the colonies. In the crisis that followed the 1773 Boston Tea Party and the passage of the British Coercive Acts, the First Continental Congress met in 1774, bringing together such leaders as Patrick Henry, Samuel Adams, John Adams, and George Washington. Americans were increasingly thinking of themselves as a united people.

C. The Great Awakening weakened American's attachment to traditional religious authorities, making them also more inclined to question British political authority. The sense that Americans were a more religious people than the British also made them more inclined to strike out on their own. The French and Indian War helped prepare the way for the American Revolution by leading to the British financial crisis that led Parliament to attempt to tax the colonies. The defeat of the French removed the major threat to the Americans, and made British military protection less important. The political and military lessons learned in the war would be important in shaping the decisions of many American leaders during the War for Independence. George Washington and a number of other American military commanders were veterans of the French and Indian War, and used the experience they gained there against the British. The acts of resistance to British taxation led directly to the American Revolution. Between the Stamp Act Congress and the First Continental Congress, Americans across the colonies grew used to coordinating their actions. The First Continental Congress created the "Association," an agreement to cease trading with Great Britain until the Coercive Acts were repealed. It also paved the way for the Second Continental Congress, which began meeting in May 1775. By then, fighting had begun outside Boston. The Second Continental Congress coordinated the American war effort, and in July 1776 declared American Independence.

4. A, B. The big battle for women at the beginning of the twentieth century was the struggle for suffrage. Carrie Chapman Catt led the mainstream National America Woman Suffrage Association. Alice Paul led the more radical Congressional Union. A number of states began to allow women to vote in state elections. The efforts of women to assist in the war effort during World War I overcame the last resistance to blocking women's suffrage. Congress passed a women's suffrage amendment which was ratified as the Nineteenth Amendment in 1920. Most women in the 1920s, such as the youthful "flappers," focused on personal self-fulfillment rather than politics, though women such as Jeanette Rankin, the first female elected to Congress, Nellie Ross of Wyoming and Miriam Ferguson of Texas, elected governors in 1924, and Frances Perkins, the first female cabinet secretary, made notable contributions to public affairs. Alice Paul lobbied for an Equal Rights Amendment, though without success. During World War II, many women made important contributions to victory by working in war industries. "Rosie the Riveter" became a celebrated image. After the war, many women left these jobs as men returned from military service. Popular culture celebrated the woman as homemaker during the 1950s. Despite this, by the end of the 1950s, about 40 percent of women were working outside the home. This was a continuation of a growing trend in women's employment that had begun early in the century. In 1963, Betty Friedan published *The Feminine Mystique*, which argued that women needed to liberate themselves from the role of housewife. In 1966, Friedan helped found the National Organization of Women (NOW), launching what is now called "Second Wave" feminism, which worked to increase the influence of women in all aspects of society. The women's movement quickly saw many victories. Title IX of the Education Amendments in 1972 opened up unprecedented opportunities for female athletes at schools receiving federal money. The Supreme Court decision *Roe v. Wade* made abortion a right. Women rapidly moved into the workforce, a trend that was accelerated by economic problems in the 1970s. One defeat for the women's movement involved the Equal Rights Amendment, which passed Congress in 1972. At first seemingly assured of ratification in the states, it ultimately failed because of the opposition of conservative activists like Phyllis Schlafly, who argued that it would lead to drafting women into the military and unisex public restrooms. Despite this, women achieved many firsts in the 1980s. Sandra Day O'Connor became the first female Supreme Court Justice in 1981. Sally Ride became the first American woman in space in 1983. Geraldine Ferraro received the Democratic nomination for Vice President in 1984. African Americans at the turn of the twentieth century faced Jim Crow laws, legalized segregation in the South, and discrimination elsewhere in the United States. Booker T. Washington, the President of the Tuskegee Institute, argued that African Americans should focus on education and economic self-empowerment instead of immediately challenging segregation. He believed that increased economic power would eventually lead to full civil rights. W.E.B. Du Bois, a Harvard University trained historian, disagreed with Washington, and wrote that African Americans should strive for full social equality. In 1910 he was one of the founders of the National Association for the Advancement of Colored People (NAACP), which would become one of the most important and effective civil rights organizations. Around the time of World War I, many African Americans left the South in the "Great Migration" to northern cities, looking for work in war industries. This led to social tensions that sometimes erupted in race riots like those in Chicago in 1919. These new centers of African American settlement also became the sources of cultural creativity, such as the Harlem Renaissance of the 1920s. Writers such as Langston Hughes and Zora Neale Hurston, and musicians such as Duke Ellington won respect across racial lines. During World War II, more African Americans moved to the North and West seeking employment in rapidly expanding industrial plants. African Americans faced discrimination in war industries. A. Philip Randolph, leader of the Brotherhood of Sleeping Car Porters, threatened a march on Washington in 1941 to protest these conditions. President Franklin Roosevelt avoided this by creating the Fair Employment Practices Commission (FEPC) to ensure that African Americans were not subject to discrimination in the military and in defense work. The FEPC could not eliminate all discrimination, but it was an important precedent. During the war, many African Americans supported the "Double V" campaign—victory over the enemy overseas, and against racism in the United States. The NAACP kept up a legal campaign against Jim Crow laws in the South. The 1944 Supreme Court decision *Smith v. Allwright* declared all-white political primaries unconstitutional. In 1948, President Harry Truman, anxious to win African American support in that year's presidential election, ordered the integration of the United States military. The 1950s saw the African American civil rights movement make great strides. Thurgood Marshall, chief counsel for the NAACP, argued crucial cases before the Supreme Court. In 1950, the Supreme Court in *Sweatt v. Painter* ruled against segregated professional schools. In 1954, in *Brown v. Board of Education of Topeka, Kansas* the Supreme Court declared that segregated schools were "inherently unequal" and therefore unconstitutional, overruling the 1896 *Plessy v. Ferguson* decision and removing the legal basis of segregation. In 1955, Rosa Parks and the Reverend Martin Luther King, Jr. led a successful campaign to integrate the buses in Montgomery, Alabama. The Montgomery bus boycott made Martin Luther King, Jr. a nationally-known civil rights leader. In 1957, when African American students were prevented from enrolling at Central High School in Little Rock, Arkansas, President Dwight D. Eisenhower sent federal troops to protect them. Civil Rights Acts were passed in 1957 and 1960. These established a Civil Rights Commission, and attempted to protect African American voting rights. Martin Luther King, Jr. founded the Southern Christian Leadership Conference (SCLC) in 1957. Other civil rights organizations followed, such as the Student Non-Violent Coordinating Committee (SNCC) in 1960. In 1960, students in Greensboro, North Carolina started the "sit-in" movement, sitting in a whites-only Woolworths lunch counter. Groups of black and white "freedom riders" rode buses into the south in an attempt to desegregate bus terminals. Many were attacked, and the Kennedy Administration had to intervene to protect them. President John F. Kennedy also had to protect James Meredith as he attempted to enroll at the University of Mississippi. The August 1963 March on Washington, with Martin Luther King, Jr.'s "I Have a Dream" speech, attempted to rally support for a new civil rights bill. Efforts to desegregate Birmingham, Alabama were met with violent action by police chief "Bull" Connor, who unleashed dogs and fire hoses on protestors. Episodes like this helped turn public opinion against the segregationists. President Lyndon B. Johnson pushed the Civil Rights Act of 1964 through Congress. This outlawed discrimination in public facilities and employment. The next year, the Voting Rights Act of 1965 made literacy tests illegal, and put the power of the federal government behind registering African American voters. The legal basis for discriminating against African Americans was overthrown by these laws. In the late 1960s, radical "Black Power" groups like the Black Panther Party promoted African American militancy and pride, but alienated many whites. By the 1920s, the Mexican American population in the United States doubled in size as people fled the violence of the Mexican Revolution or looked for work in the United States. In the depths of the Great Depression, some Mexican Americans were deported, as local authorities in the Southwest attempted to protect jobs for white Americans. During World War II, demand increased for Mexican American labor. Many Mexican Americans found work in war industries. The Bracero Program brought Mexican contract laborers into the United States to work in agriculture. Tensions between Mexican Americans and whites in Los Angeles, California boiled over in the 1943 "Zoot Suit" Riots. After reports that Latino youths wearing gaudy "zoot suits" had insulted men in uniform, sailors from a nearby Navy base surged into Mexican American neighborhoods and beat up young men wearing the distinctive clothing. The Mexican American population continued to grow. In 1954, the government launched "Operation Wetback" and rounded up and deported up to a million illegal immigrants. In 1960, Mexican American leaders formed the Mexican American Political Association (MAPA) to increase their political influence. Soon Mexican Americans were being elected to a variety of local, state, and federal offices. In 1965, Cesar Chavez formed the United Farm Workers to improve conditions for Mexican American farm workers. His efforts brought the plight of poor Mexican Americans to national attention.

C. Early feminists were influenced by the gains African Americans made during Reconstruction. They argued that if African American men had the vote, white women should have it as well. The feminist movement was also influenced by the struggles of African Americans during the civil rights movement. Some female members of the civil rights movement joined the feminist movement. Feminists staged protests and marches modeled on those of the civil rights movement. The Equal Rights Amendment was an effort to gain a statutory victory akin to the Civil Rights Act of 1964. Cesar Chavez and Chicano activists were also inspired by the civil rights movement. Like Martin Luther King, Jr., Cesar Chavez emphasized non-violence in his strikes and boycotts. Some Mexican American activists imitated the African American exponents of greater militancy and ethnic pride. Reies Tijerina led a group that occupied the Kit Carson National Forest to protest historic wrongs against Hispanics in the Southwest. "Brown Panthers" were modeled on the Black Panthers. *La Raza Unida* (The Race United) was founded to promote Hispanic interests.

Explanation for the Document-Based Question

The thesis should focus on a historical analytical skill, in this case **Comparing historical events**. Support your thesis with evidence drawn from at least six of the seven documents. Analyze more fully at least four of the documents, discussing one or more of the following: the point of view of the author, the purpose of the author, the intended audience of the document, the historical context of the document. As you construct your argument, make connections between the documents. Note differences and agreements between them that help you strengthen your analysis. Be sure to bring in outside knowledge that you can relate to your analysis of the documents and that contributes to your argument. Simply dropping names is not enough. Demonstrate an understanding of the wider context of the subject of the question. With this question such context could include debates over the role of the courts and their power of judicial review, debates over the American government's role in encouraging economic prosperity, and factors encouraging the rise of Progressivism.

Students should begin with a discussion of the Interstate Commerce Act (1887) and Sherman Antitrust Act (1890). The Interstate Commerce Act attempted to regulate railroad companies. It required railroads to submit their fare schedules with the federal government and publicize their rates. The act created an Interstate Commerce Commission (ICC) to monitor the industry. The Sherman Act declared illegal all combinations "in restraint of free trade." It empowered the Justice Department to bring suit and break up such monopolies. However, these acts would have to pass the scrutiny of the Supreme Court. Students might comment upon the composition of the Court during the period. They might explain how a conservative Court could thwart the efforts of reformers. Students should discuss the labor movement during the Progressive Era. Several strikes occurred in this period, including the Great Railway Strike (1877), Haymarket Affair (1886), and the Homestead Strike (1892). Students must examine the Pullman Strike (1894), in which railroad workers and the American Railway Union, led by Eugene Debs, crippled traffic in several states and territories. Many governors sided with the railroad companies by employing state troops to disperse the strikers. One notable exception was John Peter Altgeld, governor of Illinois. Railroad operators in Chicago appealed to President Cleveland and Attorney General Richard Olney to intercede on their behalf. The president ordered 2,000 federal troops to break up the strike. The Supreme Court further solidified the position of the railroad corporations by applying the Sherman Antitrust Act against unions that threatened free trade (Document A). In *E. C. Knight Company v. U.S.*, the Court further inhibited efforts to regulate corporations by putting manufacturing companies outside the purview of the Sherman Act (Document B). Thus, companies continued to form monopolies in various industries that fixed prices without competition. The Court undermined the Interstate Commerce Commission's authority to determine fair railroad rates by applying the "due process" clause of the Fourteenth Amendment to corporations (Document C). Progressives seeking to limit the hours of labor met with mixed results. In *Holden v. Hardy* (1898) the Court affirmed the right of state legislatures to regulate maximum hours in the interests of workers' health. Seven years later, the Court again reinterpreted the Fourteenth Amendment to cast aside a state law. The Lochner decision asserted that legislation not directly related to health concerns violated the rights of workers (Document D). However, reformers gained a partial victory in *Muller v. Oregon* (1908), which sustained the legislature's authority to pass regulatory legislation to protect women's health (Document E). Students might comment upon the double standard applied to men and women in the early twentieth century. Students might refer to the Elkins (1903) and Hepburn (1906) Acts, which intended to further the federal government's ability to regulate railroads. Others might explain how presidential leadership advanced the cause of reform by briefly discussing Theodore Roosevelt, William Howard Taft, or Woodrow Wilson. Some students might touch upon how the Roosevelt administration implemented the Sherman Act in *Northern Securities Company v. United States* (1904) to set the stage for an examination of the decentralization of monopolies. The Court furthered its position by ordering the Standard Oil Company to break up its monopoly of the oil refining industry (Document F). Students may compare the decision with the Court's response to Swift and American Tobacco. To conclude the essay, students might discuss how the Court endorsed the Adamson Act, which established an eight-hour day for interstate railway workers (Document G).

Explanations for the Long Essay Questions

2. The student could begin with a brief discussion of the debate concerning the ratification of the Constitution. Antifederalists represented a significant number of people in the United States, perhaps even a majority, and their concerns that the new central government would prove as tyrannical as the British had been touched a chord. Crucial in winning passage of the Constitution was the promise that it would be amended with a bill of rights, a promise that James Madison kept when the new Congress met in 1789. The antifederalists demonstrated that there was a strong desire across the country for limited national government and a respect for local and state's rights. Thoroughly out of sympathy with such views was President George Washington's brilliant Secretary of the Treasury Alexander Hamilton. Dubious about the ability of the common man to rule, and convinced that the government should play a leading role in encouraging economic prosperity, Hamilton shocked many with his 1790 *First Report on the Public Credit*. In it, he called for the new government to pay off the debt of the United States at its full face value, and for the federal assumption of state debts from the Revolutionary era. The purpose of this was to establish the good credit of the United States, and to win the support of the propertied classes for the government. Longer term, the federal debt would become the engine for commercial development in the United States. Many southern states opposed the assumption of state debts because they were already paying off their debts. They feared that Hamilton's plans would favor the northern commercial states over the agrarian south. James Madison was concerned about full payment of the debt, because many original bondholders had been forced to sell to speculators at a steep discount and he did not want to reward such sharp dealing. In the end, a compromise was worked out whereby Hamilton's fiscal program went through and the new national capital was located in the South along the Potomac River. The next year, Hamilton proposed a national bank. The bank would be a place where the government could deposit its funds. The bank could also stimulate the economy by making loans and by putting into circulation a reliable supply of paper money. Washington asked his cabinet to state their opinions on the constitutionality of such a measure. Secretary of State Thomas Jefferson strongly objected. Taking a "strict constructionist," or literal reading of the Constitution, he argued that there was no mention of a bank in the founding document. He believed state banks could fulfill all the functions that Hamilton desired. Hamilton countered by making a "loose constructionist," or nonliteral interpretation of the Constitution. He argued that the bank would further enumerated tasks of the government, and that the "necessary and proper" clause of the Constitution allowed the government to use implied powers to create institutions like the bank. Hamilton won the argument and the first Bank of the United States was chartered in 1791. But the constitutional disagreements between Jefferson and Hamilton were merging with sectional concerns and traditional worries about the power of the government to create two emerging blocs in the government. In 1791, Jefferson and Madison traveled to New York and New England and made contact with former antifederalists there. Newspapers for each side began editorializing against each other. The personal relations between Jefferson and Hamilton deteriorated. The coming of the French Revolution added a foreign policy dimension to the differences between the two camps. Jefferson favored the French in their quarrels with the rest of Europe, while Hamilton sympathized with their British antagonists. While both men favored Washington's Neutrality Declaration, Hamilton used the Citizen Genet affair to embarrass Jefferson. Hamilton's economic program was funded by a system of tariffs and excise taxes, including a tax on whiskey. Distilling grain into whiskey was the only way that frontier farmers could get their crops safely to a market, and they greatly resented the tax. In 1794, farmers in western Pennsylvania rose up in rebellion. They were suppressed by a military force led by Washington himself. Jefferson's supporters saw this as the repression of liberty and as an example of the way that Hamilton's program sacrificed the agrarian interests of the common man to the needs of the commercial elite. That same year foreign policy further divided the two sides. American shipping was caught between the British and the French as they waged a naval war against each other. American ships were being seized. Washington sent John Jay to London to work out an arrangement with Britain. The resulting Jay's Treaty was unsatisfactory. The British agreed to leave their posts in the American Northwest, something they would have to do anyway after Anthony Wayne's victory at Fallen Timbers. Jay won little in the way of commercial concessions. The British did agree to compensate Americans for seized ships, but Jay had to agree to the repayment of American debts dating to the pre-Revolutionary period. The treaty led to a firestorm of criticism. Southerners, who owed much of the old debt, were outraged, and again saw themselves as being subordinated to northern commercial interests. Jefferson's supporters attacked the treaty, while Hamilton defended it, believing that it was necessary to maintain good relations with Britain. The Treaty passed, but by the time Washington left office early in 1797, there were two clearly demarcated factions contending for power. Jeffersonians, known as Democratic-Republicans, distrusted a powerful government, supported a strict construction of the Constitution, and celebrated the common man and agrarian interests. Hamiltonians, known as Federalists, wanted a stronger central government, accepted a loose construction of the economy, and supported a mixed economy, with strong governmental support of commercial interests. These factions emerged more fully as parties during John Adams' term as President as a result of the X,Y, and Z Affair and the resulting troubles with France. In 1797, Adams sent a delegation to France to settle relations with that country. French representatives refused to negotiate until they received a bribe. This outraged the diplomats and public opinion at home. An undeclared naval war with France was fought at sea. At home, the Federalists attempted to use the anti-French feeling to crush their Francophile Democratic-Republican opponents. They passed the Alien and Sedition Acts, which were used to stifle opposition to government policy. Under the Sedition Act, editors defaming the government could be fined and imprisoned. The Democratic-Republicans responded with the Virginia and Kentucky Resolutions. The Virginia resolution was written by Madison, and Jefferson drafted the Kentucky resolutions. Both declared the Alien and Sedition Acts to be unconstitutional, and argued for state's rights. The Kentucky resolutions even argued that a state could nullify a law that it believe to be unconstitutional, a position later elaborated upon by John C. Calhoun. In the end, differences between John Adams and Hamilton led Adams to make peace, ending the crisis. In the election of 1800, Jefferson and his Democratic-Republicans would emerge victorious, setting up the first transfer of power between parties in American history. By this point, party politics had become a fixture of American political life, and differing interpretations of the Constitution would be an integral component of party ideology.

3. The student can construct an argument making use of information that can include the following. A variety of reform movements flourished in the United States in the period from 1820-1860. The Second Great Awakening began in Kentucky in the early 1800s. Initially a phenomenon of enthusiastic frontier camp meetings, this new religious revival soon spread across the country. The preachers of the Second

Great Awakening fostered a vibrant evangelical Protestantism that emphasized the importance of personal conversion and an intense, often more openly emotional, relationship with God. One of the most famous evangelists of the Second Great Awakening was Charles Grandison Finney, a brilliant orator who abandoned a career in the law after being "saved." Many people touched by the Second Great Awakening found spiritual homes in the Baptist and Methodist Churches, but new religious groupings also appeared, such as the Millerites, or Adventists, who expected the imminent arrival of Jesus Christ. The Church of Jesus Christ of Latter-Day Saints, or Mormons, founded by the visionary Joseph Smith, emerged during this period of religious enthusiasm, though it was deemed heretical by more orthodox Christian Churches. Facing increasing hostility, the Mormons began moving to Utah in 1846. They were led by Brigham Young after Joseph Smith was murdered by a mob. The Second Great Awakening intensified the religious character of people in the United States. By 1840, nearly half of the population was formally connected to a church. Women played a prominent role in the Second Great Awakening, making up the majority of congregations, and actively supporting a growing range of charitable organizations. A "Benevolent Empire" of such organizations attempted to spread the Christian message by supporting moral reforms or missionary activity at home and abroad. The American Bible Society (1816) and the American Tract Society (1825) were typical manifestations of the "Benevolent Empire," distributing Bibles and other religious writings everywhere in the United States. The temperance movement combined some of the religious fervor of the Second Great Awakening with a more strictly secular concern about the social cost of heavy drinking. The American Temperance Society appeared in 1826. The politician and businessman Neal S. Dow was the sponsor of the 1851 Maine Law that prohibited the sale and manufacture of liquor in that state. Prohibition remained a political issue throughout the nineteenth century. In this period, educational reform was spurred by the efforts of Horace Mann, who promoted public education for all children. Educators like Catherine Beecher established private schools designed for girls and young women. William H. McGuffey began publishing his phenomenally popular *McGuffey's Readers* in the 1830s. Large numbers of colleges, usually associated with religious denominations, appeared across the country. Oberlin College in Ohio began educating women as well as men in 1837. Efforts in these years were made to improve conditions in prisons. Alexis de Toqueville, the French author of *Democracy in America* (two volumes, 1835 and 1840), first visited the United States to study its prisons. Dorothea Dix became famous for her work to reform the treatment of the mentally ill in asylums. Various utopian communities sprang up in the United States. In 1825, Robert Owen founded a communal society at New Harmony in Indiana. The Oneida Community, established in New York in 1848, scandalized people by experimenting with "free love" and eugenics. Lucretia Mott and Elizabeth Cady Stanton began the women's rights movement by calling for women's suffrage. They helped organize a conference at Seneca Falls, New York in 1848 that issued a famous "Declaration of Sentiments" that demanded equal rights and the vote for women. Abolitionism grew in strength in the 1820s and 1830s. William Lloyd Garrison began publishing his abolitionist paper *The Liberator* in 1831. In 1833, Garrison, Lewis Tappan, and Theodore Weld founded the American Anti-Slavery Society. Abolitionists began an increasingly vocal campaign against slavery, infuriating many Southerners. Abolitionism was concentrated in the North, but some Southerners, such as the South Carolinian sisters Angelina and Sarah Grimke spoke out against the institution of slavery. African Americans like the escaped slave Frederick Douglass also joined the cause.

In addition to agitating against slavery, abolitionists organized the Underground Railroad to help slaves make their way to freedom. The former slave Harriet Tubman helped "conduct" many African Americans along the Underground Railroad. Abolitionists were often very unpopular, even in the North. Garrison was attacked by a Boston mob in 1835, and in 1837 the abolitionist editor Elijah Lovejoy was murdered in Alton, Illinois. Despite this, the abolitionists succeeded in making slavery a major political issue, exemplified by the creation of the Liberty Party in 1844, and the Free Soil Party in 1848. Political abolitionism would set the stage for the emergence of the Republican Party in the 1850s.

4. A starting point for the student is the evolving attitude toward women of the 1890s. The role of women for much of the nineteenth century had been dominated by the "cult of domesticity," which saw a woman's place as the guardian of the home and the keeper of moral and cultural values. This did not disappear entirely in the period from 1900-1930, but was already being modified by the turn of the century. The "New Woman" of the 1890s challenged older stereotypes of women as weak and passive. Symbolic of the "New Woman" was illustrator Charles Dana Gibson's "Gibson Girl," who was beautiful, athletic, and strong-willed. By the turn of the century, many women were receiving a higher education, at all-women's colleges such as Vassar or at coeducational institutions. A number of these women went into social work and became prominent progressive reformers. Emblematic of these was Jane Addams. A graduate of Rockford College, she cofounded Hull House in 1889. Hull House was a settlement house on the south side of Chicago that met many needs of the neighboring immigrant population. By the early twentieth century Addams was famous, and helped found the Progressive Party with Theodore Roosevelt in 1912. Many women were working outside of the home, most out of economic necessity, many by choice. Recent inventions like the switchboard and typewriter opened up new professions for women. The outbreak of war in 1917 opened up opportunities for women in the workplace, as they took the places of men called into the military. Although this movement into the workforce was not as massive as that of World War II, it was still significant, involving many thousands of women. For the first time, women were allowed into the American military. Many served as nurses. The contributions of women to the war effort proved decisive in convincing President Wilson, Congress, and the nation that women should get the vote. Critical in facilitating this was the work of Carrie Chapman Catt, leader of the National American Woman Suffrage Association. Congress sent the Nineteenth Amendment to the states on June 4, 1919, and it was ratified on August 18, 1920. American women would be able to vote in the 1920 presidential election. The 1920s was a time of contrasts for women. Margaret Sanger campaigned for birth-control. Alice Paul's National Woman's Party fought for an Equal Rights Amendment to the Constitution. Yet for many women, especially younger women, political struggle would not be a priority. The dominant image of females in the Jazz Age would be that of "flaming youth." Illustrator John Held's "flappers," with their bobbed hair, short skirts, boyish figures, cigarettes, and garter flasks, became the incarnation of the latest version of the new woman. Many women in the 1920s focused on the personal freedoms opening up to them in the postwar world. The woman of 1930 was very different from that of 1900, and in more ways than the amount of clothing that she wore.

5 Minutes to a 5

180 Daily Questions and Activities

5 Minutes a Day

INTRODUCTION

Welcome to *5 Minutes to a 5: 180 Questions and Activities!* This bonus section is another tool for you to use as you work toward your goal of achieving a 5 on the AP exam in May. It includes 180 AP questions and activities that cover the most essential course materials and are meant to be completed in conjunction with the 5 Steps book.

One of the secrets to excelling in your AP class is spending a bit of time *each day* studying the subject(s). The questions and activities offered here are designed to be done one per day, and each should take 5 minutes or so to complete. (Although there might be exceptions. Depending on the exam—some exercises may take a little longer, some a little less.) You will encounter stimulating questions to make you think about a topic in a big way, and some very subject-specific activities, which cover the main book's chapters; some science subjects will offer at-home labs, and some humanities subjects will offer ample chunks of text to be read on one day, with questions and activities for follow-up on the following day(s). There will also be suggestions for relevant videos for you to watch, websites to visit, or both. Most questions and activities are linked to the specific chapters of your book so that you are constantly fortifying your knowledge.

Remember—approaching this section for 5 minutes a day is much more effective than bingeing a week's worth in one sitting! So if you practice all the extra exercises in this section and reinforce the main content of this book, we are certain you will build the skills and confidence needed to succeed on your exam. Good luck!

—Editors of McGraw-Hill Education

Check off each activity as it is completed.

1. ❑	46. ❑	91. ❑	136. ❑
2. ❑	47. ❑	92. ❑	137. ❑
3. ❑	48. ❑	93. ❑	138. ❑
4. ❑	49. ❑	94. ❑	139. ❑
5. ❑	50. ❑	95. ❑	140. ❑
6. ❑	51. ❑	96. ❑	141. ❑
7. ❑	52. ❑	97. ❑	142. ❑
8. ❑	53. ❑	98. ❑	143. ❑
9. ❑	54. ❑	99. ❑	144. ❑
10. ❑	55. ❑	100. ❑	145. ❑
11. ❑	56. ❑	101. ❑	146. ❑
12. ❑	57. ❑	102. ❑	147. ❑
13. ❑	58. ❑	103. ❑	148. ❑
14. ❑	59. ❑	104. ❑	149. ❑
15. ❑	60. ❑	105. ❑	150. ❑
16. ❑	61. ❑	106. ❑	151. ❑
17. ❑	62. ❑	107. ❑	152. ❑
18. ❑	63. ❑	108. ❑	153. ❑
19. ❑	64. ❑	109. ❑	154. ❑
20. ❑	65. ❑	110. ❑	155. ❑
21. ❑	66. ❑	111. ❑	156. ❑
22. ❑	67. ❑	112. ❑	157. ❑
23. ❑	68. ❑	113. ❑	158. ❑
24. ❑	69. ❑	114. ❑	159. ❑
25. ❑	70. ❑	115. ❑	160. ❑
26. ❑	71. ❑	116. ❑	161. ❑
27. ❑	72. ❑	117. ❑	162. ❑
28. ❑	73. ❑	118. ❑	163. ❑
29. ❑	74. ❑	119. ❑	164. ❑
30. ❑	75. ❑	120. ❑	165. ❑
31. ❑	76. ❑	121. ❑	166. ❑
32. ❑	77. ❑	122. ❑	167. ❑
33. ❑	78. ❑	123. ❑	168. ❑
34. ❑	79. ❑	124. ❑	169. ❑
35. ❑	80. ❑	125. ❑	170. ❑
36. ❑	81. ❑	126. ❑	171. ❑
37. ❑	82. ❑	127. ❑	172. ❑
38. ❑	83. ❑	128. ❑	173. ❑
39. ❑	84. ❑	129. ❑	174. ❑
40. ❑	85. ❑	130. ❑	175. ❑
41. ❑	86. ❑	131. ❑	176. ❑
42. ❑	87. ❑	132. ❑	177. ❑
43. ❑	88. ❑	133. ❑	178. ❑
44. ❑	89. ❑	134. ❑	179. ❑
45. ❑	90. ❑	135. ❑	180. ❑

CHAPTER 6

Go to the website for the Cahokia Mounds State Historic Site: http://cahokiamounds.org/explore/. Click on "Learn" and then "Explore." Read the Timeline, click on some of the pictures of the mounds, and navigate the interactive map at the bottom of the page.

What important insights does this page give us into the civilization of the Mississippian people who lived at Cahokia?

Place the following European explorers in chronological order: Christopher Columbus, Marco Polo, Vasco Nuñez de Balboa.

Why are each of these explorers important?

Connect the following events with the proper decade.

Events:

The Spanish conquest of Mexico

The Portuguese explorations of the African coast and discovery of the Cape of Good Hope

The Spanish conquest of Peru

The first exploration of Christopher Columbus

Spanish expeditions into the American Southwest

Decades:

1480–1490

1490–1500

1520–1530

1530–1540

1540–1550

Day 4

"His character is marked with the most opposite traits, embracing qualities apparently the most incompatible. He was avaricious, yet liberal; bold to desperation, yet cautious and calculating in his plans; magnanimous, yet very cunning; courteous and affable in his deportment, yet inexorably stern; lax in his notions of morality, yet (not uncommon) a sad bigot. The great feature in his character was constancy of purpose; a constancy not to be daunted by danger, nor baffled by disappointment, nor wearied out by impediments and delays. He was a knight-errant, in the literal sense of the word. Of all the band of adventurous cavaliers whom Spain, in the sixteenth century, sent forth on the career of discovery and conquest, there was none more deeply filled with the spirit of romantic enterprise than Hernando Cortés."

William Hickling Prescott summarizing the character of Hernando Cortés in *The History of the Conquest of Mexico*, 1843

How does the nineteenth-century American historian see the conquistador Hernando Cortés? Is his assessment fully positive or negative?

Place the following terms in chronological order: encomienda, astrolabe, Crusades

Why are each of these important?

"From the fact that the Indians are barbarians it does not necessarily follow that they are incapable of government and have to be ruled by others, except to be taught about the Catholic faith and to be admitted to the holy sacraments. They are not ignorant, inhuman, or bestial. Rather, long before they had heard the word *Spaniard* they had properly organized states, wisely ordered by excellent laws, religion, and custom."

Bartolomé de Las Casas, *In Defense of the Indians*, 1550

What is Las Casas's argument? What would he have thought of the behavior of Spanish settlers in the New World?

Day 7

Visit the website for the Castillo de San Marcos National Monument: http://www.nps.gov/casa/index.htm

Look at pictures of the Castillo, and explore the pages describing its history.

What does the Castillo de San Marcos tell you about Spanish settlement in the New World?

CHAPTER 7

Connect the following events with the proper decade:

Events:

The English and French establish their first permanent colonies in North America.

The Pilgrims and Puritans settle in Massachusetts.

Maryland is founded by the Calvert family.

Pennsylvania is founded by William Penn.

The first colonial legislature meets in Virginia.

Decades:

1600–1610

1610–1620

1620–1630

1630–1640

1680–1690

Day 9

How did the Spanish, French, and English differ in their treatment of Native Americans? Give examples to illustrate the differences.

Place the following European explorers in chronological order: Robert La Salle, Henry Hudson, Jacques Cartier.

Why are each of these explorers important?

Go to the History.com website for Thanksgiving: http://www.history.com/topics/thanksgiving.

Explore some of the videos explaining different aspects of the story of the Pilgrims, the first Thanksgiving, and the history of the national holiday.

What was the purpose of the first Thanksgiving? How has the meaning of the holiday changed over time?

"Men's consciences ought in no sort to be violated, urged, or constrained. And whenever men have attempted anything by this violent course, whether openly or by secret means, the issue has been pernicious, and the cause of great and wonderful innovations in the principallest and mightiest kingdoms and countries."

Roger Williams, *The Bloudy Tenent of Persecution, for Cause of Conscience* (1644)

What point is Williams making in this passage? Why is this important for American history?

Day 13

Place the following figures from seventeenth-century English colonial history in chronological order: Anne Hutchinson, John Smith, Squanto.

Why are each of these people important?

Distinguish between Roman Catholicism, the Church of England, and Puritanism. How did these influence English colonization in America?

CHAPTER 8

Connect the following events with the proper decade:

Events:

King George's War

The beginning of the Great Awakening

King William's War

Queen Anne's War

The Stono Rebellion

Decades:

1690–1700

1700–1710

1720–1730

1730–1740

1740–1750

The dramatist Arthur Miller wrote his play *The Crucible* (1953) about the Salem Witch Trials as a commentary on the anti-Communist fears of the Second Red Scare.

At one point, the play's protagonist declares:

> "A fire, a fire is burning! I hear the boot of Lucifer, I see his filthy face! And it is my face, and yours, Danforth! For them that quail to bring men out of ignorance, as I have quailed, and as you quail now when you know in your black hearts that this be fraud—God damns our kind especially, and we will burn, we will burn together!"

Why did Miller see a similarity between the Salem Witch Trials and the Second Red Scare? Why does he have his protagonist condemn himself as well as his judges?

5 Minutes to a 5

Place the following events in English political history in chronological order: the Acts of Union between England and Scotland, the Glorious Revolution, the English Civil War.

Why are these events important?

Day 18

Visit the website for Historic Westover Plantation: http://westover-plantation.com/.

Explore the linked web pages, focusing on the Byrd family's Westover. What does Westover tell you about the life of a wealthy planter family in Virginia in the eighteenth century?

Day 19

What is the difference between mercantilism and free trade? What are some examples of mercantilism in action in the seventeenth and eighteenth centuries? Who was the greatest eighteenth-century British advocate of free trade?

"And . . . you are to serve your owners with cheerfulness, respect, and humility, not grumbling, or giving any saucy answers, but doing your work with readiness, mildness, and good nature; because your sauciness and grumbling is not so much against your owners, as it is against God himself, who hath placed you in that service, and expects you will do the business of it as he hath commanded you."

Thomas Bacon, *Sermon to Negro Slaves*, 1743

Thomas Bacon was a minister in Maryland. What point is Bacon making to his congregation? What does this tell you about the attitudes of some colonists in eighteenth-century Maryland?

Place the following figures into chronological order: Nathaniel Bacon, Jonathan Edwards, Sir Edmund Andros

Why are each of these people important?

CHAPTER 9

Connect the following events with the proper year:

Events:

    Boston Massacre

    Albany Congress

    Stamp Act Congress

    Boston Tea Party

    First Continental Congress

Years:

    1754

    1765

    1770

    1773

    1774

Distinguish between the roles played by George Washington, the Marquis de Montcalm, and William Pitt in the French and Indian War. Why were each of these men important?

Day 24

Visit the website for Fort Ticonderoga: http://www.fortticonderoga.org/.

Explore the pages on the fort's history. Why was this fort important? What does it tell you about warfare in America during the eighteenth century?

Place the following groups of colonists in chronological order: minutemen, Sons of Liberty, Committees of Correspondence.

Why were these groups important?

"Our patriots have been so intent on building up American rights, that they have overlooked the rights of Great-Britain, and our own interest. Instead of proving that we are entitled to privileges that our fathers knew our situation would not admit us to enjoy, they have been arguing away our most essential rights. If there be any grievance, it does not consist in our being subject to the authority of parliament, but in our not having an actual representation in it. Were it possible for the colonies to have an equal representation in parliament, and were refused it upon proper application, I confess I should think it a grievance; but at present it seems to be allowed by all parties, to be impracticable, considering the colonies are distant from Great-Britain a thousand transmarine leagues."

Daniel Leonard, "Letters Addressed to the Inhabitants of the Province of Massachusetts Bay," January 9, 1775

What point is Leonard making? Why is this perspective important?

Many American colonists supported the slogan "no taxation without representation." The British government argued that the colonists enjoyed "virtual representation." Distinguish between these two positions. Why was the difference important?

Day 28

Go to the website for Colonial Williamsburg: https://www.colonialwilliamsburg.com/.

Click on "Learn," and then go to the "History" page. Look at the various pages there, paying particular attention to the portrayal of African Americans. Colonial Williamsburg attempts to portray colonial slavery accurately. Is this a good idea? Are there some aspects of the past that should not be re-created at popular historical and tourist sites?

CHAPTER 10

Day 29

Connect the following events with the proper year:

Events:

   Declaration of Independence

   Alliance with France

   Battle of Yorktown

   Battle of Saratoga

   Second Continental Congress

Years:

   1775

   1776

   1777

   1778

   1781

Place the following legislative enactments in chronological order: the Northwest Ordinances, the Articles of Confederation, the Treaty of Paris.

Why are these important?

Day 31

Look up "Benedict Arnold" in various online dictionaries. To do a "Benedict Arnold" is to betray or sell out a person or a cause. Who was Benedict Arnold? Why has his name become a synonym for traitor in the United States?

Day 32

Distinguish between the contributions of Thomas Paine and Thomas Jefferson to the Declaration of Independence. Why were they important?

Day 33

Go to the National Park Service's website for Independence Hall: https://www.nps.gov/inde/planyourvisit/independencehall.htm.

Click on "Learn About the Park" to "History and Culture" to "Places," and then scroll down and click on "Independence Hall." Explore the pages describing the history and architecture of Independence Hall. What makes Independence Hall a remarkable site in American history?

"It now rests with the Confederated Powers, by the line of conduct they mean to adopt, to make this Country great, happy, and respectable; or to sink it into littleness; worse, perhaps, into Anarchy and Confusion; for certain I am, that unless adequate Powers are given to Congress for the general purposes of the Federal Union that we shall soon moulder into dust and become contemptible in the Eyes of Europe."

George Washington, Letter to William Gordon, July 8, 1783

What point is Washington making? Why is this perspective important?

Distinguish between the actions of Massachusetts farmers at Lexington in 1775 and during Shays's Rebellion in 1786. Why is this distinction important?

CHAPTER 11

Connect the following events with the proper year:

Events:

Beginning of the French Revolution

The Virginia Plan

The XYZ Affair

Report on the Public Credit

The Whisky Rebellion begins

Years:

1787

1789

1790

1794

1798

Place the following documents in chronological order: the Bill of Rights, the Kentucky and Virginia Resolves, *The Federalist Papers*.

Why are these important?

"The mode in which this constitution is recommended to the people to judge without either the advice of Congress, or the legislatures of the several states is very reprehensible—it is an attempt to force it upon them before it could be thoroughly understood, and may leave us in that situation, that in the first moments of slavery in the minds of people agitated by the remembrance of their lost liberties, will be like the sea in a tempest, that sweeps down every mound of security."

Mercy Otis Warren, *Observations on the New Constitution, and on the Federal and State Conventions*, 1788

What point is Mercy Otis Warren making? Why is this perspective important?

"Clear. mrs Springer grew very ill about 1 O Clok ys morn. Calld her women and was Safe Deliverd at 11 of a fine Son. I left her comfortable & returnd at 3 pm. mrs Bisbee & Lidia Came home with me. mrs Voce here Bakeing. old mr Cowen & wife & Son Drank Tea here. Georg Couch Departed this Life last wednsday Eving."

    Martha Ballard, Diary, June 8, 1787

Martha Ballard was a midwife who lived in Maine. At the age of 50, she began a diary, which she maintained for 27 years until her death. In this diary, Ballard kept a brief record of her daily activities, including visits to women in childbirth and ailing neighbors, and also the comings and goings of family members, friends, and neighbors. The historian Laurel Thatcher Ulrich used the diary to write a biography of Ballard entitled *A Midwife's Tale* (1990) that was awarded the Pulitzer Prize and several other awards. Clearly a source like Martha Ballard's diary is not as easy to read as the public papers and memoirs left by important leaders. Why are sources like this diary important?

Place the following events in American foreign policy in chronological order: the Quasi-War with France, Jay's Treaty, the Declaration of Neutrality.

Why are these important?

Day 41

Distinguish between the constitutional ideas of Thomas Jefferson and Alexander Hamilton. Why is this distinction important?

Day 42

Go to the National Park Service's website for the Fallen Timbers Battlefield and Fort Miamis National Historic Site: https://www.nps.gov/fati/index.htm.

Explore the pages discussing the Battle of Fallen Timbers and Fort Miamis. Why were these important?

Day 43

CHAPTER 12

Connect the following events with the proper year:

Events:

   Treaty of Ghent

   Louisiana Purchase

   Twelfth Amendment

   Battle of Tippecanoe

   Second National Bank

Years:

   1803

   1804

   1811

   1814

   1816

Place the following in chronological order: Non-Intercourse Act, Embargo of 1807, Hartford Convention.

Why are these important?

"It is emphatically the province and duty of the Judicial Department to say what the law is. Those who apply the rule to particular cases must, of necessity, expound and interpret that rule. If two laws conflict with each other, the Courts must decide on the operation of each.

So, if a law be in opposition to the Constitution, if both the law and the Constitution apply to a particular case, so that the Court must either decide that case conformably to the law, disregarding the Constitution, or conformably to the Constitution, disregarding the law, the Court must determine which of these conflicting rules governs the case. This is the very essence of judicial duty.

If, then, the Courts are to regard the Constitution, and the Constitution is superior to any ordinary act of the Legislature, the Constitution, and not such ordinary act, must govern the case to which they both apply."

John Marshall, *Marbury v. Madison*, 1803

What point is Chief Justice John Marshall making in this Supreme Court decision? Why is it important?

Distinguish between the positions on Westward Expansion of Tecumseh and Andrew Jackson. Why is this distinction important?

Go to the website for Thomas Jefferson's home Monticello: https://www.monticello .org/.

Explore the pages discussing Thomas Jefferson, the architecture of the house, and the free and unfree people who once worked there. What does this house tell you about Thomas Jefferson?

Place the following in chronological order: Lewis and Clark Expedition, Era of Good Feelings, Battle of New Orleans.

Why are these important?

"Yet however idle the American sometimes appeared, and however large the class of tavern loafers may have actually been, the true American was active and industrious. No immigrant came to America for ease or idleness. If an English farmer bought land near New York, Philadelphia, or Baltimore, and made the most of his small capital, he found that while he could earn more money than in Surrey or Devonshire, he worked harder and suffered greater discomforts. The climate was trying; fever was common; the crops ran new risks from strange insects, drought, and violent weather; the weeds were annoying; the flies and mosquitoes tormented him and his cattle; laborers were scarce and indifferent. . . . Life was more exacting, and every such man in America was required to do, and actually did, the work of two such men in Europe."

Henry Adams, *History of the United States during the Administrations of Thomas Jefferson*, 1889

What point is Adams making in this passage of his history? What widespread view of American life does this passage reflect?

Day 50

CHAPTER 13

Connect the following events with the proper year:

Events:

  Monroe Doctrine

  Indian Removal Act

  Missouri Compromise

  Nullification Crisis

  Completion of the Erie Canal

Years:

  1820

  1823

  1825

  1830

  1832

Place the following in chronological order: Bank War, Specie Circular, Panic of 1837. Why are these important?

Day 52

Go to the National Park Service's website for the Trail of Tears National Historic Trail: https://www.nps.gov/trte/index.htm.

Click on "Learn About the Park" and explore the pages on history and culture. Why was the Trail of Tears important?

5 Minutes to a 5

Day 53

Distinguish between the ideas of Henry Clay and Andrew Jackson on the economy and government. Why is this distinction important?

The Election of 1840 is remembered for the hoopla associated with its electioneering rather than any political issues. Give examples of the creative use of political image-making in this election. Why is this important?

Day 55

"Almost all the religion in the world has been produced by revivals. God has found it necessary to take advantage of the excitability there is in mankind, to produce powerful excitements among them, before he can lead them to obey. Men are so sluggish, there are so many things to lead their minds off from religion, and to oppose the influence of the gospel, that it is necessary to raise an excitement among them, till the tide rises so high as to sweep away the opposing obstacles. They must be so excited that they will break over these counteracting influences, before they will obey God."

Charles Grandison Finney, *Lectures on Revivals of Religion*, 1835

What early nineteenth-century religious phenomenon is Finney referring to? Why was it important?

Place the following in chronological order: Gag Rule, Nat Turner's Rebellion, the American Colonization Society.

Why are these important?

CHAPTER 14

Connect the following events with the proper year:

Events:

    The Mexican War

    The Alamo

    The California Gold Rush

    The Admission of Texas into the Union

    The Fugitive Slave Act

Years:

    1836

    1845

    1846

    1848

    1850

Distinguish between Manifest Destiny and the Wilmot Proviso. Why is this distinction important?

Day 59

Go to the National Park Service's website for the Women's Rights National Historical Park: https://www.nps.gov/wori/index.htm.

Click on "Learn About the Park," and explore the pages on history and culture. Why was the Seneca Falls Women's Rights Convention important?

"The words 'people of the United States' and 'citizens' are synonymous terms, and mean the same thing. They both describe the political body who, according to our republican institutions, form the sovereignty and who hold the power and conduct the Government through their representatives. . . . The question before us is whether the class of persons described in the plea of abatement compose a portion of this people, and are constituent members of this sovereignty? We think they are not, and that they are not included, and were not intended to be included, under the word 'citizens' in the Constitution, and can therefore claim none of the rights and privileges which that instrument provides for and secures to citizens of the United States. On the contrary, they were at the time considered as a subordinate and inferior class of beings who had been subjugated by the dominant race, and, whether emancipated or not, yet remained subject to their authority, and had no rights or privileges but such as those who held the power and the Government might choose to grant them."

Roger B. Taney, *Dred Scott v. Sandford*, 1857

What point is Chief Justice Roger B. Taney making in this Supreme Court decision? Why is this important?

Day 61

Place the following in chronological order: Harper's Ferry Raid of John Brown, "Bleeding Kansas," Kansas-Nebraska Act.

Why are these important?

Go to the website for the Alamo: http://www.thealamo.org/.

Click on "Remember" and explore some of the pages dealing with the history and the architecture of the Alamo. If you scroll to the bottom of these pages, you will find the slogan "Remember the Alamo!" Why do we remember the Alamo?

5 Minutes to a 5

Distinguish between the views of Stephen A. Douglas and Abraham Lincoln on the issue of slavery in the western territories. Why is this distinction important?

CHAPTER 15

Connect the following events with the proper year:

Events:

  Preliminary Emancipation Proclamation

  Crittenden Plan

  Draft Riots in New York City

  South Carolina Secedes from the Union

  Sherman's March to the Sea

Years:

  1860

  1861

  1862

  1863

  1864

Day 65

Place the following military events in chronological order: Fort Sumter, Appomattox, Battle of Gettysburg.

Why are these military events important?

Go onto the Internet and visit Civil War reenacting websites. Look at videos of Civil War reenactors on Youtube.com. Why is Civil War reenacting so popular? Is this something that you would like to do? Do you find this inappropriate?

Day 67

"But slavery is the cause of the war. Why? Because the South obstinately and wickedly refused to restrict or abolish it at the demand of the philosophers or fanatics or demagogues of the North and West. Then, sir, it was abolition, the purpose to abolish or interfere with and hem in slavery, which caused disunion and war. Slavery is only the subject, but Abolition the cause of this civil war. It was the persistent and determined agitation in the free States of the question of abolishing slavery in the South, because of the alleged 'irrepressible conflict' between the forms of labor in the two sections . . . that forced a collision of arms at last . . . ."

Congressman Clement Vallandigham, January 14, 1863

What point is Congressman Vallandigham making? Why is his perspective important?

Day 68

Place the following military events in chronological order: Fall of Atlanta, Battle of Shiloh, Battle of Vicksburg.

Why are these military events important?

Distinguish between the military approaches of the Federal commanders George McClellan and Ulysses S. Grant. Why is this distinction important?

Day 70

Go to the website for Ford's Theatre: http://www.fords.org/.

Click on "Lincoln's Assassination," and browse the pages on the assassination of President Abraham Lincoln and the history of Ford's Theatre. Why was the assassination of President Lincoln so traumatic for Americans in 1865?

"Begin my visits among the camp hospitals in the army of the Potomac. Spend a good part of my day in a large brick mansion on the banks of the Rappahannock, used as a hospital since the battle—seems to have receiv'd only the worst cases. Out doors, at the foot of a tree, within ten yards of the front of the house, I notice a heap of amputated feet, legs, arms, hands &c., a full load for a one-horse cart. Several dead bodies lie near, each cover'd with its brown woolen blanket. In the door-yard, towards the river, are fresh graves, mostly of officers, their names on pieces of barrel-staves or broken boards, stuck in the dirt. . . . The large mansion is quite crowded upstairs and down, everything impromptu, no system, all bad enough, but I have no doubt the best that can be done; all the wounds pretty bad, some frightful, the men in their old clothes, unclean and bloody."

> Walt Whitman, recording a visit to a military hospital at Falmount, Virginia, opposite Fredericksburg, December 21, 1862

What is Whitman's perspective on what he sees? Why is this important?

CHAPTER 16

Connect the following events with the proper year:

Events:

    Thirteenth Amendment

    Wade-Davis Act

    Ten Percent Plan

    Impeachment of President Andrew Johnson

    Tenure of Office Act

Years:

    1863

    1864

    1865

    1867

    1868

Place the following in chronological order: Reconstruction Act, Compromise of 1877, Fifteenth Amendment.

Why are these important?

D. W. Griffith's 1915 film *The Birth of a Nation* is an epic recounting of the Civil War and Reconstruction. This was the first great American feature film, and for many technical and artistic reasons it is a landmark in the history of cinema. Unfortunately, Griffith's film was controversial even in 1915 for its portrayal of Reconstruction. The heroes at the end of the movie are members of the Ku Klux Klan rescuing white Southerners from freedmen and carpetbaggers. The film can be seen in whole or in part at Youtube.com. What does this film tell us about changes in our understanding of Reconstruction? How does it illustrate changes in our understanding of race relations?

Distinguish between the positions of President Andrew Johnson and the Radical Republicans on Reconstruction. Why is this distinction important?

"Question. What did you discover in relation to the colored people?

Answer. I discovered that they were in a state of ignorance, generally, at that time of their own condition as freedmen. Some of them knew it. They all, of course, mistrusted it. They had all heard it from one another. A few knew it from their masters, and only a few; and what they did hear they had very little confidence to believe. Hearing that a party of Yankees, and especially a Yankee lady, was there, and they commenced to gather around me for the facts, asking me their little questions in their own way, which was to the effect, if they were free, and if Abraham Lincoln was really dead. They had been told that he was dead; that he had been killed; but at the same time they had been informed that, now that he was dead, they were no longer free, but would be all slaves again; and with that had come the suspicion, on their part, that he was not dead, but that it was a hoax to hold them in slavery."

Clara Barton, Testimony before Congress, February 21, 1866

What does Barton reveal about attitudes among the freedmen shortly after the conclusion of the Civil War? Why is this important?

Day 77

Go to the National Park Service's website for the Tuskegee Institute: https://www.nps.gov/tuin/index.htm

Click on "Learn About the Park" and explore the pages on history and culture. Why was the Tuskegee Institute important?

What is the distinction between a carpetbagger and a scalawag? Why is this distinction important?

CHAPTER 17

Connect the following events with the proper year:

Events:

Battle of the Little Bighorn

Homestead Act

Dawes Act

Timber and Stone Act

Ghost Dance

Years:

1862

1876

1878

1887

1890

Day 80

Place the following in chronological order: Sherman Antitrust Act, completion of the transcontinental railroad, Interstate Commerce Act.

Why are these important?

"You wonder, perhaps, at the zeal and enthusiasm of the Western women in this reform movement. . . . We endured hardships, dangers and privations; hours of loneliness, fear and sorrow; our little babes were born upon these wide, unsheltered prairies; and there, upon the sweeping prairies beneath the cedar trees our hands have planted to mark the sacred place, our little ones lie buried. We toiled in the cabin and in the field; we planted trees and orchards; we helped our loved ones to make the prairie blossom as the rose. The neat cottage took the place of the sod shanty, the log-cabin and the humble dug-out.

Yet, after all our years of toil and privation, dangers and hardships upon the western frontier, monopoly is taking our homes from us by an infamous system of mortgage foreclosures, the most infamous that has ever disgraced the statutes of a civilized nation."

Mary E. Lease, speech to the national convention of the Woman's Christian Temperance Union, 1891

What does Lease reveal about the perspective of many women living on Western farms in 1891? Why is this perspective important?

5 Minutes to a 5

Distinguish between the positions of William Jennings Bryan and William McKinley on currency issue in the election of 1896. Why is this distinction important?

Place the following in chronological order: invention of barbed wire, the first "long drive" of cattle, the opening of "Buffalo Bill's Wild West Show."

Why are these important?

Day 84

Go to the National Park Service's website for the Homestead National Monument of America: https://www.nps.gov/home/index.htm.

Click on "Learn About the Park," and explore the pages on history and culture. Why did the U.S. government honor the Homestead Act with a national monument?

Day 85

On July 12, 1893, a young scholar named Frederick Jackson Turner gave an address to a meeting of the American Historical Association at the World Columbian Exposition in Chicago. His talk was entitled "The Significance of the Frontier in American History." Here Turner laid the foundation for his famous "Frontier Thesis," which argued that the frontier experience was the most important force shaping American life. He wrote, "The frontier is the line of most rapid and effective Americanization. American social development has been continually beginning over again on the frontier. This perennial rebirth, this fluidity of American life, this expansion westward with its new opportunities, its continuous touch with the simplicity of primitive society, furnish the forces dominating American character . . . ." Turner's thesis made him one of the most influential historians in American history. Why did Turner's view of Western history prove so compelling to his contemporaries?

CHAPTER 18

Connect the following events with the proper year:

Events:

Opening of Ellis Island to process immigrants on the East Coast

Knights of Labor founded

Coxey's Army

Haymarket Square bombing

Chinese Exclusion Act

Years:

1869

1882

1886

1892

1894

"Inquire from the thousands of women and children whose husbands or fathers were suffocated or crushed in the mines through the rapacious greed of stockholders clamoring for more dividends. Investigate the sweating dens of the large cities. Go to the mills, factories, through the country. Visit the modern tenement houses or hovels in which thousands of workers are compelled to eke out an existence. Ask these whether the conqueror (monopoly) cares whether his trophy (the laborers) is destroyed or preserved. Ascertain from employers whether the laborer is not regarded the same as a machine, thrown out as soon as all the work possible has been squeezed out of him."
  Samuel Gompers, Letter to Judge Peter Grosscup, September 1894

What is the perspective of AFL president Samuel Gompers in this passage? Why is this perspective important?

Place the following in chronological order: *Looking Backward*, by Edward Bellamy; *How the Other Half Lives*, by Jacob Riis; *Progress and Poverty*, by Henry George.

Why are these books important?

Day 89

Go to the National Park Service's website for the Statue of Liberty National Monument: https://www.nps.gov/stli/index.htm.

Click on "Learn About the Park," and explore the pages on history and culture. Why has the Statue of Liberty become such an important symbol?

In 1873, Mark Twain and Charles Dudley Warner published a novel entitled *The Gilded Age*. The novel was a satire of contemporary America, condemning what the authors' saw as a post-war riot of greed and public corruption. The title came from Shakespeare: "To gild refined gold, to paint the lily . . . is wasteful and ridiculous excess." Twain and Warner achieved something unusual for novelists; they gave a name to a period of history. Why is the period of the late nineteenth century in the United States called the "Gilded Age"?

Distinguish between vertical integration and horizontal integration. Why is this distinction important?

"An army led by a council seldom conquers; it must have a commander-in-chief, who settles disputes, decides in emergencies, inspires fear or attachment. The head of the Ring is such a commander. He dispenses places, rewards the loyal, punishes the mutinous, concocts schemes, negotiates treaties. He generally avoids publicity, preferring the substance to the pomp of power, and is the more dangerous because he sits, like a spider, hidden in the midst of his web. He is a Boss."

Lord James Bryce, *The American Commonwealth*, 1888

Lord Bryce was a British analyst of American political institutions. What late nineteenth-century political phenomenon is he discussing here?

CHAPTER 19

Connect the following events with the proper year:

Events:

Spanish–American War

Purchase of Alaska from Russia

Overthrow of the Kingdom of Hawaii

Platt Amendment

Publication of *The Influence of Sea Power upon History*

Years:

1867

1890

1893

1898

1901

Place the following in chronological order: Great White Fleet, Open Door Note, Boxer Rebellion.

Why are these important?

Go to the website for the Hearst Castle: http://hearstcastle.org/.

The newspaper magnate William Randolph Hearst built a huge estate near San Simeon, California. Here he gathered treasures from around the world and entertained lavishly. Hearst's life and home were the inspiration for Orson Welles's classic film *Citizen Kane* (1941). Click on "History" and explore the pages devoted to Hearst and his home. Why was Hearst important for American foreign policy in the 1890s?

Day 96

Distinguish between the positions of supporters and opponents of imperialism following the Spanish–American War. Why is this distinction important?

Place the following in chronological order: Roosevelt Corollary, acquisition of the Panama Canal Zone, Dollar Diplomacy.

Why are these important?

"What is needed in Cuba at present is firm but liberal government of the people, for the people and by the people, under American military supervision, for the time being. . . . It must also be fully realized by those in charge that the Army of the United States is not in Cuba for the purpose of suppressing civil law and civil rights; but on the contrary, for the purpose of restoring and establishing civil law; that it stands inactive so long as the civil officers are able to execute the laws, and interferes only when they are unable to do so."

> Major-General Leonard Wood, Military Governor of Santiago de Cuba, "The Existing Conditions and Needs in Cuba," *The North American Review*, May 1899

Leonard Wood was Theodore Roosevelt's partner in creating the 1st Volunteer Cavalry, the famous "Rough Riders." During the Spanish–American War he was rapidly promoted, and after the conflict he became the military governor of Cuba. What is Wood's perspective on his role as military governor? What insight does this give us into American imperial attitudes?

Go to this Library of Congress page on the Panama Canal: https://www.loc.gov/item/mp76000330/

This page features a silent film on the making of the Panama Canal that was produced in the 1920s. What perspective does the film take toward Theodore Roosevelt and his efforts to build a canal? What is the perspective of the film on the American role in building the canal?

CHAPTER 20

Connect the following events with the proper year:

Events:

    Woodrow Wilson elected president

    Theodore Roosevelt elected president

    William Howard Taft elected president

    The Hepburn Act

    The foundation of the NAACP

Years:

1904

1906

1908

1909

1912

5 Minutes to a 5

Place the following in chronological order: Pure Food and Drug Act, Federal Trade Commission Act, Clayton Antitrust Act.

Why are these important?

"So multifarious have become corporate affairs, so many concessions and privileges have been accorded them by legislation . . . that their specially retained representatives are either elected to office, directly in their interests, or maintained in a perpetual lobby to serve them. Hence it is that the corporation does not limit its operations to the legitimate conduct of its business. Human nature everywhere is selfish, and with the vast power which consolidated capital can wield, with the impossibility of fixing any personal or moral responsibility for corporate acts, its commands are heard and obeyed in the capitals of the state and nation. But in a government where the people are sovereign why are these things tolerated. Why are there no remedies promptly applied and the evils eradicated?"

> Robert La Follette, "The Danger Threatening Representative Government," July 4, 1897

What problem is La Follette highlighting in this passage? Why is La Follette's perspective important?

Go to the website for Hull House: http://www.hullhousemuseum.org/.

In 1889, Jane Addams and Ellen Gates Starr founded Hull House as a settlement house in a poor neighborhood of Chicago. Click on "About" and learn more about Jane Addams. Browse the site and see what activities are still going on at Hull House. What role did settlement houses play in the late nineteenth and early twentieth centuries?

Look up the definition of *muckraker*. The term received its modern meaning from President Theodore Roosevelt in a speech on April 14, 1906. While Roosevelt approved of journalistic exposures of corruption, he cautioned that too many reporters could not tear themselves away from raking muck, like a character in John Bunyan's *Pilgrim's Progress* (1678). Despite, Roosevelt's criticism, the term *muckraker* soon became a source of pride to investigative journalists. Why were muckrakers important in the Progressive Era?

Place the following in chronological order: Ballinger-Pinchot Affair, Northern Securities Case, Sixteenth Amendment.

Why are these important?

"At 4:40 o'clock, nearly five hours after the employes (sic) in the rest of the building had gone home, the fire broke out. The one little fire escape in the interior was never resorted to by many of the doomed victims. Some of them escaped by running down the stairs, but in a moment or two this avenue was cut off by flame. The girls rushed to the windows and looked down at Greene Street, 100 feet below them. Then one poor, little creature jumped. There was a plate glass protection over part of the sidewalk, but she crashed through it, wrecking it and breaking her body into a thousand pieces.

Then they all began to drop. The crowd yelled "Don't jump!" but it was jump or be burned, the proof of which is found in the fact that fifty burned bodies were taken from the ninth floor alone.

They jumped, they crashed through broken glass, they crushed themselves to death on the sidewalk. Of those who stayed behind, it is better to say nothing . . . ."
New York Times, March 26, 1911

This passage is a newspaper account of the Triangle Shirtwaist Fire. Because of poor safety conditions, including doors to stairwells that had been chained shut to prevent possible thefts, 146 workers, mostly young women, died when fire swept through the Triangle Shirtwaist Company on the eighth, ninth, and tenth floors of the Asch Building in New York City. What were some of the consequences of this tragedy?

Day 107

Distinguish between Theodore Roosevelt's New Nationalism and Woodrow Wilson's New Freedom. Why is this distinction important?

CHAPTER 21

Connect the following events with the proper year:

Events:

    Zimmerman Telegram

    Outbreak of War in Europe

    Treaty of Versailles

    Announcement of the Fourteen Points

    Sussex Pledge

Years:

    1914

    1916

    1917

    1918

    1919

Day 109

Go to the website for the American Battle Monuments Commission: https://www
.abmc.gov/cemeteries-memorials#.WA0HHI2Qzcs.

The American Battle Monuments Commission was established by Congress in 1923
to address an unprecedented issue for Americans—how to memorialize war dead
who were buried overseas. The Commission created a system of cemeteries and war
memorials notable for their beauty and artistic distinction. Explore the pages describing some of the World War I cemeteries and war memorials. What would have been
some of the challenges facing those who were charged with creating these cemeteries
and memorials?

"The world must be made safe for democracy. Its peace must be planted upon the tested foundations of political liberty. We have no selfish ends to serve. We desire no conquest, no dominion. We seek no indemnities for ourselves, no material compensation for the sacrifices we shall freely make. We are but one of the champions of mankind. We shall be satisfied when those rights have been made as secure as the faith and freedom of nations can make them."

President Woodrow Wilson, War Message to Congress, April 2, 1917

When he asked Congress to declare war on Imperial Germany, what did Woodrow Wilson believe the United States should be fighting for? Why is this important?

Place the following in chronological order: *Lusitania*, Meuse-Argonne Offensive, Lever Food and Fuel Control Act.

Why are these important?

Day 112

Go to the website for the National World War I Museum and Memorial: https://www.theworldwar.org/.

Click on "Explore," and browse through some of the current and online exhibitions. What made the Great War different from wars that had gone before?

"Section 3. Whoever, when the United States is at war, shall willfully make or convey false reports or false statements with intent to interfere with the operation or success of the military or naval forces of the United States, or to promote the success of its enemies . . . or shall willfully utter, print, write, or publish any disloyal, profane, scurrilous, or abusive language about the form of government in the United States, or the Constitution, of the United States, or the military or naval forces of the United States . . . or shall willfully display the flag of any foreign enemy, or shall willfully . . . urge, incite, or advocate any curtailment of production . . . or advocate, teach, defend or suggest the doing of any of the acts or things in this section enumerated and whoever shall by word or act support or favor the cause of any country with which the United States is at war or by word or deed oppose the cause of the United States therein, shall be punished by a fine of not more than $10,000 or imprisonment for not more than twenty years, or both . . . ."

   The United States Sedition Act, May 16, 1918

What was the purpose of Congress in passing the Sedition Act? What does this tell us about the United States during World War I?

Distinguish between the supporters of the League of Nations and "reservationists." Why is this distinction important?

CHAPTER 22

Connect the following events with the proper year:

Events:

    Washington Disarmament Conference

    Start of Prohibition

    Lindbergh Flight across the Atlantic

    Stock Market Crash

    Scopes Trial

Years:

    1920

    1921

    1925

    1927

    1929

The writer F. Scott Fitzgerald entitled a 1922 collection of shorts stories *Tales of the Jazz Age*. This helped popularize a term that became associated with the 1920s. Why is the "Jazz Age" an appropriate name for the decade that followed the conclusion of World War I?

Place the following in chronological order: execution of Sacco and Vanzetti, National Origins Act, Palmer Raids.

Why are these important?

"The expenses of government reach everybody. Taxes take from everyone a part of his earnings and force everyone to work for a certain part of his time for the government. . . . I want the people of America to be able to work less for the government—and more for themselves. I want them to have the rewards of their own industry. This is the chief meaning of freedom. . . . When the government effects a new economy, it grants everybody a life pension with which to raise the standard of existence. It increases the value of everybody's property, raises the scale of everybody's wages. One of the greatest favors that can be bestowed upon the American people is economy in government."

President Calvin Coolidge, August 11, 1924

What is President Coolidge's point in this speech? What does this say about the governing philosophy of the Republican presidential administrations of the 1920s?

Go to the Charles Lindbergh website: http://www.charleslindbergh.com/history/.

Explore some of the pages describing Charles Lindbergh's solo flight across the Atlantic Ocean and its aftermath. Why did Lindbergh become an international hero? What was the significance of his achievement?

Day 120

Distinguish between the views of Herbert Hoover and Alfred "Al" Smith concerning Prohibition in the 1928 presidential election. Why is this distinction important?

"Supposedly 'nice' girls were smoking cigarettes—openly and defiantly, if often rather awkwardly and self-consciously. They were drinking—somewhat less openly but often all too efficaciously. There were stories of daughters of the most exemplary parents getting drunk—'blotto,' as their companions cheerfully put it—on the contents of hip-flasks of the new prohibition regime, and going out joyriding with men at four in the morning. And worst of all, even at well-regulated dances they were said to retire where the eye of the most sharp-sighted chaperon could not follow, and in darkened rooms or in parked cars to engage in the unspeakable practice of petting and necking."

Frederick Lewis Allen, *Only Yesterday*, 1931

What social development is Frederick Lewis Allen describing in an early popular history of the 1920s? Why was this important?

CHAPTER 23

Connect the following events with the proper year:

Events:

    End of Prohibition

    Hawley-Smoot Tariff

    Scottsboro Boys Trial

    Reconstruction Finance Corporation

    Formation of the Congress of Industrial Organization (CIO)

Years:

    1930

    1931

    1932

    1933

    1935

Place the following in chronological order: Social Security Act, Justice Reorganization Bill, National Industrial Recovery Act (NIRA).

Why are these important?

"Wearing our shade hats, with handkerchiefs tied over our faces and Vaseline in our nostrils, we have been trying to rescue our home from the accumulations of wind-blown dust which penetrates wherever air can go. It is an almost hopeless task, for there is rarely a day when at some time the dust clouds do not roll over. 'Visibility' approaches zero and everything is covered again with a silt-like deposit which may vary in depth from a film to actual ripples on the kitchen floor. I keep oiled cloths on the window sill and between the upper and lower sashes. They help a little to retard or collect the dust. Some seal the windows with gummed-paper strips used in wrapping parcels, but no method is fully effective. We buy what appears to be red cedar sawdust with oil added to use in sweeping our floors, and do our best to avoid inhaling the irritating dust."

Mrs. Caroline A. Henderson, Letter, June 30, 1935

Mrs. Henderson lived in Oklahoma. What phenomenon is she describing? Why was it important?

Distinguish between the approaches of Herbert Hoover and Franklin D. Roosevelt in combating the Great Depression. Why is this distinction important?

Day 126

Go to the National Park Service's website for the Home of Franklin D. Roosevelt National Historic Site: https://www.nps.gov/hofr/index.htm.

Click on "Learn About the Park," and explore the pages on history and culture. Why was Franklin D. Roosevelt so effective as a leader?

Day 127

"I must believe that Willie Stark was a great man. What happened to his greatness is not the question. Perhaps he spilled it on the ground the way you spill a liquid when the bottle breaks. Perhaps he piled up his greatness and burnt it in one great blaze in the dark like a bonfire and then there wasn't anything but dark and the embers winking. Perhaps he could not tell his greatness from ungreatness and so mixed them together so that what was adulterated was lost. But he had it. I must believe that."
    Robert Penn Warren, *All the King's Men*, 1946

Robert Penn Warren's great novel *All the King's Men* was about a southern politician loosely based on Louisiana's Huey P. Long. In the passage above, the novel's narrator Jack Burden reflects on Willie Stark, his former boss. Why would a figure like Huey P. Long evoke such mixed emotions?

"Unionization, as opposed to communism, presupposes the relation of employment; it is based upon the wage system and it recognizes fully and unreservedly the institution of private property and the right to investment profit. It is upon the fuller development of collective bargaining, the wider expansion of the labor movement, the increased influence of labor in our national councils, that the perpetuity of our democratic institutions must largely depend.

   The organized workers of America, free in their industrial life, conscious partners in production, secure in their homes and enjoying a decent standard of living, will prove the finest bulwark against the intrusion of alien doctrines of government."

   John L. Lewis, "The Rights of Labor," September 6, 1937

What point is the labor leader John L. Lewis making in the passage above? Why did he feel that he had to make this point?

Day 129

Distinguish between the First and Second New Deals. Why is this distinction important?

CHAPTER 24

Connect the following events with the proper year:

Events:

First Neutrality Act

German Invasion of Poland

Lend-Lease Act

Destroyers for Bases Agreement

Internment Camps for Japanese established

Years:

1935

1939

1940

1941

1942

5 Minutes to a 5

Place the following in chronological order: Battle of the Bulge, Battle of Midway, Battle of Guadalcanal.

Why are these important?

"When the World War came to an end, with its appalling waste of human life and of material resources as well, with its aftermath of depression from which we are still suffering, we were all resolved never to let it happen again. . . . Today, we in America are not so certain that we have a mission to perform in settling the quarrels of the Old World. We are not even sure that we are competent to decide in all cases as to the justice of the dispute: we are, however, profoundly convinced that the method of war is no way to bring about the establishment of justice, political freedom, or peace itself. The best place for us to exert our influence to establish these blessings is in our own country. . . . But I should like to ask what possible shame can attach to America for taking advantage of both her geographical and historical position to keep out of the present chaos in Europe? What shame is there in trying to limit the area of conflict rather than extend it? What ethical obtuseness in attempting to keep one clear pool of sanity in the world?"

Senator Gerald P. Nye, "Is Neutrality Possible for America?," in *Tomorrow in the Making*, edited by John N. Anderson, and Carl A. Marsden, 1939

What foreign policy position is Senator Nye taking in the passage above? How influential was this perspective?

Day 133

Go to the National Park Service's website for the World War II Valor in the Pacific National Monument: https://www.nps.gov/valr/index.htm.

Click on "Learn About the Park," and explore the pages on history and culture. Why is what happened on December 7, 1941, so important?

Place the following in chronological order: Beginning of the draft, G.I. Bill, Revenue Act of 1942.

Why are these important?

Day 135

Distinguish between the narrow front and broad front strategies in the European Theater of World War II. Why is this distinction important?

> "When the atomic bombs were dropped and news began to circulate that 'Operation Olympic' would not, after all, be necessary, when we learned to our astonishment that we would not be obliged in a few months to rush up the beaches near Tokyo assault-firing while being machine-gunned, mortared, and shelled, for all the practiced phlegm of our tough facades we broke down and cried with relief and joy. We were going to live. We were going to grow to adulthood after all."
>
> Paul Fussell, "Thank God for the Atomic Bomb," *The New Republic*, August 1981

Paul Fussell was a distinguished professor of literature and writer, who in his youth had served as an infantry officer in the European Theater of World War II. His essay "Thank God for the Atomic Bomb" was a response to critics who argued that the dropping of the atomic bombs on Hiroshima and Nagasaki was immoral. What is his perspective, and why is it significant?

CHAPTER 25

Connect the following events with the proper year:

Events:

    Federal Employee Loyalty Program

    Winston Churchill's "Iron Curtain" Speech

    Start of the Korean War

    Yalta Conference

    Establishment of the Communist People's Republic of China

Years:

    1945

    1946

    1947

    1949

    1950

Day 138

Place the following in chronological order: Marshall Plan, NATO, Truman Doctrine. Why are these important?

"In these circumstances it is clear that the main element of any United States policy toward the Soviet Union must be that of a long-term, patient but firm and vigilant containment of Russian expansive tendencies. It is important to note, however, that such a policy has nothing to do with outward histrionics: with threats or blustering or superfluous gestures of outward 'toughness.' While the Kremlin is basically flexible in its reaction to political realities, it is by no means unamenable to considerations of prestige. . . . For these reasons, it is a sine qua non of successful dealing with Russia that the foreign government in question should remain at all times cool and collected and that its demands on Russian policy should be put forward in such a manner as to leave the way open for a compliance not too detrimental to Russian prestige."

 George F. Kennan, "The Sources of Soviet Conduct," *Foreign Affairs*,
 July 1947

What foreign policy approach is George F. Kennan advocating? Why is this important?

Day 140

Distinguish between the positions of President Harry Truman and Senator Joseph McCarthy regarding Soviet espionage in the United States. Why is this distinction important?

Place the following in chronological order: Soviet downing of a U-2 plane, Geneva Accords, *Sputnik*.

Why are these important?

Go to the National Park Service's website for the Minuteman Missile National Historic Site: https://www.nps.gov/mimi/index.htm.

Click on "Learn About the Park," and explore the pages on history and culture. Why is this site important for understanding the history of the Cold War?

5 Minutes to a 5

"Q. Robert Richards, Copley Press: Mr. President, would you mind commenting on the strategic importance of Indochina to the free world? I think there has been, across the country, some lack of understanding on just what it means to us.

THE PRESIDENT: You have, of course, both the specific and the general when you talk about such things.

First of all, you have the specific value of a locality in its production of materials that the world needs.

Then you have the possibility that many human beings pass under a dictatorship that is inimical to the free world.

Finally, you have broader considerations that might follow what you would call the "falling domino" principle. You have a row of dominoes set up, you knock down the first one, and what will happen to the last one is a certainty that it will go over very quickly. So you could have a beginning of a disintegration that would have the most profound influences."

President Dwight D. Eisenhower, President's News Conference, April 7, 1954

What famous foreign policy theory did President Eisenhower articulate in this news conference? Why is it important?

Day 144

In the 1960s a new generation of "revisionist" historians questioned Cold War orthodoxy and argued against the belief that the Soviet Union was solely responsible for the Cold War, instead contending that the United States, pursuing expansive strategic and economic interests, made the dominant contribution to the onset of the struggle. A later generation of "post-revisionist" scholars challenged this interpretation and said that while both superpowers contributed to the coming of the Cold War, the "revisionists" downplayed the effects of Soviet policies in precipitating conflict.

Why did the disputes between historians of the Cold War take on a greater significance than the usual academic debates over the past?

CHAPTER 26

Connect the following events with the proper year:

Events:

    Interstate Highway Act

    Taft-Hartley Act

    Publication of *On the Road*

    Checkers Speech

    Fair Deal

Years:

    1947

    1949

    1952

    1956

    1957

Distinguish between the positions of President Harry Truman and South Carolina Governor Strom Thurmond on civil rights in 1948. Why is this distinction important?

"In our nation work and wealth abound. Our population grows. Commerce crowds our rivers and rails, our skies, harbors and highways. Our soil is fertile, our agriculture productive. The air rings with the song of our industry—rolling mills and blast furnaces, dynamos, dams and assembly lines—the chorus of America the beautiful."

President Dwight D. Eisenhower, Second Inaugural Address, January 21, 1957

What social and economic reality is reflected in President Eisenhower's Second Inaugural?

In the 1998 film *Pleasantville*, the 1950s is presented as a time of repression, especially for African Americans and women. That women were all forced to be housewives is a widespread view of the era. Yet, by 1957 more women were working than during World War II. By 1960, 40 percent of women held a job. Why does the less-complicated view of women's roles in the 1950s persist? Why is this important?

Day 149

Go to the State Museum of Pennsylvania's website for Levittown, PA: http://statemuseumpa.org/levittown/.

Explore the pages of the exhibit. Why were Levittown and developments like it important?

Place the following in chronological order: Montgomery Bus Boycott, *Brown v. Board of Education*, Little Rock Nine.

Why are these important?

"Even before the joint began to jump, there was trouble at the National Guard Armory in Washington, D.C. As 5,000 people, mostly teenagers, poured in for some rock'in'roll, knives flashed and one young man was cut in the arm. Inside the auditorium, 25 special officers waited tensely for Bill Haley and his Comets to swing into 'big beat' . . . .

Some of the kids danced, some scuffed, fights broke out, a chair flew. William Warfield, 17, a high-school junior, was hit. Suffering from a brain concussion and a severe cut over one eye, he was rushed to the hospital. 'Before I knew it, everybody was pounding everybody', he later said.

'It's that jungle strain that gets 'em all worked up,' said Armory manager Arthur (Dutch) Bergmann.

While parents and police viewed with alarm, one sociologist tried to pin down the cause: 'Rock and roll fever is caused by the same virus which induces panty raids and goldfish swallowing. When kids run wild, any stimulus will do.'"

"Rock and Roll Fever," St. Louis *Post-Dispatch*, June 13, 1956

What is the perspective of this passage from a news report? Why is it important?

CHAPTER 27

Connect the following events with the proper year:

Events:

Bay of Pigs

Sit-ins begin

Assassination of President John F. Kennedy

Cuban Missile Crisis

Gulf of Tonkin Resolution

Years:

1960

1961

1962

1963

1964

"Increasingly . . . government has been absorbing or controlling more and more of our resources, our energy, and our ambition. Today you work from January through April just to provide government with the money it spends. Until early February you are working to pay the expenses of local and state government. For twice as long thereafter you are working to pay the expenses of the Federal Government. Only then do you work for money that you yourself can use for what you yourself choose.

This cancerous growth of the Federal Government must and shall be stopped."

Senator Barry Goldwater, Opening Campaign Speech, September 3, 1964

What is the perspective of Senator Goldwater? Why is it important?

Go to the website for the Smithsonian National Museum of African American History and Culture: https://nmaahc.si.edu/.

Click on the "Explore Full Collection" button at the bottom of the page, and then explore the pages in the Civil Rights section. Why were the 1960s so important to the Civil Rights Movement?

Day 155

Distinguish between "Old Left" and "New Left." Why is this distinction important?

Place the following in chronological order: Tet Offensive, Woodstock Music Festival, Medicare.

Why are these important?

Day 157

"Why are we in South Viet-Nam? . . . We are . . . there because there are great stakes in the balance. Let no one think for a moment that retreat from Viet-Nam would bring an end to conflict. The battle would be renewed in one country and then another. The central lesson of our time is that the appetite of aggression is never satisfied. To withdraw from one battlefield means only to prepare for the next. We must say in Southeast Asia—as we did in Europe—in the words of the Bible: "Hitherto shalt thou come, but no further.""

President Lyndon B. Johnson, "American Policy in Vietnam," April 7, 1965

What is the perspective of President Johnson in this passage? Why is it important?

Day 158

Go to the National Park Service's website for the Vietnam Veterans Memorial: https://www.nps.gov/vive/index.htm.

Click on "Learn About the Park," and go to the page on photos and multimedia. How does the memorial capture Americans' complex feelings about the Vietnam War?

Go to the website for the Andy Warhol Museum: http://www.warhol.org/.

Click on "Education," and then "Lessons and Resources." Explore the pages on Andy Warhol's life and art. Why was Andy Warhol an important figure in the counterculture of the 1960s?

Day 160

CHAPTER 28

Connect the following events with the proper year:

Events:

    Fall of South Vietnam

    Resignation of President Richard Nixon

    Iran Hostage Crisis begins

    Roe v. Wade

    Camp David Accords

Years:

    1973

    1974

    1975

    1978

    1979

Distinguish between the foreign policy approach of President Richard M. Nixon and his predecessors. Why is this distinction important?

Go to the website for the Richard Nixon Presidential Library and Museum: https://www.nixonlibrary.gov/.

Browse through "The Life," "The Times," and "Virtual Library." Presidential libraries are designed as monuments to presidents as well as places to facilitate research into their presidencies. What special challenge is faced by the curators of the Richard Nixon Presidential Library and Museum?

"I don't think there's any doubt that, in the future, the cost of oil is going to go up. What I've had as a basic commitment since I've been President is to reduce our dependence on foreign oil. It can only be done in two ways: one to conserve energy—to stop the waste of energy—and, secondly, to produce more American energy. We've been very successful in both cases. We've now reduced the importing of foreign oil in the last year alone by one-third. We imported today 2 million barrels of oil less than the same date a year ago."

    President Jimmy Carter, debate between Jimmy Carter and Ronald Reagan, October 28, 1980

What problem is President Carter referring to in this passage? Why is this important?

Place the following in chronological order: Tax Reform Act, Strategic Defense Initiative, INF Treaty.

Why are these important?

Day 165

"We must remember a simple truth. The creativity and ambition of the American people are the vital forces of economic growth. The motivation and incentive of our people—to supply new goods and services and earn additional income for their families—are the most precious resources of our Nation's economy. The goal of this Administration is to nurture the strength and vitality of the American people by reducing the burdensome, intrusive role of the Federal Government; by lowering tax rates and cutting spending; and by providing incentives for individuals to work, to save, and to invest. It is our basic belief that only by reducing the growth of government can we increase the growth of the economy."

President Ronald Reagan, "White House Report on the Program for Economic Recovery," February 18, 1981

What perspective on government does President Reagan express in this passage? Why is this important?

Go to the website for the Lucas Museum of Narrative Art: http://lucasmuseum.org/museum.

The Lucas Museum of Narrative Art features "visual art that tells a story." It was endowed by George Lucas, the creator of *Star Wars*. Click on "The Collection," and then "View the Art of Cinema." Browse through the pages in this section, focusing on *Star Wars* and other movies of the 1970s and 1980s. Why were the films of directors like George Lucas and Steven Spielberg important to the culture of the late 1970s and 1980s?

5 Minutes to a 5

CHAPTER 29

Connect the following events with the proper year:

Events:

Fall of the Berlin Wall

Operation Desert Shield

Fall of the Soviet Union

Passage of NAFTA

Election of Bill Clinton

Years:

1989

1990

1991

1992

1993

"We gather tonight at a dramatic and deeply promising time in our history and the history of man on Earth. For in the past 12 months, the world has known changes of almost biblical proportions. . . . But the biggest thing that has happened in the world in my life, in our lives, is this: By the grace of God, America won the Cold War."

President George H. W. Bush, "State of the Union Address," January 28, 1992

President Bush in the passage above expressed the euphoria at the end of the Cold War. Americans began to expect a "peace dividend" in the form of decreased defense spending. The scholar Francis Fukuyama published a widely discussed book entitled *The End of History and the Last Man* (1992) in which he argued that with the demise of Communism, humanity had reached the end of its ideological evolution, and the world would gradually adopt Western liberal democracy. Was Fukuyama's prediction of an end of ideological struggle borne out by events?

Day 169

Go to the website for the George Bush Presidential Library and Museum: http://bush41.org/.

Click on "George Bush," and read his biography. Explore other pages at the site. George H. W. Bush was the last president from the "World War II generation." Why is this important?

Place the following in chronological order: Kosovo War, Contract with America, Personal Opportunity and Work Opportunity Reconciliation Act.

Why are these important?

"We are determined to help Americans succeed in the workplace, to raise well-educated, healthy kids, and to help Americans succeed at the toughest job of all, that of being a parent. . . . Now, I have to get back to work on my State of the Union speech. And I worked on it until pretty late last night. But I want to say one thing to the American people. I want you to listen to me. I'm going to say this again. I did not have sexual relations with that woman, Miss Lewinsky. I never told anybody to lie, not a single time—never. These allegations are false. And I need to go back to work for the American people."

President Bill Clinton, Response to the Lewinsky Allegations, January 26, 1998

What allegation is President Clinton referring to in this passage? Why is it important?

Day 172

Distinguish between traditional Democrats in the early 1990s and Bill Clinton's position as a "New Democrat." Why is this distinction important?

"The collapse of these new-economy stocks is both a predictable and rational phase of economic development—though it may not feel so rational if you've been burned by them. Launching a dotcom company in recent years has been a bit like getting a license to collect money. Venture capitalists showered you with cash, and Wall Street snapped up your stock at five or ten times the offering price—sometimes all in the same day—in the hope that you would soon become the next Intel or Microsoft. That money was a magnet for executives of boring old-economy companies, who joined dotcom start-ups for the thrill of working 20-hour days in return for wheelbarrowfuls of options. And certainly, lots of people got filthy rich."

John Greenwald, "Doom Stalks the Dotcoms," *Time*, April 17, 2000

In the passage above, journalist John Greenwald notes that before the dotcom stock crash of 2000, enormous fortunes had been made in the emerging industry that serviced the Internet. How did the dotcom boom reflect the larger economy during the 1990s?

CHAPTER 30

Connect the following events with the proper year:

Events:

    Affordable Care Act

    Hurricane Katrina

    Troubled Asset Relief Program (TARP)

    Invasion of Afghanistan

    Creation of the Department of Homeland Security

Years:

    2001

    2002

    2005

    2008

    2010

Go to the website for the 9/11 Memorial: https://www.911memorial.org/.

Explore the pages describing the Memorial and Museum. How does the memorial commemorate the tragedy of 9/11?

"The other choice is to let the American people spend their own money to meet their own needs. I hope you will join me in standing firmly on the side of the people. You see, the growing surplus exists because taxes are too high and Government is charging more than it needs. The people of America have been overcharged, and on their behalf, I am here asking for a refund.

   Some say my tax plan is too big. Others say it is too small. I respectfully disagree. [*Laughter*] This plan is just right. I didn't throw darts at a board to come up with a number for tax relief. I didn't take a poll or develop an arbitrary formula that might sound good. I looked at problems in the Tax Code and calculated the cost to fix them.

   A tax rate of 15 percent is too high for those who earn low wages, so we must lower the rate to 10 percent. No one should pay more than a third of the money they earn in Federal income taxes, so we lowered the top rate to 33 percent. . . .

   In my plan, no one is targeted in or targeted out. Everyone who pays income tax will get relief."

   President George W. Bush, "Address Before a Joint Session of the Congress on Administration Goals," February 27, 2001

What policy initiative was President Bush promoting in the passage above? Why is it important?

Day 177

Place the following in chronological order: President Bush's "Surge" in Iraq, the ISIS conquest of Mosul, Operation Iraqi Freedom.

Why are these important?

Day 178

Distinguish between the positions of 2012 presidential candidates President Barack Obama and Mitt Romney on the issue of gay marriage. Why is this distinction important?

"Now, as I said in my speech on the economy yesterday, it makes no sense to expel talented young people who, for all intents and purposes, are Americans. They've been raised as Americans, understand themselves to be part of this country. To expel these young people who want to staff our labs or start new businesses or defend our country simply because of the actions of their parents or because of the inactions of politicians—in the absence of any immigration action from Congress to fix our broken immigration system, what we've tried to do is focus our immigration resources in the right places. So we prioritize border security, putting more boots on the southern border than at any time in our history."

President Barack Obama, "Transcript of Obama's Speech on Immigration Policy," *New York Times*, June 15, 2012

In the passage above, what is President Obama's perspective on immigration policy? Why is this important?

Day 180

Go to the website for the Supreme Court of the United States: https://www.supremecourt.gov/.

Click on "About the Court" and explore the pages on the function and history of the Supreme Court. The composition of the Supreme Court has become a political issue in recent years as the Court has ruled on controversial laws and social questions. What were some important Supreme Court rulings made during the years of the Obama administration?

Answers

Day 1

As the website points out, in AD 1250 Cahokia was larger than London. The Mississippians developed a highly sophisticated urban culture that thrived centuries before the arrival of the Europeans. The mounds builders help illustrate the wide variety of cultures and levels of development among Native American peoples.

Day 2

The proper chronological order is Polo, Columbus, Balboa. Marco Polo was a Venetian merchant who traveled to China in the late 1200s. When Polo's account of his voyage was published many years later in 1477, it spurred European desires to find a way to the rich markets of the Far East. Looking for Asia by sailing west across the Atlantic, Columbus instead discovered a New World in 1492. This opened up the Americas to European exploration and settlement. Balboa crossed the isthmus of Panama in 1513 and saw the Pacific Ocean.

Day 3

Portuguese mariners were exploring the Atlantic coastline of Africa in the 1480s. In 1488 Bartolomeu Dias discovered the Cape of Good Hope. Columbus first reached the western hemisphere in 1492. Hernando Cortès captured the Aztec capital of Tenochtitlan in 1521. This broke the power of the Aztec empire and secured his conquest of Mexico. Francisco Pizarro landed a small army in Peru in 1531; by 1533 he had completed the conquest of the Inca Empire. Francisco Vasquez de Coronado explored the American Southwest between 1540 and 1542. He unsuccessfully sought rumored cities of gold.

Day 4

Prescott's *The History of the Conquest of Mexico* combines excellent scholarship with a nineteenth-century Romantic sensibility that makes it a dramatic and colorful narrative. Prescott admires Cortès and sees him as a great Romantic hero, bending events to his will. However, as a nineteenth-century man, Prescott deplores the conquistador's cruelty and religious fanaticism. Ultimately Prescott sees Cortès as a brilliant product of a harsh time.

Day 5

The proper chronological order is Crusades, astrolabe, encomienda. The Crusades were religious wars waged by Christian Europeans in the Middle Ages. The Europeans hoped to stop Islamic territorial advances and to win back control of the Holy Land. The astrolabe was a navigational device that helped European mariners calculate their latitude. It helped make possible the fifteenth- and sixteenth-century voyages of discovery. The encomienda system emerged during the sixteenth-century Spanish conquests in Central and South America. Native Americans were forced to work for Spanish colonists in exchange for "protection."

Day 6

Bartolomé de Las Casas was a Dominican friar who opposed the mistreatment of Native Americans and in person and in print defended their humanity and rights. While Las Casas had some influence on government policy, his attitudes had little impact on most Spanish settlers. Aside from converting Native Americans to Christianity, the settlers were intent on using conquered peoples as a source of labor.

Day 7

The Castillo de San Marcos is an imposing edifice that tells someone looking at it that the Spanish came to stay in America. The Castillo also tells the observer that the Spanish settlers lived in a dangerous world. The Castillo was attacked several times over the years. The Castillo is the oldest surviving fort in North America.

Day 8

The English settled Jamestown in 1607. This was the first successful English colony in America. Samuel de Champlain founded the French settlement of Quebec in 1608. The Virginia House of Burgesses, the first colonial legislature, began meeting in 1619. The Pilgrims landed at Plymouth in 1620. The Puritans established the Massachusetts Bay Colony in 1629. The first settlers arrived in Maryland in 1634. Maryland was intended as a refuge for English Catholics. William Penn founded Pennsylvania in 1681. Penn, a Quaker, established religious freedom for all Christians in Pennsylvania.

Day 9

All Europeans, whatever their nationality, regarded the Native Americans as heathen barbarians. The Spanish attempted to convert the Native Americans to Christianity, and then integrate them as workers in the colonial economic and social structure.

Examples would be the encomiendas of early Spanish settlers and the missions established by the Franciscans and other religious orders in the Southwest and California. The French also wanted to convert the Native Americans to Catholicism. Jesuit missionaries went to live among the Native Americans. Because the French were mostly interested in fur trading, they did not require much land from the Native peoples they encountered, and so caused less disruption to their ways of life. The English were interested in converting the Native Americans to Protestant Christianity, but went at this less systematically than did the Spanish and French. Because the English needed land for their growing agricultural population, they engaged in many wars with local Native Americans, notably the brutal Pequot War of 1634–1638.

Day 10

The proper chronological order is Cartier, Hudson, and La Salle. Jacques Cartier made three voyages to Canada in the 1530s and 1540s, exploring the Gulf of St. Lawrence and the St. Lawrence River. His voyages helped lay the foundation for New France. Henry Hudson was an English sea captain working for the Dutch East India Company. In 1609, Hudson explored Manhattan and the river that would be named after him. In 1610–1611, he discovered what is now called Hudson Bay in Canada. Hudson's first voyage opened the way for Dutch settlement in North America. Robert La Salle was a French explorer who sailed down the Mississippi River to the Gulf of Mexico in the 1680s. He established French outposts along the way and claimed the Mississippi River Valley for France, naming it Louisiana after King Louis XIV.

Day 11

The first Thanksgiving took place in November 1621, when the Pilgrims, with some Wampanoag Indian guests, celebrated a good harvest after the hardships that they had suffered in their first year in America. Thanksgiving did not become a national holiday until 1863, following a proclamation by President Abraham Lincoln. Now, in addition to being a time for Americans to reflect on their blessings, Thanksgiving is a time for family gatherings, parades, and football.

Day 12

Roger Williams was a Puritan minister and theologian who came to believe that church and state should be separated. His criticism of the Puritan establishment in Massachusetts led to the colony's authorities ordering his banishment in 1635. In 1636, Williams and some followers established a new settlement at Providence in what became the colony of Rhode Island. Settlers here were assured freedom of conscience. Williams helped lay the foundation of the American tradition of religious liberty and the separation of church and state.

Day 13

The proper chronological order is John Smith, Squanto, Anne Hutchinson. John Smith was the military man whose leadership contributed to the survival of the English colony at Jamestown, Virginia. He claimed that after being captured by Native American members of the Powhatan Confederacy, his life was saved by Pocahontas, the daughter of their chief. Squanto was a member of the Patuxet tribe. He learned English after being captured by English explorers. Squanto was able to return home and helped the Pilgrims at Plymouth adjust to the new world, teaching them Native American methods of agriculture. Anne Hutchinson and her family settled in the Massachusetts Bay Colony in 1634. Here Hutchinson criticized the ministerial establishment of the colony and questioned their teachings on divine grace. Hutchinson was banished from the colony in 1638, and she moved to Rhode Island.

Day 14

Roman Catholicism was the Christian church of Europe before the Reformation. The clergy of the Church were organized hierarchically, with the Pope at their head. Roman Catholicism emphasized regular attendance at the Mass and other liturgies, sacraments, and the performance of good works as a means to salvation. King Henry VIII created the Church of England when he broke with the Catholic Church in the 1530s. The Church of England looked to the king, rather than the Pope, as its head. The Church of England maintained the episcopal structure of the Catholic Church and kept the Mass and other sacraments. Puritans were followers of John Calvin and held the doctrine of predestination. They wanted to "purify" the Church of England of its "Catholic" elements. The Church of England became the established church in Virginia and most of the southern colonies. Puritans settled in Massachusetts and initially dominated in the New England colonies. In the seventeenth century, Catholics were persecuted in England. The aristocratic Calvert family founded Maryland in the 1630s as a refuge for English Catholics.

Day 15

King William's War began in 1688 and raged until 1697. In Europe it was known as the War of the League of Augsburg. Queen Anne's War began in 1702 and ended in 1713. In Europe it was known as the War of the Spanish Succession. The religious revival of the Great Awakening began in the 1720s and lasted into the 1740s. The Stono Rebellion, a slave uprising in South Carolina, took place in 1739. King George's War began in 1744 and ended in 1748. It was the American phase of the European War of the Austrian Succession, which ran from 1740–1748.

Day 16

Arthur Miller saw the Salem Witch Trials and the Second Red Scare as comparable because he believed both were hysterical reactions against imaginary threats. He opposed the investigations of the House Un-American Activities Committee (HUAC) into the political beliefs of filmmakers, writers, and actors. Miller has his protagonist condemn himself for not speaking out earlier because he criticized HUAC witnesses who named names of former Communist associates to save their own careers. He, himself, was cited for contempt of Congress in 1957 for refusing to do this.

Day 17

The proper chronological order is the English Civil War, the Glorious Revolution, and the Act of Union between England and Scotland. The English Civil War lasted from 1642 to 1651 and resulted in the execution of King Charles I and the establishment of a Puritan dictatorship under Oliver Cromwell. The Glorious Revolution took place in 1688, when the Catholic King James II was overthrown by his Protestant daughter Mary and her husband, the Dutch stadtholder William III. As the price of obtaining the kingdom, William and Mary agreed to the 1689 Bill of Rights, which limited the power of the monarchy and codified the rights of Parliament; this established a constitutional monarchy in England. The Acts of Union were passed by the English Parliament in 1706 and the Scottish Parliament in 1707, and unified the two countries into Great Britain, with one British Parliament.

Day 18

The Byrd family's mansion of Westover was built around 1750. It is a magnificent example of Georgian architecture. Westover testifies to the wealth of some Virginia planters. It also testifies to the high level of culture of some planters; the Byrd library was once one of the largest in America.

Day 19

Mercantilism was an economic theory that encouraged governments to increase their share of limited global wealth by maintaining a favorable balance of trade. This was accomplished by regulations that encouraged exports while restricting imports from foreign countries with high tariffs. Colonies provided raw materials and staple products that were turned into finished goods by the mother country. Examples of legislation furthering mercantilism were the Navigation acts of the 1660s and the Molasses Act of 1733. Proponents of free trade believe that general prosperity is encouraged by the abolition of restrictions on exports and imports of goods. The great eighteenth-century British advocate of free trade was Adam Smith in his book *The Wealth of Nations* (1776).

Day 20

Bacon was telling his congregation of African American slaves that they should accept their station in life. They were to perform their duties willingly and without complaint. They were to do this because their station in life was the will of God and to object would be to defy God's authority. This sermon demonstrates that in the eighteenth century some colonists in Maryland believed that the institution of slavery was sanctioned by God and reflected a divine order in the world. Bacon sees society divided into defined classes, much like European aristocrats. Interestingly, though the Reverend Bacon obviously saw African Americans as social inferiors, he did think it important that they embrace Christianity.

Day 21

The proper chronological order is Nathaniel Bacon, Sir Edmund Andros, and Jonathan Edwards. Nathaniel Bacon was a Virginia planter who led a rebellion against the Royal Governor William Berkeley in 1676. Bacon was protesting the inability of Berkeley to protect settlers on the frontier from Native American attacks. After initial success, Bacon died and Berkeley reasserted control over Virginia. Sir Edmund Andros was an English colonial administrator who in the seventeenth century served as governor of New York and other colonies. In 1686, King James II appointed Andros governor of the Dominion of New England, which combined New York, New Jersey, and the

New England colonies. When word of the Glorious Revolution reached the colonies, Andros was overthrown and the Dominion dissolved. Jonathan Edwards was a minister who played a leading role in the Great Awakening. He delivered his famous sermon "Sinners in the Hands of an Angry God" in 1741.

Day 22

The Albany Congress was convened in 1754 to address western settlement and the issues this raised with Native Americans. The Stamp Act Congress was held in 1765 to protest the Stamp Act and lobby for its repeal. The Boston Massacre took place in 1770 as British sentries fired into a crowd of unruly American colonists. The Boston Tea Party took place in 1773 when colonists dressed as Native Americans dumped East India Company tea into Boston Harbor. The First Continental Congress gathered in 1774 to coordinate resistance to the Intolerable Acts passed by Parliament after the Boston Tea Party.

Day 23

In 1754, Governor Robert Dinwiddie of Virginia sent George Washington, a young militia officer, to evict the French from Fort Duquesne, which they had built on the site of present day Pittsburgh. Washington was overwhelmed and defeated. He served bravely with General Edward Braddock in 1755 and helped rally the survivors of that general's defeat. Following this, Washington commanded Virginia troops on the frontier and became one of the most experienced American military commanders. The Marquis de Montcalm was the commander of French forces in Canada during the French and Indian War. He won important victories with the capture of Fort William Henry in 1757 and the successful defense of Fort Carillon (later Ticonderoga) in 1758. He was defeated and killed at the fall of Quebec in 1759. William Pitt became a leader of the British government in 1757. He devised an ambitious strategy to expand the British Empire. He sent large military reinforcements and capable commanders to North America, leading to the complete defeat of the French in Canada.

Day 24

In the eighteenth century, there were few roads in America. The easiest and fastest way to get around was by water. Lake Champlain was important because it provided an invasion route to and from Canada. Forts on the lake helped control this strategic waterway for the French, British, and later, the Americans. The French Fort Carillon was renamed Ticonderoga after it was captured by the British in 1759. It illustrates the enormously sophisticated nature of eighteenth-century fortifications, which were designed to bog attackers down in long and costly sieges.

Day 25

The proper chronological order is Sons of Liberty, Committees of Correspondence, minutemen. All these were groups of Americans resisting the policies of the British government. The Sons of Liberty were organized by Sam Adams in 1765 to resist the Stamp Act. The Sons of Liberty remained active after the Stamp Act crisis. Adams helped found a Massachusetts Committee of Correspondence in 1772 to express opposition to British actions and share ideas on methods of resistance. Soon other Committees of Correspondence emerged across the colonies. Minutemen were members of the militia charged with being ready for action at brief notice. In 1774, the Massachusetts Provincial Congress, which refused to recognize the military government imposed by the British, called on the militia to form companies of minutemen. The minutemen played an important role in the opening battles of the Revolutionary War at Lexington and Concord.

Day 26

Daniel Leonard was a wealthy and successful lawyer in Massachusetts. He opposed the agitation against Parliament and British policy, and skillfully criticized it in his "Letters," which were published in a newspaper between December 1774 and April 1775. His writings remind us that many American colonists remained loyal to the British government. During the Revolutionary War perhaps as many as 20 percent of Americans were Loyalist in their sympathies.

Day 27

Traditionally in English history, kings had to go to parliament to raise taxes, establishing the precedent that taxpayers had to have a say on taxes that affected them. The 1689 English Bill of Rights codified the principle that all taxes had to be approved by Parliament. During the long period of Salutary Neglect, the American colonists became accustomed to paying taxes voted by their legislatures. Once the British government began directly taxing the colonists with the Stamp Act (1765), it seemed to the colonists that their rights as Englishmen were being denied. They were being taxed without their legislative consent. The British government responded with the argument that American received "virtual representation" in Parliament; this assumed that members of Parliament represented all British subjects, not just the people of their electoral constituency. American critics of British policy did not find this persuasive. Increasingly influenced by the writings of thinkers like John Locke, they believed that "taxation without representation" violated their natural rights. This difference in outlooks led to the American Revolution.

Day 28

From its inception in the 1930s until 1979, Colonial Williamsburg focused on the stories of white colonists. Then it began to hire African American actors to portray slaves. In 1999, an effort to depict the darker side of slavery, such as a slave auction, led to protests. It can still be difficult to find African Americans willing to dress up and act like eighteenth-century slaves. The dilemma faced by the reenactors at Colonial Williamsburg reflects the difficulty of re-creating a history that is intensely painful for many people.

Day 29

The Second Continental Congress convened in May 1775 and was faced with carrying on the war that had just begun with Great Britain. The Declaration of Independence was signed on July 2, 1776, and formally announced on July 4. The Battle of Saratoga resulted in the surrender of an entire British army on October 17, 1777. The victory at Saratoga convinced the French government that it would be safe to intervene on the side of the American rebels. France and the United States signed a formal treaty of alliance on February 6, 1778. The Battle of Yorktown resulted in the surrender of another British army on October 19, 1781. This battle ensured that the United States would become independent and was the last major battle of the Revolutionary War.

Day 30

The proper chronological order is the Articles of Confederation, the Treaty of Paris, the Northwest Ordinances. The Articles of Confederation was a constitution for the United States that the Second Continental Congress submitted to the thirteen states on 1777 and which was finally ratified in 1781. The weakness of the central government under the Articles of Confederation led to the convening of the Constitutional Convention in 1787. The Treaty of Paris ending the Revolutionary War and recognizing the independence of the United States was signed on September 3, 1783. It was ratified by Congress on January 14, 1784. The Northwest Ordinances refer to the Land Ordinance of 1784, the Land Ordinance of 1785, and the Northwest Ordinance of 1787. Collectively they set forth procedures for governance and land sales in the western territories. The Northwest Ordinance created the Northwest Territory and stated that once a territory reached a population of 60,000 it could apply for statehood. The Northwest Ordinance also prohibited slavery in the Northwest Territory, making the Ohio River a boundary between slave and free states.

Day 31

During the first years of the Revolutionary War, Benedict Arnold was one of the bravest and most effective combat generals in the Continental Army. He led a heroic march to Canada to Quebec in 1775 and was wounded leading an assault on that British-held city. The next year he prevented a British invasion of the United States from Canada by fighting a naval battle on Lake Champlain. He played a leading role in the victory at Saratoga in 1777 and once again was badly wounded. Despite his merit, a promotion for Arnold was held up for political reasons. He grew increasingly disillusioned with the American cause and more anxious to improve his financial situation. In 1780 he conspired with the British to surrender the vital strongpoint of West Point for a large sum of money. He hoped that this would result in the capture of the garrison and possibly George Washington. Arnold's plot was discovered when his British contact was captured with incriminating documents in his boot. Arnold escaped and for the rest of the war served as a British officer. Had Arnold succeeded in his treasonous plot, the history of the Revolutionary War might have been very different. This is why he is the most infamous traitor in American history.

Day 32

Thomas Paine's pamphlet *Common Sense* was published in January 1776 and made a powerful case for American independence from Great Britain. *Common Sense* was a publishing sensation. It had an immense circulation and to this day holds the record for being the best-selling title in American history. Paine's arguments in his pamphlet helped prepare Americans for independence later in the year. Thomas Jefferson was a member of the Second Continental Congress. In June, 1776, he was appointed to a five-member committee charged with writing a declaration of independence. The committee selected Jefferson to compose the first draft. In his draft, Jefferson justified American independence with an appeal to the natural rights described by the English philosopher John Locke, and a long list of the ways that Great Britain had abused the colonies.

After some revisions made by the committee and Congress, the Declaration of Independence was released to the world on July 4, 1776.

Day 33

Independence Hall played a pivotal role in American history. It was where Congress met for much of the Revolutionary War. It was the place where George Washington was appointed the commander of the Continental Army, and the Declaration of Independence was signed. In 1787, it was the meeting place where delegates gathered to frame and sign the Constitution of the United States.

Day 34

Washington in this letter is arguing that the United States needs a strong government for the new nation to become great. Without a strong government the United States will be treated contemptuously by the European powers and might even fall apart. This perspective is important because it reveals the concerns about the weakness of the Articles of Confederation that would eventually result in the calling of the Constitutional Convention. George Washington would chair the Constitutional Convention.

Day 35

In both 1775 at Lexington, and in 1786 during Shays's Rebellion, Massachusetts farmers were resisting taxation that they believed was unfair. In 1775, the farmers were standing up to the British government and "no taxation without representation." In 1786, the rebelling farmers were protesting the tax policies of their own state legislature, which was dominated by merchant interests. The farmers at Lexington helped spark the start of the Revolutionary War. Shays's Rebellion convinced many Americans that the government under the Articles of Confederation had become too weak. This spurred the convening of the Constitutional Convention.

Day 36

The Virginia Plan, proposing a bicameral national legislature with all representatives allocated by proportional representation, was submitted to the Constitutional Convention in 1787. The French Revolution began in 1789, at the same time as the new American government under the Constitution was getting established. Secretary of the Treasury Alexander Hamilton proposed to stabilize the finances of the United States by having the federal government assume all state and Revolutionary War debts in his *Report on the Public Credit* in 1790. The Whiskey Rebellion began in 1794 as farmers in western Pennsylvania protested a new federal tax on distilled spirits. For many farmers far from urban markets, distilling grain was the only practical way to get their products to a market. The XYZ Affair occurred in 1798 when American diplomats refused to pay bribes to the emissaries of French Foreign Minister Talleyrand.

Day 37

The proper chronological order is *The Federalist Papers*, the Bill of Rights, the Kentucky and Virginia Resolves. *The Federalist Papers* were a series of articles published by James Madison, Alexander Hamilton, and John Jay intended to persuade the people of New York to support the proposed Constitution. Over time, these articles became seen as a profound commentary on the Constitution. The Bill of Rights comprises the first ten amendments to the Constitution and places limits on the federal government, guaranteeing basic rights of the American people. Supporters of the Constitution promised a bill of rights to persuade doubters to support the Constitution. James Madison proposed most of these amendments to Congress in 1789, and the ten amendments of the Bill of Rights were ratified by 1791. The Kentucky and Virginia Resolves were responses to the 1798 Alien and Sedition Acts, which gave the president the power to deport "dangerous" immigrants and shut down "seditious" newspapers. Thomas Jefferson wrote the Kentucky Resolution, and James Madison was the author of the Virginia Resolution. These resolutions argued that states could declare federal laws unconstitutional.

Day 38

Mercy Otis Warren was the sister of James Otis and the wife of James Warren, both prominent leaders in the resistance to British policies. During the Revolution she produced various writings supportive of the Patriot cause. Warren later wrote one of the first histories of the American Revolution. Warren was an anti-Federalist who opposed the ratification of the new Constitution. In the quotation she criticizes the system that was set up to ratify the Constitution through special state conventions, with the affirmative vote of nine of these making the Constitution the law of the land. Warren believed that this was an inappropriate end-run around the sitting Congress and state legislatures. Warren's work is a reminder that many people opposed the ratification of the Constitution, fearing that the strengthened federal government would become tyrannical.

Day 39

Sources like Martha Ballard's diary, if studied carefully, can give historians valuable insights into the lives of ordinary men and women. Martha Ballard's record of her daily activities is especially useful for shedding light on the lives of women on the American frontier in the late eighteenth century, providing important information on people whose lives were generally ignored by contemporary historians. The more we appreciate the way ordinary people lived in the past, the better we can understand the social, cultural, and intellectual context of more prominent figures.

Day 40

The proper chronological order is the Declaration of Neutrality, Jay's Treaty, the Quasi-War with France. George Washington issued the Declaration of Neutrality in 1793. He hoped that the United States could avoid involvement in the war being waged between the Republic of France and Great Britain and its allies. With relations deteriorating between the United States and Great Britain, President Washington sent Chief Justice John Jay to London to negotiate with the British government. The resulting Jay's Treaty was signed in 1794 and ratified in 1795. The British made few concessions to the United States, but tensions were eased between the two countries. Thomas Jefferson and his followers opposed the treaty. The Quasi-War broke out between the United States and France following the XYZ Affair. It was fought at sea. The newly revived U.S. Navy distinguished itself, winning a number of ship-to-ship battles.

The war ended with the Convention of 1800, signed September 30, 1800. The Convention of 1800 also officially ended the Revolutionary War alliance between the United States and France.

Day 41

Thomas Jefferson took a strict constructionist view of the Constitution. He believed that the federal government could not take any action that was not explicitly spelled out in the Constitution. Hence he opposed Alexander Hamilton's plan for a Bank of the United States, because there is nothing in the Constitution about a national bank. Alexander Hamilton took a loose constructionist view of the Constitution. He believed that a broader interpretation of the Constitution allowed the federal government to take actions not literally spelled out in the document. He held that the "necessary and proper" clause allowed the government to take steps necessary to carry out its enumerated tasks. Hence Hamilton believed that the federal government could create a Bank of the United States to help transact federal financial business. The constitutional differences between Jefferson and Hamilton helped create the first party system. Thomas Jefferson became the leader of the Democratic-Republicans. Hamilton was the guiding force behind the Federalists.

Day 42

Following the Revolutionary War, the British did not evacuate all their forts from what had become the northwestern territories of the United States. The British provided support to the Native Americans who were resisting American efforts to assert control over this region. In 1790 and 1791, two American armies were defeated by the Native Americans as they attempted to march into the Northwest Territory. President Washington appointed General Anthony Wayne commander of the Legion of the United States in 1792. After training his men for nearly two years, Wayne began moving into the territory controlled by the Native Americans, building forts along the way to protect his line of communication and supply. On August 20, 1794, Wayne decisively defeated the Native Americans at the Battle of Fallen Timbers, near present-day Toledo, Ohio. The retreating Native Americans hoped to find shelter in the nearby British Fort Miamis, but the fort's commander dared not let them in. On August 3, 1795, Wayne and Native American leaders signed the Treaty of Greenville, which opened up much of Ohio to American settlement. The United States had asserted its authority in its western territory.

Day 43

The Louisiana Purchase occurred in 1803. President Thomas Jefferson purchased the Louisiana Territory from France for $15 million, doubling the size of the United States. The Twelfth Amendment was ratified in 1804. It was designed to avoid the electoral tie between Thomas Jefferson and his running mate Aaron Burr in 1800, and stipulated that voters in the Electoral College vote separately for the president and vice president. The Battle of Tippecanoe took place in 1811, when William Henry Harrison, governor of the Indiana Territory, led a force against the Native American village of Prophetstown established by Tecumseh and his brother the Prophet. The Native Americans were defeated and the village was destroyed. The Treaty of Ghent, which ended the War of 1812, was signed on December 24, 1814. The Second Bank of the United States was chartered in 1816. It was intended to further economic growth after the War of 1812.

Day 44

The proper chronological order is Embargo of 1807, Non-Intercourse Act, Hartford Convention. The Embargo Act was a response to years of British impressment of American sailors, interference with American trade, and the 1807 attack on USS *Chesapeake* by HMS *Leopard*. President Thomas Jefferson hoped that an embargo on American trade would persuade the warring European powers to respect American rights. The Embargo Act hurt American merchants and shippers and became very unpopular in New England and in coastal areas. The 1810 Non-Intercourse Act was an attempt to alleviate the situation by allowing trade with all countries but Great Britain and France. These policies failed to prevent war with Great Britain in 1812. The War of 1812 was very unpopular in Federalist-dominated New England. In 1814, a group of Federalists convened the Hartford Convention, where they discussed their grievances and brought up the nullification of federal laws and even, briefly, secession. The subsequent end of the war discredited this gathering.

Day 45

In the *Marbury v. Madison* decision, Marshall made the case that since the Constitution is the supreme law of the land, the courts could void laws that conflict with the Constitution. This established the principle of judicial review, giving the courts the power to review the constitutionality of laws. This ruling enhanced the prestige and power of the judiciary.

Day 46

Tecumseh was a Shawnee war leader and diplomat who in the early nineteenth century attempted to create a tribal confederacy to oppose further American settlement on Native American lands. He made it a principle that the land belonged to all Native Americans, and so no individual or group of individuals could sell parts of it to the U.S. government. Andrew Jackson was a supporter of American westward expansion. During the War of 1812, he inflicted severe defeats on the portions of the Creek tribe that supported the British. Later, as president, he pushed for the removal of eastern tribes to lands west of the Mississippi River. The defeat and death of Tecumseh in the War of 1812 and the ascendency of American leaders like Andrew Jackson, meant the end of Native American power in the eastern United States.

Day 47

Thomas Jefferson started building a house on the site of Monticello in 1768. He began extensive remodeling in 1794 that lasted until 1809. This did not stop him from making improvements on the house until his death. For Jefferson, Monticello was always a work in progress. The house illustrates Jefferson's gifts as an architect and a designer. It reflects the gracious life of a well-to-do Virginia planter. The historical material on the website reminds viewers of the labors of the slaves who sustained this estate.

Day 48

The proper chronological order is Lewis and Clark Expedition, Battle of New Orleans, Era of Good Feelings. President Thomas Jefferson sent Captain Meriwether Lewis and Second Lieutenant William Clark on an expedition to explore the Louisiana Territory. Their journey lasted from May 1804 to September 1806. Lewis and Clark reached the Pacific Ocean, claimed the territory for the United States, and brought back a wealth of information about the geography and resources of the west. On January 8, 1815, General Andrew Jackson severely defeated a British army attempting to take control of the strategic city of New Orleans. The Battle of New Orleans foiled the last major British offensive of the War of 1812. This spectacular victory spurred American patriotism and confidence in the aftermath of the war. The Era of Good Feelings was the period during the presidency of James Monroe when post-war nationalism was the predominant sentiment in the United States. The first party system disappeared with the collapse of the Federalist Party, leaving the Democratic-Republicans in largely unchallenged control of the nation.

Day 49

Adams is making the point that most Americans worked very hard in the early nineteenth century. They made more money than people in Europe, but had to deal with harsher living conditions. This ties into the traditional view that if you work hard in America, you can make your fortune. One of the most famous manifestations of this were the books for children written by Horatio Alger in the late nineteenth century. In these books young boys avoided temptations, worked hard, and made their way up in the world.

Day 50

The Missouri Compromise was designed to keep a balance between free and slave states. In 1820, Missouri was admitted as a slave state, and Maine as a free state. The compromise, engineered by Henry Clay, drew a line through the Louisiana Territory; areas north of the line would become free states and those south of the line would become slave states. The Monroe Doctrine was issued in 1823, and warned European powers against imposing colonial rule on territories in the western hemisphere. The Erie Canal was completed in 1825. It provided a waterway between New York City and the Great Lakes, enabling western farmers to get their crops to market. The Removal Act of 1830 gave the president the power to purchase the lands of eastern Native American tribes and move them across the Mississippi River. The Nullification Crisis occurred in 1832 when South Carolina nullified federal tariffs. President Jackson threatened to use force against the state. Henry Clay defused the crisis by persuading Congress to lower the tariff rates.

Day 51

The proper chronological order is Bank War, Specie Circular, Panic of 1837. Henry Clay saw the Second Bank of the United States as a centerpiece of his American System. In 1832, as he prepared to run for the presidency, he attempted to have its charter renewed early by Congress. President Andrew Jackson opposed the bank as a tool of special interests. He vetoed the rechartering bill. The next year, in an attempt to kill the bank, Jackson withdrew all federal money from it and placed these funds in state and local banks, termed "Pet Banks" by his opponents. The Specie Circular was an executive order issued by President Jackson in 1836 requiring that federal land be paid for with gold or silver coins. This was an attempt to cut back on land speculation. The Panic of 1837 was a severe economic downturn in the United States that lasted into the 1840s. Although international financial dislocations contributed to the crash, Americans blamed the panic on credit problems caused by the Bank War and the Specie Circular.

Day 52

The Trail of Tears was the culmination of efforts by settlers to acquire the lands lived on by Native Americans in the Eastern United States. The Cherokee tribe fought back in court. In the 1831 Supreme Court decision *Cherokee Nation v. Georgia*, Chief Justice John Marshall ruled that the tribe had rights to the land that the state of Georgia was attempting to force them from. This court decision had no effect because President Andrew Jackson was unwilling to enforce it. The Removal Act of 1830 gave the federal government the authority to negotiate the removal of tribes to lands west of the Mississippi River. Tribes began moving in 1831. The removal of the Cherokee took place in 1838. One-third of the tribe died of disease as they trekked west. The path of their journey became known as the Trail of Tears.

Day 53

Following in the tradition of Alexander Hamilton, Henry Clay believed that the government could play a role in promoting economic growth. His "American System" called for a high protective tariff to encourage the growth of American industry, a Bank of the United States to provide credit and facilitate business transactions, and government support for internal improvements like roads and canals to help businessmen and farmers get their goods to markets. Andrew Jackson followed the tradition of Thomas Jefferson. He was a believer in limited government, and opposed direct government assistance to business. He killed the Bank of the United States because he thought it a corrupt bastion for the privileged. He discouraged federal funding for internal improvement projects, fearing that they would become expensive supports for special interests. Clay's ideas were adopted by the Whig Party, while Jackson's economic perspective dominated the Democratic Party.

Day 54

In the election of 1840, the Whig Party was determined to win the presidency. Looking for their own Andrew Jackson, they nominated William Henry Harrison, another aging hero of the War of 1812. They came up with a brilliant campaign slogan that reminded voters of Harrison's 1811 victory over the Indians, as well as his vice presidential running mate, John Tyler—"Tippecanoe and Tyler Too!" Instead of stressing a political program, the Whigs focused on selling the American people an image of the aristocratic Harrison as a man of the people. He was portrayed as a candidate willing to sit in front of a log cabin sipping hard cider. Copious quantities of hard cider were distributed at Harrison rallies. Groups of young Whigs rolled large balls across the countryside, supposedly until Harrison was elected. This helped popularize the expression "Keep the Ball Rolling." The success of the Whig campaign in 1840 illustrates the power of image and marketing in American elections.

Day 55

Charles Grandison Finney was one of the greatest preachers of the Second Great Awakening. The Second Great Awakening was a Protestant religious revival movement that began in the 1790s and persisted through the 1830s. This revival emphasized a more personal and emotional religious experience. The intensification of religious feeling across the United States spurred reform movements such as those for temperance and the abolition of slavery.

Day 56

The proper chronological order is American Colonization Society, Nat Turner's Rebellion, Gag Rule. The American Colonization Society was an antislavery society founded in 1817. Members of the society believed that blacks and whites could not live together peacefully in the United States and worked to send freed slaves to new homes in Africa. In 1831, Nat Turner led a bloody slave revolt in Virginia. Around 60 white men, women, and children were killed. The revolt was brutally suppressed. At least 100 slaves were killed as the authorities hunted down the rebels. Turner and 55 other slaves who had participated in the insurrection were executed. Beginning in 1831, abolitionists sent petitions to the House of Representatives opposing slavery. In 1836, Southern representatives took the lead in imposing a Gag rule that automatically tabled all antislavery petitions. The Gag rule lasted until it was overturned in 1844.

Day 57

The Battle of the Alamo took place in March 1836 as part of the Texan War of Independence. After a period of independence as the Lone Star Republic, Texas was admitted to the Union in 1845. The Mexican War began in 1846 as Mexican forces challenged the American claim for the southern border of Texas. California was part of the territory won from Mexico during the war. In 1848, gold was discovered in California, leading to a rush of prospecting and settlement. The desire of California to enter the Union as a free state led to the Compromise of 1850. The Fugitive Slave Act of 1850 was part of the compromise and a Northern concession to the South.

Day 58

Manifest Destiny was a term coined by the Democratic journalist John O'Sullivan in 1845. It referred to the belief that it was the God-given mission of the United States to expand across the continent to the Pacific Ocean. Manifest Destiny appealed to both Northerners and Southerners. In the election of 1844, the Democratic presidential candidate James K. Polk called for the United States to acquire both slaveholding Texas and all of the Oregon Territory. A Democratic Congressman named David Wilmot proposed what came to be known as the Wilmot Proviso in 1846. He called for a prohibition of slavery in any territory conquered from Mexico during the Mexican War. He expressed the view of many Northerners that the United States should expand its territory, but that the expansion of slavery should be halted. The Wilmot Proviso began a debate over the nature of American expansionism and the issue of slavery in the western territories that would last into the 1850s.

Day 59

The Seneca Falls Women's Rights Convention took place on July 19–20, 1848. It was attended by such well-known activists as Elizabeth Cady Stanton and Lucretia Mott. The African American abolitionist Frederick Douglass was also one of the attendees. The convention issued a Declaration of Sentiments that called for the right of women to vote. The convention helped spur further discussion of women's rights.

Day 60

Dred Scott was a Missouri slave who sued for his freedom because his master had taken him for a time to live in free parts of the United States. Chief Justice Roger Taney and the Supreme Court ruled that African Americans, whatever their legal status, could not be citizens. The Court also ruled that Congress could not prohibit slavery in the federal territories. This decision deepened sectional differences over the issue of slavery. Abolitionists were infuriated by the decision. Many Northerners were outraged at the prospect of slavery being allowed to expand throughout the western territories.

Day 61

The proper chronological order is Kansas-Nebraska Act, "Bleeding Kansas," the Harpers Ferry Raid of John Brown. The 1854 Kansas-Nebraska Act was sponsored by Senator Stephen A. Douglas of Illinois as a way to rapidly organize these western territories and promote a transcontinental railroad based in Chicago. To win Southern support for his scheme, Douglas's bill provided that the settlers of these territories could vote on whether they wanted slavery or not. This provision angered many Northerners because these territories were above the Missouri Compromise line, and slavery should have been prohibited there. There was never any doubt that Nebraska would be free of slavery. Kansas was a different story. Proslavery and antislavery settlers flooded into Kansas and engaged in a sometimes violent conflict over a constitution for the territory, giving the territory the name "Bleeding Kansas." John Brown was a fanatic antislavery activist who engaged in this violence and eventually had to flee after murdering five proslavery settlers. On October 16, 1859, John Brown and a band of 18 followers attacked the federal arsenal at Harpers Ferry, Virginia. He hoped to start a slave insurrection. He and his men were soon overpowered by federal troops. Brown was hanged for treason.

Day 62

During the Texas Revolution, rebels occupied the Alamo mission in San Antonio. From February 23 to March 6, 1836, the Texas garrison of around 200 men was besieged by an army led by General Antonio López de Santa Anna that eventually numbered over 3,000. Among the defenders were such well-known frontiersmen as Jim Bowie and David Crockett. Santa Anna launched his final assault early on the morning of March 6. All the Texans were killed, and the Mexicans suffered around 600 casualties. The heroic defense of the Alamo inspired Texan resistance to the Mexicans. When Sam Houston's Texan army defeated and captured Santa Anna at the Battle of San Jacinto on April 21, some of the Texans reportedly cried, "Remember the Alamo!" as they hunted fleeing Mexican soldiers. The Alamo has become a symbol of courage against great odds as well as Texan pride. The Alamo has also become a source of controversy as historians argue over the number of casualties and the fate of individual members of the garrison. Some Mexican accounts of the battle differ in important respects from the popular perception of the battle. While the broad outline of the Alamo battle is clear, its story demonstrates how difficult it is to sometimes reconstruct all the details of an event when many participants are dead and political passions color memories.

Day 63

Stephen Douglas ran for reelection to the U.S. Senate as a Democrat in 1858. His Republican opponent was Abraham Lincoln. During the political campaign, Douglas and Lincoln debated at seven locations in Illinois. Douglas defended his belief in popular sovereignty, holding that the citizens of a territory should be able to decide whether they wanted slavery or not. In the wake of the Supreme Court's 1857 *Dred Scott v. Sandford* decision, he proposed his Freeport Doctrine, arguing that even if it was technically illegal to exclude slavery from a territory, the residents of that territory could keep slavery out by legislating onerous regulations that would discourage slave owners. Abraham Lincoln opposed the extension of slavery into the territories under any circumstances. Before the Seventeenth Amendment was adopted in 1913, voters were not able to directly vote for and therefore elect a U.S. Senator. Instead, it was the state legislature that elected the senators from their state. Therefore, Douglas won the Senate campaign because the Democrats kept control of the Illinois legislature. Douglas's Freeport Doctrine angered Southern Democrats, split the party, and crippled his presidential candidacy in 1860. Though he lost the Senate race, Lincoln attained national prominence and won the Republican nomination and the presidency in 1860.

Day 64

South Carolina responded to the election of Abraham Lincoln as president by seceding from the Union in December 1860. The 1861 Crittenden Plan was Senator John Crittenden of Kentucky's effort to save the Union through a compromise. He called for the federal government to guarantee the future of slavery where it already existed and for a return to the Missouri Compromise line in the west, with it being extended all the way to the Pacific Ocean. Abraham Lincoln issued the Preliminary Emancipation on September 22, 1862, following the Union victory at Antietam. It warned the Confederate States that if they did not return to the Union, he would issue an Emancipation Proclamation freeing the slaves in rebellious states on January 1, 1863. The New York City Draft Riots took place in July 1863 as Irish immigrants and other working men violently protested the imposition a federal military draft. Sherman's March to the Sea took place from November 15 to December 21, 1864, as General William Tecumseh Sherman marched an army across Georgia from Atlanta to Savannah, living off the land and demonstrating the weakness of the Confederate government.

Day 65

The proper chronological order is Fort Sumter, Battle of Gettysburg, Appomattox. Fort Sumter was a federal fort in Charleston Harbor. The Confederate decision to bombard the fort into surrender started the fighting in the Civil War. The Battle of Gettysburg took place on July 1–3, 1863. The Federal Army of the Potomac under General George Meade defeated General Robert E. Lee's Confederate Army of

Northern Virginia, ending Lee's invasion of Pennsylvania. This was the bloodiest battle of the Civil War; never again would Lee be able to launch an offensive into the North. Appomattox, Virginia, was the place where Federal forces under General Ulysses S. Grant cornered Lee's retreating army and forced Lee to surrender on April 9, 1865. Within two months, all other major Confederate forces surrendered.

Day 66

Civil War reenacting is very popular because it allows people to re-create aspects of one of the most dramatic and important events in American history. Civil War reenactors take pride in their historical heritage, and honor the fighters on both the Northern and Southern sides. While men can dress as soldiers, many women take part in Civil war reenactments, wearing 1860s costumes. Reenactors often put on historical demonstrations at Civil War battlefields and other locations. Many have acted as extras in movies. Some question whether it is appropriate to dress as Confederate soldiers and display the Confederate battle flag in a historical context, because the Confederate army was defending slave owners.

Day 67

Congressman Clement Vallandigham was a leading Northern Democratic opponent of the Civil War. Northern Democrats who opposed the war were known as Copperheads. President Abraham Lincoln took vigorous action against these Southern sympathizers. Over 14,000 were jailed without trial. President Lincoln suspended the writ of habeas corpus to keep some of these individuals in prison indefinitely. In 1863, Vallandigham was arrested and tried by a military court for treasonable utterances. He was convicted and banished to the Confederacy.

Day 68

The proper chronological order is Battle of Shiloh, Battle of Vicksburg, Fall of Atlanta. The Battle of Shiloh was a major battle that took place in the western theater of the war on April 6–7, 1862. General Ulysses S. Grant repulsed a Confederate attack in a hard-fought battle that badly mauled his army. General Grant began a long offensive against the Confederate strongpoint of Vicksburg, Mississippi, the last important Confederate outpost on the Mississippi River. After months of maneuvering and fighting, Grant put the city under siege on May 18, 1863. When Vicksburg surrendered on July 4, Federal forces controlled the entire span of the Mississippi River, splitting the Confederacy. In May 1864, General William Tecumseh Sherman launched a campaign to capture the important Confederate manufacturing and railroad center of Atlanta, Georgia. After months of hard fighting, the city surrendered on September 2. The fall of Atlanta encouraged Northern voters, persuading them that an end to the war was in sight, and ensured the reelection of Abraham Lincoln.

Day 69

General George McClellan wanted to fight a limited war. He wanted to restore the Union, but did not want to interfere with Southern institutions like slavery. As a general, he was very cautious and slow, and hoped to outmaneuver his enemies rather than engaging in bloody, head-on battles. General Ulysses S. Grant gradually came to realize that the war would be long and hard, and that the Confederates would have to be worn down before they admitted defeat. Although capable of brilliant maneuvers, Grant knew that the Confederate armies would have to be destroyed by hard fighting. In 1864–65, Grant never let his forces lose contact with Lee's army in Virginia. The casualties were enormous, but he knew that he could afford losses better than Lee and that he was bringing the end of the war closer. Grant also allowed subordinates like William Tecumseh Sherman and Philip Sheridan to ravage enemy territory, waging psychological and economic war against Southern civilians that was a precursor of the total war of the twentieth century.

Day 70

President Abraham Lincoln was assassinated by the actor John Wilkes Booth on April 14, 1865, while attending the play *Our American Cousin* at Ford's Theatre. Booth was a Southern sympathizer who headed a conspiracy to kill the leading members of the federal government. The other conspirators failed in their efforts to murder Vice President Andrew Johnson and Secretary of State William H. Seward. Being killed at the moment of victory made Lincoln a martyr in the eyes of Northerners. There was a national outpouring of grief as Lincoln's body was taken to Springfield, Illinois, for burial. Many Americans came to believe that Lincoln would have done a much better job than his successor in guiding the United States through Reconstruction.

Day 71

Walt Whitman was shocked by the conditions of the hospital treating men wounded at the Battle of Fredericksburg, which took place December 11–15, 1862. The place that he visited was probably a triage point, treating the most badly wounded. Whitman realized that the people running the hospital were doing the best that they could. His experience near Fredericksburg inspired Whitman to travel to Washington, D.C., and volunteer as a nurse in Army hospitals. Whitman's description is a vivid reminder of the hardships faced by wounded soldiers in a period before antibiotics. Whitman noticed the results of many amputations. For Civil War doctors, amputation was often the best way to save the life of a man with a shattered arm or leg likely to develop a deadly infection.

Day 72

President Abraham Lincoln proposed his Ten Percent Plan for reconstructing the Union in 1863. When ten percent of registered voters in a former Confederate state swore allegiance to the federal government, they could form a new state government. The Wade-Davis Bill was a Radical Republican measure passed by Congress in 1864. This bill made the reorganization of state governments in former Confederate states conditional on a majority of voters swearing that they had never been disloyal. Practically, this meant that large numbers of freed slaves would have to be added to voter rolls. The Thirteenth Amendment abolishing slavery everywhere in the United States was ratified in 1865. The Tenure of Office Act was passed by the Radical Republican–dominated Congress in 1867. It prohibited the president from summarily firing cabinet officers who had been confirmed by Congress. This measure was intended to protect Radical Republican–leaning cabinet officers like Secretary of War Edwin Stanton from being fired by President Andrew Johnson. President Johnson defied Congress by firing

Stanton anyway. The House of Representatives voted articles of impeachment in 1868. Johnson survived his impeachment trial in the Senate by just one vote.

Day 73

The proper chronological order is Reconstruction Act, Fifteenth Amendment, Compromise of 1877. The Reconstruction Act was passed by the Radical Republican–dominated Congress in 1867. It divided the former Confederacy into five military districts, each governed by an army general. If former Confederate states were to form new governments, they had to give freedmen equal rights and allow them to vote. The Fifteenth Amendment furthered Radical Republican Reconstruction by ensuring that no one could be denied the right to vote "on account of race, color, or previous condition of servitude." The Compromise of 1877 was a deal worked out between Republicans and Democrats after the contested presidential election of 1876. The Republican candidate, Rutherford B. Hayes would be sworn in as president, but the remaining federal troops in the South would be withdrawn, leading to the collapse of the last Republican governments in the region. This marked the end of Reconstruction.

Day 74

D. W. Griffith based the latter part of *The Birth of a Nation* on *The Clansman* (1905), a racist novel by Thomas F. Dixon, Jr., which celebrated the Ku Klux Klan. The son of a former Confederate officer, Griffith was not sensitive to the appalling racism of his source material. Striving for historical accuracy, he had one of his film's intertitles quote a history of the United States written by President Woodrow Wilson when he was still a university professor. Wilson, like most historians of the time, regarded Radical Reconstruction as a mistaken failure. In addition to its sympathy for the Klan, Griffith's film reflected the racism of the Jim Crow era in other ways. Some of the African American characters are played by white actors in blackface. Though *The Birth of a Nation* was a huge box-office success, it roused a storm of criticism. Defensive about these attacks, Griffith released another epic film in 1916. Titled *Intolerance*, it ambitiously looked at religious and economic intolerance at four different periods of history. Ironically, for all his sympathy for the old South, Griffith regarded Abraham Lincoln as a hero and portrayed him as such in the first half of *The Birth of a Nation*. He later made a film about Lincoln's life.

Day 75

President Andrew Johnson attempted to follow what he thought was Abraham Lincoln's approach to Reconstruction. He wanted to allow the Southern states to be reorganized on lenient terms. Aside from ex-Confederate political and military leaders, and the largest plantation owners, he was willing to offer pardons to former rebels willing to swear their allegiance to the federal government. The Radical Republicans believed that Johnson's easy terms would allow former Confederates to return to power. They were appalled by the Black Codes that Southern states were creating to control the freedmen. The Radical Republicans wanted to empower the former slaves. They established the Freedman's Bureau to help them adjust to their new status. They believed that giving the freedmen the vote would enable them to protect themselves from the former Confederates, and would help create new Republican political majorities in the Southern states. The struggle between Johnson and the Radical Republicans led to the impeachment crisis in 1868. Although Radical Reconstruction was eventually dismantled, it provided a precedent for government action to promote the welfare of disadvantaged groups.

Day 76

Clara Barton's congressional testimony reveals that there was a great deal of confusion among freedmen shortly after the Civil War. They were not getting good information from their former masters and were subject to conflicting rumors, such as the possibility of being re-enslaved because of the death of Abraham Lincoln. When Clara Barton arrived on a tour of Georgia, she was seen as a source of truthful information by the local freedmen. What she saw clearly revealed that the former slaves valued their freedom and worried about losing it. Barton's report helped justify support for federal initiatives such as the Freedman's Bureau, which provided assistance to the former slaves.

Day 77

The Tuskegee Institute was founded by Booker T. Washington in 1881. Washington was a former slave who believed that the best way forward for African Americans was through economic self-reliance. His school taught students practical skills in farming and the trades. Students built many of the early buildings at Tuskegee. The school also prepared teachers to take knowledge back to their fellow African Americans. Among the teachers at Tuskegee was George Washington Carver, who became famous for his work with peanuts and other agricultural alternatives to cotton. Tuskegee was one of a number of educational institutions created in the nineteenth century to serve African Americans.

Day 78

A carpetbagger was a Northerner who moved to the South after the Civil War. Many were looking for economic opportunity . Others took part in the politics of Reconstruction, playing an important role in the Republican party in the Southern states. Scalawags were Southerners who cooperated with the Republican Reconstruction governments. Both *carpetbagger* and *scalawag* were pejorative terms for most Southerners, and for many years after Reconstruction these Northern and Southern collaborators with the Reconstruction governments in the South were looked upon as questionable participants in a doomed social experiment. Since the time of the Civil Rights Movement of the 1950s and 1960s, the historical assessment of these people has changed, and they are now seen as important allies for African Americans in the struggle for equal rights for all during Reconstruction.

Day 79

The federal government encouraged Western settlement. The 1862 Homestead Act granted 160 acres of land to a settler willing to farm it for five years. The Battle of the Little Bighorn took place on June 25–26, 1876. A large force of Sioux and Northern Cheyenne defeated a detachment of U.S. cavalry commanded by General George Armstrong Custer. Custer and 267 of his men were killed. This was the last great victory for Native Americans in the Plains Wars. The 1878 Timber and Stone Act made land deemed unsuitable for farming inexpensively available to businessmen interested in logging and mining. The 1887 Dawes Act was sponsored by reformers hoping to help Native Americans adjust to "civilized" life. Reservations were divided into plots of land for individual Native Americans so they would have land to farm. In the end, a lot of this land ended up being sold to speculators. The Ghost Dance was a religious movement that became popular among some Plains tribes in 1890. Ghost Dancers believed that their dancing would lead to the departure of the white man, the return of the buffalo, and a new era of peace and plenty. The attempt of a band of Ghost Dancers to leave the Sioux reservation led to the carnage at Wounded Knee.

Day 80

The proper chronological order is completion of the transcontinental railroad, Interstate Commerce Act, Sherman Antitrust Act. The Central Pacific and Union Pacific Railroads met at Promontory Summit, Utah, on May 10, 1869. The railroads became a major driver of Western settlement and were vital to the economic interests of Western farmers. Concerns that the railroads were abusing their power led to the 1887 Interstate Commerce Act, which gave the federal government some authority to regulate railroad rates. Fears that large businesses and monopolies were getting too powerful led to the 1890 Sherman Antitrust Act, which made business combinations "in restraint of trade" illegal.

Day 81

Mary E. Lease was a fiery spokeswoman for the Farmers' Alliances and later the Populist Party. She expressed the concerns of Western farmers who were being squeezed by falling prices, and often found themselves unable to pay their mortgages. These farmers blamed their predicament on business monopolies and the gold standard, which contributed to a tighter money supply. Lease is also important as a feminist who spoke up for the right of women to vote and defend their interests in public debate.

Day 82

William Jennings Bryan was a former congressman from Nebraska who captured the 1896 Democratic presidential nomination by giving a speech at the convention in which he declared, "You shall not crucify mankind upon a cross of gold!" Bryan was a spokesman for the Western farmers who believed that their economic situation was being ruined by tariffs that made prices for goods higher, and the gold standard with its tight money policy supported by lawmakers in Washington. They demanded a lower tariff and the free coinage of silver to inflate the currency, raise agricultural prices, and reduce the value of mortgages. William McKinley was a former congressman and governor of Ohio. He defended the interests of industry and industrial workers. He supported a high tariff to protect American industries and manufacturing jobs. He supported the gold standard to avoid inflation that would hurt businesses and undermine the purchasing power of workers. In the election of 1896, McKinley's base of support in the cities and the manufacturing centers of the East and Midwest proved decisive, and he won the election. The election of 1896 signaled a shift in power from rural to urban America.

Day 83

The proper chronological order is the first "long drive" of cattle, the invention of barbed wire, and the opening of "Buffalo Bill's Wild West Show." The first "long drive" of cattle took place in 1866, when Texas ranchers banded together and drove their herds to the railhead at Sedalia, Missouri. From there the cattle could be shipped to Chicago and Eastern markets. This began the great era of Western cattle drives that lasted for around twenty years. Joseph Glidden invented barbed wire in 1873. The ready availability of barbed wire allowed Western farmers to enclose their lands, marking the beginning of the end of the open range phase of cattle herding. William "Buffalo Bill" Cody was a former buffalo hunter and Army scout. He became famous when the writer Ned Buntline loosely based a dime novel on his exploits. Developing skills as a showman, Cody began his "Buffalo Bill's Wild West Show" in 1883. Featuring real cowboys and Indians, as well as stars such as the sharpshooter Annie Oakley, Cody's show was immensely popular for decades, and created an image of the "Wild West" that would endure in Western movies, television shows, and novels for a century and more.

Day 84

The Homestead National Monument was created in 1936 on the site of the farm of Daniel Freeman at Beatrice, Nebraska. Freeman was one of the first people to take advantage of the 1862 Homestead Act, submitting his claim a few minutes after midnight on January 1, 1863. The Homestead Act played an important part in the settlement of the West as many thousands of people took advantage of its provisions to obtain land. The Homestead Act helped make it possible for people of ordinary means to settle in the West. By 1900, 610,000 lots of land had been transferred to homesteaders. These farmers encountered many challenges on the Great Plains. Some became prosperous, while others failed. Writers such as Willa Cather and O. E. Rolvaag described the range of experiences faced by these settlers.

Day 85

For all of American history up through the late nineteenth century, there had been a frontier offering Americans a chance at a new life. Following the 1890 census, the Census Bureau announced that there no longer was a continuous American frontier. This occurred just as the United States was becoming a great industrial power, with more and more Americans living in cities. The rapid urbanization of the United States was worrisome to many Americans. Turner's thesis aggravated these worries. People asked how American democracy could continue if the frontier that had nurtured it was disappearing. Would the American character remain the same in an urbanized and industrialized nation? The response of some Americans like Theodore Roosevelt was to conserve what was left of the American wilderness and to open up a new frontier through imperialism in the Philippines and elsewhere. The idea of the frontier remained compelling to Americans in the twentieth century. President John F. Kennedy labeled his program of domestic and foreign policies the "New Frontier." At the same time, many people saw the exploration of space as opening a new frontier.

Day 86

The Knights of Labor was founded in 1869. The Knights of Labor was a union that was open to all workers. The 1882 Chinese Exclusion Act prohibited the immigration of all Chinese laborers. This act was a response to anti-Chinese feeling in California and elsewhere. The Haymarket Square bombing took place on May 4, 1886, in Chicago, Illinois. As police arrived to break up a labor rally, someone threw a bomb at them. Following the explosion the police shot into the crowd. Seven police and four workers were killed. Seven anarchists were accused of the crime. All were convicted. Five were sentenced to death. One committed suicide in prison, and the other four were hanged. Ellis Island was opened as an immigrant inspection station in 1892. It operated until 1954. Coxey's Army was a march of unemployed workers organized by Jacob Coxey, an Ohio businessman. The march was intended to publicize hardships experienced by working men as a result of the depression that began in 1893. The march began in Ohio. Participants marched to Washington, D.C., where they dispersed after a speech by Coxey.

Day 87

Samuel Gompers was president of the American Federation of Labor, which was composed of unions serving skilled workers. In 1894, the American Railway Union went on strike to protest conditions at the Pullman Company, which made railroad sleeping cars. Union members refused to work on trains carrying Pullman cars. This caused chaos on the railroads. The federal government intervened against the strike. Attorney General Richard Olney encouraged federal judges like Judge Peter Grosscup to issue injunctions against the strikers. Federal troops helped put down the strike. Eugene V. Debs, the head of the American Railway Union, was sent to prison for six months for violating the injunction. In the passage, Gompers is chastising Judge Grosscup for taking action against the strikers. He accuses the judge of failing to appreciate the conditions that led workers to unionize and strike for better working conditions. Gompers argues that workers have to join unions because business owners treat them like disposable machines.

Day 88

The proper chronological order is *Progress and Poverty*, by Henry George; *Looking Backward*, by Edward Bellamy; *How the Other Half Lives*, by Jacob Riis. George's *Progress and Poverty* (1879) attempted to explain why poverty persisted in a time of technological progress. George argued that landowners benefitted disproportionately from social progress, enabling them to charge higher rents, hurting wage-earners. He called for a single tax on land values to redress the balance. In his novel *Looking Backward* (1888), Bellamy envisioned a future where all Americans had peacefully joined together to create a socialist utopia. Riis in *How the Other Half Lives* (1890) graphically described the slums of the Lower Side in New York City and offered suggestions to improve the lives of the people living in the tenements.

Day 89

The Statue of Liberty, or *Liberty Enlightening the World*, was conceived of as a gift of the French people to the United States. It was designed by Frederic Auguste Bartholdi and was constructed by Gustave Eiffel. Americans paid for the statue's pedestal, with the money being raised by subscription. The statue was dedicated October 28, 1886. The statue was originally intended to celebrate American freedom and the centennial of American independence. It gained new meaning as a symbol of welcome to immigrants fleeing hardship and tyranny abroad. To help raise money for the pedestal, Emma Lazarus wrote a poem entitled "The New Colossus," which included the lines:

"Give me your tired, your poor—Your huddled masses yearning to breathe free." In 1903, a plaque bearing Lazarus's poem was placed on the statue's pedestal.

Day 90

The late nineteenth century in the United States is called the Gilded Age because it was a time of extremes. Businessmen and industrialists made enormous fortunes while many American lived in poverty. It was a time of intense political participation by many Americans but also a time of widespread political corruption, with political machines dominating many localities. Because of this, social critics could assert that the booming and bustling American society of the day was not experiencing a golden age, but instead was a period of a baser material, gilded to look golden. Historians debate the justice and accuracy of such a judgment of the period.

Day 91

Vertical integration and horizontal integration refer to ways in which late nineteenth-century companies structured their production. Vertical integration refers to a company controlling every phase of production from the acquisition of raw materials through manufacturing, to marketing and distribution. Horizontal integration involves a company controlling production by purchasing or merging with competitors. Andrew Carnegie's Carnegie Steel is a famous example of vertical integration. John D. Rockefeller's Standard Oil is a well-known example of horizontal integration. Eventually Carnegie engaged in horizontal integration by purchasing other steel companies, and Rockefeller pursued vertical integration through buying up oilfields.

Day 92

Lord Bryce in this passage is referring to the increasing prevalence of political machines in late nineteenth-century America. Most, though not all, political machines were located in large cities. Political machines were run by bosses, most of whom, as Bryce notes, preferred to operate behind the scenes, though some bosses held elective office. Political machines financed themselves through their control of public contracts, often receiving kickbacks from contractors as the price of business. Political machines kept the loyalty of voters by distributing jobs and favors. For immigrants in the big cities, often the only forms of welfare help available to them were the benefits that they received from machines in exchange for their votes. The most famous and long-lasting of these political organizations was Tammany Hall, the Democratic machine in New York City.

Day 93

The United States purchased Alaska from Russia in 1867. Unaware of Alaska's potential resources, many critics termed the purchase "Seward's Folly" after Secretary of State William H. Seward. Captain Alfred Thayer Mahan's *The Influence of Sea Power upon History* was published in 1890. Its argument for the importance of a large navy persuaded Theodore Roosevelt and other American policymakers to push for increases in the size of the United States Navy. When Queen Liliuokalani of Hawaii attempted to revise the Hawaiian constitution to limit the powers of the influential American planters on the islands, they organized a successful coup in January 1893. The planters ruled a republic of Hawaii until the United States annexed Hawaii in 1898. The Spanish–American War was fought from April 21 to August 13, 1898. The United States forced Spain to relinquish Cuba and acquired Puerto Rico, Guam, and the Philippines. The Platt Amendment was part of an Army appropriations bill in 1901. It prohibited Cuba from entering into agreements with other countries without American permission, and gave the United States the right to intervene in Cuban politics "when necessary."

Day 94

The proper chronological order is Open Door Note, Boxer Rebellion, Great White Fleet. Secretary of State John Hay sent his first Open Door Note to the other great powers on September 6, 1899. He proposed that the powers allow all countries to trade in China without interference. This became the foundation of the U.S. Open Door policy in China. The Boxer Rebellion was an uprising of Chinese nationalists angered by the growing influence of foreign powers in China. In 1900, Boxer rebels and elements of the Chinese army besieged the Legation Quarter in the capital of Beijing. American forces joined an international army that rescued the besieged in Beijing and suppressed the uprising. The Great White Fleet was organized by President Theodore Roosevelt. He sent a powerful fleet of 16 battleships and their escorts, all painted white to show their peaceful intentions, on a goodwill tour around the world that lasted from December 16, 1907, to February 22, 1909. The Great White Fleet was a public relations success that also demonstrated American naval power.

Day 95

William Randolph Hearst was the son of George Hearst, who made a fortune mining and became a U.S. senator. Hearst developed an interest in newspapers. After running a newspaper in San Francisco, Hearst bought the *New York Morning Journal* in 1895. Here Hearst engaged in a circulation war with Joseph Pulitzer and his *New York World*. As they competed for readers, both editors pioneered what came to be known as "Yellow Journalism," emphasizing sensationalism, human interest stories, and innovations like comic strips. As part of this competition, Hearst published lurid, and often inaccurate, stories about the Spanish war against revolutionaries in Cuba. Hearst and Pulitzer played a major role in convincing the American people that the United States should go to war with Spain.

Day 96

With victory in the Spanish–American War, Americans had to decide what to do about the Philippines after Commodore George Dewey won the Battle of Manila Bay. Supporters of a new American imperial role in the world believed that the United States should claim the Philippines. Theodore Roosevelt believed that the island chain offered the United States commercial advantages in the Asian market. He also saw the Philippines as a new frontier to replace the one that had closed in the West. Ultimately, President William McKinley decided to take the Philippines because he believed that if the United States walked away, other imperial powers like Japan and Germany would move in and claim the islands. Anti-imperialists like William Jennings Bryan, Andrew Carnegie, and Mark Twain believed that administering an imperial possession and a subject people would violate American traditions of liberty. Others worried that an empire would prove too expensive or worried about economic competition from colonized peoples with a lower standard of living. Bryan ran on an anti-imperialism platform against McKinley in the presidential election of 1900 and lost. In the Philippines, the United States had to fight a bloody war to suppress a Filipino insurrection that lasted from 1899 to 1902.

Day 97

The proper chronological order is acquisition of the Panama Canal Zone, Roosevelt Corollary, Dollar Diplomacy. The United States wanted to construct a canal through the isthmus of Panama connecting the Atlantic and Pacific oceans. In 1902, when a treaty purchasing a canal zone from Colombia fell through, President Theodore Roosevelt supported a revolution that made Panama independent. The United States quickly concluded a treaty with the new Panamanian government allowing the construction of a canal. In 1902–1903, Venezuela was blockaded by warships from Britain, Germany, and Italy to compel the government there to pay overdue debts. Disturbed by this European activity in the Western Hemisphere, in 1904 President Theodore Roosevelt announced his Roosevelt Corollary to the Monroe Doctrine; the United States would intervene in any Caribbean or Latin American country where disorder threatened to bring on European military action. This made the United States the "policeman" of the Western Hemisphere. President William Howard Taft, who came to office in 1909, hoped to replace military incursions with American economic investment designed to stabilize countries wracked with unrest. This policy came to be known as "Dollar Diplomacy."

Day 98

Leonard Wood saw the role of the U.S. Army as supporting the Cuban people as they created civil government after years of rule by Spain. As governor of Cuba, Wood not only fostered the beginnings of democratic institutions, he also launched a public health campaign that greatly reduced the dangers posed by diseases like yellow fever. Wood is seen as a sort of Progressive reformer who operated overseas. Although broadly benevolent in their approach to the Cubans, the Americans put limits on Cuban sovereignty with the Platt Amendment in 1901, which set constraints on Cuban foreign policy and allowed the United States to intervene in Cuba when thought necessary. The Americans were prepared to give the Cubans many liberties, but not enough freedom to oppose vital American interests. After leaving in 1902, American troops returned in 1906 when the Cuban government fell apart. They stayed until 1909. The United States would not abandon its paternalistic policies toward Cuba until the presidencies of Herbert Hoover and Franklin D. Roosevelt.

Day 99

The film takes a very positive perspective on Theodore Roosevelt's role in building the Panama Canal. Roosevelt is seen as completing Christopher Columbus's mission of discovery and exploration, looking for a route to the Indies. The canal is seen as a triumph of American energy, enterprise, and engineering. The film sees the canal as a measure of the U.S. position at the forefront of progress. At the end of the film, President Calvin Coolidge pays tribute to Theodore Roosevelt for his work in making the canal possible.

Day 100

Vice President Theodore Roosevelt became president when William McKinley was assassinated in 1901. He was elected president in his own right in 1904, defeating the Democratic candidate Judge Alton B. Parker. The 1906 Hepburn Act gave the Interstate Commerce Commission greater regulatory authority over railroads, including the power to set maximum railroad rates. William Howard Taft was Theodore Roosevelt's handpicked successor. He defeated third-time Democratic presidential candidate William Jennings Bryan in the election of 1908. The National Association for the Advancement of Colored People (NAACP) was founded in 1909 by a group of African American and white civil rights activists that included W.E.B. Du Bois. The NAACP quickly became the most influential civil rights organization in the United States. Woodrow Wilson was elected president in 1912. He was the first Democrat to be elected president since Grover Cleveland in 1892. He benefited from a split in the Republican Party. He defeated William Howard Taft, the Republican candidate; Theodore Roosevelt, the candidate of the Progressive (Bull Moose) Party; and Eugene V. Debs, the candidate of the Socialist Party.

Day 101

The proper chronological order is Pure Food and Drug Act, Federal Reserve Act, Clayton Antitrust Act. The 1906 Pure Food and Drug Act gave the U.S. government the authority to regulate foods and drugs for purity and safety. The act required manufacturers to list active ingredients on labels and gave the Food and Drug Administration the power to test products. Reformers like Dr. Harvey Wiley had been pushing for such a law, but the revelations of Upton Sinclair's *The Jungle* (1906) hastened passage of the legislation. The 1913 Federal Reserve Act addressed the longstanding issue of creating a central banking system and a flexible currency for the United States. This legislation established a Federal Reserve System, with a Federal Reserve Board to act as a governing body and 12 regional Federal Reserve Banks. The Federal Reserve System issues Federal Reserve Notes to act as American currency. This is still the system in the United States. The 1914 Clayton Antitrust Act strengthened the laws against monopolistic and illegal practices by corporations. The Clayton Act exempted labor unions from these provisions, giving a boost to the labor movement.

Day 102

After serving three terms in the U.S. House of Representatives, Robert La Follette became concerned about the power wielded by business interests in his state of Wisconsin. He organized an insurgent group within the Wisconsin Republican party, and in 1900 was elected governor. In office, La Follette enacted a series of reforms, including greater regulation of railroad rates. In 1906, La Follette moved on to the U.S. Senate, where he remained until his death in 1925. La Follette embodied the Progressive Movement's effort to exert greater public control over corporations. This was a battle that was waged on the state as well as national levels.

Day 103

Settlement houses were established by middle class reformers to provide services to the urban poor. Hull House helped recent immigrants adjust to life in the United States.

Among the services Hull House provided were classes on language, domestic skills, and the arts. Hull House also sponsored clubs, concerts, and other recreational activities. Reformers living at Hull House also conducted studies of the neighborhood to aid in social planning and advocating for new public institutions such as a juvenile court.

Day 104

Muckrakers played an important role in publicizing corporate abuses, political malfeasance, and other social problems during the Progressive Era. They helped mobilize public opinion behind progressive reforms. Although muckrakers published in a variety of venues, some periodicals such as *McClure's Magazine* became famous for their investigative journalism. Famous muckrakers include Ida M. Tarbell, who wrote a critical history of John D. Rockefeller's Standard Oil, and Lincoln Steffens, who exposed the workings of urban political machines.

Day 105

The proper chronological order is Northern Securities Case, Ballinger-Pinchot Affair, and Sixteenth Amendment. The Northern Securities Company was organized in 1901 by James J. Hill, E. H. Harriman, and J. P. Morgan, and controlled a number of railroads. In 1902, President Theodore Roosevelt directed the Justice Department to sue for the dissolution of the company under the Sherman Antitrust Act. The directors of the Northern Securities Company fought back in court until 1904, when the Supreme Court ruled in favor of the government, and the company was dissolved. The Northern Securities Case was the first of a number of Progressive Era prosecutions of "trusts" that breathed life into the Sherman Antitrust Act. The 1909–1910 Ballinger-Pinchot Affair began with a dispute between Secretary of the Interior Richard Ballinger and Gifford Pinchot, the head of the U.S. Forest Service, over the opening of public land in Alaska to coal mining. President Taft ultimately sided with Ballinger and fired Pinchot, a close friend of Theodore Roosevelt. This well-publicized dispute contributed to the eventual political rupture between Roosevelt and Taft. The Sixteenth Amendment, ratified in 1913, gave Congress the power to levy an income tax. This taxing power enabled Congress to vastly increase federal spending over the course of the twentieth century.

Day 106

The disastrous Triangle Shirtwaist Fire shocked the nation in 1911. It had immediate consequences in New York. After an investigation, new workplace safety laws were enacted in New York. The New York legislature also passed a bill to shorten workers' hours. These bills became models for other states. The tragedy also proved a spur to unionization. Many garment workers joined the growing International Ladies' Garment Workers' Union (ILGWU).

Day 107

Theodore Roosevelt began promulgating his New Nationalism in 1910, and it became the basis of his run for the presidency in 1912 as the candidate of the Progressive (Bull Moose) party. Roosevelt called for an expanded role for the federal government in regulating business and the economy. Roosevelt argued that government had to grow to match the power of the big corporations that were central to the economic future of the United States. He also believed that the government should take the lead in promoting greater social justice. Elements of the New Nationalism included a federal income tax, a federal securities commission, social insurance, the eight-hour day, and suffrage for women. Woodrow Wilson's New Freedom rejected Roosevelt's big-government solutions to social problems and his assumption that big corporations were inevitable. Wilson called for a reduction in the protective tariff, a more aggressive antitrust policy, and banking reform to reduce the power of Wall Street. Wilson won the election of 1912 when Roosevelt and President William H. Taft split the Republican vote. Once in office, Wilson moved closer to the regulatory vision of the New Nationalism with laws such as the Federal Trade Commission Act of 1914.

Day 108

World War I broke out in August 1914, following a diplomatic crisis precipitated by the assassination of the Austrian Archduke Franz Ferdinand. The 1916 Sussex Pledge was a reaction of the Imperial German government to American criticism of its campaign of unrestricted submarine warfare against the British and French. The Germans had recently sunk the *Sussex*, with the loss of 50 lives. The Germans promised not to sink passenger ships and to only sink enemy merchant ships after their crews had been allowed to escape in lifeboats. The breaking of the Sussex Pledge by the Germans in early 1917 led to American participation in the war. The 1917 Zimmerman Telegram was a message from the German foreign minister to the Mexican government. In the event of war with the United States, the Germans offered a military alliance to the Mexicans and stated that they would not object if the Mexicans reconquered lands lost in the Mexican War of the 1840s. The British intercepted this message and gave it to the U.S. government. Publication of the telegram angered Americans and helped prepare them for war with Germany. The Fourteen Points were a list of war objectives issued by President Woodrow Wilson in January, 1918. Among these objectives were freedom of the seas, national self-determination, and a league of nations. President Wilson saw the Fourteen Points as a basis for the postwar peace. The Treaty of Versailles was signed in 1919. While it did not embody all of Wilson's Fourteen Points, it did include a League of Nations.

Day 109

The American Battle Monuments Commission faced many challenges. They had to relocate the bodies of American soldiers killed in many battles to these new cemeteries. In many cases, they could not identify the dead. They also had to arrange the cemeteries and memorials in a way that was tasteful and respectful of the dead. They also had to memorialize a war that meant many things to many people. Most scholars believe that the Commission did an excellent job balancing its different responsibilities.

Day 110

President Woodrow Wilson's War Message to Congress envisioned a very idealistic war. The United States went to war because of the German submarine campaign and questions of the freedom of the seas. Wilson was interested in ensuring the freedom of the seas, but he also wanted to see a new, more democratic world emerge from the conflict. He embodied his ideas on a just peace in his Fourteen Points. Such an idealistic understanding of the war caused problems when the Treaty of Versailles failed to live up to all the ideals in the Fourteen Points. Many Americans became disillusioned with the outcome of the war. This was intensified when Wilson refused to compromise with the Senate majority over the League of Nations, leading to the failure of the Treaty of Versailles in the Senate. Postwar writers such as Ernest Hemingway questioned whether the idealistic rhetoric of Woodrow Wilson justified the bloody horrors experienced by soldiers in the war.

Day 111

The proper chronological order is *Lusitania*, Lever Food and Fuel Control Act, Meuse-Argonne Offensive. The *Lusitania* was a British passenger liner that was sunk by a German submarine off the coast of Ireland on May 7, 1915. 1,198 passengers and crew lost their lives, including 128 Americans. This sinking outraged American public opinion and led to a diplomatic crisis with Germany. With the Sussex pledge the following year, the Germans would temporarily back off from their full submarine campaign. The 1917 Lever Food and Fuel Control Act gave the president the power to regulate the production, transportation, and price of food and fuel during the war. Herbert Hoover was named the head of the U.S. Food Administration charged with implementing the production and allocation of food. This law reflected the total war mobilization of all American resources for the war effort. The Meuse-Argonne Offensive was the last and largest major offensive of the American Expeditionary Force in World War I. The offensive began on September 26, 1918, and continued to the end of the war on November 11. Over a million American soldiers took part and 26,000 lost their lives. The American attack cut crucial German supply lines and helped convince the Germans to call for an armistice.

Day 112

The National World War I Museum and Memorial exhibitions give a good sense of the vast scale of the Great War. The fighting was deeply influenced by technological advances such as machine guns and artillery on recoilless platforms that literally drove armies underground into trenches. Weapons such as poison gas, tanks, airplanes, and submarines were deployed to break the stalemate on the Western Front. Initially these proved indecisive and added to the casualties. World War I was a total war that required the full mobilization of a nation's resources. During the war, the U.S. government took control of industrial production, food production, and transportation, running the railroads. Another consequence of this vast mobilization was the movement of women into jobs previously held by men. The significant contributions of women to the war effort helped pave the way for the passage of women's suffrage in 1919.

Day 113

The 1918 Sedition Act was an expansion of the 1917 Espionage Act. It was designed to quell dissent and actions that might interfere with the war effort. It was also intended to end vigilante actions by citizens against supposed traitors by giving the government the power to prosecute them. The law reflected the widespread intolerance for dissenting viewpoints on the war. A notable figure prosecuted under the Sedition Act was the Socialist party leader Eugene V. Debs, who was sentenced to 10 years in prison for advocating resistance to the draft. The Sedition Act was repealed in December 1918.

Day 114

President Woodrow Wilson and supporters of the League of Nations believed that the international organization would prevent any more conflicts like World War I. Operating under the principle of collective security, member states would act to resolve international disputes and oppose unprovoked aggressions. Supporters of the League believed that it would eventually rectify problems created by the harsh terms imposed by the Treaty of Versailles on the defeated nations. "Reservationists" were concerned that the League of Nations threatened aspects of American sovereignty. They feared the League's collective security provisions threatened congressional war powers. They also believed that the League posed problems for such traditional pillars of American foreign policy as the Monroe Doctrine. The "reservationists" were prepared to support the Treaty of Versailles and the League, but only if reservations about these concerns were attached to the document. This distinguished them from a handful of "irreconcilables" in the Senate who opposed any sort of American participation in the League. In the end, President Wilson refused to compromise, and the Treaty of Versailles never received enough votes, with or without reservations, to be ratified.

Day 115

A constitutional amendment to introduce national prohibition was passed by Congress in 1917 and was ratified by the states in 1919. The Volstead Act to enforce prohibition passed Congress on October 28, 1919. Prohibition went into effect on January 1, 1920. The Washington Disarmament Conference convened on November 12, 1921. It resulted in treaties that limited naval construction, maintained the territorial status-quo in the Pacific, and upheld the Open Door in China. The 1925 Scopes Trial resulted from a challenge to a Tennessee law that prohibited the teaching of evolution in that state's schools. The presence of William Jennings Bryan on the prosecution team and Clarence Darrow on the defense team helped make the trial a national sensation. At the trial the law was upheld, but religious fundamentalism was criticized by the defense. Charles Lindbergh became an international hero when he became the first person to make a solo flight across the Atlantic Ocean in his plane the *Spirit of St. Louis* on May 20–21, 1927. After several bumps, the stock market crashed in October 1929. This set in motion an economic crisis that resulted in the Great Depression.

Day 116

The name "Jazz Age" is appropriate for the 1920s in part because this was a time when jazz music became very popular. Both African American musicians like Louis Armstrong and white jazz musicians such as the bandleader Paul Whiteman enjoyed a great deal of success. Serious composers like George Gershwin wrote music heavily influenced by jazz. The name "Jazz Age" is also appropriate because jazz music helped capture the cultural rebelliousness and excitement about change that was very prominent in the 1920s.

Day 117

The proper chronological order is Palmer Raids, National Origins Act, execution of Sacco and Vanzetti. Attorney General A. Mitchell Palmer launched the Palmer Raids between November 1919 and January 1920. These were a response to terrorist bombings. The raids rounded up thousands of left-wing radicals, and 500 were deported. This was a major moment in the first Red Scare. The National Origins Act was part of the larger Immigration Act of 1924. It was a response to concerns about high immigration that were intensified by the Red Scare. This limited immigration to 2 percent of the number of any ethnic group living in the United States in 1890. This greatly reduced immigration, especially from Southern and Eastern Europe. Nicola Sacco and Bartolomeo Vanzetti were two Italian-born anarchists who were convicted of a 1920 payroll robbery murder. Some observers believed that the men were innocent and were victims of a prejudiced trial during the Red Scare. After many protests, the men were executed in 1927.

Day 118

In this speech, Coolidge is making the point that decreases in government spending benefit ordinary Americans by reducing taxes, which allows them to keep more of their money. Like his predecessor Warren G. Harding, Coolidge believed in limited government. Both Harding and Coolidge cut government spending and lowered taxes. They agreed with Secretary of the Treasury Andrew Mellon that lowered tax rates would increase prosperity and raise actual tax revenues. The 1920s did see a period of dramatic economic growth in the country. Coolidge significantly reduced the national debt in his time in office.

Day 119

In May 1927, Charles Lindbergh became the first person to make a solo flight across the Atlantic in his plane *The Spirit of St. Louis*. Lindbergh was honored for his courage and skill in singlehandedly accomplishing a feat that had cost other pilots their lives. Lindbergh increased the esteem of his contemporaries through his modesty and unwillingness to financially capitalize on his achievement. Many Americans saw Lindbergh as a person who was carrying on the pathfinding tradition of the American pioneers, and in doing so demonstrating that traditional American virtues were possible in the modern era. Lindbergh was also seen as a harbinger of a new era of technological possibilities. His close identification with his plane made him seem a cutting-edge figure in a decade experiencing rapid technological change.

Day 120

Governor Alfred "Al" Smith of New York was the Democratic nominee for president in 1928. A native of New York City, and in his early career associated with the Tammany Hall political machine, Smith vehemently opposed Prohibition. Herbert Hoover, the Republican nominee, expressed some support for Prohibition, calling it an "experiment noble in purpose." Hoover, famous as a philanthropist and energetic public servant, easily won the election. Smith's desire to repeal Prohibition, along with his Roman Catholicism, hurt him with rural voters who were still a powerful political force. Smith did very well in the big cities and laid the groundwork for the coalition of urban, ethnic voters who would be a political mainstay of Franklin D. Roosevelt's New Deal.

Day 121

Frederick Lewis Allen is describing changes in the behavior of young women in the 1920s. Women had received the vote in 1920, but one of the most conspicuous developments of the decade was the growing social freedom of women. Women shed their corsets and long, heavy dresses and embraced makeup. The "flapper," with her bobbed hair, short dress, and mannish figure became the symbol of the age. As Allen points out, many young women joined young men in smoking and drinking. Some women took advantage of decreasing parental controls, and the freedom provided by the automobile, to partake in sexual experimentation. This behavior contributed to the reputation of the 1920s as the "Jazz Age."

Day 122

The 1930 Hawley-Smoot Tariff was intended to protect American industries and jobs by making foreign goods more expensive. It had the unintended effect of leading other countries to increase their tariffs, hurting foreign trade and Americans who worked in industries that exported goods. The 1931 Scottsboro Boys Trial involved nine African American teenagers who were convicted of raping two white women on a train. The trial, held in segregated Alabama, was widely thought to be unfair. The young men are now believed to have been innocent. Created in 1932, the Reconstruction Finance Corporation (RFC) was an effort by President Herbert Hoover and Congress to combat the Great Depression. The RFC lent money to banks and other businesses. Prohibition ended in 1933. The Twenty-first Amendment repealing the Eighteenth Amendment was ratified on December 5, 1933. The Congress of Industrial Organizations (CIO) was organized in 1935. The CIO unionized many unskilled workers in large industries.

Day 123

The proper chronological order is National Industrial Recovery Act (NIRA), Social Security Act, Justice Reorganization Bill. The 1933 NIRA was a centerpiece of the First New Deal. The NIRA attempted to restore industrial prosperity by encouraging industries to set standards for prices and competition, while also protecting the rights of workers. The NIRA also set up a Public Works Administration (PWA) to provide work for the unemployed. The 1935 Social Security Act was a centerpiece of the Second New Deal. It helped lay the foundations for the modern American welfare state by creating a retirement plan for older Americans and unemployment insurance for workers who lost their jobs. The 1937 Justice Reorganization Bill was an attempt by President Franklin D. Roosevelt to increase the size of the Supreme Court so he could appoint justices favorable to the New Deal. A coalition of conservative Democrats, many of them from the South, and Republicans defeated this bill because it seemed to place too much power in Roosevelt's hands.

Day 124

Mrs. Henderson's letter is referring to the effects of the Dust Bowl. Beginning in 1934, a series of droughts in the 1930s dried out soil that had been exposed by years of farming in the Lower Plains states and produced immense clouds of dust. Many people lost their farms. By 1940, 3.5 million people moved away from the affected area. Many moved to California, where they were known as "Okies." John Steinbeck chronicled the plight of such people in his novel *The Grapes of Wrath* (1939).

Day 125

It is not true that President Herbert Hoover did nothing to help people during the Great Depression. He actively used the power of the federal government to combat the depression. He cut taxes and launched public works to provide employment. He signed legislation such as the Hawley-Smoot Tariff and helped create the Reconstruction Finance Corporation (RFC) to pump money into the economy by lending money to banks and businesses. Hoover feared that too much government involvement in people's lives would undermine American individualism. He worked hard to organize local private charities to provide relief for the unemployed. Franklin Roosevelt and his New Deal built on the foundation established by Hoover and agencies like the RFC. Roosevelt was willing to go further than Hoover in expanding the reach of government, and used government agencies to provide direct relief to the unemployed and poor. Roosevelt brought an experimental approach to fighting the depression, and created many different sorts of agencies, such as the Agricultural Adjustment Administration (AAA) and the Tennessee Valley Authority (TVA) in an effort to improve the situation.

Day 126

Although Franklin D. Roosevelt's New Deal failed to end the Great Depression, he did build a New Deal Coalition that endured for many decades. Born to wealth, as his home indicates, FDR had a capacity to empathize and communicate with ordinary Americans. Some scholars attribute this to his long struggle with the polio that crippled his legs. FDR spoke directly to the American people in radio addresses that became known as his "Fireside Chats." This way he became a reassuring presence in many people's homes. FDR gave the impression that he cared about ordinary Americans. Although the New Deal did not solve the nation's economic problems, it provided relief and a measure of security to millions.

Day 127

Huey P. Long served as governor of Louisiana from 1928–1932, and as U.S. senator from 1932–1935. Long built a political machine in Louisiana that made him the virtual dictator of the state. He remained very popular in Louisiana because he spoke up for the poor, built a string of charity hospitals, and expanded schools, with free textbooks for schoolchildren. As an ambitious senator, Long aimed for the presidency. He won favor with millions by promoting a "Share Our Wealth" program that would cap personal fortunes at $50 million and provide an annual income of $2,000–3,000 for every family. Many observers believed that Long was a dangerous demagogue. FDR's Second New Deal was intended in part to curb his popular appeal. A Louisiana doctor who opposed Long's actions assassinated him in September 1935.

Day 128

President Franklin D. Roosevelt and his New Deal provided increased legal support to the labor movement. The 1935 Wagner Act affirmed the right of workers to unionize and bargain collectively. The Wagner Act also outlawed certain labor practices and established the National Labor Relations Board (NLRB) to enforce the labor laws. This led to an effort to expand unionization. John L. Lewis, the president of the United Mine Workers (UMW), helped found the Congress of Industrial Workers

(CIO) in 1935. The CIO worked to unionize unskilled workers in large industries. In 1936 and 1937 there was a wave of strikes in the automobile and steel industries. Workers in the automobile industry staged "sit-down" strikes, where they occupied manufacturing plants. This tactic seemed radical to many Americans. The intense labor strife in this period was also disturbing. This is why Lewis went on to the radio to reassure his listeners that the striking union members were not radicals influenced by communistic ideas, but could, if treated fairly, become mainstays of the American free enterprise system.

Day 129

President Franklin D. Roosevelt promoted recovery, relief, and reform in his New Deal Program. The First New Deal of 1933–1934 emphasized recovery and relief, with agencies such as the National Recovery Administration (NRA), Civilian Conservation Corps (CCC), and the Agricultural Adjustment Administration (AAA). Elements of reform in the First New Deal were the Federal Deposit Insurance Corporation (FDIC) and the Securities and Exchange Commission (SEC). The Second New Deal, launched in 1935, was in part a response to challenges from leaders like Huey Long and his "Share Our Wealth" Plan and Francis Townshend with his "Townshend Plan" of old-age pensions. The Second New Deal emphasized reform though legislation like the Social Security Act, which provided aid to the aged, children, and the unemployed, and the Wagner Act, which provided government protections to organized labor.

Day 130

The Neutrality Act of 1935 was an effort to keep the United States out of a conflict like World War I. The law established a six-month moratorium on American trade in weapons or military supplies with warring countries. Following the signing of a nonaggression pact with the Soviet Union, Germany invaded Poland on September 1, 1939, beginning World War II. The Destroyers for Bases Agreement was concluded between the United States and Great Britain on September 2, 1940. The United States gave Great Britain 50 retired destroyers in exchange for bases in British territories in the Western Hemisphere. The British needed the ships to fight submarines, while the United States was interested in building up its defenses. Technically, the agreement was a violation of American neutrality. The 1941 Lend-Lease Act provided military supplies to countries resisting Nazi Germany. Promoted as a self-defense measure, the Lend-Lease Act was an expression of growing American opposition to the Axis Powers. Internment camps for Japanese were established in 1942, after the December 1941 bombing of Pearl Harbor. Japanese living on the West Coast of the United States, citizens and noncitizens alike, were regarded as a security threat and moved to internment camps. Although the Supreme Court upheld the constitutionality of this war measure in 1944, it is now regarded as an unnecessary violation of these people's rights.

Day 131

The proper chronological order is Battle of Midway, Battle of Guadalcanal, and Battle of the Bulge. The Battle of Midway, fought June 4–7, 1942, turned the tide of the war in the Pacific Theater. In a battle dominated by aircraft carriers, the Americans sank four Japanese aircraft carriers while losing one aircraft carrier of their own.

After this defeat, the Japanese were forced on the defensive. The Battle of Guadalcanal was fought from August 7, 1942, to February 9, 1943. The American landing on the island of Guadalcanal was the first American offensive of the Pacific War. In a series of battles on the island and in the waters surrounding it, American land, air, and naval forces inflicted heavy losses on the Japanese and forced them to fall back. The Battle of the Bulge, fought from December 16, 1944, to January 25, 1945, resulted from a desperate German offensive that aimed at inflicting such a defeat on the Allies that they would be forced to make a compromise peace. After being caught by surprise, American forces stopped the Germans and forced them back, inflicting losses the Germans could no longer afford.

Day 132

Senator Gerald P. Nye of North Dakota was an influential isolationist. From 1934 to 1936, Nye headed a Senate investigation into the munitions industry to see if prominent American businesses had helped lead the United States into World War I. He played an important role in passing the neutrality laws designed to keep the United States out of another war. Nye opposed American intervention in World War II. He was not alone. The America First organization, founded in 1940, became an influential force in American politics. Isolationists remained vocal until the Japanese attack on Pearl Harbor on December 7, 1941.

Day 133

The World War II Valor in the Pacific National Monument lies above the resting place of the USS *Arizona*. During the December 7, 1941, Japanese attack on Pearl Harbor, the *Arizona*, an American battleship, was sunk with the loss of 1,177 men. In all, during the Japanese assault, 2,403 Americans were killed and 1,178 were wounded. The United States and Japan disagreed over Japanese conquests in China and Indochina. The Japanese attacked because they resented American economic sanctions, which cut them off from supplies of American oil and metals. The Japanese believed that they could capture sources of these resources from the British and Dutch possessions in Asia. To do this safely, they had to neutralize the American fleet. The Japanese surprise attack infuriated Americans. The Pearl Harbor attack failed to catch the American aircraft carriers, which were out of port, and failed to destroy Pearl Harbor as a functioning naval base. The United States would soon be able to launch a series of counterattacks that eventually destroyed the Japanese Empire.

Day 134

The proper chronological order is beginning of the draft, Revenue Act of 1942, G.I. Bill. In 1940, in response to the security threat posed by the outbreak of World War II and Axis victories, the United States launched a massive rearmament program to build up American defenses. Part of this program was the institution of a draft to build up the army. The Selective Training and Service Act of 1940 was the first peacetime draft in American history. The Revenue Act of 1942 was a wartime measure to help raise funds for the war. The number of Americans paying income tax was increased. The top tax rate on excess profits was raised to 90 percent. The Serviceman's Readjustment Bill of 1944, popularly known as the G.I. Bill, provided benefits to returning members of the armed services. Benefits included low-interest loans to purchase homes and start businesses, as well as funds to help pay for education. These benefits helped many veterans successfully reenter civilian life and played a significant role in spurring postwar prosperity.

Day 135

Following the Allied breakout from the D-Day beachhead in July, 1944, a dispute arose over the best way to complete the rout of the German armies and end the war. The Allied armies moved so fast that they began to outrun available supplies, especially gasoline. The British General Bernard Montgomery argued for a narrow front thrust into Germany by his forces. He believed that this would disrupt the German defenses and bring on a German surrender. Such an attack would require giving him most of the available fuel, bringing American operations to a halt. General Dwight D. Eisenhower, the Supreme Commander of Allied forces in Europe, preferred a broad front strategy that would have all his armies advance. Debate over the narrow versus broad front strategies continues to this day. Proponents of the narrow front strategy argue that the broad front advance delayed victory, while proponents of the broad front strategy argue that a narrow thrust would have been overwhelmed by the Germans.

Day 136

By August 1945, Japan was isolated and objectively beaten. Despite this, the military rulers of Japan declared that they would fight on and were gathering large forces to resist an American invasion. The Americans were preparing Operation Olympic, an assault on the Japanese home islands. Given the ferocity of the Japanese resistance in the bloody battles of Iwo Jima and Okinawa, the Americans were expecting heavy casualties. With Germany defeated, troops in Europe, including Paul Fussell, were slated to be shipped to the Pacific and the climactic battle for Japan. Fussell's reaction to the dropping of the atomic bombs was similar to that of many American soldiers— relief that they would not have to fight a harrowing battle that might have cost their lives. In his essay, Fussell responds to critics of the atomic bombing by pointing out that a rapid conclusion to the war in the Pacific not only prevented a bloody invasion of Japan that would have killed untold numbers of Americans and Japanese, but it also ended the many deaths from ongoing fighting and from Japanese cruelties in the lands that they occupied.

Day 137

The February 1945 Yalta Conference between President Franklin D. Roosevelt, British Prime Minister Winston Churchill, and Soviet Premier Josef Stalin discussed post-war conditions in Europe. Stalin promised free elections in Poland, a pledge he later broke. On March 5, 1946, Winston Churchill, now out of office, gave his "Iron Curtain" speech while visiting the United States. His vision of Europe divided between Communist and democratic nations was a rhetorical acknowledgment of the beginning of the Cold War. The Federal Employee Loyalty program was introduced in 1947. It was a reaction to the recognition that Soviet spies had infiltrated the American government. Loyalty Review Boards attempted to root Communists and Communist sympathizers out of government employment. The People's Republic of China was established on October 1, 1949, after the Communist forces of Mao Zedong won the Chinese Civil War. The Korean War began on June 25, 1950, when Communist North Korean forces invaded South Korea. The United States rapidly entered the conflict to support the South Koreans.

Day 138

The proper chronological order is Truman Doctrine, Marshall Plan, NATO. In early 1947, the British told the American government that they could no longer protect Greece and Turkey from Communist threats. In gathering Congressional support to take over for the British, President Harry Truman announced what came to be known as the "Truman Doctrine" on March 12, 1947. Truman promised American aid to any country being threatened by Communist aggression or internal subversion. The Marshall Plan was launched in 1948. Named after Secretary of State George Marshall, this was a plan to help restore Western European prosperity and weaken the appeal of Communism through American economic aid. The plan, which encouraged greater European economic integration, proved very successful. Because of concerns about the military threat posed by the Soviet Union, the United States, Canada, and 10 European nations formed the North Atlantic Treaty Organization in 1949. This was the first formal alliance for the United States since it ended its Revolutionary War alliance with France in 1800.

Day 139

George F. Kennan was an American diplomat with extensive experience in the Soviet Union by the mid-1940s. In his "Long Telegram" sent to Washington on February 22, 1946, and his 1947 *Foreign Affairs* article, initially published anonymously and signed "X," Kennan formulated the policy of containment. Kennan's superiors in the Truman Administration found his writings very useful in clarifying their thought and adopted and elaborated on his policy of containment. Kennan believed that Soviet expansionism should be contained through adroit diplomacy. Much to Kennan's dismay, as time went on American administrations looked to military means of containment.

Day 140

Both President Harry Truman and Senator Joseph McCarthy believed that Soviet spies had infiltrated the American government. Revelations about Soviet spying, including in the atomic bomb program, became public in the late 1940s and early 1950s. President Truman responded to this with his Federal Employee Loyalty program, which established a Loyalty Review Board to sift security risks out of the federal bureaucracy. He believed that this program effectively addressed the problem. On February 9, 1950, Senator McCarthy achieved notoriety by giving a speech claiming that a large number of Communists were serving in the State Department. From that point, McCarthy became influential by accusing the government of harboring Communists and launching Senate investigations of government officials. This infuriated Truman, who regarded McCarthy as an irresponsible demagogue and political partisan. Following maneuvers by the Eisenhower Administration, McCarthy was censured by the Senate on December 2, 1954.

Day 141

The proper chronological order is Geneva Accords, *Sputnik*, the Soviet downing of a U-2 plane. The Geneva Accords were announced on July 21, 1954. They were the result of a conference called to determine the future of Indochina. While the conference was ongoing, on May 7, the French were forced to surrender the remains of an army at Dien Bien Phu. The Geneva Accords divided Vietnam into North Vietnam controlled by Ho Chi Minh and his predominantly Communist forces and South Vietnam, controlled by anti-Communist Vietnamese. On October 4, 1957, the Soviet Union launched *Sputnik*, the first human-made satellite, into space. This technological and public-relations triumph led to dismay in the United States and a greater emphasis on math and science in American education. Anxious to avoid a costly arms race, President Dwight D. Eisenhower sponsored the development of the U-2 spy planes, which could do high-altitude reconnaissance flights over the Soviet Union and monitor Soviet missile installations. On May 1, 1960, the Soviets shot down a U-2 plane with a missile, capturing its pilot, Captain Francis Gary Powers. At first the Eisenhower Administration tried to deny that it had been spying in this way on the Soviet Union. When the Soviets produced Captain Powers, the Americans had to admit that they had been doing so. This incident led to the failure of a summit meeting between President Eisenhower and the Soviet premier Nikita Khrushchev, and a deterioration in relations between the United States and the Soviet Union.

Day 142

During the 1950s, the United States began deploying Intercontinental Ballistic Missiles (ICBMs) as part of its nuclear deterrent against the Soviet Union. In the mid-1950s development began on the solid-fuel Minuteman missile. ICBMs, capable of carrying increasingly destructive nuclear warheads, were the most deadly weapons ever created. Fears grew of a "missile gap" with the Soviet Union and became a political issue. The first Minuteman missiles went into service in 1962. The Minuteman Missile National Historic Site offers insight into the bases where, for decades, men and women remained on alert, ready to fire these ICBMs in the event of a nuclear confrontation with the Soviet Union.

Day 143

In this news conference President Dwight D. Eisenhower articulated the "Domino Theory." This argues that if one country in a region falls to Communism, other neighboring countries will succumb as well, like a line of falling dominoes. This formulation is important because it became an underpinning of American involvement in Indochina in the 1950s and 1960s. The United States supported South Vietnam in its struggle with the Viet Cong and North Vietnam in order to prevent Communism from spreading to other countries in East Asia.

Day 144

The disputes over the origins of the Cold War took on greater significance than usual academic debates over the past because they often reflected deep political divisions. The Cold War lasted over 40 years. It was still ongoing when many of these historical debates took place. The understanding of the past was thought to have relevance for present and future policy. Many of the "revisionists" were angered by American policy in Vietnam, and reflected the anti-establishment sentiments that emerged in the 1960s. "Post-revisionism" emerged in the aftermath of the tumult of the 1960s and reflected a more critical view of the Soviet Union that emerged in the increasingly conservative 1970s and 1980s.

Day 145

The 1947 Taft-Hartley Act was passed over President Harry Truman's veto in a brief interval between 1947 and 1949 when the Republicans controlled Congress. The law placed some limits on union activity and required union leaders to declare that they were not Communists. Newly elected President Truman proposed an ambitious program of legislation that he called the Fair Deal in 1949. Among other things, Truman called for a universal health care law and the repeal of the Taft-Hartley Act. A coalition of Republicans and Southern Democrats prevented Truman from getting much Fair Deal legislation enacted. In 1952, Republican vice presidential candidate Richard Nixon was accused of benefitting from an illegal campaign fund. Nixon went on television and gave a speech defending himself during which he referenced a dog named Checkers that had been given to his daughter. The Checkers Speech was a great success and Nixon saved his political career. The 1956 Interstate Highway Act was a recognition of the growing importance of automobiles in American life. It laid the foundations for the modern interstate highway system. Beat writer Jack Kerouac published his novel *On the Road* in 1957. The tale of two friends road-tripping across the country together, *On the Road* helped inspire the counterculture of the 1960s.

Day 146

In 1948, facing a strong challenge from the Republicans and New York Governor Thomas E. Dewey, President Harry Truman appealed to African American voters by proposing laws to extend greater civil rights protections to them. At the Democratic Convention, he supported a plank favoring greater civil rights for African Americans. This alienated many Southern Democrats. They formed the States' Rights Democratic Party (Dixiecrats) and nominated South Carolina Governor Strom Thurmond for president. During the campaign, Thurmond defended segregation. Truman won the presidential election, but Thurmond carried four states with a total of 39 electoral votes.

Day 147

President Eisenhower's Second Inaugural reflects a widespread American prosperity in the 1950s. Prosperity began after World War II, with unemployment falling to 2 percent in 1948. With many competitors hobbled by wartime damage, American industry dominated the world. In 1950, American industries produced 6.2 million automobiles, 6.2 million refrigerators, and 14.6 million radios. The American GNP increased 25 percent from 1953–1961. In 1954, stock prices finally regained the levels last seen in 1929. While poverty persisted in many parts of the United States, for many people the 1950s were indeed "happy days."

Day 148

One reason for the *Pleasantville* view of women in the 1950s is that the popular culture of the time exalted the role of woman as homemaker. Many women's magazines, movies, and television shows persistently portrayed women as happy in the home. A good example of this would be the hit sitcom *Leave It to Beaver*, which first aired in 1957. Critics of this role for women helped shape the current view in the 1960s. Betty Friedan in *The Feminine Mystique* (1963) led a reaction against the role of housewife for women. The women's movement of the 1960s and 1970s, as well as economic change, sparked dramatic differences in women's expectations for employment.

Day 149

William Levitt was a developer who created seven "Levittowns" in the post-war years. His developments utilized assembly-line construction techniques perfected during World War II to quickly produce communities of largely identical homes that were comfortable and reasonably priced. Levitt's developments helped spur the rapid growth of the suburbs in the late 1940s and 1950s, as married couples looked for places to raise their families. Levittowns and other suburban developments enabled many Americans to own their own homes in a time of growing prosperity. These suburban communities also reflected the demographic effects of the post-war baby boom with their emphasis on yards and room for children.

Day 150

The proper chronological order is *Brown v. Board of Education*, Montgomery Bus Boycott, Little Rock Nine. The 1954 *Brown v. Board of Education* Supreme Court decision was a landmark in the African American struggle for civil rights. The Supreme Court ruled against segregation in schools by declaring that "separate but equal" was illegal. In 1955, Rosa Parks refused to surrender her seat on a Montgomery, Alabama, bus to a white man. She was arrested. This led to an African American boycott of the Montgomery bus system. One of the leaders of the boycott was a minister named Martin Luther King, Jr. The boycott eventually succeeded when the Supreme Court ruled that segregation on city buses was illegal. In 1957, Central High School in Little Rock, Arkansas, was about to be integrated by the admission of nine African American students. This was opposed by many white citizens and Arkansas Governor Orval Faubus, who ordered National Guardsmen to prohibit the Little Rock Nine from entering the school. President Dwight D. Eisenhower federalized the National Guard and deployed Army troops to escort the Little Rock Nine into Central High School.

Day 151

The news story from the St. Louis *Post-Dispatch* reflects a critical attitude toward rock and roll. The new music, being popularized by bands like Bill Haley and his Comets, is seen as encouraging violent behavior. Many adults in the 1950s believed that rock and roll was "devil's music," and associated it with immorality. Rock and roll was embraced by a baby-boom generation of young people who saw it as central to an emerging youth culture. Rooted in jazz, and joining African American and white musical styles, rock music appealed to a broad cross-section of American teenagers. Rock musicians like Chuck Berry and Elvis Presley bridged the racial divide.

Day 152

Sit-ins as a tactic for civil rights protesters began in 1960. African American students staged a sit-in at a segregated lunch counter at a Greensboro, North Carolina, Woolworth store. In an attempt to overthrow the Communist regime of Fidel Castro in Cuba, the United States landed a force of anti-Castro Cubans at the Bay of Pigs in Cuba on April 17, 1961. The invasion was a disaster and the American-backed force was defeated and captured. To provide greater support for the Castro regime after the Bay of Pigs invasion, the Soviet Union began to build sites capable of launching nuclear missiles at the United States. American U-2 surveillance fights discovered these sites. This led to the Cuban Missile Crisis, which lasted from October 16–28, 1962. The United States blockaded Cuba. This raised international tensions and the specter of nuclear war. In the end the United States and Soviet Union reached an agreement—the Soviet Union pulled its missiles out of Cuba and the United States secretly dismantled missile sites in Turkey. The United States pledged to respect the sovereignty of Cuba. President John F. Kennedy was assassinated by Lee Harvey Oswald on November 22, 1963. In early August 1964, an American destroyer was engaged by North Vietnamese torpedo boats in the Gulf of Tonkin. In reporting the incident to Congress, President Lyndon B. Johnson did not reveal that the ship had been on an electronic intelligence mission to monitor North Vietnamese communications. Congress passed the Gulf of Tonkin Resolution on August 7, 1964, authorizing the president to "take all necessary steps" to protect American forces and American allies in Southeast Asia. This resolution provided legal support for President Johnson's intervention in the Vietnam War.

Day 153

Senator Barry Goldwater of Arizona won the Republican nomination for president in 1964. Goldwater was a conservative who rejected the political legacy of the New Deal. He called for a return to limited government and promised a more robust military and diplomatic response to Communist aggression. In the general election Goldwater was heavily defeated by President Lyndon B. Johnson, who worked to characterize Goldwater as a political extremist. Johnson's landslide helped him push forward his Great Society expansion of government. Though Goldwater lost in 1964, his campaign is seen as laying the foundation for a conservative revival under one of his supporters, Ronald Reagan.

Day 154

In the 1950s the Eisenhower Administration began to put the federal government behind the Civil Rights Movement with its support of the Little Rock Nine and the Civil Rights Acts of 1957 and 1960. The African American struggle for civil rights continued in the 1960s with sit-ins and Freedom Rides on interstate buses. Dr. Martin Luther King, Jr., made a powerful appeal to the American people with his "I Have a Dream" speech during the March on Washington on August 28, 1963. President Lyndon B. Johnson helped pass the important Civil Rights Act of 1964, which outlawed discrimination by employers and in public locations. 1965 saw the passage of the Voting Rights Act, which removed impediments to African American voting. Following these great victories, a cultural movement toward "Black Power" began with some African Americans, inspired in part by the black nationalism of Malcolm X.

Riots against unequal conditions in Northern and Western cities became part of the political turmoil of the later 1960s. The 1960s were a time of dramatic change for African Americans.

Day 155

The "Old Left" was associated with loyalty to the Communist Party and an approach to politics that emphasized ideological discipline and a hierarchical organization. The young founders of the "New Left" rejected this approach. They stressed "participatory democracy" and individual control of one's life. A key document of the New Left was the 1962 Port Huron Statement issued by the Students for a Democratic Society (SDS). This criticized American materialism and called for nonviolent action to spur reform. The SDS became a leading force on many campuses in opposing the Vietnam War. The SDS broke up in the late 1960s, with some of its members joining the radical Weather Underground organization.

Day 156

The proper chronological order is Medicare, Tet Offensive, and Woodstock Music Festival. Medicare was passed in 1965 as part of President Lyndon B. Johnson's Great Society. Medicare is a federal program that provides medical insurance to Americans aged 65 and older. The Tet Offensive was a massive series of Communist attacks that were launched all across South Vietnam beginning on January 30, 1968. After some initial successes, the Communists were repulsed with heavy losses. Despite this military success, many in the United States began to doubt the Johnson administration's predictions of imminent victory. President Johnson and many of his advisors also lost confidence in their prospects in Vietnam. The Woodstock Music Festival took place from August 15–18, 1969, in a rural area of upstate New York. Over 400,000 young people gathered to hear 32 acts perform. Among the famous musicians who appeared were Janis Joplin and Jimi Hendrix. The immense gathering at the Woodstock Music Festival became a highpoint for the 1960s counterculture.

Day 157

In this passage, President Lyndon B. Johnson is defending American involvement in Vietnam. At this point, the United States was supporting South Vietnam against an insurgency being waged by Viet Cong guerillas and soldiers from North Vietnam. In March, Johnson had sent a contingent of Marines into Vietnam to protect the American airbase at Danang. Later in the year, Johnson sent more troops and widened their mission into combat operations against the Communists. Based on the experience of World War II, Johnson believed that you could not appease aggressors. He assumed that if you give ground, they will merely attack somewhere else. Hence he believed that the United States had to resist the Communists in South Vietnam to prevent a "domino theory" spread of Communism into other parts of Southeast Asia.

Day 158

The Vietnam Veterans Memorial was designed by a young artist named Maya Lin and was dedicated on November 13, 1982. The design, two long black walls etched with the names of the 58,000 Americans who lost their lives in the Vietnam War, was controversial because some critics thought it was too modest and somber and did not celebrate the achievements of the memorialized servicemen and women. As a compromise, a statuary group created by Frederick Hart depicting three soldiers was placed to the side of the memorial in 1984. In 1993, a statuary group created by Glenna Goodacre depicting three nurses and a wounded soldier was placed near the memorial to honor female veterans of the Vietnam War. Though controversial at first, the Vietnam Veterans memorial has been embraced by most Americans. Family members trace the names of their loved ones at the memorial and leave commemorative mementos and flowers. The contemplative atmosphere of the Vietnam Veterans Memorial, with its mix of monuments, reflects the complex feelings Americans have about the Vietnam War.

Day 159

Andy Warhol was an important countercultural figure in the 1960s. He was a pioneer of "Pop Art," which employed imagery drawn from popular culture or advertising in artistic works. Warhol created reproductions of Brillo detergent boxes and painted Campbell's Soup cans and Coca-Cola bottles. He produced silkscreen images of iconic figures such as Marilyn Monroe and Elvis Presley. Warhol branched into filmmaking, and produced a long string of experimental films. At his studio, known as "The Factory," he hosted parties that attracted many celebrities, as well as a following of countercultural figures whom he featured in his movies. Warhol also sponsored the development of the cult rock band the Velvet Underground.

Day 160

The 1973 *Roe v. Wade* Supreme Court decision argued that women had a right to an abortion before fetal viability. This set off a long-standing political battle over abortion. President Richard M. Nixon resigned on August 9, 1974. He was in danger of being impeached for obstruction of justice in the Watergate scandal, and his political situation had become untenable. South Vietnam fell to a military offensive by North Vietnam. The South Vietnamese government surrendered on April 30, 1975. President Jimmy Carter brokered a peace deal between Israeli Prime Minister Menachem Begin and Egyptian President Anwar El Sadat at the Camp David presidential retreat. The Camp David Accords were signed on September 17, 1978, and provided a framework for a formal peace treaty between Israel and Egypt. Following his overthrow in 1979, the former Shah of Iran, Mohammad Reza Pahlavi was allowed into the United States for medical treatment. In response, a mob of Iranian students supported by the revolutionary Iranian government of the Ayatollah Ruhollah Khomeini stormed the American embassy and took the staff hostage on November 4, 1979. A few female and African American hostages were released. The Iranians continued to hold 52 others. An American rescue mission in April 1980 was a failure. The hostage crisis was seen as sign of American weakness. The hostages were not released until January 20, 1981, the date of the inauguration of President Ronald Reagan.

Day 161

President Richard M. Nixon was innovative in his foreign policy initiatives. He launched a new phase of the Vietnam War with his policy of "Vietnamization," which consisted of turning more of the fighting over to the South Vietnamese while gradually pulling out American troops. Nixon supported the South Vietnamese with training, supplies, and a massive bombing campaign. This eventually led to the signing of the Paris Peace Accords on January 27, 1973, and the end of American fighting in the war. Nixon and his national security advisor, and later secretary of state, Henry Kissinger were practitioners of "realpolitik" or balance of power international relations. They sought to check the threat posed by their leading Cold War rivals by improving relations with both, putting pressure on the Soviet Union and China, who disliked each other, to look to the United States for support. They initiated a policy of "détente" with the Soviet Union. At the same time, Nixon and Kissinger reversed decades of American foreign policy by opening diplomatic relations with Communist China. Nixon made an unprecedented trip to China in February 1972.

Day 162

The Richard Nixon Presidential Library and Museum has the challenge of commemorating a president who was forced to resign because of his actions in the Watergate Scandal. The curators of the library meet this challenge by being scrupulously fair about the scandal in their exhibits and forthcoming with documentation about Watergate. President Nixon himself helped mitigate memories of his disgrace and resignation through a long post-presidential career of writing about international relations, restoring his reputation as an expert on foreign policy.

Day 163

President Jimmy Carter was referring to the energy crisis of the 1970s. The world faced shortages of oil as a result of the Arab Oil Embargo in the aftermath of the 1973 Yom Kippur War and the 1979 Iranian Revolution. In 1973 American drivers for a time had to submit to gas rationing. In 1974, Congress passed a law setting the national speed limit at 55 miles per hour. Americans began to purchase fuel-efficient foreign cars, leading to severe problems for the American automobile industry. President Carter tried to institute an ambitious program of energy conservation that met with only limited success.

Day 164

The proper chronological order is Strategic Defense Initiative, Tax Reform Act, and INF Treaty. Under President Ronald Reagan Cold War tensions intensified as he accelerated an arms buildup begun under President Jimmy Carter. Reagan also ramped up rhetorical attacks on the Soviet dictatorship. Reagan believed that the Cold War was not a permanent feature of world affairs and that the United States could prevail in this struggle. The heightening of the Cold War in Reagan's first term led to fears of a nuclear war. To help allay these fears, Reagan launched the Strategic Defense Initiative (SDI), popularly known as "Star Wars," a program to provide the United States with defense systems that could shoot down enemy nuclear missiles in space. The Tax Reform Act of 1986 was a continuation of the tax cutting begun in Reagan's first term. This legislation reduced the top tax rate from 50 percent to 28 percent. By the later 1980s the Soviet leadership realized that the Soviet Union's economy was crumbling and that they could no longer compete in a Cold War with the United States. This led to diplomatic actions to thaw relations between the superpowers. The 1987 Intermediate-Range Nuclear Forces Treaty (INF Treaty), signed by President Reagan and Soviet leader Mikhail Gorbachev, eliminated a whole class of shorter-range nuclear missiles.

Day 165

President Ronald Reagan believed that prosperity came from Americans pursuing their economic goals as free as possible from government intervention. To encourage this, Reagan attempted to cut the size of government and turn back some services to the states with his plan for a New Federalism. He also cut tax rates and promoted the policy of deregulation in the energy and transportation industries. Though Reagan was not able to achieve all his goals in reducing government, the general prosperity of the 1980s made his ideas the foundation for American conservatives for the next two decades.

Day 166

The late 1960s and early 1970s saw the production of many films that emphasized serious and socially conscious themes such as *Midnight Cowboy* (1969) and *Chinatown* (1974). Steven Spielberg's *Jaws* (1975) ushered in a new era of escapist cinematic blockbusters that often emphasized action and special effects. *Star Wars* (1977) was the most successful of these, inspiring sequels and a merchandizing line that continues to this day. The popularity of these films reflected the political mood in the country, which was drawing back from the political activism of the previous decade and was growing more conservative.

Day 167

The Berlin Wall was broken down in 1989 as the Soviet Union weakened and the people of Eastern Europe began to overthrow their Soviet-imposed Communist governments. Operation Desert Shield was implemented by President George Herbert Walker Bush to protect Saudi Arabia after Iraq invaded and conquered Kuwait in August 1990. The next year, in Operation Desert Storm, the United States and a large coalition of allies drove the Iraqi forces out of Kuwait. Soviet hardliners attempted to overthrow President Mikhail Gorbachev in August 1991. Boris Yeltsin led the resistance to the coup, which collapsed. Yeltsin ended the Soviet Union on December 24, replacing it with the Russian Federation. Bill Clinton was elected president in 1992, taking political advantage of a recession that ended earlier in the year and a desire on the part of the American people to enjoy a "peace dividend" with the conclusion of the Cold War. President Bush negotiated the North American Free Trade Agreement (NAFTA) in 1992. This agreement ended most tariffs between the United States, Canada, and Mexico. President Clinton successfully pushed for the passage of a congressional bill enabling the implementation of NAFTA in 1993.

Day 168

The end of the Cold War was a watershed event. The American people wanted to enjoy their "peace dividend" and move in new directions. In the election of 1992, President George Herbert Walker Bush was replaced by the much younger William Jefferson (Bill) Clinton. While scholars debated Francis Fukuyama's thesis on the "end of history," most Americans enjoyed the prosperity of the 1990s. Comparatively little attention was paid to ominous signs in other parts of the world, especially the Middle East. Arguably the escape from "history" ended with the Al Qaeda attack on the United States on September 11, 2001, which opened up a new era of warfare.

Day 169

George H. W. Bush served bravely during World War II as a naval pilot. At one point, he was the youngest pilot in the service. Bush came of political age during the Cold War, which helped shape his career as he served at ambassador to the United Nations, envoy to China, Director of Central Intelligence, and vice president. As president, Bush played an important diplomatic role in peacefully winding down the Cold War. Once the Cold War was won, and other international crises like the Gulf War were seemingly resolved, Bush appeared distant and out of touch to Americans interested in focusing on the economy and domestic affairs. Bush's defeat by Bill Clinton was regarded by many as a symbolic moment, with power passing from a World War II veteran to the first baby-boom president.

Day 170

The proper chronological order is Contract with America, Personal Responsibility and Work Opportunity Reconciliation Act, Kosovo War. The 1994 Contract with America was written by Republican congressmen Newt Gingrich and Dick Armey. It was signed by almost all Republican congressional candidates and laid out a detailed platform of objectives, including welfare reform and tax cuts. The Contract with America proved to be an effective and popular program. In the 1994 elections, the Republicans recaptured control of the House of Representatives for the first time since the 1952 election. Gingrich became the Speaker of the House, and Armey, the House Republican Leader. The Personal Responsibility and Work Opportunity Reconciliation Act, better known as the Welfare Reform Act of 1996, put time limits on welfare assistance and added work requirements for those receiving assistance. This bill reflected the increasingly conservative mood in the nation and a sense that earlier welfare policies had not worked well. President Bill Clinton signed the bill as part of his political move to the middle during the election of 1996. President Clinton had ended the 1992–1995 Bosnian War in the former Yugoslavia with a brief bombing campaign near the end. The peace was negotiated at Dayton, Ohio. In 1998, the Federal Republic of Yugoslavia began a war with Albanian rebels in the territory of Kosovo. After reports of government atrocities, the United States led NATO in a bombing campaign against the Federal Republic of Yugoslavia from March to June 1999. The bombing forced Yugoslav forces out of Kosovo; they were replaced by international peacekeepers. The Kosovo War confirmed a popular American belief at the time that wars could be won with few or no casualties through technology and airpower.

Day 171

Because of continuing allegations of corruption about a land deal involving the Whitewater Development Corporation during President Bill Clinton's time as governor of Arkansas, Ken Starr was appointed as an independent counsel to investigate his involvement. Over time, Starr's investigation was broadened to include other matters, including the firing of the White House travel staff and allegations that Clinton had sexually harassed an Arkansas employee named Paula Jones. During the investigation of the Paula Jones case, Starr learned that Clinton had carried on an affair with a young White House intern named Monica Lewinsky. Pressed on this, Clinton lied about the matter in public and was evasive in sworn testimony. Starr decided that Clinton had committed perjury and obstructed justice by trying to influence Ms. Lewinsky's testimony. The Republican-dominated House of Representatives voted to impeach Clinton. After a trial in the Senate, the Senate voted on February 12, 1999; 67 votes, or two thirds, would have been necessary to remove the president from office. On the perjury charge the Senate voted 45 for conviction and 55 against. On obstruction of justice, the vote was 50 to 50. Clinton survived the impeachment crisis, but dealing with the Lewinsky scandal ate up much of his second term. Clinton was later cited for contempt by a federal judge over his testimony in the Paula Jones case and ordered to pay a $90,000 fine. Before leaving office, Clinton accepted a further penalty of being disbarred from legal practice in Arkansas. He paid Paula Jones $850,000 in an out-of-court settlement. These scandals hurt Vice President Al Gore in the 2000 election.

Day 172

Democrats running as traditional liberals supporting an expansion of government programs to meet social problems lost the elections of 1984 and 1988. This led some Democrats to argue that the party needed to move closer to the political center. In 1985 the Democratic Leadership Council (DLC) was founded to promote this approach. Governor Bill Clinton of Arkansas was a member of the DLC and served for a time as its chairman. In 1992, Clinton ran for president as a "New Democrat." He portrayed himself as more economically conservative than liberal Democrats, being open to middle-class tax cuts and welfare reform. In office, Clinton supported NAFTA. In 1996, Clinton declared that "the era of big government is over," and worked with Republicans to pass tax cuts and welfare reform.

Day 173

Overall, the decade of the 1990s was prosperous, with the last years of the decade especially so. Americans benefitted from lower taxes, lower energy prices, and the emergence of new industries like the dotcom companies pioneering the developing Internet. Following the recession of 1992, the unemployment rate fell to 4 percent by the end of the decade. The absence of perceived foreign threats helped contribute to an optimistic economic atmosphere. The collapse of the overinflated dotcom boom in 2000 was a harbinger of harder economic times.

Day 174

The United States attacked Afghanistan on October 7, 2001. The United States invaded Afghanistan to overthrow the Taliban government that was sheltering Osama bin Laden and other Al Qaeda figures implicated in the 9/11 attacks on the United States. President George W. Bush created an Office of Homeland Security shortly after the 9/11 attacks. The Department of Homeland Security was formally established by the passage of the Homeland Security Act of 2002. The mission of the new department was to provide greater security against terrorism and other threats. In August 2005, Hurricane Katrina caused extensive damage and the loss of 1,254 lives along the Gulf Coast of the United States. The City of New Orleans was especially hard hit because of the failure of levees. The Bush administration was criticized because of its difficulties in getting relief to the area. The Troubled Asset Relief Program (TARP) of 2008 was an effort to bolster banks and other financial institutions following the subprime mortgage crisis. The federal government helped these institutions by purchasing "troubled assets." The goal of President Bush in signing this legislation was to head off a greater financial crisis that might lead to a depression. He secured the support of both 2008 presidential candidates, Senators John McCain and Barack Obama. The Patient Protection and Affordable Care Act, better known as the Affordable Care Act (ACA) or Obamacare, was signed into law by President Barack Obama. Passed with only Democratic votes, it was an effort to provide health care for more Americans while improving care quality and lowering costs. The law was controversial from its inception and spurred political opposition throughout President Obama's presidency.

Day 175

The September 11, 2001, terrorist attack by Al Qaeda operatives flying hijacked airliners killed 2,996 people. The attacks destroyed the Twin Towers of the World Trade Center in New York City and damaged the Pentagon. Resistance by the passengers of United Flight 93 led the terrorists flying that plane to crash it near Shanksville, Pennsylvania. The terrorists probably intended to fly that plane into a government building in Washington, D.C. The 9/11 Memorial and the 9/11 Museum are dedicated to bearing "solemn witness" to the terrorist attacks. They commemorate the people who died that day and celebrate the achievements of the first responders who saved many lives. The memorial bears the names of all the victims of 9/11 and has two waterfalls and reflecting pools in the places where the Twin Towers stood. Nearby, as a sign of hope and reconstruction, stands One World Trade Center (Freedom Tower), the replacement for the World Trade Center.

Day 176

In this speech before a Joint Session of Congress, President Bush was arguing for his program of tax cuts. Bush believed that these cuts would stimulate the economy following a recession caused by the collapse of the dotcom boom. Bush secured tax cuts in 2001 and 2003. These cut the highest tax rate to 35 percent. The Bush tax cuts were intended to expire in 2010. That year President Barack Obama and Congress agreed to extend the Bush rates for two years. In 2012, President Obama and Republicans in Congress compromised on the American Taxpayer Relief Act. The Bush tax cuts were made permanent for individuals earning less than $400,000 and couples earning less than $450,000; for individuals and couples earning more than that, the highest tax rate returned to the pre-Bush rate of 39.6 percent. For most Americans, Bush's tax cuts proved an enduring legacy.

Day 177

Following 9/11, the U.S. government and its allies grew concerned about the Iraqi dictator Saddam Hussein. They held him to be in noncompliance with UN Security Council Resolutions passed since the Gulf War. President George W. Bush, British Prime Minister Tony Blair, and other leaders believed that Saddam Hussein was stockpiling weapons of mass destruction. Saddam Hussein himself contributed to this impression by not cooperating with UN inspectors. On October 16, 2002, large majorities in Congress approved a Joint Resolution giving President Bush authority to use force against Iraq. Operation Iraqi Freedom was launched on March 20, 2003. Saddam Hussein was rapidly overthrown by an invasion of American, British and allied forces. A bloody insurgency against coalition forces and a new Iraqi government ensued. After years of frustration in combating the insurgency, in 2007 President Bush ordered a surge of 20,000 troops into Iraq. In cooperation with Iraqi forces, the "surge" was militarily successful, suppressing the insurgents and bringing a degree of stability to Iraq. In 2011, President Barack Obama withdrew the last American forces from Iraq, declaring that they were leaving behind a "sovereign, stable, and self-reliant Iraq." Soon afterward the Iraqi government fell into sectarian conflict. A successor group to the old Al Qaeda insurgency, the Islamic State of Iraq and Syria (ISIS) emerged as a powerful force in Iraq and in neighboring Syria, which was divided by a civil war. Promoting a fundamentalist form of Sunni Islam, ISIS forces captured large amounts of territory in Syria and Iraq in 2014, including the large Iraqi city of Mosul.

Day 178

In May 9, 2012, President Barack Obama publically announced support for gay marriage. Former Massachusetts governor Mitt Romney, his Republican opponent in the 2012 presidential election, opposed gay marriage and supported a proposed constitutional amendment to limit marriage to one man and one woman. Gay marriage was a divisive social issue until the Supreme Court held that same-sex couples had a right to marry in the 2015 *Obergefell v. Hodges* decision.

Day 179

Immigration and immigration reform were contentious political issues during the Bush and Obama Administrations. Immigration reform legislation failed to pass out of Congress. President Barack Obama was reluctant to deport law-abiding illegal immigrants. He supported the Development, Relief, and Education for Alien Minors Act (Dream Act), which would have provided resident status to illegal immigrants who came to the United States before the age of 16 and who graduated from an American high school and passed a criminal check. This law did not pass Congress. President Obama responded by announcing on June 15, 2012, that his administration would cease deporting people who met the Dream Act criteria.

Day 180

The Supreme Court made a number of important rulings during the Obama years. The 2010 *Citizens United v. FEC* decision prohibited government limits on political spending by nonprofit corporations, arguing that such limits violated the right to freedom of speech. The 2014 *National Federation of Independent Business v. Sebelius* decision upheld most provisions of the Patient Protection and Affordable Care Act (ACA). This legislation, popularly known as "Obamacare," was President Barack Obama's most important legislative achievement, and a subject of intense partisan debate between Democrats and Republicans. The 2015 *Obergefell v. Hodges* decision legalized gay marriage across the United States.

GLOSSARY

Abolitionist movement Movement dedicated to the abolition of slavery that existed primarily in the North in years leading up to the Civil War and consisted of both white and black members.

advertising age Term first used to describe America's consumer culture of the 1920s, when advertising began to influence the choices of purchasers.

affirmative action Policies that began in the 1970s to make up for past discrimination and give minorities and women advantages in applying for certain jobs and in applying for admission to certain universities.

affluent society Term used by economist John Kenneth Galbraith to describe the American economy in the 1950s, during which time many Americans became enraptured with appliances and homes in the suburbs.

Agricultural Adjustment Administration (AAA) Established by the Agricultural Act of 1932, a New Deal bureau designed to restore economic position of farmers by paying them *not* to farm goods that were being overproduced.

Agricultural Marketing Act of 1929 Act championed by Herbert Hoover that authorized the lending of federal money to farmer's cooperatives to buy crops to keep them from the oversaturated market; program hampered by lack of adequate federal financial support.

Albany Congress (1754) Meeting of representatives of seven colonies to coordinate their efforts against French and Native American threats in the Western frontier regions.

Alien and Sedition Acts Proposed and supported by John Adams, gave the president the power to expel aliens deemed "dangerous to the country's well-being" and outlawed publication and public pronouncement of "false, scandalous, and malicious" statements about the government.

Allied Powers Coalition of nations that opposed Germany, Italy, and Japan in World War II; led by England, the Soviet Union, and the United States. In World War I, the coalition consisted of France, Russia, and Great Britain. This group opposed the Central powers (Germany, Austria-Hungary, and Italy).

America First Committee Isolationist group in America that insisted that America stay out of World War II; held rallies from 1939 to 1941; argued that affairs in Europe should be settled by Europeans and not Americans and stated that the Soviet Union was a greater eventual threat than Nazi Germany.

American Colonization Society Formed in 1817, stated that the best way to end the slavery problem in the United States was for blacks to emigrate to Africa. By 1822, a few American blacks emigrated to Liberia. Organization's views were later rejected by most abolitionists.

American Expeditionary Force Official title of American army sent to Europe to aid England and France after United States entered World War I; army was commanded by General John J. Pershing.

American Federation of Labor (AFL) National labor union founded by Samuel Gompers in 1886; original goal was to organize skilled workers by craft. Merged with Congress of Industrial Organizations (CIO) in 1955.

American Indian Movement (AIM) Native American organization founded in 1968 to protest government policies and injustices suffered by Native Americans; in 1973 organized armed occupation of Wounded Knee, South Dakota.

American Liberty League Formed in 1934 by anti-New Deal politicians and business leaders to oppose policies of Franklin Roosevelt; stated that New Deal policies brought America closer to fascism.

American System Economic plan promoted by Speaker of the House Henry Clay in years following the War of 1812, which promoted vigorous growth of the American economy and the use of protective tariffs to encourage Americans to buy more domestic goods.

Anaconda Copper Company Large mining syndicate typical of many companies involved in mining in the western United States in the 1860s and 1870s; used heavy machinery and professional engineers. Many prospectors who found gold, silver, or copper sold their claims to companies such as this.

Anaconda Plan Critical component of initial Union plans to win the Civil War; called for capture of critical Southern ports and eventual control of the Mississippi River, which would create major economic and strategic difficulties for the Confederacy.

Antifederalists Group that opposed the ratification of the proposed Constitution of the United States in 1787; many feared that strong central government would remove the processes of government "from the people" and replicate the excesses of the British monarchy.

Anti-Imperialist League Organization formed in 1898 to oppose American annexation of the Philippines and American imperialism in general; focused the public on the potential financial, military, and especially moral costs of imperialism.

Anti-Saloon League Organization founded in 1893 that increased public awareness of the social effects of alcohol on society; supported politicians who favored prohibition and promoted statewide referendums in Western and Southern states to ban alcohol.

Appomattox In the courthouse of this Virginia city Robert E. Lee surrendered his Confederate army to Ulysses S. Grant on April 9, 1865.

Army-McCarthy hearings 1954 televised hearings on charges that Senator Joseph McCarthy was unfairly tarnishing the U.S. Army with charges of Communist infiltration into the armed forces; hearings were the beginning of the end for McCarthy, whose bullying tactics were repeatedly demonstrated.

Articles of Confederation Ratified in 1781, this document established the first official government of the United States; allowed much power to remain in the states, with the federal government possessing only limited powers. Articles replaced by the Constitution in 1788.

astrolabe Instrument that enabled navigators to calculate their latitude using the sun and the stars; allowed more accuracy in plotting routes during the Age of Discovery.

Atlantic, Battle of the Began in spring 1941 with the sinking of an American merchant vessel by a German submarine. Armed conflict between warships of America and Germany took place in September 1941; American merchant vessels were armed by 1942.

Atlantic Charter Fall 1941 agreement between Franklin Roosevelt and Winston Churchill, stating that America and Great Britain would support a postwar world based on self-determination and would endorse a world body to ensure "general security." U.S. agreement to convoy merchant ships across part of Atlantic inevitably drew America closer to conflict with Germany.

Aztecs Advanced Indian society located in central Mexico; conquered by Spanish conquistador Cortes. The defeat of the Aztecs was hastened by smallpox brought to Mexico by the Spanish.

baby boom Large increase in birthrate in United States that began in 1945 and lasted until 1962; new and larger families fueled the move to suburbia that occurred in the 1950s and produced the "youth culture" that would become crucial in the 1960s.

Ballinger-Pinchot Affair Crisis that occurred when William Howard Taft was president, further distancing him from Progressive supporters of Theodore Roosevelt. Richard Ballinger, Taft's secretary of the interior, allowed private businessmen to purchase large amounts of public land in Alaska. Forest Service head Gifford Pinchot (a Roosevelt supporter) protested to Congress and was fired by Taft.

Bank War Political battles surrounding the attempt by President Andrew Jackson to greatly reduce the power of the Second Bank of the United States. Jackson claimed the bank was designed to serve special interests in America and not the common people.

Bataan Death March Forced march of nearly 75,000 American and Filipino soldiers captured by the Japanese from the Bataan Peninsula in early May 1942; over 10,000 soldiers died during this one-week ordeal.

Bay of Pigs Failed 1961 invasion of Cuba by United States–supported anti-Castro refugees designed to topple Castro from power; prestige of the United States, and of the newly elected president, John Kennedy, was damaged by this failed coup attempt.

Bear Flag Republic Declaring independence from Mexican control, this republic was declared in 1846 by American settlers living in California. This political act was part of a larger American political and military strategy to wrest Texas and California from Mexico.

Beat Generation Literary movement of the 1950s that criticized the conformity of American society and the ever-present threat of atomic warfare; *On the Road* by Jack Kerouac, *Howl* by Allen Ginsberg, and *Naked Lunch* by William Burroughs were key works of the Beat Generation.

Berlin Airlift American and British pilots flew in food and fuel to West Berlin during late 1948 and early 1949 because the Soviet Union and East Germany blockaded other access to West Berlin (which was located in East Germany); Stalin ended this blockade in May 1949. Airlift demonstrated American commitment to protecting Western Allies in Europe during the early cold war period.

Berlin Wall Concrete structure built in 1961 by Soviets and East Germany physically dividing East and West Berlin; to many in the West, the Wall was symbolic of Communist repression in the cold war era. The wall was finally torn down in 1989.

Bessemer steel First produced in 1856 in converter (furnace) invented by Henry Bessemer; was much more durable and harder than iron. Steel was a critical commodity in the Second Industrial Revolution.

bias No historical writing can be totally objective; observers are always influenced by either conscious or unconscious bias. Conscious bias might be a flattering biography of Lincoln written by an abolitionist in 1865, or an unflattering biography of Lincoln written by a southerner in the same year. Unconscious bias may be created by one's education, predispositions toward the subject, or even one's race or gender.

bicameral legislature A legislative structure consisting of two houses, this was adopted by the authors of the U.S. Constitution; membership of the states in one house (the House of Representatives) is determined by population, while in the other house (the Senate) all states have equal representation.

Bill of Rights Added to the Constitution in 1791, the first 10 amendments protected freedom of speech, freedom of the press, the right to bear arms, and other basic rights of American citizens.

Birth of a Nation Epic movie released in 1915 by director D. W. Griffith; portrayed the Reconstruction as a period when Southern blacks threatened basic American values, which the Ku Klux Klan tried to protect. The film was lauded by many, including President Woodrow Wilson.

Black Codes Laws adopted by the Southern states in the Reconstruction era that greatly limited the freedom of Southern blacks. In several states blacks could not move, own land, or do anything but farm.

black nationalism Spurred by Malcolm X and other black leaders, a call for black pride and advancement without the help of whites; this appeared to be a repudiation of the calls for peaceful integration urged by Martin Luther King, Jr. Race riots in Northern cities in mid-1960s were at least partially fueled by supporters of black nationalism.

Black Panthers Group originally founded in Oakland, California, to protect blacks from police harassment; promoted militant black power; also ran social programs in several California cities. Founded by Bobby Seale and Huey P. Newton.

black power Movement of black Americans in the mid-1960s that emphasized pride in racial heritage and black economic and political self-reliance; term coined by black civil rights leader Stokely Carmichael.

blacklist Prevented persons accused of being Communists from getting work in entertainment and other industries during the period of anti-Communist fervor of the late 1940s and early 1950s; some entertainers waited until the mid-1960s before working publicly again.

"Bleeding Kansas" As a result of the Kansas-Nebraska Act of 1854, residents of Kansas territory could decide if territory would allow slavery or not. As a result, both pro and antislavery groups flooded settlers into Kansas territory. Much violence followed very disputed elections in 1855.

bonanza farms Large farms that came to dominate agricultural life in much of the West in the late 1800s. Instead of plots farmed by yeoman farmers, large amounts of machinery were used, and workers were hired laborers, often performing only specific tasks (similar to work in a factory).

Bonus Army Group of nearly 17,000 veterans who marched on Washington in May 1932 to demand the military bonuses they had been promised; this group was eventually driven from their camp city by the United States Army. This action increased the public perception that the Hoover administration cared little about the poor.

Boston Massacre Conflict between British soldiers and Boston civilians on March 5, 1770. After civilians threw rocks and snowballs at the soldiers, the soldiers opened fire, killing five and wounding six.

Boston Tea Party In response to the Tea Act and additional British taxes on tea, Boston radicals disguised as Native Americans threw nearly 350 chests of tea into Boston Harbor on December 16, 1773.

Brown v. Board of Education 1954 Supreme Court decision that threw out the 1896 *Plessy v. Ferguson* ruling that schools could be "separate but equal." The ruling began the long and painful process of school desegregation in the South and other parts of America.

Bulge, Battle of the December 1944 German attack that was the last major offensive by the Axis powers in World War II. Germans managed to push forward into Belgium but were then driven back. Attack was costly to the Germans in terms of material and manpower.

Bull Moose party Name given to the Progressive party in the 1912 presidential campaign. Bull Moose candidate ex-president Theodore Roosevelt ran against incumbent president William Howard Taft and Democrat Woodrow Wilson, with Wilson emerging victorious.

Bull Run, First Battle of July 21, 1861 Confederate victory over Union forces, which ended in Union forces fleeing in disarray toward Washington. This battle convinced Lincoln and others in the North that victory over the Confederates would not be as easy as they initially thought.

Bull Run, Second Battle of Decisive victory by General Robert E. Lee and Confederate forces over the Union army in August 1862.

Bunker Hill, Battle of In June 1775, the British attacked colonial forces at Breed's Hill outside Boston; despite frightful losses, the British emerged victorious in this battle.

Calvinism Protestant faith that preached salvation "by faith alone" and predestination; desire by Calvinists in England to create a "pure church" in England was only partially successful, thus causing Calvinist Puritans to come to the New World starting in 1620.

Camp David Accords Treaty between Egypt and Israel brokered by President Jimmy Carter and signed in early 1979; Israel agreed to give back territory in the Sinai Peninsula to Egypt, while Egypt agreed to recognize Israel's right to exist as a nation.

carpetbaggers Term used by Southerners to mock Northerners who came to the South to gain either financially or politically during the Reconstruction era.

Central Powers The alliance of Germany, Austria-Hungary, the Ottoman Empire, and Bulgaria that opposed England, France, Russia, and later the United States in World War I.

Chancellor of the Exchequer During the era prior to and during the Revolutionary War, this was the head of the department in the British government that issued and collected taxes. Many acts issued by the Chancellor of the Exchequer created great resentment in the American colonies.

Chancellorsville, Battle of Brilliant Confederate attack on Union forces led by Stonewall Jackson and Robert E. Lee on May 2 to 3, 1863. Union defeat led to great pessimism in the North and convinced many in the South that victory over the North was indeed possible.

Chateau-Thierry, Battle of One of the first 1918 World War I battles where soldiers of the American Expeditionary Force fought and suffered severe casualties.

Checkers Speech Speech made by Richard Nixon on national television on September 23, 1952, where he defended himself against charges that rich supporters had set up a special expense account for his use; by the speech Nixon saved his spot on the 1952 Republican ticket (he was running for vice president, with Eisenhower running for president) and saved his political career.

Cherokee Nation v. Georgia (1831) Supreme Court case in which the Cherokee tribe claimed that Georgia had no right to enforce laws in Cherokee territory, since Cherokees were a sovereign nation. This ruling by John Marshall stated that Cherokees were a "domestic dependent nation" and had no right to appeal in federal court.

Church of England Also called the Anglican church, this was the Protestant church established by King Henry VIII; religious radicals desired a "purer" church that was allowed by monarchs of the early seventeenth century, causing some to leave for the Americas.

Circular Letter In reaction to the 1767 Townshend Acts, the Massachusetts assembly circulated a letter to the other colonies, asking that they work together and jointly issue a petition of protest. Strong-willed response of British authorities to the letter influenced the colonial assemblies to work together on a closer basis.

Civil Rights Act of 1866 Act that struck down Black Codes and defined the rights of all citizens; also stated that the federal government could act when civil rights were violated at the state level. Passed by Congress over the veto of President Andrew Johnson.

Civil Rights Act of 1964 Key piece of civil rights legislation that made discrimination on the basis of race, sex, religion, or national origin illegal; segregation in public restrooms, bus stations, and other public facilities also was declared illegal.

Civil Service Commission Created by the Pendleton Civil Service Act of 1883, this body was in charge of testing applicants and assigning them to appropriate government jobs; filling jobs on the basis of merit replaced the spoils system, in which government jobs were given as rewards for political service.

Civilian Conservation Corps (CCC) New Deal program that began in 1933, putting nearly 3 million young men to work; workers were paid little, but worked on conservation projects and maintaining beaches and parks. CCC program for young women began in 1937.

Clayton Antitrust Act of 1914 Act designed to strengthen the Sherman Antitrust Act of 1890. Certain activities previously committed by big businesses, such as not allowing unions in factories and not allowing strikes, were declared illegal.

cold war Period between 1945 and 1991 of near-continuous struggle between the United States and its Allies and the Soviet Union and its Allies; cold war tensions were made even more intense by the existence of the atomic bomb.

colonial assemblies Existed in all of the British colonies in America; House of Burgesses in Virginia was the first one. Members of colonial assemblies were almost always members of the upper classes of colonial society.

Columbian Exchange The exchange of crops, animals (as well as diseases), and ideas between Europe and the Western Hemisphere that developed in the aftermath of the voyages of Columbus.

Committee on Public Information Created by Woodrow Wilson during World War I to mobilize public opinion for the war, this was the most intensive use of propaganda until that time by the United States. The image of "Uncle Sam" was created for this propaganda campaign.

Committees of Correspondence First existed in Massachusetts, and eventually in all of the colonies. Leaders of resistance to British rule listed their grievances against the British and circulated them to all of the towns of the colony.

Common Sense Very popular 1776 publication in the colonies written by Englishman Thomas Paine, who had come to America in 1774; repudiated the entire concept of government by monarchy. After publication of this document, public sentiment in the colonies turned decisively toward a desire for independence.

Compromise of 1850 Complex agreement that temporarily lessened tensions between Northern and Southern political leaders, and prevented a possible secession crisis; to appease the South, the Fugitive Slave Act was strengthened; to appease the North, California entered the Union as a free state.

Compromise of 1877 Political arrangement that ended the contested presidential election of 1876. Representatives of Southern states agreed not to oppose the official election of Republican Rutherford B. Hayes as president despite massive election irregularities. In return, the Union army stopped enforcing Reconstruction legislation in the South, thus ending Reconstruction.

Concord, Battle of Occurred on April 19, 1775, between British regulars and Massachusetts militiamen. Almost 275 British soldiers were wounded or died; as a result, a wider conflict between the colonies and the British became much more probable.

Confederate States of America Eventually made up of 11 former states with Jefferson Davis as its first and only president; was unable to defeat the North because of lack of railroad lines, lack of industry, and an inability to get European nations to support their cause.

Congress of Industrial Organizations (CIO) Group of unions that broke from the AFL in 1938 and organized effective union drives in automobile and rubber industries; supported sit-down strikes in major rubber plants. Reaffiliated with the AFL in 1955.

conscription Getting recruits for military service using a draft. This method was used by the American government in all of the wars of the twentieth century. Conscription was viewed most negatively during the Vietnam War.

consumer society Many Americans in the 1950s became infatuated with all of the new products produced by technology and went out and purchased more than any prior generation. Consumer tastes of the decade were largely dictated by advertising and television.

containment policy Formulated by George Kennan, a policy whereby the United States would forcibly stop Communist aggression whenever and wherever it occurred; containment was the dominant American policy of the cold war era, and forced America to become involved in foreign conflicts such as Vietnam.

Continentals Soldiers in the "American" army commanded by George Washington in the Revolutionary War. Victory at the Battle of Trenton on December 16, 1776, did much to raise the morale of the soldiers (and convince many of them to reenlist). Also a term used for paper money printed in 1781 that was soon made worthless by inflation.

Contract with America (1994) Pledge by Republican candidates for House of Representatives; led by Newt Gingrich, candidates promised to support term limits, balancing the budget, and lessening the size of the federal government. In 1994 Congressional elections, Republicans won both houses of Congress for the first time in 40 years.

convoy system System used to protect American ships carrying materials to Great Britain in 1940 and 1941; merchant ships were protected by American warships. Firing took place between these ships and German submarines, with American losses. Also used in World War I by the navy to allow American shipping to Europe.

Copperheads Democrats in Congress in the first years of the Civil War who opposed Abraham Lincoln and the North's attack on the South, claiming that the war would result in massive numbers of freed slaves entering the North and a total disruption of the Northern economy.

Coral Sea, Battle of the May 1942 American naval victory over the Japanese; prevented Japanese from attacking Australia. First naval battle where losses on both sides came almost exclusively from bombing from airplanes.

counterculture Youth of the 1960s who espoused a lifestyle encompassing drug use, free love, and a rejection of adult authority; actual "hippies" were never more than a small percentage of young people.

Coxey's Army Supporters of Ohio Populist Jacob Coxey who in 1894 marched on Washington, demanded that the government create jobs for the unemployed; although this group had no effect whatsoever on policy, it did demonstrate the social and economic impact of the Panic of 1893.

creationism Belief in the biblical account of the origin of the universe and the origin of man; believers in creationism and believers in evolution both had their day in court during the 1925 Scopes Trial.

Crittenden Plan (1860) Compromise proposal on the slavery issue designed to defuse tension between North and South; would have allowed slavery to continue in the South and would have denied Congress the power to regulate interstate slave trade. On the advice of newly elected President Lincoln, Republicans in Congress voted against it.

Crusades From these attempts to recapture the Holy Land, Europeans acquired an appreciation of the benefits of overseas expansion and an appreciation of the economic benefits of slavery.

Cuban Missile Crisis (1962) Conflict between the United States and the Soviet Union over Soviet missiles discovered in Cuba; Soviets eventually removed missiles under American pressure. Crisis was perhaps the closest the world came to armed conflict in the cold war era.

Currency Act of 1764 British act forbidding the American colonies to issue paper money as legal tender; act was repealed in 1773 by the British as an effort to ease tensions between themselves and the colonies.

dark horse candidate A candidate for office with little support before the beginning of the nomination process. James K. Polk was the first dark horse candidate for president in 1844.

Dawes Act of 1887 Act designed to break up Native American tribes, offered Native American families 160 acres of farmland or 320 acres of land for grazing. Large amounts of tribal lands were not claimed by Native Americans, and thus were purchased by land speculators.

Declaration of Neutrality Issued by President Woodrow Wilson after the outbreak of World War I in Europe in 1914, stating that the United States would maintain normal relations with and continue to trade with both sides in the conflict; factors including submarine warfare made it difficult for America to maintain this policy. Also declared by George Washington in 1793 to allow American merchants to trade with those on both sides of the French Revolution.

Declaration of Rights and Grievances (1774) Measure adopted by the First Continental Congress, stating that Parliament had some rights to regulate colonial trade with Britain, but that Parliament did not have the right to tax the colonies without their consent.

Declaratory Act of 1766 British law stating that the Parliament had absolute right to tax the colonies as they saw fit and to make laws that would be enacted in the colonies. Ironically, issued at the same time as the repeal of the Stamp Act.

deficit spending Economic policy whereby government spends money that it "doesn't have," thus creating a budget deficit. Although "conventional" economic theory disapproves of this, it is commonplace during times of crisis or war (e.g., the New Deal; post–September 11, 2001).

Democratic party Had its birth during the candidacy of Andrew Jackson; originally drew its principles from Thomas Jefferson and advocated limited government. In modern times many Democrats favor domestic programs that a larger, more powerful government allows.

Democratic-Republicans Believed in the ideas of Thomas Jefferson, who wrote of the benefits of a limited government and of a society dominated by the values of the yeoman farmer. Opposed to the Federalists, who wanted a strong national state and a society dominated by commercial interests.

détente The lessening of tensions between nations. A policy of détente between the United States and the Soviet Union and Communist China began during the presidency of Richard Nixon; the architect of policy was National Security Advisor Henry Kissinger.

Dien Bien Phu, Battle of (1954) Victory of Vietnamese forces over the French, causing the French to leave Vietnam and all of Indochina; Geneva Peace Accords that followed established North and South Vietnam.

direct primary Progressive-era reform adopted by some states that allowed candidates for state offices to be nominated by the rank-and-file party members in statewide primaries instead of by the party bosses, who had traditionally dominated the nominating process.

Dollar Diplomacy Foreign policy of President William Howard Taft, which favored increased American investment in the world as the major method for increasing American influence and stability abroad; in some parts of the world, such as in Latin America, the increased American influence was resented.

domesticity Social trend of post–World War II America; many Americans turned to family and home life as a source of contentment. Emphasis on family as a source of fulfillment forced some women to abandon the workforce and achieve "satisfaction" as homemakers.

Dominion of New England Instituted by King James II in 1686. Sir Edmund Andros governed the colonies of Massachusetts, Connecticut, Rhode Island, New York, Plymouth, and New Hampshire as a single entity without an elective assembly; Andros was finally overthrown by militiamen in Boston in April 1689 (after the Glorious Revolution).

domino theory Major tenet of cold war containment policy of the United States held that if one country in a region turned Communist, other surrounding countries would soon follow; this theory convinced many that to save all of Southeast Asia, it was necessary to resist Communist aggression in Vietnam.

Double V campaign World War II "policy" supported by several prominent black newspapers, stating that blacks in America should work for victory over the Axis powers but at the same time work for victory over oppression at home; black leaders remained frustrated during the war by continued segregation of the armed forces.

***Dred Scott* case** Supreme Court case involving a man who was born a slave but had then lived in both a nonslave state and a nonslave territory and was now petitioning for his legal freedom; in 1857 the Court ruled that slaves were not people but were property, that they could not be citizens of the United States, and thus had no legal right to petition the Court for anything. Ruling also stated that the Missouri Compromise, which banned slavery in the territories, was unconstitutional.

Dust Bowl Great Plains region that suffered severe drought and experienced massive dust storms during the 1930s. Because of extreme conditions many who lived in the Dust Bowl left their farms and went to California to work as migrant farmers.

Eisenhower Doctrine Policy established in 1957 that promised military and economic aid to "friendly" nations in the Middle East; the policy was established to prevent communism from gaining a foothold in the region. The policy was first utilized later that year when the United States gave large amounts of aid to King Hussein of Jordan to put down internal rebellion.

Electoral College Procedure outlined in the Constitution for the election of the president; under this system, votes of electors from each state, and not the popular vote, determine who is elected president. As was demonstrated in 2000 presidential election, this system allows a person to be elected president who does not win the nationwide popular vote.

Emancipation Proclamation Edict by Abraham Lincoln that went into effect on January 1, 1863, abolishing slavery in the Confederate states. The proclamation did not affect the four slave states that were still part of the Union (so as not to alienate them).

Embargo of 1807 Declaration by President Thomas Jefferson that banned all American trade with Europe. As a result of the war between England and Napoleon's France, America's sea rights as a neutral power were threatened. Jefferson hoped the embargo would force England and France to respect American neutrality.

Emergency Quota Act Also called the Johnson Act, this 1921 bill limited immigration from Southern and Eastern Europe by stating that in a year, total immigration from any country could only equal 3 percent of the number of immigrations from that country living in the United States in 1910.

encomienda system American natives were given over to Spanish colonists, who in exchange for their labor, promised to "protect" them.

enlightenment Eighteenth-century European intellectual movement that attempted to discover the natural laws that governed science and society and taught that progress was inevitable in the Western world. Americans were greatly influenced by the Enlightenment, especially by the ideas of John Locke, who stated that government should exist for the benefit of the people living under it.

Enola Gay The name of the American bomber that on August 6, 1945, dropped the first atomic bomb on the city of Hiroshima, thus initiating the nuclear age.

environmentalists They broadly support the goals of environmentalism—a broad philosophy, ideology, and social movement that advocates preservation, restoration, and/or improvement of the natural environment by, in part, controlling pollution and protecting plant and animal diversity.

Era of Good Feelings Term used by a newspaper of the period to describe the years between 1816 and 1823, when after the end of the War of 1812 the United States remained generally free of foreign conflicts and when political strife at home was at a bare minimum (because of the collapse of the Federalist party).

Espionage Act World War I era regulation passed in 1917 that ordered severe penalties for citizens who criticized the war effort or the government. Mandatory prison sentences were also proclaimed for those who interfered with the draft process. Nearly 700 Americans were arrested for violating this act.

Essex Junto Group of Massachusetts Federalists who met to voice their displeasure with the policies of Thomas Jefferson during Jefferson's second term, and proposed that the New England states and New York secede from the Union.

Exodusters Large number of Southern blacks who left the South and moved to Kansas for a "better life" after Reconstruction ended in 1877; many failed to find satisfaction in Kansas because of lack of opportunities and open hostility from Kansas residents.

Fair Deal A series of domestic programs proposed to Congress by President Harry Truman that included a Fair Employment Practices Act, a call for government construction of public housing, an extension of Social Security, and a proposal to ensure employment for all American workers.

Farmers' Alliances After the decline of Grange organizations, these became the major organizations of farmers in the 1880s; many experimented with cooperative buying and selling. Many local alliances became involved in direct political activity with the growth of the Populist party in the 1890s.

Federal Deposit Insurance Corporation (FDIC) Passed during the first Hundred Days of the administration of Franklin Roosevelt, this body insured individual bank deposits up to $2,500 and helped to restore confidence in America's banks.

Federal Reserve System Established by the Federal Reserve Act of 1913, this system established 12 district reserve banks to be controlled by the banks in each district. In addition, a Federal Reserve Board was established to regulate the entire structure. This act improved public confidence in the banking system.

Federal Trade Commission Authorized after the passage of the Clayton Antitrust Act of 1914, it was established as the major government body in charge of regulating big business. The FTC investigated possible violations of antitrust laws.

Federalists During the period when the Constitution was being ratified, these were the supporters of the larger national government as outlined in the Constitution; the party of Washington and John Adams, it was supported by commercial interests. Federalists were opposed by Jeffersonians, who favored a smaller federal government and a society dominated by agrarian values. Federalist influence in national politics ended with the presidential election of 1816.

Feminine Mystique, The Betty Friedan's 1963 book that was the bible of the feminist movement of the 1960s and 1970s. Friedan maintained that the post–World War II emphasis on family forced women to think of themselves primarily as housewives and robbed them of much of their creative potential.

feminist movement Movement dedicated to the belief that women should have the same rights and benefits in American society that men do. Feminism gained many supporters during the Progressive Era, and in the 1960s drew large numbers of supporters. The National Organization for Women (NOW) was established in 1966 by Betty Friedan and had nearly 200,000 members in 1969.

Fifteenth Amendment Ratified in 1870, this amendment stated that a person could not be denied the right to vote because of the color of their skin or whether or not they had been a slave. This extended the rights of blacks to vote to the North (which the Emancipation Proclamation had not done); some in the women's movement opposed the amendment on the grounds that it did nothing for the rights of women.

Final Solution The plan of Adolf Hitler and Nazi Germany to eliminate Jewish civilization from Europe. By the end of the war in 1945, nearly 6 million Jews had been executed. The full extent of Germany's atrocities was not known in Europe and the United States until near the end of World War II.

fireside chats Broadcasts on the radio by Franklin Roosevelt addressed directly to the American people that made many Americans feel that he personally cared about them. FDR did 16 of these in his first two terms. Many Americans in the 1930s had pictures of Roosevelt in their living rooms. In addition, Roosevelt received more letters from ordinary Americans than any other president in American history.

First Continental Congress A 1774 meeting in Philadelphia at which colonists vowed to resist further efforts to tax them without their consent.

First Great Awakening A religious revival in the American colonies that lasted from the 1720s through the 1740s; speakers like Jonathan Edwards enraptured speakers with sermons such as "Sinners in the Hands of an Angry God." Religious splits in the colonies became deeper because of this movement.

flapper A "new woman" of the 1920s, who wore short skirts and bobbed hair and rejected many of the social regulations that controlled women of previous generations.

Force Act of 1832 Legislation that gave President Andrew Jackson the power to invade any state if that action was necessary to enforce federal law. The bill was in response to nullification of federal tariff regulation by the legislature of South Carolina.

Fordney-McCumber Tariff of 1922 Act that sharply increased tariffs on imported goods. Most Republican leaders of the 1920s firmly believed in "protectionist" policies that would increase profits for American businesses.

Fort Sumter Federal fort located in Charleston, South Carolina, that was fired on by Confederate artillery on April 12, 1861; these were the first shots actually fired in the Civil War. A public outcry immediately followed across the Northern states, and the mobilization of a federal army began.

Fourteen Points Woodrow Wilson's view of a post–World War I that he hoped the other Allied powers would endorse during the negotiations for the Treaty of Versailles. Wilson's vision included elimination of secret treaties, arms reduction, national self-determination, and the creation of a League of Nations. After negotiations, only the League of Nations remained (which the United States never became part of).

Fourteenth Amendment Ratified in 1868, this amendment stated that "all persons born or naturalized in the United States" were citizens. In addition, all former Confederate supporters were prohibited from holding office in the United States.

Franciscans Missionaries who established settlements in the Southwestern United States in the late 1500s; at their missions Christian conversion was encouraged, but at the same time Native Americans were used as virtual slaves. Rebellions against the missions and the soldiers sent to protect them began in 1598.

Fredericksburg, Battle of Battle on December 13, 1862, where the Union army commanded by General Ambrose Burnside suffered a major defeat at the hands of Confederate forces.

Free Speech Movement Protests at the University of California at Berkeley in 1964 and 1965 that opposed the control that the university, and "the establishment" in general, had over the lives of university students. Protesters demanded changes in university regulations and also broader changes in American society.

free trade The philosophy that trade barriers and protective tariffs inhibit long-term economic growth; this philosophy was the basis for the 1994 ratification by the United States of the North American Free Trade Agreement (NAFTA), which removed trade restrictions between the United States, Mexico, and Canada.

freedmen Term used for free blacks in the South after the Civil War. Freedmen enjoyed some gains in terms of education, the ability to hold office, and economic well-being during the Reconstruction era, although many of these gains were wiped out after the Compromise of 1877.

Freedom Rides Buses of black and white civil rights workers who in 1961 rode on interstate buses to the Deep South to see if Southern states were abiding by the 1960 Supreme Court ruling banning segregation on interstate buses and in waiting rooms and restaurants at bus stations. Buses met mob violence in numerous cities; federal marshals were finally called in to protect the freedom riders.

Freeport Doctrine Introduced by Stephen Douglas in the Lincoln-Douglas debates, the idea that despite the *Dred Scott* Supreme Court decision, a territory could still prevent slavery by electing officials who were opposed to it and by creating laws and regulations that would make slavery impossible to enforce.

Free-Soil party Political party that won 10 percent of the vote in the 1848 presidential election. They were opposed to the spread of slavery into any of the recently acquired American territories. Free-Soil supporters were mainly many former members of the Whig party in the North.

French and Indian War Called the Seven Years' War in European textbooks. In this war, the British and the French fought for the right to expand their empire in the Americas. Colonists and Native Americans fought on both sides, and the war eventually spread to Europe and elsewhere. The English emerged victorious, and in the end received all of French Canada.

Fugitive Slave Act Part of the Compromise of 1850, this legislation set up special commissions in Northern states to determine if an accused runaway slave really was one. According to regulations, after the verdict, commissioners were given more money if the accused was found to be a runaway than if he or she was found not to be one. Some Northern legislatures passed laws attempting to circumvent the Fugitive Slave Act.

Gadsden Purchase Strip of territory running through Arizona and New Mexico that the United States purchased from Mexico in 1853. President Pierce authorized this purchase to secure that the southern route of the transcontinental railroad (between Texas and California) would be in American territory.

Geneva Accords After the French were defeated in Vietnam, a series of agreements made in 1954 temporarily divided Vietnam into two parts (along the 17th parallel) and promised nationwide elections within two years. To prevent Communists from gaining control, the United States installed a friendly government in South Vietnam and saw that the reunification elections never took place.

Gettysburg Address Speech made by Abraham Lincoln at dedication ceremony for a cemetery for Union soldiers who died at the Battle of Gettysburg. In this November 19, 1863 speech Lincoln stated that freedom should exist in the United States for *all* men, and that "government of the people, by the people, for the people, shall not perish from the earth."

Gettysburg, Battle of The most important battle of the Civil War, this July 1863 victory by Union forces prevented General Robert E. Lee from invading the North. Defeat at Gettysburg, along with defeat at the Battle of Vicksburg during the same month, turned the tide of war firmly in the direction of Union forces.

Ghent, Treaty of (1814) Treaty between the United States and Great Britain ending the War of 1812; treaty restored diplomatic relations between the two countries but did nothing to address the issues that had initially caused the war.

Ghost Dances Religion practiced by Lakota tribesmen in response to repeated incursions by American settlers. Ghost dancers thought that a Native American messiah would come and banish the whites, return the buffalo, and give all former Native American land back to the Native Americans. Worried territorial officials had Sitting Bull arrested (he was later killed under uncertain circumstances) and killed another 240 Lakota at Wounded Knee Creek.

GIs Popular term for an American servicemen during World War II; refers to the fact that virtually anything worn or used was "government issued."

GI Bill Officially called the Serviceman's Readjustment Act of 1944, this legislation gave many benefits to returning World War II veterans, including financial assistance for veterans wanting to go to college or enter other job training programs, special loan programs for veterans wanting to buy homes or businesses, and preferential treatment for veterans who wished to apply for government jobs.

Gilded Age, The Some historians describe the late nineteenth century in this manner, describing it as an era with a surface of great prosperity hiding deep problems of social inequity and shallowness of culture. The term comes from the title of an 1873 Mark Twain novel.

globalization Belief that the United States should work closely with other nations of the world to solve common problems; this was the foreign policy approach of President Clinton. Policies that supported this approach included the ratification of NAFTA, the United States working more closely with the United Nations, and "nation building" abroad. Many policies of globalization were initially rejected by Clinton's successor, George W. Bush.

Glorious Revolution English revolution of 1688 to 1689 when King James II was removed from the throne and his Protestant daughter Mary and her Dutch husband William began to rule. Reaction to this in the American colonies was varied: There was a revolt against appointed Catholic officials in New York and Maryland, and in Massachusetts the governor was sent back to England with the colonial demand that the Dominion of New England be disbanded.

gold standard Economic system that based all currency on gold, meaning that all paper currency could be exchanged at a bank for gold. Business interests of the late nineteenth century supported this. William Jennings Bryan ran for president three times opposing the gold standard, and supported the free coinage of silver instead.

"Gospel of Wealth" The philosophy of steel magnate Andrew Carnegie, who stated that wealthy industrialists had an obligation to create a "trust fund" from their profits to help their local communities. By the time of his death, Carnegie had given over 90 percent of his wealth to various foundations and philanthropic endeavors.

Grange Initially formed in 1867, the Grange was an association of farmers that provided social activities and information about new farming techniques. Some local Grange organizations became involved in cooperative buying and selling.

Great Compromise Plan drafted by Roger Sherman of Connecticut that stated one house of the U.S. Congress would be based on population (the House of Representatives), while in the other house all states would be represented equally with two representatives per state (the Senate). This compromise greatly speeded the ratification of the Constitution.

Great Migration Migration of large numbers of American blacks to Midwestern and Eastern industrial cities that began during World War I and continued throughout the 1920s. Additional workers were needed in the North because of the war and during the 1920s because of immigration restrictions. Blacks were willing to leave the South because of continued lynchings there and the fact that their economic situation was not improving.

Great Society Aggressive program announced by President Lyndon Johnson in 1965 to attack the major social problems in America; Great Society programs included the War on Poverty, Medicare and Medicaid programs for elderly Americans, greater protection for and more legislation dealing with civil rights, and greater funding for education. Balancing the Great Society and the war in Vietnam would prove difficult for the Johnson administration.

Greenback party Political party of the 1870s and early 1880s that stated the government should put more money in circulation and supported an eight-hour workday and female suffrage. The party received support from farmers but never built a national base. The Greenback party argued into the 1880s that more greenbacks should be put in circulation to help farmers who were in debt and who saw the prices of their products decreasing annually.

"greenbacks" Paper money issued by the American government during and immediately after the Civil War that was not backed up by gold or silver.

gridlock Situation when the president is a member of one political party and the U.S. Congress is controlled by the other party, causing a situation where little legislation is actually passed. This is how some describe the situation with President Clinton and the Republican-controlled Congress after the 1994 congressional elections.

Guadalcanal, Battle of Battle over this Pacific island lasted from August 1942 through February 1943. American victory against fierce Japanese resistance was the first major offensive victory for the Americans in the Pacific War.

Guadalupe Hidalgo, Treaty of Treaty ending the war with Mexico that was ratified by the Senate in March 1848 and for $15 million gave the United States Texas territory to the Rio Grande River, New Mexico, and California.

Gulf of Tonkin Resolution (1964) Congressional resolution that gave President Johnson the authority to "take all necessary measures to repel" attacks against American military forces stationed in Vietnam. Later, critics would charge, this resolution allowed the president to greatly expand the Vietnam War without congressional oversight.

Harlem Renaissance Black literary and artistic movement centered in Harlem that lasted from the 1920s into the early 1930s that both celebrated and lamented black life in America; Langston Hughes and Zora Neale Hurston were two famous writers of this movement.

Hartford Convention Meeting of New England Federalists in the closing months of the War of 1812 where they threatened that New England would secede from the United States unless trade restrictions imposed by President Madison were lifted. American victory in the war made their protests seem pointless.

Hawley-Smoot Tariff In response to the initial effects of the Great Depression, Congress authorized this tariff in 1930; this established tariff rates on imported goods at the highest level of any point in U.S. history. Some American companies benefited in the short term, although the effect on world trade was disastrous, as many other countries erected tariff barriers on American imports.

Haymarket Square Location in Chicago of labor rally called by anarchists and other radical labor leaders on May 2, 1886. A bomb was hurled toward police officials, and police opened fire on the demonstrators; numerous policemen and demonstrators were killed and wounded. Response in the nation's press was decidedly antiunion.

Head Start One of Lyndon Johnson's War on Poverty programs that gave substantial funding for a nursery school program to prepare children of poor parents for kindergarten.

heavy industry The production of steel, iron, and other materials that can be used for building purposes; great increase in heavy industry fueled the massive industrial growth that took place in the last half of the nineteenth century.

Hessians German troops who fought in the Revolutionary War on the side of Great Britain; Hessian troops were almost all paid mercenaries.

Historiography The study of history and how it is written. Students of historiography would analyze various historical interpretations and the viewpoints of historians. This field is not as concerned with historical events themselves as it is with how these events are interpreted.

holding company A company that existed to gain monopoly control over an industry by buying large numbers of shares of stock in as many companies as possible in that industry. The best example in American history was John D. Rockefeller's Standard Oil corporation.

Holocaust Historical term used for the extermination of 6 million Jewish victims by Nazi Germany during World War II. Much has been written on the reasons for the Holocaust and why it occurred in Germany.

Homeland Security Act of 2002 States that it is the mission of the Department of Homeland Security to prevent terrorist attacks within the United States, reduce the vulnerability of the United States to terror, and minimize the damage and assist in the recovery from a terrorist attack that might occur in the United States.

Homestead Act of 1862 Enactment by Congress that gave 160 acres of publicly owned land to a farmer who lived on the land and farmed it for two years. The provisions of this bill inspired hundreds of thousands of Americans to move westward in the years after the Civil War.

Hoovervilles Groups of crude houses made of cardboard and spare wood that sprang up on the fringes of many American cities during the first years of the Great Depression. These shacks were occupied by unemployed workers; the name of these communities demonstrated the feeling that President Hoover should have been doing more to help the downtrodden in America.

horizontal integration The strategy of gaining as much control over an entire single industry as possible, usually by creating trusts and holding companies. The most successful example of horizontal integration was John D. Rockefeller and Standard Oil, who had at one point controlled over 92 percent of the oil production in the United States.

HUAC (House Un-American Activities Committee) Committee of the House of Representatives that beginning in 1947 investigated possible Communist infiltration of the entertainment industry and, more importantly, of the government. Most famous investigations of the committee were the investigation of the "Hollywood Ten" and the investigation of Alger Hiss, a former high-ranking member of the State Department.

Huguenots Protestants in France, who by the 1630s were believers in Calvinism. Few Huguenots ended up settling in the Americas, as French officials feared they would disrupt the unity of colonial settlements.

Hull House Established by Jane Addams and Ellen Gates Starr in Chicago in 1889, this was the first settlement house in America. Services such as reading groups, social clubs, an employment bureau, and a "day care center" for working mothers could be found at Hull House. The Hull House model was later copied in many other urban centers.

"Hun" Term used in Allied propaganda during World War I to depict the German soldier; Germans were portrayed as bloodthirsty beasts. World War I was the first war where propaganda was used on a widespread scale.

Hundred Days The period from March through June 1933; the first 100 days of the New Deal presidency of Franklin Roosevelt. During this period programs were implemented to assist farmers, the banks, unemployed workers, and businessmen. In addition, Prohibition was repealed.

hunter-gatherers Early civilizations that existed not by farming but by moving from region to region and taking what was necessary at the time from the land; some early Native American tribes in northern New England lived as hunter-gatherers.

hydrogen bomb Atomic weapons much more powerful than those used at Hiroshima and Nagasaki; these were developed and repeatedly tested by both the United States and the Soviet Union in the 1950s, increasing dramatically the potential danger of nuclear war.

impeachment The process of removing an elected public official from office. During the Progressive Era several states adopted measures making it easier to do this. Presidents Andrew Johnson and William Jefferson Clinton were both impeached by the House of Representatives, but neither was convicted by the U.S. Senate (the procedure outlined in the Constitution of the United States).

impressment British practice of forcing civilians and ex-sailors back into naval service. During the wars against Napoleon. The British seized nearly 7,500 sailors from American ships, including some that had actually become American citizens. This practice caused increased tensions between the United States and Great Britain and was one of the causes of the War of 1812.

Inca empire Advanced and wealthy civilization centered in the Andes mountain region; aided by smallpox, Francisco Pizarro conquered the Incas in 1533.

indentured servants Legal arrangement when an individual owed compulsory service (in some cases only 3 years, in others up to 10) for free passage to the American colonies. Many of the early settlers in the Virginia colony came as indentured servants.

Industrial Workers of the World (IWW) Established in 1905, this union attempted to unionize the unskilled workers who were usually not recruited by the American Federation of Labor. The IWW included blacks, poor sharecroppers, and newly arrived immigrants from Eastern Europe. Members of the union were called "Wobblies," and leaders of the union were inspired by Marxist principles.

Influence of Sea Power upon History, The Very influential 1890s book by Admiral Alfred Thayer Mahan, which argued that throughout history the most powerful nations have achieved their influence largely because of powerful navies. Mahan called for a large increase in the size of the American navy, the acquisition of American bases in the Pacific, and the building of the Panama Canal.

initiative process Procedure supported by the Populist party in the 1890s by which any proposed law could go on the public ballot as long as a petition with an appropriate number of names is submitted beforehand supporting the proposed law.

internment camps Controversial decision was made after the bombing of Pearl Harbor to place Japanese Americans living on the West Coast in these camps. President Roosevelt authorized this by Executive Order #9066; this order was validated by the Supreme Court in 1944. In 1988 the U.S. government paid compensation to surviving detainees.

Interstate Commerce Act Passed in 1887, the bill created America's first regulatory commission, the Interstate Commerce Commission. The task of this commission was to regulate the railroad and railroad rates, and to ensure that rates were "reasonable and just."

Intolerable Acts Term used by anti-British speakers across the colonies for the series of bills passed in Great Britain to punish the Massachusetts colony for the Boston Tea Party of December 1773. These including the closing of Boston harbor, prohibiting local meetings, and mandatory quartering of troops in the homes of Massachusetts residents.

Iran-Contra Affair During the second term of the Reagan administration, government officials sold missiles to Iran (hoping that this would help free American hostages held in Lebanon); money from this sale was used to aid anti-communist Contra forces in Nicaragua. Iran was a country that was supposed to be on the American "no trade" list because of their taking of American hostages, and congressional legislation had been enacted making it illegal to give money to the Contras. A major scandal for the Reagan administration.

Iranian Hostage Crisis On November 4, 1979, Islamic Fundamentalists seized the American embassy in Tehran, Iran, and took all Americans working there hostage. This was a major humiliation for the United States, as diplomatic and military efforts to free the hostages failed. The hostages were finally freed on January 20, 1981, immediately after the inauguration of Ronald Reagan.

iron curtain In a March 5, 1946, speech in Fulton, Missouri, Winston Churchill used this term to describe the division that the Soviet Union had created between itself and its Eastern European Allies and Western Europe and the United States. Churchill emphasized the need for the United States to stand up to potential Soviet aggression in the future.

ironclad ship Civil War-era ships that were totally encased in iron, thus making them very difficult to damage; the ironclad of the Confederate army was the *Virginia* (it had been the *Merrimac* when it was captured from the Union), whereas the Union ship was the *Monitor*. The two ships battled each other in March 1862, with both being badly damaged.

"irreconcilables" After World War I, a group of U.S. senators who were opposed to a continued U.S. presence in Europe in any form. This group was influential in preventing the passage of the Versailles Treaty in the Senate.

island-hopping A successful American military tactic in the Pacific in 1942 and 1943 of taking strategic islands that could be used as staging points for continued military offensives. Increasing American dominance in air power made this tactic possible.

isolationism A policy of disengaging the United States from major world commitments and concentrating on the U.S. domestic issues. This was the dominant foreign policy of the United States for much of the 1920s and the 1930s.

Jay's Treaty of 1794 Treaty between the United States and Great Britain designed to ease increasing tensions between the two nations. The British did make some concessions to the Americans, including abandoning the forts they occupied in the interior of the continent. However, Britain refused to make concessions to America over the

rights of American ships. Tensions over this issue would eventually be a cause of the War of 1812.

Jazz Age Term used to describe the image of the liberated, urbanized 1920s, with a flapper as a dominant symbol of that era. Many rural, fundamentalist Americans deeply resented the changes in American culture that occurred in the "Roaring 20s."

Jazz Singer, The 1927 film starring Al Jolson that was the first movie with sound. Story of the film deals with a young Jewish man who has to choose between the "modern" and his Jewish past.

Jesuits Missionary group who established settlements in Florida, New Mexico, Paraguay, and in several areas within French territory in North America. Jesuits were organized with military precision and order.

jingoism American foreign policy based on a strident nationalism, a firm belief in American world superiority, and a belief that military solutions were, in almost every case, the best ones. Jingoism was most evident in America during the months leading up to and during the Spanish-American War.

judicial review In the 1803 *Marbury v. Madison* decision, Chief Justice John C. Marshall stated that the U.S. Supreme Court ultimately had the power to decide on the constitutionality of any law passed by the U.S. Congress or by the legislature of any state. Many had argued that individual states should have the power to do this; the *Marbury* decision increased the power of the federal government.

Judiciary Act of 1801 Bill passed by the Federalist Congress just before the inauguration of President Thomas Jefferson; Federalists appointed by this bill attempted to maintain control of the judiciary by reducing the number of Supreme Court judges (so Jefferson probably wouldn't be able to name a replacement) and by increasing the number of federal judges (who President Adams appointed before he left office). Bill was repealed by new Congress in 1802.

Justice Reorganization Bill Franklin Roosevelt's 1937 plan to increase the number of Supreme Court justices. He claimed that this was because many of the judges were older and needed help keeping up with the work. In reality he wanted to "pack the court" because the Court had made several rulings outlawing New Deal legislation. Many Democrats and Republicans opposed this plan, so it was finally dropped by Roosevelt.

kamikaze pilots 1945 tactic of Japanese air force where pilots flew at American ships at full speed and crashed into them, in several cases causing ships to sink. This tactic showed the desperate nature of the Japanese military situation at this time. By July 1945, kamikaze attacks were no longer utilized, as Japan was running out of airplanes and pilots.

Kansas-Nebraska Act of 1854 Compromise legislation crafted by Stephen Douglas that allowed the settlers in the Kansas and Nebraska territories to decide if those territories would be slave or free. Bill caused controversy and bloodshed throughout these territories; in the months before the vote in Kansas, large numbers of "settlers" moved in to influence the vote, and after the vote (won by proslavery forces), violence between the two sides intensified.

Kent State University Site of May 1970 antiwar protest where Ohio National Guardsmen fired on protesters, killing four. To many, this event was symbolic of the extreme political tensions that permeated American society in this era.

Kentucky and Virginia Resolves Passed by the legislatures in these two states, these resolutions maintained that the Alien and Sedition Acts championed through Congress by John Adams went beyond the powers that the Constitution stated belonged to the federal government. These resolves predated the later Southern argument that individual states could "nullify" federal laws deemed unconstitutional by the states.

Kerner Commission Established in 1967 to study the reason for urban riots, the commission spoke at length about the impact of poverty and racism on the lives of urban blacks in America, and emphasized that white institutions created and condoned the ghettoes of America.

King-Crane Commission The American commission that went into various regions of the Middle East immediately after World War I to discover what political future was desired by residents of the region. It was determined that many did not want to be controlled by Britain and France, and saw the United States in a favorable light. Predictably, the British and French saw to it that the findings of the commission were largely kept quiet.

King William's War Colonial war against the French that lasted from 1689 to 1697; army from New England colonies attacked Quebec, but were forced to retreat because of the lack of strong colonial leadership and an outbreak of smallpox among colonial forces.

Kitchen Cabinet An informal group of advisors, with no official titles, who the president relies on for advice. The most famous Kitchen Cabinet was that of Andrew Jackson, who met with several old political friends and two journalists for advice on many occasions.

Knights of Labor The major labor union of the 1880s; was not a single large union, but a federation of the unions of many industries. The Knights of Labor accepted unskilled workers. Publicity against the organization was intense after the Haymarket Square riot of 1886.

Know-Nothing party Political party developed in the 1850s that claimed that the other political parties and the entire political process were corrupt, that immigrants were destroying the economic base of America by working for low wages, and that Catholics in America were intent on destroying American democracy. Know-Nothings were similar in many ways to other nativist groups that developed at various points in America's history.

Korean War (1950 to 1953) War in which American and other UN forces fought to stop Communist aggression against South Korea. U.S. entry into the Korean War was totally consistent with the U.S. cold war policy of containment. Negotiated settlement divided Korea along the 38th parallel, a division that remains today.

Ku Klux Klan Organization founded in the South during the Reconstruction era by whites who wanted to maintain white supremacy in the region. The KKK used terror tactics, including murder. The Klan was revitalized in the 1920s; members of the 1920s Klan also opposed Catholics and Southern and Eastern European immigrants. The KKK exists to this day, with recent efforts to make the Klan appear to be "respectable."

labor movement The drive that began in the second half of the nineteenth century to have workers join labor unions. Divisions existed in nineteenth-century unions as to whether unions should focus their energies on political gains for workers or on "bread and butter" issues important to workers. In the twenty-first century, unions have broad political powers, as most endorse and financially support candidates in national and statewide elections.

laissez-faire economic principles Economic theory derived from eighteenth-century economist Adam Smith, who stated that for the economy to run soundly the government should take a hands-off role in economic matters. Those who have favored policies such as high import tariffs do *not* follow laissez-faire policies; a policy like NAFTA has more support among the "free market" supporters of Adam Smith.

land speculation The practice of buying up land with the intent of selling it off in the future for a profit. Land speculation existed in the Kentucky territory in the 1780s, throughout the West after the Homestead Act, and in Florida in the 1920s, when hundreds bought Florida swampland hoping to later sell it for a profit.

League of Nations International body of nations that was proposed by Woodrow Wilson and was adopted at the Versailles Peace Conference ending World War I. The League was never an effective body in reducing international tensions, at least partially because the United States was never a member of it.

Lend-Lease Act Legislation proposed by Franklin Roosevelt and adopted by Congress in 1941, stating that the United States could either sell or lease arms and other equipment to any country whose security was vital to America's interest. After the passage of this bill, military equipment to help the British war effort began to be shipped from the United States.

Letters from a Farmer in Pennsylvania A 1767 pamphlet by Pennsylvania attorney and land-owner John Dickinson, in which he eloquently stated the "taxation without representation" argument, and also stated that the only way that the House of Commons could represent the colonies in a meaningful way would be for actual colonists to be members of it.

Lever Food and Fuel Control Act August 1917 measure that gave President Wilson the power to regulate the production and consumption of food and fuels during wartime. Some in his administration argued for price controls and rationing; instead, Wilson instituted voluntary controls.

Levittown After World War II, the first "suburban" neighborhood; located in Hempstead, Long Island, houses in this development were small, looked the same, but were perfect for the postwar family that wanted to escape urban life. Levittown would become a symbol of the post–World War II flight to suburbia taken by millions.

Lewis and Clark Expedition (1804 to 1806) Mission sent by Thomas Jefferson to explore and map the newly acquired Louisiana territory and to create good relations with various Native American tribes within the territory. Reports brought back indicated that settlement was possible in much of the region, and that the Louisiana territory was well worth what had been paid for it.

Lexington Massachusetts town where the first skirmish between British troops and colonial militiamen took place; during this April 19, 1775, "battle," eight colonists were killed and another nine were wounded.

Liberator, The The radical abolitionist journal of William Lloyd Garrison that was first published in 1831. Garrison and his journal presented the most extreme abolitionist views during the period leading up to the Civil War.

Liberty Bonds Sold to United States civilians during World War I. A holder who paid $10 for a bond could get $13 back if the holder held on to the bond until it matured. Bonds were important in financing the war effort, and celebrities such as Charlie Chaplin made short films encouraging Americans to buy them.

Little Bighorn, Battle of the (1876) Montana battle where Colonel George Custer and more than 200 of his men were killed by a group of Cheyenne and Lakota warriors. This was the last major victory by Native American forces over a U.S. army unit.

London Company In 1603 King James I gave the London Company a charter to settle the Virginia territory. In April 1607, the first settlers from this company settled at Jamestown.

"Lost Generation" Group of American intellectuals who viewed America in the 1920s as bigoted, intellectually shallow, and consumed by the quest for the dollar. Many became extremely disillusioned with American life and went to Paris. Ernest Hemingway wrote of this group in *The Sun Also Rises*.

Louisiana Purchase The 1803 purchase of the huge Louisiana territory (from the Mississippi River out to the Rocky Mountains) from Napoleon for $15 million. This purchase made eventual westward movement possible for vast numbers of Americans.

Lowell System Developed in the textile mills of Lowell, Massachusetts, in the 1820s. In these factories as much machinery as possible was used, so that few skilled workers were needed in the process, and the workers were almost all single young farm women who worked for a few years and then returned home to be housewives. Managers found these young women were the perfect workers for this type of factory life.

Loyalists Individuals who remained loyal to Great Britain during the years up to and during the Revolutionary War. Many who were Loyalists were from the higher strata of colonial society; when war actually broke out and it became apparent that the British were not going to quickly win, almost all went to Canada, the West Indies, or back to Great Britain.

Loyalty Review Board This were established in 1947 in an effort to control possible Communist influence in the American government. These boards were created to investigate the possibility of "security risks" working for the American government, and to determine if those "security risks" should lose their jobs. Some employees were released because of their affiliation with "unacceptable" political organizations or because of their sexual orientation.

Lusitania British passenger liner with 128 Americans on board that was sunk off the coast of Ireland by a German U-boat on May 7, 1915. This sinking caused outrage in the United States and was one of a series of events that drew the United States closer to war with Germany.

Man in the Gray Flannel Suit, The Early 1950s book and movie that compares the sterility, sameness, and lack of excitement of postwar work and family life with the vitality felt by many World War II veterans during their wartime experiences.

Manhattan Project Program begun in 1942 to develop an atomic weapon for the United States. The project was aided by German scientists added to the research team who had been working on a similar bomb in Germany. First test of the bomb took place in New Mexico on July 16, 1945.

Manifest Destiny Term first used in the 1840s, the concept that America's expansion westward was as journalist John O'Sullivan said, "the fulfillment of our Manifest Destiny to overspread the continent allotted by Providence for the free development of our yearly multiplying millions."

Marbury v. Madison (**1803**) Decision of this case written by Chief Justice John Marshall established the principle of judicial review, meaning that the Supreme Court ultimately has the power to decide if any federal or state law is unconstitutional.

March on Washington Over 200,000 came to Washington for this August 1963 event demanding civil rights for blacks. A key moment of the proceedings was Martin Luther King's "I have a dream" speech; the power of the civil rights movement was not lost on Lyndon Johnson, who pushed for civil rights legislation when he became president the following year.

Marshall Plan Plan announced in 1947 whereby the United States would help to economically rebuild Europe after the war; 17 Western European nations became part of the plan. The United States introduced the plan so that communism would not spread across war-torn Europe and bring other European countries into the Communist camp.

martial law During a state of emergency, when rule of law may be suspended and government is controlled by military or police authorities. During the Civil War, Kentucky was placed under martial law by President Lincoln.

Massacre at Wounded Knee December 28, 1890, "battle" that was the last military resistance of Native Americans of the Great Plains against American encroachment. Minneconjou Indians were at Wounded Knee Creek. American soldiers attempted to take their arms from them. After shooting began, 25 American soldiers died, along with more than 200 men, women, and children of the Indian tribe.

massive retaliation Foreign policy officials in the Eisenhower administration believed the best way to stop communism was to convince the Communists that every time they advanced, there would be massive retaliation against them. This policy explains the desire in this era to increase the nuclear arsenal of the United States.

McCarran Internal Security Act Congressional act enacted in 1950 that stated all members of the Communist party had to register with the office of the Attorney General and that it was a crime to conspire to foster communism in the United States.

McCarran-Walter Act of 1952 Bill that limited immigration from everywhere except Northern and Western Europe and stated that immigration officials could turn any immigrant away that they thought might threaten the national security of the United States.

McCarthyism Named after Wisconsin Senator Joseph McCarthy, the title given for the movement that took place during the late 1940s and early 1950s in American politics to root out potential Communist influence in the government, the military, and the entertainment industry. Harsh tactics were often used by congressional investigations, with few actual Communists ever discovered. This period is seen by many today as an era of intolerance and paranoia.

Meat Inspection Act Inspired by Upton Sinclair's *The Jungle,* this 1906 bill established a government commission that would monitor the quality of all meat sold in America and inspect the meatpacking houses for safety and cleanliness.

Medicare Part of Lyndon Johnson's Great Society program, this program acted as a form of health insurance for retired Americans (and disabled ones as well). Through Medicare, the federal government would pay for services received by elderly patients at doctor's offices and hospitals.

mercantilism Economic policy practiced by most European states in the late seventeenth century that stated the power of any state depended largely on its wealth; thus it was the state's duty to do all that it could to build up wealth. A mercantilist country would not want to import raw materials from other countries; instead, it would be best to have colonies from which these raw materials could be imported.

Merrimack Union ironclad ship captured by Confederates during the Civil War and renamed the *Virginia*.

Meuse-Argonne Offensive American forces played a decisive role in this September 1918 Allied offensive, which was the last major offensive of the war and which convinced the German general staff that victory in World War I was impossible.

Mexican-American War War fought over possession of Texas. The settlement ending this war gave the United States the northern part of Texas territory and the territories of New Mexico and California.

Middle Passage The voyage across the Atlantic Ocean taken by slaves on their way to the Americas. Sickness, diseases, and death were rampant as slave ships crossed the Atlantic; on some ships, over 20 percent of slaves who began the journey were dead by the time the ship landed.

"midnight appointments" Judicial or other appointments made by an outgoing president or governor in the last hours before he or she leaves office. The most famous were the judicial appointments made by John Adams in the hours before Thomas Jefferson was inaugurated as president.

Midway, Battle of June 4, 1942, naval battle that crippled Japanese offensive capabilities in the Pacific; American airplanes destroyed four aircraft carriers and over 200 Japanese planes. After Midway, Japanese military operations were mainly defensive.

Missouri Compromise In a continued effort to maintain a balance between free and slave states, Henry Clay proposed this 1820 compromise, which admitted Maine to the Union as a free state, Missouri to the Union as a slave state, and stated that any part of the Louisiana Territory north of 36 degrees, 30 minutes would be nonslave territory.

Model T Automobile produced by Ford Motor Company using assembly line techniques. The first Model Ts were produced in 1907; using the assembly line, Ford produced half of the automobiles made in the world between 1907 and 1926.

Molasses Act In the early 1700s colonists traded for molasses with the French West Indies. British traders wanted to reduce trade between the colonies and the French; in 1733 they pressured Parliament to pass this act, which put prohibitively high duties on imported molasses. Colonists continued to smuggle French molasses into the Americas in spite of British efforts to prevent this.

Monitor Union ironclad ship utilized during the Civil War; fought one battle against the *Virginia*, the South's ironclad ship, and never left port again.

Monroe Doctrine President James Monroe's 1823 statement that an attack by a European state on any nation in the Western Hemisphere would be considered an attack on the United States; Monroe stated that the Western Hemisphere was the hemisphere of the United States and not of Europe. Monroe's statement was scoffed at by certain European political leaders, especially those in Great Britain.

Montgomery bus boycott Year-long refusal by blacks to ride city buses in Montgomery, Alabama, because of their segregation policies. Boycott began in December 1955; Supreme Court finally ruled that segregation on public buses was unconstitutional. Rosa Parks began the protest when she was arrested for refusing to give up her seat for a white man, and Martin Luther King was a young minister involved in organizing the boycott.

Morrill Land-Grant Act (1862) Federal act designed to fund state "land-grant" colleges. State governments were given large amounts of land in the western territories; this land was sold to individual settlers, land speculators, and others, and the profits of these land sales could be used to establish the colleges.

Ms. Founded in 1972 by Gloria Steinem, this glossy magazine was aimed at feminist readers.

muckrakers Journalists of the Progressive era who attempted to expose the evils of government and big business. Many muckrakers wrote of the corruption of city and state political machines. Factory conditions and the living and working conditions of workers were other topics that some muckrakers wrote about.

My Lai Massacre In 1968 a unit under the command of Lieutenant William Calley killed over 300 men, women, and children in this small Vietnamese village. The antiwar movement took the attack as a symbol of the "immorality" of U.S. efforts in Vietnam.

NAFTA (North American Free Trade Agreement) Ratified in 1994 by the U.S. Senate, this agreement established a free trade zone between the United States, Mexico, and Canada. Critics of the agreement claim that many jobs have been lost in the United States because of it.

napalm Jellylike substance dropped from American planes during the Vietnam conflict that horribly burned the skin of anyone who came into contact with it. On several occasions, napalm was accidentally dropped on "friendly" villages.

Nation of Islam Supporters were called Black Muslims; this group was founded by Elijah Muhammad and preached Islamic principles along with black pride and black separatism. Malcolm X was a member of the Nation of Islam.

National American Woman Suffrage Association The major organization for suffrage for women, it was founded in 1890 by Susan B. Anthony and Elizabeth Cady Stanton. It supported the Wilson administration during World War I and split with the more radical National Woman's Party, which, in 1917, began to picket the White House because Wilson had not forcefully stated that women should get the vote.

National Association for the Advancement of Colored People (NAACP) Formed in 1909, this organization fought for and continues to fight for the rights of blacks in America. The NAACP originally went to court for the plaintiff in the *Brown v. Board of Education* case, and Thurgood Marshall, the NAACP's chief counsel and later a Supreme Court justice, was the main attorney in the case.

national bank Planned by Alexander Hamilton to be similar to the Bank of England, this bank was funded by government and private sources. Hamilton felt a national bank would give economic security and confidence to the new nation. Republicans who had originally opposed the bank felt the same way in 1815 when they supported Henry Clay's American System.

National Consumers League Formed in 1899, this organization was concerned with improving the working and living conditions of women in the workplace.

national culture When a general unity of tastes and a commonality of cultural experience exist in a nation; in a general sense, when a country starts to "think the same." This occurred in America for the first time in the 1920s; as many people saw the same movies, read the same magazines, and heard the same things on the radio, a national culture was born.

National Industrial Recovery Act (NIRA) (1933) New Deal legislation that created the Works Progress Administration (WPA) that created jobs to put people back to work right away and the National Recovery Administration (NRA), who worked in conjunction with industry to bolster the industrial sector and create more long-lasting jobs.

National Labor Relations Board (NLRB) Part of the 1935 Wagner Act, which was a huge victory for organized labor. The NLRB ensured that factory owners did not harass union organizers, ensured that collective bargaining was fairly practiced in labor disputes, and supervised union elections. The NLRB was given the legal "teeth" to force employers to comply with all of the above.

National Origins Act Very restrictive immigration legislation passed in 1924, which lowered immigration to 2 percent of each nationality as found in the 1890 census. This lowered immigration dramatically and, quite intentionally, almost eliminated immigration from Eastern and Southern Europe.

National Security League Organization founded in 1914 that preached patriotism and preparation for war. In 1915, they successfully lobbied government officials to set up camps to prepare men for military life and combat. The patriotism of this group became more strident as the war progressed. In 1917, they lobbied Congress to greatly limit immigration into the country.

National Woman's Party Formed by Alice Paul after women got the vote, this group lobbied unsuccessfully in the 1920s to get an Equal Rights Amendment for women added to the Constitution. Desire for this amendment would return among some feminist groups in the 1970s.

nativist Nativist sentiment was especially strong in the 1920s. Nativism states that immigration should be greatly limited or banned altogether, since immigrants hurt the United States economically and also threaten the social well-being of the country. Nativist groups and parties have developed on several occasions in both the nineteenth and the twentieth centuries.

NATO (North Atlantic Treaty Organization) Collective alliance of the United States and most of the Western European nations that was founded in 1949; an attack of one member of NATO was to be considered an attack on all. Many U.S. troops served in Europe during the cold war era because of the NATO alliance. To counter NATO, the Soviet Union created the Warsaw Pact in 1955.

Naval Act of 1900 Legislation that authorized a large increase in the building of ships to be used for offensive purposes; this measure helped ensure the creation of a world-class American navy.

Navigation Acts of 1660 Measures passed by Charles II that were designed to increase the dependence of the colonies on England for trade. Charles mandated that certain goods produced in the colonies, such as tobacco, should be sold only to England; that if the colonies wanted to sell anything to other countries it had to come through England first; and that all trade by the colonies to other countries would have to be done in English ships. These measures could have been devastating to the colonies; however, British officials in the colonies did not enforce them carefully.

Neoconservativism Modern American political philosophy that opposes big-government approaches to domestic issues yet favors an interventionist and aggressive foreign policy; most neoconservatives advocated American intervention in Iraq in 2003.

Neoconservatives (neocons) Group who wanted to use American might to remake the Middle Eastern region into a democracy. Neocons believed that to accomplish this, Saddam Hussein had to be removed from power in Iraq.

Neutrality Act of 1935 To prevent the United States from being drawn into potential European conflicts, this bill said that America would not trade arms with any country at war, and that any American citizen traveling on a ship of a country at war was doing so at his or her own risk.

Neutrality Act of 1939 Franklin Roosevelt got Congress to amend the Neutrality Act of 1935; new legislation stated that England and France could buy arms from the United States as long as there was cash "up front" for these weapons. This was the first military assistance that the United States gave the Allied countries.

New Deal Series of policies instituted by Franklin Roosevelt and his advisors from 1933 to 1941 that attempted to offset the effects of the Great Depression on American society. Many New Deal policies were clearly experimental; in the end it was the onset of World War II, and not the policies of the New Deal, that pulled the United States out of the Great Depression.

New Deal Coalition The coalition of labor unions and industrial workers, minorities, much of the middle class, and the Solid South that carried Franklin Roosevelt to victories in 1936 and 1940 and that was the basis of Democratic victories on a national level until this coalition started to break up in the late 1960s and early 1970s. A sizable number of this group voted for Ronald Reagan in the presidential elections of 1980 and 1984.

New Democrat Term used to describe Bill Clinton and his congressional supporters during his two terms in office. A New Democrat was pragmatic, and not tied to the old Democratic belief in big government; New Democrats took both Democratic and Republican ideas as they crafted their policies. Some in the Democratic party maintained that Clinton had actually sold out the principles of the party.

New Federalism A series of policies during the administration of Ronald Reagan that began to give some power back to the states that had always been held by the federal government. Some tax dollars were returned to state and local governments in the form of "block grants"; the state and local governments could then spend this money as they thought best.

New Freedom policy An approach favored by Southern and Midwestern Democrats, this policy stated that economic and political preparation for World War I should be done in a decentralized manner; this would prevent too much power falling into the hands of the federal government. President Wilson first favored this approach, but then established federal agencies to organize mobilization.

New Frontier The program of President John Kennedy to revitalize America at home and to reenergize America for continued battles against the Soviet Union. Kennedy asked young Americans to volunteer for programs such as the Peace Corps; as he said in his inaugural speech: "Ask not what your country can do for you—ask what you can do for your country."

"new immigrants" Immigrants that came from Southern and Eastern Europe, who made up the majority of immigrants coming into the United States after 1900. Earlier immigrants from Britain, Ireland, and Scandinavia appeared to be "like" the groups that were already settled in the United States; the "new immigrants" were very different. As a result, resentment and nativist sentiment developed against this group, especially in the 1920s.

New Jersey Plan As the U.S. Constitution was being debated and drafted, large and small states each offered proposals on how the legislature should be structured. The New Jersey Plan stated that the legislature should have a great deal of power to regulate trade, and that it should consist of one legislative house, with each state having one vote.

New Nationalism The series of Progressive reforms supported by Theodore Roosevelt as he ran for president on the Progressive or Bull Moose ticket in 1912. Roosevelt said that more had to be done to regulate big business and that neither of his opponents were committed to conservation.

New Right The conservative movement that began in the 1960s and triumphed with the election of Ronald Reagan in 1980. The New Right was able to attract many middle-class and Southern voters to the Republican party by emphasizing the themes of patriotism, a smaller government, and a return to "traditional values."

New South Concept promoted by Southerners in the late 1800s that the South had changed dramatically and was now interested in industrial growth and becoming a part of the national economy. A large textile industry did develop in the South beginning in the 1880s.

Nez Perce Plains Native American tribe that attempted to resist reservation life by traveling 1,500 miles with American military forces in pursuit. After being tracked and suffering cold and hardship, the Nez Perce finally surrendered and were forced onto a reservation in 1877.

Non-Intercourse Act In response to the failure of France and Britain to respect the rights of American ships at sea, President Madison supported this legislation in 1809, which authorized trade with all countries except Britain and France, and stated that trade exist with those countries as soon as they respected America's rights as a neutral power. The British and the French largely ignored this act.

Northwest Ordinances Bills passed in 1784, 1785, and 1787 that authorized the sale of lands in the Northwest Territory to raise money for the federal government; these bills also carefully laid out the procedures for eventual statehood for parts of these territories.

NOW (National Organization for Women) Formed in 1966, with Betty Friedan as its first president. NOW was at first interested in publicizing inequalities for women in the workplace; focus of the organization later turned to social issues and eventually the unsuccessful effort to pass an Equal Rights Amendment for women.

nuclear proliferation The massive buildup of nuclear weapons by the United States and the Soviet Union in the 1950s and into the 1960s; in the United States this was fostered in the belief that the threat of "massive retaliation" was the best way to keep the Soviet Union under control. The psychological effects of the atomic bomb on the populations of the Soviet Union and the United States were also profound.

nullification The belief that an individual state has the right to "nullify" any federal law that the state felt was unjust. Andrew Jackson was able to resolve a Nullification Crisis in 1832, but the concept of nullification was still accepted by many Southerners, and controversy over this was a cause of the Civil War.

Ocala Platform Platform of the Farmer's Alliances, formulated at an 1890 convention held in Ocala, Florida. This farmer's organization favored a graduated income tax, government control of the railroad, the unlimited coinage of silver, and the direct election of U.S. senators. Candidates supporting the farmers called themselves Populists and ran for public offices in the 1890s.

Old Age Revolving Pension Plan Conceived by California doctor Francis Townsend in 1934, this plan would give every retired American $200 a month, with the stipulation that it would have to be spent by the end of the month; Townsend claimed this would revitalize the economy by putting more money in circulation. A national tax of 2 percent on all business transactions was supposed to finance this plan. A large number of Townsend clubs were formed to support this plan.

"on the margin" The practice in the late 1920s of buying stock and only paying in cash 10 percent of the value of that stock; the buyer could easily borrow the rest from his or her stockbroker or investment banker. This system worked well as long as investors could sell their stocks at a profit and repay their loans. After the 1929 stock market crash, investors had to pay these loans back in cash.

OPEC Acronym for Organization of Petroleum Exporting Countries, this organization sets the price for crude oil and determines how much of it will be produced. The decision of OPEC to raise oil prices in 1973 had a dramatic economic impact in both the United States and the rest of the world.

Open Door policy The policy that China should be open to trade with all of the major powers, and that all, including the United States, should have equal rights to trade there. This was the official American position toward China as announced by Secretary of State John Hay in 1899.

Operation Desert Shield After Iraq invaded Kuwait on August 2, 1990, President Bush sent 230,000 American troops to protect Saudi Arabia.

Operation Desert Storm February 1991 attack on Iraqi forces in Kuwait by the United States and other allied forces; although Iraq was driven from Kuwait, Saddam Hussein remained in power in Iraq.

Oregon Trail Trail that took settlers from the Ohio River Valley through the Great Plains and the Rocky Mountains to Oregon. Settlers began moving westward along this trail in 1842; by 1860 over 325,000 Americans had traveled westward along the trail.

Oregon Treaty Both the United States and Great Britain claimed the Oregon territory; in 1815 they agreed to jointly control the region. In 1843 the settlers of Oregon declared that their territory would become an independent republic.

Palmer Raids Part of the Red Scare, these were measures to hunt out political radicals and immigrants who were potential threats to American security. Organized by Attorney General A. Mitchell Palmer in 1919 and 1920 (and carried out by J. Edgar Hoover), these raids led to the arrest of nearly 5,500 people and the deportation of nearly four hundred.

Panama Canal Crucial for American economic growth, the building of this canal was begun by American builders in 1904 and completed in 1914. The United States had to first engineer a Panamanian revolt against Colombia to guarantee a friendly government in Panama that would support the building of the canal. In 1978 the U.S. Senate voted to return the Panama Canal to Panamanian control.

panic of 1837 The American economy suffered a deep depression when Great Britain reduced the amount of credit it offered to the United States. American merchants and industrialists had to use their available cash to pay off debts, thus causing businesses to cut production and lay off workers.

Paris, Treaty of The treaty ending the Revolutionary War, and signed in 1783. By the terms of this treaty, the United States received the land between the Appalachian Mountains and the Mississippi River. The British did keep their Canadian territories.

Pendleton Civil Service Act of 1883 Act that established a civil service system. There were a number of government jobs that were filled by civil service examinations and not by the president appointing one of his political cronies. Some states also started to develop professional civil service systems in the 1880s.

Pentagon Papers A government study of American involvement in Vietnam that outlined in detail many of the mistakes that America had made there. In 1971, a former analyst for the Defense Department, Daniel Ellsberg, released these to the *New York Times*.

Platt Amendment For Cuba to receive its independence from the United States after the Spanish-American war, it had to agree to the Platt Amendment, which stated that the United States had the right to intervene in Cuban affairs if the Cuban government could not maintain control or if the independence of Cuba was threatened by external or internal forces.

Plumbers A group of intelligence officials who worked for the committee to reelect Richard Nixon in 1972; the job of this group was to stop leaks of information and perform "dirty tricks" on political opponents of the president. The Plumbers broke into the office of Daniel Ellsberg's psychiatrist, looking for damaging information against him and totally discredited the campaign of Democratic hopeful Edmund Muskie.

pocket veto A method a president can use to "kill" congressional legislation at the end of a congressional term. Instead of vetoing the bill, the president may simply not sign it; once the congressional term is over, the bill will then die.

political machine An organization that controls the politics of a city, a state, or even the country, sometimes by illegal or quasi-legal means. A machine employs a large number of people to do its "dirty work," for which they are either given some government job or are allowed to pocket government bribes or kickbacks. The "best" example of a political machine was the Tammany Hall organization that controlled New York City in the late nineteenth century.

Populist party Party that represented the farmers who scored major electoral victories in the 1890s, including the election of several members of the U.S. House of Representatives and the election of one U.S. senator. Populist candidates spoke against monopolies, wanted government to become "more democratic," and wanted more direct government action to help the working classes.

Port Huron Statement The manifesto of Students for a Democratic Society, a radical student group formed in 1960. The *Port Huron Statement* called for a greater role for university students in the nation's affairs, rejected the traditional role of the university, and rejected the foreign policy goals that America was embracing at the time.

Postmodernism A recent trend in cultural and historical study that doubts the existence of absolute historical certainties. It is impossible to know, for example, what "really happened" in the past; therefore, how individuals observe and interpret the past becomes a valuable source of analysis. Postmodernists would also reject statements such as "democracy is best for all nations of the world," and would emphasize the study of various historical viewpoints.

Potsdam Conference July 1945 conference between new president Harry Truman, Stalin, and Clement Atlee, who had replaced Churchill. Truman took a much tougher stance toward Stalin than Franklin Roosevelt had; little substantive agreement took place at this conference. Truman expressed reservations about the future role of the Soviet Union in Eastern Europe at this conference.

Powhatan Confederacy Alliance of Native American tribes living in the region of the initial Virginia settlement. Powhatan, leader of this alliance, tried to live in peace with the English settlers when they arrived in 1607.

primary source Actual documents or accounts from an era being studied, these are invaluable to historians. Almost all true historical research involves analysis of primary source documents. Examples would be a letter written by Napoleon, an account of someone who knew Napoleon personally, or a newspaper account from Napoleon's time.

professional bureaucracy Government officials that receive their positions after taking competitive civil service tests; they are not appointed in return for political favors. Many government jobs at the state and national level are filled in this manner beginning in the 1880s.

progressivism A movement that desired political and social reform, and was most influential in America from the 1890s up until World War I. Most popular Progressive causes included reforming city government, better conditions for urban workers, the education of newly arrived immigrants, and the regulation of big businesses.

proportional representation The belief that representation in a legislature should be based on population; the states with the largest populations should have the most representatives. When the Constitution was being formulated, the larger states wanted this; the smaller states favored "one vote per state." The eventual compromise, termed the Connecticut plan, created a two-house legislature.

proprietorships Settlements in America that were given to individuals who could govern and regulate the territory in any manner they desire. Charles I, for example, gave the Maryland territory to Lord Baltimore as a proprietorship.

Pure Food and Drug Act of 1906 Bill that created a federal Food and Drug Administration; example of consumer protection legislation of the Progressive Era, it was at least partially passed as a result of Upton Sinclair's novel *The Jungle*.

Puritans Group of religious dissidents who came to the New World so they would have a location to establish a "purer" church than the one that existed in England. The Puritans began to settle the Plymouth Colony in 1620 and settled the Massachusetts Bay Colony beginning in 1630. Puritans were heavily influenced by John Calvin and his concept of predestination.

putting-out system The first textile production system in England, where merchants gave wool to families who, in their homes, created yarn and then cloth. The merchants would then buy the cloth from the families and sell the finished product. Textile mills made this procedure more efficient.

Quartering Act of 1765 British edict stating that to help defend the empire, colonial governments had to provide accommodations and food for British troops. Many colonists considered this act to be the ultimate insult; they perceived that they were paying for the troops that were there to control the colonies.

Queen Anne's War (1702 to 1713) Called the War of the Spanish Succession in European texts, pitted England against France and Spain. Spanish Florida was attacked by the English in the early part of this war, and Native Americans fought for both sides in the conflict. The British emerged victorious and in the end received Hudson Bay and Nova Scotia from the French.

Radical Republicans Group of Republicans after the Civil War who favored harsh treatment of the defeated South and a dramatic restructuring of the economic and social systems in the South; favored a decisive elevation of the political, social, and economic position of former slaves.

ratifying conventions In late 1787 and in 1788 these were held in all states for the purpose of ratifying the new Constitution of the United States. In many states, approval of the Constitution was only approved by a small margin; in Rhode Island ratification was defeated. The Founding Fathers made an intelligent decision in calling for ratifying conventions to approve the Constitution instead of having state legislatures do it, since under the system proposed by the Constitution, some of the powers state legislatures had at the time would be turned over to the federal government.

ration cards Held by Americans during World War II, these recorded the amount of rationed goods such as automobile tires, gasoline, meat, butter, and other materials an individual had purchased. Where regulation in World War I had been voluntary, consumption in World War II was regulated by government agencies.

realpolitik Pragmatic policy of leadership, in which the leader "does what he or she has to do" in order to be successful. Morality has no place in the mindset of a leader practicing realpolitik. The late nineteenth-century German chancellor Otto von Bismarck is the best modern example of a leader practicing realpolitik.

Rebel Without a Cause 1955 film starring James Dean exploring the difficulties of family life and the alienation that many teenagers felt in the 1950s. Juvenile delinquency, and the reasons for it, was the subtext of this film, as well as the source of countless other 1950s-era movies aimed at the youth market.

recall process One of a number of reforms of the governmental system proposed by progressive-era thinkers. By the process of recall, the citizens of a city or state could remove an unpopular elected official from office in midterm. Recall was adopted in only a small number of communities.

reconcentration (1896) Spanish policy designed to control the Cuban people by forcing them to live in fortified camps; American outrage over this led some politicians to call for war against Spain.

Reconstruction Act Plan of Radical Republicans to control the former area of the Confederacy and approved by Congress in March 1867. The former Confederacy was divided into five military districts, with each controlled by a military commander (Tennessee was exempt from this). Conventions were to be called to create new state governments (former Confederate officials could not hold office in these governments).

Reconstruction Era The era following the Civil War where Radical Republicans initiated changes in the South that gave newly freed slaves additional economic, social, and political rights. These changes were greatly resented by many Southerners, causing the creation of organizations such as

the Ku Klux Klan. Reconstruction ended with the Compromise of 1877.

Reconstruction Finance Corporation Established in 1932 by Herbert Hoover to offset the effects of the Great Depression; the RFC was authorized to give federal credit to banks so that they could operate efficiently. Banks receiving these loans were expected to extend loans to businesses providing jobs or building low-cost housing.

Red Scare Vigorous repression of radicals, "political subversives," and "undesirable" immigrants groups in the years immediately following World War I. Nearly 6,500 "radicals" were arrested and sent to jail; some sat in jail without ever being charged with a crime, while nearly 500 immigrants were deported.

referendum process One of a series of progressive-era reforms designed to improve the political system. According to this referendum, certain issues would not be decided by elected representatives, but voters are called upon to approve or disapprove specific government programs. Consistent with populist and progressive era desire to return government "to the people."

religious right Primarily Protestant movement that greatly grew beginning in the 1970s and pushed to return "morality" to the forefront in American life. The religious right has been especially active in opposing abortion, and since the 1980s has extended its influence in the political sphere by endorsing and campaigning for specific candidates (e.g., during the 2004 campaign of President George W. Bush).

Removal Act of 1830 Part of the effort to remove Native Americans from "Western" lands so that American settlement could continue westward, this legislation gave the president the authorization (and the money) to purchase from Native Americans all of their lands east of the Mississippi, and gave him the money to purchase lands west of the Mississippi for Native Americans to move to.

***Report on the Public Credit* (1790)** Report by Secretary of the Treasury Alexander Hamilton, in which he proposed that the federal government assume the entire amount of the nation's debt (including state debt), and that the federal government should have an increased role in the nation's economy. Many of America's early leaders vigorously opposed the expansion of federal economic power in the new republic and the expansion of American industry that Hamilton also promoted.

Republican party Formed in 1854 during the death of the Whig party, this party attracted former members of the Free-Soil party and some in the Democratic party who were uncomfortable with the Democratic position on slavery. Abraham Lincoln was the first Republican president. For much of the twentieth century, the party was saddled with the label of being "the party of big business," although Richard Nixon, Ronald Reagan, and others did much to pull middle class and Southern voters into the party.

"reservationists" This group in the United States Senate was led by Henry Cabot Lodge and was opposed to sections of the Versailles Treaty when it was brought home from Paris by President Woodrow Wilson in 1919. Reservationists were especially concerned that if the United States joined the League of Nations, American troops would be used to conduct League of Nations military operations without the approval of the Congress.

Resettlement Administration In an attempt to address the problems of Dust Bowlers and other poor farmers, this 1935 New Deal program attempted to provide aid to the poorest farmers, resettle some farmers from the Dust Bowl, and establish farm cooperatives. This program never received the funding it needed to be even partially successful, and in 1937 the Farm Security Administration was created to replace it.

Revenue Act of 1935 Tax legislation championed by Franklin Roosevelt that was called a "soak the rich" plan by his opponents. Under this bill, corporate, inheritance, and gift taxes went up dramatically; income taxes for the upper brackets also rose. By proposing this, Roosevelt may have been attempting to diffuse the popularity of Huey Long and others with more radical plans to redistribute wealth.

Revenue Act of 1942 Designed to raise money for the war, this bill dramatically increased the number of Americans required to pay income tax. Until this point, roughly 4 million Americans paid income tax; as a result of this legislation, nearly 45 million did.

"revisionist" history A historical interpretation not found in "standard" history books or supported by most historians. A revisionist history of the origins of the cold war, for example, would maintain that the aggressive actions of the United States forced the Soviet Union to seize the territories of Eastern Europe for protection. Historical interpretations that may originally be revisionist may, in time, become standard historical interpretation.

revival meetings Religious meetings consisting of soul-searching, preaching, and prayer that took place during the Second Great Awakening at the beginning of the nineteenth century. Some revival meetings lasted over one week.

Rio Pact (1947) Treaty signed by the United States and most Latin American countries, stating that the region would work together on economic and defense matters and creating the Organization of American States to facilitate this cooperation.

***Roe v. Wade* (1973)** Supreme Court decision that made abortion legal (except in the last months of pregnancy). Justices voting in the majority in this 5-to-2 decision stated that a woman's right to privacy gave her the legal freedom to choose to have an abortion. Abortion has remained one of the most hotly debated social issues in America.

Roosevelt Corollary An extension of the Monroe Doctrine, this policy was announced in 1904 by Theodore Roosevelt. It firmly warned European nations against intervening in the affairs of nations in the Western Hemisphere, and stated that the United States had the right to take action against any nation in Latin America if "chronic wrongdoing" was taking place. The Roosevelt Corollary was used to justify several American "interventions" in Central America in the twentieth century.

Rosie the Riveter Image of a woman factory worker drawn by Norman Rockwell for the *Saturday Evening Post* during World War II. Women were needed to take on factory jobs that had been held by departing soldiers; by 1945 women made up nearly 37 percent of the entire domestic workforce.

"Rough Riders" A special unit of soldiers recruited by Theodore Roosevelt to do battle in the Spanish-American War. This unit was composed of men from many backgrounds, with the commanding officer of the unit being Roosevelt (after he resigned as assistant secretary of the navy). The most publicized event of the war was the charge of the Rough Riders up San Juan Hill on July 1, 1898.

Salem Witch Trials 120 men, women, and children were arrested for witchcraft in Salem, Massachusetts, in 1692; 19 of these were executed. A new governor appointed by the Crown stopped additional trials and executions; several historians note the class nature of the witch trials, as many of those accused were associated with the business and/or commercial interests in Salem, while most of the accusers were members of the farming class.

SALT I (Strategic Arms Limitation Talks) 1972 treaty signed by Richard Nixon and Soviet premier

Leonid Brezhnev limiting the development of additional nuclear weapon systems and defense systems to stop them. SALT I was only partially effective in preventing continued development of nuclear weaponry.

"salutary neglect" British policy announced at the beginning of the eighteenth century stating that as long as the American colonies remained politically loyal and continued their trade with Great Britain, the British government would relax enforcement of various measures restricting colonial activity that were enacted in the 1600s. Tensions between the colonies and Britain continued over British policies concerning colonial trade and the power of colonial legislatures.

satellite countries Eastern European countries that remained under the control of the Soviet Union during the cold war era. Most were drawn together militarily by the Warsaw Pact. Satellite nations that attempted political or cultural rebellion, such as Hungary in 1956 or Czechoslovakia in 1968, faced invasion by Soviet forces.

"Saturday Night Massacre" October 20, 1973, event when Richard Nixon ordered the firing of Archibald Cox, the special investigator in charge of the Watergate investigation. Attorney General Elliot Richardson and several others in the Justice Department refused to carry out this order and resigned. This event greatly damaged Nixon's popularity, both in the eyes of the public and in the Congress.

scalawags Term used by Southerners in the Reconstruction era for fellow Southerners who either supported Republican Reconstruction policies or gained economically as a result of these policies.

Scopes Trial of 1925 Tennessee trial where teacher John Scopes was charged with teaching evolution, a violation of state statutes. The American Civil Liberties Union hired Clarence Darrow to defend Scopes, while the chief attorney for the prosecution was three-time presidential candidate William Jennings Bryan. While Scopes was convicted and ordered to pay a small fine, Darrow was able to poke holes in the theory of creationism as expressed by Bryan.

Scottsboro Boys Nine black young men who were accused of raping two white women in a railway boxcar in Scottsboro, Arizona, in 1931. Quick trials, suppressed evidence, and inadequate legal council made them symbols of the discrimination that faced blacks on a daily basis during this era.

Scramble for Africa The competition between the major European powers to gain colonial territories in Africa that took place between the 1870s and the outbreak of World War I. Conflicts created by competing visions of colonial expansion increased tensions between the European powers and were a factor in the animosities that led to World War I.

secession A single state or a group of states leaving the United States of America. New England Federalists threatened to do this during the first administration of Thomas Jefferson. Southern states did this in the period prior to the Civil War.

Second Continental Congress Meeting of delegates from the American colonies in May 1775. During the sessions some delegates expressed hope that the differences between the colonies and Britain could be reconciled, although Congress authorized that the Continental army be created and that George Washington be named commander of that army.

Second Great Awakening Religious revival movement that began at the beginning of the nineteenth century. Revivalist ministers asked thousands of worshippers at revival meetings to save their own souls. This reflected the move away from predestination in Protestant thinking of the era.

Second Industrial Revolution The massive economic growth that took place in America from 1865 until the end of the century that was largely based on the expansion of the railroad, the introduction of electric power, and the production of steel for building. By the 1890s America had replaced Germany as the major industrial producer in the world.

Second National Bank Bank established by Congress in 1816. President Madison had called for the Second Bank in 1815 as a way to spur national economic growth after the War of 1812. After an economic downturn in 1818, the bank shrank the amount of currency available for loans, an act that helped to create the economic collapse of 1819.

Second New Deal Beginning in 1935, the New Deal did more to help the poor and attack the wealthy. One reason Roosevelt took this path was to turn the American people away from those who said the New Deal wasn't going far enough to help the average person. Two key legislative acts of this era were the Social Security Act of May 1935 and the June 1935 National Labor Relations Act (also called the Wagner Act), which gave all Americans the right to join labor unions. The Wealth Tax Act increased the tax rates for the wealthiest Americans.

secondary source A historical account written after the fact; a historian writing a secondary source would analyze the available primary sources on his/her topic. Examples would be a textbook, a biography written today of Napoleon, or a new account of the Black Death.

Separatists Religious group that opposed the Church of England. This group first went to Holland, and then some went on to the Americas.

settlement houses Centers set up by progressive-era reformers in the poorest sections of American cities. At these centers, workers and their children might receive lessons in the English language or citizenship; while for women, lessons in sewing and cooking were often held. The first settlement house was Hull House in Chicago, established by Jane Addams in 1889.

Seventeenth Amendment Ratified in 1913, this amendment allowed voters to directly elect U.S. senators. Senators had previously been elected by state legislatures. This change perfectly reflected the spirit of progressive-era political reformers who wanted to do all they could to put political power in the hands of the citizenry.

Sherman Antitrust Act of 1890 Congressional legislation designed to break up industrial trusts such as the one created by John D. Rockefeller and Standard Oil. The bill stated that any combination of businesses that was "in the restraint of trade" was illegal. Because of the vagueness of the legislation and the lack of enforcement tools in the hands of the federal government, few trusts were actually prosecuted as a result of this bill.

Shiloh, Battle of Fierce Civil War battle in Tennessee in April 1862. Although the Union emerged victorious, both sides suffered a large number of casualties in this battle. Total casualties in this battle were nearly 25,000. General Ulysses S. Grant commanded the Union forces at Shiloh.

Sioux Plains tribe that tried to resist American westward expansion; after two wars, the Sioux were resettled in South Dakota. In 1876, Sioux fighters defeated the forces of General Custer at the Battle of the Little Bighorn. In 1890, almost 225 Sioux men, women, and children were killed by federal troops at the Massacre at Wounded Knee.

sit-down strikes A labor tactic where workers refuse to leave their factory until management meets their demands. The most famous sit-down strike occurred at the General Motors plant in Flint, Michigan, beginning in December 1936. Despite efforts by company guards to end the strike by force, the workers finally saw their demands met after 44 days.

sit-in Tactic used by the civil rights movement in the early 1960s; a group of civil rights workers would typically occupy a lunch counter in a segregated establishment in the South and refuse to leave, thus disrupting normal business (and profits) for the segregated establishment. During sit-ins civil rights workers often suffered physical and emotional abuse. The first sit-in was at the Woolworth's store in Greensboro, North Carolina, on February 1, 1960.

Sixteenth Amendment (1913) Amendment that instituted a federal income tax. In debate over this measure in Congress, most felt that this would be a fairer tax than a national sales tax, which was proposed by some.

Smith-Connally Act of 1943 Legislation that limited the nature of labor action possible for the rest of the war. Many in America felt that strikes, especially those organized in the coal mines by the United Mine Workers, were detrimental to the war effort.

Social Darwinism Philosophy that evolved from the writings of Charles Darwin on evolution that stated people inevitably compete with each other, as do societies; in the end the "survival of the fittest" would naturally occur. Social Darwinism was used to justify the vast differences between the rich and the poor in the late nineteenth century, as well as the control that the United States and Europe maintained over other parts of the world.

Social Gospel movement Late nineteenth-century Protestant movement preaching that all true Christians should be concerned with the plight of immigrants and other poor residents of American cities and should financially support efforts to improve the lives of these poor urban dwellers. Progressive-era settlement houses were often financed by funds raised by ministers of the Social Gospel movement.

Social history The field of history that analyzes the lives and beliefs of common people in any historical era. In American history, this field has grown dramatically since the 1960s. Social historians believe that we can get a more accurate view of the civil rights movement, by for example, studying the actions of civil rights workers in Mississippi than we can by studying the actions and pronouncements of leaders of the civil rights movement who were active on the national stage.

Social Security Act Considered by many to be the most important act passed during the entire New Deal, this 1935 bill established a system that would give payments to Americans after they reached retirement age; provisions for unemployment and disability insurance were also found in this bill. Political leaders of recent years have wrestled with the problem of keeping the Social Security system solvent.

Sons of Liberty Men who organized opposition to British policies during the late 1760s and 1770s. The Sons of Liberty were founded in and were most active in Boston, where in response to the Stamp Act they burned the local tax collector in effigy and burned a building that he owned. The Sons of Liberty also organized the Boston Tea Party. Samuel Adams was one of the leaders of this group.

"Southern Strategy" Plan begun by Richard Nixon that has made the Republican party dominant in many areas of the South that had previously voted Democratic. Nixon, Ronald Reagan, and countless Republican congressional candidates had emphasized law and order and traditional values in their campaigns, thus winning over numerous voters. Support from the South had been part of the New Deal Democratic coalition crafted by Franklin Roosevelt.

Spanish-American War War that began in 1898 and stemmed from furor in America over treatment of Cubans by Spanish troops that controlled the island. During the war the American navy led by Admiral Dewey destroyed the Spanish fleet in the Pacific, the American ship the U.S.S *Maine* was sunk in Havana harbor, and Teddy Roosevelt led the Rough Riders up San Juan Hill. A major result of the war was the acquisition by the United States of the Philippines, which made America a major power in the Pacific.

speakeasies Urban clubs that existed in the 1920s where alcohol was illegally sold to patrons. The sheer number of speakeasies in a city such as New York demonstrated the difficulty of enforcing a law such as prohibition.

special prosecutor An official appointed to investigate specific governmental wrongdoing. Archibald Cox was the special prosecutor assigned to investigate Watergate, while Kenneth Starr was the special prosecutor assigned to investigate the connections between President Clinton and Whitewater. President Nixon's order to fire Cox was the beginning of the famous 1973 "Saturday Night Massacre."

speculation The practice of purchasing either land or stocks with the intent of selling them for a higher price later. After the Homestead Act and other acts opened up the western United States for settlement, many speculators purchased land with no intent of ever settling on it; their goal was to later sell the land for profit.

spoils system Also called the patronage system, in which the president, governor, or mayor is allowed to fill government jobs with political allies and former campaign workers. Political reformers of the 1880s and 1890s introduced legislation calling for large numbers of these jobs to be filled by the merit system, in which candidates for jobs had to take competitive examinations. President Andrew Jackson began the spoils system.

Sputnik First man-made satellite sent into space, this 1957 scientific breakthrough by the Soviet Union caused great concern in the United States. The thought that the United States was "behind" the Soviet Union in anything worried many, and science and mathematics requirements in universities across the country increased as a result.

Square Deal The philosophy of President Theodore Roosevelt; included in this was the desire to treat both sides fairly in any dispute. In the coal miner's strike of 1902 he treated the United Mine Workers representatives and company bosses as equals. This approach continued during his efforts to regulate the railroads and other businesses during his second term.

stagflation A unique economic situation faced political leaders in the early 1970s, where inflation and signs of economic recession occurred at the same time. Previously, in times of inflation, the economy was improving, and vice versa. Nixon utilized wage and price controls and increased government spending to address this problem.

Stamp Act To help pay for the British army in North America, Parliament passed the Stamp Act in 1765, under which all legal documents in the colonies had to be issued on officially stamped paper. A tax was imposed on all of these documents, as well as on all colonial newspapers. The resistance to the Stamp Act was severe in the colonies, and it was eventually repealed.

Stamp Act Congress Representatives of nine colonies went to this meeting held in New York in October 1765; the document produced by this congress maintained the loyalty of the colonies to the Crown but strongly condemned the Stamp Act. Within one year the Stamp Act was repealed.

states' rights The concept that the individual states, and not the federal government, have the power to decide whether federal legislation or regulations are to be enforced within the individual states. The mantle of states' rights would be taken up by New England Federalists during the presidency of Thomas Jefferson, by many Southern states in the years leading up to the Civil War, and by some Southern states again in response to federal legislation during the civil rights era of the 1960s.

Stono Rebellion of 1739 Slave rebellion in South Carolina where over 75 slaves killed white citizens and marched through the countryside with captured guns. After the rebellion was quashed, discipline imposed by many slave owners was much harsher. This was the largest slave rebellion of the 1700s in the colonies.

Students for a Democratic Society (SDS) Founded in 1960, this group was part of the "New Left" movement of the 1960s. SDS believed in a more participatory society, in a society that was less materialistic, and in university reform that would give students more power. By 1966 SDS concentrated much of its efforts on organizing opposition to the war in Vietnam. The *Port Huron Statement* was the original manifesto of SDS and was written by SDS founder Tom Hayden.

suburbia The area outside of the cities where massive numbers of families flocked to in the 1950s and 1960s. Suburban parents often still worked in the cities, but the suburban lifestyle shared little with urban life. Critics of 1950s suburbia point to the sameness and lack of vitality noted by some suburban residents and to the fact that suburban women often had to forget past dreams to accept the role of "housewife."

Suffolk Resolves These were sent from Suffolk County, Massachusetts, to the meeting of the First Continental Congress in September 1774 and called for the citizens of all of the colonies to prepare to take up arms against the British. After much debate, the First Continental Congress adopted the Suffolk Resolves.

Sugar Act Another effort to pay for the British army located in North America, this 1764 measure taxed sugar and other imports. The British had previously attempted to halt the flow of sugar from French colonies to the colonies: By the Sugar Act they attempted to make money from this trade. Another provision of the act harshly punished smugglers of sugar who didn't pay the import duty imposed by the British.

supply-side economics Economic theory adopted by Ronald Reagan stating that economic growth would be best encouraged by lowering the taxes of wealthy businessmen and investors; this would give them more cash, which they would use to start more businesses, make more investments, and in general stimulate the economy. This theory of "Reaganomics" went against economic theories going

back to the New Deal that claimed to efficiently stimulate the economy, more money needed to be held by consumers (who would in turn spend it).

Sussex Pledge A torpedo from a German submarine hit the French passenger liner the *Sussex* in March 1916, killing and injuring many (including six Americans). In a strongly worded statement, President Wilson demanded that the Germans refrain from attacking passenger ships. In the Sussex Pledge the Germans said that they would temporarily stop these attacks, but that they might have to resume them in the future if the British continued their blockade of German ports.

Taft-Hartley Act of 1947 Congressional legislation that aided the owners in potential labor disputes. In key industries the president could declare an 80-day cooling off period before a strike could actually take place; the bill also allowed owners to sue unions over broken contracts, and forced union leaders to sign anti-Communist oaths. The bill was passed over President Truman's veto; Truman only vetoed the bill for political reasons.

Tammany Hall Political machine that ran New York City Democratic and city politics beginning in 1870, and a "model" for the political machines that dominated politics in many American cities well into the twentieth century. William Marcy "Boss" Tweed was the head of Tammany Hall for several years and was the most notorious of all of the political bosses.

Tariff of 1816 An extremely protectionist tariff designed to assist new American industries in the aftermath of the War of 1812. This tariff raised import duties by nearly 25 percent.

Tax Reform Act of 1986 The biggest tax cut in American history, this measure cut taxes by $750 billion over five years and cut personal income taxes by 25 percent. Tax cuts were consistent with President Reagan's belief that more money in the hands of the wealthy would stimulate the economy. Critics of this tax cut would argue that the wealthy were the ones that benefited from it, as little of the money that went to the hands of the rich actually "trickled down" to help the rest of the economy. Critics would also argue that the national deficits of the late 1980s and early 1990s were caused by these tax cuts.

Taylorism Following the management practices of Frederick Winslow Taylor, the belief practiced by many factory owners beginning in 1911 (when Taylor published his first book) that factories should be managed in a scientific manner, with everything done to increase the efficiency of the individual worker and of the factory process as a whole. Taylor describes the movements of workers as if they were machines; workers in many factories resisted being seen in this light.

Tea Act of 1773 Act by Parliament that would provide the American colonies with cheap tea, but at the same time would force the colonists to admit that Parliament had a right to tax them. The Sons of Liberty acted against this measure in several colonies, with the most dramatic being the Boston Tea Party. Parliament responded with the harsh Coercive Acts.

Teapot Dome Scandal One of many scandals that took place during the presidency of Warren G. Harding. The Secretary of the Interior accepted bribes from oil companies for access to government oil reserves at Teapot Dome, Wyoming. Other cabinet members were later convicted of accepting bribes and using their influence to make millions. The Harding administration was perhaps the most corrupt administration in American political history.

Teller Amendment As Americans were preparing for war with Spain over Cuba in 1898, this Senate measure stated that under no circumstances would the United States annex Cuba. The amendment was passed as many in the muckraking press were suggesting that the Cuban people would be better off "under the protection" of the United States.

temperance movement Movement that developed in America before the Civil War that lamented the effect that alcohol had on American society. After the Civil War, members of this movement would become especially concerned about the effect of alcohol on immigrants and other members of the urban poor. Out of the temperance movement came the drive for nationwide prohibition.

Ten Percent Plan Abraham Lincoln's plan for Reconstruction, which would have offered full pardons to persons living in Confederate states who would take an oath of allegiance to the United States (former Confederate military officers and civilian authorities would not be offered this possibility). Once 10 percent of the citizens of a state had taken such an oath, the state could take steps to rejoin the Union. Radical Republicans in the U.S. Senate felt that this plan was much too lenient toward the South.

tenant farmers In the Reconstruction South, a step up from sharecropping. The tenant farmer rented his land from the landowner, freeing him from the harsh supervision that sharecroppers suffered under.

Tennessee Valley Authority Ambitious New Deal program that for the first time provided electricity to residents of the Tennessee Valley; the TVA also promoted agricultural and industrial growth (and prevented flooding) in the region. In all, residents of seven states benefited from the TVA.

Tenure of Office Act (1867) Congressional act designed to limit the influence of President Andrew Johnson. The act took away the president's role as commander in chief of American military forces and stated that Congress had to approve the removal of government officials made by the president. In 1868, Johnson attempted to fire Secretary of War Stanton without congressional approval, thus helping set the stage for his impeachment hearings later that year.

Tet Offensive January 1968 attack launched on American and South Vietnamese forces by North Vietnamese and Vietcong soldiers. Although Vietcong troops actually occupied the American embassy in Vietnam for several hours, the end result was a crushing defeat for the anti-American forces. However, the psychological effect of Tet was exactly the reverse: Vietcong forces were convinced they could decisively strike at South Vietnamese and American targets, and many in America ceased to believe that victory was "just around the corner."

Thirteenth Amendment (1865) Amendment abolishing slavery in the United States and all of its territories (the Emancipation Proclamation had ended slavery only in the Confederate states). Final approval of this amendment depended on ratification by newly constructed legislatures in eight states that were former members of the Confederacy.

38th parallel The dividing line between Soviet-supported North Korea and U.S.-backed South Korea both before and as a result of the Korean War. American forces have been stationed on the southern side of this border continually since the Korean War ended in 1953.

Three-Fifths Compromise As the new Constitution was being debated in 1787, great controversy developed over how slaves should be counted in determining membership in the House of Representatives. To increase their representation, Southern states argued that slaves should be counted as people; Northerners argued that they should not count, since they could not vote or own property. The compromise arrived at was that each slave would count as three-fifths of a free person.

"tight money" Governmental policy utilized to offset the effects of inflation. On numerous occasions the Federal Reserve Board has increased the interest rate on money it loans to member banks; these higher interest rates are passed on to customers of member banks. With higher interest rates, there are fewer loans and other business activity, which "slows the economy down" and lowers inflation.

Timber and Stone Act of 1878 Bill that allowed private citizens to purchase forest territory in Oregon, Washington, California, and Nevada. Although the intent of the bill was to encourage settlement in these areas, lumber companies purchased large amounts of these land claims from the individuals who had originally purchased them.

Townshend Acts of 1767 Parliamentary act that forced colonists to pay duties on most goods coming from England, including tea and paper, and increased the power of custom boards in the colonies to ensure that these duties were paid. These duties were despised and fiercely resisted in many of the colonies; in Boston resistance was so fierce that the British were forced to occupy Boston with troops. The acts were finally repealed in 1770.

Trail of Tears Forced march of 20,000 members of the Cherokee tribe to their newly designated "homeland" in Oklahoma. Federal troops forced the Cherokees westward in this 1838 event, with one out every five Native Americans dying from hunger, disease, or exhaustion along the way.

Trenton, Battle of December 26, 1776, surprise attack by forces commanded by George Washington on Hessian forces outside of Trenton, New Jersey. Nearly 950 Hessians were captured and another 30 were killed by Washington's forces; three Americans were wounded in the attack. The battle was a tremendous psychological boost for the American war effort.

Triangle Shirtwaist Fire March 1911 fire in New York factory that trapped young women workers inside locked exit doors; nearly 50 ended up jumping to their death, while 100 died inside the factory. Many factory reforms, including increasing safety precautions for workers, came from the investigation of this incident.

triangular trade system The complex trading relationship that developed in the late seventeenth century between the Americas, Europe, and Africa. Europeans purchased slaves from Africa to be resold in the Americas, raw materials from the Americas were exported to European states, while manufactured products in Europe were sold throughout the Americas.

Truman Doctrine Created in response to 1947 requests by Greece and Turkey for American assistance to defend themselves against potentially pro-Soviet elements in their countries. This policy stated that the United States would be ready to assist any free nation trying to defend itself against "armed minorities or . . . outside pressures." This would become the major American foreign policy goal throughout the cold war.

trusts Late nineteenth-century legal arrangement that allowed owners of one company to own stock in other companies in the same industry. By this arrangement, John D. Rockefeller and Standard Oil were able to buy enough stock to control other oil companies in existence as well. The Sherman Antitrust Act and the Clayton Antitrust Act were efforts to "break up" the numerous trusts that were created during this period.

Turner Thesis Published by Frederick Jackson Turner in 1893, "The Significance of the West in American History" stated that western expansion had played a fundamental role in defining the American character, and that the American tendencies toward democracy and individualism were created by the frontier experience.

Twelfth Amendment of 1804 Amendment that established separate balloting in the Electoral College for president and vice president. This amendment was passed as a result of the electoral deadlock of the 1800 presidential election, when Thomas Jefferson and his "running mate" Aaron Burr ended up with the same number of votes in the Electoral College; the House of Representatives finally decided the election in favor of Jefferson.

U-2 American reconnaissance aircraft shot down over the Soviet Union in May 1960. President Eisenhower initially refused to acknowledge that this was a spy flight; the Soviets finally produced pilot Francis Gary Powers, who admitted the purpose of the flight. This incident created an increase in cold war tensions at the end of the Eisenhower presidency.

Uncle Tom's Cabin 1852 novel by Harriet Beecher Stowe that depicted all of the horrors of Southern slavery in great detail. The book went through several printings in the 1850s and early 1860s and helped to fuel Abolitionist sentiment in the North.

unicameral legislature A governmental structure with a one-house legislature. As written in the Articles of Confederation, the United States would have a unicameral legislature, with all states having equal representation.

United Farm Workers Organized by Cesar Chavez in 1961, this union represented Mexican Americans engaged in the lowest levels of agricultural work. In 1965 Chavez organized a strike against grape growers that hired Mexican-American workers in California, eventually winning the promise of benefits and minimum wage guarantees for the workers.

U.S. Forest Service Created during the presidency of Theodore Roosevelt, this body increased and protected the number of national forests and encouraged through numerous progress the efficient use of America's natural resources.

Universal Negro Improvement Association Black organization of the early 1920s founded by Marcus Garvey, who argued that, however possible, blacks should disassociate themselves from the "evils" of white society. This group organized a "back to Africa" movement, encouraging blacks of African descent to move back there; independent black businesses were encouraged (and sometimes funded) by Garvey's organization.

unrestricted submarine warfare The German policy announcement in early 1917 of having their U-boats attack all ships attempting to land at British or French ports, despite their origin or purpose. Because of this policy, the rights of the United States as a neutral power were being violated, stated Woodrow Wilson in 1917, and America was forced to declare war on Germany.

U.S.S *Maine* American ship sent to Havana harbor in early 1898 to protect American interests in period of increased tension between Spanish troops and native Cubans. On February 15 an explosion took place on the ship, killing nearly 275 sailors. Later investigations pointed to an internal explosion on board, but all of the muckraking journals of the time in the United States blamed the explosion on the Spanish, which helped to develop intense anti-Spanish sentiment in the United States.

Valley Forge Location where General Washington stationed his troops for the winter of 1777 to 1778. Soldiers suffered hunger, cold, and disease: nearly 1,300 deserted over the course of the winter. Morale of the remaining troops was raised by the drilling and discipline instilled by Baron von Steuben, a former Prussian officer who had volunteered to aid the colonial army.

vertical integration Type of industrial organization practiced in the late nineteenth century and pioneered by Andrew Carnegie and United States Steel. Under this system all of the various business activities needed to produce and sell a finished product (procuring the raw materials, preparing them, producing them, marketing them, and then selling them) would be done by the same company.

Vicksburg, Battle of After a lengthy siege, this Confederate city along the Mississippi River was finally taken by Union forces in July 1863. This victory gave the Union virtual control of the Mississippi River and was a serious psychological blow to the Confederacy.

Vietcong During the Vietnam war, forces that existed within South Vietnam that were fighting for the victory of the North Vietnamese. Vietcong forces were pivotal in the initial successes of the Tet Offensive, which did much to make many in America question the American war effort in Vietnam and played a crucial role in the eventual defeat of the South Vietnamese government.

Vietnamization The process begun by Richard Nixon of removing American troops from Vietnam and turning more of the fighting of the Vietnam war over to the South Vietnamese. Nixon continued to use intense bombing to aid the South Vietnamese efforts as more American troops were being pulled out of Vietnam. In 1973, a peace treaty was finally signed with North Vietnam, allowing American troops to leave the country and all American POWs to be released. In March 1975, North Vietnamese and Vietcong forces captured Saigon and emerged victorious in the war.

Virginia Plan A concept of government crafted by James Madison and adopted by delegates to the convention that created the U.S. Constitution; this plan proposed a stronger central government than had existed under the Articles of Confederation to prevent too much power being placed in the hands of one person or persons. The plan also proposed that the powers of the federal government be divided among officials of executive, judicial, and legislative branches.

VISTA (Volunteer in Service to America) Program instituted in 1964 that sent volunteers to help poor Americans living in both urban and rural settings; this program was sometimes described as a domestic peace corps. This was one of many initiatives that were part of Lyndon Johnson's War on Poverty program.

voluntarism The concept that Americans should sacrifice either time or money for the well-being of their country. A sense of voluntarism has permeated America during much of its history, especially during the Progressive Era and during the administration of John Kennedy ("ask not what your country can do for you—ask what you can do for your country"). President George W. Bush called for a renewed sense of voluntarism in the aftermath of the attacks of September 11, 2001.

Wade-Davis Act Congress passed this bill in 1864 in response to the "10 Percent Plan" of Abraham Lincoln; this legislation set out much more difficult conditions than had been proposed by Lincoln for Southern states to reenter the Union. According to Wade-Davis, all former officers of the Confederacy would be denied citizenship; to vote, a person would have to take an oath that he had never helped the Confederacy in any way, and half of all white males in a state would have to swear loyalty to the Union before statehood could be considered. Lincoln prevented this from becoming law by using the pocket veto.

Wagner Act Also called the National Labor Relations Act, this July 1935 act established major gains for organized labor. It guaranteed collective bargaining, prevented harassment by owners of union activities, and established a National Labor Relations Board to guarantee enforcement of its provisions.

war bonds Also called Liberty Bonds, these were sold by the United States government in both World War I and World War II and used by the government to finance the war effort. A person purchasing a war bond could make money if he or she cashed it in after 5 or 10 years; in the meantime, the government could use the money to help pay its bills. In both wars, movie stars and other celebrities encouraged Americans to purchase war bonds.

War of 1812 War between the British and Americans over British seizure of American ships, connections between the British and Native-American tribes, and other tensions. Treaty ending war restored diplomatic relations between the two countries.

War Industries Board Authorized in 1917, the job of this board was to mobilize American industries for the war effort. The board was headed by Wall Street investor Bernard Baruch, who used his influence to get American industries to produce materials useful for the war effort. Baruch was able to increase American production by a staggering 22 percent before the end of the war.

Warren Commission The group that carefully investigated the assassination of John F. Kennedy. After hearing much testimony, the commission concluded that Lee Harvey Oswald acted alone in killing the president. Even today many conspiracy theorists question the findings of the Warren Commission, claiming that Oswald was part of a larger group who wanted to assassinate the president.

Warsaw Pact Defensive military alliance created in 1955 by the Soviet Union and all of the Eastern European satellite nations loyal to the Soviet Union; the Warsaw Pact was formed as a reaction against NATO and NATO's 1955 decision to invite West Germany to join the organization.

Washington Conference of 1921 Conference where the United States, Japan, and the major European powers agreed not to build any no more warships for 10 years. In addition, the nations agreed not to attack each other's territories in the Pacific. This treaty came from strong post–World War I sentiment that it was important to avoid conflicts between nations that might lead to war.

Watergate Affair The break-in into Democratic campaign headquarters was one of a series of "dirty tricks" carried out by individuals associated with the effort to reelect Richard Nixon president in 1972. Extensive efforts were also made to cover up these activities. In the end, numerous government and campaign officials spent time in jail for their role in the Watergate Affair, and President Nixon was forced to resign in disgrace.

Webb Alien Land Law (1913) California law that prohibited Japanese who were not American citizens from owning farmland in California. This law demonstrates the nativist sentiment found in much of American society in the first decades of the twentieth century.

Webster-Hayne Debate (1830) Senate debate between Senator Daniel Webster of Massachusetts and Senator Robert Hayne of South Carolina over the issue of state's rights and whether an individual state has the right to nullify federal legislation. Webster skillfully outlined the dangers to the United States that would be caused by the practice of nullification; this debate perfectly captured many of the political divisions between North and South that would increase in the 1830s through the 1860s.

Whig party Political party that came into being in 1834 in opposition to the presidency of Andrew Jackson. Whigs opposed Jackson's use of the spoils system and the extensive power held by President Jackson; for much of their existence, however, the Whigs favored an activist federal government (while their opponents, the Democrats, favored limited government). William Henry Harrison and Zachary Taylor were the two Whigs elected president. The Whig party dissolved in the 1850s.

Whiskey Rebellion Many settlers in Western frontier territory in the early 1790s questioned the power that the federal power had over them. In 1793 settlers in the Ohio territory refused to pay federal excise taxes on whiskey and attacked tax officials who were supposed to collect these taxes;

large numbers of "whiskey rebels" threatened to attack Pittsburgh and other cities. In 1794 President Washington was forced to send in federal troops to put down the rebellion.

"White Man's Burden" From the poem of the same name by Rudyard Kipling, this view justified imperialism by the "white man" around the world, but also emphasized the duty of the Europeans and Americans who were occupying new territories to improve the lives of those living in the newly acquired regions.

Whitewater The name of the scandal that got President Bill Clinton impeached but not convicted. Whitewater was the name of a real-estate deal in Arkansas that Clinton and his wife Hillary Rodham Clinton were both involved in; opponents claimed the actions of the Clintons concerning Whitewater were illegal, unethical, or both. Independent Counsel Kenneth Starr expanded the investigation to include the suicide of Clinton aide Vincent Foster, missing files in the White House, and the relationship of President Clinton with a White House intern, Monica Lewinsky.

Wilmot Proviso In the aftermath of the war with Mexico, in 1846 Representative David Wilmot proposed in an amendment to a military bill that slavery should be prohibited in all territories gained in the treaty ending that war. This never went into law, but in the debate over it in both houses, Southern representatives spoke passionately in defense of slavery; John C. Calhoun even suggested that the federal government had no legal jurisdiction to stop the existence of slavery in any new territory.

Woodstock Music Festival (1969) Event that some perceive as the pinnacle of the 1960s counterculture. 400,000 young people came together for a weekend of music and a relative lack of hassles or conflict. The difficulty of mixing the 1960s counterculture with the radical politics of the era was demonstrated when Peter Townshend of the Who kicked Abbie Hoffman off the Woodstock stage.

Works Progress Administration (WPA) New Deal program established in 1935 whose goal was to give out jobs as quickly as possible, even though the wages paid by the WPA were relatively low. Roads and public buildings were constructed by WPA work crews. At the same time, WPA authors wrote state guidebooks, artists painted murals in newly constructed public buildings, and musicians performed in large cities and small towns across the country.

writ of habeas corpus Allows a person suspected of a crime not to simply sit in jail indefinitely. Such a suspect must be brought to court and charged with something, or he or she must be released from jail. Abraham Lincoln suspended the right of habeas corpus during the Civil War so that opponents of his policies could be contained.

Yalta Conference Meeting between Stalin, Churchill, and Roosevelt held two months before the fall of Nazi Germany in February 1945. At this meeting Stalin agreed to assist the Americans against the Japanese after the Germans were defeated; it was decided that Germany would be divided into zones (each controlled by one of the victors), and Stalin promised to hold free elections in the Eastern European nations the Soviet army had liberated from the Nazis. Critics of the Yalta agreement maintain that Roosevelt (he was only months from his own death) was naïve in his dealings with Stalin at this meeting, and that Churchill and Roosevelt essentially handed over control of Eastern Europe to Stalin.

yellow journalism This method uses accounts and illustrations of lurid and sensational events to sell newspapers. Newspapers using this strategy covered the events in Cuba leading up to the Spanish-American War, and did much to shift American opinion toward desiring war with Spain. Some critics maintain that many tactics of yellow journalism were used during the press coverage of the Whitewater investigation of Bill Clinton.

Yorktown, Battle of The defeat of the forces of General Cornwallis in this battle in October 1781 essentially ended the hopes of the British for winning the Revolutionary War. American and French troops hemmed the British in on the peninsula of Yorktown, while the French navy located in Chesapeake Bay made rescue of the British troops by sea impossible.

Zimmermann Telegram January 1917 telegram sent by the German foreign minister to Mexico suggesting that the Mexican army should join forces with the Germans against the United States. When the Germans and Mexicans were victorious, the Mexicans were promised most of the southwestern part of the United States. The British deciphered the code of this telegram and turned it over to the United States; the release of its content caused many in America to feel that war against the Germans was essential.

BIBLIOGRAPHY

To get the "perfect 5" on the AP exam you should read this study guide thoroughly. In addition, read all of the assignments your teacher gives you from the textbook. She/he will undoubtedly give you primary source readings and additional readings; these are also critical to your success. Remember, the more you read about American history, the more prepared you will be for the exam!

On this page, we have also included a number of topics that you will study in an AP U.S. History course and books that have been helpful to us in studying each particular topic. This is a totally subjective list; your teacher would probably recommend other books for some of the topics. Nevertheless, if you feel weak in a particular subject (or if you want to learn more about it) read all or a part of the books we have recommended. We are confident that you will not be disappointed.

The Age of Jackson: *Waking Giant: America in the Age of Jackson* by David S. Reynolds (Harper, 2008).

America and World War I: *The Illusion of Victory: America in World War I* by Thomas Fleming (Basic Books, 2004).

The American Revolution: *The American Revolution: A History* by Gordon S. Wood (Modern Library, 2003).

The Civil Rights Movement: *Eyes on the Prize: America's Civil Rights Years, 1954–1965* by Juan Williams (Penguin, 1988).

The Civil War: *Battle Cry of Freedom: The Civil War Era* by James M. McPherson (Oxford University Press USA, 2003).

The Clinton Era: *The Natural: The Misunderstood Presidency of Bill Clinton* by Joe Klein (Broadway, 2003).

The Cold War: *The Cold War: A History* by Martin Walker (Holt Paperbacks, 1995).

Colonial Settlement and the Environment: *Changes in the Land: Indians, Colonists, and the Ecology of New England* by William Cronon (Hill and Wang, 2003).

The Constitution: *A Brilliant Solution: Inventing the American Constitution* by Carol Berkin (Harvest Books, 2003).

Early Industrialization: *What Hath God Wrought: The Transformation of America, 1815–1848* by Daniel Walker Howe (Oxford University Press USA, 2007).

George Washington: *His Excellency: George Washington* by Joseph J. Ellis (Vintage, 2005).

The Gilded Age: *America in the Gilded Age* by Sean Cashman (NYU Press, 1993).

The Great Depression: *The Forgotten Man: A New History of the Great Depression* by Amity Shlaes (Harper Perennial, 2008).

Imperialism: *A People's History of American Empire* by Howard Zinn, Mike Konopacki, and Paul Buhle (Metropolitan Books, 2008).

1920s: *New World Coming: The 1920s and the Making of Modern America* by Nathan Miller (Da Capo Press, 2004).

1950s: *The Fifties* by David Halberstam (Ballantine Books, 1994).

1960s: *The Sixties: Years of Hope, Days of Rage* by Todd Gitlin (Bantam, 1993).

1970s: *It Seemed Like Nothing Happened: America in the 1970s* by Peter N. Carroll (Rutgers University Press, 1990).

Origins of the Civil War: *The Impending Crisis, 1848–1861* by David M. Potter (Harper Perennial, 1977).

Progressivism: *A Fierce Discontent: The Rise and Fall of the Progressive Movement in America, 1870–1920* by Michael McGerr (Oxford University Press USA, 2005).

The Reagan Era: *Transforming America: Politics and Culture During the Reagan Years* by Robert M. Collins (Columbia University Press, 2006).

The Reconstruction Era: *Reconstruction: America's Unfinished Revolution, 1863–1877* by Eric Foner (Harper Perennial Modern Classics, 2002).

The Settlement of the American Colonies: *American Colonies: The Settling of North America* by Alan Taylor (Penguin, 2002).

Slavery: *Slavery and the Making of America* by James Oliver Horton and Lois E. Horton (Oxford University Press USA, 2006).

Thomas Jefferson: *Thomas Jefferson: Author of America* by Christopher Hitchens (Eminent Lives, 2005).

The 2008 Elections: *The 2008 Elections and American Politics* by James W. Ceaser, Andrew E. Busch, and John J. Pitney (Rowman & Littlefield Publishers, 2009).

The War on Terror: *The Dark Side: The Inside Story of How the War on Terror Turned into a War on American Ideals* by Jane Mayer (Anchor, 2009).

Westward Expansion: *The American West: A New Interpretive History* by Robert V. Hine and John Mack Faragher (Yale University Press, 2000).

World War II: *The American People in World War II: Freedom from Fear, Part Two* by David M. Kennedy (Oxford University Press USA, 2003).

WEBSITES

There are literally thousands of sites on the web where you can get valuable information on aspects of American history. Historical figures, historical events, and historic sites all have websites with specific information; in addition, there are hundreds of websites with a vast variety of information and resources on topics of U.S. history. If you want to start somewhere, we would recommend two sites. One is a University of Delaware Library site, entitled "Internet Resources for U.S. History." This is found at University of Delaware's "Websites for US History" page and the Internet Public Library's "United States History" page.

Do some more exploring, and you will be utterly amazed at what you can find. In addition, go to your state and local historical society sites; here you will find information about the connections between the history of your town and state and the larger historical themes that you have studied in your AP U.S. History class.